S0-BSJ-824

THE NEW PHRYNICHUS

THE NEW PHRYNICHUS

BEING A REVISED TEXT OF THE ECLOGA OF THE GRAMMARIAN PHRYNICHUS

With introductions and commentary by

W. GUNION RUTHERFORD

1968

GEORG OLMS VERLAGSBUCHHANDLUNG
HILDESHEIM

Reprografischer Nachdruck der Ausgabe London 1881
Printed in Germany
Herstellung: Druckerei Lokay, 6101 Reinheim / Odw.
Best.-Nr. 5101 885

TO

BENJAMIN JOWETT,

MASTER OF BALLIOL COLLEGE,

REGIUS PROFESSOR OF GREEK IN THE UNIVERSITY OF OXFORD,

DOCTOR IN THEOLOGY OF THE UNIVERSITY OF LEYDEN,

THIS BOOK IS DEDICATED

BY

A FORMER PUPIL.

DATE.

Ἤκμασεν ὁ ἀνὴρ ἐν τοῖς χρόνοις Μάρκου βασιλέως Ῥωμαίων καὶ τοῦ παιδὸς αὐτοῦ Κομμόδου.

PHOTIUS, *Bibliotheca.*

WORKS.

Φρύνιχος, Βιθυνὸς σοφιστὴς ἔγραψεν Ἀττικιστήν, περὶ Ἀττικῶν Ὀνομάτων βιβλία β, τιθεμένων συναγωγήν, Σοφιστικῆς Παρασκευῆς βιβλία μζ΄, οἱ δὲ οδ΄.

SUÏDAS.

PREFACE.

In the progress of a long and exacting study of the Attic verb it was my fortune to discover that before the inquiry could be placed upon a scientific basis it would be necessary to reconsider some of the received opinions regarding the language of the Athenian people, and to subject to unflinching criticism the recognised claims of certain writers to a place in Attic literature. For a time my attention was withdrawn from the more special aspect of the question to which it had for several years been devoted, and directed to the prosecution of the wider inquiry, which was to provide a starting point scientifically important, and suggest a more comprehensive and intelligent method. The results obtained were in my judgment of such value that it seemed desirable to find a means of making them public, which would at the same time assist my cherished ulterior project of an authoritative work on the Attic verb.

Augustus Lobeck's edition of the Ecloga of Phrynichus had long been familiar to me, and the suggestion of the High Master of Saint Paul's School that a new edition of the second century Atticist would be of service in calling attention to the peculiar characteristics of Attic Greek received the consideration which his judgment commands.

There is no Grammarian to whose work so high a value

attaches as to that of Phrynichus, the Bithynian, and a perusal of the articles in the Ecloga, crude, fragmentary, and corrupt as they are, will yet prove that the writer regarded Attic Greek from a truer standpoint than more recent Grammarians, and one which students of Greek, subjected since Hermann's time to the thraldom of minute psychological annotation, have often strangely ignored.

It is not my purpose to reprehend the careful and pains-taking study of Greek texts. Accuracy, rigid and uncompromising, is demanded of every student of Greek, but it must be combined with an appreciation of the relative value of facts. The precision of a scholar is one thing, and that of a scholiast another. Details are only valuable as a basis for generalisation, and the study of isolated phenomena without any reference to general principles is as puerile and futile in the student of language as in the questioner of Nature. Grammatical inquiry, however, has one difficulty to encounter which is unknown in the laboratory of the Chemist or the Physicist. To a law of Nature there is in the last resort no exception, but a grammatical rule cannot fail to be sometimes contravened, as long as the human mind is subject to mistake.

There are errors in grammar in all writers, but little is gained by trying to discover the state of mind which produced them. Certainly, in a language so signally accurate and regular as Attic Greek such errors may be remarked upon when encountered, but otherwise left to shift for themselves. Eliminate the innumerable and gross corruptions which transmission by the hand of copyists through a score of centuries necessarily entails, and the texts of Attic writers would present as few errors in syntax and in the forms of words as the best French classics.

As to Syntax, Professor Goodwin's judgment will be considered final by most scholars. In the preface to his well-known work on the Greek Moods and Tenses he states the case against Hermann with the vigorous common sense which marks his scholarship. 'One great cause of the obscurity which has prevailed on this subject is the tendency of so many scholars to treat Greek syntax metaphysically rather than by the light of common sense. Since Hermann's application of Kant's *Categories of Modality* to the Greek Moods, this metaphysical tendency has been conspicuous in German grammatical treatises, and has affected many of the grammars used in England and America more than is generally supposed. The result of this is seen not merely in the discovery of hidden meanings which no Greek writer ever dreamed of, but more especially in the invention of nice distinctions between similar or even precisely equivalent expressions. A new era was introduced by Madvig, who has earned the lasting gratitude of scholars by his efforts to restore Greek syntax to the dominion of common sense.'

It is this same common sense which gives the work of Phrynichus its importance, and although the plan of the Ecloga is unsatisfactory in the extreme, and proves that its author had not attained to the highest view of the scholar's functions, yet its general tone testifies to scholarly instincts. The dedication to Cornelianus contains the creed of a genuine scholar. 'Ἡμεῖς οὐ πρὸς τὰ διημαρτημένα ἀφορῶμεν, ἀλλὰ πρὸς τὰ δοκιμώτατα τῶν ἀρχαίων, and similar maxims occur repeatedly in the work itself. With Phrynichus it was not a mere theory but a practical rule, and no better illustration could be given of scholarly nerve and wholesome masculine common sense than the article in which he contemptuously disregards the few unimportant exceptions to the general rule that μέλλειν in the sense of 'intend' or 'be about' is followed only by the future or present infinitive. To his mind the aorist infinitive after μέλλειν was simply a mistake, and to pay any attention to the examples of it in Attic writers would have appeared as serious an error of judgment as to attempt to distinguish between μέλλω ποιεῖν and μέλλω ποιήσειν.

Questions of Syntax, however, are rarely discussed by Phrynichus, his attention being occupied for the most part with the use of words and their genuine forms. As to these points his testimony is peculiarly valuable, since on the one hand he had access to a very large number of works which have been subsequently lost, and on the other he lived at an age when if due care was used it was still possible even from the manuscripts to discover the inflexions employed by the original writer. The evidence supplied by his dicta I have used to the best of my ability, adding to it all that could be derived from other sources, and endeavouring by its help to make some impression upon the enormous mass of corrupt forms which disfigure all the texts of Attic writers.

Much, indeed, has already been done in this way, and there are unmistakeable indications of a growing tendency to return to the old traditions of scholarship as represented in the work of Bentley, Porson, Elmsley, and Dawes, by adding to the all-important study of syntax a scientific study of words and the orthography of words[1]. In his preface to 'Greek Verbs Irregular and Defective' Dr.

[1] A striking instance of the development of this tendency is the remarkable article by Mr. A. W. Verrall which appeared in No. XVII of the Journal of Philology, entitled 'On a Chorus of the Choephorae, with Remarks upon the verb τοπάζω and its cognates.'

William Veitch long ago suggested the track which such an inquiry should take, and in the book itself supplied a storehouse of materials without which the inquiry itself would be impracticable.

To another scholar, however, my chief acknowledgment is due. Everyone who has taken an interest in the recent history of Greek criticism is familiar with the 'Variae Lectiones,' 'Novae Lectiones,' and the other articles of C. G. Cobet in the Mnemosyne Journal. There are few pages of the present work in which his influence may not be traced, and even in those cases in which my conclusions differ most widely from those of the veteran critic the line of reasoning which produced the divergence was not seldom suggested by writings of his own. A familiar apophthegm of Menander furnishes Greek criticism with an apt watchword, and from Cobet's lips I for one have learned the import of these words—

ἐλευθέρως δούλευε, δοῦλος οὐκ ἔσει.

W. G. R.

1 KING'S BENCH WALK, TEMPLE,
May, 1881.

CORRIGENDA.

Page 25, note 1, *read* προσιόντα.
„ 40, „ 1, *read* art. 38.
„ 47, line 20, *read* art. 73.
„ 129, „ 2, *read* εἴποις.
„ 186, „ 28, *read* ἀποκρίνεται.
„ 194, „ 14, *read* ἀκρατὴς.
„ 204, „ 16, *read* texts of Herodotus.
„ 211, „ 22, *read* ἰχθύες.
„ 224, „ 18, *read* ὑδαρὲς.
„ 225, „ 22, *read* πλεῖον.
„ 234, note, *read* κείμενον.
„ 250, line 13, *read* manuscript.
„ 272, extr., *read* 'Αττικός. διὰ τοῦ ο δ'Ἴων, λαγός.
„ 276, line 14, *read* ἄρ' ἦν.
„ 287, „ 10, *read* ὀπωροπώλης.
„ 288, „ 21, *read* ἐκτρώσασαν.
„ 313, „ 9, *read* immorality but.
„ 324, „ 14, *read* ἐπαρίστερος.
„ 325, lines 8, 9, *read* στυππέϊνον, στύππινον.
„ 325, line 11, *read* στύππινος or στύπινος.

THE NEW PHRYNICHUS.

THE GROWTH OF THE ATTIC DIALECT.

THE interest of the Δαιταλῆς—the first play of Aristophanes—lies in the disappointment felt by an Athenian of a rural deme in the education which his son has received in the city. He asks him to dig, and the boy shows him hands accustomed to no rougher labour than fingering the flute and the lyre. The farmer prays for a sturdy drinking song by Alcaeus or Anacreon, but his cultured son,—

λεῖος ὥσπερ ἔγχελυς, χρυσοῦς ἔχων κικίννους,—

knows none but modern airs. When the old man would test his knowledge of Homer—and Homer was to the Greek much that the Bible in a higher sense was to the Jew—his questions as to the meaning of Homeric phrases are answered by counter-questions on the sense which certain words bear in Attic law.

This play was written just in the middle of the great literary period of Athens. About one hundred years earlier Tragedy earned a place in literary history, and before the close of the next century Athens had left her genius on the field of Chaeronea. Aeschylus was born a few years after the rude stage of Thespis first courted the Dionysiac crowd, and Demosthenes survived the national independence by only fifteen years. Yet, in this short space, the Athenian tongue was able to mould the

Greek language into the most perfect vehicle of thought known to literature.

The fragment of the Δαιταλῆς already referred to demonstrates the fact that much of Homer was as unintelligible to an Athenian of the best days, as Chaucer is to an ordinary Englishman of the present century. In fact the Attic even of the Μαραθωνομάχαι was as far removed from the Greek of Homer as the English of Milton from that of Chaucer[1], and if the lapse of time is alone considered it must have been more so. But if Homer was often hard for them to understand, the debased forms and mixed vocabulary of the common dialect would have struck the contemporaries of Aristophanes and Plato as little better than the jargon of the Scythian policemen who kept order in the market-place.

In the Δαιταλῆς the master of Attic Comedy brought the old and the new in Athens face to face. The boy's grandfather might well have heard Thespis in his first rude attempts at tragedy, and his grandson have been forced to doubt whether it was life that imitated Menander, or Menander who imitated life. Now the forces which in this Comedy Aristophanes represents as acting upon the young men of his day had been at work for years, not only in modifying the national character, but also in moulding the speech of the Athenians. There is little in the Attic of Aristophanes or the Orators which would indicate that it is only a development of Ionic, and a genuine descendant of the Greek which Homer wrote. So great has been the influence of the democratic institutions

[1] The lines in question are preserved in a fragmentary state by the Physician Galen in his Lexicon to Hippocrates:—

Father. Πρὸς ταῦτα σὺ λέξον Ὁμήρου ἐμοὶ γλώττας,
τί καλοῦσι κόρυμβα;
Father. τί καλοῦσ' ἀμένηνα κάρηνα;
Son. ὁ μὲν οὖν σός, ἐμὸς δ' οὗτος ἀδελφὸς φρασάτω,
τί καλοῦσιν ἰδυίους;
Son. τί καλοῦσιν ὀπυίειν (ἀποινᾶν Mke. conj.);

and free city life—the δικαστήρια and ἀγορά—on the one hand, the arrogance of empire and foreign commerce—the ἡγεμονία and Πειραεύς—on the other. But that this was certainly the case is proved not only by many phenomena of form and expression, but also by a literary fact which has never received the serious attention which it merits.

It is strange that Tragedy which, rightly considered, sheds more light than aught else on the history of the Attic dialect, should have been the occasion of concealing its purity. Among other causes which have prevented Attic from being thoroughly understood, none can equal the mistake of regarding the Tragic diction as only an elevated modification of ordinary Attic. This conviction is of the same kind as that arising from the concomitant study of several Hellenic dialects, namely, that Greek as a whole is markedly irregular. As a matter of fact nothing is further from the truth.

It is a well-known characteristic of Greek literature that different kinds of composition had a tendency to adhere generally to the dialect in which they started. Epic verse did not deviate from that use of words which Homer had discovered to be most suitable to the genius of hexameter metre. Even in Comedy, when there was occasion to use hexameters, old words and forms, unused in the Attic of the day, were liberally introduced. Choric poetry had its rise among the Dorians, and Doric was the vehicle of expression used in all choric verse ever afterwards, and in Comedy no less than in Tragedy the choral odes were couched in Doric.

By considering Tragedy with reference to this fact it is possible at once to account for the striking discrepancy which exists, both in vocabulary and accidence, between tragedies and comedies of precisely the same date. *The basis of the language of Tragedy is the Attic of the time when Tragedy sprang into life.*

Accordingly, in the Tragic Dialect is discovered what might otherwise have been lost, the missing link between Ionic proper and that modification of it which is called Attic. It must however be remembered, at the same time, that the Tragic poetry of Athens, like that of all other nations, contained words, expressions, and metaphors which it would be ridiculous to employ in other species of composition or in the course of ordinary conversation. In Greek, indeed, this was especially the case. Tragedy was intimately associated with religion, and had in fact developed itself from a rude religious ceremonial. Moreover, the characters were gods and demigods, and the poet took as much care to elevate his diction above that of common life as the actor to increase the proportions of his figure and the sonorousness of his voice.

A careful comparison of the diction of Herodotus and the Attic tragedians confirms in a marvellous degree this theory as to the peculiar characteristics of the latter.

Even if the choric odes and other lyrical passages are left unregarded—and throughout this inquiry they have been altogether set aside—there remains in the senarii alone a very large number of words which are found elsewhere only in Ionic.

In the first place, a writer of Tragedy used at pleasure many forms of words unknown in Comedy or Prose but normal in Ionic. Thus, while in Attic *ἐκεῖνος* was the only form known, the tragedians, like Herodotus, use *κεῖνος* or *ἐκεῖνος* indifferently. The shorter form never occurs in Comedy except[1] in Arist. Pax 46, as an intended Ionicism—

> Ἰωνικός τίς φησι παρακαθημένος,
> δοκέω μέν, ἐς Κλέωνα ταῦτ' αἰνίσσεται
> ὡς κεῖνος ἀναιδέως τὴν σπατίλην ἐσθίει.

[1] In Vesp. 751. it occurs in a chorus, and it is cited from the comic poet Phrynichus. But the line, if not hopelessly corrupt, is meant for Ionic,—

> κείνη μεμνήσθω με ξύλον ὑποτεταγός.

The Ionic ξυνός (=κοινός), Hdt. 4. 12; 7. 53, etc., is found in Aesch. Sept. 76, Supp. 367.

ἀείδω (=ᾄδω), Hdt. 1. 24; 2. 60, etc., occurs in Aesch. Agam. 16. Similarly ἀοιδή (=ᾠδή) in Hdt. 2. 79, and Soph. Ant. 883. ἀοιδός (=ᾠδός) in Hdt. 1. 24; Soph. O. R. 36; Eur. Heracl. 403, et al.

ἀείρω=αἴρω, Hdt. 2. 125; 4. 150; Soph. Ant. 418.

ἀΐσσω=ᾄσσω, Hdt. 4. 134; 9. 62; Aesch. Pers. 470; Eur. Hec. 31.

γούνατος, γούνατα, etc.,=γόνατος, γόνατα, Hdt. 2. 80; 4. 152; 9. 76, etc.; Soph. O. C. 1607; Eur. Hec. 752, etc.

ζόη=ζωή, Hdt. 1. 32, 85, 157, etc.; Soph. Fr. 509.

ζα- for δια- in compounds, as ζάπλουτος, Hdt. 1. 32; Eur. Andr. 1283. Cp. ζαχρεῖος, Aesch. Supp. 194; ζαπληθής, Pers. 316; ζάθεος, Eur. freq.; ζάχρυσος, Eur.

These instances are but typical of a large class which even a careless student of Tragedy will be able to extend at pleasure. It is sufficient here to indicate the relation which such variations from ordinary usage bear to the question under discussion. Another important class consists of words used in Tragedy and Ionic in the simple form, but which in Attic are invariably compounded.

In Attic there is not a single instance of the simple verb ἀντιοῦμαι, 'I oppose.' The compound ἐναντιοῦμαι has taken its place. But to the numerous instances afforded by Ionic, Hdt. 1. 76, 207; 4. 1, 3, 126; 7. 9, 139, 168; 8. 100; 9. 26; Aeschylus, in Supp. 389, presents a parallel,—

. . τίς ἂν τοῖσδ' ἀντιωθῆναι θέλοι;

For the Ionic ὀχλῶ (Hdt. 5. 41) Attic writers used the compound ἐνοχλῶ, but the simple verb is found both in Aeschylus and Sophocles (P. V. 1001; O. R. 446).

Still more marked is the case of αἰνῶ, which in Hdt. 3. 76; 5. 113; Soph. Aj. 526, Phil. 451, 889, and in Euripides and Aeschylus repeatedly, is used for the Attic ἐπαινῶ.

Other instances are ἄγνυμι for κατάγνυμι[1], ἀντῶ for ἀπαντῶ[2], ἕζομαι for καθέζομαι[3], ἱκνοῦμαι for ἀφικνοῦμαι[4], and the list might easily be increased. Some care, however, must be taken to select only well-marked instances for purposes of speculation. Thus the simple form of ἀράσσω, which is common enough in Tragedy[5], is found in Prose only in Hdt. 6. 44, but the line of Aristophanes (Eccl. 977),—

A. καὶ τὴν θύραν γ' ἤραττες. B. ἀποθάνοιμ' ἄρα,

puts it beyond a doubt that the word might, on occasion, have been used in prose, as it was certainly employed in every-day life.

On the other hand, Ionic writers and Tragedians frequently use a compound word in cases in which an Attic prose author would prefer the simple form. Before a language is matured, and that feeling of language developed, which sees in a common word the most suitable expression for a common action or fact, there is a tendency to make work-a-day words more expressive by compounding with a preposition. This stage of language still existed in Attica towards the close of the sixth century, and became one of the mannerisms of Tragic composition, being in this way carried on in literature to a time when such a tendency had disappeared from Attic employed under ordinary conditions. Ionic never got beyond this stage.

[1] Hdt. 1. 185; Eur. Hel. 410.

[2] Hdt. 1. 114; 2. 119; Aesch. Supp. 323; Soph. Aj. 533, Trach. 902; Eur. Ion 802.

[3] Hdt. 4. 85; 8. 22; Aesch. Eum. 3; Soph. O. R. 32, O. C. 100; Eur. Heracl. 344, Ion 1202, El. 109, 1259, etc.

[4] Hdt. 1. 216; very frequent in all three Tragedians. In Thuc. 1. 99, the simple is used in the peculiar sense of *be suitable*, which is also found in Hdt. 2. 36; 6. 57, 84.

[5] Aesch. P. V. 58, Pers. 460; Soph. O. R. 1276, Ant. 52, Aj. 725, Phil. 374; Eur. Hec. 1044, I. T. 327. The compounds are comparatively common in Prose and Comedy, the following passages being cited by Veitch:—ἐξαράξει, Ar. Thesm. 704; ἐξήραξα, Eq. 641; κατήραξε, Dem. 675. 19; ἐπήραξε, Plato, Prot. 314 D; ἀπαράξητε, Thuc. 7. 63; κατηράχθη, Thuc. 7. 6.

The preposition ἐκ, ἐξ is of all the most frequently employed in thus extending verbs. In Sophocles especially it would almost seem as if any verb might be compounded with it. He is the only Greek writer who uses ἐκθεᾶσθαι, ἐκλήγειν, ἐκπροτιμᾶν, ἐκσημαίνειν, ἐκστέλλεσθαι (of dress), ἐκχρῆν (of the responses of Apollo), ἐξανάγεσθαι, ἐξατιμάζειν, ἐξεφίεσθαι (=προστάττειν), none of which differ at all from the simple verbs, except in being in a slight degree more picturesque. Similarly there is as little difference between ἐκθύειν, ἐκλαγχάνειν, ἐκμανθάνειν, ἐκπείθειν, ἐκπυνθάνεσθαι, ἐκσώζειν, ἐκτιμᾶν, ἐκφοβεῖσθαι, ἐξαιτεῖν, ἐξακούειν, ἐξαναγκάζειν, ἐξανέχεσθαι, ἐξαπαλλάσσεσθαι, ἐξαποφθείρειν, ἐξελευθεροστομεῖν, ἐξεπίστασθαι, ἐξικετεύειν, and the forms not compounded with this preposition. The verbs ἐξαπολλύναι, ἐξεμπολᾶν, and ἐξημεροῦν for ἀπολλύναι, ἐμπολᾶν, and ἡμεροῦν, are a few out of many instances common to the Tragedians with Herodotus[1]. Of compounds with other prepositions, ἀνακαίειν[2] and ἀνακλαίειν[3] for κάειν and κλάειν might be mentioned if the case of ἀπολαγχάνειν for the simple λαγχάνειν did not present itself as a deterrent. The compound occurs repeatedly in Herodotus, and once in Euripides[4], but in Attic Prose only in Lys. 101. 3, and not in Comedy at all. But that it was really not uncommon in both these kinds of composition is attested by Harpocration in his Lexicon to the Ten Orators—'Απολαχεῖν: ἀντὶ ἁπλοῦ τοῦ λαχεῖν 'Αντιφῶν ἐν τῷ κατὰ Φιλίνου, Λυσίας κατὰ Ποσειδίππου, 'Αριστοφάνης Ταγηνισταῖς. In fact this feeling towards picturesque compounds is one which, though especially characteristic of the immaturity of a language, can never be said to have

[1] ἐξαπόλλυμι, Hdt. 1. 92, 2. 171; Aesch. Agam. 528; Soph. El. 588; Eur. Tro. 1215, Heracl. 950. ἐξεμπολῶ, Hdt. 1. 1; Soph. Ant. 1036, Phil. 303. ἐξημερῶ, Hdt. 1. 126; Eur. H. F. 20, 852.

[2] ἀνακαίω, Hdt. 4. 145; 5. 19; 8. 19; Eur. Cycl. 383; Xenophon has it, Anab. 3. 1. 3, ἀνέκαυσαν τὸ πῦρ.

[3] ἀνακλαίω, Hdt. 3. 14, 66; Soph. Phil. 939; Antiphon uses it, 119. 23, τὰς παρούσας ἀτυχίας ἀνακλαύσασθαι πρὸς ὑμᾶς.

[4] Hdt. 4. 114, 115, 145; 5. 57; 7. 23; Eur. H. F. 331.

wholly disappeared from it. All that it is necessary to demonstrate in the present case is that it had become exceedingly rare in Attic at a time when it was still in full force in Tragedy and the Ionic dialect.

But to pass to another feature which these present in common. Words rare in prose occur with frequency both in Herodotus and the Tragic poets, which is equivalent to saying that words in common use in the Attic of the time when Tragedy became a distinct style retained a literary status as long as the Tragic drama continued, although, for all other purposes, they were practically obsolete in Attic speech and writing. Such a word is the adverb *κάρτα*. It occurs with extraordinary frequency[1] in Ionic and in Tragedy, but hardly at all in Attic Comedy or Prose. In Plat. Tim. p. 25 D, *πηλοῦ κάρτα βραχέος*, it has been perhaps rightly restored from the Parisian manuscript for the vulgate *καταβραχέος*, but it would be difficult to discover another Prose instance. Of the two times which it occurs in Aristophanes, one at least proves its un-Attic character. In Ach. 544—

> *καθῆσθ' ἂν ἐν δόμοισιν; ἦ πολλοῦ γε δεῖ·*
> *καὶ κάρτα μέντἂν εὐθέως καθείλκετε—*

the preceding words *ἦ πολλοῦ γε δεῖ·* certainly come from the Telephus of Euripides, as do several more clauses and lines immediately before and after, and if *καὶ κάρτα μέντἂν* is not directly from the same source, the word *κάρτα* is beyond question intended to harmonize with the parody.

For the other instance—

> *ταῦτα μὲν ληρεῖς ἔχων*
> *κάρτα· πῶς κλαύσει γὰρ ἣν ἅπαξ γε τὠφθαλμὼ 'κκοπῇς;*—
> Av. 342.

there must be some similar reason, as in the only other

[1] Hdt. 1. 71, 88; 3. 80, 104; 7. 16, etc.; Hippocrates, p. 393. 51, 394. 53, etc. In Aeschylus over thirty times, in Sophocles about twenty times, and in Euripides fourteen or fifteen times.

passage of Comedy in which the word occurs—Ameipsias in Athen. 11. 783 E.—

A. αὔλει μοι μέλος,
σὺ δ' ᾆδε πρός· τήνδ' ἐκπίομαι δ' ἐγὼ τέως.
B. αὔλει σύ, καὶ σὺ τὴν ἄμυστιν λάμβανε,
"οὐ χρὴ πόλλ' ἔχειν θνητὸν ἄνθρωπον
ἀλλ' ἐρᾶν καὶ κατεσθίειν· σὺ δὲ κάρτα φείδει"—

it forms part of a drinking song, like Iago's,

'Then take thine *auld* cloak about thee.'

Another word almost equally significant is φρήν. In Herodotus it is found in 3. 134; 7. 13; 9. 10[1]; and in Tragedy repeatedly—about two hundred times in all. Of the numerous Aristophanic instances all occur either in the lyrical passages, in parody, or in paratragedy, except Nub. 153—

ὦ Ζεῦ βασιλεῦ, τῆς λεπτότητος τῶν φρενῶν—

and Thesm. 291, Ran. 534, Lys. 432; where it forms part of the phrase νοῦς καὶ φρένες, which is a survival of the old Ionic Attic, and common even in Prose, as in Dem. de Cor. 332. 20, μάλιστα μὲν καὶτούτοις βελτίω τινὰ νοῦν καὶ φρένας ἐνθεῖτε, Ib. 780. 11, νοῦ καὶ φρενῶν ἀγαθῶν καὶ προνοίας πολλῆς. A similar survival is its use with words like συμφορά to denote aberration of intellect, as in Andoc. 20. 29. It is found twice in Plato, but in a connection which strengthens this account of the history of the word. In both cases, Theaet. 154 D, Conviv. 199 A[2], it refers to the famous line in the Hippolytus of Euripides—

ἡ γλῶσσ' ὀμώμοχ', ἡ δὲ φρὴν ἀνώμοτος—

so often parodied by Aristophanes.

The survival of φρήν in the phrase νοῦς καὶ φρένες has

[1] Cp. φρενήρης, Hdt. 3. 25, 30; 5. 42; 9. 55; Eur. Heracl. 150, El. 1053.

[2] The passages are, Theaet. ἀτάρ, ὡς ἔοικεν, ἐὰν ἀποκρίνῃ ὅτι ἔστιν, Εὐριπίδειόν τι συμβήσεται· ἡ μὲν γὰρ γλῶττα ἀνέλεγκτος ἡμῖν ἔσται, ἡ δὲ φρὴν οὐκ ἀνελέγκτος ... εἰ μὲν δεινοὶ καὶ σοφοὶ ἐγώ τε καὶ σὺ ἦμεν, παντὰ τὰ τῶν φρενῶν ἐξητάκοτες: Conviv. ἡ γλῶττα οὖν ὑπέσχετο, ἡ δὲ φρὴν οὔ.

many parallels, and Comedy is often very useful in preserving these remnants of every-day language in cases in which there was naturally little occasion for their appearance in Prose. Thus the old word σθένος survives in Prose[1] only in the phase παντὶ σθένει, but Comedy has preserved a similar use of the verb σθένω—

οὐ γὰρ προσήκει τὴν ἐμαυτοῦ μοι πόλιν
εὐεργετεῖν, ὦ κέπφε καθ' ὅσον ἂν σθένω;
Ar. Plut. 912.

The same is true of θείνω, which, like the simple ἀράσσω already mentioned (p. 6), occurs out of Tragedy only in Comic verse—

οὗτος σὺ ποῖ θεῖς; οὐ μενεῖς; ὡς εἰ θενεῖς
τὸν ἄνδρα τοῦτον, αὐτὸς ἀρθήσει τάχα.
Arist. Ach. 564.

ἀλλ' οἶσθ' ὃ δράσον; τῷ σκέλει θένε τὴν πέτραν.
Av. 54.

But of all these survivals perhaps the most interesting is that of the aorist ἐμάστιξα. Every one will remember its use in Homer—

μάστιξεν δ' ἐλάαν· καναχὴ δ' ἦν ἡμιόνοιϊν·

but it will surprise many to hear that it had become a term of the kitchen. Athenaeus (7. 322 d,) quotes from the Leuce of Alexis the lines—

A. ἐπίστασαι τὸν σαῦρον ὡς δεῖ σκευάσαι;
B. ἀλλ' ἂν διδάσκῃς. A. ἐξελὼν τὰ βραγχία,
πλύνας, περικόψας τὰς ἀκάνθας τὰς κύκλῳ,
παράσχισον χρηστῶς, διαπτύξας θ' ὅλον
τῷ σιλφίῳ μάστιξον εὖ τε, καὶ καλῶς
τυρῷ τε σάξον ἁλσί τ' ἠδ'[2] ὀριγάνῳ—

[1] Dem. 30. 12; Thuc. 5. 23; Plat. Legg. 646 A, 854 B; Xen. Cyrop. 6. 1. 42; 8. 5. 25, Hell. 6. 5. 2, Rep. Lac. 4. 5. In Plato, Phaedr. 267 C, τὸ τοῦ Χαλκηδονίου σθένος in humorous passage = ὁ Χαλκηδόνιος.

[2] ἠδέ is certainly corrupt here. We must read ἁλσὶν εἶτ' ὀριγάνῳ, or some such word.

in which a master is giving directions to his new cook how he likes a fish of a certain kind dressed. After being boned it is to be well *whipped* or dusted with silphium and stuffed with cheese, salt, and marjoram.

Another passage indicates that it was probably the word used by boys when spinning tops. In the Baptae of Eupolis[1] occur the words—

ὦ ῥύμβοισι μαστίξας ἐμέ·

but the context is required to make them quite clear.

It is in this way that the use of ῥύεσθαι in Thucydides ought probably to be explained. The word is otherwise unknown in Attic, and when Thucydides represents Agis (5. 63) as promising ἔργῳ ἀγαθῷ ῥύσεσθαι τὰς αἰτίας στρατευσάμενος, he is probably only giving a metaphorical turn to a word in common use among the tradesmen in the agora to denote their goods bringing down the weights on the opposite scale of the balance[2].

Ἀκτή is another word which almost by itself might demonstrate the truth of the theory at present under discussion. Though found repeatedly in Homer[3] in the sense of 'rocky foreland,' and in Herodotus[4] with the meaning 'littoral tract,' it is in Attic confined to Tragedy[5], except in one case, namely, when it refers to the coast-district of Attica. Harpocration tells us that Hyperides so used it: Ἀκτή, ἐπιθαλαττίδιός τις μοῖρα τῆς Ἀττικῆς· Ὑπερείδης ἐν τῷ περὶ τοῦ ταρίχους, and in Dinarchus, 110. 2, it is found

[1] Quoted Fr. Com. 2. 452. The ῥύμβος was in this 'a metal top,' used in celebrating the orgies of Kotytto by her 'licentiates' the Baptae.

[2] ῥύομαι, Hdt. 3. 119, 132; 4. 164, 187, etc.; Aesch. Eum. 232, 300, Supp. 509 et al.; Soph. O. C. 285, Aj. 1276, O. R. 72, 312, 313; Eur. Alc. 11, et freq.

[3] Il. 2. 395; 20. 50; Od. 5. 405; 10. 89, etc.

[4] Hdt. 4. 38; 7. 183. Xenophon, un-Attic as usual, employs it in An. 6. 2. ἐθεώρουν τὴν Ἰασονίαν ἀκτήν.

[5] Aesch. Pers. 303, 421, 449, Eum. 10, Ag. 493, and freq. in ch.; Soph. Phil. 1, 272, 1017; Aeg. fr. 19. 3; Captiv. fr. 42, and in chor.; Eurip. Hec. 778, Hipp. 1199, and very frequently.

in a suggestive series: ἐν οἷς (sc. τοῖς χρήμασι) καὶ ἡ ἀκτὴ καὶ οἱ λιμένες εἰσὶ καὶ τὰ νεώρια ἃ οἱ πρόγονοι ὑμῖν κατασκευάσαντες κατέλιπον[1].

No evidence could be more distinct. It was plainly a word in daily use in Attica before the Ionic then spoken had gone far in the peculiar path which was to end in the Attic dialect, and its application to the coast-district began at that time. In the sixth century it was dropping out of use, but received a new lease of life from becoming part of the literary dialect of Tragedy.

Exactly the same history belongs to another old Attic word. Its attachment to a natural feature of the country preserved it un-modified, just as the peculiar Greek tendency of literary styles to become permanent brought it down in Tragedy to a period when it had disappeared in all other literature but the Ionic. The name ζωστήρ, the Ionic and old Attic equivalent of ζώνη, had at an early date been bestowed upon a tongue of land between the Piraeus and Sunium[2], which resembled the ζωστήρ in shape, and is mentioned under that name both by Herodotus and Xenophon[3]. Thus even the stones cry out against regarding the peculiarly Tragic forms of words as due to no more than a craving for elevation of style.

Of a piece with the use of compound verbs for simple, already discussed, is the preference for picturesque words with a dash of metaphor in them over their more tame

[1] Strabo, 9. 391 b, thus describes the district, ἀκτὴ δ' ἐστὶν ἀμφιθάλαττος, στενὴ τὸ πρῶτον, εἶτ' εἰς τὴν μεσογαίαν πλατύνεται, μηνοειδῆ δ' οὐδὲν ἧττον ἐπιστροφὴν λαμβάνει πρὸς Ὠρωπὸν τῆς Βοιωτίας, τὸ κυρτὸν ἔχουσα πρὸς θαλάττῃ.

[2] Strabo, 398.

[3] Hdt. 8. 107, ἐπεὶ δὲ ἀγχοῦ ἦσαν Ζωστῆρος πλεόντες οἱ βάρβαροι κτε.: Xen. Hell. 5. 1. 9, ἐπεὶ δὲ ἦσαν αἱ (νῆες) τοῦ Εὐνόμου πρὸς τῇ γῇ περὶ Ζωστῆρα τῆς Ἀττικῆς κτε. A surname of Apollo, viz. Ζωστήριος, was probably derived from a temple on this spot. Cp. Πορθμός, a town in Euboea, mentioned by Dem. 248. 15; 119. 21; 125. 26; 133. 21: πορθμός is old Attic for πόρος. Ἄρειος πάγος: πάγος for *hill* is never once found in Attic prose or comedy, but occurs in Aesch. P. V. 20, 270, Supp. 189, etc.; Soph. O. C. 1601; Ant. 411, etc.; Eur. El. 1271, etc.

equivalents. Take, for instance, αἰχμή. Even in its ordinary sense[1] the word was probably un-Attic, having been replaced by δόρυ, but in the signification of *war* it had certainly disappeared altogether. Yet that with that meaning it had once been in common use is proved by the compound αἰχμάλωτος, which must have had an emphatically metaphorical origin. From the development of Attic such a metaphorical use had become impossible in that dialect; but it had been, as it were, crystallised in Tragedy, and remained in use in Ionic. Thus Herodotus could say not only (5. 94), Σίγειον εἶλε Πεισίστρατος αἰχμῇ, but even (7. 152), ἐπειδή σφι πρὸς τοὺς Λακεδαιμονίους κακῶς ἡ αἰχμὴ ἑστήκεε, and in Tragedy occur the expressions αἰχμὴν εἰς μίαν καθέστατον for εἰς μονομαχίαν (Eur. Phoen. 1273); κακοὶ ὄντες πρὸς αἰχμήν (Soph. Phil. 1306); and αἰχμὴ θηρῶν (Eur. H. F. 158), a 'battle with wild beasts.'

Εὐφρόνη is another of these words. No Attic writer would have used it for νύξ; but not only does it occur in Herodotus more frequently than the soberer term, but even a scientific writer like Hippocrates employs it[2].

Again, if we compare the usage of πάλος[3] and κλῆρος, it will be seen that the more picturesque of the two words has in all Attic, but that of Tragedy, been ousted by the colourless term, though in Ionic prose the former remained the commoner. And that πάλος really retained much of its primitive colour is proved by the line of Euripides

[1] Hdt. 1. 8, 39, 52; 3. 78. 128; 5. 49; 7. 61, 64, 69, 77, etc. and in the Tragedians very frequently. Xenophon has it, Cyr. 4. 6. 4; 8. 1. 8. μεταίχμιον did not survive in Attic, but occurs, Hdt. 6. 77, 112, cp. 8. 140; Aesch. Sept. 197; Eur. Phoen. 1240, 1279, 1361, Heracl. 803.

[2] Hdt. 7. 56, διέβη δὲ ὁ στρατὸς αὐτοῦ ἐν ἕπτα ἡμέρῃσι καὶ ἐν ἕπτα εὐφρόνῃσι: 9. 37, τρίτῃ εὐφρόνῃ, so 7. 12, 188; 8. 12, 14; 9. 39; Hippocrates, 588. 42, δύο ἡμέρας καὶ δύο εὐφρόνας: id. 1275. 32, ἡμέρην καὶ εὐφρόνην: Aesch. P. V. 655, Pers. 180. 221, Agam. 265, 279, 337, 522; Soph. El. 19, 259, Fr. 521, 11; Eur. Hec. 828, I. A. 109, 1571, Rh. 92, 518, 617, Tro. 660, etc.

[3] Hdt. 3. 80; 4. 94, 153; Aesch. Sept. 55, 376, Agam. 333, Pers. 779, Eum. 32, 742, 753; Soph. Ant. 275; Eur. I. A. 1151, Tro. 263, Ion 416, Heracl. 546.

(Iph. Aul. 1151), where Clytemnestra addresses Agamemnon in the words—

βρέφος τε τοὐμὸν σῷ προσουρίσας πάλῳ
μαστῶν βιαίως τῶν ἐμῶν ἀποσπάσας.

But it would be tedious to discuss each separate instance of this one characteristic of immaturity in language. There are still too many points to consider which throw light on the way in which the old Ionic of Attica developed into a language of such marvellous precision and strength as the Attic dialect certainly is. But it is hard to refrain from enumerating, however cursorily, a few more old Ionicisms like εὐφρόνη and αἰχμή. Such are ἀγορᾶσθαι[1] in the sense of λέγειν or εἰπεῖν, ἁμαξευμένος in the sense of 'provided with carriage roads[2],' ἀμφιδέξιος, *ambiguous*[3], ἀπότιμος[4] for ἄτιμος, ἄρθμιος[5] for φίλος, ἁρμόζεσθαι[6] for γαμεῖν, ἄρουρα[7] for γῆ, ἄτρυτος[8] for ἰσχυρός or μέγας, ἐγχρίμπτειν[9] for ἐφάπτεσθαι, ἐκπαγλεῖσθαι[10] for θαυμάζειν, ἐλαστρῶ[11] for

[1] Hdt. 6. 11; Soph. Tr. 601, ἕως σὺ ταῖς ἔξωθεν ἠγορῶ ξέναις.

[2] Hdt. 2. 108, Αἴγυπτον ἱππάσιμον καὶ ἁμαξευμένην, followed by Αἴγυπτος ἐοῦσα πεδιὰς πᾶσα ἄνιππος καὶ ἀναμάξευτος γέγονε: Soph. Ant. 251, στυφλὸς δὲ γῆ καὶ χέρσος ἀρρὼξ οὐδ' ἐπημαξευμένη τροχοῖσιν, where observe the Ionicism for ἐφημαξευμένη.

[3] ἀμφιδέξιος, lit. of a man who can use his left hand as dexterously as his right; opp. ἀμφαρίστερος. Hdt. 5. 92, χρηστήριον ἀμφιδέξιον, *an ambiguous response:* Aesch. Frag. 259, ἀμφιδεξίως ἔχει, *it is indifferent.* In Eur. Hipp. 780 = ἀμφηκής, ἀμφιδέξιον σίδηρον: Soph. O. C. 1112 uses the sing. in the signification *both.*

[4] Hdt. 2. 167; Soph. O. R. 215.

[5] Hdt. 6. 83, 7. 101, 9. 9, 37. So ἀρθμός = φιλία in Aesch. P. V. 191.

[6] Hdt. 3. 137; 5. 32, 47; 6. 65; Soph. Ant. 570; cp. ἁρμόζω = 'give in marriage,' Hdt. 9. 108; Eur. Phoen. 411.

[7] Hdt. 2. 14; Aesch. Pers. 595; Soph. Tr. 32, Aj. 1286; Eur. Or. 553, H. F. 369.

[8] Hdt. 9. 52, ἄτρ. πόνος: Aesch. Eum. 403, ἄτρ. πόδα: Soph. Aj. 788, ἄτρ. κακόν.

[9] Hdt. 2. 60, 93; 3. 85; 4. 113; 9. 98; Hippocr. de Artic. p. 800, B, de Oss. nat. 280. 12, de Morb. mul. 2. p. 654, 23; Soph. El. 898. The simple χρίμπτω, χρίμπτομαι, occurs Aesch. Eum. 185, P. V. 713; Soph. El. 721.

[10] Hdt. 7. 181; 8. 92; 9. 48; Aesch. Cho. 217; Eur. Or. 890, Tro. 929, Hec. 1157. Confined to the participle.

[11] Hdt. 2. 158; 7. 24; Eur. I. T. 934, 971. Cp. βωστρέω for βοῶ.

ἐλαύνω, ἐμπρέπειν[1] for φανερὸς εἶναι, φονεύω[2], or καταφονεύω[3], for ἀποκτείνω, ἐρείπια[4] for λείψανα, ἐφέστιος[5] for ἱκέτης, θεήλατος[6], *sent from heaven*=θεῖος, στρατηλατῶ[7] for στρατεύομαι, θεοπρόπος[8] for θέωρος, θωκῶ[9] for καθῆμαι, ἰθαγενής[10] for αὐτόχθων, κασίγνητος[11] for ἀδελφός, κέρτομος[12] for ὑβριστικός, κληδών[13] for φήμη, μόρος[14] for θάνατος, μυσαρός[15] for μιαρός, ὅμαιμος[16] for συγγενής,

[1] Hdt. 7. 67, 83; Aesch. Ag. 6, 1428; Soph. El. 1187; Eur. Heracl. 407.

[2] Hdt. 1. 211; 8. 53 Soph. O. R. 716, 1411, Ant. 1174, El. 34; Eur. Andr. 412, Or. 1193, etc. In Plat. Legg. 871 D, 873 E, in legal language.

[3] Hdt. 1. 106, 165; 2. 45; 3. 157; Eur. Or. 536, 625.

[4] Hdt. 2. 154; 4. 124; Aesch. Agam. 660, Pers. 425; Soph. Aj. 308; Eur. Bac. 7, etc. ἐρείπω, *throw down*, is found in Hdt. 1. 164; 9. 70; Hippocrates, Epid. 6. 1174 G; Soph. Aj. 309, O. C. 1373; Xen. Cyr. 7. 4. 1.

[5] Hdt. 1. 35; Aesch. Supp. 365, 503, Eum. 577, 669; Soph. Trach. 262.

[6] Hdt. 7. 18; Aesch. Agam. 1297; Soph. O. R. 255, Ant. 278; Eur. Or. 2, Andr. 851, Ion 1306, 1392.

[7] Hdt. 1. 124, 154; 4. 118; 5. 31; 7. 5, 10; Aesch. Pers. 717, Eum. 690; Eur. Or. 717, Supp. 234, I. A. 1195, Heracl. 465, et al.

[8] Hdt. 1. 48, 67, 78, and frequently; Aesch. P. V. 659.

[9] Hdt. 2. 173. Tragic θακῶ, Aesch. P. V. 313, 389; Soph. O. R. 20, O. C. 340, Aj. 325, 1173, Tr. 23; Eur. Heracl. 239.

[10] Hdt. 2. 17; 6. 53; Hippocrates, de Morb. mul. 1. 70, de Infaec. 16; Aesch. Pers. 306.

[11] Hdt. 1. 171; Aesch. P. V. 347, Sept. 632, Agam. 327; Soph. and Eurip. very frequently. It occurs in Comic senarii in Arist. Thesm. 900, but in παρατραγῳδία with πόσις to keep it in countenance.

[12] Hdt. 5. 83; Eur. Alc. 1125, Fr. 495. The tragedians also use κερτομῶ, Aesch. P. V. 986; Soph. Phil. 1235; Eur. Bac. 1294, Hel. 619; and κερτόμησις is found in Soph. Phil. 1236.

[13] Hdt. 5. 72; 9. 91, 101; Aesch. Agam. 863, 874, Cho. 853, etc.; Soph. O. C. 258, Phil. 255; Eur. Alc. 315, etc. The only instance in Attic is Andocides, 17. 9, **κληδὼν** ἐν ἁπάσῃ τῇ πόλει κατέσχεν . . . . πῶς οὖν ἡ **φήμη** ἡ τότε οὖσα κτε.; which probably indicates that the word was still in use among the people.

[14] Hdt. 1. 117; 3. 65, etc., and very frequently in all three tragedians. Similarly **μόρσιμος** occurs, Hdt. 3. 154; Aesch. P. V. 933, Sept. 263, 281, etc.; Soph. Ant. 236; Eur. Rh. 636, Al. 939, etc.

[15] Hdt. 2. 37; Eur. Or. 1624, et al. It occurs in Ar. Lys. 340, but in a chorus.

[16] Hdt. 1. 151; 8. 144; and very freq. in all three tragedians. On the authority of an anonymous Grammarian, Cramer, Anecd. 3. 195, the lines—

οὐδεὶς ὁμαίμου συμπαθέστερος φίλος,
κἂν ᾖ τοῦ γένους μακράν,

are assigned to the comic poet Plato; but on his own confession the Grammarian preserved neither λέξις nor μέτρον, only τὸν νοῦν τοῦ βιβλίου ἀποτεταμίευκε.

ὁμῆλιξ[1] for *ἡλικιώτης*, *στρατάρχης*[2] for *στρατηγός*, *φατίζω*[3] for *λέγω*. The significance of *χειρῶναξ* and its derivations is too great to allow of no more than a Nota bene. No words could be more picturesque, yet they are used in sober, every-day language in Ionic. Herod. 2. 167, *τοὺς δὲ ἀπαλλαγμένους τῶν χειρωναξιέων, γενναίους νομίζοντας εἶναι*, and Hippocrates, 384. 46, 391. 45. In Attic *χειρωναξία* is simply *τέχνη* and *χειρῶναξ*, *χειροτέχνης*, but in Tragedy the old highly-coloured expressions have been preserved without modification[4]. There can be no explanation of facts so anomalous, but the one which can not be reiterated too often, namely, that, if allowance is made for the peculiarities of metrical composition, Tragedy can supply the student of Attic with many of the most essential characteristics of that dialect during the sixth century[5].

Picturesqueness of metaphor is another quality which is not so much inherent in Attic Tragedy as Tragedy, but derived from the tendency of language at the time when the Tragic diction was formed. It is difficult to reach certainty in a speculation of this sort if only the more general aspects of the question are considered; accordingly,

Moreover *συμπαθέστερος* is probably a late word. Similarly *ὁμαίμων*, Hdt 5. 49; Trag. frequently.

[1] Hdt. 1. 99; Eur. Hipp. 1098, Alc. 953, Tro. 1183, Bac. 201.

[2] Hdt. 3. 157; 8. 45; Aesch. Fr. 176.

[3] Hdt. 5. 58; Eur. I. A. 135, 936.

[4] *χειρωναξία*, Hdt. 2. 167; Aesch. P. V. 45, Cho. 761. *χειρῶναξ*, Hdt. 1. 93; 2. 141; Eur. Fr. 793.

[5] Additional instances of these highly-coloured words are these:—**ἀλλόθροος**, Hdt. 1. 78; 3. 11; Aesch. Ag. 1200; Soph. Phil. 540. **δυσπετέως** = *χαλεπῶς*, Hdt. 3. 107; Hippocr. 456. 22; Aesch. P. V. 752; adj. Soph. Aj. 1046. **ὁδόω** = *put on the right road*, Hdt. 4. 139; Aesch. P. V. 498, 813. **σέλας** = *bright light*, Hdt. 3. 28; Tragedy very freq. It occurs in Plato, Crat. 409 B, but simply in the linguistic statement *σέλας καὶ φῶς ταὐτόν*. **ὑπερτέλλω**, *rise above* = Att. *ἐξέχω*, Hdt 3. 104; Eur. Or. 6, Hec. 1010, Phoen. 1007. Words which are Attic in other significations have a specially picturesque meaning in Ionic and Tragedy. As *κάμνω* = *χαλεπῶς φέρω*, Hdt. 1. 118; Eur. H. F. 293, Med. 1138. *κατεργάζομαι* = *ἀποκτείνω*, Hdt. 1. 24; Soph. Trach. 1094; Eur. Hipp. 888, I. T. 1173 (Xen. Cyr. 4. 6. 4). *ἐξεργάζομαι* = id., Hdt. 3. 52; 4. 134; 5. 19; Eur. Hel. 1098. *νομός* = *dwelling place*, Hdt. 5. 92 et al.; Eur. Rhes. 477.

the following instances have been selected to show that in the metaphorical use of particular words Ionic and the Tragic dialect stand by themselves. Take the two compounds of *ζέω*, boil, *ἐκζέω*, boil over, and *ἐπιζέω*, boil up, seethe. In 4. 205, Herodotus employs the horribly suggestive sentence, *οὐ μὲν οὐδὲ ἡ Φερετίμη εὖ τὴν ζόην κατέπλεξε. ὡς γὰρ δὴ τάχιστα ἐκ τῆς Λιβύης τισαμένη τοὺς Βαρκαίους ἀπενόστησε ἐς τὴν Αἴγυπτον, ἀπέθανε κακῶς· ζῶσα γὰρ εὐλέων ἐξέζεσε, ὡς ἄρα ἀνθρώποισι αἱ λίην ἰσχυραὶ τιμωρίαι πρὸς θεῶν ἐπίφθονοι γίνονται.* The whole is oriental enough to come from the Old Testament, and in this question of metaphorical usage geographical considerations are not to be wholly disregarded. In Aesch. Sept. 709 the word is not too strong—

ἐξέζεσεν γὰρ Οἰδίπου κατεύγματα.

Again in Herod. 7. 13, *ἀκούσαντί μοι τῆς Ἀρταβάνου γνώμης παραυτίκα μὲν ἡ νεότης ἐπέζεσε*, the metaphor may be paralleled from Euripides—

δεινόν τι πῆμα Πριαμίδαις ἐπέζεσεν.

Hec. 583.

δεινή τις ὀργὴ δαιμόνων ἐπέζεσε[1].

I. T. 987.

Another excellent instance is afforded by the use of the verb *ἐκτρίβω*, which occurs repeatedly in Herodotus and the Tragedians, but in a metaphorical sense is never used elsewhere. In Herodotus, 6. 37, Croesus threatens the people of Lampsacus in words that hardly required the brutal jest on *Πιτυοῦσσα*, the ancient name of their city, to make them effective: *εἰ δὲ μή, σφέας πίτυος τρόπον ἀπείλεε ἐκτρίψειν. πλανωμένων δὲ τῶν Λαμψακηνῶν ἐν τοῖσι λόγοισι τὸ θέλει τὸ ἔπος εἶναι τό σφι ἀπείλησε ὁ Κροῖσος πίτυος τρόπον ἐκτρίψειν, μόγις κοτὲ μαθὼν τῶν τις πρεσβυτέρων εἶπε τὸ ἐόν, ὅτι πίτυς μούνη πάντων δενδρέων ἐκκοπεῖσα βλαστὸν οὐδένα*

[1] Arist. Thesm. 468 is paratragedic, while Ach. 321, *θυμάλωψ ἐπέζεσεν*, is evidently a burlesque on some Tragedian's *θυμὸς ἐπέζεσεν*, and proves that the metaphor in Herodotus was felt to be too strong for common use.

μετίει, ἀλλὰ πανώλεθρος[1] ἐξαπόλλυται. And in a later chapter (86) of the same book, is narrated the fulfilment of a doom prophesied by the Pythia, Γλαύκου νῦν οὔτε τι ἀπόγονόν ἐστι οὐδέν, οὔτ' ἱστίη οὐδεμία νομιζομένη εἶναι Γλαύκου, ἐκτέτριπταί τε πρόρριζος ἐκ Σπάρτης[2].

Now the Tragedians are the only Attic writers in whom a similar usage is discovered—

Ζεύς σ' ὁ γεννήτωρ ἐμὸς
πρόρριζον ἐκτρίψειεν οὐτάσας πυρί.
Eur. Hipp. 683.

κατεύχομαι δὲ τὸν δεδρακότ', εἴτε τις
εἷς ὢν λέληθεν εἴτε πλειόνων μέτα,
κακὸν κακῶς νιν ἄμορον ἐκτρῖψαι βίον.
Soph. O. R. 246.

Further on (O. R. 428) Teiresias ends his outburst of indignation at the charges of Oedipus in words that were too surely fulfilled—

πρὸς ταῦτα καὶ Κρέοντα καὶ τοὐμὸν στόμα
προπηλάκιζε. σοῦ γὰρ οὐκ ἔστιν βροτῶν
κάκιον ὅστις ἐκτριβήσεταί ποτε.

An aspect of the inquiry which has occasionally presented itself in considering other points, itself merits some attention. Words which, on the testimony of Tragedy, must have been used in old Attic, and which were never superseded in Ionic proper, were in the matured dialect of Attica replaced by other terms. These new words were either from the same root as the primitive ones, or of an origin altogether distinct. Of substantives of the former class πάτρα is a marked example. Herodotus never uses πατρίς, but πάτρη occurs in 6. 126, ἐνθαῦτα Ἑλλήνων ὅσοι σφίσι τε αὐτοῖσι ἦσαν καὶ πάτρῃ ἐξογκωμένοι, ἐφοίτεον μνηστῆρες, of the suitors for the hand of Aganiste, which Hippoclides

[1] Cp. Soph. El. 1009, πανωλέθρους . . . . ἡμᾶς τ' ὀλέσθαι.
[2] Cp. 4. 120, τὴν ποίην ἐκ τῆς γῆς ἐκτρίβειν.

was to win and humorously lose. In Tragedy it is found repeatedly, but in Attic prose not once, and the instances in Comedy are conclusive evidence that the word was considered merely a literary survival on the one hand, or an Ionicism on the other. Thus, Ar. Thesm. 136, Ran. 1163, and 1427, are all parodies of Tragedy, while in Ach. 147 there is a ludicrous point in the boy who has just been initiated at the great Ionic[1] festival of the Ἀπατούρια, and gorged with the sausages that symbolised Athenian citizenship, addressing his father in Ionic heroics, and calling upon him *βοηθεῖν τῇ πάτρᾳ*[2].

Other instances are *αἰγυπιός*[3] for *γύψ*, *γνῶμα*[4] for *γνώρισμα*, *γόνος*[5] for *γονή*, *δράμημα*[6] for *δρόμος*, *εἶμα*[7] for *ἔσθης*, *ζεύγλη*[8] for *ζύγον*, *ζωστήρ*[9] for *ζώνη*, *ἱππότης*[10] for *ἱππεύς*, *κλώψ*[11] for

[1] *Εἰσὶ δὲ πάντες Ἴωνες, ὅσοι ἀπ' Ἀθηνέων γεγόνασι καὶ Ἀπατούρια ἄγουσι ὁρτήν. ἄγουσι δὲ πάντες πλὴν Ἐφεσίων καὶ Κολοφωνίων· οὗτοι γὰρ μοῦνοι Ἰώνων οὐκ ἄγουσι Ἀπατούρια κτε.*, Hdt. 1. 147.

[2] The old term also supplied the poets of later comedy with material for a wretched pun, as Alexis quoted by Athenaeus, 3. 100. c.—

> *ὑπὲρ* **πάτρας** *μὲν πᾶς ἀποθνήσκειν θέλει,*
> *ὑπὲρ δὲ* **μήτρας** *Καλλιμέδων ὁ Κάραβος*
> *ἐφθῆς ἴσως προσεῖτ' ἂν ἄλλως ἀποθανεῖν.*

There is a similar pun on the words *μητρόπολις*, *πατρόπολις*, *μήτρα*, **Μητρᾶς**, and *ἔμμητρος*, in a fragment of Antiphanes, also preserved by Athenaeus in the same passage, 100. d.

[3] Hdt. 3. 76; Aesch. Ag. 49; Soph. Aj. 169. It is probably this fact that is referred to in Suidas, **αἰγυπιόν**· *οὕτως οἱ παλαιοί, ἀλλ' οὐ γῦπα*, and Bekk. An. 354. 28, for Arist. Av. 1181 is conclusive proof that *γύψ* was the Attic term.

[4] Hdt. 7. 52, *τῶν ἔχομεν γνῶμα μέγιστον*, and Soph. Trach. 593, *οὐδ' ἔχοις ἂν γνῶμα μὴ πειρωμένη.*

[5] In the sense of *proles, suboles*, Hdt. 1. 108, 109; 3. 66; 5. 92, etc.; Trag. frequently.

[6] Hdt. 8. 98; Aesch. Pers. 247; Eur. Tro. 688, et al.

[7] Hdt. 1. 10; 2. 155, et freq.; Hippocrates, de Morb. mul. 2. 640, 16; Aesch. Agam. 1383, Cho. 81; Soph. Aj. 1145, O. R. 1268, Fr. 451; Eur. Hec. 342, I. A. 73, Hel. 1574.

[8] Hdt. 1. 31; Aesch. P. V. 463; Eur. Med. 479, Hel. 1536.

[9] Hdt. 1. 215; 4. 9, 10; 9. 74; Soph. Aj. 1030; Eur. Heracl. 217 (see supra p. 12.)

[10] Substantive, Hdt. 9. 49, 69; Soph. O. C. 59; (Xen. Cyr. 1. 4. 18; 8. 8. 20.)

[11] Hdt. 1. 41; 2. 150; 6. 16; Eur. Alc. 766, Cycl. 223, Hel. 553, Rhes. 709; (Xen Cyr. 2. 4. 23; An. 4. 6. 17).

κλέπτης, ναυτίλος [1] for *ναύτης, ὅρισμα* [2] for *ὅρος, ὅριον, ὀφρύη* [3] for *ὀφρύς, ὄχος* [4] for *ὄχημα, παρηΐς* [5] for *παρειά, πορθμός* [6] for *πόρος, ῥεῖθρον* [7] for *ῥεῦμα, φάτις* [8] for *φήμη, φοναί* [9] for *φόνος, φόρτος* [10] for *φορτίον, χόλος* [11] for *χολή.*

The instances of adjectives of an older formation which have given place to those of a newer from the same stem are not so numerous, but there are still some marked examples, such as *ἄμωμος* [12] for *ἄμεμπτος, βιώσιμος* [13] for *βιωτός,* and conversely *εὐξύμβλητος* [14] for *εὐσύμβολος, νεοχμός* [15] for *νέος, πέτρινος* [16] for *πετρώδης,* and *χέρσος* [17] for *ξηρός.* A

[1] Hdt. 2. 43; Aesch. P. V. 468, Agam. 899, 1234, Cho. 202; Soph. Aj. 1146, Trach. 537; Eur. Hec. 1273, et al. In Arist. Ran. 1207, it is from Euripides. *ναυτίλλομαι,* which occurs in Hdt. 1. 163; 2. 5, 178; 3. 6; and in Soph. Ant. 717; Eur. fr. 791, is only found once in Attic Prose, Plat. Rep. 551 C.

[2] Hdt. 2. 17; 4. 45; Eur. Hec. 16, Hipp. 1459, Andr. 969, I. A. 952, Rhes. 437.

[3] Hdt. 4. 181, 182, 185; Eur. Heracl. 394.

[4] Hdt. 8. 124; Aesch. P. V. 710, Agam. 1070, Eum. 405; Soph. O. R. 808, El. 708, 727; Eur. frequently.

[5] Hdt. 2. 121; Aesch. Sept. 534; Eur. Hec. 274, et al.

[6] Hdt. 8. 76; Aesch. Pers. 722, 799, Agam. 307; Eur. Hel. 127, 532, Cycl. 108 (see p. 12, note 3).

[7] Hdt. 1. 75, 186, 191, and freq.; Aesch. P. V. 790, Pers. 497; Soph. Ant. 712; Eur. El. 794. In Aesch. Pers. 497 even the uncontracted Ionic form *ῥέεθρον* is retained. Antiphanes (quoted by Athenaeus 1. 22, f.) uses *ῥεῖθρον,* but in a parody of Soph. Ant. quoted.

[8] Hdt. 1. 60, 122; 7. 189 γ; 8. 94; 9. 84. Very frequently in all three tragedians.

[9] Hdt. 9. 76; Soph. Ant. 696, 1003, 1314; Eur. Hel. 154.

[10] Hdt. 1. 1; Soph. Tr. 537. In Eur. I. T. 1306, Supp. 20 = 'burden.' In the sense of *wretched stuff, chaff,* the word is good Attic, Ar. Pax 748, Plut. 796. Cp. *φορτικός.*

[11] Hdt. 1. 118; 6. 119; 8. 27; Aesch. P. V. 29, 199, 370, 376; Soph. Aj. 41, 744, Trach. 269, Phil. 328.

[12] Hdt. 2. 177; Aesch. Pers. 135.

[13] Hdt. 1. 45; 3. 109; Soph. Ant. 566; Eur. Heracl. 606.

[14] Hdt. 7. 57, *εὐξύμ. τέρας, easy to divine*; Aesch. P. V. 775, *ἥδ' οὐκέτ' εὐξύμβλητος ἡ χρησμῳδία.*

[15] Hdt. 9. 99, 104; Hippocr. 651, 36; 598, 12; Aesch. Pers. 693; Soph. Phil. 751; Eur. I. T. 1162, et al. Like many others of this class of words, it occurs in the Chorus in Aristophanes and other Comic writers, as Thesm. 701, Ran. 1372; Cratinus Fr. Com. 2. 101.

[16] Hdt. 2. 8; Eur. I. T. 290, et al.

[17] Hdt. 2. 99; 4. 123; Aesch. Agam. 558, Eum. 240, Supp. 178; Soph. Ant. 251, O. R. 1502; Eur. El. 325, etc.

class by itself consists of forms used adjectively, which in Attic were only substantival, as Ἑλλάς [1] for Ἑλληνική, Ἰλιάς [2] for Ἰλιακή, ἱππότης [3] for ἱππικός, and Περσίς [4] for Περσική. In the case of πίσυνος [5] an adjective is used where an Attic writer would prefer a participle, πιστεύων. Of verbs which became modified in Attic some have been already considered, but to these may be added ἀντιάζω [6] to ἀπαντῶ, πλάζομαι [7] to πλανῶμαι, and πτώσσω [8] to πτήσσω. Adverbs are more numerous, such as ἀγχοῦ [9], ἄγχιστα [10], ἀνέκαθεν [11], ἀρχῆθεν [12], μεταῦθις [13], πάγχυ [14], πέρ [15], σαφηνῶς [16]. Why these words and others like them were modified as the Attic dialect developed its more distinctive features it would be useless to discuss. The fact of their modification exists, and may be theorised upon by those who have the mind. But the field is a dangerous one to tread, and justifies the caution of the old proverb, ὑπὸ παντὶ λίθῳ σκορπίον φυλάσσεο. But if it is difficult to give a reason for mere alterations in the forms of words, in what way are

[1] Hdt. 4. 78; 6. 98; Aesch. Supp. 243, Pers. 186, 809; Soph. Phil. 223; Eur. I. T. 17, et al.

[2] Hdt. 7. 43; Eur. repeatedly.

[3] Hdt. 4. 136; Soph. O. C. 899; Eur. Supp. 660.

[4] Hdt. 6. 29; Aesch. Pers. repeatedly.

[5] Hdt. 1. 66, 73, 92; 2. 141; 7. 10, 85; 9. 143; Eur. Or. 905, Supp. 121. It is found, however, *once* in Attic prose, Thuc. 5. 14, τοῖς ἔξω πίσυνοι.

[6] Hdt. 1. 166; 4. 8; 9. 6; Aesch., Soph., Eur.

[7] Hdt. 2. 116; Eur. Or. 56, Rhes. 283, H. F. 1188.

[8] Hdt. 9. 48; Eur. Bacch. 223.

[9] In Att. ἐγγύς, Hdt. 1. 190; 3. 78, 85, 111; 6. 77; Soph. Frag. 69 (D).

[10] Hdt. 1. 134; 4. 81; 5. 79; Aesch. Supp. 1036. In Hdt. 2. 143, it is used of time, ὁ ἄγχιστα ἀποθανών, a sense which is also found in Antiphon, 115. 25, a signification also attaching to the Attic ἐγγύτατα. For Antiphon see p. 30, and note 2.

[11] Attic ἄνωθεν: Hdt. 4. 57; Aesch. Cho. 427, Eum. 369.

[12] Attic ἐξ ἀρχῆς. See infra, Phrynich. Art. 73.

[13] Attic αὖθις: Hdt. 1. 62; Aesch. Eum. 478.

[14] Attic πάνυ: Hdt. 4. 135, etc.; Aesch. Theb. 641. It is found in Ar. Ran. 1531, but in hexameters.

[15] Attic καίπερ: Hdt. 3. 131; Aesch. Agam. 1084, 1203, Sept. 1038, Cho. 570; Soph. Phil. 1068; Eur. Alc. 2.

[16] Attic σαφῶς: Hdt. 1. 140; 3. 122; 6. 82. Herodotus has not the adj. σαφηνής, but it is found in Aesch. Pers. 634 (chor.), and Soph. Trach. 892 (chor.).

we to explain the replacement of one term by another etymologically far removed from it? Yet such substitution can be demonstrated beyond debate, and with a precision which in such subjects is rarely attainable. Take for example the compound ἀμφίπολος, which is found constantly in Homer in the sense of handmaiden. There is no trace of it in Attic prose or Comedy, though it survived in Ionic, and is again and again encountered in Tragedy[1]; θεράπαινα had driven it from the field. Now θεράπαινα was quite a recent formation from the old masculine word θεράπων, which, though met with as early as ἀμφίπολος, had nevertheless not only managed to keep its ground, but driven out a fellow of its own, namely, ὀπάων[2]. Like ἀμφίπολος, however, ὀπάων enjoyed all its old vitality in Ionic, and its ostracism from Attic was compensated by the dignified retirement of Tragedy.

The large mantle which for centuries formed the outer covering of Greeks, and admitted of so many gracefnl adjustments, was in the Homeric age designated as φᾶρος, but in Attic invariably ἱμάτιον. Herodotus and the Tragedians, however, employ φᾶρος[3], and ignore ἱμάτιον[4] altogether. True, φᾶρος is read in a passage of the Comic poet Philetaerus quoted by Athenaeus (1. 21, c.), ἀμφὶ στέρνοις φᾶρος οὐ καθήσεις, τάλαν, μηδ' ἀγροίκως ἄνω γόνατος ἀμφέξει, but Cobet is right in regarding the initial words as mutilated and corrupt, though perhaps Naber's conjecture

[1] Hdt. 2. 131; 5. 92; 9. 76; Eur. Supp. 1115, I. T. 1114, Alc. 59, Or. 1417. It occurs twice in Aristophanes, Ran. 1337 (chorus), and in a fragment (Fr. Com. 2. 947) in a pseudo-oracle.

[2] Hdt. 5. 111; 9. 50; Aesch. Supp. 492, 954, Cho. 769; Soph. O. C. 1103, Ant. 1108; Eur. Tro. 880, El. 1135.

[3] Hdt. 2. 122; 9. 109; Aesch. Cho. 11, 1011; Soph. Trach. 916, Fr. 332, 272, 343; Eur. Supp. 286.

[4] ἱμάτιον occurs in Herodotus thrice, 1. 9; 2. 47; and 4. 23, but in the two first cases in the plural as equivalent to *clothes* (Att. ἐσθής), and in the last in the singular for *rag* or *cloth*. Nauck justly rejects the only case of the word's occurrence in Tragedy, viz. in a so-called fragment of the Colchides of Sophocles, Fr. Trag. Soph. 317.

of *σφυροῖς* does not offer the best means of emending the passage [1].

To take another instance, *ἄγγος*, a vessel, was in Ionic a word of very general import, and almost as familiar to the surgery as to the pantry [2]. Now in all senses but the medical [3] its place was in Attic usurped by *ὑδρία*, although *ἄγγος* remained in Tragedy [4]. In Aristophanes *ὑδρία* has not only its original sense of waterpot or pitcher (Eccl. 678, 738, Vesp. 926), but also those of a winepot (Fr. 183), pot of money (Av. 602), and cinerary urn (Av. 601). Menander and Antiphanes each wrote a play called *Ὑδρία*, probably in the sense of Money-bags, and the term was the recognised designation of the balloting urn [5] in the Law Courts. Of these meanings, of the very word itself there is not a trace in any dialect but Attic. It is a growth peculiarly Attic, and dating from a time posterior to that in which the Tragic dialect became fixed. There could not be a more striking instance of the vigour, thoroughness, and rapidity, with which the people of Attica recast their old language, and replaced worn and stiff terms by crisp and flexible innovations.

[1] Cobet arranges the words as cretics—

οὐ καθήσεις, τάλαν,
μηδ' ἀγροίκως ἄνω τοῦ γόνατος ἀμφιεῖ.

Naber, with doubts about the metre, accepts Cobet's second line, and thus supplements the first—

ἀμφὶ περὶ τοῖς σφυροῖς οὐ καθήσεις, τάλαν.

[2] In Od. 16. 13, for wine; Od. 2. 289, for general goods; Od. 9. 222, of household vessels; Il. 16. 643, for milk; Hdt. 1. 113 = *a cinerary urn*; 5. 12, *a water jar*; in Hippocrates freq. of the vessels of the body.

[3] *ἄγγος* itself does not happen to occur with this signification in Attic prose or comedy, but that it was so used may be inferred from *κεναγγία*, *fast*, being employed by the comic poet Plato. For most purposes *φλέψ* would be preferred.

[4] El. 1118, 1205, *a cinerary urn*; Eur. I. T. 953, *a wine flagon*; Ion 32, 1337, 1398, 1412, *a cradle* (*ἀντίπηξ*); El. 55, *a water jar*.

[5] Isocr. Trapez. 365 C: *τίς οὐκ οἶδεν ὑμῶν πέρυσιν ἀνοίξαντα τὰς ὑδρίας καὶ τοὺς κριτὰς ἐξελόντα τοὺς ὑπὸ τῆς βουλῆς εἰσβληθέντας; .... ταύτας ὑπανοίγειν ἐτόλμησεν αἳ σεσημασμέναι μὲν ἦσαν ὑπὸ τῶν πρυτάνεων, κατεσφραγισμέναι δ' ὑπὸ τῶν χορηγῶν, ἐφυλάττοντο δ' ὑπὸ τῶν ταμιῶν κτε.* Cp. Xen. Hell. 1. 7, 6.

A word even more instructive is ὄργια. That it was once in use in Attica is proved beyond question by its derivatives ὀργεών and ὀργιάζω. The latter term is good classical Attic occurring repeatedly in Plato[1], and the former form, becoming attached to an official[2] position, was retained in that connection till long after it was superseded for ordinary purposes by ἱερεύς. According to Suidas, ὀργεῶνες were those οἱ συλλόγους ἔχοντες περί τινας ἥρωας ἢ θεούς[3], and in that sense occurs four times in the speech of Isaeus concerning the inheritance of Menekles (2. 14, 16, 17, 45). Another of his speeches was addressed πρὸς Ὀργεῶνας, and Harpocration quotes the word from Lysias. It is another instance of crystallisation not dissimilar to ἀκτή and ζωστήρ, and, like both these terms, survived in its original sense in the literary trustee of the Attic of the sixth and preceding century—the Tragic dialect. In a fragment of the Mysi[4] of Aeschylus it is used as ἱερεύς—

ποταμοῦ Καΐκου χαῖρε πρῶτος ὀργεών,
εὐχαῖς δὲ σώζοις δεσπότας παιωνίαις.

But ὄργια itself was uncompromisingly disfranchised, and but for Ionic[5], Tragedy, and the Chorus of Comedy would have disappeared altogether; so assiduously do Attic writers substitute μυστήρια or τελεταί for the older word.

[1] Plat. Legg. 10. 910, τὸν ἱερὰ ὀργιάζοντα: Id. Phaedr. 250 C, τελετὴν ὠργιάζομεν; cp. 252 D, Legg. 4. 717 B twice; Isocr. Anop. 145 C, καὶ πρῶτον μὲν τὰ περὶ τοὺς θεοὺς οὐκ ἀνωμάλως οὐδ' ἀτάκτως οὔτ' ἐθεράπευον οὔτ' ὠργίαζον.

[2] Another survival from a similar cause is the spelling ξυμβάλλεσθαι for συμβάλλεσθαι, in the phrase γνώμην ξυμβάλλεσθαι τῆς βουλῆς εἰς τὸν δῆμον, of communicating a probouleuma of the Senate to the Ecclesia. Up to about 416 B.C. ξύν is invariably used in Inscriptions, but within ten years from that date its place is usurped, in all cases except the phrase in question, which occurs very frequently, but hardly ever with σ.

[3] So Pollux, 8. 107, **ὀργεῶνες**· οἱ κατὰ δήμους ἐν τακταῖς ἡμέραις θύοντες θυσίας τινάς.

[4] Phot. Lexic. p. 344, 19; Suidas, s. v. ὀργεῶνες; Harpocr. s. v. ὀργεῶνας (p. 344. 7) is wrong in considering this use an instance of poetical substitution of the particular for the general.

[5] Hdt. 2. 51; 5. 61; Soph. Trach. 765; Eur. Bac. freq., H. F. 613.

The only instance of ὄργια in the senarii of Comedy is curiously significant. The lines[1] are either paratragedic, or quoted directly from Tragedy, as the lengthening of the υ in Κύπρου and the occurrence of μεδέουσα distinctly prove.

Other substantives similarly eclipsed in Attic are very numerous, such as ἀλκή[2] by βοήθεια, ἄρδις[3] by ἀκίς, δειρή or δερή[4] by τράχηλος, δῶμα[5] by οἶκος or οἰκία, κοτόπτης[6] by κατάσκοπος, κῦδος[7] by δόξα or εὐδοξία, λιταί[8] by εὐχαί, ὄλβος[9] by εὐδαιμονία, ὄχθος[10] by the neuter of ἄκρος or ὑψηλός, ποινή[11] by δίκη, σποδός[12] by κόνις,

[1] Ar. Lys. 831—

Ἄνδρ' ἄνδρ' ὁρῶ προσιόντα παραπεπληγμένον,
τοῖς τῆς Ἀφροδίτης ὀργίοις εἰλημμένον.
ὦ ποτνία Κύπρου καὶ Κυθήρων καὶ Πάφου
μεδέουσ'. ἴθ' ὀρθὴν ἥνπερ ἔρχει τὴν ὁδόν.

[2] Hdt. 3. 110; 4. 125; Aesch. Sept. 76, et freq.; Soph. O. C. 459, 1524; Eur. freq. It occurs occasionally also in the early prose of Thucydides, as 2. 34. Its other signification of *strength* had disappeared still sooner, being replaced by ῥώμη, but in the derivatives ἄλκιμος and ἄναλκις lingered on. For ἄλκιμος see p. 50. ἄναλκις is equally un-Attic: Hdt. 2. 103; Aesch. Agam. 1224, P. V. 870; Soph. El. 301; (Xen. Cyr. 7. 5. 62; 8. 1 45.) The discussion of Xenophon's style is reserved.

[3] Hdt. 4. 81; Aesch. P. V. 880.

[4] Hdt. 1. 51; Aesch. Agam. 329, 875, Eum. 592; Eur. Hec. 154; (Xen. Cyr. 1. 3. 2; 5. 1. 7.)

[5] Hdt. 2. 62. In Tragedy with extraordinary frequency. The many passages in which it is found in Comedy are all burlesques of the tragic dialect, as Ach. 479, 1072, Thesm. 871.

[6] Hdt. 3. 17, 21; Aesch. Sept. 41, 369; Eur. Rhes. 632.

[7] Hdt. 7. 8; Aesch. Pers. 455.

[8] Hdt. 1. 105, 116; 6. 69; in all three tragedians repeatedly. λίσσομαι occurs in Hdt. 1. 24, and frequently in Tragedy. It is also found in Plato, Rep. 366 A, in a poetical passage, and in Arist. Pax 382 for comic effect.

[9] Hdt. 1. 86, and frequently in Tragedy. Cp. ἀνόλβιος, Hdt. 1. 32, thrice; Eur. Antig. Fr. 175; and ἄνολβος is very common in Tragedy. (Xen. Cyr. 1. 5. 9; 4. 2. 44.)

[10] Hdt. 4. 203; 8. 52; 9. 25, 56, 59; Aesch. Pers. 467, Cho. 4; Eur. Supp. 655; (Xen. Hipparch. 6. 5; 8. 3; Re. Eq. 3. 7.) In Aristophanes it is met with in Thesm. 1105, and Ran. 1172, but the latter is from Aesch. Cho. 4, as the former is from Euripides.

[11] Hdt. 2. 134; 7. 134; Aesch. P. V. 112, 223, 620, et al.; Soph. El. 564; Eur. Tro. 360, et al.; (Xen. Cyr. 6. 1. 11; Antiphon, 120, 25, see p. 30.) Compare ἄποινα, *compensation for injury done*, Hdt. 9. 120; Aesch. Pers. 808, Agam. 1420; Eur. Alc. 7, Bacch. 516.

[12] Hdt. 2. 100, 140; 4. 35, 172; Aesch. Agam. 820, Cho. 687; Soph. O. R. 21, Ant. 1007, El. 758, 1122, 1198.

τέρμα[1] by τελευτή, and φορβή[2] by τροφή or σῖτος. With reference to ποινή and its fellow ἄποινα, it is worthy of remark that their survival as legal technical terms supplies another argument as to the constitution of old Attic of a similar kind to those suggested by ἀκτή and ὀργεών. Its legal status made ἄποινα as durable as if it had been rooted to the soil like ἀκτή, or like ζωστήρ founded on a rock. In explaining a law of Solon[3], Demosthenes (630. 28) has the words τὸ δέ, μηδ' ἀποινᾶν, μὴ χρήματα πράττεσθαι· τὰ γὰρ ἄποινα χρήματα ὠνόμαζον οἱ παλαιοί, and ἄποινα is with this legal sense used in two passages of Plato[4].

Of superseded adjectives, αἰνός[5], λαβρός[6], ὑπέροχος[7], ἀτρέκης[8], πρόνους[9], and ἄελπτος[10], will serve as specimens. Their Attic equivalents were δεινός, σφοδρός, παχύς, ἀκριβής, προμηθής, and ἀπροσδόκητος. The negatives, ἄνιππος[11] and ἄφθογγος[12], were used in Ionic and Tragedy in the sense of πεζός and σιγῶν respectively.

Of adverbs which were rejected in mature Attic none

1 Hdt. 2. 8; 4. 52; 3. 97; and frequently in all three tragedians; (Xen. Cyr. 8. 3. 25; Rep. Lac. 10. 1.)

2 Hdt. 1. 202, 211; 4. 122; 7. 50, 107, 119; Soph. Ant. 775, Aj. 1065, Phil. 43.

3 The law he quotes in 629. 22, τοὺς δ' ἀνδροφόνους ἐξεῖναι ἀποκτείνειν ἐν τῇ ἡμεδαπῇ καὶ ἀπάγειν· λυμαίνεσθαι δὲ μή, μηδ' ἀποινᾶν. Cp. Suid. s. Gramm. Bekk. p. 428, 9, Ἄποινα, λύτρα ἃ δίδωσί τις ὑπὲρ φόνου ἢ σώματος· Οὕτω Σόλων ἐν νόμοις.

4 Legg. 9. 862 C, τὸ ἀποίνοις ἐξιλασθέν: Rep. 3. 393 E, δεξαμένους ἄποινα.

5 Hdt. 4. 31, 61. 76; Soph. Aj. 706; Aesch. Pers. 930.

6 Hdt. 4. 50; 8. 12; Soph. Aj. 1147; Eur. I. T. 1393, Cycl. 403, H. F. 253, Or. 697.

7 Hdt. 5. 92; Soph. Trach. 1096.

8 Hdt. 3. 98, etc.; Eur. Hipp. 261, 1115.

9 Hdt. 3. 36; Soph. Aj. 119.

10 Hdt. 1. 111: Aesch. Supp. 342, and freq.; Soph. O. C. 1120, Trach. 203; Eur. freq.

11 Hdt. 1. 215, ἱππόται εἰσὶ καὶ ἄνιπποι: Soph. O. C. 899, λεὼν ἄνιππον ἱππότην τε. Cp. Hdt. 2. 108, Αἴγυπτος ἐοῦσα πεδιὰς πᾶσα ἄνιππος καὶ ἀναμάξευτος γέγονε.

12 Hdt. 1. 116; Aesch. Pers. 206; Soph. Aj. 314; Eur. Or. 956, Tro. 690, etc. It occurs in Plato, but only in the technical sense of consonant as opposed to vowel.

were subjected to so great a reverse of fortune as κάρτα, the history of which has already occupied our attention. It was not, however, an isolated case. Ἔνερθε is one member of a family of words never once met with either in Attic Prose or Comedy, their place having been taken by others. As an adverb ἔνερθε gave place to κάτω, and as a preposition to ὑπό, while οἱ ἔνεροι and οἱ ἐνέρτεροι or νέρτεροι were replaced by οἱ κάτω or οἱ νεκροί. In Herodotus ἔνερθε governs the genitive in the sense of κάτω in phrases like πᾶν τὸ ἔνερθε τῶν ὀφρύων[1], and in Sophocles it is actually transferred to moral subjection when Philoctetes addresses Neoptolemus in the words—

> ὃς τῶν ἐμῶν
> ἐχθρῶν μ' ἔνερθεν ὄντ' ἀνέστησας πέρα.

But in true Attic there is not a trace of ἔνερθε, νέρθε, ἐνέρτερος, νέρτερος, or ἔνεροι. Accordingly, when Naber would alter νεωτέρων to ἐνερτέρων in the lines of Aristophon—

> ἐσθίουσι δὲ
> λάχανά τε καὶ πίνουσιν ἐπὶ τούτοις ὕδωρ·
> φθεῖρας δὲ καὶ τρίβωνα τήν τ' ἀλουσίαν
> οὐδεὶς ἂν ὑπομείνειε τῶν νεωτέρων—

his ingenuity may be admired, but it has introduced into Comic Verse a word utterly uncongenial to its style. The lines are preserved by Diogenes Laertius (8. 38), and, from a longer fragment which precedes, it is clear that they form part of an account of the world below given by one who was fortunate enough to be only a sojourner there. He describes the squalor of the Pythagorean shades as peculiarly grateful to Pluto, and speaks of them and their fellows as οἱ κάτω or οἱ νεκροί—both genuine Attic expressions. But to take ἐνέρτεροι from its fit home in

[1] Hdt. 4. 65; 2. 13 bis. So Aesch. P. V. 500, Pers. 228, Cho. 125, Eum. 1023; Soph. Phil. 666; Eur. Phoen. 505, Tro. 459, H. F. 263. It is also very frequent in all three tragedians = οἱ κάτω.

Tragedy and from associates like βέλος in the Aeschylean trimeter (Cho. 286)—

τὸ γὰρ σκοτεινὸν τῶν ἐνερτέρων βέλος—

and place it among the moderns in Comedy is one of those errors almost inseparable from critical inquiry, but which the present work is to some extent intended to minimise.

Of Attic writers Thucydides alone uses ἕκας, and that only coupled with the negative, as οὐχ ἕκας, in two passages[1]. The word occurs in Ionic and Tragedy as the equivalent of the Attic πόρρω[2]. This is one out of several examples which tend to prove that Attic prose as written by Thucydides was not yet matured.

It was from a different cause that Xenophon's use of words uncongenial to Attic arose, and in the adverbial use of the neuter adjective μέγα[3] he supplies another instance of the injury which his sojourn abroad did to the purity of his style.

The use of ἦμος[4] for ἡνίκα, and of ὥστε[5] for ὥσπερ, ἅτε, ὡς, merits a passing notice, as does also the employment of πέλας[6] with a genitive in the sense of the Attic ἐγγύς. The word is common enough in Prose and Comedy in the meaning of πλήσιον, but on no occasion does it govern the genitive case or stand alone without the definite article to give it an adjectival force.

But as πέλας had in the development of Attic been to a great extent superseded by πλήσιον, so its congener

[1] Thuc. 1. 69, 80.

[2] ἕκας: Hdt. 8. 144, οὐχ ἕκας χρόνου πάρεσται: Aesch. Agam. 292, 1650; Soph. Phil. 41, O. C. 1668; Eur. Heracl. 673, H. F. 198, El. 246; ἑκαστέρω, Hdt. 2. 169; 3. 89, etc.; Eur. H. F. 1047.

[3] Xen. Cyr. 3. 2. 4, μέγα σύμμαχον: 5. 1. 28, μεγ' εὐδαίμονας: Hdt. 1. 32, μέγα πλούσιος: Aesch. P. V. 647, μέγ' εὐδαίμων: Eur. Hec. 493, Or. 1338. The case is different with verbs, as μέγα φέρει, which is good Attic, Plat. Rep. 449 D.

[4] Hdt. 4. 28; Hippocr. 85 E, 599. 40; Soph. Trach. 155, 531, O. R. 1134.

[5] Hdt. 5. 19, 83; 1. 8, 6, 94, etc.; Aesch. P. V. 452, Sept. 62, etc.; Soph. Ant. 1033, etc.; Eur. freq.

[6] Hdt. 8. 39, 138; Aesch. Pers. 684, and very frequent in all three tragedians.

πελάζω[1] had altogether given way to πλησιάζω. For, though quoted from Plato, Symp. 413 B, it there occurs in a proverb again referred to in Rep. 371, ὁ γὰρ παλαιὸς λόγος εὖ ἔχει, ὡς ὅμοιον ὁμοίῳ ἀεὶ πελάζει.

The two verbs μηνίω[2] and χολοῦμαι[3] sank their differences in the Attic θυμοῦμαι—as δαίνυμι[4] and θοινῶ[5] were combined in ἑστιῶ. The same law of parsimony is observed persistently at work in rejecting useless synonyms throughout the whole period during which the Athenians were new-modelling their language. The verb σείω drove out δονῶ[6] and πάλλω[7], while of the pairs θρώσκω[8] and πηδῶ, πατέομαι[9] and γεύομαι, θαμβῶ[10] and θαυμάζω, ἁνδάνω[11] and ἀρέσκω, αὐδῶ[12] and λέγω, στείχω[13] and ἔρχομαι, ἄνωγα[14] and κελεύω, ἔρδω[15] and ποιῶ, θεσπίζω[16] and μαντεύομαι, the

[1] Hdt. 2. 19; 4. 181; 9. 74; Aesch. P. V. 712, 807, Supp. 300; Soph. O. C. 1107; Eur. Hec. 1289, Phoen. 279, Med. 91, etc.; (Xenophon, Cyr. 1. 4. 7, 20, etc.).

[2] Hdt. 5. 84; 7. 229; 9. 7; Aesch. Eum. 101; Soph. O. C. 965, 1274, Ant. 1177, Trach. 274, El. 570. Cp. ἀμήνιτος, Hdt. 9. 94; Aesch. Agam. 64?; Supp. 975.

[3] Hdt. 7. 31; Soph. Ant. 1235, Phil. 374; Eur. Alc. 5, Tro. 730.

[4] Hdt. 1. 162; Aesch. Eum. 305; Eur. Or. 15; cp. I. A. 707. *Mid.* Hdt. 1. 211; 2. 100; 3. 18; Soph. Trach. 771, 1088, etc.; Eur. Tro. 770, Cycl. 326.

[5] Hdt. 1. 129; Eur. Ion 982, Alc. 549, Cycl. 248, 373, 550, El. 836.

[6] Hdt. 4 2; 7. 1; Aesch Fr., δονοῦσα καὶ τρέπουσα τύρβ' ἄνω κάτω.

[7] Hdt. 1. 141; 3. 128; 7. 140; 8. 120; Aesch. Cho. 524; Soph. El. 710, Ant. 396; Eur. freq.

[8] ὑπερθρώσκω, Hdt. 2. 66; 3. 134; Aesch. Ag. 297, 827; Eur. Hec. 823.

[9] Hdt. 1. 73; 2. 37, 47, 66, 187; Aesch. Agam. 1408; Soph. Ant. 203. In Arist. Pax 1092, it occurs in a comic adaptation from Homer.

[10] Hdt. 1. 113 γ; Soph. Ant. 1246; Eur. I. A. 1561.

[11] Hdt. 1. 151; 2. ?5; 8. 29, etc.; Soph. Ant. 89, 504; Eur. freq.

[12] Hdt. 2. 57, etc.; Aesch., Soph., Eur.

[13] Hdt. 1. 9; 3. 76; 9. 11. Very frequent in all three tragedians. So ἀποστείχω = ἀπέρχομαι, in Hdt. 9. 56; Aesch. Supp. 769; Soph. El. 799, Trach. 693.

[14] Hdt. 3. 81; 7. 104, etc.; Aesch. P. V. 947; Soph. Trach. 1247; Eur. Or. 119, et al.

[15] Hdt. 1. 119, 131, 137; 2. 121; 7. 83, etc.; Aesch. Agam. 933, 1649, and freq.; Soph. Trach. 935, and freq.

[16] Hdt. 1. 47, 48; 4. 61, 67, 155; 8. 135; Aesch. Agam. 1210, 1213; Soph. O. C. 388, 1428, 1516, Ant. 1054, 1091, Phil. 610, El. 1425; Eur. Andr. 1161,

latter alone survived in each. The same law is exemplified in the disappearance from Attic of the weak aorist of *βαίνω*. That tense, with its causal signification, is familiar to every student of Ionic[1] and the Tragic poets, but it is not encountered in any Attic writer of higher authority than Xenophon. A synonym to *βιβάζω* was regarded as unnecessary. But marked as this law of parsimony is in Attic, it is occasionally violated, sometimes accidentally, sometimes from *malice prepense*, by acknowledged masters of Attic diction. Antiphon's style is not so far removed from suspicion that *ἀσπαίρω*[2] can be regarded as a case in point. Like Thucydides, he wrote at a period when Attic had not reached its full strength, and now and again lapsed into old faults; but in the vigorous rhetoric of his junior, Andocides, it is strange to meet with a term like *ἐπαυρέσθαι*[3]. Yet the word occurs in the beginning of his speech on his Recall (20. 2), *καί μοι μέγιστον θαῦμα παρέστηκε τί ποτε οὗτοι οἱ ἄνδρες δεινῶς οὕτω περικάονται εἴ τι ὑμᾶς χρὴ ἀγαθὸν ἐμοῦ ἐπαυρέσθαι*, and ought to be carefully marked. It is a distinct instance of an old word quite uncalled for, and stands on a very different footing from the Ionic and old-Attic *ἀριστεύς*[4], which is appropriately used in speaking of the siege of Troy in a funeral oration ascribed, though perhaps erroneously, to Demosthenes (1392. 4), *τοσούτῳ γὰρ ἀμείνους τῶν ἐπὶ Τροίαν στρατευσαμένων νομίζοιντ' ἂν εἰκότως, ὅσον οἱ μὲν ἐξ ἁπάσης Ἑλλάδος ὄντες ἀριστεῖς δέκ' ἔτη τῆς Ἀσίας ἓν χωρίον πολιορκοῦντες μόλις εἷλον κτε.* In ordinary

Phoen. 1598, etc. *θέσπισμα*, for the Attic *μαντεῖον*, is found Hdt. 1. 29; Aesch. Frag. 81; Soph. O. R. 971; Eur. freq.

[1] In a causal sense are used *ἐμβῆσαι* in Hdt. 1. 46; Eur. Cycl. 467, Heracl. 845: *ἀναβῆσαι*, in Hdt. 1. 80: *ἀποβῆσαι*, in 5. 63, etc.: *ἐκβῆσαι*, in Eur. Hel. 161 : *εἰσβῆσαι*, Alc. 1055, Bacch. 466.

[2] Antipho, 119, 39, *ἀωρὶ τῆς νυκτὸς νεκροῖς ἀσπαίρουσι συντυχών*: Hdt. 1. 111; 9. 120; Aesch. Pers. 976; Eur. I. A. 1157, El. 843.

[3] Hdt. 7. 180; Hippocr. de Morb. 4. 498, 29, 32; 502. 5; 503. 25; 504. 22, 25, 47; Aesch. P. V. 28; Eur. I. T. 529, Hel. 469.

[4] Hdt. 6. 81; Aesch. Pers. 306; Soph. Aj. 1304; Eur. I. A. 28, Phoen. 1226, 1245, Rhes. 479, Ion 416.

circumstances the use of such a word would form a strong argument against the genuineness of the work, but as it is, ἀριστεύς is here natural and effective.

It has been a difficult task to conduct this inquiry with the sobriety which such questions demand. There is no limit to the extraordinary results which might have been obtained by allowing the imagination to run riot over the whole field of Greek life in the period under consideration. But the results would, for all practical purposes, have been valueless. The habit of generalising without a basis of facts, and of theorising on vague impressions, affords agreeable occupation to one who has acquired it, but brings little instruction to others. The study of Greek has suffered severely from a want of that definiteness which was at one time the peculiar honour of English scholarship, and it is the aim of this work to help, in its modest way, towards a rigidly scientific study of the phenomena of the Greek language.

THE LESSONS OF COMEDY.

THE position taken up in the preceding pages regarding the diction of Tragedy receives singularly striking confirmation from an enlightened study of the eleven complete plays of Aristophanes and the Fragments of that master and the other writers of Comedy who preceded or followed him. The language of Comedy is the language of everyday life, but in the case of the Attic stage this fact has a significance of its own. No citizen of Athens is ever represented as abusing his mother tongue in the way that Dogberry or Dame Quickly abuses the King's English. Even the slaves of Athenian households have excellent Attic put into their mouths. But a stranger, if introduced on the stage, is always represented as talking the language or dialect of the people to which he belongs, or, like Parson Evans, as modifying Attic by retaining the vocal peculiarities of his countrymen. Such treatment always adds colour to the Comedian's work, and beyond question Aristophanes would not have spared his contemporaries if, as usually spoken, their language had contained vulgarisms either in vocabulary or pronunciation. The same concentration which brought about so extraordinarily rapid a development of the Attic dialect, as has been already indicated, was also the occasion of its being used with propriety. It was not the speech of a numerous, widely-extended, variously educated people with a vast variety of opposing interests, but it was one out of many dialects of a common language, and was confined to a race of one origin located in an area so limited that every one of its inhabitants was constantly coming into more or less immediate contact with every other. It was, moreover, the language at once of a democracy and an imperial people placed in that position which, in peoples no less than in individuals, developes signally dignified and commanding qualities. The lesson of enterprise once taught, as to the Athenians it was taught by Marathon, the resolve to venture all—

ὥστ' ἢ γεγονέναι λαμπρὸς ἢ τεθνηκέναι—

becomes paramount and brings out the grander, if not the higher, side of human nature. The Athenian government was a democracy, but it was not one in the ordinary sense of the term. There was not a member of it but would have rejected, as an insult to his understanding, any proposal to give slaves or aliens a voice in the state, or to place him as an Athenian on the same level as an Islander, a Boeotian, or an Oriental. The state was to him more of a reality than it has ever been to any citizen since. The collective will of his fellows supplied in the Athenian, as in every other Greek of that age, the directing and restraining power which the individual conscience supplies in us. To a Greek the State was Conscience; and Socrates did not alter this fact, although the higher rule of personal responsibility made part of his teaching.

These facts explain the phenomenon that an Athenian comic poet had no occasion to deviate from literary Attic in giving a faithful representation of his countrymen; and accordingly the testimony of a writer like Aristophanes, with regard to the dialect of Attica at his own time, is much more straightforward than in other circumstances would have been possible. In fact without Comedy it would be impracticable to decide with accuracy many questions affecting the purity of Attic. Prose was corrupted and interpolated with impunity by consecutive generations of ignorant critics and negligent copyists, but by the rules of verse the scholar is enabled, in most cases, at once to detect late alterations, and the information acquired by a study of verse-corruptions is invaluable in tracking the corruptions which disfigure the text of prose writers.

A different position in regard to Attic Comedy has been taken up by some scholars, but by none whose judgment is worthy of attention. Here, as in other cases which will come under our notice, Veitch[1] has been misled by attending to the letter divorced from the spirit. No one will insist that every word, expression, or construction which occurs in the pages of Comedy necessarily belongs to Attic Greek, but it will be easy to demonstrate that there is no variation from Attic usage which, if rightly considered, has not some lesson to teach us with reference to the development and completed facts of the Athenian language.

Thus one set of facts securely establishes the literary phenomenon so well known as affecting Greek as a whole, and on which the theory of Tragic diction propounded in the last chapter is based. The chorus is couched in that literary modification of Doric in which all choric poetry was always written. Hexameter verse was, from its traditions and necessities, similarly, though not equally, privileged, and, though not composed in Epic, yet admitted of words and forms of words unknown in genuine Attic. Even in Anapaestic verse a few Epic irregularties were allowed. No evidence could be more conclusive that the existence, side by side even in the same play, of three or four distinct literary dialects was to an Athenian perfectly natural, and that the change from one set of grammatical forms to another was for him as easy to make as the change from one metrical system to another. Certainly it must have appeared to an Athenian no more extra-

[1] Greek Verbs, Irregular and Defective, 3rd ed., p. 536.

ordinary to hear a chorus in Doric than to have a Dorian introduced as talking his mother tongue, to listen to a Tragic poet or a character from Tragedy conversing on the comic stage in phraseology otherwise obsolete in Attica, than to understand the Ionicisms of the Islanders who did business with him in the Piraeus. The ability to keep all these styles distinct indicates a sense of language highly developed, and is a fact that ought never to be lost sight of in the critical study of Greek literature. It makes the isolated appearance of an un-Attic form or expression, in a writer otherwise careful, a very suspicious circumstance, and raises the study of Attic almost to the dignity of an exact science.

The consideration of un-Attic words and phrases in Aristophanes will be serviceable in two ways. It will bring into bold relief the fact, which cannot too often be affirmed, that the diction of Tragedy was essentially a survival, and not merely a highly poetical mode of expression; and, on the other hand, it will explain to some extent the rapidity with which a diction formulated in one century was left behind by the living speech in another.

Aristophanes seldom let slip an opportunity of ridiculing Euripides, and Cratinus invented the verb Εὐριπιδαριστοφανίζειν to express uncompromising lampoon. The method employed was parody; and either in parody or caricature the Tragic dialect is repeatedly presented to the student of Comedy side by side with the ordinary Attic mode of expression. True, Euripides introduced many modernisms into his verse, such as the more frequent use of βούλομαι for ἐθέλω and δεῖ for χρή: but, at the same time, he tried to disguise these innovations by antique mannerisms like the employment of σέθεν and ἐμέθεν for the possessive pronouns, and ποτί for πρός. This fact should be kept in mind in reading the pages that follow; but it does not to any great degree affect the point under discussion—the contrast between the Attic and Tragic dialects as illustrated by parody.

It will be convenient to treat the question of parody in Attic Comedy as a whole, and to consider, not only those passages in which Tragedy is caricatured, but also the few others in which the Epic and Lyric styles are introduced into the regular metres for purposes of comic effect. Parody, as found in the chorus, does not much concern us, and may be dismissed with a short notice.

Parody in the Choric passages occurs occasionally in Aristophanes and other Comic poets. In Ran. 1309 ff. Aeschylus strings together many lines from the choric songs of different plays of Euripides—κερκίδος ἀοιδοῦ μελέτας coming from the Meleager, the three following lines from the Electra, and οἰνάνθας γάνος ἀμπέλου and περίβαλλ', ὦ τέκνον, ὠλένας from the Hypsipyle, while line 1339—

ἀλλά μοι, ἀμφίπολοι, λύχνον ἅψατε,

is derived from the Temenidae of the same Tragic poet. A fragment of another lost play of Euripides is inserted bodily in Acharnians 659–662. The passage as preserved by Clement of Alexandria[1]—

πρὸς ταῦθ' ὅ, τι χρῂ καὶ παλαμάσθω,
καὶ πᾶν ἐπ' ἐμοὶ τεκταινέσθω·
τὸ γὰρ εὖ μετ' ἐμοῦ
καὶ τὸ δίκαιον ξύμμαχον ἔσται,
κοὐ μήποθ' ἁλῶ κακὰ πράσσων,

was by Aristophanes only slightly altered to suit his purpose. Similarly, the first few lines of the strophe in Pax 775, and the antistrophe in 796, are from the Oresteia of Stesichorus, as two lines of the Knights (1263–1265) are parodied from Pindar. Beginning with the exact words of Stesichorus and Pindar, Aristophanes in each case ends with a frëer parody. The lines of Pindar—

[1] Cicero quotes ll. 1–3 in Ep. ad Att. 8. 8. 2, and l. 3 in ib. 6. 1. 8.

τί κάλλιον ἀρχομένοισιν ἢ καταπαυομένοισιν
ἢ βαθύζωνόν τε Λατὼ καὶ θοᾶν ἵππων
ἐλάτειραν ἀεῖσαι;

are quoted direct to καταπαυομένοισιν, but the rest are only represented by ἢ θοᾶν ἵππων ἐλατῆρας ἀείδειν, and the passage from the Oresteia is similarly modified, as is seen from comparing the parody with the original words as given by the Scholiast—

τοιάδε χρὴ Χαρίτων δαμώματα καλλικόμων
ὑμνεῖν Φρύγιον μέλος ἐξευρόντα ἁβρῶς
ἦρος ἐπερχομένου.

Examples of less distinct parody, when little more was intended than to suggest a well-known passage of Tragedy, are found in Eq. 973—

ἥδιστον φάος ἡμέρας,

and in Av. 1470—

πολλὰ δὴ καὶ καινὰ καὶ θαυ-
μάστ' ἐπεπτόμεσθα, καὶ
δεινὰ πράγματ' εἴδομεν·
ἔστι γὰρ δένδρον πεφυκός κτε.

In the former Aristophanes had in mind the beginning of the first chorus of the Antigone of Sophocles, and in the latter the beginning of the second, while in its fourth line he went on to suggest the famous chorus in the Oedipus Coloneus.

But, as the discussion of parody in the chorus does not materially affect the present inquiry, it is necessary to refrain from further details, and to devote the space so saved to the more important question of the kinds of parody encountered in the regular metrical systems of Comedy.

With those parodies in which the sentiment merely and not the words is parodied, we have nothing to do. Strattis, in a passage preserved by Pollux (9. 124)—

εἶθ' ἥλιος μὲν πείθεται τοῖς παιδίοις
ὅταν λέγωσιν, "Ἔξεχ', ὦ φίλ' ἥλιε·"—

ridiculed the lines of the Phoenissae, in which Euripides introduced Jocasta as expostulating with Eteocles (l. 546)—

εἶθ' ἥλιος μὲν νύξ τε δουλεύει βροτοῖς,
σὺ δ' οὐκ ἀνέξει δωμάτων ἔχειν ἴσον;

but he did not retain their Tragic colour, as would have been the case if πείθεται had not been substituted for δουλεύει. To bring the children's catch[1], corresponding to that of the English nursery rhyme—

'Rain, rain, go away,
Come again another day,'

into association with what were probably two well-known lines of Euripides, was sufficient for his purpose.

The diction of Tragedy, however, is parodied in two ways. Either lines are quoted without alteration from the Tragic poets, in humorous contrast with the circumstances with which they are associated, or the dialect of Tragedy is put into the mouth of a writer of Tragedy, or a god, or hero. Occasionally also expressions are used for no other reason but to caricature the grandiose style of the older rival of Comedy on the Attic stage. Consequently, the most practicable plan of approaching the fact of distinctions of dialect presented by parody in Comic dialogue, is to trace the use of questionable words, forms, or expressions; and in all cases it will be seen that modes of expression inadmissible in Prose were equally inadmissible in Comedy, except when they were employed from *malice prepense* and to give colour to the work.

Attic writers used ἀπέθανον, ἀποθάνω, ἀποθάνοιμι, ἀπο-

[1] The catch occurs again in the Νῆσοι of Aristophanes—

λέξεις ἄρα
ὥσπερ τὰ παιδί', "Ἔξεχ', ὦ φίλ' ἥλιε."

The passage is quoted by Suidas, who adds, κωλάριόν τι παροιμιῶδες ὑπὸ τῶν παιδίων λεγόμενον ὅταν ἐπινεφῇ ψύχους ὄντος.

θανεῖν, ἀποθανών, never ἔθανον, θάνω, etc., κατέθανον, κατθανών, etc. Yet in Aristophanes κατθανεῖν occurs in Ran. 1477, ἔθανον in Thesm. 865, θανών in Ach. 893. But if in these three passages it is proved that the Comic poet was parodying Euripides, not only are the rules of Attic vindicated, but some light is thrown upon the history of the Attic dialect.

The senarii in Ran. 1477—

τίς οἶδεν εἰ τὸ ζῆν μέν ἐστι κατθανεῖν,
τὸ πνεῖν δὲ δειπνεῖν, τὸ δὲ καθεύδειν κῴδιον;

had their prototype in the Polyidus of Euripides—

τίς οἶδεν εἰ τὸ ζῆν μέν ἐστι κατθανεῖν,
τὸ κατθανεῖν δὲ ζῆν κάτω νομίζεται[1];

lines which are quoted by Plato in the Gorgias (492, E), and from Ran. 1082, are proved to have been spoken by a woman. They were probably the words of Pasiphaë discussing the fate of Glaucus, her son by Minos, who, unknown to his parents, had been drowned in a vessel of honey, but was restored to life by Polyidus. As to Thesm. 865—

ψυχαὶ δὲ πολλαὶ δι' ἔμ' ἐπὶ Σκαμανδρίαις
ῥοαῖσιν ἔθανον—

the words are those of Helen in the play of Euripides named after her (ll. 52, 53), and repeated, with the necessary alterations, by the messenger who reports (ll. 609, 610) to Menelaus her miraculous disappearance—

τοσόνδε λέξασ', ὦ ταλαίπωροι Φρύγες,
τάλανές τ' Ἀχαιοί, δι' ἔμ' ἐπὶ Σκαμανδρίοις
ἀκταῖσιν Ἥρας μηχαναῖς ἐθνήσκετε.

The third passage forms the last words of the enthusiastic

[1] Cp. Eur. Fr. 830 (Phrixus)—

τίς δ' οἶδεν εἰ ζῆν τοῦθ' ὃ κέκληται θανεῖν,
τὸ ζῆν δὲ θνήσκειν ἐστί; πλὴν ὅμως βροτῶν
νοσοῦσιν οἱ βλέποντες, οἱ δ' ὀλωλότες
οὐδὲν νοσοῦσιν οὐδὲ κέκτηνται κακά.

address of Dicaeopolis in the Acharnians to an eel from lake Copais—

μηδὲ γὰρ θανών ποτε
σοῦ χωρὶς εἴην ἐντετευτλιωμένης [1],

and is a brutal parody on the words of Admetus in the Alcestis (l. 367)—

μηδὲ γὰρ θανών ποτε
σοῦ χωρὶς εἴην, τῆς μόνης πιστῆς ἐμοί.

This adaptation of Aristophanes was in turn referred to by Philetaerus in a couple of lines quoted by Athenaeus (7. 280 D) from his Comedy Οἰνοπιών—

οὐ γὰρ θανὼν δήπουθ' ἂν ἔγχελυν φάγοις [2],
οὐδ' ἐν νεκροῖσι πέττεται γαμήλιος.

Similar results are obtained by a consideration of the Ionic [3] and Tragic verb στυγῶ. The word is quite unknown to Attic prose, but nevertheless occurs three times in Aristophanes,—Ach. 33, Ib. 472, and Thesm. 1144. The last quotation is from the chorus, and may be disregarded, but the other two lines are iambic trimeters. The latter—

καὶ γάρ εἰμ' ἄγαν
ὀχληρός, οὐ δοκῶν με κοιράνους στυγεῖν,

is from the Oeneus of Euripides; and besides στυγεῖν contains the Tragic word κοίρανος. Of the former line—

στυγῶν μὲν ἄστυ, τὸν δ' ἐμὸν δῆμον ποθῶν,

the Scholiast remarks, ὁ στίχος ἐκ τραγῳδίας, and he is undoubtedly right.

The thoroughly un-Attic word ἀλύω [4] is found in the senarii in Vesp. 112—

[1] The true reading, see Phryn. Art. 36. fin.

[2] There is no necessity to read, with Naber, οὐκ ἀποθανὼν γὰρ ἂν ποτ' ἔγχελυν φάγοις, as his chief objection, namely the occurrence of θανών, is made invalid by the circumstances stated above. The MSS. have οὐ γὰρ θανών γε δήπουθ' ἔγχελυν φάγοις, which Porson emended. The simple ἔθανον, etc. became common enough in post-Macedonian Comedy, but not before.

[3] στυγῶ, Hdt. 7. 236; Aesch. P. V. 37, 46, Sept. 410, 1046, etc.; Soph. Phil. 87, etc.; Eur. freq. ἀποστυγῶ, Hdt. 2. 47; 6. 129; Eur. Ion 488 (chor.).

[4] The word is also Ionic. Hippocr. Περὶ Παρθεν. p. 563, ὑπὸ δὲ τῆς κακίης

τοιαῦτ' ἀλύει, νουθετούμενος δ' ἀεὶ
μᾶλλον δικάζει.

It comes from the Sthenoboea of Euripides, quoted by the Scholiast and by Plutarch—

τοιαῦτ' ἀλύει· νουθετούμενος δ' Ἔρως
μᾶλλον πιέζει [1].

In trochaic tetrameters, in Ach. 690, Meineke reads—

εἶτ' ἀλύει καὶ δακρύει καὶ λέγει πρὸς τοὺς φίλους.

but the mere word of the Scholiast [2] must not be allowed to outweigh both manuscript authority and the distinct testimony of all other Attic literature against the verb ἀλύω. Aristophanes, beyond question, wrote what the manuscripts give, εἶτα λύζει.

Another signally instructive word is the aorist ἔμολον. No Attic prose writer of authority [3] uses it; and yet it occurs in Aristophanes nine times, and in other Comic poets twice. Of the Aristophanic instances three are met with in lyrical passages (Av. 404, Thesm. 1146, 1155) and require no discussion. Its use in Lys. 743—

ὦ πότνι' Εἰλείθυι', ἐπίσχες τοῦ τόκου,
ἕως ἂν εἰς ὅσιον μόλω 'γὼ χωρίον,

is to be explained in the same way as ὀργίοις, μεδέουσα, and Κύπρου in 832–34 of the same play (see p. 25). It is a burlesque imitation of Tragic diction.

The play upon words would be sufficient reason for its repeated appearance in Eq. 15–26, even if the whole passage was not a comic extension of the lines in the Hippolytus (345–351) in which Phaedra discusses with the Nurse her unnatural passion.

τοῦ αἵματος ἀλύων καὶ ἀδημονέων ὁ θυμὸς κακὸν ἐφέλκεται: Aesch. Sept. 391; Eur. Cycl. 434, Or. 277, Hipp. 1182.

[1] Cp. Aesch. Sept. 391—

τοιαῦτ' ἀλύων ταῖς ὑπερκόπαις σαγαῖς.

[2] Ἐὰν διὰ τοῦ ζ, ὀλολύζει, ἐὰν δὲ χωρὶς τοῦ ζ, ἀλύει.

[3] Xen. An. 7. 1. 32.

Plutarch, in Mor. p. 220 E, 225 E, puts the word into the mouth of Lacedaemonians; and that he did so justly is proved by Ar. Lys. 984, where the Lacedaemonian herald is represented as saying—

κᾶρυξ ἐγών, ὦ κυρσάνιε, ναὶ τὼ σιὼ
ἔμολον ἀπὸ Σπάρτας περὶ τᾶν διαλλαγᾶν·

and by Ib. 1263 and 1297 in a choric song recited by Lacedaemonians. The remaining passages—a fragment of Cratinus, one of Strattis, and another of Aristophanes (Fr. Com. 2. 85, 778, 1201),—would certainly be explicable in a similar way if their context was known. The existence of the compounds *αὐτόμολος* and *αὐτομολῶ*, and the frequency with which the simple word is met with in Tragedy, makes it evident that the word was in common use in Attica at a period not very far removed from the date of the great Attic writers in Prose and Comedy.

The word *ἀλγύνω* is a stranger to Attic prose[1], but it is nevertheless encountered in the couplet of Eupolis—

οὐ γάρ, μὰ τὴν Μαραθῶνι τὴν ἐμὴν μάχην,
χαίρων τις αὐτῶν τοὐμὸν ἀλγυνεῖ κέαρ[2],

which Longinus, in his work De Sublimitate (16. 3), records as the origin of the famous adjuration of Demosthenes, *μὰ τοὺς Μαραθῶνι προκινδυνεύσαντας*[3]. Be this as it may, the verses are a parody on the lines of the Medea (394–397) in which she invokes Hecate—

οὐ γάρ, μὰ τὴν δέσποιναν ἣν ἐγὼ σέβω
μάλιστα πάντων καὶ ξυνεργὸν εἱλόμην,
Ἑκάτην, μυχοῖς ναίουσαν ἑστίας ἐμῆς,
χαίρων τις αὐτῶν τοὐμὸν ἀλγυνεῖ κέαρ.

[1] Xenophon (Apol. 8) not only employs this word, but actually of physical pain, *νόσοις ἀλγυνόμενος*, a sense otherwise unknown.

[2] From the *Δῆμοι*, and probably the words of Miltiades—

'Nae per Marathone quod commisi proelium
Gaudebit nemo cor meum qui afflixerit.' *Grotius.*

[3] De Corona, 297. 11.

But of all un-Attic words λάσκω deserves most notice. Here, if anywhere, is a well-marked instance of Εὐριπιδαριστοφανισμός. Of Comic poets Aristophanes, as far as we know, alone used the verb, and it is quite alien to Attic prose; but that the term was a favourite with Euripides was reason sufficient why it should not be rare in Aristophanes. In Ach. 410 the question, τί λέλακας; is appropriately put into the mouth of Euripides, who, throughout the scene with Dicaeopolis, consistently talks in the Tragic dialect, as τὰ ποῖα τρύχη; 418; λακίδας πέπλων, 423; τὰ δυσπινῆ πεπλώματα, 426; Τηλέφου ῥακώματα, 432; ὦ Ζεῦ διόπτα καὶ κατόπτα πανταχῇ, 435; πυκνῇ γὰρ λεπτὰ μηχανᾷ φρενί, 445; ἄπελθε λαΐνων σταθμῶν, 449; τί δ', ὦ τάλας, σε τοῦδ' ἔχει πλέκους χρέος; 454, etc.

As belonging to the language of deities and heroes it falls with propriety from the lips of Dionysus in Ran. 97—

> γόνιμον δὲ ποιητὴν ἂν οὐχ εὕροις ἔτι
> ζητῶν ἄν, ὅστις ῥῆμα γενναῖον λάκοι,

and of Hermes in Pax 381—

> ἀλλ', ὦ μέλ', ὑπὸ τοῦ Διὸς ἀμαλδυνθήσομαι,
> εἰ μὴ τετορήσω ταῦτα καὶ λακήσομαι.

The mortal Trygaeus shrinks from hearing the God elevating his voice and deprecating him in the words, μή νυν λακήσῃς, λίσσομαί σ', ὡρμίδιον, turns to the Chorus, demanding that they also should take measures to prevent so tragic a catastrophe—

> εἰπέ μοι, τί πάσχετ', ὦνδρες; ἕστατ' ἐκπεπληγμένοι.
> ὦ πονηροί, μὴ σιωπᾶτ'· εἰ δὲ μὴ λακήσεται.

Like ἀμαλδυνθήσομαι and the ridiculous τετορήσω, the aorist ἔλακον and the future λακήσομαι belong to the language of Olympus, and accordingly the Scholiast's remark on Plut. 39—

τί δῆτα Φοῖβος ἔλακεν ἐκ τῶν στεμμάτων[1];

is almost unnecessary—*τραγικώτερον ἀπεφήνατο προσδιασύρων, ὥς φασιν, Εὐριπίδην.* In Ach. 1046, *λάσκων* is uttered by the Chorus, and in Eq. 1018 is part of a pseudo-oracle, couched in hexameter verse, and containing words and forms like *φράζευ, ἴαχεν, ἀδύτοιο, σέθεν,* just as in another such oracle a few lines on (1036–1040) *τέξει* is found where *τέξεται* would be required in Attic. The same peculiarities of diction, arising from the same cause, are encountered in a passage ascribed by Athenaeus (6. 241 C) to Cratinus the younger—

Κόρυδον τὸν χαλκοτύπον πεφύλαξο·
οὐ μή σοι νομιεῖς αὐτὸν μηδὲν καταλείψειν,
μηδ' ὄψον κοινῇ μετὰ τούτου πώποτε δαίσῃ,
τοῦ Κορύδου· προλέγω σοι· ἔχει γὰρ χεῖρα κραταιὰν
χαλκῆν, ἀκάματον, πολὺ κρείττω τοῦ πυρὸς αὐτοῦ.

Other examples of the Olympian and Tragic speech, almost as striking as *λάσκω*, will be readily noted in reading Aristophanes, as, for instance, in the dialogue between Iris and Pisthetaerus in Av. 1200 ff. Pisthetaerus talks excellent Attic, but Iris Olympic—

μηλοσφαγεῖν τε βουθύτοις ἐπ' ἐσχάραις
κνισᾶν τ' ἀγυιάς.
1232.

δείσασ' ὅπως μή σου γένος πανώλεθρον
Διὸς μακέλλῃ πᾶν ἀναστρέψει δίκη,
λιγνὺς δὲ σῶμα καὶ δόμων περιπτυχὰς
καταιθαλώσει σου λικυμνίαις βολαῖς.
1239.

Similarly the women in the Thesmophoriazusae talk Attic, but Mnesilochus and Euripides employ the *Tragic* dialect, as in 871—

[1] Cp. Eur. I. T. 976—

ἐντεῦθεν αὐδὴν τρίποδος ἐκ χρυσοῦ λακὼν
Φοῖβός μ' ἔπεμψε δεῦρο κτε.

Εὐρ. Τίς τῶνδ' ἐρεμνῶν δωμάτων ἔχει κράτος,
ὅστις ξένους δέξαιτο ποντίῳ σάλῳ
κάμνοντας ἐν χειμῶνι καὶ ναυαγίαις;
Μνησ. Πρωτέως τάδ' ἐστὶ μέλαθρα, κτε.,

and this is sustained throughout the whole passage.

In his Χείρων Pherecrates (as quoted by Plutarch, de Mus. p. 1146) introduces Mousike as complaining to Dikaiosune of her fallen estate. Her first words are a burlesque of Tragic diction—

λέξω μὲν οὐκ ἄκουσα, σοί τε γὰρ κλύειν
ἐμοί τε λέξαι θυμὸς ἡδονὴν ἔχει.

Occasionally some exceptionally forced metaphor of Tragedy, or some other mode of expression unusually grandiloquent, is singled out by the poet for ridicule. There is no special propriety in the Sycophant of the Plutus (l. 854 ff) departing from ordinary language, but Aristophanes seized the opportunity of casting merited ridicule on such expressions as δειλαίᾳ συγκέκραμαι δύᾳ in the Antigone (l. 1311), and Τέκμησσαν οἴκτῳ τῷδε συγκεκραμένην in the Ajax (l. 895) of Sophocles—

οἴμοι κακοδαίμων, ὡς ἀπόλωλα δείλαιος,
καὶ τρὶς κακοδαίμων καὶ τετράκις καὶ πεντάκις
καὶ δωδεκάκις καὶ μυριάκις· ἰού, ἰού,
οὕτω πολυφόρῳ συγκέκραμαι δαίμονι.

Reasons equally just and good might be given for every Tragic form or expression occurring in Comedy, but it would be tedious and useless to enumerate all. Again and again the question recurs in the critical study of Attic Greek, and it is no rare experience to find the most distinguished critics advocating an alteration of all the manuscripts, simply because they have never tried to estimate, as is done in this inquiry, the extraordinary ease with which an Athenian of the best age moved among the various co-existent literary dialects of his time.

There is a curious example of the way in which mere caricature affects the language of Comedy in the case of the aged 'amante' in the Plutus. In order to delineate her affectation and intenseness, Aristophanes puts exceptional words into her mouth. The adjective ἐκνόμιος in Classical Greek is found only in one passage, namely, Pindar—

ἔστα δὲ θάμβει δυσφόρῳ
τέρπνῳ τε μιχθείς· εἶδε γὰρ ἐκνόμιον
λῆμα τε καὶ δύναμιν
υἱοῦ·

Nem. 1. 56.

and the adverb occurs nowhere but in two lines of this play. In l. 981 the lady complains—

καὶ γὰρ ἐκνομίως μ' ᾐσχύνετο,

and Chremylus repeats the word in chaff in l. 992, and in a form even more intense—

λέγεις ἐρῶντ' ἄνθρωπον ἐκνομιώτατα.

It is of a piece with her love for diminutives [1], and very telling.

The parodies in hexameter verse are of little importance compared with those which the senarii afford. They are numerous enough, and not uninteresting, but a careful study of them would be of no value in the present inquiry as to the facts which affect the purity of the Attic dialect in Comedy. The presence of a word in Comic hexameter verse can never enfranchise it as Attic, and consequently little can be gained by pointing out those passages in which the eccentricities of the hexameter metre are exaggerated.

The case of pseudo-oracles has already been discussed,

[1] The marked caricature in which the old woman is depicted forms an excellent argument for avoiding a solecism by reading in 1020 που for μου. ὄζειν τε τῆς χρόας ἔφασκεν ἡδύ που, *sweetly, really.* M and Π are frequently confounded in MSS., as in Eur. I. A. 761, παντόσυνοι in several MSS. for μαντόσυνοι.

and with these may go the utterance of the seer Hierocles in Pax 1075—

> οὐ γάρ πω τοῦτ' ἐστὶ φίλον μακάρεσσι θεοῖσιν,
> φυλόπιδος λῆξαι πρίν κεν λύκος οἶν ὑμεναιοῖ·

regarding which Trugaeus inquires—

> καὶ πῶς, ὦ κατάρατε, λύκος ποτ' ἂν οἶν ὑμεναιοῖ;

but the rest of the scene, from l. 1064 to 1115, is pure Epic parody.

From the Φορμοφόροι of Hermippus, Athenaeus (1. p. 27, d) quotes over twenty lines of Epic verse beginning—

> ἔσπετε νῦν μοι, Μοῦσαι Ὀλύμπια δώματ' ἔχουσαι,

and containing many expressions taken direct from Homer. As might be expected, the Χείρων of Pherecrates supplies several specimens of Epic parody, as the lines—

> μηδὲ σύ γ' ἄνδρα φίλον καλέσας ἐπὶ δαῖτα θάλειαν
> ἄχθου ὁρῶν παρέοντα· κακὸς γὰρ ἀνὴρ τόδε ῥέζει,
> ἀλλὰ μάλ' εὔκηλος τέρπου φρένα τέρπε τ' ἐκεῖνον·

which, according to Athenaeus (8. 364 B), had their prototype in the Eoeae of Hesiod, and, if we trust Phrynichus (see art. 71), Aristophanes used the words καὶ κόσκινον ἠπήσασθαι in his Δαιταλῆς, in a parody on that didactic poet.

It is rare that parodies of Homer or Hesiod occur in the senarii of Comedy, but there is no doubt that the line—

> δώσει δέ σοι γυναῖκας ἑπτὰ Λεσβίδας,

quoted by the Scholiast on Arist. Ran. 1343 as from the Χείρων of Pherecrates, was intended to suggest the offer of Agamemnon in the Πρεσβεία πρὸς Ἀχιλλέα—

> δώσει δ' ἑπτὰ γυναῖκας ἀμύμονα ἔργ' εἰδυίας
> Λεσβίδας,
>
> Il. 9. 270.

In such cases an Epic word might readily be used, as in

the Clouds (l. 30) Aristophanes boldly inserted a choric fragment of Euripides in the line—

ἀτὰρ τί χρέος ἔβα με μετὰ τὸν Πασίαν,

and in Ach. 883 made a Boeotian burlesque Aeschylus in his own patois. In the Ὅπλων κρίσις Thetis was addressed as—

δέσποινα πεντήκοντα Νηρῄδων κορῶν,

which, in the mouth of a country poulterer, as he draws a splendid eel from his basket, becomes—

πρέσβειρα πεντήκοντα Κωπᾴδων κορᾶν,
ἔκβαθι τεῖδε κὴπιχάριτται τῷ ξένῳ.

The form πρίασο, which occurs a few lines before, must not be regarded, as Veitch insists, as good Attic, simply because it is found in the senarii of Comedy. Whether it was or was not recognized will be discussed at another time; but as for Veitch, he might, with equal justice, claim as Attic every word used by the Scythian policeman in the Thesmophoriazusae, and with better right enfranchise both οἰκέω and πωλήσω for οἰκῶ and ἀποδώσομαι, because Cratinus puts the one word into Solon's[1] mouth, and Aristophanes the other into an Ionian's[2].

The verb κικλήσκω was probably once used in Attica, because it is found in Tragedy and in other Greek dialects, but it had disappeared from the mature language. Strattis, however, used it in senarii in his Μακεδόνες ἢ Παυσανίας, but the lines themselves show that it is a Macedonian who employs the term—

[1] The lines are quoted from the Χείρωνες by Diogen. Laert. 1. 62—

οἰκέω δὲ νῆσον, ὡς μὲν ἀνθρώπων λόγος,
ἐσπαρμένος κατὰ πᾶσαν Αἴαντος πόλιν.

Plutarch, Sol. 14, makes Solon use δοκέω, and in id. 32 narrates the fact referred to in the words of Cratinus, ἡ δὲ δὴ διασπορὰ κατακαυθέντος αὐτοῦ τῆς τέφρας περὶ τὴν Σαλαμινίων νῆσον, ἔστι μὲν διὰ τὴν ἀτοπίαν ἀπίθανος παντάπασι καὶ μυθώδης, ἀναγέγραπται δ' ὑπὸ ἄλλων ἀνδρῶν ἀξιολόγων καὶ Ἀριστοτέλους τοῦ φιλοσόφου.

[2] ap. Athen. 12, 525 A. In Av. 1039 πωλήσων is employed for antithetic effect.

A. ἡ σφύραινα δ᾽ ἐστὶ τίς;

B. κέστραν μὲν ὔμμες, ὦττικοί, κικλήσκετε[1].

The Doric σιδάρεος, for σιδηροῦς, is always retained in speaking of the iron coinage of the Dorian colony, Byzantium. In Arist. Nub. 249, to the quandary of Socrates—

ποίους θεοὺς ὀμεῖ σύ; πρῶτον γὰρ θεοὶ
ἡμῖν νόμισμ᾽ οὐκ ἔστι—

Strepsiades replies—

τῷ γὰρ ὄμνυτ᾽; ἢ
σιδαρέοισιν ὥσπερ ἐν Βυζαντίῳ;

and the Scholiast on that passage quotes from the Comic writer, Plato—

χαλεπῶς ἂν οἰκήσαιμεν ἐν Βυζαντίοις,
ὅπου σιδαρέοις νομίζουσιν[2].

It was shown how the immature speech of Attica had been crystallised in names of places, in religious formulae, and in official names, no less than in the diction of Tragedy. But no method of crystallisation could be more effective than a proverbial saying, and accordingly most of the proverbs which occur in Aristophanes contain words which had dropped out of use in the developed dialect of Attica.

Ἔρδω is of frequent occurrence in Ionic and Tragedy[3], but there is no trace of it in Attic except in a proverb found in Ar. Vesp. 1431—

ἔρδοι τις ἣν ἕκαστος ἂν εἰδείη τέχνην,

[1] Quoted by Athenaeus (7. 323, b). In Ar. Nub. 565 it occurs in a chorus, and in a line of Cratinus quoted by Hesychius under κύβηλις—

χαλκίδα κικλήσκουσι θεοί, ἄνδρες δὲ κύβηλιν·

which is a parody of Homer Il. 14. 291—

χαλκίδα κικλήσκουσι θεοί, ἄνδρες δὲ κύμινδιν.

[2] Pollux (9. 78) describes the σιδάρεος as νόμισμά τι λεπτόν, and quotes an obscure and corrupt couplet from the Myrmidons of Strattis—

ἐν τοῖς βαλανείοις προκέλευθος ἡμέρα
ἀπαξάπασα γῆ στρατιαὶ σιδαρέων.

[3] Hdt. 1. 119, 131, 137; 2. 121; 7. 33, etc.; Aesch. Agam. 933, 1649, and freq.; Soph. Trach. 935, and freq.

and somewhat resembling another—

τί δῆτα χεῖρες οὐκ ἂν ἐργασαίατο;

which Aristophanes adapted in Av. 1147—

τί δῆτα πόδες ἂν οὐκ ἂν ἐργασαίατο;

and Lys. 42—

τί δ' ἂν γυναῖκες φρόνιμον ἐργασαίατο;

The old Attic ἄλκιμος survived in the proverb—

πάλαι ποτ' ἦσαν ἄλκιμοι Μιλήσιοι,

which occurs twice in the Plutus (ll. 1003, 1075), and is referred to in Vesp. 1033.

The aged lover in the Plutus (1036) swears that her misplaced affection is killing her, and describes her emaciation in the line—

διὰ δακτυλίου μὲν οὖν ἔμεγ' ἂν διελκύσαις·

but the words διὰ δακτυλίου ἂν διελκύσαις were beyond question proverbial, which accounts for the monosyllabic ending of διελκύσαις. As from a proverb, too, the form ἐωνήσατο for ἐπρίατο ought not to condemn Athenaeus of inaccuracy when he quotes (6. 266 F), Χῖος δεσπότην ὠνήσατο, as a proverbial expression used by Eupolis in his play of 'the Friends.' Eupolis may well have written ὠνήσατο.

The Ionic and old Attic[1] word ἕρπω is four times encountered in Aristophanes, but in three out of the four in the one phrase ὁ πόλεμος ἑρπέτω—

οὐ δεόμεθα σπονδῶν· ὁ πόλεμος ἑρπέτω.
Eq. 673.

A. οὐκ ἂν ποιήσαιμ', ἀλλ' ὁ πόλεμος ἑρπέτω.
B. μὰ Δί', οὐδ' ἐγώ γ' ἄν, ἀλλ' ὁ πόλεμος ἑρπέτω.
Lys. 129, 130.

From the first passage it is reasonable to infer that the

[1] Hippocr. 6. 480, 490; Aesch. Eum. 39, etc.; Soph. O. C. 1551, and very freq.; Eur. freq.

phrase was a common cry in Athens during the Peloponnesian war, and the lines from the Lysistrata confirm this view. The fourth instance occurs in an isolated trimeter of the Δαιταλῆς quoted by Harpocration[1]—

ὁ δ' ἡλιαστὴς 'εἶρπε πρὸς τὴν κιγκλίδα,

and without context affords no clue. But the word was, like ἀράττω, μαστίζω, and others already discussed, most probably a colloquial survival of the older language.

The occurrence of a word, or form of a word, in the anapaestic verse of Comedy is no proof of its Attic character. If there are fewer Epic irregularities in the anapaests than in the hexameters, yet, in a question of this kind, one distinct anomaly is sufficient to destroy their authority. As a matter of fact the irregularities are very marked. Thus, in Vesp. 662 in anapaestic tetrameters catalectic, the third person plural of the Aorist Passive Indicative ends in -εν instead of -ησαν[2]—

ἐξ χιλιάσιν, κοὔπω πλείους ἐν τῇ χώρᾳ κατένασθεν.

The Dative singular of proper names in -κλῆς (from -κλέης) invariably undergoes in Attic a double contraction, but in Av. 567, Ἡρακλέει occurs in place of Ἡρακλεῖ—

ἢν δ' Ἡρακλέει θύῃσι λάρῳ ναστοὺς θύειν μελιτοῦντας,

and the same line supplies the Epic θύῃσι for θύῃ. More instances may be gleaned by the most cursory reader.

The purpose of this inquiry has been fulfilled if it has been made clear that Comedy must not be regarded as invariably presenting only Attic forms, Attic words, and

[1] Κιγκλίς. αἱ τῶν δικαστηρίων θύραι κιγκλίδες ἐκαλοῦντο. Ἀριστοφάνης Δαιταλεῦσιν· Ὁ δ' κτε.

[2] The form is found in Tragedy. Eur. Hipp. 1247—

ἵπποι δ' ἔκρυφθεν καὶ τὸ δύστηνον τέρας:

Phoen. 1246—

ἔσταν δὲ λαμπρὼ χρῶμά τ' οὐκ ἠλλαξάτην,

both of which Nauck wrongly tries to alter,—a striking inconsistency when he replaces πληροῦσιν in Hec. 574 by a late absurdity like ἐπλήρουσαν. In choric passages are found, ἔβαν, Aesch. Pers. 18; Eur. Andr. 287, etc.; κατέβαν, Soph. Trach. 504; ἀπέδραν, Aj. 167.

Attic constructions. The choric passages on the one hand, and the hexameter and anapaestic metres on the other, had each literary sympathies uncongenial to Attic, while even in the Iambic and Trochaic parts, un-Attic phrases, words, and forms, were, under certain conditions, necessarily employed. But these conditions are capable of being accurately classified; and such classification not only prevents the student of Attic from misconception, but actually introduces him to many new aspects of the language, giving him glimpses into its history and nature, and providing him with rules by which he may bring to nothingness many of the most unquestioned emendations of great critical scholars.

ΦΡΥΝΙΧΟΥ

ΕΚΛΟΓΗ

ΡΗΜΑΤΩΝ ΚΑΙ ΟΝΟΜΑΤΩΝ

ΑΤΤΙΚΩΝ.

ΦΡΥΝΙΧΟΣ ΚΟΡΝΗΛΙΑΝΩΙ ΕΥ ΠΡΑΤΤΕΙΝ.

Τήν τε ἄλλην σου παιδείαν θαυμάζω, ἣν διαφερόντως ὑπὲρ ἅπαντας ὅσοις ἐγὼ ἐνέτυχον πεπαίδευσαι, καὶ δὴ καὶ τοῦτο θαυμάσας ἔχω, τὸ περὶ τὴν τῶν καλῶν καὶ δοκίμων ὀνομάτων κρίσιν. Ταῦτ' ἄρα κελεύσαντος σοῦ τὰς ἀδοκίμους τῶν φωνῶν ἀθροισθῆναι, πάσας μὲν οὐχ οἷός τε ἐγενόμην τανῦν περιλαβεῖν, τὰς δὲ ἐπιπολαζούσας, μάλιστα καὶ τὴν ἀρχαίαν διάλεξιν ταραττούσας καὶ πολλὴν αἰσχύνην ἐμβαλλούσας. Οὐ λανθάνει δὲ σέ, ὥσπερ οὐδ' ἄλλο τι τῶν κατὰ παιδείαν, ὥς τινες ἀποπεπτωκότες τῆς ἀρχαίας φωνῆς, καὶ ἐπὶ τὴν ἀμαθίαν καταφεύγοντες πορίζουσι μάρτυράς τινας τοῦ προειρῆσθαι ὑπὸ τῶν ἀρχαίων τάσδε τὰς φωνάς· ἡμεῖς δὲ οὐ πρὸς τὰ διημαρτημένα ἀφορῶμεν, ἀλλὰ πρὸς τὰ δοκιμώτατα τῶν ἀρχαίων. καὶ γὰρ αὐτοῖς εἴ τις αἵρεσιν προθείη, ποτέρως ἂν ἐθέλοιεν διαλέγεσθαι ἀρχαίως καὶ ἀκριβῶς ἢ νεοχμῶς καὶ ἀμελῶς, δέξαιντ' ἂν ἀντὶ παντὸς ἡμῖν σύμψηφοι γενόμενοι τῆς ἀμείνονος γενέσθαι μοίρας· οὐ γάρ τις οὕτως ἄθλιος, ὡς τὸ αἰσχρὸν τοῦ καλοῦ προτιθέναι. Ἔρρωσο.

ΦΡΥΝΙΧΟΥ ΕΚΛΟΓΗ.

Τμῆμα πρῶτον.

"Οστις ἀρχαίως καὶ δοκίμως ἐθέλει διαλέγεσθαι τάδ' αὐτῷ φυλακτέα [1].

I.

Ἑκοντὴν οὐ χρὴ λέγειν, ἀλλ' ἐθελοντήν.

This rule is absolute, not only for Attic, but also for Classical Greek as a whole. *ἑκοντής* is not met with till after Christ, but *ἐθελοντής* is used by Thucydides, 1. 60; 2. 96; 3. 20; Lysias, 181. 36; 182. 9; Isocrates, 221; Demosthenes, 247. 24, and by Xenophon and Herodotus. It means one who volunteers for a military enterprise or perilous civil duty.

The form *ἐθελοντήρ* occurs in the Odyssey, 2. 291—

ἐγὼ δ' ἀνὰ δῆμον ἑταίρους
αἶψ' ἐθελοντῆρας συλλέξομαι·

and was beyond question that employed in early Attic. At all events the termination *-τηρ* confronts the student of

[1] For the bearing of these words on the Ecloga as a whole, see Appendix A.

Attic in such words as would naturally retain their primitive shape, namely, those used in the common business and amusements of life, such as κρατήρ, *a wine-bowl*, ποδανιπτήρ, *a foot-bath*, ῥυτήρ, *a strap*, τριπτήρ, *a pestle*, τροπωτήρ, *an oar-thong*, ἀστραφιστήρ, *a surveyor's level* or *sight*, μυκτήρ, *nose*, *nosel*, and others. The same story is told by words like βασανιστήριον, δικαστήριον, βασανίστρια, ναύτρια, by the side of βασανιστής, δικαστής, ναύτης, etc. Certain officers at Athens retained the name of ἁρμοστῆρες till the end of the fifth century B. C. or later, as they are mentioned by Plato, the Comic poet, in his play of the 'Ambassadors[1].' In the same way κλητήρ survived as a law term, and never passed into κλητής[2].

Tragedy—that storehouse of early Attic—has preserved very many of the old forms in -τηρ, such as οἰκητήρ, οἰκιστήρ, μηνυτήρ: πρακτήριος in Aeschylus carries us back to πρακτήρ, just as φυλακτήριον implies φυλακτήρ. Both πρακτήρ and φυλακτήρ occur in the Homeric poems. But side by side with the forms in -τηρ, Tragedy supplies a large number in -τωρ, ἁρμόστωρ, ἀκέστωρ, κράντωρ, σημάντωρ, πράκτωρ, and others. That this was no so-called poetical licence is clearly established. Certain revenue officers at Athens were called πράκτορες (Antiphon, 147. 14); Ἀκέστωρ was not only a surname of Apollo, but was a well-known proper name both in Athens and in cities of other Greek peoples (Diod. Sic. 11. 51; 19. 5). Homer used ῥητήρ, but ῥήτωρ took its place in Attic. In fact euphony, or

[1] See Meineke, Frag. Com. 2. 658, ὅθεν καὶ ἁρμοστῆρας πάλιν ἐκάλουν Ἀθηναῖοι τοὺς εἰς τὸ εὖ ζῆν διατάττοντας ὡς σαφῶς Πλάτων ὁ κωμικὸς δηλοῖ ἐν Πρέσβεσι τῷ δράματι. πάλιν should there be replaced by πάλαι. As instructors of manners they were probably the same as the κοσμηταί or σωφρονισταί. Meineke errs in suggesting Λακεδαιμόνιοι for Ἀθηναῖοι. The corresponding magistrates at Sparta had a different name, viz. Ἁρμόσυνοι, Hesych. s. voc.

[2] Schol. Ar. Vesp. 189, κλητῆρες οἱ καλοῦντες ἐς τὸ δικαστήριον πάντας· σημαίνει δὲ ἡ λέξις καὶ τὸν μάρτυρα. In the latter sense κλήτωρ is found occasionally in Demosthenes in the oblique cases, but never without the variant κλητήρ, which must be read.

mere accident, seems, in many cases, to have determined the form ultimately assumed. If ῥητήρ passed into ῥήτωρ, how is it that throughout Greek literature σωτήρ remained without a rival? There is no question that -της is later than -τηρ, but the existence of -tor as a common Latin termination, dator, stator, amator, venator, etc., seems to prove the existence of -τωρ in Greek of a very early date. The Attic ῥήτωρ, however, by the side of the Homeric ῥητήρ, does not stand alone. In the Odyssey *the drawer of a bow* is ῥυτὴρ βιοῦ, in Aristophanes ῥύτωρ τόξου. In the Odyssey *a defender* is ῥυτήρ, in Aeschylus ῥύτωρ.

The old termination survived in other dialects even in words which in Attic had lost it irreclaimably. Hippocrates speaks of the wisdom-teeth as σωφρονιστῆρες, and they were also called κραντῆρες and φραστῆρες. Passing from the dialects, these forms appeared in the Common dialect, and Plutarch employs σωφρονιστήρ in the sense of the Attic σωφρονιστής (Cato Maj. 27). Xenophon, whose style was distinctly an anticipation of the Common dialect, was significantly fond of the forms in -τηρ, e.g. θεραπευτήρ for θεραπευτής, in Cyr. 7. 5. 65; λυμαντήρ for λυμαντής in Hiero 3. 3; and ἁρμοστήρ for ἁρμοστής in Hell. 4. 8. 39. Although ἁρμοστῆρες was certainly the Lacedaemonian name for the officers there referred to, correct Attic writers invariably spoke of them as ἁρμοσταί.

Thomas Magister (p. 285) repeats the rule of Phrynichus, μὴ εἴπῃς ἑκοντής, ἀλλ' ἐθελοντής, ὡς πάντες οἱ δοκιμώτατοι, but adds the erroneous statement, ἐπὶ δὲ τοῦ ἐπιρρήματος ἀμφότερα λέγε καὶ ἐθελοντὶ καὶ ἑκοντί. There was no such adverb as ἑκοντί in Classical Greek, and even in Arist. Rhet. 3. 15; (1416. 16,) οὐ γὰρ ἑκόντι εἶναι αὐτῷ ὀγδοήκοντα ἔτη, the word is the dative of the adjective. Thucydides, however, uses ἐθελοντί in 8. 2, ἐθελοντὶ ἰτέον ἐπὶ τοὺς Ἀθηναίους, and ἐθελοντηδόν in a later chapter (9) of the same book.

The form ἐθελοντήν in Xenophon (Mem. 2. 1. 3) is simply one of the Ionicisms so frequent in his style (Hdt. 1. 5; 6. 25).

On the other hand, ἑκούσιος and ἀκούσιος, with their adverbs, were recognized Attic words, while ἐθελούσιος and ἐθελουσίως have no better authority than that of Xenophon.

II.

Ὄπιθεν ἄνευ τοῦ σ μηδέποτε εἴπῃς, ὄπισθεν δέ.

In such a question manuscript authority is valueless. Thus the un-Attic ἄποθεν often replaces the genuine ἄπωθεν in the manuscripts of Attic books, as in most at Thucydides, 2. 81, and in some at 3. 111; 4. 67, 92, 115, 120, 125, 126; 6. 58, 77; 8. 69. The testimony of verse makes the long penult absolutely secure—

κἄστ' οὐ μακρὰν ἄπωθεν, ἀλλ' ἐνταῦθά που.
Ar. Av. 1184.

ὀλίγον ἄπωθεν τῆς κεφαλῆς τοῦ γρᾳδίου.
Plut. 674.

Similarly ὄπισθεν is placed beyond question by lines like—

A. ποῦ ποῦ 'στιν; B. ἐξόπισθεν. A. ἐξόπισθ' ἴθι.
Ar. Ran. 286.

In a choric passage of Aeschylus ὄπιθεν is encountered, but there is no other instance even in Tragedy—

τροχηλάτοισιν ὄπιθεν ἑπόμενοι.
Pers. 1002.

The metre demands ὄπιθεν, and yet the manuscripts exhibit ὄπισθεν without a variant. That in Attic texts ὄπισθεν remains uncorrupted is due to the fact that, even in the Common dialect, it vigorously held its own against the forms with the short penult. The affinity of theta for sigma—always present in Greek from the earliest period—

rather increased than lessened as the language aged, and is a fact which must be carefully observed by the student of Greek forms.

III.

Ἱκεσία· καὶ τοῦτο ἀδόκιμον, ἱκετεία δέ.

The former word is the older, being found in Tragedy and in a religious formula in Aeschines (70. 33). In the 'Apparatus Sophistae' Phrynichus supplements this statement (44. 5): *ἱκετεία· διὰ τοῦ τ, οὐ διὰ τοῦ σ· ἱκεσίους μέντοι λιτὰς καὶ λόγους ἱκεσίους*, and unintentionally sets the inquirer on the right road. To the grammarian *ἱκεσία* was a late form; and he did not accept the lesson which the adjective *ἱκέσιος* might have taught him, namely, that, like many other *un-Attic* words employed in the Common dialect, it was in existence, not only in other dialects, but had also a place in undeveloped Attic itself. As a matter of fact *ἱκεσία* and *ἱκέσιος* bear the same relation to *ἱκέτης*, *ἱκετεύω* as *δημόσιος* to *δημότης*, *δημοτεύω*, and *προστάσιος* to *προστάτης*, *προστατεύω*. Accordingly, there might have been a *δημοτεῖν* and a *ἱκετεῖν* by the side of *δημοτεύειν* and *ἱκετεύειν* as well as a *προστατεῖν* by the side of *προστατεύειν*. *ἱκετήρ* is not found even in Homer, although Hesychius has preserved a form *ἱκετορεύω* from *ἱκέτωρ*. Moreover, *ἱκετήσιος* by the side of *ἱκετήριος* seems to indicate that the change from *ἱκετήρ* to *ἱκέτης* took place early.

Most verbs in *-εύω* are of a comparatively late origin. The ending is simply that of the naturally-formed *ἁλιεύω*, *βασιλεύω*, *ἱππεύω*, and the like, applied to other stems. The verbs *εὔω*, *δεύω*, *νεύω*, *κελεύω*, *θεραπεύω* stand on a different footing and must be eliminated from the inquiry. Apart from them there are over two hundred verbs in *-εύω*, and of these little more than twenty belong to the group regularly formed from substantives in -εύς. These, however, are mostly old words found in the Homeric poems, while a very large proportion of the others is not found till long after that date. Most are from substantives in -ος, -ον, like δεσμεύω, δουλεύω, κινδυνεύω, μεταλλεύω from δεσμός, δοῦλος, κίνδυνος, and μέταλλον, a few from adjectives in -ος, like περισσεύω from περισσός, and πτωχεύω from πτωχός, while the other two declensions are fairly represented.

The group which contains ἱκετεύω is not large—ἀλητεύω, γοητεύω, δημοτεύομαι, δυναστεύω, ἐμβατεύω, ἐποπτεύω, ἰδιωτεύω, ληστεύω, μαστεύω, μνηστεύω, ὁπλιτεύω, πολιτεύω, προστατεύω, προφητεύω, πυκτεύω, σοφιστεύω, τραπεζιτεύω, ὑποπτεύω. The verb ξενιτεύομαι, *serve as a mercenary*, is a remarkable instance of formation by false analogy. Forms like ξενίτης from ξένος are quite unknown to Greek, and the verb could never have been used except ὁπλιτεύω and τραπεζιτεύω had prepared the way for it.

IV.

Ὑπόδειγμα· οὐδὲ τοῦτο ὀρθῶς λέγεται· παράδειγμα λέγε.

Xenophon (Eq. 2. 2) anticipates the Common dialect in using ὑπόδειγμα for παράδειγμα. In Attic ὑποδείκνυμι was never used except in its natural sense of *show by implication;* but in Herodotus and Xenophon it signifies *to mark out*, *set a pattern*. Herod. 1. 89, κατέτεινε σχοινοτενέας ὑποδέξας διώρυχας: Xen. Mem. 4. 3. 13, αὐτοὶ οἱ θεοὶ οὕτως ὑποδεικνύουσιν.

This comparison of the half-hearted ὑπόδειγμα, with the masculine and straightforward παράδειγμα, well brings out the distinction between the Attic dialect on the one hand, and the Ionic and the Common dialect on the other. There is more tone about ὑπόδειγμα, but παράδειγμα has common sense to recommend it.

V.

Ὠνάμην, ὤνασο, ὤνατο πάντα ἀδόκιμα ὅταν διὰ τοῦ α. τὰ γὰρ ἀρχαῖα διὰ τοῦ η, ὠνήμην, ὤνησο, ὤνητο.

The Indicative forms in alpha came at a late date from the genuine *ὀναίμην* and *ὄνασθαι*, and were sometimes imported into Attic texts, as in Eur. H. F. 1368—

ἀπώλεσ', οὐδ' ὤνησθε τῶν ἐμῶν καλῶν·

where the manuscripts exhibit *ὤνασθε*. The true form was preserved by the metre in Alc. 335—

θεοῖς γενέσθαι· σοῦ γὰρ οὐκ ὠνήμεθα.

Veitch has treated the verb with his usual care. It is observable that Xenophon has in one passage coined *ὠνήθην*, although *ὠνήμην* was ready to his hand.

The aorist *ὠνήμην*, from *ὀνίνημι*, may be instructively compared with *ἐπλήμην*, from *πίμπλημι*, which, compounded with *ἐν*, was in common use at Athens—

ἀποδρὰς γὰρ ἐς τὴν γωνίαν, τυρὸν πολὺν
κατεσικέλιζε κἀνέπλητ' ἐν τῷ σκότῳ.

Ar. Vesp. 910.

εὐθὺς γὰρ ὡς ἐνέπλητο πολλῶν κἀγαθῶν.

Id. 1304.

In its imperative, *ἔμπλησο* (Vesp. 603), and its participle, *ἐμπλήμενος* (Vesp. 424, 984, Eccl. 51, Eq. 935), it corresponded with *ὀνίνημι*; but its infinitive was undoubtedly *ἐμπλῆσθαι*, and its optative, *ἐμπλῄμην* (Ach. 236), followed the analogy of the perfect optatives *βεβλῄμην* and *μεμνῄμην*.

Cobet is unquestionably right in restoring *ἐνέπλητο* for *ἐνεπέπλητο* in Lysias, 180. 5 (28. 6), *οὕτως, ὦ ἄνδρες Ἀθηναῖοι, ἐπειδὴ τάχιστα ἐνέπλητο καὶ τῶν ὑμετέρων ἀπέλαυσαν κτε.*

VI.

Μέχρις καὶ ἄχρις σὺν τῷ σ, ἀδόκιμα· μέχρι δὲ καὶ ἄχρι λέγε.

The question has been settled by Wecklein in Curae Epigraphicae, p. 51, where he quotes from Attic inscriptions, *μέχρι ἑξακοσίων* (bis), *μέχρι ἀνδρῶν*, *μέχρι τοῦ τεταγμένου*, and *ἄχρι τῆς συναγωγῆς*. Stone records exhibit no instances of the forms with sigma even before a vowel, and the same lesson is taught by metre. The words are unknown to Tragedy, except that *μέχρις* occurs in a desperately corrupt line of Sophocles—

> *τὸν παῖδα τόνδε πρὸς δόμους ἐμοὺς ἄγων*
> *Τελαμῶνι δείξει μητρί τ', Ἐριβοίᾳ λέγω,*
> *ὥς σφιν γένηται γηροβοσκὸς εἰσαεί·*
> *μέχρις οὗ μυχοὺς κίχωσι τοῦ κάτω θεοῦ.*
>
> Ajax 571.

Most manuscripts have *μέχρις οὗ*, the Cod. Ven. *μέχρι*, others *μέχρις ἄν*, which has the questionable support of Suïdas, sub vocibus *γηροβοσκῶ* and *μυχός*. Though the broken anapaest *μέχρις οὗ* may pass as an extension of the licence allowed even in Tragedy to prepositions followed immediately by their case, yet the variety of readings justify *ἔστ' ἂν μυχούς*, the conjecture of Hermann, *μέχρις οὗ, μέχρις, μέχρι* having crept into the text from the margin. In Aesch. P. V. 376, *μέχρις* is a manuscript gloss on the primitive *ἔστ' ἄν*, but has not replaced the latter in the text.

In Comedy there is not one instance of *ἄχρις* or *μέχρις* demanded by the metre, but even if lines like Eq. 964—

> *ψωλὸν γενέσθαι δεῖ σε μέχρι τοῦ μυρρίνου,*

are not regarded as absolutely conclusive, there is still a line of Antiphanes (Ath. 10. 441) in which *μέχρις* could certainly not stand—

μέχρι γὰρ τριῶν δεῖν φασὶ τιμᾶν τοὺς θεούς.

In the New Comedy, by which time *μέχρι ἂν* with the mood of a verb was not only a tolerated but a recognised construction, the hiatus is in manuscripts sometimes avoided by reading *μέχρις*, but that form was certainly never used even by the latest writers of Comic verse—

καὶ τοῦτο πωλεῖν μέχρι ἂν ὥσπερ ἐν ἐράνῳ
εἷς λοιπὸς ᾖ κάπηλος ἠδικημένος
ὑπ' οἰνοπώλου.

Diphilus (Athen. 11. 499 D.).

The grammarians are singularly at one on this point. Moeris, p. 34, *ἄχρι, ἄνευ τοῦ σ Ἀττικῶς, ἄχρις Ἑλληνικῶς*: Herodian, Philet. 451, *ἄχρι καὶ μέχρι ἄνευ τοῦ σ· τὸ δὲ σὺν τῷ σ Ἰωνικόν*: Thomas Mag. 135, *ἄχρι καὶ μέχρι Θουκυδίδης ἀεὶ λέγει, οὐ μόνον ἐπαγομένου συμφώνου, ἀλλὰ καὶ φωνήεντος*, and although he adds, *οἱ δὲ ἄλλοι, ἐπαγομένου μόνου φωνήεντος, καὶ μετὰ τοῦ σ καὶ χωρὶς τοῦ σ γράφουσιν οἷον ἄχρις οὗ καὶ ἄχρι οὗ*, there is no doubt that to all Attic texts the shorter forms should be restored, without any regard to manuscripts, as even in Thucydides the copyists followed no rule, but wrote either indifferently.

VII.

Ἀπίναι, προσίναι, ἐξίναι, κατίναι, πάντα ἀδόκιμα ἄνευ τοῦ ε λεγόμενα. χρὴ γὰρ σὺν τῷ ε ἀπιέναι, ἐξιέναι λέγειν.

VIII.

Εἰσιέτω· καὶ περὶ τούτου οὕτως ἔσχε. Λολλιανὸς ἀκούσας ὅτι χρὴ σὺν τῷ ε εἰσιέναι λέγειν εἶτα ὑπέλαβε καὶ τὸ εἰσίτω εἰσιέτω δεῖν λέγεσθαι.

That Lollianus was himself a Greek and taught at

Athens shortly before Phrynichus wrote, vividly illustrates the condition into which the Attic dialect had fallen in the first half of the second century A.D. Those who desire more information about Lollianus may consult Philostratus, de Vitis Sophistarum, I. 23. 526, but he gets more than his due in Suïdas: *Λολλιανός. Ἐφέσιος, σοφιστής, μαθητὴς Ἰσαίου τοῦ Ἀσσυρίου· γεγονὼς ἐπὶ Ἀδριανοῦ τοῦ Καίσαρος· ἔγραψε πολλά.*

IX.

Ἐμπτύει μου μηδαμῶς λέγε, ἀλλὰ καταπτύει μου, καὶ κατέπτυσα αὐτοῦ.

Scaliger proposed to substitute *μοι* for *μου* after *ἐμπτύει*, in spite of the fact that *ἐμπτύει μου* seems quite possible in late Greek.

In the Septuagint and the New Testament, *ἐμπτύω* is frequently encountered in the sense of the Attic *καταπτύω*. Mk. 10. 34, *καὶ ἐμπαίξουσιν αὐτῷ καὶ μαστιγώσουσιν αὐτὸν καὶ ἐμπτύσουσιν αὐτῷ, καὶ ἀποκτενοῦσιν αὐτόν*: id. 14. 65, *καὶ ἤρξαντό τινες ἐμπτύειν αὐτῷ*: id. 15. 19, *καὶ ἐνέπτυον αὐτῷ*. Lobeck quotes from Galen, 13. 940 D, *ἐμπτύει τοῖς σώμασι τὸν ἰόν.*

In Attic *ἐμπτύω* could only be used of spitting *in a vessel*, etc., like *ἐνουρῶ*, whereas *καταπτύω, καταγελῶ, καθυβρίζω*, corresponded to *κατουρῶ*.

It is the same difference which confronts us in *ἐγχέω* and *καταχέω*. *ἐγχεῖν* is legitimately used with the dative in the meaning *pour in*—

μέθυ δ' ἐκ κρητῆρος ἀφύσσων
οἰνοχόος φορέῃσι καὶ ἐγχείῃ δεπάεσσιν·
Od. 9. 10.

φέρε τὴν οἰνήρυσιν
ἵν' οἶνον ἐγχέω λαβὼν ἐς τοὺς χόας·
Ar. Ach. 1067.

and καταχέω with the genitive in the sense of *pour over*,—

σφωϊν μάλα πολλάκις ὑγρὸν ἔλαιον
χαιτάων κατέχευε.

Il. 23. 282.

ἀλλ' ἱππερών μου κατέχεεν τῶν χρημάτων.

Ar. Nub. 74.

ἀλλ' ἐγὼ εἶδον ὄναρ, καὶ μοὐδόκει ἡ θεὸς αὐτὴ
τοῦ δήμου καταχεῖν ἀρυταίνῃ πλουθυγίειαν.

Eq. 1090.

Plato, Legg. 800 D, ἐνίοτε πᾶσαν βλασφημίαν τῶν ἱερῶν καταχέουσι. In Rep. 398 A, the preposition is expressed, τὸν μύρον κατὰ τῆς κεφαλῆς καταχέαντες. In late Greek, however, ἐγχέω was used for καταχέω, just as ἐμπτύω for καταπτύω. Synes. Ep. 140, p. 276 C, τί οὖν ποτνιᾷ, καὶ ταῖς ἐπιστολαῖς τῶν δακρύων ἐγχεῖς; in such words ἐν has never the force of *on*, *at*, *over*, in Attic Greek, but, when it does not mean *in*, is simply intensive. Thus ἐνορῶ is justly used in Ar. Ach. 1129—

ἐν τῷ χαλκίῳ
ἐνορῶ γέροντα δειλίας φευξούμενον,

and in Plato, Gorg. 447 B, ἐν χρημάτων κατασκευῇ κακίαν ἄλλην τινὰ ἐνορᾷς ἢ πενίαν; Dem. 401. 17, ἤρετο τίνα ἐν αὐτῷ μικροψυχίαν ἐνεωρακὼς εἴη. But no genuine Attic writer could have used it as Xenophon does in Cyr. 1. 4. 27, ἐνεώρας μοι, 'you looked *at* me,' though such a use would have been tolerated in Ionic and late Greek. On the other hand, ἐν intensive was frequently added to the simple verb by the best Attic writers, as ἐνήλλετο in Ar. Vesp. 1305—

ὥσπερ καχρύων ὀνίδιον εὐωχημένον
ἐνήλλετ', ἐσκίρτα, 'πεπόρδει, κατεγέλα.

ἔντραγε in Eq. 51—

ἐνθοῦ, ῥόφησον, ἔντραγ', ἔχε τριώβολον,

and in some words the simple form had completely disappeared before the compound, as in ἐμπίπρημι, ἐνοχλῶ, ἐναντιοῦμαι, etc. In some cases the analogy of the Latin *in* is so likely to suggest itself, that it is not surprising to find ἐγγελῶ generally regarded as the equivalent of *irrideo*, and ἐμπαίζω of *illudo*, etc. As a matter of fact, it will be difficult to discover a single instance, in Attic Prose or Comedy, of ἐμπαίζω in the sense of προσπαίζω or καταπαίζω, of ἐγγελῶ in that of προσγελῶ or καταγελῶ, and of ἐμπνέω in that of καταπνέω.

In Aristophanes the ἐν in ἐνυβρίζω, Thesm. 719, is simply intensive—

> ἀλλ' οὐ μὰ τὼ θεὼ τάχ' οὐ χαίρων ἴσως
> ἐνυβριεῖ λόγους λέξεις τ' ἀνοσίους·

and ἐνυβρίζω might be followed by κατά to convey the meaning of καθυβρίζομαι, just as κατά is used after ἐγγελῶ by Sophocles—

> ὁ δ' ἐν δόμοις τύραννος, ὦ τάλας ἐγώ,
> κοινῇ καθ' ἡμῶν ἐγγελῶν ἁβρύνεται.
> O. C. 1339.

In Tragedy as in Ionic there is no question that ἐν in compounds had occasionally a force similar to that of κατά or πρός, but such a use must be distinctly denied in genuine Attic writers. Accordingly, if Porson's conjecture of ἐγγελῶσι for ἀγγελοῦσι be admitted in the lines of Eubulus, quoted by the Scholiast on Eurip. Med. 476, the word is intended as a hit at Tragic diction—

> Εὐριπίδου δ' ἔσωσας ὡς ἴσασι σοι
> . . . . .
> καὶ τοῖς ἐμοῖσιν ἐγγελῶσι πήμασιν
> τὸ σῖγμα συλλέξαντες ὡς αὐτοὶ σόφοι.

X.

Εὐκοίτει· καὶ τοῦτο ἀποτρέπου.

This is the only place in which the word εὐκοιτεῖν is found, although μονοκοιτοῦμεν occurs in Aristophanes (Lys. 592), σκληροκοιτεῖν in Hippocrates (338. 23), στιβαδοκοιτεῖν in Polybius (2. 17. 10), and Strabo (3. 155), αἰθριοκοιτεῖν in Theocritus (8. 78). Phrynichus himself has preserved φορμοκοιτεῖν (App. Soph. 70. 5): Φορμοκοιτεῖν· τὸ ἐπὶ φορμοῦ καθεύδειν. Φορμὸς δέ ἐστι πλέγμα τι ἐκ φλέω. Τάττεται ἐπὶ λυπρῶς καὶ κακῶς κοιμωμένων, οὐδ' ἐχόντων κνάφαλλον. Here some particular usage of εὐκοιτεῖν is doubtless reprehended. Lobeck supposes that Phrynichus is deprecating the use of its imperative in the sense of *good night.* Had such a usage been classical, it would certainly have been referred to by Lucian in his discussion of the different forms of address (Ὑπὲρ τοῦ ἐν τῇ προσαγορεύσει πταίσματος), along with χαῖρε, ὑγίαινε, ἔρρωσο.

XI.

Εὐχαριστεῖν οὐδεὶς τῶν δοκίμων εἶπεν, ἀλλὰ χάριν εἰδέναι.

The word εὐχάριστος is of some interest. In pure Attic writers it occurs neither in the sense of *gracious* nor *grateful*, but Xenophon employs it in both these meanings, Cyr. 2. 2. 1, ἀεὶ μὲν οὖν ἐπεμέλετο ὁ Κῦρος ὅπως εὐχαριστότατοί τε ἅμα λόγοι ἐμβληθήσονται: Cyr. 8. 3. 49, καὶ γὰρ βέλτιστον πάντων τῶν ζῴων ἡγεῖτο ἄνθρωπον εἶναι καὶ εὐχαριστότατον. Even εὐχαριστεῖν, *to be grateful*, εὐχαριστία, *gratitude*, would not have been out of place in his style The meaning *gratias agere* is first attached to the verb in Polybius, e.g. 16. 25. 1, ὁ τῶν Ἀθηναίων δῆμος ἐξέπεμπε πρεσβευτὰς πρὸς Ἄτταλον τὸν βασιλέα τοὺς ἅμα μὲν εὐχαριστήσοντας ἐπὶ τοῖς γεγόνοσι κτε., and became frequent after his time.

XII.

Ἄρτι ἥξω μηδέποτε εἴπῃς ἐπὶ τοῦ μέλλοντος ἀλλ' ἐπὶ τοῦ ἐνεστηκότος καὶ τοῦ παρῳχημένου, ἄρτι ἥκω, ἄρτι ἀφικόμην.

Two instances of ἄρτι with the future used to be quoted from Attic writers, one from Plato, Charm. 172 D, σκεψώμεθα εἰ ἄρτι καὶ ἡμᾶς ὀνήσει, the other from Antiphanes (Athen. 8. 338 E)—

ὦ Ζεῦ, τίς ποτε,
ὦ Καλλιμέδων, σὲ κατέδετ' ἄρτι τῶν φίλων;

but ἄρα τι has been restored to Plato with manuscript authority, and Meineke is unquestionably right in reading κατέδετἄρα τῶν φίλων in the Comic poet. The word does not occur in Homer, and appears first in literature in Theognis 997—

ἦμος δ' ἠέλιος μὲν ἐν αἰθέρι μώνυχας ἵππους
ἄρτι παραγγέλλοι, μέσσατον ἦμαρ ἔχων.

Attic writers frequently add νῦν or νυνί, as Ar. Lys. 1008, ἄρτι νυνὶ μανθάνω. ἄρτι corresponds exactly to the English adverb *just*, and, like it, may be used both of past and present time. ἔναγχος, on the other hand, is always attached to past tenses—

ἔναγχος γάρ ποτε
ὑπ' ἀλφιταμοιβοῦ παρεκόπην διχοινίκῳ.
Ar. Nub. 639.

It never occurs in Tragedy, νεωστί being used instead. The latter word is, however, itself an excellent prose form. The synonym προσφάτως, so frequent in the Common dialect, is unknown to Attic, although it doubtless existed in other dialects in pre-Macedonian times. Pindar, Pyth. 4.

extr. has the neuter of the adjective in an adverbial sense, *πρόσφατον Θήβᾳ ξενωθείς*.

Sophocles is the first author in whose writings *ἀρτίως* is encountered as an equivalent of *ἄρτι*. In writers posterior to him both forms are found. The circumstance that in Sophocles *ἀρτίως* occurs thirty-three times, *ἄρτι* only thirteen times, while in Euripides *ἄρτι* is met with as often as *ἀρτίως*, and in other writers more often, adds some colour to the opinion that *ἀρτίως* was first coined by Sophocles. Certainly Aeschylus never employs the term, and that Xenophon eschews it goes to prove that it was a peculiarly Attic formation. In another passage (App. Soph. 11. 19) Phrynichus tells us that the Atticists distinguished between *ἄρτι* and *ἀρτίως*, but no distinction is traceable in Attic writers.

The word *ἄρτι* is never equivalent to *νῦν* in Classical Greek. Accordingly, the Anti-atticist in Bekk. An. 79 must be in error: Ἀπάρτι· ἀντὶ τοῦ ἄρτι ἀπὸ νῦν. Πλάτων Σοφισταῖς. The meaning of *ἀπαρτί* is in Attic very different. The preposition has the same strengthening force that is seen in *ἀπεργάζεσθαι, ἀπανδροῦν*. The primitive meaning *exactly*, is not found in Attic, but occurs in Ionic. Its Attic signification, *just the reverse*, *quite the contrary*, is of course due to irony, and *ἀπαρτί* belongs to that considerable class of expressions by which Athenian vivacity lent colour to dialogue and repartee. For example, when the Nurse in the Medea would call the Paedagogus a fool for estimating their mistress' passion too lightly, she uses a phrase which was probably familiar even to vulgar ears, and from attrition had lost the *τοῦ νοῦ* which originally belonged to it—

ζηλῶ σ'· ἐν ἀρχῇ πῆμα κοὐδέπω μεσοῖ.

Eur. Med. 60.

So firmly attached had its secondary meaning become to *ἀπαρτί*, that it retained it even in the middle of a sentence, and to qualify a verb—

οὐκ, ὦ κακόδαιμον, ἀλλὰ τοὺς χρηστοὺς μόνους
ἔγωγε, καὶ τοὺς δεξιοὺς καὶ σώφρονας
ἀπαρτὶ πλουτῆσαι ποιήσω.

Ar. Plut. 388.

There is a lucid note on this word in Bekk. An. I. 418, which bears the marks of being by an early and able hand: Ἀπαρτί· παρ' Ἡροδότῳ σημαίνει τὸ ἀπηρτισμένως καὶ ἀκριβῶς. ἀπὸ τούτου εἰσὶ στάδιοι χίλιοι ἀπαρτὶ εἰς τὸν Ἀραβικὸν κόλπον[1]. παρὰ δὲ τοῖς Κωμικοῖς, τὸ ἐκ τοῦ ἐναντίου. Φερεκράτης Κραταπάλλοις—

A. τί δαί; τί σαυτὸν ἀποτίνειν τῷδ' ἀξιοῖς[2]; φράσον μοί.
B. ἀπαρτὶ δή που προσλαβεῖν παρὰ τοῦδ' ἔγωγε μᾶλλον.

Κοριαννοῖ—

ἀπαρτὶ μὲν οὖν ἐμοὶ μὲν εἰκός ἐστ' ἐρᾶν,
σοὶ δ' οὐκέθ' ὥρα.

Πλάτων Κλεοφῶντι—

ἀλλ' αὐτὸς ἀπαρτὶ τἀλλότρι' οἰχήσει φέρων.

τάχα δὲ ὁ Τηλεκλείδης ὁμοίως τῷ Ἡροδότῳ κέχρηται·

σὺ δὲ φρόνιμος αὐτὸς ὢν
ἀπαρτὶ ταύτης τῆς τέχνης,

μήποτ' οὖν τὸ μὲν πλῆρες καὶ ἀπηρτισμένον ὅταν σημαίνῃ ὀξυτονεῖται, τὸ δ' ἐναντίον βαρύνεται. It is quite possible that Teleclides, an early comic poet, used the word in its primitive sense; but in the passage quoted by the Grammarian the context is required to prove that it does not bear its ordinary Attic signification.

XIII.

Τέμαχος κρέως ἢ πλακοῦντος ἢ ἄρτου οὐκ ὀρθῶς ἐρεῖ τις, ἀλλὰ τόμος κρέως ἢ πλακοῦντος· τὸ δὲ τέμαχος μόνον ἐπὶ ἰχθύος.

This usage, inculcated again by Phrynichus in App.

[1] Hdt. 2. 158; cp. id. 5. 53, ἀναισιμοῦνται ἡμέραι ἀπαρτὶ ἐνενήκοντα: Hippocr. 390. 46, ὡς ἐπὶ τὸ πουλὺ ἀπαρτὶ ἐν τοῖσι καιροῖσι μεταβάλλουσι ἐς τὰ ῥοφήματα ἐκ τῆς κενεαγγείης.

[2] MSS. τίς αὐτὸν ἀποκτείνει τὸ δ' ἀξιοῖς; emendavit Lobeck.

Soph. 65, and by Thomas and Suïdas, is never departed from till post-Attic times—

ἄρτον καὶ κρέας καὶ τέμαχος.

Ar. Eq. 283.

ἄρτους, τεμάχη, μάζας.

Eccl. 606.

πολὺ χρῆμα τεμαχῶν καὶ κρεῶν ὠπτημένων.

Plut. 894.

κεστρᾶν τεμάχη μεγαλᾶν ἀγαθᾶν κρέα τ' ὀρνίθεια κιχηλᾶν.

Nub. 339.

How large a place fish occupied in the dietary of the Athenians may be indirectly illustrated by the well-known saying of Aeschylus given by Athenaeus (8. 347 E), τὰς αὑτοῦ τραγῳδίας τεμάχη εἶναι ἔλεγε τῶν Ὁμήρου μεγάλων δείπνων.

In Attic writers τόμος occurs with the following genitives: ἀλλᾶντος, *sausage*, Pherecrates, Eubulus, Aristophanes, Mnesimachus; φύσκης, *large sausage*, Pherecrates, Mnesimachus; χορδῆς, *small sausage*, Cratinus, Axionicus, Mnesimachus; χορδαρίου, *id.*, Alexis; τυροῦ, *cheese*, Eubulus, Ephippus; μήτρας, *swine's paunch*, Teleclides; ἠνύστρου, *tripe*, Mnesimachus; πλακοῦντος, *cake*, Ar. Eq. 1190. The distinction between the words is brought into relief in Ar. Eq. 1177 ff.—

Παφλαγών.

τουτὶ τέμαχός σοὔδωκεν ἡ Φοβεσιστράτη.

Ἀλλαντοπώλης.

ἡ δ' Ὀβριμοπάτρα γ' ἑφθὸν ἐκ ζωμοῦ κρέας,
καὶ χόλικος, ἠνύστρου τε, καὶ γαστρὸς τόμον.

Probably Attic stood alone in thus differentiating these two kindred words. At all events, in the Common dialect the distinction was not observed. The value of a language as a vehicle of expression is enhanced by adroit manipulation of superfluous forms. English has been greatly enriched in this way, as is indicated by the presence in literary English, in distinct senses, of elder, older, eldest, oldest, later, latter, last, latest, brothers, brethren, and many other words originally identical in signification. In fact, there are few better tests of a language than the way in which it utilises its waste.

XIV.

Ἄμυναν μὴ εἴπῃς, ἀλλ' εἰς ῥῆμα μεταβάλλων, ἀμύνασθαι· πάντα γὰρ τὰ τοῦ ῥήματος εὐδόκιμα, ἀμυνοῦμαι, ἀμύνασθαι, ἠμυνάμην, ἀμυνοῦμεν.

Like πλύνω, and a few other verbs in -ύνω, ἀμύνω has no noun from which it may be considered to be derived. Verbs in -ύνω are few in number, and nine tenths of them are, like βαθύνω from βαθύς, κακύνω from κακός, αἰσχύνω from αἶσχος, formed from an existing noun by the help of the suffix -ύνω. The α in ἀμύνω is beyond question euphonic, as is seen from the Homeric μύνη (Od. 21. 111), in the sense of a *putting off*, ἀλλ' ἄγε, μὴ μύνῃσι παρέλκετε κτε., and the verb μύνομαι, employed by Alcaeus in a similar sense, οὐδέ τι μυνάμενος ἄλλο νόημα. The root is of extraordinary fertility in Latin, moenia, munio, immunis, etc.

There are two ways of accounting for the substantive ἄμυνα, which, according to Lobeck, is first found in writers of the first century A. D., such as Philo and Plutarch. Either it entered the Common dialect from the dialects—a supposition which is supported by the existence of μύνη—or it was formed at a late date on the analogy of εὔθυνα. Of the forty or so verbs in -ύνω which are found in Attic, εὐθύνω is differentiated from the others by having an adjective εὔθυνος allied to it, and in this respect another verb, namely, αἰσχύνω, meets it half way by having a substantive αἰσχύνη among its kin. As has been shown, ἀμύνω stands on a different footing from either of these words; but yet it is quite possible that ἄμυνα was due to a false derivation.

εὐθύνω	εὔθυνος	εὔθυνα	εὐθυντήρ
αἰσχύνω		αἰσχύνη	αἰσχυντήρ
ἀμύνω		ἄμυνα	ἀμυντήρ.

The former explanation is, however, the more probable, and receives valuable support from the form χειμάμυνα, Pollux 7. 61, τὸ χειμερινὸν ἱμάτιον χείμαστρον ἂν λέγοις, καὶ χλαῖναν δὲ παχεῖαν ἣν χειμάμυναν μὲν Αἴσχυλος, Ὅμηρος δὲ ἀλεξάνεμον κέκληκεν.

XV.

Ἀποτάσσομαί σοι ἔκφυλον πάνυ. χρὴ λέγειν ἀσπάζομαί σε. οὕτω γὰρ καὶ οἱ ἀρχαῖοι εὑρίσκονται λέγοντες ἐπειδὰν ἀπαλλάττωνται ἀλλήλων.

The sense of ἀποτάσσειν in pre-Alexandrine Greek is *to assign.* Plato, Theaet. 153 E, μηδέ τιν' αὐτῷ χῶρον ἀποτάξῃς: Dem. 238. 8, ἐν τοῖς φρουρίοις ἀποτεταγμένοι, *having posts assigned them, stationed.* The use of the preposition is identical with that in ἀποβλέπω, and ἀφορῶ, ἀποτάσσειν meaning, *to post in one place,* disregarding all others, as ἀποβλέπειν and ἀφορᾶν mean, *to look in one direction,* disregarding all others.

The usage referred to by Phrynichus is very frequent in late writers, as Nov. Test. Luc. 9. 61, πρῶτον δὲ ἐπίτρεψόν μοι ἀποτάξασθαι τοῖς εἰς τὸν οἶκόν μου: Acts 18. 18, ὁ δὲ Παῦλος τοῖς ἀδέλφοις ἀποταξάμενος ἐξέπλει εἰς τὴν Συρίαν.

Still more strangely, συντάσσομαι seems to have been employed in a similar signification, Pallad. Anth. Pal. 9. 171, λόγοι, συντάσσομαι ὑμῖν. In the Pseudosophist, Lucian tells us how his friend Socrates took off a stranger who used the word in this absurd sense (566), λέγοντος δέ τινος, Συνετάξατό μοι· καὶ λόχον δέ, ἔφη, Ξενοφῶν εἶπε συνετάξατο.

XVI.

Σημᾶναι, ἐσήμαναν, καὶ θερμᾶναι, ἐθέρμαναν, καὶ καθᾶραι, ἐκάθαραν· καὶ ταῦτα παρὰ τὴν ἀρχαίαν χρῆσιν διὰ τοῦ α. λέγομεν δὲ διὰ τοῦ η, σημῆναι, θερμῆναι, καθῆραι.

XVII.

Ἐφλέγμανε, φλεγμᾶναι· καὶ ταῦτα διὰ τοῦ η.

These remarks of Phrynichus start a question of some importance and of great difficulty. As regards verbs in *-αίρω* there can be no doubt about the Attic rule; the aorist is invariably formed in eta, as *αἴρω, ἦρα, ἐχθαίρω, ἤχθηρα, καθαίρω, ἐκάθηρα, σαίρω, ἔσηρα, τεκμαίρομαι, ἐτεκμηράμην*. But with verbs in *-αίνω* the case is different. As far as the statement of Phrynichus goes it is absolute, for verbs in which the *-αίνω* is preceded by mu take eta without exception in the aorist tense—

ἐκμαίνω	ἐξέμηνα	πημαίνω	ἐπήμηνα
θερμαίνω	ἐθέρμηνα	ποιμαίνω	ἐποίμηνα
κυμαίνω	ἐκύμηνα	σημαίνω	ἐσήμηνα
λυμαίνομαι	ἐλυμηνάμην	φλεγμαίνω	ἐφλέγμηνα.

With those verbs in *-αίνω* which his note does not embrace there is more difficulty. Two classes, however, are uniform, namely, verbs in *-ραίνω* and verbs in *-ιαίνω*. In the aorist of verbs in *-ραίνω* the alpha of the present is invariably retained—

δυσχεραίνω	ἐδυσχέρανα	ξηραίνω	ἐξήρανα
ἐρυθραίνω	ἠρύθρανα	περαίνω	ἐπέρανα
εὐφραίνω	ηὔφρανα	πικραίνω	ἐπίκρανα
ἐχθραίνω	ἤχθρανα	ῥαίνω	ἔρρανα
κηραίνω	ἐκήρανα	ὑγραίνω	ὕγρανα
μαραίνω	ἐμάρανα	ὑδραίνω	ὕδρανα
μωραίνω	ἐμώρανα	χραίνω	ἔχρανα.

When Veitch, sub *μαραίνω*, says, 'In the aorist of this

verb even the Attics retain *α*,' he adds one more to the long list of erroneous remarks which disfigure a work of incalculable utility and enormous labour. It is true that *διετετρήνατο* occurs in Aristophanes, but it is there employed to produce a burlesque effect—

> *ἀκοῇ δὲ χοάνην*[1] *ὦτα διετετρήνατο.*
>
> Thesm. 18.

It is only one instance out of many in which *Εὐριπιδαριστοφανισμός* has misled grammarians who regard rather the letter than the spirit of Attic law. 'In the beginning,' Euripides is represented as saying, 'Ether drilled ears, a channel for hearing,' and he aptly uses the Homeric *ἐτετρήνατο*, going even in language as near the beginning as he can. The Attic form was *ἔτρησα, ἐτρησάμην*.

The verb *τρυφεραίνομαι* is a passive deponent, and *ὀσφραίνομαι* has for aorist *ὠσφρόμην*.

The rule as to verbs in *-ιαίνω* is equally stringent—

ἀγριαίνω	*ἠγρίανα*
μιαίνω	*ἐμίανα*
πιαίνω	*ἐπίανα*
ὑγιαίνω	*ὑγίανα*
χλιαίνω	*ἐχλίανα.*

Homer uses *ἐδίηνα*, as he uses *ἐμίηνα, ὕδρηνα*, etc., but if an Attic writer, even a Tragic poet, had had occasion to use the aorist of *διαίνω*, he would have replaced *ἐδίηνα* by *ἐδίανα*, just as Euripides replaced *ἐμίηνα* by *ἐμίανα*, and *ὑδρηνάμην* by *ὑδρανάμην*.

Of the five verbs in *-λαίνω* one only is found in the aorist, namely, *κοιλαίνω*, and that has indisputably *ἐκοίλανα*. Accordingly, the aorists of the others may be safely formed on its analogy—

δυσκολαίνω	*ἐδυσκόλανα*
χωλαίνω	*ἐχώλανα*
μελαίνω	*ἐμέλανα.*

[1] The accepted emendation of Dobree for the MSS. *ἀκοὴν δὲ χοάνης*.

The fifth verb, *ἀλαίνω*, goes no further than the present stem.

The same method will, on the analogy of *κατεγλυκάνατο*[1] and *ὤργανα*, supply an aorist *ἐλεύκανα* to *λευκαίνω*, *ἐκάλχανα* to *καλχαίνω*, *ἠσέλγανα* to *ἀσελγαίνω*, and *ἐβάσκανα* to *βασκαίνω*.

The few that remain admit of no classification. Aeschylus has *ἀπανηναμένας* (Eum. 972), Euripides *ἀνήνασθαι* (Med. 237), but *ἴσχνανα* occurs in the same play of Aeschylus (267), and in Aristophanes (Ran. 941). Isocrates employs *χαλεπήναντες* (62. a.), but Aristophanes *πεπᾶναι* (Vesp. 646), and Axionicus *λιπάνας* (Athen. 8. 342 B).

Ought *παπτήνας* in Sophocles (Ant. 1231), and *ἐτεκτήναντο* in Euripides (I. T. 951), to set the law to *λιταίνω*, *ἀκολασταίνω*, and *ἀμαθαίνω*, or should the last be seriated with *ἐκέρδανα*, a common form in Attic? Were the aorists of *κραδαίνω* and *χλιδαίνομαι*, *ἐκράδηνα*, *ἐχλιδηνάμην* or *ἐκράδανα*, *ἐχλιδανάμην*, and did *λεαίνω* and *δυσμενεαίνω* form their aorist with alpha or eta? These questions will always remain unanswerable. This, however, is certain, that in Attic Greek the four verbs *σαίνω*, *ξαίνω*, *ὑφαίνω*, *φαίνω*, preferred eta—

ξαίνω	*ἔξηνα*	*ὑφαίνω*	*ὕφηνα,*
σαίνω	*ἔσηνα*	*φαίνω*	*ἔφηνα*

and in the same series the Euripidean word *πυρσαίνω* may be placed, whereas *πυρραίνω*, if used in Attic, certainly formed an aorist *ἐπύρρανα*.

XVIII.

Διωρία ἐσχάτως ἀδόκιμον. ἀντ' αὐτοῦ δὲ προθεσμίαν ἐρεῖς.

The *ἐσχάτως* is certainly not out of place. It is difficult

[1] In the *Πτωχοί* of Chionides, quoted by Athen. 14. 638 D—

ταῦτ' οὐ μὰ Δία Γνήσιππος, οὐδὲ Κλεομένης,
ἐν ἐννέ' ἂν χορδαῖς κατεγλυκάνατο.

κατεγλυκήνατο is merely a conjecture of Porson's.

to discover how διωρία came to take the place of προθεσμία, and to discuss the question would demand an acquaintance with the slums of language which few would care to possess.

XIX.

Ἀνεῖναι ἐλαίῳ ἢ ὄξει ἢ ἄλλῳ τινὶ λέγουσιν οἱ ἰατροί, πάνυ ἀμαθῶς· δεῖ γὰρ διεῖναι λέγειν.

From the literal signification of *let run through*, διιέναι readily came to mean *steep*, *saturate*—

ἔπειτ' ἔφλα
ἐν τῇ θυίᾳ συμπαραμιγνύων ὀπὸν
καὶ σχῖνον· εἶτ' ὄξει διέμενος Σφηττίῳ,
κατέπλασεν αὐτοῦ τὰ βλέφαρα κτε.
Ar. Plut. 720.

Alexis, Πονηρά (Ath. 4. 170 C)—

τὸ τρίμμ' ἐπιπολῆς εὐρύθμως διειμένον
ὄξει, σιραίῳ χρωματίσας κτε.

Sotades, Ἐγκλειόμεναι (Ath. 7. 293 D)—

θρίοισι ταύτην (ἀμίαν) ἅλις ἐλαδίῳ διείς.

The word is frequently so used by Hippocrates, but later scientific writers, like Galen, employ ἀνιέναι, which, if ever equivalent to διιέναι, must have developed such a meaning from that of *dissolve*, *break up*.

XX.

Περιέσσευσεν ἀλλοκότως· ἐχρῆν γὰρ ἐπερίσσευσε λέγειν.

The word περισσεύω is one of the few verbs which are not included in the Attic rule, that, whether a verb is compounded with a preposition, or only appears to be so compounded, it takes the augment after the prepositional or pseudo-prepositional syllable or syllables. So accustomed had the ear become to encounter the augment after the prepositions that it was still placed after *πρό, ἐκ, ὑπέρ, περί, ἐπί*, etc., in verbs directly formed from substantives and adjectives compounded with them, and even in verbs beginning with syllables identical in sound with prepositions, but really in no way related to them. Thus, there is no *φητεύω, στατῶ, σπονδῶ, μαχῶ, σιτῶ, φασίζομαι*, but nevertheless the genius of the Greek language demanded *προεφήτευσα* or *προὐφήτευσα, ἐπεστάτουν, παρεστάτησα, προὐστάτουν, παρεσπόνδηκα, ὑπερεμάχουν, συνεσίτουν, προὐφασιζόμην*, although the verbs came from *προφήτης, ἐπιστάτης, παραστάτης, παράσπονδος, ὑπερμάχος, σύσσιτος*, and *πρόφασις*. There is no *ὠπιάζω*, but the verb formed from *ὑπώπιον*, *a black eye*, nevertheless retains its first syllable short in the tenses which require the augment—

καὶ ταῦτα δαιμονίως ὑπωπιασμέναι.
Ar. Pax 541.

ἐπιδορπίζομαι is formed from *ἐπιδόρπιον*, *dessert*, but its aorist is *ἐπεδορπισάμην*, not *ἠπιδορπισάμην*. It is not surprising therefore that verbs like *ἐπακρίζω, ἐπαμφοτερίζω*, which come directly from the phrases *ἐπ' ἄκρον* and *ἐπ' ἀμφότερα*, should form aorists *ἐπήκρισα* and *ἐπημφοτέρισα*.

The word *ἐπιτηδεύω* is an excellent instance of a verb which augments as if it were a compound with a preposition, and yet it is formed from the mysterious *ἐπιτηδές*, which may or may not be connected with the preposition *ἐπί*. It is, however, consistent, and puts to shame several verbs in which the prepositional origin of their first syllables is beyond dispute.

There are many facts which indicate that, notwithstanding the above rule, the place of the augment was in some verbs determined by the vividness with which the meaning of the prepositional element was recognized.

The history of the augmentation of ἐναντιοῦμαι puts this fact in a very striking light. In a line of Aristophanes—

> ἀλλὰ μὴν οὐδ' ἄλλο σοί πω πρᾶγμ' ἐνηντιώμεθα,
>
> Av. 385.

all the manuscripts read ἠναντιώμεθα in unabashed disregard for the rules of metre. Bentley restored the true reading, and Porson went with him. But in Attic texts there is no other instance of this method of augmenting ἐναντιοῦσθαι. Hesychius, however, proves that ἐνηντιώμεθα[1] should be restored to Thucydides, as it has been restored to Aristophanes: Thuc. 2. 40, καὶ τὰ ἐς ἀρετὴν ἠναντιώμεθα τοῖς πολλοῖς. It is very probable that in many more passages forms of ἐναντιοῦμαι with post-prepositional augment were originally read, but it is now quite impossible to detect the blunder. The comparison of these two passages with others from Demosthenes and the Orators, in which the verb certainly augments on the first syllable, clearly proves that the two elements of ἐναντιοῦμαι, still separable in the time of Thucydides and Aristophanes, ultimately coalesced to form a thoroughly agglutinative word. There is a similar period of uncertainty in many English compound words. At one time written with a hyphen, and pronounced with the emphasis equally distributed over each element, they ultimately become agglutinative compounds and receive the accent as far back as possible. It is in this way that καθήμην and ἐκαθήμην, χρῆν and ἐχρῆν, ἀφίει and ἠφίει, καθῖζον and ἐκάθιζον are to be explained. Aeschylus seems even to have used ἠφευμένος as the perfect participle of ἀφεύω—

> λευκός, τί δ' οὐχί; καὶ καλῶς ἠφευμένος
> ὁ χοῖρος· ἕψου, μηδὲ λυπηθῇς πυρί.
>
> Athen. 9. 375 E.

In fact, just as ἐνάντιος came to be regarded not as a com-

[1] The gloss in Hesychius has got mixed with another, ἠντίασεν, ἀπήντησεν. ἱκέτευσε. Θουκυδίδης δὲ τὸ ἠντιώμεθα ἐπὶ τῷ ἐναντιώμεθα, but it is plain that ἐνηντιώμεθα should be restored for ἠντιώμεθα.

pound of *ἐν* with *ἄντιος*, but as itself a simple word, so *κάθημαι, καθίζειν*, etc., ended in being considered not compounds of simple verbs with prepositions, but as themselves simple words. This at once explains the consistency with which *ἐμπολῶ* and *ἐγγυῶ* take the temporal rather than the syllabic augment. It is true that manuscripts often exhibit forms like *ἐνεγύα, ἐνεγύησα*, but only in the simple verb, and they are easily explained by other corruptions, such as *ἐγγύων* and *ἐγγύησα*. The temporal augment was in copying carelessly dropped, and in later transcripts was ignorantly replaced as a syllabic one.

In such questions manuscript authority merits little consideration. Thus, inscriptions prove that *ἀναλίσκω* did, like *ἐπιτηδεύω*, augment after the first syllable, not on it; and yet, even in the same author, the same manuscript will sometimes exhibit the genuine *ἀνήλωσα, ἀνήλωκα, ἀνηλώθην* by the side of the corrupt *ἀνάλωσα, ἀνάλωκα, ἀναλώθην*.

'Εμπολῶ, formed from *ἐμπολή*, as *ἐγγυῶ* from *ἐγγύη*, ought, like *ἐγγυῶ*, always to receive the temporal augment. In *ἐγκωμιάζω*, on the other hand, the syllabic augment is uniformly employed, *ἐνεκωμίαζον, ἐνεκωμίασα*, but never *ἠγκωμίαζον, ἠγκωμίασα*, although the verb is not a compound of *κωμιάζω*, but derived from *ἐγκώμιον*. In regard to *ἐκκλησιάζω*, manuscripts offer such conflicting evidence that it is impossible to decide finally upon the true method of augmenting the verb. To my own mind forms like *ἐξεκλησίασα, ἐξεκλησίαζον*, recommend themselves, but perhaps *ἐκκλησιάζω*, like *ἐναντιοῦμαι*, augmented in different ways at different periods. This only is certain, that in a language so precise as Attic the same writer did not, as manuscripts would indicate, use two kinds of augment in the same work and the same page of that work.

These two opposing tendencies—the feeling that the augment should follow syllables like *ἐν, πρό, ὑπέρ*, etc., and the desire to treat verbs like *κάθημαι*, not as compounds, but as simples—naturally led to many irregularities, the most marked of which was that of double augmentation. Forms like *ἀνειχόμην* and *ἀμπισχόμην* came to be regarded as simple words; and the natural result was the addition of the temporal augment to the initial syllable, *ἀνειχόμην* and *ἀνεσχόμην* becoming *ἠνειχόμην* and *ἠνεσχόμην*, *ἀμπειχόμην* and *ἀμπεσχόμην* ending in *ἠμπειχόμην* and *ἠμπεσχόμην*. These verbs in their turn led to the same treatment of others, as in Attic Greek analogy played a singularly important part.

The verbs in which Attic writers employed a double augment are eleven in number—

ἀντιβολεῖν,	entreat,	ἠντεβόλουν.
ἀντιδικεῖν,	dispute,	ἠντεδίκουν.
ἀμφισβητεῖν,	dissent,	ἠμφεσβήτουν.
ἀμφιγνοεῖν,	doubt,	ἠμφεγνόουν.
διαιτᾶν,	arbitrate,	ἐδιῄτων.
διακονεῖν,	serve,	ἐδιηκόνουν.
ἐνοχλεῖν,	trouble,	ἠνώχλουν.
παροινεῖν,	act as if drunk,	ἐπαρῴνουν.
ἀνοιγνύναι,	open,	ἀνέῳγον.
ἀνέχεσθαι	endure,	ἠνειχόμην.
ἀμπέχεσθαι,	have on,	ἠμπειχόμην.

Pierson on Moeris (p. 17, cp. p. xv) long ago observed that in Photius and Suïdas there was a distinct class of glosses—'per totum opus veluti totidem gemmulae dispersae'—easily distinguishable from the rest, not only by their inherent excellence, but also by outward marks, such as the precise and scholarly way in which confirmatory quotations are made. Cobet has demonstrated what Pierson suggested, namely, that these are both in Photius and Suïdas (and sometimes in other lexica) derived from the Ἀττικὰ Ὀνόματα of Aelius Dionysius, a rhetorician who flourished in the early part of the second century A. D.

In the present question his glosses are of incalculable value as the verbs do not happen to occur in stone monuments, and metre, for various reasons, is of little service, while the remarks of other grammarians are as foolish and unintelligible as the manuscripts of Attic texts are contradictory and corrupt.

In Photius, sub *ἠνείχετο*, is a gloss evidently from the pen of Dionysius: *Ἠνείχετο καὶ ἠνώχλει καὶ ἠκηκόει καὶ ἠντεβόλει· κοινὸν τῶν Ἀττικῶν ἰδίωμα.* Even here the copyists exhibit *ἠντιβόλει*, as they do in Aristophanes, Eq. 667—

ὁ δ' ἠντεβόλει γ' αὐτοὺς ὀλίγον μεῖναι χρόνον,

and in a fragment of the same writer preserved in Ath. 12, p. 525 A—

ἐπηκολούθουν κἠντεβόλουν προσκειμένοι.

The Etymologicum Magnum, however, p. 112. 52, puts it beyond question that Aristophanes used the forms with two augments. After quoting *ἀντεβόλησεν* from Pindar (Olym. 13. 43), and from Homer (Il. 16. 847)—

τοιοῦτοι δ' εἴ πέρ μοι ἐείκοσιν ἀντεβόλησαν,

it adds the words, *τὸ δὲ παρ' Ἀριστοφάνει ἐν Ἀμφιαράῳ διὰ τοῦ ε, ἠντεβόλησε, δύο κλίσεις ὑπέστη.*

The evidence of a scholar like Dionysius, who wrote at a time far anterior to all our manuscripts, is quite convincing, especially as there is the confirmatory evidence of the Etymologicum Magnum (11th century A. D.), also older than most of our texts, and the authority, such as it is, of the best manuscripts, for the double augment of the verbs *ἀντιδικῶ* and *ἀμφισβητῶ* in Demosthenes, and *ἀμφιγνοῶ* in Plato[1].

[1] *ἠντεδίκει*, best MS., S in Dem. 1006. 2; 1013. 23. *ἠμφεσ.* S alone or with others in Dem. 818. 9; 820. 26; 899. 11; 1000. 3, etc. Observe the place of the second augment, *ἠμφ-ε-ς-βήτει*. *ἀμφεσβήτει*, in Inscript. from Priene, of date between Ol. 133 and Ol. 160, confutes any who may choose to deny such a position for an augment. *ἠμφέγνοει* in best MSS. of Plato, Soph. 236, and *ἠμφεγνόησε* in id. 228, Polit. 291; the others, *ἀμφε-*, *ἀμφη-*, *ἠμφη-*.

Another of the glosses of Dionysius, in Suïdas under Ἀνεῴγεισαν, and in Bekker's Anecdota, p. 399. 24, establishes the Attic usage as regards ἀνοίγνυμι: Ἀνέῳγεν, οὐχὶ ἤνοιγε, καὶ ἀνεῴγετο, καὶ Θρασυλέοντι γ ἢ δ—

ἡ δ' ἀνέῳγε τὴν θύραν·

Θετταλῇ—

καὶ τὸ κεράμιον
ἀνέῳχας· ὄζεις, ἱερόσυλ', οἴνου πολύ·

Εὔπολις Πόλεσιν—

ὃν οὐκ ἀνέῳξα πώποτ' ἀνθρώποις ἐγώ·

Φερεκράτης Κραπατάλλοις—

οὐδεὶς γὰρ ἐδέχετ', οὐδ' ἀνέῳγέ μοι θύραν.

There is no difficulty about παροινῶ [1], ἐνοχλῶ, and ἀμπέχομαι [2]. Double augmentation is in their case allowed by all; but some Grammarians throw doubts upon it in the remaining verbs, διαιτῶ, διακονῶ, and ἀνέχομαι. There are numerous instances of the imperfect and aorist of ἀνέχομαι, in both Tragic and Comic verse, but they are found under circumstances which give little or no indication of Attic usage. Thus either single or double augmentation is possible in the lines Arist. Nub. 1363, 1373, Thesm. 593, Eq. 412, Ach. 709; Aesch. Cho. 747, Agam. 905, 1274; Soph. Trach. 276, Phil. 411, etc.; while Arist. Lys. 507; Soph. Ant. 467, are too corrupt to be used on either side. It is true that ἀνεσχόμην must be read in Arist. Pax 347—

πολλὰ γὰρ ἀνεσχόμην πράγματα κτε.

but its position in a paeonic hexameter at once takes it out of the inquiry.

The question is, however, set at rest by Euripides. He

[1] Moeris, p. 332, πεπαρῴνηκεν Ἀττικοί, παροίνικεν (sic) Ἕλληνες.

[2] Gramm. Coislin. Bekk. Anecd. 3. 1285, ἀμπέχομαι, ἠμπειχόμην, καὶ ἠμπεσχόμην.

uses, it is true, the old form ἀνεσχόμην when his verse demands it—

σὺ δ' οὐκ ἀνέσχου· τοιγὰρ οὐκέτ' εὐκλεεῖς,
Hipp. 687.

just as he uses, like other Tragic poets, old words like ἔρχωμαι, ἔρχου, ἔρχεσθαι, τέξω, στείχω, etc., by the side of ἴω, ἴθι, ἰέναι, τέξομαι, ἔρχομαι, but the occurrence in his verse of the unquestionably new formation ἠνεσχόμην proves that the manuscripts are right in generally exhibiting ἠνειχόμην and ἠνεσχόμην—

Ὄλυμπον ἠνέσχοντο θ' ἡμαρτηκότες.
H. F. 1319.

The case for διαιτῶ depends upon a fragment of the 'Hyperbolus' of the Comic poet Plato, preserved in Herodian (Περὶ λέξεως μονήρους, p. 20. 1)—

ὁ δ' οὐ γὰρ ἠττίκιζεν, ὦ Μοῖραι φίλαι,
ἀλλ' ὁπότε μὲν χρείη 'διῃτώμην λέγειν,
ἔφασκε δη τω μην, ὅποτε δ' εἰπεῖν δέον
ὀλίγον, ὁ λι ον ἔλεγεν.

The point lies in the attempt to reproduce the deliberate and cautious pronunciation of one unfamiliar with the dialect, who, nevertheless, misses those refined sounds which his ear is not yet sufficiently trained to catch—the γ between two vowels in ὀλίγος, and the light vowels before and after the δ in ἐδιῃτώμην. To the prominent sounds he gives more than their due emphasis.

The Attic forms of the augmented tenses of διακονῶ are dependent merely upon the argument from seriation, which in Attic Greek is of no small authority. In Eur. Cycl. 406, for καὶ διηκόνουν, κἀδιηκόνουν should be read—

ἐχριμπτόμην Κύκλωπι κἀδιηκόνουν.

With these eleven verbs the compound of ὀρθῶ with ἐπί and ἀνά may best be classed. That ἐπηνώρθουν, ἐπηνώρθωκα, ἐπηνωρθούμην, ἐπηνωρθωσάμην, ἐπηνώρθωμαι, and ἐπηνωρθώθην were the only forms known to Attic, is never called in question. It is, however, the only compound of ὀρθῶ which has this peculiarity.

XXI.

Σπῖλος· καὶ τοῦτο φυλάττου, λέγε δὲ κηλίς.

The forbidden word should probably be written σπίλος, as in its compound ἄσπιλος the iota is short.

In the sense of κῆλις the word is unquestionably late; but Hesychius quotes it in the sense of *rock*, from the Omphale of the Tragic poet Ion—σπίλον Παρνασσίαν—a usage also found in Aristotle, de Mund. 3. 392. b30, and Arrian (?), Peripl. Maris Rubri. p. 12, while σπιλώδης in Polybius shows that σπίλος was to him also equivalent to σπιλάς. The words of Hesychius, s. v., are, σπῖλος· κῆλις, ῥύπος ἱματίου, πέτρα πωρώδης, γῆ κεραμική, and they suggest one plausible origin for the late meaning κῆλις. Originally meaning *rock*, it came to signify successively *porous rock*, *rotten-stone*, *clay*, and *clay-stain*, till Paul could employ it metaphorically, as in Ephes. 5. 27, τὴν ἐκκλησίαν μὴ ἔχουσαν σπίλον ἢ ῥυτίδα, and Dionysius of Halicarnassus apply it to men with the meaning *dregs of humanity*, Ant. 4. 24. 698, εἰς τούτους μέντοι τοὺς δυσεκκαθάρτους σπίλους ἐκ τῆς πόλεως ἀποβλέποντες οἱ πολλοὶ δυσχεραίνουσι καὶ προβέβληνται τὸ ἔθος.

Without doubt there is an enormous gulf between these meanings and that of the Homeric σπιλάς, as seen in Od. 3. 298—

αἱ μὲν ἄρ' ἔνθ' ἦλθον, σπουδῇ δ' ἤλυξαν ὄλεθρον
ἄνδρες, ἀτὰρ νῆάς γε ποτὶ σπιλάδεσσιν ἔαξαν
κύματ'·

but even σπιλάς is used by Theophrastus, C. P. 2. 4. 4,

in the sense of clay, and the Latin *pumex* passed through some of the same stages of meaning. J. H. Heinrich Schmidt, in his Synonymik der Greich. Sprache 51, though evidently considering the two meanings, 'stone' and 'stain,' as belonging to two distinct words, yet bridges the gulf between them by quoting the following passages:—Strabo, 16. 4. 18, ὄρος γὰρ παρατείνει τραχὺ καὶ ὑψηλόν· εἶθ' ὑπώρειαι σπιλαδώδεις μέχρι τῆς θαλάττης: Polyb. 10. 10. 7, τὰ δὲ λοιπὰ περιέχεται λόφοις δυσὶ μὲν ὀρεινοῖς καὶ τραχέσιν, ἄλλοις δὲ τρισὶ πολὺ μὲν χθαμαλωτέροις, σπιλώδεσι δὲ καὶ δυσβάτοις: Arist. H. An. 5. 15 fin., φύεται μὲν οὖν τὰ ὄστρια καθάπερ εἴρηται, φύεται δ' αὐτῶν τὰ μὲν ἐν τενάγεσι, τὰ δ' ἐν τοῖς αἰγιαλοῖς, τὰ δ' ἐν τοῖς σπιλώδεσι τόποις, ἔνια δ' ἐν τοῖς σκληροῖς καὶ τραχέσι. The variants for σπιλώδεσι in the last passage, viz. πηλώδεσι and πνελώδεσι, are evidently glosses, but correct glosses, that have crept into the text.

Against this view, that σπίλος and σπιλάς, originally meaning *hard stone*, degenerated in meaning as the language aged, may be set another, namely, that σπίλος = κῆλις came into the Common dialect from some unregarded corner of Greece, in which it survived as another form of πίνος. Curtius supports the latter view by the Bohemian word 'spina,' which forms a connecting link between πίνος and σπίλος.

The former view is unquestionably the true one. There is no trace of σπίλος = πίνος, κῆλις till a late period; we can track σπίλος, *rock*, through an easy gradation of meanings historically consecutive, from the beginning to the close of Greek literature, and surely the degradation of ἄρτι, ἀποτάσσομαι, and ἐμπτύω, to limit ourselves to words already discussed, is sufficiently marked to make that of σπίλος neither surprising nor impossible.

XXII.

Ἀνειλεῖν βιβλίον διὰ τοῦ ἑτέρου λ, κάκιστον· ἀλλὰ διὰ τῶν δύο, ἀνείλλειν.

It is possible that in this passage Phrynichus wrote ἀνίλλειν, as in the next remark but one ἀλήλιπται should replace ἀλήλειπται. In the App. Soph. 20. 1, the true form of the latter word has been preserved, and in 19. 14, ἀνίλλειν is read: Ἀνίλλειν βιβλίον· οἱ μὲν ἄλλοι περισπῶσι τὴν λέξιν, καὶ δι' ἑνὸς λ γράφουσιν· οὕτω καὶ τὸ ἐξίλλειν. It is no rare error for copyists to go further still, and to substitute for the true word the very form against which a grammarian is warning his readers. Cobet, Var. Lect. 361, is very confident: 'Εἴλλειν et εἶλαι et composita saepe apud Hesychium leguntur, cui redde εἰσίλλειν· εἰσάγειν, εἰσελαύνειν pro εἰσηλεῖν, et ἐξίλλειν· ἐκβαλεῖν pro ἐξειλεῖν, et κατίλλειν pro κατειλεῖν, et συνιλλόμενα· συστρεφόμενα pro συνειλόμενα, et συνίλας· συνειλήσας pro συνείλας. Vera forma conspicitur nunc in pulchro Euripidis senario de Sphinge,

οὐρὰν ὑπίλασ' ὑπὸ λεοντόπουν βάσιν,

ubi in libris est ὑπήλλασα et ὑπήλασ'. Verum vidit Valckenarius in Diatr. p. 193. Aristophani in Ranis vs. 1066, pro ῥακίοις περιειλλόμενος redde περιϊλάμενος ex Photii annotatione: περιειλάμενος· περιειλησάμενος, quod ex illo loco sumptum est, ut centena ex Aristophane vocabula in Photii Lexico sine Poetae nomine explicantur ex antiquis Scholiis, quae nescio unde Photius nactus est multo meliora nostris. In Euripidis *Helena*, vs. 452,

ἃ μὴ προσείλει χεῖρα μηδ' ὤθει βίᾳ,

legendum arbitror μὴ πρόσιλλε χεῖρα.'

The forms in -έω are of course past praying for, and must be banished without recall, not only from Attic writers, but also from the texts of Homer and Herodotus. They are as desperately late as ἀλήθειν for ἀλεῖν, καλινδῶ or καλίω for καλίνδω, νιφῶ for νίφω, νήθειν for νῆν, λούομαι for λοῦμαι, χώννυμι for χόω, and many others which now disfigure the pages of Classical writers. The evidence for the spelling εἴλλω is, however, much greater than that for ἴλλω. It is true that in Ar. Nub. 762 the Ravenna has ἴλλε, not εἴλλε, which the other manuscripts exhibit; but in Plato, Tim. 40 B, they are by no means the best codices which present ἰλλομένην. The utter futility of regarding manuscript authority in a question of this kind will be acknowledged by any one who studies the variants in this passage of Plato, or in Tim. 76 B, 86 E. The readings in 40 B are these, εἰλλομένην, εἱλλομένην, ἰλλομένην, ἱλλομένην, εἰλομένην, εἰλουμένην, εἱλουμένην.

The word does not seem to occur in Attic Inscriptions, but the authentic history of the aorist of τίνω is strongly in favour of the diphthongal spelling. The aorist of τίνω, ἀποτίνω, etc., is in stone records always represented with a diphthong, τεῖσαι, ἀποτεῖσαι, ἐκτεῖσαι, etc., down to the second century B.C., at which date forms like ἀποτίσασθαι begin to appear. Admirable confirmatory evidence is afforded by the proper names Τεισάμενος, Τείσανδρος, Τεισίας, Τεισίμαχος, Τεισίλαος, which in stone records appear consistently with the diphthong, whereas codices prefer the simple vowel. The same is true of Τείθρας and Τειθράσιος [see Herwerden, Test. Lapid. pp. 36, 66]. As to the *spiritus asper*, the compounds ὑπίλλω and κατίλλω are hardly necessary to prove its non-existence. It was a pastime of inferior Grammarians like George Choeroboscus —the ἔτυμον of his name is worthy of remark—to exercise their ignorant ingenuity in making two words out of one, and differentiating its meaning by the breathing. Inscriptions demonstrate that the Athenians often blundered in their h's, but they did not make the error scientific.

XXIII.

Πιοῦμαι σὺν τῷ υ λέγων, οὐκ ὀρθῶς ἐρεῖτε· πίομαι γάρ ἐστι τὸ ἀρχαῖον, καὶ πιόμενος ἄνευ τοῦ υ. Δίων δὲ ὁ φιλόσοφος σὺν τῷ υ λέγων ἁμαρτάνει.

The same statement is made by other Grammarians, and Athenaeus (10. 446 E) adds instances from the Poets: *Πίομαι δὲ ἄνευ τοῦ υ λεκτέον, ἐκτείνοντας δὲ τὸ ι. Οὕτω γὰρ ἔχει καὶ τὸ Ὁμηρικόν—*

πιόμεν' ἐκ βοτάνης·

καὶ Ἀριστοφάνης Ἱππεῦσι—

κοὔποτ' ἐκ ταὐτοῦ μεθ' ἡμῶν πίεται ποτηρίου·

καὶ ἐν ἄλλοις—

πικρότατον οἶνον τήμερον πίει τάχα[1].

ἐνίοτε δὲ καὶ συστέλλουσι τὸ ι, ὡς Πλάτων ἐν Ταῖς ἀφ' ἱερῶν—

οὐδ' ὅστις αὐτῆς ἐκπίεται τὰ χρήματα·

καὶ ἐν Σύρφακι—

καὶ πίεσθ' ὕδωρ πολύ.

Probably *πιοῦμαι* should be removed even from Xenophon (Symp. 4. 7), but in writers like Aristotle it should doubtless be retained. In another place of the Symposium the future *παιξοῦμαι* occurs (9. 2), but in the mouth of a Syracusan. The Attic form was doubtless *παίσομαι*, as all forms with *ξ*, like *παίξας* and *πέπαιγμαι*, were unquestionably un-Attic, and should be removed, with manuscript authority, from such passages as Plato, Euthyd. 278 C. In genuine Doric writers the case is different, as in Theocr. 14. 22, "*λύκον εἶδες;*" *ἔπαιξέ τις.*

In Ar. Pax 1081, *κλαυσούμεθα* occurs in hexameters,

[1] Even into the text of Athenaeus copyists have imported the late *πιεί*, adding the gloss *ὡς ἀπὸ τοῦ πιοῦμαι* before *ἐνίοτε*. This is a signal instance of the transcribers' habit, already mentioned, of altering the text of Grammarians so as to present the very forms on which an interdict is being put.

and alongside of forms like μακάρεσσι, κεν, ὑμεναιοῖ (opt.), φυλόπιδος, and others. It was, of course, as unknown to Attic as πιοῦμαι. The future of the unsavory χέζω must be left unsettled. There is no line of verse in which χέσομαι may not be read as easily as χεσοῦμαι (Ar. Pax 1235, Vesp. 941, Lys. 440, 441, Fr. 207), but the latter has the manuscript influence on its side. That, however, is absolutely valueless in such questions. In Alexis (Ath. 12, 516 D)—

ἐὰν παραθῶ σοι, προσκατέδει τοὺς δακτύλους,

almost all the codices read προσκατεδεῖ, although no fact is better established than that ἔδομαι, not ἐδοῦμαι, was the Attic future of ἐσθίω. Moreover, the only exceptions to one of the most comprehensive facts of the Attic dialect—the fact that all verbs denoting bodily or functional activity are either deponents throughout or deponents in the future tense—are due to the copyists importing the late Active forms into our texts by adding a sigma to the second person singular. What dependence can be put on leaders like these? The Attic future of νέω, *swim*, was unquestionably νεύσομαι, but in Xen. An. 4. 3. 12, ἐκδύντες ὡς νευσόμενοι, the original νευσόμενοι supported by Hesychius—

νευσόμεθα, νήξομεθα,

appears in the manuscripts as νευσούμενοι, πευσόμενοι, σπευσόμενοι. From the last two words the true form may be elicited.

As long as the metre protects πνεύσομαι it is safe—

ἐμπνεύσομαι τῇδ᾽· εἰπέ, τίνι δίκῃ χέρας.
Eur. Andr. 555.

ταχὺ δὲ πρὸς πατρὸς τέκν᾽ ἐκπνεύσεται.
H. F. 886.

When that support fails, πνευσοῦμαι at once appears—

τὸ ληκύθιον γὰρ τοῦτο πνεύσεται πολύ,
Ar. Ran. 1221.

where all the manuscripts have πνευσεῖται. In Theocritus, as a Doric writer, πλευσοῦμαι is in place, 14. 55—

πλευσοῦμαι κἠγὼν διαπόντιος, οὔτε κάκιστος·

but it must be carefully corrected in the texts of Attic writers. It is absurd to read πλεύσομαι and πλευσοῦμαι in different passages of Thucydides, and of Demosthenes, and other Orators. It is but another instance of the ignorant uncertainty of transcribers which was above (p. 60) so clearly demonstrated in the case of ἄπωθεν. No editor would now vary with the manuscripts in reading ἄποθεν or ἄπωθεν indifferently, and why should a verb receive different treatment from an adverb? The Attic future of πλέω was πλεύσομαι, as the Attic form of the adverb was ἄπωθεν. Ἄποθεν and πλευσοῦμαι are equally late.

In Theocr. 3. 50—

ὃς τοσσῆν' ἐκύρησεν, ὅσ' οὐ πευσεῖσθε βέβαλοι,

the Doric future πευσοῦμαι is as much in place as the Doric present πεύθομαι in 13. 36 (12. 37)—

χρυσὸν ὁποίῃ
πεύθονται, μὴ φαῦλος ἐτήτυμον, ἀργυραμοιβοί·

but in an Attic writer πευσοῦμαι is intolerable. Accordingly, it must be removed from the only passage of Attic in which it occurs. All manuscripts of Aeschylus exhibit the genuine form πεύσει in P. V. 963, Ag. 266, Eum. 415, 419, 454; πεύσομαι in Ag. 599; πεύσεται in Eum. 503; and πεύσεσθε in P. V. 642: but, by some unaccountable fatality, πευσεῖσθαι has manuscript authority in P. V. 988—

εἰ προσδοκᾷς ἐμοῦ τι πεύσεσθαι πάρα,

although, fortunately for the text of those nerveless editors who justly trust the pen of a nodding transcriber in preference to their own reason, some codices have retained πεύσεσθαι.

The future of φεύγω has escaped corruption almost by a miracle. In Thucydides and Xenophon φεύξομαι is always read; in Demosthenes, who uses it with frequency, the manuscripts consistently exhibit the genuine form, except in one passage (990. 4), in which *φευξεῖσθαι* appears by the side of *φεύξεσθαι*. In Plato the corrupt *φευξοῦμαι* seldom presents itself, perhaps only in three places, Legg. 635 C, *φευξεῖται*: id. 762 B, *ἀποφευξεῖσθαι*: Rep. 432 D, *ἐκφευξεῖσθαι*: and these must be at once corrected to harmonize with *φεύξομαι*, Apol. 29 B; *φεύξει*, Crit. 53 C; *φεύξεται*, Rep. 592 A; *φευξόμεθα*, Theaet. 181 A; *φεύξονται*, id. 168 A; *ἀποφεύξεται*, Apol. 39 A; *ἐκφεύξεται*, Soph. 235 B; *ἐκφεύξεσθαι*, Symp. 189 B, etc. As to the Poets, Aeschylus and Sophocles are free from corruption, but the texts of both Euripides and Aristophanes have been tampered with. These writers certainly employ the Doric future of this verb when the verse demands it—

ἐνορῶ γέροντα δειλίας φευξούμενον.
Ar. Ach. 1129.

ἔρημον ἀπολιπόντε ποι φευξούμεθα.
Plut. 447.

εἰ μή τί γ' αὐτῷ δόντες ἀποφευξούμεθα.
Av. 932.

καὶ ξυμπερᾶναι φροντίδ' ᾗ φευξούμεθα.
Eur. Med. 341.

τοὐμοῦ γὰρ οὔ μοι φροντίς, εἰ φευξούμεθα.
Id. 346.

ἡμεῖς δέ σοι μενοῦμεν, οὐ φευξούμεθα.
Bac. 659.

οὐδ' αὖ τὸ δεινὸν προσπόλου φευξούμεθα.
Hel. 500.

πείσαιμ' ἄν· ἀλλὰ τίνα φυγὴν φευξούμεθα;
Id. 1041.

This licence may be regarded as the converse of that which even Comic poets did not scruple to use in the case of datives plural in -*αισι(ν)*, -*οισι(ν)*, third persons plural optative middle in -*οίατο*, and the insertion of *σ* before -*θα* of the first person plural middle and passive. The latter was a licence derived from an old stage of the language, the former, which embraces futures like *φευξοῦμαι*, was an anticipation of later usage. But just as -*αισι(ν)*, -*οισι(ν)*, -*οίατο*, -*μεσθα* never appear except when the metre absolutely demands them, so *φευξοῦμαι* was undoubtedly never employed *citra necessitatem.* And in Ar. Ach. 203—

ἐγὼ δὲ φεύξομαί γε τοὺς Ἀχαρνέας,

as in Eur. Bacch. 798, Med. 604, and Hipp. 1093, no attention should be paid to the codices.

This is not the only instance in which a general rule can be elicited from a particular statement of Phrynichus. Just as in Arts. 16, 17 above his particular rule was shown to be general, namely, *Verbs in* -μαίνω *and* -αίρω *form their aorists with* eta, *not* alpha, so here his dictum as to the future of *πίνω* has been proved to be generally true. The Doric future in -*οῦμαι* was practically unused by Attic writers.

XXIV.

Ἤλειπται, κατώρυκται οὐ χρή, ἀλλὰ διπλασίαζε τὴν φωνὴν ὥσπερ οἱ Ἀθηναῖοι, ἀλήλειπται, κατορώρυκται.

XXV.

Ὤμοκε τελέως ἄηθες· χρὴ γὰρ ὀμώμοκε λέγειν.

These two paragraphs put in a very clear light the character of the work of Phrynichus. As just stated, it is fragmentary to a degree, and his rules are rarely general. To learn facts in this way is not only difficult but puerile, and the aim of this book will have been attained if it demonstrates that there are certain general facts relating to the Attic dialect which explain many phenomena in its literature, and introduce law and symmetry into the language itself.

The perfects with the so-called Attic reduplication are these—

ἀκούω	ἀκήκοα	
ἀλείφω	ἀλήλιφα	ἀλήλιμμαι
ἀλῶ		ἀλήλεμαι
ἀρῶ		ἀρήρομαι
ἐγείρω		ἐγήγερμαι
ἔδω	ἐδήδοκα	ἐδήδεσμαι
ἐλαύνω	ἐλήλακα	ἐλήλαμαι
ἐλέγχω		ἐλήλεγμαι
ἔρχομαι	ἐλήλυθα	
ὄλλυμι	ὀλώλεκα	ὄλωλα
ὄμνυμι	ὀμώμοκα	ὀμώμομαι
ὀρύσσω	ὀρώρυχα	ὀρώρυγμαι
[φέρω]	ἐνήνοχα	ἐνήνεγμαι.

The peculiarity of the reduplication consists in the fact that, after augmenting in the ordinary way, they place their initial vowel with the following consonant before the augment. Thus, *ὤρυχα, ὤρυγμαι,* would be the regular perfects of *ὀρύσσω*, but in Attic the syllable *ὀρ-* was thrown before each. In the perfect passive of *ἀκούω* this was not done, but the simple augment sufficed, *ἤκουσμαι.*

There can be no question that *ἀλήλεκα* and *ἀρήροκα,* though not found in our texts, were yet in ordinary use ; but it is not so certain what was the active perfect of *ἐλέγχω*. It is well known that *ἤνεγκας* and *ἠνέγκατε* were common Attic forms, but the fact that in the two large classes of verbs—those in *-ύνω* and *-αίνω*—together numbering over one hundred verbs, only one perfect active regularly formed occurs, brings into suspicion all perfect active forms not found in Classical texts in which the combination *-γκα* is found.

Moreover, the one exception referred to, namely, *ἀποπέφαγκα*, occurs only in one writer, Dinarchus, who wrote towards the close of the Attic period, after which perfects of the objectionable kind like *ᾔσχυγκα, κεκέρδαγκα* became common enough. For this reason a just suspicion must rest upon *ἐλήλεγκα*.

A similar difficulty confronts us in *ἐγείρω*. There may have been an *ἐγήγερκα* in use, as even the passive perfect has been preserved only in one passage (Thuc. 7. 51), but it is always difficult to reconstruct a verb not perfectly regular. Of all regular vowel verbs, and of verbs in -*ίζω* and -*άζω*, the perfect may be confidently used, whether or not it happens to occur in Classical Greek. However sesquipedalian, such forms were never eschewed, *γεγυμνασιάρχηκα, κεκαλλιέρηκα*, and similar words being employed as often as their need was felt. By the sober use of the theory of probabilities the existence of many forms not found in our texts will ultimately be established; but this is not the place to start so tedious and intricate an inquiry.

The question of the insertion of sigma before the terminations of the perfect indicative passive is one of great difficulty; occasionally verse establishes the true form, as in the case of *ὄμνυμι*—

> *τουτὶ τὸ πρᾶγμα πανταχόθεν ξυνομώμοται.*
>
> Ar. Lys. 1007.
>
> *ὀμώμοται γὰρ ὅρκος ἐκ θεῶν μέγας.*
>
> Aesch. Ag. 1284.

But the untrustworthiness of manuscripts is demonstrated by the circumstance that, as soon as the support of metre is withdrawn, the sigma appears—

> *εὖ νυν τόδ' ἴστε, Ζεὺς ὀμώμοσται πατήρ.*
>
> Eur. Rhes. 816.

In Dem. 505. 29 it is only the best manuscript (Paris S.) which has retained the primitive hand *ἐν ᾗ γέγραπται καὶ ὀμώμοται.* The true form of the perfect passive of *ἀλῶ* has barely escaped corruption in a passage of the *Γυναικομανία* of Amphis, quoted by Athenaeus, 14. 642 A—

> A. *ἤδη ποτ' ἤκουσας βίον*
> *ἀληλεμένον*; B. *ναί.* A. *τοῦτ' ἐκεῖν' ἔστιν σαφῶς·*
> *ἄμητες, οἶνος ἡδύς, ᾠά, σησαμαῖ,*
> *μύρον, στέφανος, αὐλητρίς.* B. *ὦ Διοσκόρω,*
> *ὀνόματα τῶν δώδεκα θεῶν διελήλυθας.*

The passage itself well explains the meaning of *βίος ἀληλεμένος*, and the explanation of Suïdas is hardly required, *ἀληλεσμένος βίος ἐπὶ τῶν ἐν ἀφθονίᾳ τῶν ἐπιτηδείων ὄντων.* Schweighaeuser and Dindorf edit—

> *ἤδη ποτ' ἤκουσας βίον ἀληλεσμένον*
> *. . . . αι τοῦτ' ἐκεῖν' ἔστιν σαφῶς·*

but the manuscripts, for a marvel, do not offer the late *ἀληλεσμένον*, and the former arrangement unquestionably restores the hand of the Comic poet. In Thuc. 4. 26, *εἰσάγειν σῖτον ἀληλεμένον*, the corrupt *ἀληλεσμένον* appears in some manuscripts. In most cases, however, verse helps the inquirer but little, as the penultimate is often long even without the sigma, and if not, the word occurs in a part of the line in which either form may stand.

Sometimes a corruption has preserved the original reading, as in a fragment of Aristophanes found in Stob. Flor. 121. 18—

> *οὐδ' ἂν ποθ' οὕτως ἐστεφανωμένοι νεκροὶ*
> *προὐκείμεθ' οὐδ' ἂν κατακεχριμένοι μύροις,*

where the codices exhibit *κατακεκριμένοι.* To all Attic writers the perfect without sigma should be restored to *χρίω*, as to *κονίω, μηνίω*, etc.—*κέχριμαι, κεκόνιμαι, μεμήνιμαι*, as *χρῖμα, μήνιμα*, etc., not *χρῖσμα, μήνισμα.*

On the other hand, *ἐχρίσθην*, not *ἐχρίθην*, was the ancient form of the aorist. It seems as if this sigma would tax the most powerful of human memories; one rule, however, of great usefulness can be formulated. *If the aorist passive has not the sigma, the perfect also is without it.* Thus the absence of the sigma in κεκόλουμαι may be proved by Thuc. 7. 66, where the genuine κολουθῶσι is preserved, not only by the better manuscripts, but also by the corruption ἀκουλῶθι. So the unquestioned ἐσώθην establishes the perfect σέσωμαι—a form which is confirmed by Photius, s. v. σέσωται: Σέσωται καὶ σεσωμένος οἱ παλαιοὶ ἄνευ τοῦ σ, καὶ διεζωμένοι φησὶ Θουκυδίδης, οἱ δὲ νεώτεροι σέσωσμαι. Now in Thuc. 1. 6, the passage referred to, all manuscripts exhibit the late διεζωσμένοι, as περιεζωσμέναι in Ar. Av. 1148, although stone records support the statement of Photius, διεζωμέναι, διέζωται, and ὑπέζωται being quoted from inscriptions of the best Attic times, whereas no form with σ is ever found. Accordingly, with manuscript authority, σέσωται has to be restored to Eur. I. T. 607, and to Plato, Crit. 109 D; 110 A. In fact, σέσωσται is as late as ὀμώμοσται and ἀληλεσμένον.

This fact, that the sigma, if unknown in the aorist, is not found in the perfect, demonstrates what might otherwise be liable to question, that the sigma in the indicative and participle of the perfect came from the infinitive, where it was always inserted before theta—ὀμώμοσθαι, ἐλήλασθαι, ἀρήροσθαι, κέκλαυσθαι, κεκέλευσθαι, κεκόλουσθαι, etc. In fact, λέλυσθαι is as unquestioned as λέλυμαι, and ὀμώμοσθαι as ὀμώμομαι, and as neither in ὄμνυμι nor λύω had the sigma passed from ὀμώμοσθαι and λέλυσθαι to ὠμόθην and ἐλύθην, still less had it passed to ὀμώμομαι and λέλυμαι. Take the two verbs γιγνώσκω and τιτρώσκω. The aorist of γιγνώσκω as certainly had the sigma, ἐγνώσθην, as that of τιτρώσκω was without it, ἐτρώθην. Accordingly, in its perfect τιτρώσκω could not have the sigma, while γιγνώσκω might either have it or want it. As a matter of fact ἔγνωσμαι is as securely established as τέτρωμαι. This rule extends the utility of verse, as, if verse shows that the aorist of a verb was without sigma, the true form of the perfect follows as a matter of course. Thus ἐλήλαμαι is proved by ἠλάθην, Aesch. Eum. 283—

Φοίβου καθαρμοῖς ἠλάθη χοιροκτόνοις,

and ἀρήρομαι by ἠρόθην, Soph. O. R. 1485—

πατὴρ ἐφάνθην ἔνθεν αὐτὸς ἠρόθην,

and ἀπήρυμαι by a line of the Δημήτριος ἢ Φιλέταιρος of Alexis (Ath. 2. 36 E)—

τούτων ἁπάντων, ἀπαρυθέντα τὴν ἄνω.

There is no exception to the law, and the inquirer will readily extend the subjoined list—

ἐλούθην	λέλουμαι	ηὐξήθην	ηὔξημαι
ἀνηλώθην	ἀνήλωμαι	ἐτμήθην	τέτμημαι
ἐκρίθην	κέκριμαι	ἐκράθην	κέκραμαι
ἐπόθην	πέπομαι	ἐστρώθην	ἔστρωμαι
ἐδόθην	δέδομαι	ἐδυνήθην	δεδύνημαι
ἐτάθην	τέταμαι	ἐβουλήθην	βεβούλημαι
ἐστάθην	ἕσταμαι	ἐβλήθην	βέβλημαι
ἐβάθην	βέβαμαι	ἐκαύθην	κέκαυμαι.
ἡμαρτήθην	ἡμάρτημαι		

A diligent searcher would perhaps find manuscripts in which each of these perfects and aorists is read with sigma, and bless Hermes for his luck. Such grammarians would have worse fortune if they searched for sparks of reason in themselves. In Dem. 214 29, ἐν τοῖς παραβεβαμένοις ὅρκοις, all the manuscripts have παραβεβασμένοις, as all but one had ὀμώμοσται in 505. 29; but can a reasonable man doubt for a moment that the form with σ was imported into the text at an age when ἐβάσθην strove for supremacy with ἐβάνθην?

To the above class, consisting of verbs which have never sigma in the aorist, and consequently are always without it in the perfect passive, belong all verbs in -εύω, except λεύω and κελεύω, all contracting verbs in -όω, except the only disyllabic one, χόω, all contracting verbs in -έω which have eta in the aorist passive, and all contracting verbs in -άω, with alpha long, except χρῶμαι and δρῶ. Wecklein would deprive even κελεύω of the sigma (Cur. Epigr. 62), but there is no question that ἐκελεύσθην and ἐλεύσθην were the genuine aorists of λεύω and κελεύω. Like γεύω, δεύω, εὕω, and νεύω, these verbs stand on a different footing from other verbs in -εύω. Photius quotes καταγευσθείς, Suïdas, εὑθείς, and ἐδεύθην is found in Hippocrates and Theophrastus, but there is no instance of the aorist of νεύω.

Ἐχρήσθην is of course undisputed, but ἐδράσθην may well be a corruption for ἐδράθην. The tense occurs only in two passages of Thucydides (3. 38; 6. 53); and in a third passage (3. 54) even the unquestioned δέδραμαι appears in the manuscripts as δέδρασμαι, just as in 3. 61, ᾐτιασμένων is exhibited for the genuine ᾐτιαμένων. On the other hand, as δραστέος occurs without variant in Plato, Phil. 20 A, Crit. 108 E, Legg. 626 A, etc.; Soph. O. R. 1443, El. 1019, etc., the aorist with sigma may well be correct.

If the alpha in the present is short the sigma invariably appears in the aorist passive—

γελῶ	ἐγελάσθην
κλῶ	ἐκλάσθην
σπῶ	ἐσπάσθην
χαλῶ	ἐχαλάσθην,

as also in the perfect indicative and participle. Of verbs in -έω, αἰδοῦμαι and ἀκοῦμαι take the sigma in the aorist, but it is never found in ᾐνέθην, ᾑρέθην, and ἐδέθην.

In the case of those verbs which have -σθην in the aorist it is often difficult to establish the true form of the perfect passive. Of some there has never been any doubt. All regular verbs in -άζω and -ίζω have sigma both in aorist and perfect. Others equally well-established are these—

κυλίνδω	*ἐκυλίσθην*	*κεκύλισμαι*
ψεύδω	*ἐψεύσθην*	*ἔψευσμαι*
σβέννυμι	*ἐσβέσθην*	*ἔσβεσμαι*
χρώζω	*ἐχρώσθην*	*κέχρωσμαι*
χόω	*ἐχώσθην*	*κέχωσμαι*
αἰδοῦμαι	*ᾐδέσθην*	*ᾔδεσμαι*
πρίω	*ἐπρίσθην*	*πέπρισμαι*
τίνω	*ἐτίσθην*	*τέτισμαι*
κατεσθίω	*κατεδέσθην*	*κατεδέδεσμαι*
σείω	*ἐσείσθην*	*σέσεισμαι*
κνῶ	*ἐκνήσθην*	*κέκνησμαι.*

On the other hand, the sigma, though found in the aorist, is absent from the perfect in the verbs—

χρῶμαι	*ἐχρήσθην*	*κέχρημαι*
[*ῥώννυμι*]	*ἐρρώσθην*	*ἔρρωμαι*
κλῄω	*ἐκλῄσθην*	*κέκλῃμαι*
κρούω	*ἐκρούσθην*	*κέκρουμαι*
μιμνήσκομαι	*ἐμνήσθην*	*μέμνημαι*
κελεύω	*ἐκελεύσθην*	*κεκέλευμαι.*

Others are disputed. To the passage already quoted on *σέσωμαι* Photius adds, *ἐπ' ἐνίων ἁπλῶς παραλείπουσι τὸ σῖγμα, κεκλειμένον, πεπρημένον.* Now the aorists were certainly *ἐκλῄσθην* and *ἐπρήσθην,* and *κέκλῃμαι* is doubted by none, yet the Ravenna codex, which alone has preserved *κεκλειμένα* in Ar. Plut. 206, falls as low as the rest in Vesp. 198, and exhibits *κέκλεισμαι.* In Vesp. 36 it is the only manuscript which presents *ἐμπεπρημένην* without the sigma. When the danger of adding the obnoxious letter was so great, the testimony of the Ravenna, combined with that of Photius, ought to be regarded as conclusive. Perhaps the aorist of *παύω* was *ἐπαύθην,* the perfect was certainly *πέπαυμαι,* and if the sigma appeared in the aorist of *κλάω,* it was beyond question absent from the perfect.

XXVI.

Ἀπελεύσομαι παντάπασι φυλάττου· οὔτε γὰρ οἱ δόκιμοι ῥήτορες, οὔτε ἡ ἀρχαία κωμῳδία, οὔτε Πλάτων κέχρηται τῇ φωνῇ· ἀντὶ δὲ αὐτοῦ τῷ ἄπειμι χρῶ καὶ τοῖς ὁμοειδέσιν ὡσαύτως.

XXVII.

Ἐπεξελευσόμενος ἄλλος οὗτος Ἡρακλῆς. τοῦτ' οὖν ἔσυρεν ἐκ τριόδου Φαβωρῖνος, χρὴ γὰρ ἐπεξιὼν εἰπεῖν· καὶ γὰρ ἐπέξειμι λέγεται, ἀλλ' οὐκ ἐπεξελεύσομαι.

Nothing can better illustrate the precision of Attic Greek than the consideration of the Greek equivalent of the English verb *to go*. Whether simple or compounded with a preposition, *εἶμι* had consistently a future signification. Its present indicative was *ἔρχομαι*, but *ἔρχομαι* did no more than fill the blank left by the preoccupation of *εἶμι*. There was no *ἔρχωμαι, ἐρχοίμην, ἔρχου, ἔρχεσθαι, ἐρχόμενος*, and no imperfect *ἠρχόμην*. *εἶμι* could well supply those forms without drawing upon another root, and all the moods of the present, except the indicative, were derived from the stem *ι*, namely, *ἴω, ἴοιμι, ἴθι, ἰέναι, ἰών*. The imperfect was *ᾖα*, not *ἠρχόμην*. *εἶμι*, however, formed no aorist or perfect; and for these tenses recourse was again had to the root *ἐρ-*, which, modified to *ἐλυθ-*, supplied the aorist and perfect tenses throughout. The following scheme represents these facts in one view:—

PRESENT.

	INDICATIVE.	CONJUNCTIVE.
S. 1.	ἔρχομαι	ἴω
2.	ἔρχει	ἴῃς
3.	ἔρχεται	ἴῃ

	INDICATIVE.	CONJUNCTIVE.
D. 2.	ἔρχεσθον	ἴητον
3.	ἔρχεσθον	ἴητον
P. 1.	ἐρχόμεθα	ἴωμεν
2.	ἔρχεσθε	ἴητε
3.	ἔρχονται.	ἴωσι(ν).

PAST.

S. 1.	ᾖα	ἴοιμι or ἰοίην
2.	ᾖεισθα	ἴοις
3.	ᾖει(ν)	ἴοι
D. 2.	ᾖτον	ἴοιτον
3.	ᾔτην	ἰοίτην
P. 1.	ᾖμεν	ἴοιμεν
2.	ᾖτε	ἴοιτε
3.	ᾖσαν.	ἴοιεν.

	IMPERATIVE.	INFINITIVE.
S. 2.	ἴθι	ἰέναι.
3.	ἴτω	
D. 2.	ἴτον	PARTICIPLE.
3.	ἴτων	ἰών, ἰοῦσα, ἰόν
P. 2.	ἴτε	ἰόντος, ἰούσης, ἰόντος.
3.	ἰόντων.	

FUTURE.

	INDICATIVE.	OPTATIVE.	INFINITIVE.	PARTICIPLE.
S. 1.	εἶμι	ἐλευσοίμην	ἐλεύσεσθαι.	ἐλευσόμενος.
2.	εἶ	ἐλεύσοιο		
3.	εἶσι(ν)	ἐλεύσοιτο		
D. 2.	ἴτον	ἐλεύσοισθον		
3.	ἴτον	ἐλευσοίσθην		
P. 1.	ἴμεν	ἐλευσοίμεθα		
2.	ἴτε	ἐλεύσοισθε		
3.	ἴασι.	ἐλεύσοιντο.		

Aorist.

	INDICATIVE.		CONJUNCTIVE.
S. 1.	ἦλθον	ἔλθω	ἔλθοιμι
2.	ἦλθες	ἔλθῃς	ἔλθοις
3.	ἦλθε(ν)	ἔλθῃ	ἔλθοι
D. 2.	ἤλθετον	ἔλθητον	ἔλθοιτον
3.	ἠλθέτην	ἔλθητον	ἐλθοίτην
P. 1.	ἤλθομεν	ἔλθωμεν	ἔλθοιμεν
2.	ἤλθετε	ἔλθητε	ἔλθοιτε
3.	ἦλθον.	ἔλθωσιν.	ἔλθοιεν.

	IMPERATIVE.	INFINITIVE.
S. 2.	ἐλθέ	ἐλθεῖν.
3.	ἐλθέτω	
D. 2.	ἔλθετον	
3.	ἐλθέτων	PARTICIPLE.
P. 2.	ἔλθετε	ἐλθών, ἐλθοῦσα, ἐλθόν
3.	ἐλθόντων.	ἐλθόντος, ἐλθούσης, ἐλθόντος.

Perfect.

S. 1.	ἐλήλυθα	ἐληλύθω	ἐληλυθοίην
2.	ἐλήλυθας	ἐληλύθῃς	ἐληλυθοίης
3.	ἐλήλυθε(ν)	ἐληλύθῃ	ἐληλυθοίη
D. 2.	ἐληλύθατον	ἐληλύθητον	ἐληλύθοιτον
3.	ἐληλύθατον	ἐληλύθητον	ἐληλυθοίτην
P. 1.	ἐληλύθαμεν	ἐληλύθωμεν	ἐληλύθοιμεν
2.	ἐληλύθατε	ἐληλύθητε	ἐληλύθοιτε
3.	ἐληλύθασι(ν).	ἐληλύθωσι(ν).	ἐληλύθοιεν.

	PLUPERFECT.	INFINITIVE.
S. 1.	εἰληλύθη	ἐληλυθέναι.
2.	εἰληλύθης	
3.	εἰληλύθει(ν)	PARTICIPLE.
D. 2.	εἰληλύθετον	ἐληλυθώς, ἐληλυθυῖα, ἐληλυθός
3.	εἰληλυθέτην	ἐληλυθότος, etc.
P. 1.	εἰληλύθεμεν	
2.	εἰληλύθετε	
3.	εἰληλύθεσαν.	

If to these are added the synonyms ἀφικόμην for the aorist, and ἀφῖγμαι and ἥκω for the perfect, ἀφίγμην and ἧκον for the pluperfect, with ἥξω for future perfect (=ἐληλυθὼς ἔσομαι), the Attic usage with regard to this verb-notion will be thoroughly understood.

It has been said that in Attic ἔρχομαι appears in no mood but the indicative, and is never used in the imperfect tense. As a matter of fact, even if Xenophon be excluded as hopelessly un-Attic, there are still five exceptions to this rule, namely, ἐπήρχοντο and προσήρχοντο in Thucydides, ἀπερχόμενοι in Lysias, ἐπεξερχόμενοι in Antiphon, and περιήρχετο in Aristophanes.

Now, even if these instances were genuine beyond question, they might be disregarded, as opposed to the infinite number of passages in which the law is observed; but all five cases are signally exceptional. Cobet, following in the track of Elmsley, considers them due to the notorious habit which copyists had of replacing genuine forms by words better known at the time when the manuscript was made. For example, in a passage of Aristophanes—

καὶ πρῶτ' ἐρήσομαί σε τουτί· παῖδά μ' ὄντ' ἔτυπτες;
Nub. 1409.

the two best manuscripts replace ἔτυπτες by ἐτύπτησας, a form not only unknown to Classical Greek, but quite incompatible with the metre. In another passage of the same play—

Στρ. ὅπως δ' ἐκείνω τὼ λόγω μαθήσεται,
τὸν κρείττον' ὅστις ἐστὶ καὶ τὸν ἥττονα,
ἐὰν δὲ μή, τὸν γοῦν ἄδικον πάσῃ τέχνῃ.
Σωκ. αὐτὸς μαθήσεται παρ' αὐτοῖν τοῖν λόγοιν,
ἐγὼ δ' ἄπειμι.
Στρ. τοῦτο νῦν μέμνησ', ὅπως
πρὸς πάντα τὰ δίκαι' ἀντιλέγειν δυνήσεται,
Nub. 883.

the manuscripts read ἀπέσομαι and assign ἐγὼ δ' ἀπέσομαι to Strepsiades. Bentley restored the text by a convincing conjecture, which has long been generally received.

The habit was certainly in existence, but critics ought to be chary of using it to explain aberrations from usage. It will be shown that ἐλεύσεσθαι, which Elmsley regarded as the product of this habit, was really used by Lysias, and not imported into his text by a late hand, and the same is true of some of the exceptions now under discussion. The participle ἐπεξερχόμενοι is merely one of the many words and forms which demonstrate that at the time at which Antiphon wrote Attic was not yet mature (Ant. 115. 9), ἡμεῖς δ' οἱ ἐπεξερχόμενοι τὸν φόνον οὐ τὸν αἴτιον ἀφέντες τὸν ἀναίτιον διώκομεν: and ἐπήρχοντο and προσήρχοντο might be granted to an Attic writer who used κάρτα and ἑκάς. It is true that, in quoting Thuc. 4. 121, ἰδίᾳ δὲ ἐταινίουν τε καὶ προσήρχοντο ὥσπερ ἀθλητῇ, Pollux used προσῄεσαν for προσήρχοντο, but he evidently quoted from memory, as he gives the passage as from Xenophon: Pollux, 3. 152, Ξενοφῶν γὰρ εἴρηκεν· ἐταινίουν τε καὶ προσῄεσαν ὥσπερ ἀθλητῇ. If critics will remove προσήρχοντο from Thucydides, they are bound to prove that in his style there is no other trace of early Attic.

'Επήρχοντο, however, at the beginning of the preceding chapter of Thucydides, stands, like ἀπερχόμενοι in Lysias, on quite a different footing. When a word is not only questionable as regards form, but also unintelligible, there is a strong case against it. The words in Lysias are these (147. 34), πολλοὶ μὲν γὰρ μικρὸν διαλεγόμενοι καὶ κοσμίως ἀπερχόμενοι μεγαλῶν κακῶν αἴτιοι γεγόνασιν, ἕτεροι δὲ τῶν τοιούτων ἀμελοῦντες πολλὰ κἀγαθὰ ὑμᾶς εἰσὶν εἰργασμένοι. The manuscripts present no variant to ἀπερχόμενοι, but no one has been able to extract from the word a meaning in unison with the context. The conjecture ἀμπεχόμενοι[1]

[1] The change from ἐχόμενος to ἐρχόμενος occurs in some MSS. of Thuc.

suggested by Dobree, and adopted by Cobet, affords an excellent sense; but for the question at issue it is sufficient to indicate that the passage is corrupt. Now the imperfect ἐπήρχοντο in Thucydides is as unintelligible as the participle ἀπερχόμενοι in Lysias: Thuc. 4. 120, περὶ δὲ τὰς ἡμέρας ταύτας αἷς ἐπήρχοντο, Σκιώνη ἐν τῇ Παλλήνῃ πόλις ἀπέστη ἀπ' Ἀθηναίων πρὸς Βρασίδαν. The verb requires both a subject and a prepositional object. Suppose these omissions supplied, as they are by the Scholiast, in the words εἰς ἀλλήλους ἑκάτεροι, and a new difficulty presents itself—the meaning of the word. In late Greek the term might perhaps pass muster in the sense of going backwards and forwards to one another, but no such sense is possible in Attic. As a matter of fact, αἷς ἐπήρχοντο originally formed part of the Scholium on περὶ δὲ τὰς ἡμέρας ταύτας, and made its way from the margin into the text, the words of Thucydides being these, περὶ δὲ τὰς ἡμέρας ταύτας Σκιώνη κτε.

The reason for περιήρχετο in Aristophanes is not far to seek—

ὁ δ' ἀνὴρ περιήρχετ', ὠκυτόκι' ὠνούμενος.
Thesm. 504.

It was used by the Comic poet in *malice prepense*, in a passage containing many other reminders of Tragic diction. It is like viewing a storm in a mill-pond to read the pages in which critics have proposed and seconded their emendations of this unhappy line. Elmsley suggested περιῇρρεν, Hamaker, περιέτρεχε, and Cobet cut the knot by reading περιῄειν. If there was any necessity to make the change, the reading of the great Dutch scholar might take its place in the line as confidently as ἄπειμι for ἀπέσομαι in the passage cited above from the 'Clouds.'

6. 3, τοῦ ἐχόμενου ἔτους. In this case there happens to be MSS. authority, but, if this had failed, timid editors would have left the text unemended. There is little doubt that ἀμπεχόμενοι passed to ἀπερχόμενοι through ἀπεχόμενοι.

The usage of Xenophon is as contradictory in this respect as in others. In some passages he follows the rules observed by pure Attic writers, in others he employs forms which they studiously avoided: Anab. 4. 7. 12, *παρέρχεται πάντας· ὁ δὲ Καλλίμαχος ὡς ἑώρα αὐτὸν παριόντα κτε.* Cp. 4. 3. 13; 3. 2. 35, etc., but An. 2. 4. 25, *παρερχομένους τοὺς Ἕλληνας ἐθεώρει*: Cyr. 8. 5. 12, *εἰς χεῖρας ἐρχόμενον.* Sometimes the manuscripts present two forms, as in Anab. 4. 6. 22, *ἀπήρχοντο* and *ᾤχοντο* have both good manuscript authority, and *ἐξέρχεται* is a variant to *ἐξέρχοιτο* in Cyr. 4. 1. 1, *μείνας δὲ ὁ Κῦρος μέτριον χρόνον αὐτοῦ σὺν τῷ στρατεύματι, καὶ δηλώσας ὅτι ἕτοιμοί εἰσι μάχεσθαι εἴ τις ἐξέρχοιτο, ὡς οὐδεὶς ἀντεξῄειν, ἀπήγαγεν κτε.* Similarly, in Cyr. 2. 4. 18, *πολλῶν βουλομένων ἕπεσθαι*, the better manuscripts read *ἀπέρχεσθαι*. The more Xenophon is studied the more difficult will it appear to find any standpoint for the criticism of his text. His verbosity, and his extraordinary disregard of the most familiar rules of Attic writing, make sober criticism almost impossible. Cobet may alter word after word, and cut down sentence after sentence, but the faults of Xenophon's style are due, not to the glosses of Scholiasts or the blunders of transcribers, but to the want of astringents in his early mental training, and the unsettled and migratory habits which he indulged in his manhood.

The only forms from the stem *ἐρχ-* which are used, in Attic of any purity, are *ἔρχομαι, ἔρχει, ἔρχεται, ἔρχεσθον, ἐρχόμεθα, ἔρχεσθε*, and *ἔρχονται*, and this is true not only of the simple verb, but also of its compounds. There is, however, one exception, namely, the compound of *ἔρχεσθαι* with *ὑπό*, which early acquired a secondary meaning never attached to *ὕπειμι*, and when used in that special sense was inflected throughout the imperfect and the moods of the present. When *ὑπέρχομαι* signified *to fawn upon, to cringe*, all the forms which, in the meaning *go under*, were not recognized in Attic, were at once ennobled; and in the metaphorical meaning, *ὑπέρχωμαι, ὑπερχοίμην, ὑπέρχου, ὑπέρχεσθαι, ὑπερχόμενος, ὑπηρχόμην*, and *ὑπελεύσομαι*, replaced the *ὑπίω, ὑπίοιμι, ὕπιθι, ὑπιέναι, ὑπιών, ὑπῇα*, and *ὕπειμι* demanded by the simple signification: Plato, Crito 53 E, *ὑπερχόμενος δὴ βιώσει πάντας ἀνθρώπους καὶ δουλεύων*: Demosth. 623. 22, *συμβέβηκε γὰρ ἐκ τούτου αὐτοῖς μὲν ἀντιπάλους εἶναι τούτους, ὑμᾶς δὲ ὑπέρχεσθαι*[1] *καὶ θεραπεύειν*: Andoc. 31. 44 (4. 21), *εἰκότως δέ μοι δοκοῦσιν οἱ κρίται ὑπέρχεσθαι Ἀλκιβιάδην, ὁρῶντες Ταυρέαν τοσαῦτα μὲν χρήματα ἀναλώσαντα προπηλακιζόμενον, τὸν δὲ τοιαῦτα παρανομοῦντα μέγιστον δυνάμενον*. The same metaphor is found in Xen. Rep. Ath. 2. 14, *ὑπερχόμενος*, and in the present indicative and aorist in Arist. Eq. 269; Dem. 1369. 20; and Xen. Rep. Lac. 8. 2[2]. It will, moreover, be observed that, even in the simple verb, the paradigm represents *ἐλεύσομαι* as correct Attic in the moods. In the indicative it was rendered unnecessary in Attic by the unconditional surrender of *εἶμι* to a future sense, but in the two moods—the optative and infinitive—and in the participle, forms from *ἐλεύσομαι* might naturally be used, as *ἴοιμι, ἰέναι*, and *ἰών* were always employed in a present signification. The future optative, as is well known, is the rarest of moods, and *ἐλευσοίμην* certainly does not happen to be found in Attic writers, but Lysias employs the infinitive *ἐλεύσεσθαι*, 165. 12 (22. 13), *ἀλλὰ γάρ, ὦ ἄνδρες δικασταί, οἴομαι αὐτοὺς ἐπὶ μὲν τοῦτον τὸν λόγον οὐκ ἐλεύσεσθαι*. Now, as in this case, if *ἐλεύσεσθαι* was questionable Attic, the Orator might easily have said, *οἴομαι ἂν αὐτοὺς . . . ἐλθεῖν*, the passage is a valuable proof that *ἐλευσοίμην, ἐλεύσεσθαι*, and *ἐλευσόμενος* were good Attic, while the indicative *ἐλεύσομαι* was, by the stringent law of

[1] In Thuc. 3. 12, *τίς οὖν αὕτη ἡ φιλία ἐγίγνετο ἢ ἐλευθερία πιστὴ ἐν ᾗ παρὰ γνωμὴν ἀλλήλους ὑπεδεχόμεθα*; Haase has conjectured, with some plausibility, *ὑπηρχόμεθα*.

[2] Compare Soph. O. R. 386, Phil. 1007; Eur. Andr. 435, I. A. 67.

parsimony which rules in Attic Greek, studiously ignored. The participle future of *βαίνω* is used in certain compounds, as *ἀποβησόμενα* in Thuc. 8. 75, and its indicative and infinitive are also occasionally encountered in the compound form; but neither *βαίνω*, nor any compound of *βαίνω*, could have supplied the place of *ἐλεύσεσθαι* in Lysias. The phrase is *ἐπὶ λόγον ἰέναι, ἐλθεῖν, ἐλεύσεσθαι, ἐληλυθέναι*: and in such a phrase, if the future optative or participle was required, *ἐλευσοίμην* or *ἐλευσόμενος* was certainly employed. Nothing proves the genuineness of the expression in Lysias so well as the conjectures which, from Elmsley's time, have been hazarded by critics. Rauch reads *οὐ καταφεύξεσθαι*, Scheibe, *οὐκέτι φεύξεσθαι*, and Cobet, *οὐ τρέψεσθαι*, and there may be others equally futile. Elmsley was led to suggest corruption in Lysias by the dictum of Phrynichus, who himself errs in giving a future sense not only to the indicative but also to the other moods of *εἶμι*. Professor Goodwin, in a book of rare merit, 'The Syntax of the Moods and Tenses of the Greek Verb,' has committed the same grave error when he says, p. 6: 'The present *εἶμι*, *I am going*, through all its moods is used like a future.' And he further errs in the remark that follows: 'Its compounds are sometimes used in the same sense.' The future signification of *εἶμι* is known only in the present, and in Attic Greek the same is always true of all its compounds.

XXVIII.

Ἀλκαϊκὸν ᾆσμα δι' ἑνὸς ι οὐ χρὴ λέγειν, ἀλλ' ἐν τοῖν δυοῖν, ἀλκαιικόν, τροχαιικόν.

On this question, how far the soft vowel of the diphthongs *αι*, *οι*, *ει*, was in Attic Greek elided before another vowel, a ponderous literature has accumulated. To any one who cares to reflect that it is practically impossible to acquire any certain knowledge of ancient Greek pronunciation, and that such knowledge, if acquired, would never commend itself as an important part of pure scholarship, the discussion of this point would prove of little interest. Moreover, it would be inconsistent with the design of the present work, which aims rather at pourtraying the extraordinary refinement and precision of the Athenian mind, during its brief imperial life, than at discussing the lisp of Alcibiades, or even the pebbles to which Demosthenes owed his fluency.

However, as often as there is any trustworthy evidence on points like these, it is worthy of consideration, and many questions of Attic orthography may be settled beyond dispute. Even in this case certainty in regard to some points is attainable, and no one would now venture to dispute that, in the old Attic of Tragedy, forms like *καίω*, *κλαίω*, *αἰετός*, *αἰεί*, *ἐλαία* were retained when *κάω*, *κλάω*, *ἀεί*, *ἐλάα*, had replaced them in ordinary speech. Perhaps of Tragedy also, the dictum of Phrynichus may have held true, but it certainly is not true of Attic generally. The history of the name of their patron goddess demonstrates the inconsistency of the Athenians in such cases. The original *'Αθηναία* is found in many inscriptions anterior to Euclides, afterwards it was reduced to *'Αθηνάα*, and ultimately to *'Αθηνᾶ*. In Tragedy, however, *'Αθηναία* is found only in three lines of Aeschylus (Eum. 288, 299, 614); elsewhere he employs, as Sophocles and Euripides always do, the distinct form *'Αθάνα*.

A very careful discussion of the whole question will be found in Konrad Zacher's monograph, 'de Nominibus Graecis in *-αιος*, *-αια*, *-αιον*,' which forms the third volume of 'Dissertationes Philologicae Halenses.' The result he arrives at is this (p. 11), 'Vides in certis quibusdam vocibus diphthongum quae ante vocalem est a poetis corripi interdum, sed saepe etiam servare longam naturam; vides aliorum in hac re alium esse usum, ut Sophocles multo saepius hac correptione utitur, quam Aeschylus vel Euripides; vides in nonnullis horum ipsorum vocabulorum interdum etiam prorsus omitti iota, sed neque in omnibus neque in illis ipsis semper et certis quibusdam legibus; vides denique titulorum scriptores valde titubasse et ante Euclidem iota saepius servasse, quam omisisse. Quid his omnibus efficitur? Nihil aliud quam quod supra jam dixi; illo tempore vocalis iota sonum in diphthongis ante vocalem sequentem admodum attenuatum esse et in multis vocibus tenerae cujusdam consonae nostro j similis naturam induisse, ita tamen ut in ipso sermone Attico magna esset inconstantia, quum iota modo vocali plenae similius sonaret, modo ad consonae sonum appropinquaret, modo fortius, modo exilius pronuntiaretur.'

XXIX.

Νηρὸν ὕδωρ μηδαμῶς, ἀλλὰ πρόσφατον, ἀκραιφνές.

Phrynichus is in error. *Νηρός*, as applied to water, was not Attic, but it was as good as *πρόσφατος* or *ἀκραιφνής*, both of which are strongly metaphorical. The Attic phrase was *καθαρὸν ὕδωρ*: Plato, Phaedr. 229 B, *καθαρὰ καὶ διαφανῆ τὰ ὑδάτια φαίνεται καὶ ἐπιτήδεια κόραις παίζειν παρ' αὐτά*:

> *καθαρῶν ὑδάτων πῶμ' ἀρυσαίμην.*
>
> Eur. Hipp. 209.

The word *νηρός*, however, is of extraordinary interest. Phrynichus doubtless considered it the same word as *νεαρός*, but there can be no question about its true origin. Its history can be traced for about 3000 years. It is presupposed by the names *Νηρεύς* and *Νηρηΐς*, and in modern Greek survives as *νερός*. The Etymologicum Magnum, s. v. Ναρόν, quotes from the Troïlus of Sophocles—

πρὸς ναρὰ καὶ κρηναῖα χωροῦμεν πότα,

and Photius from Aeschylus—

ναρᾶς τε Δίρκης,

and the former writer adds that, even in Hellenistic Greek, the word had become *νερός* : *ἡ συνήθεια, τρέψασα τὸ α εἰς ε, λέγει νερόν.*

It is one of that class of words which, though often hardly represented in literature, live persistently in the mouth of the people; and in many a rural deme of Attica the word was undoubtedly used when it was lost to literary Attic, except in the representative of the dialect in its ancient form, the language of Tragedy.

XXX.

Ποῖ ἄπει; οὕτω συντάσσεται διὰ τοῦ ι· ποῦ δὲ ἄπει; διὰ τοῦ υ, ἁμάρτημα. εἰ δὲ ἐν τῷ υ, ποῦ διατρίβεις;

As frequently happens, a general rule underlies the special instance of the grammarian. In late Greek the distinction between *ποῖ ποῦ*, *οἶ οὗ*, *ὅπου ὅποι*, *ἐκεῖ* and *ἐκεῖσε*, practically disappeared, and transcribers brought the careless and ignorant usage of their own day into the texts of Classical writers. The older and more reliable a manuscript is, the less frequently does the corruption occur in its pages. The fault must in every case be ascribed to the copyists. An Attic writer would as readily have used *οἴκοι* for *οἴκαδε*, as *ποῦ* for *ποῖ*, or *ἐκεῖ* for *ἐκεῖσε*, and *οἴκαδε* for *οἴκοι* would have seemed little less absurd than *ποῖ* for *ποῦ*, or *ἐκεῖσε* for *ἐκεῖ*.

Ordinary intelligence must, however, be exercised in applying this rule, as many verbs of rest may, without violence, receive a modified signification of motion. Thus in Eur. H. F. 74—

ὦ μῆτερ, αὐδᾷ, ποῖ πατὴρ ἄπεστι γῆς;

the use of ποῖ is natural and correct, but in Arist. Av. 9, Dawes was certainly right in altering οὐδὲ πῆ, or οὐδὲ ποῖ, to οὐδ' ὅπου—

ἀλλ' οὐδ' ὅπου γῆς ἐσμὲν οἶδ' ἔγωγ' ἔτι.

In Plutus 1055—

A. βούλει διὰ χρόνου πρὸς ἐμὲ παῖσαι;
B. ποῖ τάλαν;
A. αὐτοῦ, λαβοῦσα κάρυα·

where Meineke edits ποῦ, the Scholiast has a plausible reason for ποῖ: Τὸ ποῖ σκωπτικόν· δηλοῖ γὰρ ἀκολασίας τόπον ζητοῦσαν. Sophocles wrote in O. C. 335—

A. οἱ δ' αὐθόμαιμοι ποῖ νεανίαι πονεῖν;
B. εἴσ' οὗπέρ εἰσι· δεινὰ δ' ἐν κείνοις τὰ νῦν·

and Euripides in Or. 1474—

ποῦ δῆτ' ἀμύνειν οἱ κατὰ στέγας Φρύγες;

There is no question that the Greek of both passages is excellent.

As usual, Xenophon must be regarded as outside the limits of Attic law. There is practically no standard of criticism possible for him, and it is quite possible that the manuscripts do not misrepresent him when they exhibit ποῦ with a verb of motion and ποῖ with a verb of rest. He even employs οἴκαδε in what is nearly the sense of οἴκοι: Cyr. I. 3, 4, δειπνῶν δὲ ὁ Ἀστυάγης σὺν τῷ Κύρῳ βουλόμενος τὸν παῖδα ὡς ἥδιστα δειπνεῖν, ἵνα ἧττον τὰ οἰκάδε ποθοίη, προσήγαγεν αὐτῷ καὶ παροψίδας. When critics erase the τά before οἴκαδε they show their ignorance of the character of Xenophon's style, and forget that the occurrence of expressions like οἴκαδε ἔχειν, in the Common dialect, is a strong argument for a similar usage in a writer who, from the circumstances of his life, was placed in a literary position resembling in many points that of men who wrote after the fall of Attic independence.

The case of ἐκεῖθεν with the article is very different. When Euripides (I. T. 1410) says—

κἀγὼ μὲν εὐθὺς πρός σε δεῦρ' ἀπεστάλην
σοὶ τὰς ἐκεῖθεν σημανῶν, ἄναξ, τύχας·

the propriety of ἐκεῖθεν is at once recognized; and the case is not different with Thuc. 8. 107, καὶ ἐς τὴν Εὔβοιαν ἀπέπεμψαν Ἱπποκράτη καὶ Ἐπικλέα κομιοῦντας τὰς ἐκεῖθεν ναῦς. Even in Thuc. 1. 62 the meaning of ἐκεῖθεν is very different from that of ἐκεῖ: καὶ τῶν ξυμμάχων ὀλίγους ἐπὶ Ὄλυνθου ἀποπέμπουσιν, ὅπως εἴργωσι τοὺς ἐκεῖθεν ἐπιβοηθεῖν,—*the people from there.* The well-known τοὐκεῖθεν in Soph. O. C. 505 is not equivalent to ἐκεῖ, but is due to the same tendency in language which made *ab illa parte*, *e regione*, etc., common expressions in Latin—

A. ἀλλ' εἶμ' ἐγὼ τελοῦσα· τὸν τόπον δ' ἵνα
χρὴ 'σται μ' ἐφευρεῖν, τοῦτο βούλομαι μαθεῖν.
B. τοὐκεῖθεν ἄλσους, ὦ ξένη, τοῦδ', κτε.

In the earliest Greek πρόσθεν and ἔμπροσθεν, ὄπισθεν and ἐξόπισθεν, are constantly encountered by a usage of which τοὐκεῖθεν ἄλσους is merely an extension, and in Attic times expressions like εἰς τὸ ἐξόπισθεν, εἰς τοὔπισθεν, were familiarly employed by the best writers.

XXXI.

Ἔκτοτε κατὰ μηδένα τρόπον εἴπῃς, ἀλλ' ἐξ ἐκείνου.

XXXII.

'Απόπαλαι καὶ ἔκπαλαι ἀμφοῖν δυσχεραίνω, ἐκ παλαιοῦ γὰρ χρὴ λέγειν.

These words of Phrynichus start an inquiry of great difficulty. It is true that ἔκτοτε does not occur in Attic, but Homer used εἰσότε, *against the time when*—

μίμνετ' ἐπειγόμενοι τὸν ἐμὸν γάμον, εἰς ὅ κε φᾶρος
ἐκτελέσω—μή μοι μεταμώνια νήματ' ὄληται—
Λαέρτῃ ἥρωι ταφήϊον, εἰς ὅτε κέν μιν
μοῖρ' ὀλοὴ καθέλῃσι τανηλεγέος θανάτοιο.

Od. 2. 99.

And Aeschines has εἰς ὁπότε, 67. 38, δεύτερον δὲ ἃ εὖ οἶδεν οὐδέποτε ἐσόμενα τολμᾷ λέγειν ἀριθμῶν εἰς ὁπότ' ἔσται. In Plato, εἰς τότε is frequently met with: Legg. 845 C, ἐὰν εἰς τότε τὰ τοιαῦτα περὶ αὐτοῦ τοὺς τότε κριτάς τις ἀναμιμνήσκῃ: 888 B, περίμεινον οὖν εἰς τότε κριτὴς περὶ τῶν μεγίστων γίγνεσθαι. In a chorus of Sophocles ἐς πότε is found—

τίς ἄρα νέατος ἐς πότε λήξει πολυπλάγκτων ἐτέων ἀριθμός;

Aj. 1185.

and even ἐξότε occurs in a choric passage of Aristophanes—

γένος ἀνόσιον, ὅπερ ἐξότ' ἐγένετ' ἐπ' ἐμοὶ
πολέμιον ἐτράφη.

Av. 334.

After the Attic period ἔκτοτε came into use. Although Lucian, in his Pseudosophist[1], ridicules the word, he yet employs it himself in his Asinus, 45. (613), κἀκ τότε ἐξ ἐμοῦ πρώτου ἦλθεν εἰς ἀνθρώπους ὁ λόγος οὗτος, 'Εξ ὄνου παρακύψεως. Moreover it is read by some manuscripts in

[1] He makes his friend Socrates ironically compliment a man for using ἔκτοτε: Τῷ δὲ λέγοντι ἔκτοτε, Καλόν, ἔφη, τὸ εἰπεῖν ἐκπέρυσι, ὁ γὰρ Πλάτων ἐς τότε λέγει. Pseudosophist, 7. (571).

Aristotle, H. A. 12. 519. 29, οὐδὲ (ἀναφύεται) τὸ κέντρον ὅταν ἀποβάλῃ ἡ μέλιττα, ἀλλ' ἐκ τότε ἀποθνήσκει. On the other hand, neither ἀπὸ τότε nor ἀφ' ὅτε is encountered till a very late date.

Throughout Greek literature ἐς is used with adverbs of time. In Homer, Od. 7. 318, it is true that the original reading was αὔριον ἐς not ἐς τῆμος—

> πομπὴν δ' ἐς τόδ' ἐγὼ τεκμαίρομαι, ὄφρ' εὖ εἰδῇς,
> αὔριον ἔς· τῆμος δὲ σὺ μὲν δεδμημένος ὕπνῳ,

for τῆμος could not be used of any but past time; but εἰς ὅτε has already been quoted, and with that may be compared the use of ἐς τί in Il. 5. 465—

> ἐς τί ἔτι κτείνεσθαι ἐάσετε λαὸν Ἀχαιοῖς;

No one needs to be reminded of the phase κτῆμα ἐς ἀεί, and ἐς ὀψέ occurs in Thucydides (8. 23), and εἰς ὀψέ in Dem. 1303. 14.

In a different sense, namely, that which appears in phrases like εἰς ἐνιαυτόν—

> τρὶς γὰρ τίκτει μῆλα τελεσφόρον εἰς ἐνιαυτόν,
> Od. 4. 86.
>
> ἥν περ γὰρ κῆταί γε τελεσφόρον εἰς ἐνιαυτόν,
> Il. 19. 32.

the preposition is also attached to adverbs of time. Some of these are ἐσάπαξ (Thuc. 5. 85; Plato, Soph. 247 E), εἰσαῦθις or εἰς αὖθις (Plato, Legg. 862 D et freq.), ἐσέπειτα (Thuc. 1. 130, etc.). The meaning of the preposition in ἐσαυτίκα is clearly indicated by Ar. Pax 366—

> A. ἀπόλωλας, ἐξόλωλας,
> B. ἐς τίν' ἡμέραν;
> A. ἐς αὐτίκα μάλα.

All Greek authors from Homer downwards use ἐσύστερον.

In both these significations εἰς was in late Greek attached

to many more adverbs than was allowable in Attic, and expressions like εἰσάγαν, εἰς ἅλις, εἰσάρτι, εἰσμάτην, εἰσάχρι, were used with freedom.

It is here necessary to make an important distinction. The meaning of εἰς and ἐξ, in the combinations discussed above, is decidedly prepositional; but it must not be forgotten that prepositions are often associated with adverbs in quite another way. In ἀπαρτί the force of the ἀπό is not prepositional, but adverbial; and the same is true of ὑποκάτω, ὑποκάτωθεν, ἐπάνω, ἐπάνωθεν, and many others. In late writers, on the other hand, an ἀπάρτι is found, in which the ἀπό has its meaning prepositional (see p. 71); but in an Attic writer such a meaning was certainly impossible.

The Homeric and late ἐξέτι has not the meaning which its form might suggest, and really has no place in this discussion, but in προσέτι the πρός is distinctly adverbial. In Attic, *two years ago* is expressed by προπέρυσιν as naturally as *a year ago* by πέρυσι, but the πρό in the former word is not a preposition, but an adverb. In ἐκπέρυσι, however, the form which Lucian indicates as little worse than ἔκτοτε, the ἐκ would not be adverbial, but prepositional.

In a Comic climax in the Knights, Aristophanes employs πρόπαλαι, l. 1153—

> A. τρίπαλαι κάθημαι βουλόμενός σ' εὐεργετεῖν.
> B. ἐγὼ δὲ δεκάπαλαί γε, καὶ δωδεκάπαλαι,
> καὶ χιλιόπαλαι, καὶ προπαλαιπαλαίπαλαι.

Like the adjective προπάλαιος, it is used in sober writing in late Greek. In no case should it be compared with ἀπόπαλαι, as the πρό is adverbial, the ἀπό prepositional.

A good instance of a compound in which both parts are distinctly adverbial is the word σύνεγγυς, which occurs in Thucydides and other Attic writers: Thuc. 4. 24, ξύνεγγυς κειμένου τοῦ τε Ῥηγίου ἀκρωτηρίου τῆς Ἰταλίας τῆς τε Μεσσήνης τῆς Σικελίας. It would be rash to found any argument upon ἔνεγγυς, which, at best, has only a precarious existence in Quintus Smyrnaeus, an epic writer of the fourth Christian century; but Aristotle unquestionably employed πάρεγγυς. The word is typical of a notable characteristic of un-Attic Greek. Instead of accepting common words as the natural exponents of common thoughts, it attempted to say more than was necessary, and in this way defeated its own aim. Σύνεγγυς supplied a distinct want; πάρεγγυς is a weaker ἐγγύς in the guise of strength, and finds fitting company in παρεκεῖ, παραυτόθεν, παραυτόθι, ἐπιπρόσω, ἀπεκεῖθεν, ἀπεντεῦθεν, and other late words. The expression 'un-Attic Greek' has been purposely used, because, even in Homer and other Classical writers outside the Attic bounds, a similar tendency of language is distinctly traceable. The words μετόπισθεν and ἀπονόσφιν, of frequent occurrence in the Homeric poems, are peculiarly in point, as they belong to the class now under discussion. Ἀπόνοσφιν is no more than νόσφιν, and μετόπισθε no more than ὄπισθε, and both words involve a violation of the law of parsimony, an instinctive principle which permeates the language of the Athenians, and not only differentiates it from all other Greek dialects, but elevates it above almost all other tongues. Προπάροιθε is another word of the same class, which may also be considered to include all such expressions as ἐκ διόθεν, and ἐξ οὐρανόθεν. In Homer forms like ὑπέκδιεκ, διαπρό, ἀποπρό, are often used with propriety, but the line ought surely to be drawn at ἀπέκ, which is met with in the Homeric Hymns—

> αὐτίκ' ἄρ' Εἰλείθυιαν ἄπεκ μεγάροιο θύραζε
> ἐκπροκαλεσσαμένη, ἔπεα πτερόεντα προσηύδα.
> Apol. 110.

A well-known feature of Euripides' style, already referred to (p. 35), is the habit of using antique words in order to balance the great number of modern expressions which he introduced into his verse The tragic dialect, which had for its basis the Attic of the period before the Persian wars, was, of course, more or less modified by every great Tragic poet; but Euripides was the first to give a firm footing to many words of modern acceptance which were either not used at all, or only tolerated by his predecessors. At the same time, a careless observer might regard his style as more than usually antiquated from the free use of such words as *σέθεν, ὑπέρφεν, ἐμέθεν, ποτί*, etc. It would often seem as if he almost consciously used Epic words to give an old-world air to his verse. Accordingly, it is not surprising to encounter in Euripides expressions like *μετόπισθε* and *ἀποπρό*, and similar reminiscences of Homer may be observed on every page.

Any freak of diction may be expected in a writer like Apollonius Rhodius, who, at an age when Greek had already lost all its great qualities, attempted to write in an old style which he little understood. He naturally makes even more blunders than are found in modern attempts to imitate Classical Greek styles, and, by misunderstanding the facts of tmesis in Homer, has been led to use many forms intrinsically absurd. In Iliad 10. 273—

> *βὰν ῥ' ἰέναι, λιπέτην δὲ κατ' αὐτόθι πάντας ἀρίστους,*

the *κάτα* belongs to *λιπέτην*, but in Apollonius *καταυτόθι* unblushingly takes the place of the simple *αὐτόθι*—

> *εὖ γὰρ ἐγώ μιν*
> *Δασκύλου ἐν μεγάροισι καταυτόθι πατρὸς ἐμοῖο*
> *οἶδ' εἰσιδών.*
>
> Ap. Rh. 2. 778.

Another kind of mistake has produced *ἐπὶ δήν* or *ἐπιδήν*—

> *οὐδ' ἐπὶ δὴν μετέπειτα κερασσάμενοι Διὶ λοιβάς.*
>
> Id. 1. 516.

> *ἔλπομαι οὐκ ἐπὶ δήν σε βαρὺν χόλον Αἰήταο*
> *ἐκφυγέειν.*
>
> Id. 4. 738.

It is an unintelligent imitation of the Homeric ἐπὶ δηρόν, which, like ἐπὶ πολὺν χρόνον, is used with propriety.

Late forms as debased as ἀπεκεῖ, ἀπεκεῖσε, ἀπονῦν, ἀποψέ, and their fellows, do not merit, and would not repay, consideration.

XXXIII.

Πηνίκα μὴ εἴπῃς ἀντὶ τοῦ πότε· ἔστι γὰρ ὥρας δηλωτικόν, οἷον εἰπόντος τινός, πηνίκα ἀποδημήσεις; ἐὰν εἴπῃς, μετὰ δύο ἢ τρεῖς ἡμέρας, οὐκ ὀρθῶς ἐρεῖς· ἐὰν δ' εἴπῃς ἕωθεν ἢ περὶ μεσημβρίαν, ὀρθῶς ἐρεῖς.

The other grammarians copy Phrynichus, and some of them extend his dictum to the correlatives ὁπηνίκα, ἡνίκα, τηνικαῦτα, and τηνικάδε. They are all more or less in error. It is true that πηνίκα and τηνικάδε are generally used in what was doubtless their genuine meaning, and that the other words are frequently so employed. Thus their primitive reference to the time of day attaches to πηνίκα and ὁπηνίκα in Arist. Av. 1498—

A. πηνίκ' ἐστὶν ἄρα τῆς ἡμέρας;
B. ὁπηνίκα; σμικρόν τι μετὰ μεσημβρίαν.

And an interesting passage of Aeschines tells the same story (2. 15), ὁ γὰρ νομοθέτης διαρρήδην ἀποδείκνυσι πρῶτον μὲν ἣν ὥραν προσήκει ἰέναι τὸν παῖδα τὸν ἐλεύθερον εἰς τὸ διδασκαλεῖον, ἔπειτα μετὰ πόσων παίδων εἰσιέναι καὶ ὁπηνίκα ἀπιέναι, καὶ τοὺς διδασκάλους τὰ διδασκαλεῖα καὶ τοὺς παιδοτρίβας τὰς παλαίστρας ἀνοίγειν μὲν ἀπαγορεύει μὴ πρότερον πρὶν ἂν ὁ ἥλιος ἀνίσχῃ, κλείειν δὲ προστάττει πρὸ ἡλίου δεδυκότος. In the only passage of Homer in which ἡνίκα is met with, it has this same limited sense—

νῦν μὲν δὴ μάλα πάγχυ, Μελάνθιε, νύκτα φυλάξεις,
εὐνῇ ἔνι μαλακῇ καταλεγμένος, ὥς σε ἔοικεν·
οὐδέ σέ γ' ἠριγένεια παρ' ὠκεάνοιο ῥοάων

λήσει ἐπερχομένη χρυσόθρονος, ἡνίκ' ἀγινεῖς
αἶγας μνηστήρεσσι, δόμον κατὰ δαῖτα πένεσθαι·

Od. 22. 198.

and naturally it never loses it throughout Greek literature. Similarly, τηνικαῦτα is employed of a point of time in the natural day by Lysias (93. 43), τούτῳ ἡλίου δεδυκότος ἰόντι ἐξ ἀγροῦ ἀπήντησα. εἰδὼς δ' ἐγὼ ὅτι τηνικαῦτα ἀφιγμένος οὐδένα καταλήψοιτο οἴκοι τῶν ἐπιτηδείων: and τηνικάδε so occurs very frequently (Plato, Phaed. 76 B, Protag. 310 B, Crit. 43 A).

With the exception of τηνικάδε, however, which does not extend its meaning till late writers like Polybius, all these words are found more or less frequently in a more general sense. Even πηνίκα certainly so occurs in Demosthenes (329. 23), ἐν τίσιν οὖν καὶ πηνίκα σὺ λαμπρός; ἡνίκ' ἂν εἰπεῖν τι κατὰ τούτων δέῃ, and in Ar. Av. 1514—

A. ἀπόλωλεν ὁ Ζεύς· B. πηνίκ' ἄττ' ἀπώλετο;

no one but a grammatical martinet would insist upon any other rendering. From its generalised meaning of *when*, which occurs with frequency, ὁπηνίκα acquired that of *since*. An example of the former signification is provided by Thucydides (4. 125), κυρωθὲν οὐδὲν ὁπηνίκα χρὴ ὁρμᾶσθαι, and of the latter by Demosthenes (527. 23), ἀλλὰ μὴν ὁπηνίκα καὶ πεποιηκώς, ἃ κατηγορῶ, καὶ ὕβρει πεποιηκὼς φαίνεται, τοὺς νόμους ἤδη δεῖ σκοπεῖν.

It is no rare experience to find ἡνίκα corresponding to τότε, Plato, Symp. 198 C, τότε . . . ἡνίκα ὑμῖν ὡμολόγουν, and still more frequently ἡνίκ' ἂν replacing ὅταν or ἐπειδάν—

ἡνίκ' ἂν πενθῶμεν ἤτοι Μέμνον' ἢ Σαρπηδόνα.

Ar. Nub. 622.

Not only does τηνικαῦτα become as general as τότε—

κᾆτα γίγνομαι παχὺς
τηνικαῦτα τοῦ θέρους,

Id. Pax 1170.

but even passes from chronology to Ethics in such passages as Ar. Pax 1142—

εἰπέ μοι, τί τηνικαῦτα δρῶμεν, ὦ Κωμαρχίδη;

XXXIV.

Ὀρθρινὸς οὔ, ἀλλ' ὄρθριος χωρὶς τοῦ ν.

XXXV.

Ὀψινός, ὁμοίως τῷ ὀρθρινὸς καὶ τοῦτο ἁμάρτημα. χρὴ οὖν ἄνευ τοῦ ν, ὄψιος.

Of the second of these words three forms occur, namely, *ὄψιμος, ὀψινός,* and *ὄψιος.* First met with in a line of the Iliad (2. 325), *ὄψιμος* does not again appear till late Greek, except in the Oeconomicus, a disputed work of Xenophon (17. 4), *ὁ πρώιμος ἢ ὁ μέσος ἢ ὁ ὀψιμώτατος σπόρος.* If the book is really Xenophon's, the words *πρώιμος* and *ὀψιμώτατος* not only afford an admirable illustration of the inconsistency of his diction, as *ὀψιαίτατοι* occurs in Hell. 5. 4. 3, and *πρῳαίτατα* in Cyr. 8. 8. 9, but may well be regarded as another proof of the position, that with an Attic basis his diction is really a composite one, being modified, both in vocabulary and syntax, by the other dialects of European and Asiatic Hellas.

Although the Latin bimus, trimus, etc., are doubtless derived from hiems, and can no more be compared with *ὄψιμος,* than hornus (ho-ver-nus) with *ὡρινός,* yet there is no reason to deny the antiquity of the suffix in *ὄψιμος, πρώιμος,* and *ὥριμος.* With the exception of *ὄψιμος,* the words are late as far as literature can inform us, but they may still have had a long and uninterrupted history in some little-regarded corner of Greece.

With ὀψινός, besides ὀρθρινός, may be compared χειμερινός, ἡμερινός, πρωινός, and the Latin vernus, diuturnus, periendinus, while with ὄψιος and ὄρθριος are comparable ὥριος, πρῷος, ἡμέριος, and χειμέριος. Attention has already been called to the way in which Attic Greek utilised superfluous forms, and some of these words illustrate this habit in an interesting manner. When an Attic writer desires to express some natural fact which takes place *in winter* he employs χειμερινός, but with reference to incidents which merely resemble those of winter χειμέριος is the term employed. Thucydides (7. 16) speaks of χειμεριναὶ ἡλίου τροπαί, and in Plato (Legg. 683 C; 915 D), the winter solstice is called τὰ χειμερινά. Any article of apparel or of domestic furniture intended for winter use has χειμερινός appropriately applied to it. On the other hand, χειμέριος is employed with propriety in Thuc. 3. 22, τηρήσαντες νύκτα χειμέριον ὕδατι καὶ ἀνέμῳ, καὶ ἅμ' ἀσέληνον: and figuratively in Arist. Ach. 1141—

νίφει, βαβαιάξ· χειμέρια τὰ πράγματα.

There can be little question that the same distinction was made between θερινός and θέρειος, and that it is merely by accident that θέρειος does not occur in Attic Greek. Similarly, ἡμερινός strictly means *of day*, as φῶς ἡμερινόν, while ἡμέριοι ἄνθρωποι, not ἡμερινοί, is the correct expression. For the poetical ἡμέριος, prose writers substituted ἡμερήσιος, as Isocr. 343 C, ἡμερήσιος λόγος, *a speech that takes a day to deliver*. Νυκτερινός and νυκτερήσιος are differentiated in the same way.

In cases in which nothing could be gained by retaining more than a single form, Attic abandoned all but one—sometimes one suffix getting the mastery, sometimes another—as ἠρινός, μεσημβρινός, ὀπωρινός, μετοπωρινός, but ὄψιος, ὄρθριος, and πρῷος.

XXXVI.

Μεσονύκτιον· ποιητικόν, οὐ πολιτικόν.

Even the adjective *μεσονύκτιος* is poetical, as Eur. Hec. 914, ch.—

μεσονύκτιος ὠλόμαν,
ἦμος ἐκ δείπνων ὕπνος κτε.

Of the substantive, Lobeck remarks that it is first met with in Hippocrates, and afterwards used by Aristotle, Diodorus, Strabo, and others. There was in Attic no word expressing for the night what *μεσημβρία* expressed for the day, the phrases *μεσούσης νυκτός, μέσης νυκτός,* and *μέσον νυκτῶν,* or *νυκτός,* being always employed instead. Even *μεσημβρία* became in late Greek *μέση ἡμέρα,* a form discovered also in the Oeconomicus (16. 14), *εἴ τις αὐτὴν ἐν μέσῳ τῷ θέρει καὶ ἐν μέσῃ τῇ ἡμέρᾳ κινοίη τῷ ζεύγει,* and doubtless owing its place in the Common dialect to Ionian influence. According to Lobeck, the first instance of the analytical form comes from Hippocrates.

In Thuc. 3. 80, *μέχρι μέσου ἡμέρας,* the *μέσου* used to be regarded as a peculiar feminine form, and not, as it really is, a substantive governing *ἡμέρας* in the genitive.

XXXVII.

Ἡ ὄμφαξ, ἡ βῶλος, θηλυκῶς δέον, οὐκ ἀρσενικῶς.

XXXVIII.

Ἡ πηλὸς Συρακούσιοι λέγοντες ἁμαρτάνουσιν.

Such remarks require no comment, except that they are

correct. In the latter, the purism of Phrynichus comes out in ἁμαρτάνουσιν, a word which Lobeck has considered worthy of half a page of small print.

It is, however, tempting to seize this opportunity of discussing the derivation of προπηλακίζω, a verb generally derived from πηλός. This is of course altogether impossible, and Curtius has accordingly to coin a form, πῆλαξ, corresponding to βῶλαξ, a side-form of βῶλος, encountered in Pindar and Theocritus. But of πῆλαξ there is no trace in Greek authors, and none even in lexicographers, and of πάλκος in Hesychius the less said the better. Moreover, why should the Greeks have gone out of their way to say προπηλακίζω, when προπηλίζω was certainly as legitimate a formation? As a matter of fact, the verb has no connection whatever with πηλός, as there is no πῆλαξ, and κάτα not πρό would have been the preposition used to bring out the signification which Suïdas assigns to the word, παρὰ τὸ πηλὸν ἐπιχρίεσθαι τὰ πρόσωπα τῶν ἀτιμίαν καὶ ὕβριν καταψηφιζομένων.

In a passage of Xenophanes of Colophon, preserved in Athenaeus (2. 54 F), the adjective πηλίκος occurs in a connection in which it must have been familiarly used—

> πὰρ πυρὶ χρὴ τοιαῦτα λέγειν χειμῶνος ἐν ὥρῃ,
> ἐν κλίνῃ μαλακῇ κατακείμενον ἔμπλεον ὄντα
> πίνοντα γλυκὺν οἶνον, ὑποτρώγοντ' ἐρεβίνθους,
> τίς πόθεν εἶς ἀνδρῶν; πόσα τοι ἔτη ἐστί, φέριστε;
> πηλίκος ἦσθ' ὅθ' ὁ Μῆδος ἀφίκετο;

Almost any phrase could be thrown into a verbal shape by the suffixing of -ίζω. From ἐς κόρακας came the verb σκορακίζω, which by Demosthenes' time had fought its way into literature (155. 15), οἱ δ' ὅταν τὰ μέγιστα κατορθώσωσι, τότε μάλιστα σκορακίζονται καὶ προπηλακίζονται παρὰ τὸ προσῆκον. Similarly, ἐπ' ἀμφότερα supplied ἐπαμφοτερίζω, and ἐπ' ἀκρόν, ἐπακρίζω. Many words of the same kind must necessarily have perished, as it is only a tithe of any argot which ever finds its way into literature proper. Even πηλικίζω, or πηλακίζω, was doubtless often used in colloquial Greek of asking a man's age; but its compound προπηλακίζω, *ask a man's age before you know him*, *begin with asking a man's age*, if not primarily so used, must soon have acquired the secondary sense which it always bears in literary Greek. The obnoxious antepenult is at once explained, and the preposition has an appropriate and usual signification, while the change of vowel presents no difficulty. The Homeric prototype of verbs of this formation, namely, ἰσοφαρίζω, itself exhibits a similar change, that of ε to α, as in πλατυγίζω from πλαταγή, α itself has been replaced by υ.

Accuracy of scholarship is checked at the outset when a boy turns up his dictionary and finds one of the meanings given for *que* is *or*, and is told that προπηλακίζω comes from πηλός, ζυγωθρίζω from ζύγον, πλαταγίζω from πλάτη, and ἐντευτλανῶ from τεῦτλον. In the latter word even the texts are in error. In the Aristophanic parody—

μηδὲ γὰρ θανών ποτε
σοῦ χωρὶς εἴην ἐντετευτλιωμένης,
Ach. 894.

the manuscripts present nothing but ἐντετευτλανωμένης, a formation altogether impossible. The Greek word for *beet* was τεῦτλον or τευτλίον, and from the latter form Aristophanes legitimately used ἐντευτλιοῦν for *to cook in beet*. Not even in its most debased period did Greek replace τεῦτλον or τευτλίον by τεύτλανον.

XXXIX.

Ποταπὸς διὰ τοῦ τ μὴ εἴπῃς, ἀδόκιμον γάρ. διὰ τοῦ δέλτα δὲ λέγων ἐπὶ γένους θήσεις, Ποδαπός ἐστι; Θηβαῖος ἢ

Ἀθηναῖος. Ἔστι γὰρ οἷον ἐκ τίνος δαπέδου. ποταπὸς δέ ἐστιν εἰ εἴποι, ποταπὸς τὸν τρόπον Φρύνιχος; ἐπιεικής· χρὴ οὖν οὕτως ἐρωτᾶν, Ποῖός τίς σοι δοκεῖ εἶναι;

It will be observed that Phrynichus begins with denying the spelling with tau altogether, but afterwards proceeds to say that, when so spelt, it has a different signification. Lobeck is wrong in considering the second half of the remark as a spurious addition. The sense is plain. 'Ποδαπός must not be written with a tau. Its only form in Attic is ποδαπός, with the meaning *of what country?* As for the other meaning now-a-days attached to ποταπός, that is no better than the spelling, and was expressed in Attic Greek by ποῖος.'

The use of his own name by Phrynichus may be paralleled from other Grammarians, and the adjective he associates with it is in keeping with the dry humour of the man.

There is no question that ποταπός is simply a degenerated form of ποδαπός. Classical texts have on the whole escaped corruption, but a few instances of the vicious spelling are found; the first traces, according to Lobeck, being met with in some codices of Herodotus, 5. 13 and 7. 218. In Alexis—

> A. ἡδύ γε τὸ πῶμα· ποδαπὸς ὁ Βρόμιος, Τρύφη;
> B. Θάσιος. A. ὅμοιον καὶ δίκαιον τοὺς ξένους
> πίνειν ξενικόν, τοὺς δ' ἐγγενεῖς ἐπιχώριον,
> (Athen. 10. 431 B.)

the manuscripts give only ποταπός or ποταμός. It is possible that the τ is due to Athenaeus, but Alexis wrote ποδαπός. Another passage of Alexis—

> τί λέγεις σύ; ποδαπὸς οὑτοσὶ
> ἄνθρωπος; οὐκ ἐπίστασαι ζῆν. ψυχρά σοι
> ἅπαντα παραθῶ;
> (Athen. 9. 386 A.)

was corrected by Dobree. The manuscripts exhibit *τί λέγεις, δέσποτα, πῶς οὑτοσί..;* The lines represent the natural surprise of a chef at the orders he receives, and the conjecture certainly restores the text.

In late Greek *ποταπός* acquired the sense of *ποῖος*, as N.T. Matth. 8. 27, *ποταπός ἐστιν οὗτος ὅτι καὶ οἱ ἄνεμοι καὶ ἡ θάλασσα ὑπακούουσιν αὐτῷ;* but that use is certainly unknown to the Attic *ποδαπός*. A natural inference from a passage of Athenaeus is that the more general signification came from Ionic: Athen. 4. 159 D, *Χρύσιππος δ', ἐν τῇ εἰσαγωγῇ τῇ εἰς τὴν περὶ ἀγαθῶν καὶ κακῶν πραγματείαν, νεανίσκον φησί τινα ἐκ τῆς Ἰωνίας σφόδρα πλούσιον ἐπιδημῆσαι ταῖς Ἀθήναις. πορφυρίδα ἠμφιεσμένον, ἔχουσαν χρυσᾶ κράσπεδα. πυνθανομένου δέ τινος αὐτοῦ, ποδαπός ἐστιν, ἀποκρίνασθαι, ὅτι πλούσιος. μήποτε τοῦ αὐτοῦ μνημονεύει καὶ Ἄλεξις ἐν Θηβαίοις, λέγων ὧδε·*

> *ἔστιν δὲ ποδαπὸς τὸ γένος οὗτος;* B. *πλούσιος·*
> *τούτους δὲ πάντες φασὶν εὐγενεστάτους*
> *εἶναι· πένητας δ' εὐπατρίδας οὐδεὶς ὁρᾷ.*

A similar line to this of Alexis is found in Ar. Pax 186—

> B. *ποδαπὸς τὸ γένος δ' εἶ; φράζε μοι.*
> A. *μιαρώτατος·*

where the joke lies in this, that poor Trugaeus is so alarmed at the terrible greeting of Hermes that, to every question put to him, he can only mutter *μιαρώτατος*, the key-word of the salutation.

The speech against Aristogiton is generally considered spurious; but, if it is a genuine work of Demosthenes, *ποδαπός* in 782. 8 is certainly not equivalent to *ποῖος*, but is used in its ordinary sense, *τί οὖν οὗτός ἐστι; κύων, νὴ Δία, φασί τινες, τοῦ δήμου. ποδαπός; οἷος οὓς μὲν αἰτιᾶται λύκους εἶναι μὴ δάκνειν· ἃ δέ φησι φύλαττειν πρόβατα, αὐτὸς κατεσθίειν.* 'Of what breed, pray? Molossian, Laconian, or what? a dog with such a temper that ——.'

XL.

Φανὸς ἐπὶ τῆς λαμπάδος ἀλλὰ μὴ ἐπὶ τοῦ κερατίνου λέγε. τοῦτο δὲ λυχνοῦχον λέγε.

In the App. Soph. p. 50. 22, Phrynichus is much more explicit: *Λυχνοῦχος, λαμπτήρ, φανὸς διαφέρει. λυχνοῦχος μέν ἐστι σκεῦός τι ἐν κύκλῳ ἔχον κέρατα, ἔνδον δὲ λύχνον ἡμμένον, διὰ τῶν κεράτων τὸ φῶς πεμπόντα. λαμπτὴρ δὲ χαλκοῦν ἢ σιδηροῦν ἢ ξύλινον λαμπάδιον ὅμοιον, ἔχον θρυαλλίδα. φανὸς δὲ φάκελός τινων συνδεδεμένος καὶ ἡμμένος· ὃ καὶ διὰ τοῦ π.* Athenaeus (15. 699 D) quotes many passages illustrative of these words. The *λυχνοῦχος* was a lantern used in the open air—

καὶ διαστίλβονθ' ὁρῶμεν,
ὥσπερ ἐν καινῷ λυχνούχῳ,
πάντα τῆς ἐξωμίδος.
Aristophanes.

ἕξουσιν οἱ πομπῆς λυχνούχους δηλαδή.
Plato.

ἄνυσόν ποτ' ἐξελθών, σκότος γὰρ γίγνεται,
καὶ τὸν λυχνοῦχον ἔκφερ', ἐνθεὶς τὸν λύχνον.
Pherecrates.

ὁ πρῶτος εὑρὼν μετὰ λυχνούχου περιπατεῖν
τῆς νυκτὸς ἦν τις κηδεμὼν τῶν δακτύλων.
Alexis.

The *φανός*, on the other hand, was a link or torch consisting of strips of resinous wood tied together—

ὁ φανός ἐστι μεστὸς ὕδατος οὑτοσί·
δεῖ τ' οὐχὶ σείειν, ἀλλ' ἀποσείειν αὐτόθεν.
Menander.

In Attic it meant a species of *λαμπάς*, but in late Greek was used for λυχνοῦχος, *lantern.* With similar inaccuracy *λαμπάς* in the Common dialect became equivalent to λύχνος, *an oil lamp*, being so used in the New Testament in the parable of the Ten Virgins.

The λυχνοῦχος must not be confused with the λυχνεῖον, which was used indoors to support or suspend one or more λύχνοι—

τῶν δ' ἀκοντίων
συνδοῦντες ὀρθὰ τρία λυχνείῳ χρώμεθα.
Antiphanes.

ἅψαντες λύχνον
λυχνεῖον ἐζητοῦμεν.
Diphilus.

XLI.

Ἐν χρῷ κουρίας φαθί, καὶ μὴ ψιλόκουρος.

The substantive κουρίας does not occur in what remains to us of Classical Greek, but may well have existed. It is employed by Lucian, Hermotimus 18. (756), ἑώρων αὐτοὺς κοσμίως βαδίζοντας, ἀναβεβλημένους εὐσταλῶς, φροντίζοντας ἀεί, ἀρρενωπούς, ἐν χρῷ κουρίας τοὺς πλείστους, and has the authoritative support of Aelius Dionysius (Eustath. 1450. 32), ἡ ἐν χρῷ κουρά, ἡ ψιλὴ κατὰ Αἴλιον Διονύσιον, καὶ πρὸς τὸν χρῶτα καὶ ἐν χρῷ δὲ κουρίας. According to Pollux, 2. 33, Pherecrates used the phrase ἐν χρῷ κουριῶντας, and in Xen. Hell. 1. 7. 8 occurs the expression ἐν χρῷ κεκαρμένους. Thucydides has ἐν χρῷ metaphorically (2. 84), ἐν χρῷ ἀεὶ παραπλέοντες: a usage which may further be exemplified by the proverb ξυρεῖ γὰρ ἐν χρῷ (Soph. Aj. 786).

XLII.

Πεινῆν, διψῆν λέγε, ἀλλὰ μὴ διὰ τοῦ α.

Besides these two verbs eight others in -άω, contracted in eta preferentially to alpha, namely—

ζῶ,	ζῆν,	live.
κνῶ,	κνῆν,	scrape.
ψῶ,	ψῆν,	rub.
σμῶ,	σμῆν,	wipe.
νῶ,	νῆν,	spin.
χρῶ,	χρῆν,	utter an oracle.
χρῶ,	χρῆν,	am eager for.
χρῶμαι,	χρῆσθαι,	use.

Many of them have escaped the altering hand of the copyists almost entirely; but it is not surprising if some of them have occasionally been altered, when forms like πεινᾷ, πεινᾶν, διψᾷς, ἐχρᾶτο, became possible in late Greek. Σμῶ and ψῶ will occupy our attention at a future time, but the others may best be considered here. In Plato (Gorg. 494 C) κνῆσθαι has escaped, but in Ar. Av. 1586, ἐπικνῇς must be restored in spite of the manuscripts. Although χρῶμαι is really only the middle voice of χρῶ, *give the use of*, yet in Attic the place of the active is usurped by κίχρημι, and the middle alone concerns the present inquiry. It is, however, reasonable to suppose that its active voice is retained in χρῶ, *utter an oracle*, the connection between the two meanings being best seen in the common notion of *furnish with anything of which one stands in need.* If this is the case, the above list ought to be reduced from ten to nine.

The verb χρῶ, *am eager for*, *wish*, is very rare, occurring only in the second and third persons singular of the present indicative. Grammarians explain χρῇς by χρῄζεις or θέλεις and χρῇ by χρῄζει or θέλει. In all Greek literature it is found only in six passages. In Sophocles, Ant. 887—

> ἄφετε μόνην ἔρημον, εἴτε χρῇ θανεῖν,
> εἴτ' ἐν τοιαύτῃ ζῶσα τυμβεύειν στέγῃ,

the manuscripts read χρή and τυμβεύει, but the gloss of the Scholiast, χρῄζει καὶ θέλει, proves that χρῇ was read by him. The same form is met with in Euripides, quoted by Cicero, Epist. ad Att. 8. 8. 2, and by Suïdas under παλαμᾶσθαι—

> πρὸς ταῦθ' ὅ τι χρῇ, καὶ παλαμάσθω
> καὶ πᾶν ἐπ' ἐμοὶ τεκταινέσθω·

while in Cratinus, as cited by Suïdas, the second person occurs—

> νῦν γὰρ δή σοι πάρα μὲν θεσμοὶ
> τῶν ἡμετέρων, πάρα δ' ἄλλ' ὅ τι χρῇς·

where Suïdas says, χρῇς τὸ χρήζεις καὶ τὸ δέῃ (but the copyists give χρῇς in both text and explanation). It is probably to the same passage that the gloss of Hesychius, χρῇς· θέλεις, χρήζεις, should be referred.

In Ar. Ach. 778, where a Megarian is speaking, the second person appears as χρῇσθα or χρῆσθα—a form like ἔφησθα, ἦσθα, ᾔδησθα, etc.—

> φώνει δὴ τὺ ταχέως χοιρίον.
> οὐ χρῆσθα; σιγῇς, ὦ κάκιστ' ἀπολουμένα.

Now, as in Ant. 887, the true reading has been preserved only in a gloss of the Scholiast, and in Cratinus only by a similar gloss of Suïdas and Hesychius, there is no doubt that it was right to restore χρῇ to Euripides; and Dindorf's χρῇς must be substituted for χρή in Soph. Aj. 1373—

> σοὶ δὲ δρᾶν ἔξεσθ' ἃ χρῇς·

and Wunder's in El. 606—

> κήρυσσέ μ' εἰς ἅπαντας, εἴτε χρῇς κακήν,
> εἴτε στόμαργον, εἴτ' ἀναιδείας πλέαν.

As it will be shown that σμῶ and ψῶ had in late Greek the un-Attic forms σμήχω and ψήχω, which have actually crept into Attic texts, so κνῶ and νῶ were in the Common dialect replaced by κνήθω and νήθω. The longer κνήθω does not once appear in the texts of Classical writers till the time of Aristotle; but νῶ has been much less fortunate.

The word is rare in Classical Greek, occurring only in the ten following places—

ἔνθα δ' ἔπειτα
πείσεται ἅσσα οἱ Αἶσα κατὰ Κλῶθές τε βαρεῖαι
γιγνομένῳ νήσαντο λίνῳ, ὅτε μιν τέκε μήτηρ.
Hom. Od. 7. 198.

γιγνομένῳ ἐπένησε λίνῳ, ὅτε μιν τέκε μήτηρ.
Id. Il. 20. 128.

τῇ γάρ τοι νεῖ (lege νῇ) νήματ' ἀερσιπότητος ἀράχνης.
Hesiod. Op. 777.

τῇ χειρὶ νῶσαι μαλθακωτάτην κρόκην.
Eupolis.

εἰ μὴ τὸν στήμονα νήσω.
Arist. Lys. 519.

Plat. Polit. 289 C, τοὺς περὶ τὸ νήθειν καὶ ξαίνειν, corresponding to a preceding 282 A, καὶ μὴν ξαντική γε καὶ νηστικὴ καὶ πάντα τὰ περὶ τὴν ποίησιν τῆς ἐσθῆτος: id. 282 E, τὰ νηθέντα.

Μᾶλις μὲν ἔννη λέπτον ἔχοισ' ἐπ' ἀτράκτῳ λίνον.
Alcaeus (?), Bgk. p. 1333.

πέπλους τε νῆσαι λινογενεῖς τ' ἐπενδύτας.
Soph. Nausicaa.

κρόκην δὴ νήσεις
καὶ στήμονα.
Menander.

Now of these ten places most help us little, for νήσω and ἔνησα may come from either of three presents, νέω, νήθω, or νάω: νηθέντα may come from νέω or νάω: νῶσαι and ἔννη from νάω only, while νεῖ in Hesiod and νήθειν in Plato stand alone. The authority of Hesychius and Photius is in favour of νῆν from νάω, and, what is more, they also prove the tendency of νῆν to be converted into νεῖν. Hesychius—

Νημερτής· ἀναμαρτής
Νεῖν· νήθειν
Νηνεμία· γαλήνη ἀνέμων.

Even the alphabetical order has not prevented the *νῆν*, which the lexicographer actually wrote, from being changed to *νεῖν*. The same liberty has been taken with Photius—

Νημερτής· ἀληθής
Νεῖν· νήθειν κρόκην
Νηνεμία· ἀνέμων ἀπουσία.

Pollux supports *νῆν*, giving *νῶσι* as the Attic of *νήθουσι*[1]. Other Grammarians supply *νῶντα*[2], *νώμενος*[3], *ἔνη*[4]. That Plato wrote *νητική* from *νῆν* in Polit. 282 A is proved by a Platonic gloss in Photius: Νητικήν· ἄνευ τοῦ σ τὴν περὶ τὸ νήθειν τέχνην: and consequently *νήθειν* in id. 289 C at last stands by itself as a solitary instance in Attic Greek of what all Grammarians combine to call an un-Attic form. Doubtless it came from the same hand as *νηστική*, while Plato himself wrote *τοὺς περὶ τὸ νῆν τε καὶ ξαίνειν*, as Hesiod long before had written *νῇ νήματα*, not, as late copyists wrote for him, *νεῖ νήματα*.

The only Classical form of the verb was *νῶ* (*-άω*), and derived from it *νῆμα, νητικός, νήσω, ἔνησα, ἐνήθην, εὔνητος*. Late transcribers substituted *νήθειν* for *νῆν* in Plato, *νηστική* for *νητική*, as in Eupolis only the best books have retained the participle *νῶσαι*, while the inferior read *νῆθε*. It is not till late that forms like *ἐνήσθην* and *νενῆσμαι* are met with. Hesychius, as was seen, has the gloss *νῶντα· νήθοντα*, Photius, *νώμενος· ὁ νηθόμενος*, and both give *νῆν· νήθειν*, though the copyists accredit them with *νεῖν*, as they accredit Herodian, and, through Herodian, accredit Hesiod with the unclassical *νεῖ*. Νῆμα, runs the gloss in the Ety-

[1] Pollux, 7. 32, ἐφ' οὗ νήθουσιν ἢ νῶσιν· οἱ Ἀττικοὶ γὰρ τὸ νήθειν νεῖν (leg. νῆν) λέγουσι: cp. 10. 125, καὶ ὄνον ἐφ' οὗ νῶσιν.

[2] Hesychius, Νῶντα· νήθοντα, ῥέοντα.

[3] Photius, νώμενος· ὁ νηθόμενος.

[4] Etym. Mag. 344. 1, Ἔννη· ἔστι (τοῦ) νῶ, σημαίνει τὸ νήθω, ὁ παρατακτικός, καὶ ἐπὶ πρώτης συζυγίας καὶ ἐπὶ δευτέρας . . . τοῦ νῶ ὁ παρατακτικὸς ἔνων, ἔνης, ἔνη καὶ πλεονασμῷ τοῦ ν, ἔννη· οὕτως Ἡρωδιανός. For whole question see Cobet, Mnem. N. S. i. 38.

mologicum Magnum, 603. 34, νῆμα· οὐκ ἔστιν ἀπὸ τοῦ νήθω, νῆσμα γὰρ ἂν ἦν, ἀλλ' ἀπὸ τοῦ νῶ, τὸ νήθω. ὅθεν καὶ

νεῖ νήματα

Ἡσίοδος, καὶ ὁ παρατακτικός—

μάλιστα μὲν ἔνη·

lege νῇ νήματα and Μᾶλις μὲν ἔννη.

XLIII.

Ἡ χάραξ ἐρεῖς τὸ τῆς ἀμπέλου στήριγμα, οὐ κατὰ τὸ ἀρρενικόν.

In the App. Soph. 72. 3, Phrynichus does not altogether disallow the masculine gender, but requires it for the meaning *palisade*: Χάραξ θηλυκῶς ἐπὶ τοῦ τῆς ἀμπέλου στηρίγματος· τὸ μέντοι χαράκωμα ἀρρενικῶς, ὁ χάραξ: and Moeris makes the same distinction (p. 410): Χάραξ ἡ μὲν πρὸς ταῖς ἀμπέλοις θηλυκῶς· ὁ δὲ ἐν τοῖς στρατοπέδοις ἀρρενικῶς, ὁ χάραξ. The Grammarians are in fact all so well-agreed on this point that it may be considered established. The rule is violated by none but late writers.

The proverb, ἡ χάραξ τὴν ἄμπελον, is worthy of some remark. The ellipse is supplied by Aristophanes—

εἶτα νῦν ἐξηπάτησεν ἡ χάραξ τὴν ἄμπελον.

Vesp. 1291.

The notion seems to have been, not that of a support failing, but of a subordinate getting the better of a superior; and the Scholiast in loco is probably right, ἀπὸ τῶν καλάμων τῶν προσδεδεμένων ταῖς ἀμπέλοις, οἳ ἐνίοτε ῥιζοβολήσαντες ὑπεραύξονται ἀμπέλων.

XLIV.

Σκίμπους λέγε, ἀλλὰ μὴ κράββατος.

The word κράββατος is not found till late; but Pollux,

10. 35, states that it was used by Crito and Rhintho, writers of the senile New Comedy: *ἀλλὰ καὶ σκίμπους τῶν ἔνδον σκευῶν, ὃς καὶ ἀσκάντης ἐστὶν εἰρημένος, καὶ σκιμπόδιον· ἐν δὲ τῇ Κρίτωνος Μεσσηνίᾳ καὶ τῷ Ῥίνθωνος Τηλέφῳ καὶ κράββατον εἰρῆσθαι λέγουσιν.* Accordingly, Salmasius (de Ling. Hell. p. 65), and Sturtz (de Dial. Maced. p. 176) are probably right in claiming it for a Macedonian word, as there is no other dialect on which to father it. It is of frequent occurrence in the New Testament and in the notes of Scholiasts.

XLV.

Ἐρεύγεσθαι ὁ ποιητής·

ὁ δ' ἐρεύγετο οἰνοβαρείων,

ἀλλ' ὁ πολιτικὸς ἐρυγγάνειν λεγέτω.

A glance at Veitch will show the truth of this statement with regard to Attic Greek; but a point of great interest has escaped the notice of Phrynichus. For *ἐρεύγομαι* Attic writers used *ἐρυγγάνω*, but the future was beyond question still derived from the rejected present—a fact curiously confirmed by a rule which is quite absolute in Attic Greek, and which will be discussed in detail in a future article. That rule may be thus stated—All verbs expressing the exercise of the senses, or denoting any functional state or process, have the inflexions of the middle voice either throughout or in the future tense. It will be seen that by its means innumerable corruptions may be banished from the text of Attic writers, and many verbs which accident has left defective may be safely reconstructed. Moreover, no inquiry is more rich in side-results, and the history of this law is the history of the Attic dialect. The importance of the generalisation cannot be overrated. It restores to the Athenian language the precision and symmetry which were peculiarly its own, and brings out its grand and simple outlines. It supplies rules for textual criticism, it sheds a new light upon the import of many words, and is of incalculable service in tracing the development of Attic speech.

XLVI.

Ὁ φάρυγξ ἀρρενικῶς μὲν ὁ Ἐπίχαρμος λέγει, ὁ δὲ Ἀττικὸς ἡ φάρυγξ.

This is one of those statements, unfortunately too common in Phrynichus, which have little but lexicographical interest. The passage of Epicharmus referred to is probably that in Athen. 10. 411 E—

πρῶτον μέν, αἴ κ' ἔσθοντ' ἴδοις νιν, ἀποθάνοις.
βρέμει μὲν ὁ φάρυξ ἔνδοθ', ἀραβεῖ δ' ἁ γνάθος.

The masculine is also demanded by the metre in Euripides—

πάρεστιν· ὁ φάρυγξ εὐτρεπὴς ἔστω μόνον·
Cycl. 215.

on the other hand, the feminine is equally beyond question in a later line of the same play—

εὐρείας φάρυγγος, ὦ Κύκλωψ,
ἀναστόμου τὸ χεῖλος
Id. 356.

The authority of Aristophanes is for the feminine gender—

ἵν' αὐτὸν ἐπιτρίψωμεν, ὦ μιαρὰ φάρυγξ.
Ran. 571.

ὁπόσον ἡ φάρυγξ ἂν ἡμῶν.
Id. 259.

Moreover, the manuscripts exhibit *ἡ φάρυγξ* in Thucydides (2. 49), *τὴν φάρυγα* in Pherecrates (Athen. 11. 481 A), and in Cratinus (Suïdas, sub v. *μαρίλη*).

Later authors appear inconsistent. For the feminine, Lobeck quotes Aristides, Pausanias, Aelian, and for the masculine, Plutarch, and Lucian. Hippocrates, Aristotle, and Galen use the two genders indifferently, both in its ordinary sense of *the throat* and in its technical signification *the common opening of the gullet and windpipe.* The authority of Phrynichus, buttressed as it is by metre in Aristophanes, must be regarded as settling the question for Attic Greek, and in Teleclides (Ath. 6. 268 C), τὴν φάρυγα must be restored for τὸν φάρυγα, and in a line of Aristophanes, preserved both by Photius and Suïdas—

τὴν φάρυγα μηλῶν δύο δραχμὰς ἕξει μόνας,

τόν, the reading of Suïdas, must be rejected. The case of Euripides is interesting; it is another instance of the strange combination of forms from two distinct strata of language in constant use side by side—a combination which is the Tragic dialect.

XLVII.

Ἀναιδίζεσθαι λέγε, μὴ ἀναιδεύεσθαι.

This is the suggestion of W. Dindorf for the reading of the manuscripts and editions, which is without meaning, αὐθαδίζεσθαι λέγε, μὴ ἀναιδεύεσθαι. There is a wide difference between the meanings of ἀναιδής and αὐθάδης, and Phrynichus knew Greek too well to think that there was not. Moreover, αὐθαδίζομαι is excellent Attic, being found in Plato, Apol. 34 D, οὐκ αὐθαδιζόμενος, and αὐθάδισμα is used by Aeschylus (P. V. 964).

On the other hand, ἀναιδεύομαι is read in Aristophanes—

ὡς δὲ πρὸς πᾶν ἀναιδεύεται κτε.
Eq. 396, ch.

and in a subsequent line of the same play (1206), Elmsley replaced ὑπεραναιδεσθήσομαι by ὑπεραναιδευθήσομαι. But a Grammarian in Bekk. Anec. p. 80. 30, supplies the note, Ἀναιδίζεσθαι, Ἀριστοφάνης Ἱππεῦσιν, and if ἀναιδίζεται is not to be restored in l. 396, certainly the later line must be read thus—

οἴμοι κακοδαίμων ὑπεραναιδισθήσομαι.

The form in -*ίζομαι* is more according to analogy and may be compared with *εὐηθίζομαι* from *εὐηθής*, *εὐμενίζομαι* from *εὐμενής*, and *αὐθαδίζομαι* from *αὐθάδης*, whereas *ἀληθεύω* from *ἀληθής* is not a deponent, and *ἐπιδαψιλεύομαι* from *ἐπιδαψιλής* is one of the un-Attic words employed by Xenophon. If the two classes, as a whole, are compared, the words *δημοτεύομαι*, *νεανιεύομαι*, *ἑβδομεύομαι*, *νωθρεύομαι*, *πονηρεύομαι*, *φιλανθρωπεύομαι*, *βωμολοχεύομαι*, *νεανισκεύομαι*, *ἀλαζονεύομαι*, *εἰρωνεύομαι*, *ἐπικηρυκεύομαι*, *μαντεύομαι*, *πραγματεύομαι*, *τερατεύομαι*, *τερθρεύομαι*, *κοβαλικεύομαι*, and *στραγγεύομαι* are far outnumbered by deponents in -*ίζομαι*—*ἀγκαλίζομαι*, *ἀνδραγαθίζομαι*, *αὐλίζομαι*, *διαγκυλίζομαι*, *κορίζομαι*, *αἰκίζομαι*, *ἀγροικίζομαι*, *ἀκρατίζομαι*, *ἀνθρωπίζομαι*, *ἐνθετταλίζομαι*, *λογίζομαι*, *ξυλίζομαι*, *οἰωνίζομαι*, *ἀκροβολίζομαι*, *ἁπλοίζομαι*, *ἐπιδορπίζομαι*, *εὐαγγελίζομαι*, *ἰσχυρίζομαι*, *λαγαρίζομαι*, *μαλακίζομαι*, *μαλθακίζομαι*, *ψελλίζομαι*, *ἀγωνίζομαι*, *ἀκκίζομαι*, *δαιμονίζομαι*, *πορπακίζομαι*, *προφασίζομαι*, *χαρίζομαι*, *χαριεντίζομαι*, and *ὠστίζομαι*.

XLVIII.

Υἱέως οἱ ψευδαττικοί φασιν, οἰόμενοι ὅμοιον εἶναι τῷ Θησέως καὶ τῷ Πηλέως.

XLIX.

Υἱέα· ἐν ἐπιστολῇ ποτε Ἀλεξάνδρου τοῦ σοφιστοῦ εὗρον τοὔνομα τοῦτο γεγραμμένον, καὶ σφόδρα ἐμεμψάμην· οὐ γάρ, ἐπεὶ υἱέος καὶ υἱεῖ ἐστίν, εὐθὺς καὶ τὸν υἱέα εὕροι τις ἄν· ἀλλὰ τὴν αἰτιατικὴν υἱόν λέγουσιν οἱ ἀρχαῖοι. τοῦτο δὲ καὶ Φιλόξενος, ἐν τοῖς ε περὶ τῆς Ἰλιάδος συγγράμμασι, δαψιλέστατα ἀπέφηνεν, ἀδόκιμον μὲν εἶναι τὸν υἱέα, δόκιμον δὲ τὸν υἱόν.

The following table exhibits the forms of *υἱός* used by Attic writers—

SINGULAR.	DUAL.	PLURAL.
υἱός	*υἱῆ*	*υἱεῖς*
υἱέ	*υἱέοιν.*	*υἱεῖς*
υἱόν		*υἱεῖς*
υἱοῦ or *υἱέος*		*υἱέων*
υἱῷ or *υἱεῖ.*		*υἱέσι(ν).*

Late forms have in several passages crept into Attic texts. In Thuc. 1. 13 the Scholiast, many editions, and one manuscript exhibit *υἱέως.* The same vicious form has manuscript authority in three places of Plato (Rep. 378 A, id. D, Legg. 687 D), in Xenophon, Hell. 4. 1. 40, and in Demosthenes, 1062, 1075, 1077; and was actually *restored* by Reiske in id. 1057.

The genitive *υἱοῦ* is found in Thuc. 5. 16, and the dative *υἱῷ* once in Antiphanes and several times in Menander; but the third declension forms are far more frequent than the second in these two cases of the singular, and are the only forms employed in the dual and plural numbers. The nominative dual appears as *υἱέε* in Plato, Apol. 20 A, *ἐστὸν γὰρ αὐτῷ δύο υἱέε*: but there can be no question that the original reading was *υἱῆ*, and that *υἱέε* is as corrupt as the *δύω*, which some manuscripts present for *δύο*. In Rep. 410 E, besides the genuine *τὼ φύση τούτω*, both *τὼ φύσεε τούτω* and *τὼ φύσει τούτω* are encountered; and in Isocrates, 44 B, there are the similar three varieties of reading—the correct *τὼ πόλη τούτω* and the two corruptions *τὼ πόλεε τούτω* and *τὰς πόλεις ταύτας.* A line of Aristophanes has preserved the original form—

> *καὶ πρός γε τούτοις ἥκετον πρέσβη δύο,*

and stone records tell the same story.

Certainly Plato did not use all three forms of the dual of *φύσις*, or Isocrates write *πόλεε*, *πόλη*, and *πόλεις*: and why should the nominative and accusative dual be exempt from a law to which every other Attic word is subject? There is no reason why scholarship should quarrel with common sense.

The late accusative singular *υἱέα*, reprehended by Phrynichus with its plural consort *υἱέας*, has not found its way into any Attic text. The dative *υἱεῦσι* has been equally considerate, but in Sophocles, Antig. 571, the Laurentian exhibits the corrupt *υἱάσιν*.

In this word it is probable that throughout the Attic period the iota was never written. At all events Herwerden (Lapid. de Dial. Att. Test. pp. 11, 12) distinctly states that in no Attic Inscription of a good age does any form but *ὑός* appear, except in verse, and even in that case *ὑός*, *ὑεῖς*, etc., are sometimes found. Accordingly, the forms without iota should be restored to all prose texts, and to Comedy, either in every case, or at least when the first syllable need not be long. The reason for the prevalence of *υἱός*, *υἱέος*, etc., in the manuscripts of Attic writers is not far to seek. Those forms gradually took the place of *ὑός*, *ὑέος*, etc., in stone records after the time of Alexander.

L.

Τελευταιότατον λέγειν ἁμάρτημα τῶν περὶ παιδείαν δοκούντων τευτάζειν. ἐπεὶ γὰρ ἀρχαιότατον εὗρον λεγόμενον παρὰ τοῖς ἀρχαίοις, ᾠήθησαν καὶ τοῦτο δεῖν λέγειν. ἀλλὰ σὺ τελευταῖον λέγε.

LI.

Ἔσχατον χρὴ λέγειν, οὐχὶ ἐσχατώτατον, εἰ καὶ μάρτυρα παρέχει τις.

LII.

Κορυφαιότατον· ἐνεκαλυψάμην εὑρὼν παρὰ Φαβωρίνῳ· λέγε οὖν κορυφαῖον.

Phaborinus would find himself in good company now-a-days, and Phrynichus might justly ask the question, Is life worth living? The *ἐπίτασις ὑπερθέσεως* is not a fault of style, but a virtue in the eyes of many nineteenth century writers. According to Suïdas[1], Phaborinus was *τὴν τοῦ σώματος ἕξιν ἀνδρόγυνος*, but the same reason will not account for Plutarch's use of the vicious superlative (Mor. p. 1115 E), or for *τελευταιότατος* in Arrian, still less for *ἐσχατώτατος* in Xenophon, Hell. 2. 3. 49, *τὰ πάντων ἐσχατώτατα παθεῖν.*

Lucian (Pseudosoph. 5) ridicules the superlative of *κορυφαῖος*: *Ἄλλου δὲ εἰπόντος, Τῶν φίλων ὁ κορυφαιότατος, χαρίέν γε, ἔφη, τὸ τῆς κορυφῆς ποιεῖν τι ἐπάνω*: and with reference to *ἐσχατώτατος*, Aristotle remarks (Metaphys. 9. 4. 1055. 20[a]), *οὔτε γὰρ τοῦ ἐσχάτου ἐσχατώτερον εἴη ἄν τι.* In this case, Xenophon is seen anticipating a usage which is rare even in the latest and most debased Greek, and of which there is certainly no trace in any Attic writer.

LIII.

Βεβίασται ἡ κόρη λεκτέον, ἀλλ' οὐχ ὥς τινες τῶν ῥητόρων ἔφθαρται.

The same statement is made by Moeris, in three different passages, p. 103, *βεβιασμένη* Ἀττικῶς, *ἐφθαρμένη* Ἑλληνικῶς: p. 106, *βιάσασθαι* Ἀττικῶς, *φθεῖραι* Ἑλληνικῶς: and

[1] *Φαβωρῖνος, Ἀρλεάτου, τῆς ἐν Γαλλίᾳ πόλεως, ἀνὴρ πολυμαθὴς κατὰ πᾶσαν παιδείαν, γεγονὼς δὲ τὴν τοῦ σώματος ἕξιν ἀνδρόγυνος, (ὅν φασιν ἑρμαφρόδιτον,) φιλοσοφίας μεστός, ῥητορικῇ δὲ μᾶλλον ἐπιθέμενος. γεγονὼς ἐπὶ Τραϊανοῦ τοῦ Καίσαρος, καὶ παρατείνας μέχρι τῶν Ἀδριανοῦ χρόνων τοῦ βασιλέως. Ἀντεφιλοτιμεῖτο γοῦν καὶ ζῆλον εἶχε πρὸς Πλούταρχον τὸν Χαιρωνέα εἰς τὸ τῶν συνταττομένων βιβλίων ἄπειρον κτε.*

p. 390, φθορέα καὶ ἐφθαρμένην οὐδεὶς τῶν παλαιῶν, ἀλλὰ τὸν βιασάμενον καὶ βεβιασμένην· φθορεὺς δὲ καὶ ἐφθαρμένη Ἑλληνικῶς.

Certainly βιάζομαι is so used in two places of Aristophanes—

ἐὰν δ' ἐμ' ἄκουσαν βιάζηται βίᾳ·
Lys. 225.

θάρρει, μὴ φόβου
οὐ γὰρ βιάσεται·
Plut. 1091.

on the latter of which the Scholiast remarks, with appreciation, ὃ ποιοῦσιν οἱ ἄνδρες, τοῦτο ἐπὶ τῆς γραός φησι.

On the other hand, if Dionysius of Halicarnassus is to be trusted, Euripides employed φθαρεῖσα, (Rhet. 9. 11), περιερχομένη γὰρ πάσας αἰτίας τοῦ σῶσαι τὰ παιδία λέγει (ἡ Μελανίππη), "εἰ δὲ παρθένος φθαρεῖσα ἐξέθηκε τὰ παιδία καὶ φοβουμένη τὸν πατέρα, σὺ φόνον δράσεις;" and in the Orators διαφθείρειν occurs not seldom, Lysias, 92. 10; 93. 16; 95. 17; 136. 3. Of course it refers primarily to moral corruption, whereas βιάζομαι denotes only the physical fact. The distinction is well brought out by a passage of Lysias, in which both verbs occur (94. 41), οὕτως, ὦ ἄνδρες, τοὺς **βιαζομένους** ἐλάττονος ζημίας ἀξίους ἡγήσατο εἶναι ἢ τοὺς **πείθοντας**· τῶν μὲν γὰρ θάνατον κατέγνω, τοῖς δὲ διπλῆν ἐποίησε τὴν βλάβην, ἡγούμενος τοὺς μὲν διαπραττομένους βίᾳ ὑπὸ τῶν βιασθέντων μισεῖσθαι, τοὺς δὲ πείσαντας οὕτως αὐτῶν τὰς ψυχὰς **διαφθείρειν**, ὥστ' οἰκειοτέρας αὐτοῖς ποιεῖν τὰς ἀλλοτρίας γυναῖκας ἢ τοῖς ἀνδράσι κτε.

In late Greek φθείρω acquired the physical reference of the classical βιάζομαι, and it is this use of the word which Phrynichus reprehends.

LIV.

Ἡ ὕσπληξ λέγεται, οὐχ ὁ ὕσπληξ.

The same statement is made by Phrynichus again (App. Soph. 69), and by Moeris (p. 376). The ὕσπληξ was distinct from the βαλβῖδες, and meant the cord or tape, breast-high, which the runner carried away with him as he passed the βαλβῖδες at the finish. The line of starting and finishing, in both foot-race and chariot-race, was the same, the starting point being βαλβῖδες, the finishing point βαλβῖδες + ὕσπληξ. A comparison of Harpocration and Moeris suggests this explanation — Βαλβῖσιν· Ἀντιφῶν περὶ ὁμονοίας ἀντὶ τοῦ ταῖς ἀρχαῖς· εἴρηται δὲ ἀπὸ τῶν δρομέων· ἡ γὰρ ὑπὸ τὴν ὕσπληγγα γινομένη γραμμὴ διὰ τὸ ἐπὶ ταύτης βεβηκέναι τοὺς δρομέας βαλβὶς καλεῖται: Moeris, p. 103, Βαλβῖδες, αἱ ἐπὶ τῶν ἀφέσεων βάσεις ἐγκεχαραγμέναι, αἷς ἐπέβαινον οἱ δρομεῖς, ἵνα ἐξ ἴσου ἵσταιντο. διὸ καὶ οἱ κήρυκες ἐπὶ τῶν τρεχόντων, "Βαλβῖδι[1] πόδας ἔνθετε, πόδα παρὰ πόδα," καὶ νῦν ἔτι λέγουσιν, Ἀττικῶς. ὕσπληξ δὲ κοινόν. The primitive term was preserved in the herald's formula, even in the Common dialect, but otherwise was replaced by ὕσπληξ. The latter word happens to occur only once in Attic Greek, Plato, Phaedr. 254 E, ὁ ἡνίοχος ὥσπερ ἀπὸ ὕσπληγος ἀναπεσών.

Two explanations of the plural βαλβῖδες suggest themselves—the one, that originally the term was applied to two poles to which two cords were attached, one at the ground, the other breast-high (ὕσπληξ). This explanation is given in Lex. Rhet. Bekk. An. 220. 31. The other is more in accord with the facts, namely, that βαλβίς primitively signified *a projecting edge*, and in the plural was applied to a piece of wood placed in front of the runners'

[1] The place is corrupt, βαλβῖδ' ἀπόδυς θέτε being the only reading. Perhaps the above conjecture restores the text.

feet, and provided with a groove to catch the toes. Schol. Ar. Eq. 1156, *τὸ ἐν τῇ ἀρχῇ τοῦ δρόμου κείμενον ἐγκαρσίως ξύλον ὅπερ . . . ἀφαιρούμενοι ἀφίεσαν τρέχειν*. This is in harmony with the usage of *βαλβιδώδης* in Hippocrates, 842 F. *τὸ δὲ πρὸς ἀγκῶνα αὐτοῦ (τοῦ βραχίονος) πλατὺ καὶ κονδυλῶδες καὶ βαλβιδῶδες καὶ στερεὸν ἔγκοιλον ὄπισθεν*, and with the glosses of Hesychius and Galen on *βαλβίς* in the same writer, Galen explaining the word by *κοιλότης παραμήκης*, and Hesychius by *τὸ ἔχον ἑκατέρωθεν ἐπαναστάσεις*. Beyond question the true origin of the plural *βαλβῖδες* is the second of the two suggested above.

LV.

Ἰλὺς οἴνου οὐκ ὀρθῶς λέγεται, ποταμοῦ μὲν γὰρ ἰλύς, οἴνου δὲ τρὺξ ἢ ὑποστάθμη.

There is no occasion to doubt the correctness of this remark, because un-Attic writers like Aristotle, Theophrastus, and Hippocrates use *ἰλύς* in a wider sense. In the Iliad and in Herodotus it is found only in the signification claimed for it in Attic by Phrynichus—

οὔτε τὰ τεύχεα καλά, τά που μάλα νειόθι λίμνης
κείσεθ' ὑπ' ἰλῦος κεκαλυμμένα· κὰδ δέ μιν αὐτὸν
εἰλύσω ψαμάθοισιν κτε.

Il. 21. 318.

Herod. 2. 7, *ἐνθεῦτεν μὲν καὶ μέχρι Ἡλίου πόλιος ἐς τὴν μεσόγαιάν ἐστι εὐρέα Αἴγυπτος, ἐοῦσα πᾶσα ὑπτίη τε καὶ ἔνυδρος καὶ ἰλύς*. Even *τρύξ*, which no Attic writer would use of anything but the lees of wine, has its meaning generalized by late writers, and is applied not only to water, but to oil, fat, and similar liquids. Dioscorides, 5. 120, actually makes it a term of metallurgy, *τοῦ κατεργαζομένου χαλκοῦ οἷον ὑποστάθμη καὶ τρύξ*. Misuse could not go further.

The generic word *ὑποστάθμη* occurs in Plato, Phaed.

109 C, *οὗ δὴ (τοῦ αἰθέρος) ὑποστάθμην ταῦτα εἶναι*, and was doubtless in constant use in cases in which special words like *ἰλύς* and *τρύξ* were out of place.

LVI.

Κόριον ἢ κορίδιον ἢ κορίσκη λέγουσι, τὸ δὲ κοράσιον οὔ.

The word *κοράσιον* occurs in some verses attributed to Plato by Diog. Laert. 3. 33, but the whole is in Doric—

Ἁ Κύπρις Μούσαισι· κοράσια, τὰν Ἀφροδίταν
τιμᾶτ' ἢ τὸν Ἔρωτ' ὔμμιν ἐφοπλίσομαι·

and therefore, even if genuine, does not affect the dictum of Phrynichus. Photius also repudiates the term, *Παιδισκάριον, κοράσιον δὲ οὐ λέγεται, ἀλλὰ καὶ κεκωμῴδηκε Φιλιππίδης ὡς ξενικόν*, and Pollux, 2. 17, characterizes it as *εὐτελές*. 'Sed si Arrianus in summa argumenti gravitate, si scriptores sacri et ecclesiastici cum nulla *εὐτελισμοῦ* significatione huc delapsi sunt, apparet eos contra cultioris sermonis leges peccasse . . . . Quod autem Phrynichus *κοράσιον* contra analogiam factum esse dicit, non eo spectat, quo Pauwius statuit, quod a *κόρα* (pro *κόρη*) derivatum sit, sed quod nullum Graecorum diminutivorum in *-ασιον* terminatur . . . *Κάππα, καππάσιον* extremae Graecitatis est, *Πρυμνάσιον* autem et *Κορυφάσιον* quae Schol. Venet. Il. 20. 404, cum *κοράσιον* componit, nullam cum eo praeter terminationis similitudinem habent, ideoque ille *κοράσιον* potius Macedonicum esse tradit.' Lobeck.

LVII.

Ἡ ῥὰξ ἐρεῖς· ὁ γὰρ ῥῶξ δύο ἔχει ἁμαρτήματα.

Eustathius has preserved the authoritative judgment of

Aelius Dionysius on this point (p. 1485. 59, cp. 1633. 42), *ὁ ῥῶξ καὶ σολοικισμὸς καὶ βαρβαρισμὸς κατὰ Αἴλιον Διονύσιον.*

The word is met with in two passages of Attic Greek—in a fragment of Sophocles—

ἦν μὲν γὰρ οἶος μαλλός, ἦν δὲ κἀμπέλου
σπονδή τε καὶ ῥὰξ εὖ τεθησαυρισμένη,
Nk. 365.

and in Plato, Legg. 8. 845 A, *ἐὰν δὲ δὴ δοῦλος μὴ πείσας τὸν δεσπότην τῶν χωρίων ἅπτηταί του τῶν τοιούτων κατὰ ῥᾶγα βοτρύων καὶ σῦκον συκῆς ἰσαρίθμους πληγὰς τούτοις μαστιγούσθω.*

There is nothing to show whether the soloecism in gender, and barbarism in form, of the late *ῥώξ* was simply due to ignorance and carelessness, or came from some of the less known dialects. For purposes of lexicography Lobeck's note is invaluable, but it is needless here to reproduce details which are not worth remembering.

LVIII.

Τάχιον οἱ Ἕλληνες οὐ λέγουσι, θᾶττον δέ.

LIX.

Βράδιον· καὶ τοῦτο Ἡσίοδος μὲν λέγει,

βράδιον δὲ Πανελλήνεσσι φαείνει,

Πλάτων δὲ καὶ Θουκυδίδης καὶ οἱ δόκιμοι βραδύτερον.

To the former of these articles most editions append the words *μᾶλλον μὲν οὖν Ἕλληνες τὸ τάχιον, θᾶττον δὲ Ἀττικοί*, which, as Scaliger pointed out, *est clausula non Phrynichi, sed Phrynichum corrigentis studiosi;* a conjecture strikingly confirmed by their absence from the best Laurentian manuscript, which also indicates their origin by omitting *οὐ* before *λέγουσι*. The meaning of *Ἕλληνες* was misunderstood.

The caution of Phrynichus, Moeris (p. 436), and other grammarians seems unnecessary now, but it must be remembered that Plutarch, Diodorus, and others use the vicious forms.

The line of Hesiod quoted may be found in Op. 528. For the superlative Homer has *βάρδιστος* (Il. 23. 310, 530), but in the fragment of Aristophanes, referred to by Liddell and Scott as authority for *βράδιστος*, the word is only a useless conjecture of Brunck's—

> ἐνταῦθα δ' ἐτυράννευεν Ὑψιπύλης πατὴρ
> Θόας, βραδύτατος ὢν ἐν ἀνθρώποις δραμεῖν.

No Attic writer could have used such a form.

The earliest instance of *τάχιον* is quoted from Menander (Gellius, Noct. Att. 2. 23), but the lines in which it is found will not scan, and baffle translation—

> παιδισκάριον θεραπευτικὸν δὲ λόγου
> τάχιον, ἀπαγέσθω δέ τις ἢ ἄρ' ἀντεισαγάγοι.

To Attic writers *θάσσων* (*θάττων*) was the only comparative, and *τάχιστος* the only superlative. Dindorf fathers *ταχύτατα* upon Antiphanes, but it is easy to settle a case of affiliation when the defendant is dead. The passage of Athenaeus, in which the lines of the Comic poet are quoted (4. 161 D), is one of a kind which has introduced into the company of their betters many forms like *ταχύτατα*. The lines are first adapted to suit the context, and scholars are not to be blamed if they exercise their ingenuity to restore them to their original form: Τούτων δ' ὑμεῖς, ὦ φιλόσοφοι, οὐδὲν ἀσκεῖτε, ἀλλὰ καὶ τὸ πάντων χαλεπώτερον λαλεῖτε περὶ ὧν οὐκ οἴδατε, καὶ ὡς κοσμίως ἐσθίοντες ποιεῖτε τὴν ἔνθεσιν κατὰ τὸν ἥδιστον Ἀντιφάνη· οὗτος γὰρ ἐν Δραπεταγωγῷ λέγει,

> κοσμίως ποιῶν τὴν ἔνθεσιν,
> μικρὰν μὲν ἐκ τοῦ πρόσθε, μεστὴν δ' ἔνδοθεν
> τὴν χεῖρα, καθάπερ αἱ γυναῖκες,

κατεφάγετε πάμπολλα καὶ ταχύτατα, ἐξὸν κατὰ τὸν αὐτὸν τοῦτον ποιητὴν ἐν Βομβυκίῳ λέγοντα δραχμῆς ὠνήσασθαι· "τὰς προσφόρους ἡμῖν τροφάς, σκόροδα, τυρόν, κρόμμυα, πάππαριν, πάντα ταῦτ' ἐστὶν δραχμῆς." The passage is at best not very intelligible, but from κοσμίως to γυναῖκες the words run tolerably well as iambics. The plural κατεφάγετε, however, corresponding to ἀσκεῖτε, λαλεῖτε, ποιεῖτε, shows that Athenaeus left Antiphanes at that point. In that case ταχύτατα has its equals in οἴδατε and ὠνήσασθαι.

In Xenophon, on the other hand, a form used by Pindar (O. 1. 125), and kept in countenance by the Herodotean ταχύτερος (3. 65; 7. 194), would not necessarily be out of place, and, accordingly, ταχύτατα may be right in Hell. 5. 1. 27, τὰς βραδύτατα πλεούσας ταῖς ἄριστα πλεούσαις ταχύτατα κατειλήφει. Cobet and L. Dindorf, however, read ταχύ with some manuscript authority.

LX.

Κωλύφιον μὴ λέγε, κωλῆνα δέ.

This is the only place in which κωλύφιον is encountered, but in Latin writers *coliphium* is met with, as Plaut. Pers. 1. 3. 12; Juv. 2. 53; Mart. 7. 67. In all these passages it is used of food for athletes, a signification which in Greek appears to have belonged to κωλῆνες. From its use by Plautus it is natural to infer that it came into the Latin vocabulary as a translation from some of his New Comedy models—a supposition that is quite consistent with the hypothesis that -ύφιον as a diminutive suffix entered the Common dialect from Macedonia. However, ξυλήφιον is exhibited in Alexis, ap. Ath. 13. 568 D, and in Hippocr. 682. 44, but it is simply impossible to decide whether ξυλήφιον, ξυλάριον, or ξυλύφιον, was the genuine classical form. Thomas has ξυλίφιον, οὐ ξυλάριον, and other grammarians are either similarly corrupt or similarly wrong. It is discreet to leave unsettled a question on which authority is so divided.

LXI.

Κακοδαιμονεῖν· οὕτως οἱ νόθως ἀττικίζοντες. Ἀθηναῖοι γὰρ διὰ τοῦ α, κακοδαιμονᾶν λέγουσιν, καὶ θαυμάσειεν ἄν τις πῶς εὐδαιμονεῖν μὲν λέγουσιν, οὐκέτι δὲ κακοδαιμονεῖν, ἀλλὰ κακοδαιμονᾶν· καὶ πῶς εὐδαιμονοῦσι μὲν λέγουσιν, οὐκέτι δὲ κακοδαιμονοῦσιν, ἀλλὰ κακοδαιμονῶσι.

As far as form goes, there is no reason why an Attic writer should not have employed *κακοδαιμονεῖν*. The adjective *κακοδαίμων*, in the sense of *unfortunate*, forms a verb *κακοδαιμονεῖν* as naturally as in the sense of *possessed by an evil genius* it forms *κακοδαιμονᾶν*. Κακοδαιμονεῖν is *to be unfortunate*, as *εὐδαιμονεῖν* is *to be fortunate*, and there is no *εὐδαιμονᾶν*, simply because the Greeks never thought of men as being possessed by a good genius.

In Xenophon, Hier. 2. 4, *κακοδαιμονεῖν* is quite correctly used, *ἔνθαπερ καὶ τὸ εὐδαιμονεῖν καὶ τὸ κακοδαιμονεῖν τοῖς ἀνθρώποις ἀποκεῖται*, but in Mem. 2. 1. 5 there is no question that *κακοδαιμονῶντος* is the true form: *καὶ τηλικούτων μὲν ἐπικειμένων τῷ μοιχεύοντι κακῶν τε καὶ αἰσχρῶν, ὄντων δὲ πολλῶν τῶν ἀπολυσόντων τῆς τῶν ἀφροδισίων ἐπιθυμίας ἐν ἀδείᾳ, ὅμως εἰς τὰ ἐπικίνδυνα φέρεσθαι, ἆρ' οὐκ ἤδη τοῦτο παντάπασι κακοδαιμονῶντός ἐστιν;*

In Demosthenes (93. 24), *κακοδαιμονῶσι* should replace *κακοδαιμονοῦσι* as the context demands: *νὴ Δία, κακοδαιμονῶσι γὰρ ἄνθρωποι καὶ ὑπερβάλλουσιν ἀνοίᾳ.*

The adjective *κακοδαίμων*, in the sense of *lost to reason*, is met with in Antiphon, 134. 25, *καίτοι τὸ εἰκὸς συμμαχόν μοι ἐστίν· οὐ γὰρ δήπου οὕτω κακοδαίμων ἐγώ, ὥστε τὸ μὲν ἀποκτεῖναι τὸν ἄνδρα προὐνοησάμην μόνος κτε.*, and in Aristophanes (Eq. 112) is jocularly used substantively = κακὸς δαίμων—

ἀτὰρ τοῦ δαίμονος
δέδοιχ' ὅπως μὴ τεύξομαι κακοδαίμονος.

The class of verbs to which κακοδαιμονᾶν belongs is a very interesting one, and comprises the following words—

ἀγωνιῶ, am in distress.
βεμβικιῶ, spin like a top.
βουλιμιῶ, am ravenous.
γειτνιῶ, am neighbour to.
γενειῶ, grow a beard.
δαιμονῶ, am possessed.
ἐνθουσιῶ, am inspired.
ἐρυθριῶ, blush.
ἑτερεγκεφαλῶ, am half-mad.
εὐρωτιῶ, am stale.
ἡβυλλιῶ, am youngish.
ἰλιγγιῶ, am dizzy.
κερουτιῶ, toss the horns.
κλαυσιῶ, desire to weep.
κνησιῶ, itch.
κομῶ, wear the hair long.
κοπιῶ, am tired.
κορυβαντιῶ, am frenzied.
κορυζῶ, have a catarrh.
κραιπαλῶ, have the headache.
κυλοιδιῶ, have swellings beneath the eyes.
λεπρῶ, am leprous.
ληματιῶ, am resolute.
λιθῶ, suffer from stone.
λιπῶ, am fat.
μαδῶ, am bald.
μαθητιῶ, wish to become a disciple.
μακκοῶ, am stupid.
μαστιγιῶ, deserve a whipping.
ματῶ, am idle.
μελαγχολῶ, am melancholy.
μεριμνῶ, am anxious.
ναρκῶ, am numb.
ναυτιῶ, am sea-sick.
ὀργῶ, am lusty.
οὐρητιῶ, micturio.
ὀφθαλμιῶ, have running eyes.
ποδαγρῶ, have the gout.
σιβυλλιῶ, play the old woman.
σκοτοδινιῶ, am dizzy.
σπαργῶ, swell.
στρηνιῶ, wax wanton.
φαρμακῶ, suffer from poison.
φονῶ, am athirst for blood.
φυσιῶ, pant.
χαλαζῶ, have pimples.
ὡρακιῶ, faint.

Perhaps words like διψῶ, πεινῶ, ἡβῶ, λυσσῶ, πινῶ, ῥυπῶ, κισσῶ, σφριγῶ, may be rightly added to the list, or they may go with the following, which are less definite in meaning—

ζῶ, live.
κυβιστῶ, tumble.
λιχμῶ, play with the tongue.
λωφῶ, take rest.
μαργῶ, rage.
μειδιῶ, smile.
μενοινῶ, am bent on.
μυδῶ, drip.
περῶ, cross.
πηδῶ, leap.
σκιρτῶ, skip.
φληναφῶ, babble.
φοιτῶ, roar.
βοῶ, shout.
ἀντῶ, meet.
ἀριστῶ, dine.
ἀσχαλῶ, grieve.
βαυβῶ, sleep.
βροντῶ, thunder.
κολυμβῶ, dive.
σιγῶ, am silent.
σιωπῶ, am silent.

No member of the former class has a middle or passive voice as the verbs denote bodily or mental *states*, but those members of the latter class which come under the law stated above on p. 138 have the middle inflexions in the future, βοήσομαι, φοιτήσομαι, πηδήσομαι, σκιρτήσομαι, just as ἀκροῶμαι, ἀλῶμαι, βληχῶμαι, βρυχῶμαι, μασῶμαι, κυυζῶμαι, and others are deponents throughout.

Naturally, verbs of the type δαιμονῶ occur principally in the present tense. It is seldom that a future or aorist is encountered, and their perfect is almost non-existent. The aorist of ἰλιγγιῶ is found in Plato, Prot. 339 E, ἐσκοτώθην καὶ ἰλιγγίασα εἰπόντος αὐτοῦ ταῦτα, and the future in Gorg. 527 A, χασμήσει καὶ ἰλιγγιάσεις. So ὀφθαλμιάσας πέρυσιν, Aristoph. Fr. ap. Poll. 4. 180; γυναιξὶ κοπιάσαισιν, id. ap. Ath. 3. 104 F; κομήσειν, Plat. Phaed. 89 C; μεμακκοακότα, Ar. Eq. 62; ἢν οὐρητιάσῃς, Vesp. 808; ὡρακιάσας, Pax 702; μεριμνήσας, Dem. 576. 24.

It is a difficult question to decide which is the true form

of many of these verbs—whether the -*άω* should or should not be preceded by an iota. On this point Photius says, *Λιθῶντας· τρισυλλάβως, οὐ λιθιῶντας· Πλάτων ια' Νόμων. καὶ βραγχᾶν λέγουσιν, οὐ βραγχιᾶν· καὶ ἕτερα τοιαῦτα.* But in the passage of Plato referred to (11. 916 A) the manuscripts read only *λίθων* or *λιθιῶν*, not *λιθῶν*: *ἀνδράποδον ἢ λιθῶν ἢ στραγγουριῶν.* There can be no question that *λιθῶν* should be read, and that the iota was inserted from false analogy with *στραγγουριῶν.* Lobeck, however, is wrong in suggesting *καρηβαρᾶν* for *καρηβαριᾶν* in Pollux, 2. 41, *καὶ καρηβαρικόν, τὸ πάθος, Τηλεκλείδης· τὸ δὲ ὑπὸ μέθης καρηβαριᾶν Ἀριστοφάνης.* Akin to *καρηβαρία*, the verb has the iota as naturally as *στραγγουριῶ* from *στραγγουρία*, and *σκοτοδινιῶ* from *σκοτοδινία*, and all verbs of this class which have such a substantive connected with them—*ἀγωνιῶ, βουλιμιῶ, ἰλιγγιῶ*, etc.

As to several of the others, it is now impossible to decide. Certainly *λιθῶ* is no isolated case, and the later Greeks often added the iota to verbs which in Attic were spelt without it. Thus Aeschylus employed *κριθῶ*, Agam. 1641, *κριθῶντα πῶλον*, but in later writers *κριθιῶντα* would have been preferred. They even increased the class by new formations which from signification had no right to a place in it. Such a word is *ἀροτριᾶν* from *ἄροτρον*—a poor substitute for the genuine and unassuming *ἀροῦν.* Of other verbs they merely modified the suffix, making in this way *μηνίειν* into *μηνιᾶν*, and *μαλκίειν* into *μαλκιᾶν.* The latter word has been peculiarly unfortunate. By Cobet's help (Mnem. 3. 306) *μαλκίω* has been restored to its just position, but till recently the word had practically disappeared. In Demosthenes, 120. 7, its place has in all manuscripts been taken by *μαλακιζόμεθα*: *ταῦτα τοίνυν πάσχοντες ἅπαντες μέλλομεν καὶ μαλκίομεν καὶ πρὸς τοὺς πλησίον βλέπομεν, ἀπιστοῦντες ἀλλήλοις.* The primitive reading has been preserved in Harpocration's invaluable *Λέξεις τῶν δέκα ῥητόρων.*

Phrynichus, in App. Soph. 51. 31, assigns the true meaning to the word—

μαλκίειν· τὸ ὑπὸ κρύους ναρκᾶν,

but the word itself has become corrupted to μαλακιῆν.

LXII.

Κόρημα χρὴ λέγειν, οὐχὶ σάρον, καὶ κορεῖν καὶ παρακορεῖν, ἀλλὰ μὴ σαροῦν.

LXIII.

Σάρωσον ἐπειδὰν ἀκούσῃς τινὸς λέγοντος, κέλευσον παρακόρησον λέγειν, ὅτι οὐδὲ σάρον λέγουσιν, ἀλλὰ κόρημα καὶ κάλλυντρον.

The word σάρον is unquestionably an old one, as in the middle of the fifth century, Ion, the Tragic poet, and Sophron, the writer of mimes, employed it. At all events, Hesychius says so, and certainly σαίρω is in constant use in Tragedy (Soph. Ant. 409; Eur. Hec. 363, Andr. 166, Cycl. 29, Ion 115, 120, 795). The words of Hesychius are, Σάρον· κάλλυντρον Βυζάντιοι. Σάρον· Ἴων Ἀργείοις—

ὡς παλαιὸν οἰκίας σάρον·

βαρυτονητέον, ὡς παρὰ Σώφρονι· θέλει δὲ λέγειν ὅτι ἀχρηστοί εἰσι διὰ τὸ γῆρας. It is one of those common words which do not die easily. Phrynichus, however, is quite right in denying it to Attic proper. Of the two verbs σαίρω and κορῶ, the Athenians, obeying the inexorable law of parsimony, selected the latter, and let σαίρω drop out of use; κορῶ occurs in the Odyssey—

> ἀγρεῖθ', αἱ μὲν δῶμα κορήσατε ποιπνύσασαι,
> 20. 149.

and is the only word known to Attic Prose and Comedy, Dem. 313. 12, of Aeschines, τὸ μέλαν τρίβων, καὶ τὰ βάθρα σπογγίζων, καὶ τὸ παιδαγωγεῖον κορῶν:

> κατάθου τὸ κόρημα, μὴ 'κκόρει τὴν Ἑλλάδα·
> Aristoph. Pax 59.

> τουτὶ λαβὼν τὸ κόρημα, τὴν αὐλὴν κόρει.
> Eupolis (Pollux, 10. 29).

Probably the substantive κόρημα was of purely Attic growth, and ought to be compared with such words as ὑδρία (p. 23), which illustrate the extraordinary formative activity of the Athenian mind during the period which began with Marathon and Salamis. It need hardly be added that σαροῦν is as debased a form as ἀροτριᾶν, ἀλήθειν, σμήχειν, ψήχειν, et hoc genus omne.

LXIV.

Ἀφῆλιξ λέγουσιν ἁμαρτάνοντες οἱ ῥήτορες· τοὐναντίον γὰρ ἢ δεῖ χρῶνται· τὸν μὲν γὰρ πρεσβύτερον ῥητέον ἀφήλικα, οἱ δ' ἐπὶ τοῦ μηδέπω τῆς ἐν νόμῳ ἡλικίας χρῶνται.

It is easy to see how these opposed meanings originated. The force of the preposition in the classical sense is the same as in such words as ἀπαρτί, ἀπακριβοῦμαι, ἀπανδροῦμαι, ἀπαρκῶ, etc.; whereas in ἀφῆλιξ, *young*, *in one's nonage*, the ἀπό bears the meaning that it has in ἀπάνθρωπος, ἀπαρέσκω, ἀποτυγχάνω, and other words.

There is no reason to believe that Pollux (2. 17) is right in enfranchising as Attic the latter of these significations: καὶ Φρύνιχος μὲν ὁ Κωμικὸς τὰς νέας ἀφήλικας λέγει, **ἦσαν δὲ καὶ γυναῖκες ἀφήλικες.** Φερεκράτης δὲ τὴν γεραιτάτην ἀφηλικεστάτην, ὡς καὶ Κρατῖνος ἀφήλικα γέροντα. Any late Greek writer was capable of misunderstanding a Classical predecessor, and the context is required to fix the meaning of the words by which Pollux confirms his assertion.

LXV.

Ἐπιτροπιάζειν· ἔτι καὶ τοῦτο διέφθαρται, καίτοι λεγόντων φανερῶς τῶν ἀρχαίων ὑποτροπιάζειν.

According to Lobeck, there is no trace of this corruption in our texts. Phrynichus himself explains the meaning of *ὑποτροπιάζειν* in App. Soph. 69. 19 by the words *ὅταν πεπαυμένης τῆς νόσου πάλιν ἐπινοσῇ τις*. The word is so used by Hippocrates, but does not occur in any extant Attic writer.

LXVI.

Προκόπτειν λέγουσι· τὸ δὲ ὄνομα προκοπὴ παρ' αὐτοῖς οὐκ ἔστι.

This is a mere question of fact. *Προκοπή* certainly does not occur in Classical Greek. Those who care may search for a reason why *προκοπή*, *ἐγκοπή*, *ἐκκοπή*, *συγκοπή*, were tabooed when *ἀποκοπή*, *παρακοπή*, and *περικοπή*, were in use among Attic writers.

LXVII.

Βιβλιαγράφος· οὕτω λέγουσιν ἐν πέντε συλλαβαῖς καὶ διὰ τοῦ α, οὐχὶ τετρασυλλάβως διὰ τοῦ ο.

In App. Soph. 29. 29 is found the dictum *βιβλιοπώλης καὶ βιβλοπώλης καὶ βιβλογράφος*. It is impossible to reconcile contradictory statements—and there is no means of arriving at the truth. There is a discussion of the question in the Parerga to Lobeck's edition, pp. 655 ff.

LXVIII.

Βασκάνιον λέγουσιν οἱ ἀρχαῖοι, οὐ προβασκάνιον μετὰ τῆς πρό.

A good notion of the meaning of the term may be got from the App. Soph. 30. 5: *Βασκάνιον· ὃ οἱ ἀμαθεῖς προβασκάνιον· ἔστι δέ τι ἀνθρωποειδὲς κατασκεύασμα, βραχὺ παρηλλαγμένον τὴν ἀνθρωπείαν φύσιν, ὃ πρὸ τῶν ἐργαστηρίων οἱ χειρώνακτες κρεμαννύουσι τοῦ μὴ βασκαίνεσθαι αὐτῶν τὴν ἐργασίαν.*

In a similiar description, Pollux, 7. 108, quotes these lines of Aristophanes—

> *πλὴν εἴ τις πρίαιτο δεόμενος*
> *βασκάνιον ἐπὶ κάμινον ἀνδρὸς χαλκέως.*

The *πρό* violates Attic usage in the same way as *σύν* in the words *συμπολίτης* and *συμπατριώτης.*

LXIX.

Νοΐδιον καὶ βοΐδιον ἀρχαῖα καὶ δόκιμα, οὐχὶ νούδιον καὶ βούδιον, διὰ τοῦ υ.

LXX.

Ῥοΐδιον διαιροῦντες λέγουσιν οἱ ἀμαθεῖς· ἡμεῖς δὲ ῥοίδιον.

The former of these articles hardly requires annotation, but the latter may even now be insisted upon with advantage.

Any one who knows anything of Attic Greek must feel convinced that the open forms are radically opposed to the genius of that dialect. In late Greek the uncontracted forms were in vogue and have crept into all manuscripts. Other grammarians besides Phrynichus saw occasion to insist upon the old genuine forms. Moeris, p. 275: Οἰστός, δισυλλάβως Ἀττικῶς, βέλος Ἑλληνικῶς. In his note on that passage Pierson showed that Attic verse often requires and always allows of the contracted forms, and that οἶς, φθοῖς, οἰζυρός, Εὐβοΐδα, διπλοΐδα, διπλοΐζω, ἀθροΐζω, καταπροΐξεται, γρᾴδιον, and the like, should be restored without any regard to codices or editions. Porson followed in his steps in his Preface to the Hecuba, and there can no longer be any doubt on the point. Transcribers wrote ὀιστός for οἰστός, ὄις for οἶς, ἐλεεινός for ἐλεινός, just as they substituted φύσεε for φύση and πόλεε for πόλη. Yet editors will still write ἐλεεινός, φύσεε, and similar forms in prose, and trust with credulity guides who, as often as there is any evidence external to themselves, are found to be consistently untrustworthy.

LXXI.

Ὀσμὴ χρὴ λέγειν διὰ τοῦ σ· διὰ γὰρ τοῦ δ, ὀδμ', Ἰώνων· παρανομεῖ γοῦν Ξενοφῶν εἰς τὴν πάτριον διάλεκτον ὀδμὴ λέγων.

It has already been observed, that Xenophon's diction is an anticipation of the Common dialect. With Attic for its basis, it allows of words from all the dialects, and is wanting in that quality which has justly been termed purity. Moreover, not only the diction, but the style as a whole lacks the masculine simplicity and manly self-restraint which marks all genuine Attic work, and has many of the characteristics of the feminine Ionic. Certainly no pure Attic writer ever recalls by faults of style the Greek of Macedonian times so frequently as Xenophon. He is wanting in dignity, loquacious, superficial, and indifferent to all that differentiates a good style from a bad. He uses different words of identical meaning in the same paragraph, and never exercises his judgment in the selection of terms. On the other hand, he does not disdain the trivial methods of ornamentation which every good style is without.

It did not escape the notice of the later Greeks that Xenophon's diction was very different from that of pure Attic writers, and there are still extant several remarks upon this point. The physician Galen, in his Commentary on Hippocrates, compares Xenophon with the great Ionic medical writer in his use of *ὀνόματα γλωσσηματικὰ καὶ τροπικά*—'foreign words and figurative expressions'—and the Grammarians use language of a similar kind. In Photius (Biblioth. p. 533. 25) are preserved the following words of Helladius, a grammarian of the fifth century A. D., *οὐδὲν θαυμαστὸν ἀνὴρ ἐν στρατείαις σχολάζων καὶ ξένων συνουσίαις εἴ τινα παρακόπτει τῆς πατρίου φώνης· διὸ νομοθέτην αὐτὸν οὐκ ἄν τις ἀττικισμοῦ παραλάβοι.* The explanation suggested by Helladius is unquestionably correct, and recommends itself to any one who studies the evidence that is still available. A busy man, living almost wholly abroad, devoted to country pursuits and the life of the camp, attached to the Lacedaemonian system of government, and detesting the Athenian, Xenophon must have lost much of the refined Atticism with which he was conversant in his youth. It is not only in the form of words that he differs from Attic writers, but he also uses many terms—the *ὀνόματα γλωσσηματικά* of Galen—altogether unknown to Attic prose, and often assigns to Attic words a meaning not actually attached to them in the leading dialect. The fact that expatriation modifies the use of one's native tongue was no less true in Greece than it is now, and may be illustrated by the lines of Solon—

> πολλοὺς δ' Ἀθήνας πατρίδ' ἐς θεόκτιτον
> ἀνήγαγον πραθέντας, ἄλλον ἐκδίκως,
> ἄλλον δικαίως, γλῶσσαν οὐκέτ' Ἀττικὴν
> ἱέντας, ὡς ἂν πολλαχῇ πλανωμένους,
>
> ap. Aristid. 2. 536.

and still more aptly by a passage of Demosthenes (p. 1304), *διαβεβλήκασί μου τὸν πατέρα ὡς ἐξένιζε*[1]· *καὶ ὅτι μὲν ἁλοὺς ὑπὸ τῶν πολεμίων ὑπὸ τὸν Δεκελεικὸν πόλεμον, καὶ πραθεὶς εἰς Λευκάδα Κλεάνδρῳ, περιτυχὼν τῷ ὑποκριτῇ πρὸς τοὺς οἰκείους ἐσώθη δεῦρο πολλοστῷ χρόνῳ, παραλελοίπασιν, ὥσπερ δὲ δέον ἡμᾶς δι' ἐκείνας τὰς ἀτυχίας ἀπολέσθαι, τὸ ξενίζειν αὐτοῦ κατηγορήκασιν· ἐγὼ δ' ἐξ αὐτῶν τούτων μάλιστ' ἂν οἶμαι ὑμῖν ἐμαυτὸν Ἀθηναῖον ὄντα ἐπιδεῖξαι· καὶ πρῶτον μὲν ὡς ἑάλω καὶ ἐσώθη, μάρτυρας ὑμῖν παρέξομαι, ἔπειθ' ὅτι ἀφικόμενος τῆς οὐσίας παρὰ τῶν θείων τὸ μέρος μετέλαβεν, εἶθ' ὅτι οὔτ' ἐν τοῖς δημόταις, οὔτ' ἐν τοῖς φράτορσιν, οὔτ' ἄλλοθι οὐδαμοῦ τὸν ξενίζοντα οὐδεὶς πώποτ' ᾐτιάσατο ὡς εἴη ξένος.*—The man had been sold from one part of Greece to another, had always lived among Greek-speaking men, and yet, when he returned to his native Attica, he no longer talked Attic.—It is a point, which cannot be insisted upon too often, that the phenomena of language presented by Greece up to the time of Alexander were exceptional to a degree. Several dialects, differing essentially in vocabulary and pronunciation, existed contemporaneously within a very limited area. Moreover, as has been shown, there were, in addition to these, what may be called literary dialects, produced by a fact almost peculiar to Greek literature—that a style of composition had a tendency to keep to the same dialect in which it started. In this way it was possible, even in the case of one people like the Athenians, to have two

[1] *ξένῃ διαλέκτῳ ἐχρῆτο.* Vid. Harpocration sub vocabulo.

stages in the history of their language represented in contemporary literature, namely, the matured Attic of the day, known to us from Comedy and the Orators, and the partially developed Ionic Attic of more than a century earlier, which is the basis of the language of Tragedy.

Now, while it has been already proved that, to an Athenian of the best age, it was as easy and natural to pass in literature from one dialect to another as from one metrical system to another, yet, at the same time, nothing but constant communion with his contemporaries could have produced that marvellous precision of language which is observable in Aristophanes, Plato, and the Orators. Such precision was only possible in a language spoken by a great people, elevated by events to a still higher intellectual level, inhabiting a limited area with few opposing interests, and thrown into constant communication with one another. No Athenian of the best days used for ordinary purposes *ἔρχηται* for *ἴῃ*, *ἐρχόμενος* for *ἰών*, *πωλήσω* for *ἀποδώσομαι*, *τέξω* for *τέξομαι*, *κάρτα* for *σφόδρα*, yet the words were known to him, and he recognized that they were in place in Tragedy, and might, for literary purposes, be employed in Comedy. But if the same man moved for a year or two among Greek peoples which used *ἔρχηται*, *ἔρχοιτο*, *πωλήσω*, *τέξω*, *ἐλεύσομαι*, and the like, there is no question that he would follow their example. Accordingly, it is contrary to all reason to treat Xenophon as a genuine Attic writer, and to apply to him the same standard that may justly be applied to Aristophanes, Plato, and the Orators. As it is, there is every reason to believe that his text has already severely suffered in this way, and that early critics have made corrections of the same kind as modern editors have recently been introducing. The word *ὀδμή* is a case in point. It is not encountered once in the present texts of Xenophon. The Attic *ὀσμή* has everywhere been substituted for it. Yet, besides that of Phrynichus, there is the testimony of other grammarians to the same effect; and their authority is far superior to that of manuscripts, more recent by many centuries. Pollux has a remark of great value: Ἡ δὲ ὀδμὴ καὶ εὐοδμία δοκεῖ μὲν τοῖς πολλοῖς εἶναι καλὰ ὀνόματα, ἔστι δὲ ποιητικά, ἐν δὲ τοῖς καταλογάδην Ἰωνικὰ καὶ Αἰωλικά. Παρὰ δὲ Ἀντιφῶντι μόνῳ ὀδμὰς καὶ εὐοδμίαν[1] εὕροι τις ἂν (2. 76). In the texts of Xenophon ὀδμή must be restored, in accordance with the authority of Grammarians; and ὀδμή and εὐοδμία are moreover guaranteed by Pollux to have survived, even in Attic, till the time of Antiphon, or the middle of the fifth century B.C., so that not only did Aeschylus use ὀδμά in a lyrical passage, P. V. 115—

τίς ἀχώ, τίς ὀδμὰ προσέπτα μ' ἀφεγγής;

but the manuscripts are probably to be trusted in exhibiting ὀδμή even in Euripidean senarii[2]—

ὦ θεῖον ὀδμῆς πνεῦμα κτε.

Hipp. 1391.

Further evidence that the text of Xenophon, as we now have it, differs in many essential points from the text of the early Christian centuries, is not wanting. Photius[3] has preserved the fact that Xenophon used ἠώς for ἕως: Ἕως, οὐχὶ ἠώς, τὸ Ἀττικόν ἐστι. Ξενοφῶν δὲ ἠὼς λέγει ποιητικῶς, κατακόρως ἐν Κύρου Παιδείᾳ ἥν πρὸς ἠῶ, ἥν τε πρὸς ἑσπέραν. Yet ἕως now appears everywhere in the manuscripts. A gloss in Suïdas is, Μάσσων, μακροτέρος: Ξενοφῶν· ἂν μὴ πολὺ μάσσων ὁδὸς ᾖ. To the examples of un-Attic

[1] The editions have ὀσμὰς καὶ εὐοσμίαν, which means nothing. Antiphon, the earliest of Attic prose writers, retains very many words and forms of words abandoned at a later period by the Attic dialect, and ὀδμή and εὐοδμία do not stand alone in his diction as indications of that earlier Attic, a still earlier stage of which became the basis of the Tragic diction.

[2] The coexistence of ὀσμή in Eur. El. 498, Cycl. 153, and in Soph. Phil. 891, Ant. 412, 1083; Fr. Philoct. 630; Synd. Fr. 141. 4, is only another instance of the combination of new and old in the Tragic diction, and of which the new νοσοίην, by the side of the old νοσοῖμι, is a striking instance.

[3] In Lex. MSS. apud Valcken. ad Eur. Hipp. 78.

words and forms in Xenophon already referred to (see p. 59), may be added the following: *γνωστήρ*=Att. *ἐγγυητής*, Cyr. 6. 2. 39; *δοτήρ, ἀποδεκτήρ*, 8. 1. 9; *ἐπιτακτήρ*, 2. 3. 4; *ὀπτήρ, φραστήρ*, 4. 5. 17; *θεραπευτήρ*, 7. 5. 65; *μνηστήρ*, 8. 4. 15; *λυμαντήρ*, Hier. 3. 3; and in alphabetical order:—

'Αγλαΐα=κοσμός, Eq. 5. 8, *δέδοται δὲ παρὰ θεῶν καὶ ἀγλαΐας ἕνεκα ἵππῳ χαίτη καὶ προκόμιόν τε καὶ οὐρά.*

'Αγρεύω, hunt=*θηρεύω, κυνηγετῶ*, Hipp. 4. 18, Cyn. 12. 6, Anab. 5. 3. 8.

'Αγχέμαχα ὅπλα=*τὰ μὴ βαλλόμενα ὅπλα*, Cyr. 1. 2. 13: Homer: Hesiod.

'Αγχιτέρμων=*γείτων*, Hier. 10. 7, *τὰς δὲ ἀγχιτέρμονας πόλεις*: Soph. Fr. Lemn. 352; Eur. Rhes. 426.

'Αδαής=*ἀσύνετος*, Cyr. 1. 6. 43, *οὐδενὸς αὐτῶν ἠμέληκας οὐδ' ἀδαὴς γεγένησαι*: Hdt. 2. 49; 5. 90; 9. 46; cp. 8. 65.

'Αλγύνομαι=*ἀνιῶμαι, λυποῦμαι*, Apol. 8, *ἀλγυνόμενος νόσοις ἢ γήρᾳ*. In Tragedy frequently, in Comedy only in parody or paratragedy.

'Αλέκω=*ἀμύνω*, if *ἀλέξομαι* is read for *ἀλεξήσομαι* in An. 7. 7. 3, so *ἠλεξάμην, ἀλέξασθαι*, An. 1. 3. 6; 3. 4. 33, etc.

'Αλέξω=*ἀμύνω*, act. Cyr. 4. 3. 2; middle, Cyr. 1. 5. 13.

'Αλεξητήρ=*βοηθός*, Oec. 4. 3, *ταῖς πατρίσιν ἀλεξητῆρες*: Hom. Il. 20. 396.

'Αλίζω=*ἀθροίζω*, Cyr. 1. 4. 14; An. 7. 3. 48; 6. 3. 3; Herod. 1. 79; 5. 15; 7. 12; Eur. Heracl. 403. It occurs in Plato, Crat. 409 A, but only in a philological argument, *ἅλιος οὖν εἴη μὲν ἂν κατὰ τὸ ἁλίζειν εἰς ταὐτὸ τοὺς ἀνθρώπους, ἐπειδὰν ἀνατείλῃ.*

"Αλκιμος=*θρασύς, μάχιμος*, Cyr. 1. 2. 10; 5. 2. 25, Anab. 4. 3. 4; 7. 7. 15, Hell. 7. 2. 16; 7. 3. 1, Oec. 4. 15, etc. In Plato, Rep. 614 B, it is used for the sake of a pun, and in Arist. Plut. 1002, in a proverb.

'Αμαυρῶ=*συγχέω, ἀφανίζω*, Cyn. 5. 4, *ἡ σελήνη ἀμαυροῖ τὰ*

ἴχνη: Ages. 11. 12, ἀμαυροῦν τὰ τῶν πολεμίων: Hdt. 9. 10; Eur. Fr. 420.

Ἄναλκις, Cyr. 7. 5. 62; 8. 1. 45, ἀνάλκιδας καὶ ἀσυντάκτους: Soph. El. 301; Hdt. 2. 102.

Ἀνιμῶ = ἀνέλκω, Anab. 4. 2. 8, Eq. 7. 1.

Ἀπαμείβομαι = ἀποκρίνομαι, Xen. An. 2. 5. 15, Τισσαφέρνης δὲ ὧδε ἀπημείφθη: otherwise only Epic.

Ἀπερύκω = κωλύω, Mem. 2. 9. 2, κύνας δὲ τρέφεις ἵνα σοι τοὺς λύκους ἀπὸ τῶν προβάτων ἀπερύκωσι . . . ἀπερύκειν: Oec. 5. 6, αἱ δὲ κύνες τά τε θηρία ἀπερύκουσαι ἀπὸ λύμης καρπῶν καὶ προβάτων. See ἐρύκω.

Ἀραιός = μανός, Lac. 11. 6, ἀραιαὶ φάλαγγες: Hom. Il. 16. 161; Hippocr. 243. 36, ἣν δὲ ξηρὰ ἔῃ καὶ ἀραιῶς κείμενα = *raris intervallis.*

Ἀρήγω, Cyr. 1. 5. 13, τοῖς φίλοις ἀρήγειν: Oec. 5. 7, ἀρήγειν τῇ χώρᾳ: Hom. Il. 1. 77, etc.; Herod. 7. 236; Hippocr. 395. 6, λουτρὸν δὲ συχνοῖσι τῶν νουσημάτων ἀρήγοι ἂν χρεομένοισι: Aesch. Eum. 571, P. V. 267, etc.; Soph. Aj. 329, etc.; Eur. Tr. 772, etc.

Ἀστυφέλικτος = ἀσφαλής, Lac. 15. 7, ἀστυφέλικτον τὴν βασιλείαν παρέχειν.

Ἀτημέλητος = ἠμελημένος, Cyr. 5. 4. 18, οὐδένα ἑκὼν ἀτημέλητον παρέλειπεν: 8. 1. 14, οὐδεὶς ἀτημέλητος γίγνεται. In an active sense, Cyr. 8. 1. 15, τῶν οἰκείων ἀτημελήτως ἔχειν: Aesch. Agam. 891.

Ἀχθεινός = λυπηρός, Mem. 4. 8. 1, τὸ ἀχθεινότατον τοῦ βίου: Hell. 4. 8. 27, οὐκ ἀχθεινῶς ἑώρα: Eur. Hipp. 94, Hec. 1240.

Ἄχος = λύπη, Cyr. 5. 5. 6, ἄχος αὐτὸν ἔλαβεν: id. 6. 1. 37, οἱ ἄνθρωποί με καταδύουσιν ἄχει: Herod. 2. 131; Trag. freq.

Βιοτή = βίος, Cyr. 7. 2. 27, μακαριωτάτην βιοτὴν . . . μακαρίαν βιοτήν: Herod. 7. 47; Trag.

Γαμέτης = ἀνήρ, Cyr. 4. 6. 3, τὸν τῆς βασιλέως θυγατρὸς γαμέτην: Aesch. P. V. 897 (ch.); Eur. Supp. 1028 (ch.), Troad. 312 (ch.).

Γαυροῦμαι = ἀγάλλομαι, ἐπαίρομαι, Hier. 2. 15, γαυροῦνται ἐπὶ τῷ ἔργῳ: Cyr. 2. 4. 30, ἐπιγαυρωθεὶς τῇ ἐντολῇ τοῦ Κύρου: Eur. Or. 1532, Bacch. 1144.

Γοῶμαι = ἀποδακρύω, Cyr. 4. 6. 9, ἡ θυγατὴρ πολλὰ γοωμένη: on which Pollux (3. 100) remarks, Ξενοφῶν δὲ γοωμένη που λέγει ποιητικώτερον: Aesch. Pers. 1072; Eur. Tro. 289; Soph. O. R. 1249, etc. In Ar. Thesm. 1036 in ch.

Γεινάμενοι οἱ = οἱ γονεῖς, Mem. 1. 4. 7, Apol. 20; Herod. 1. 120, 122; 4. 10; 6. 52.

Δαήμων = ἐπιστήμων, Cyr. 1. 2. 12, δαημονέστατοι καὶ ἀνδρικώτατοι: Od. 8. 159.

Δάπεδον = ἔδαφος, de Re Eq. 1. 3, αἱ ὑψηλαὶ ὁπλαὶ πόρρω ἀπὸ τοῦ δαπέδου ἔχουσι τὴν χελιδόνα καλουμένην: id. ὥσπερ γὰρ κύμβαλον ψοφεῖ πρὸς τῷ δαπέδῳ ἡ κοίλη ὁπλή: Anab. 4. 5. 6, διατηκομένης τῆς χιόνος βόθροι ἐγίγνοντο μεγάλοι ἔστε ἐπὶ τὸ δάπεδον: Cyr. 8. 8. 16, Oec. 8. 17; Homer; Eur. Hipp. 230 (ch.), Alc. 594 (ch.). In Ar. Plut. 515 in paratragedy.

Δαψιλής = ἄφθονος, Anab. 4. 2. 22, καλαῖς οἰκίαις καὶ ἐπιτηδείοις δαψιλέσι, 4. 4. 2: ἐπιτήδεια δ' ἦν δαψιλῆ: Mem. 2. 7. 6, Cyr. 1. 6. 17; Herod. 3. 130. The word occurs in middle Comedy, Sophilus (in Ath. 3. 100 a), by the side of χορτασθήσομαι, and στρηνιῶ. Antiphanes in Ath. 1. 23).

Δειπνίζω = ἑστιῶ, Mem. 1. 3. 7, Oec. 2. 5, Cyr. 4. 5. 5; Hom. Od. 4. 535, etc.; Herod. 7. 118.

Δεσπόσυνος = δεσποτικός, Oec. 9. 16; 14. 2; Aesch. Pers. 587; Eur. Hec. 101, I. T. 439; and in Ar. Thesm. 42 in paratragedy.

Δουπῶ = κρούω, which occurs in An. 1. 8. 18, although in itself quite in keeping with Xenophon's style, evidently belongs to a gloss; but δοῦπος is met with in An. 2. 2. 19, θόρυβος καὶ δοῦπος ἦν οἷον εἰκὸς φόβου ἐμπεσόντος: Homer; Aesch. Cho. 375; Soph. Aj. 633; Eur. Ion 516. In Thuc. 3. 22. 5, κατέβαλε γάρ τις κεραμίδα ἣ πεσοῦσα *ψόφον ἐποίησεν*, an excellent MS. has *δοῦπον*, which may be right—an indication of the immaturity of Attic in the historian's time.

Δρύπτομαι = *σπαράσσομαι*, Cyr. 3. 1. 13, *γυναῖκες ἀναβοήσασαι ἐδρύπτοντο*: id. 3. 3. 67, *καταρρηγνύμεναί τε πέπλους καὶ δρυπτόμεναι*: Hom. Od. 2. 153; Eur. El. 150, Hec. 655.

Δύσελπις = *ἀνέλπιστος, ἀνελπίστως ἔχων*, Vect. 3. 7, Hell. 5. 4. 31; Aesch. Cho. 412 (ch.).

Δώρημα = *δῶρον*, Hier. 8. 4; Aesch. P. V. 626, Pers. 523; Soph. Aj. 662; Eur. Hel. 883, etc.

Ἔκπαγλος = *θαυμαστός*, Hier. 11. 3, *ὅπλοις δὲ τοῖς ἐκπαγλοτάτοις αὐτὸς κατακεκοσμημένος*: Homer freq.; Aesch. Ag. 862, Cho. 548; Soph. El. 204; Herod. 9. 48 has the verb *ἐκπαγλεόμενοι*, and Eur. Or. 890, Tro. 929, Hec. 1157.

Ἐμπολή = *ὤνια, φορτία*, Hell. 5. 1. 23, *ὁλκάδας γεμούσας τὰς μέν τινας σίτου, τὰς δὲ καὶ ἐμπολῆς*: = *ὠνή*, Cyr. 6. 2. 39, *εἰ δέ τις χρημάτων προσδεῖσθαι νομίζει εἰς ἐμπολήν . . . λαμβάνειν*: Soph. Fr. Scyr. Nk. 508; Eur. I. T. 1111.

Ἐξαλαπάζω = *ἐκπορθῶ*, Ar. 7. 1. 29, *Ἑλληνίδα δὲ εἰς ἣν πρώτην πόλιν ἤλθομεν, ταύτην ἐξαλαπάξομεν*: Il. 1. 129.

Ἐπαρήγω = *ἐπικουρῶ*, Cyr. 6. 4. 18, *οἱ ἀπὸ τῶν πύργων ἡμῖν ἐπαρήξουσι*: Il. 1. 408, et freq.; Aesch. Cho. 725; Soph. El. 1197; Eur. El. 1350; Aristoph. Vesp. 402, in anapaests.

Ἐπιδαψιλεύομαι (vid. *δαψιλής* supra), Cyr. 2. 2. 15, *ἡμῖν γέλωτος ἐπιδαψιλεύσει*: Herod. 5. 20.

Ἐρείπω, Cyr. 7. 4. 1, *ὁ δὲ Κῦρος μηχανὰς ἐποιεῖτο ὡς ἐρείψων τὰ τείχη*: Homer freq.; Herod. 9. 70; Soph. Ant. 596, O. C. 1373, Aj. 309.

Ἐρύκω, Anab. 3. 1. 25, *ἐρύκειν ἀπ' ἐμαυτοῦ τὰ κακά* (see *ἀπερύκω*): Hom. freq.; Herod. 9. 49; Aesch. Sept. 1075; Soph. Tr. 120, Phil. 1153; Eur. H. F. 317.

Εὐθημοσύνη, Cyr. 8. 5. 7, *καλὸν ἡγεῖτο ὁ Κῦρος ἐν οἰκίᾳ εἶναι ἐπιτήδευμα τὴν εὐθημοσύνην κτε.*: Hesiod, Op. 471: *εὐθημών*, Aesch. Cho. 84.

Εὐνάζω, Cyn. 9. 3, οὗ ἂν μέλλῃ ἑκάστη τὸν ἑαυτῆς εὐνάσειν (νέβρον): id. 12. 2, εὐνάζεσθαι σκληρῶς δυνατοὶ ἔσονται καὶ φύλακες εἶναι ἀγαθοί: Soph. Trach. 1242, O. R. 982; Eur. Med. 18, Rhes. 611, 762.

Ἐχθραίνω = μισῶ, Ag. 11. 5, τῶν παρρησιαζομένων οὐδένα ἤχθραινεν: Soph. Ant. 93 (v. l. ἐχθαίρω).

Ἠϊών, Hell. 1. 1. 5, κατὰ τὴν ἠϊόνα: Hom. freq.; Herod. 8. 96; Aesch. Ag. 1159 (ch.); Eur. Or. 995 (ch.), Tro. 827 (ch.).

Ἠλίβατος, Anab. 1. 4. 4, ὕπερθεν δὲ ἦσαν πέτραι ἠλίβατοι: Hom. Il. 15. 619, ἠΰτε πέτρη ἠλίβατος: id. 16. 35, Od. 9. 243; 10. 88; 13. 196; Hesiod, Theog. 786, Scut. 422; Theognis, 176; Pindar, Ol. 6. 110; Aesch. Suppl. 351; Eur. Hipp. 732; Ar. Av. 1732 (ch.). In late prose writers, as Polybius, 4. 41. 9; Plutarch, Mor. 163 C, 935 E; Strabo, 17, 818.

Θάλπω = θερμαίνω, Cyr. 5. 1. 11, μηδὲ ῥιγῶν τοῦ χειμῶνος μηδὲ θάλπεσθαι τοῦ θέρους: Hom. Od. 21. 179; Hesiod, Theog. 864; Aesch. P. V. 590, 650, 878; Soph. Tr. 697, 1082, Phil. 38, El. 888, Ant. 417; Eur. Hel. 183. In Ar. Eq. 210, αἴ κα μὲ θαλφθῇ λόγοις, in pseudo-oracle.

Θήγω = ὀξύνω, Cyr. 1. 2. 10, τὴν ψυχὴν θήγεσθαι: 1. 6. 41, εὖ μὲν τὰ σώματα ἠσκημένα, εὖ δὲ αἱ ψυχαὶ τεθηγμέναι: 2. 1. 11, τὰς ψυχὰς θήγειν: 2. 1. 13, θήγειν τὸ φρόνημα: 2. 1. 20, θήγειν τὰς ψυχὰς εἰς τὰ πολεμικά: Mem. 3. 3. 7, θήγειν τὰς ψυχὰς τῶν ἱππέων: Hom. Il. 2. 382, etc.; Aesch. Ag. 1262, P. V. 311, Sept. 715; Soph. Aj. 584, etc.; Eur. Or. 51. 1036, 1625, El. 1142, etc. In Ar. Lys. 1255, in the χόρος Λακώνων.

Θιγγάνω = ἅπτομαι, Cyr. 1. 3. 5, ὅταν τούτων τινὸς θίγῃς: 5. 1. 16, πυρὸς θιγόντα: 6. 4. 9, θιγὼν αὐτῆς τῆς κεφαλῆς: Hippocr. 8. 88; 6. 90; 3. 272, etc.; Aesch. P. V. 849, Sept. 44, 258, Ag. 432, 663, etc.; Soph. O. R. 760, 1413, 1469, O. C. 330, 470, etc.; Eur. Hec. 605, Or. 218, 382, 1602, Hipp. 310, etc. It is not found in Comedy, except once in anapaests in Pherecrates, Ath. 6. 263 B, and in Lacedaemonian form, σιγῆν = θιγεῖν, in Ar. Lys. 1004. In Antiphanes, Ath. 15. 667 A, θίγῃ is merely a conjecture of Jacobs' for τύχῃ.

Ἱππότης = ἱππεύς, Cyr. 1. 4. 18, σὺν τοῖς παρατυχοῦσιν ἱππόταις: 8. 8. 20; de Re Eq. 8. 10, δύο ἱππότα συντιθεμένω: Hom. Il. 2. 336, et freq.; Herod. 9. 69, οἱ τῶν Θηβαίων ἵπποται: Aesch. Sept. 80 (ch.); Soph. O. C. 899; Eur. Phoen. 1095, etc.

Καίνω = ἀποκτείνω, Cyr. 4. 2. 24, οὗτοι δὲ καινόντων [so κατακαίνω = ἀποκτείνω very frequently in Xenophon alone of *Classical* authors]: Aesch. Ag. 1562, Sept. 347, 630, Cho. 930; Soph. O. C. 994, El. 820, Ant. 1319; Eur. H. F. 865, I. T. 27, 1252, etc.

Κλῄζω = καλῶ, Cyr. 1. 2. 1, Περσεῖδαι ἀπὸ Περσέως κλῄζονται: Hippocr. 3. 191; Aesch. Ag. 631; Soph. O. R. 48, 1171, 1451, etc.; Eur. Phoen. 10, H. F. 340, Bac. 1180, etc. In Ar. Thesm. 116 in chorus; so in Av. 1745: but in id. 905, 921 in the mouth of the ποιητής.

Κλωπεύω = κλέπτω, An. 6. 1. 1, ἐκλώπευον εὖ μάλα τοὺς ἀποσκεδαννυμένους: Lac. 2. 7. Suïdas has the gloss, ἐκλώπευον, ἔκλεπτον· Ξενοφῶν ἐν τῇ Ἀναβάσει.

Κοινών = κοινωνός, Cyr. 7. 5. 35, κοινῶνας τῶν καταπεπραγμένων: 8. 1. 16, 36, 40. Pollux says, 8. 134, οἱ κοινῶνες, Ξενοφῶντος ἴδιον: but Pindar uses the word in Pyth. 3. 28, and κοινεών is an excellent emendation of Scaliger's for τὸν νεών in Eur. H. F. 340—

> ὦ Ζεῦ, μάτην ἄρ' ὁμόγαμόν σ' ἐκτησάμην,
> μάτην δὲ παιδὸς τὸν νεὼν ἐκλῄζομεν.

Cp. ξυνεών, ξυνήων.

Κυδρός, Apol. 29, ὁ μὲν ἀνὴρ ὅδε κυδρός: de Re Eq. 10. 16, κυδρῷ τῷ σχήματι, of a horse: Hom. Od. 11. 580; Aesch. Fr. 162 (Nk.).

Λάφυρα = λεία, Hell. 5. 1. 24, καὶ ἀποδόμενος τὰ λάφυρα: cp.

λαφυροπωλοῦντες in An. 6. 6. 38: λαφυροπώλης, Anab. 7. 7. 56; Hell. 4. 1. 26; Aesch. Sept. 278, Ag. 578; Soph. Tr. 646, Aj. 93; Eur. Rhes. 179, H. F. 416.

Λάχος = μέρος, An. 5. 3. 9, τῶν θυομένων λάχος καὶ τῶν θηρευομένων: Aesch. Eum. 5, 310, 335, 344, etc.; Soph. Ant. 1303.

Λεηλατῶ = λειὰν ποιοῦμαι, etc., Cyr. 1. 4. 17, λεηλατεῖν ἐκ τῆς Μηδικῆς: 1. 4. 20; Hell. 4. 4. 15, et freq.: cp. λεηλασία, Hier. 1. 36; Hdt. 2. 152; Soph. Aj. 343; Eur. Rhes. 293, Hec. 1143. In Dem. 280. 8 it is in a letter of Philip.

Λέχριος = πλάγιος, Cyn. 4. 3, ἰχνευόντων τιθεῖσαι τὰς κεφαλὰς ἐπὶ γῆν λεχριάς, Soph. O. C. 195; Eur. Med. 1168: Hec. 1025.

Λεωργός = κακοῦργος, πανοῦργος, Mem. 1. 3. 9, θερμουργότατον καὶ λεωργότατον: Aesch. P. V. 5.

Ληΐς = λειά, Rep. Lac. 13. 11, ληΐδα ἄγων: Hom. Od. 3. 106, etc.: Aesch. Sept. 331 (ch.).

Λυμαντήρ = λυμεών, Hier. 3. 3, λυμαντῆρας τῆς τῶν γυναικῶν φιλίας πρὸς τοὺς ἄνδρας: Soph. Tr. 793, λυμαντής.

Μαστεύω = ζητῶ, Anab. 5. 6. 25; 7. 3. 11, Ages. 1. 23; 9. 3, etc.; Aesch. Ag. 1099; Soph. O. T. 1052; Eur. Phoen. 416. The companion form ματεύω is also unknown to Attic prose and Comedy.

Μήκιστος = μακρότατος, Ages. 10. 4, ἀφικόμενος ἐπὶ τὸ μήκιστον ἀνθρωπίνου αἰῶνος: id. 11. 15, Cyr. 4. 5. 28; Hom. Il. 7. 155, etc.; Aesch. Frag. 275 (Nk.); Soph. O. T. 1301, Phil. 849.

Μηρύω = συνάγω, συνστέλλω, etc., An. 6. 5. 22, θᾶττον γὰρ ἀθρόον ἐδόκει ἂν οὕτω πέραν γενέσθαι τὸ στράτευμα ἢ εἰ κατὰ τὴν γέφυραν ἐξεμηρύοντο: Hom. Od. 12. 170; Hes. Op. 538; Soph. ap. Ath. 3. 99 D, ναῦται δ' ἐμηρύσαντο νηὸς ἰσχάδα.

Μόχθος = πόνος, Conv. 2. 4, ἀπὸ τῶν ἐλευθερίων μόχθων: 8. 40, σῶμα ἱκανὸν μόχθους ὑποφέρειν: Hes. Sc. 306; Aesch.

P. V. 99, 244, 314, 383, etc.; Soph. O. C. 105, 329, Tr. 1170, etc.; Eur. Hipp. 52, Phoen. 695, Med. 1261, etc. Μοχθῶ, however, though rare, is good Attic.

Μυσάττομαι=βδελύττομαι, Cyr. 1. 3. 5, *μυσαττόμενον ταῦτα τὰ βρώματα*: Hippocr. 477. 25, *μυσάττεται τὸ σίαλον*: Eur. Med. 1149.

Νεογνός=νεογενής, Cyn. 5. 14, *τὰ λίαν νεογνά*: 10. 23, *νεογνοὶ νεβροί*: Oec. 7. 21, *νεογνῶν τέκνων*: id. 24, *νεογνὰ βρέφη*: Her. 2. 2; Aesch. Agam. 1163; Eur. Ion 31.

Νέομαι is read by one manuscript in Cyr. 4. 1. 11, *οὓς μάλιστα καιρὸς ἦν ἢ λαβεῖν ἢ κατακανεῖν, οὗτοι ἐφ' ἵππων νέονται οὓς ἡμεῖς τρέπεσθαι μὲν σὺν τοῖς θεοῖς ἱκανοί, διώκοντες δὲ αἱρεῖν οὐχ ἱκανοί.* Most manuscripts read *ἔσονται*. There is little question that the *νέονται* is right, and that *ἔσονται* is an ancient emendation, no more worthy of being received into the text than the *ὀχοῦντοι* of Cobet (Mnem. N. S. 3. 389). Xenophon used *νέονται* as he used *ἠρώτησα* for *ἠρόμην* (Cyr. 4. 5. 21), *ἐρχόμενος* for *ἰών* (see p. 109), and such like words and forms. The present inquiry will have served its purpose if it puts an end to unwarranted emendations in the text of Xenophon.

Νοσφίζω=ὑφαιρῶ, Cyr. 4. 2. 42, *χρήματα οὐκ ἀγνοῶ ὅτι δυνατὸν ἡμῖν νοσφίσασθαι ὁπόσα ἂν βουλώμεθα*: Eur. Supp. 153; Aesch. Cho. 620; Soph. Phil. 1427, etc.

Ὄλβος=εὐδαιμονία, Xen. Cyr. 1. 5. 9, where it forms one of the series *ὄλβος, εὐδαιμονία, τιμαί*: 4. 2. 44 (no Attic writer could have distinguished between *ὄλβος* and *εὐδαιμονία*); Hdt. 1. 86, very freq. in all three Tragedians.

Ὄχθος, Hipparch. 6. 5; 8. 3; de Re Eq. 3. 7; Hdt. 4. 203; 8. 52; 9. 25; 56. 99; Aesch. Supp. 467, Cho. 4; Eur. Supp. 655. In Ar. Thesm. 1105, and Ran. 1172, in parody.

Ὄψιμος, see p. 124.

Παλαμναῖος=ἀλάστωρ, Cyr. 8. 7. 18, *οἵους μὲν φόβους τοῖς*

μιαιφόνοις ἐμβάλλουσιν, οἵους δὲ παλαμναίους τοῖς ἀνοσίοις ἐπιπέμπουσιν: Eur. I. T. 1218—

A. τί χρή με δρᾶν;
B. πέπλον ὀμμάτων προθέσθαι.
A. μὴ παλαμναῖον λάβω;

According to the Etym. Mag., Zeus had this surname in Chalcis, 647. 43, ὁ γὰρ τοὺς αὐτοχειρὶ φονεύσαντας τιμωρούμενος Ζεὺς παλαμναῖος. Λέγεται καὶ ἐν Χαλκίδι Παλαμναῖος. In the other sense of αὐτόχειρ, it does not occur in Xenophon, but, according to Harpocration, sub voc., in Hyperides ἐν τῷ κατὰ Δημάδου, and it is put in Hermes' mouth by Phrynichus, Com. (Plutarch. Alc. 20). The word is well known in Tragedy, Aesch. Eum. 448; Soph. El. 587.

Πέπαμαι=κέκτημαι, An. 1. 9. 10, ὥστε ἐκτῶντο καὶ ὃ ἐπέπατο αὖ τις ἥκιστα Κῦρον ἔκρυπτεν: 3. 3. 18, πέπανται σφενδόνας: 6. 1. 12; Aesch. Agam. 835, πεπαμένος. Aesch. has also the future πάσομαι in Eum. 177, and the aorist ἐπάσω=ἐκτήσω in Frag. 211 (Nk.). In Soph. O. C. 528—

ἦ ματρόθεν, ὡς ἀκούω,
δυσώνυμα λέκτρ' ἐπλήσω;

Nauck is probably right in reading ἐπάσω.

Περιέπω=θεραπεύω, χρῶμαι, Mem. 2. 9. 5, μάλα περιεῖπεν αὐτόν: Conv. 8. 38, τοῦτον ταῖς μεγίσταις τιμαῖς περιέπειν: Cyr. 4. 4. 12, τοῦτον ὡς εὐεργέτην καὶ φίλον οὐχ ὡς δοῦλον περιέψομεν: Hell. 3. 1. 16, οἱ Ἕλληνες οὐ πάνυ τι καλῶς περιείποντο: Herod. 1. 73, and very frequently.

Πορσύνω=εὐτρεπίζω, παρασκευάζω, Cyr. 4. 2. 47, πορσύνοντες τὰ ἐπιτηδεῖα; 7. 5. 17, τὸ τοῦ ποταμοῦ οὕτως ἐπορσύνετο, etc.: Hdt. 9. 7, et al.; Aesch. Cho. 911, 1041; Ag. 1251, 1374, etc.; Soph. O. C. 341, El. 670, etc.; Eur. Med. 1020, etc.

Πρώιμος, see supra, p. 124.

Ῥεῖθρον=ῥεῦμα, Cyn. 5. 15, 34; 9. 11; Hdt. 1. 75, 186,

191, et al.; Aesch. P. V. 790, Pers. 497; Soph. Ant. 712; Eur. El. 794.

Σαφηνίζω, Cyr. 8. 7. 9, *τὴν βασιλείαν σαφηνίσαντα καταλιπεῖν*: Hell. 7. 5. 21; Mem. 4. 3. 4, Oec. 20. 13, etc.; Aesch. P. V. 228. Σαφηνής = *σαφής* is found in Hdt. 1. 140, etc.; Aesch. Pers. 634, 738, etc.; Soph. Trach. 892.

Σαώτερος, Cyr. 6. 3. 4, *ἅπαντα καὶ σαώτερα ἦν*: Hom. Il. 1. 32, *ἀλλ' ἴθι μή μ' ἐρέθιζε, σαώτερος ὥς κε νέηαι.* This comparative is formed from *σάος*, which, when contracted, gave the Attic *σῶς*.

Σηκάζω, Hell. 3. 2. 4, *τέλος δὲ ὥσπερ ἐν αὐλίῳ σηκασθέντες κατηκοντίσθησαν*: Hom. Il. 8. 131.

Τάραχος = *ταραχή*, Anab. 1. 8. 2, Cyr. 7. 1. 32, Oec. 8. 10, de Re Eq. 9. 4; Hippocr. 300. 41, *ὑπηρετοῦντος τῷ θορύβῳ καὶ ταράχῳ τοῦ κύματος.*

Ὑπόδειγμα = *παράδειγμα*, see p. 62.

Ὑποθημοσύνη = *παραίνεσις*, Mem. 1. 3. 7, *Ἑρμοῦ ὑποθημοσύνῃ*: Hom. Il. 15. 412, *ὑποθημοσύνῃσιν Ἀθήνης.*

Φθίμενοι οἱ, Cyr. 8. 7. 18; Hom. Od. 24. 436, etc.; Aesch. Pers. 626, etc.; Soph. Tr. 1161; Eur. Tro. 1083.

Φρενῶ = *νουθετῶ*, Mem. 2. 6. 1, *δοκεῖ δέ μοι καὶ εἰς τὸ δοκιμάζειν, φίλους ὁποίους ἄξιον κτᾶσθαι, φρενοῦν, τοιάδε λέγων*: Aesch. Agam. 1183, etc.; Soph. Ant. 754, etc.; Eur. Ion 526, etc.

Φύρδην = *ἀναμίξ*, Cyr. 7. 1. 37, *φύρδην ἐμάχοντο καὶ πεζοὶ καὶ ἱππεῖς*: Aesch. Pers. 812.

LXXII.

Βελόνη καὶ βελονοπώλης ἀρχαῖα, ἡ δὲ ῥαφὶς τί ἐστιν οὐκ ἂν τις γνοίη.

Of these two words *ῥαφίς* was undoubtedly the older, *βελόνη* standing in the same relation to *ῥαφίς* as *κόρημα* to *σάρον*, and *ὑδρία* to *ἄγγος*. Helladius (p. 17) has the following interesting note on this point: *τὸ μάκτραν καλεῖν ἐν αἷς τὰς μάζας μάττουσιν, Ἀττικὸν καὶ οὐχ, ὡς ἔνιοι δοκοῦσιν, ἰδιωτικόν. ἀλλὰ καὶ ἡ ξύστρα τῆς στλεγγίδος καὶ τοῦ ὀχετοῦ ἡ ὑδρορροὴ καὶ ὁ ἀλετὼν τοῦ μύλου καὶ τῆς βελόνης ἡ ῥαφὶς παλαιότερον.* According to a grammarian in Bekk. Anecd. 113, Epicharmus employed *ῥαφίς,—ῥαφίδα· τὴν βελόνην Ἐπίχαρμος,* and Pollux, 10. 136, quotes the word from Archippus—

ῥαφίδα καὶ λίνον λαβὼν
τόδε ῥῆγμα σύρραψον.

In Attic, however, *βελόνη* replaced the earlier word. Pollux, 10. 136, *καὶ βελόνης δὲ τοὔνομα ἐν Εὐπόλιδος Ταξιάρχοις*—

ἐγὼ δέ γε στίξω σε βελόναισιν τρισίν,

καὶ βελονίδες, ὡς Ἕρμιππος ἐν Μοίραις. Aeschines uses *βελόνη* in 77. 28, and Aristophanes *βελονοπώλης* in Plut. 175. For *βελοπώλιδας* in Pollux, 7. 200, *βελονοπώλιδας* should be read.

LXXIII.

Ἀκεστὴς λέγουσιν οἱ παλαιοί, οὐκ ἠπητής. Ἔστι μὲν ἠπήσασθαι ἅπαξ παρ' Ἀριστοφάνει ἐν Δαιταλεῦσι, παίζοντι τὰς Ἡσιόδου ὑποθήκας—καὶ κόσκινον ἠπήσασθαι—σὺ δὲ λέγε ἀκέσασθαι τὸ ἱμάτιον.

Phrynichus was before some of our present-day scholars in recognizing that its use, even in the senarii of Comedy, did not necessarily enfranchise a word as Attic, and he explains correctly the occurrence of *ἠπήσασθαι* in Aristophanes. The word continued in use outside Attica till it became a synonym of *ἀκεῖσθαι* in the Common dialect, and accordingly there is no reason why Xenophon should not have employed it. In Cyr. I. 6. 16 the better manuscripts read *ἤπηταί* where others exhibit *ἀκεσταί*: *ὥσπερ ἱματίων ῥαγέντων εἰσί τινες ἠπηταί, οὕτω καὶ οἱ ἰατροὶ ὅταν τινὲς νοσήσωσι, τότε ἰῶνται τούτους,* and in spite of the fact that in the *Συναγωγὴ λέξεων χρησίμων* (Bekk. An. 364. 15), *ἀκεσταί* is recommended,—'*Ακεσταί· οἱ τὰ ἱμάτια ἀκούμενοι· Ξενοφῶν· ὥσπερ ἱματίων ῥαγέντων εἰσί τινες ἀκεσταί,* it is likely that the latter word is simply an alteration of some critic who considered Xenophon an Attic writer. All grammarians, Moeris (p. 48), Photius, Aelius Dionysius (in Eustath. 1647, 57), and others reject both the verb and the substantives *ἠπητής* and *ἠπήτρια,* and it was probably from trust in their authority that some mistaken copyist substituted *ἀκεσταί* for *ἠπηταί* in the Cyropaedia.

LXXIV.

'Αγαθὸς μᾶλλον λέγε, μὴ ἀγαθώτερος, καὶ ἀντὶ τοῦ ἀγαθώτατος, ἀγαθὸς μάλιστα.

There is no instance of the regular comparative and superlative of *ἀγαθός* till the Common dialect, and the dictum of Aelius Dionysius may be accepted as final: *ἀγαθώτερος καὶ ἀγαθώτατος παρ' οὐδενὶ τῶν Ἑλλήνων κεῖται* (ap. Eustath. 1384. 50). Unknown to any dialect of Classical Greek, they were the product of a degenerate age.

LXXV.

'Αρχῆθεν ποιηταὶ λέγουσι, τῶν δὲ καταλογάδην δοκίμων οὐδείς, ἀλλ' ἐξ ἀρχῆς.

The same statement is found in the App. Soph. 7,

'Αρχῆθεν παρὰ μὲν ταῖς ἄλλαις διαλέκτοις εὑρίσκεται· 'Αττικοῖς δὲ οὐ φίλον· διὸ οὔτε Πλάτωνα οὔτε Θουκυδίδην ἔστιν εὑρεῖν λέγοντα τοῦτο: and in the Συναγωγὴ λέξεων χρησίμων (450. 4) there is a very fertile remark on this word: 'Αρχῆθεν οὐκ ἔστι παρὰ τοῖς 'Αττικοῖς, πλὴν παρ' Αἰσχύλῳ· παρ' Ἡροδότῳ δὲ ἔστι καὶ τοῖς Ἴωσι.

The lexicography of the word in Classical times is as follows: Hdt. 1. 131; 3. 25, 80; 5. 18; 7. 104; 8. 22; Hippocrates, 1195 init.; Pindar, Ol. 9. 81, Isthm. 4. 11; Aeschylus; Sophocles, in Frag. Androm. ap. Hesychium, voc. κούριον (Nk. 122).

In fact, the history of ἀρχῆθεν is like that of a very large proportion of the words in a Greek Lexicon. Used in early times, and appearing both before and after the Attic period, it was rejected by Attic writers as unnecessary; but its existence in early Attic is demonstrated by its appearance in the verse of the Tragedians and in Ionic writers contemporary with the fastidious masters of Athenian Prose and Comedy.

Lobeck's note shows that ἀρχῆθεν and its fellows—ἀγρόθεν, οὐρανόθεν, μακρόθεν, γῆθεν, πυργόθεν, etc.—were of frequent occurrence in the Common dialect. In Attic this class of words is singularly small, and, if proper names like 'Αθήνηθεν, 'Αγκυλῆθεν, Κονδυλῆθεν, Κριῶθεν, Πεντελῆθεν, and adverbs like πόρρωθεν, ἐκεῖθεν, χαμᾶθεν, are excepted, few are left to claim Attic citizenship except πατρόθεν, οἴκοθεν, ἔωθεν, θύραθεν. Though μητρόθεν does not happen to occur in pure Attic, it was doubtless in use in genealogical formulae, and should take a place by the side of πατρόθεν.

LXXVI.

Γαστρίζειν ἐπὶ τοῦ ἐμπίπλασθαι λέγουσιν Ἀθηναῖοι, οὐκ ἐπὶ τοῦ τὴν γαστέρα τύπτειν.

It is true that Pollux refers to Comedy the meaning here assigned by Phrynichus to *γαστρίζειν* (2. 168), *γαστριμαργία καὶ γαστρίμαργος, γαστροβόρος, καὶ γαστρισμός, καὶ γαστρίσαι καὶ γαστρίδιον οἱ κωμικοί . . . καὶ ὑπεγαστρίζετο, τὸ ἐχορτάζετο, ἡ κωμῳδία*, but in the Attic which has come down to us the verb is used only in the sense which the Grammarian reprehends—

ὦ πόλις καὶ δῆμ', ὑφ' οἵων θηρίων γαστρίζομαι.
Ar. Eq. 273.

παῖ' αὐτὸν ἀνδρειότατα καὶ
γάστριζε καὶ τοῖς ἐντέροις κτε.
Id. 454.

στρόβει, παράβαινε κύκλῳ καὶ γάστρισον σεαυτόν.
Vesp. 1529.

Perhaps in this place, as certainly in some others, the text of Phrynichus has been tampered with, and the words discussed transposed; but the alteration, if made at all, must have been made at an early date, as Thomas Mag. 182 reproduces the dictum of Phrynichus as it is printed above.

In either case the remark is of no value. Γαστρίζειν is one of a large class of Greek verbs which have their meaning defined by the context. Thus the verb *καρκινοῦν* naturally means, *to make into a crab* or *make crab-like*, just as *δουλῶ* means, *to make into a slave*, *enslave*, and, with a slight modification, it is so used by Antiphanes (Athen. 15. 667 A) in describing the game of cottabos—

αὐλητικῶς δεῖ καρκινοῦν τοὺς δακτύλους,
οἶνόν τε μικρὸν ἐγχέαι καὶ μὴ πολύν.

In the passive it is frequently applied to the roots of

trees, *to become tangled*, and might be employed of any object which possessed any of the marks of a crab. One of these, however, is so obtrusive that it puts the rest out of count, and καρκινοῦν has consequently few modifications of meaning. The corresponding form from ταῦρος should be more prolific, and, as a matter of fact, its signification covers a wide ground. Hesychius has preserved the active voice, and the primary meaning, in the gloss ταύρωσον· ταῦρον ποίησον, and the passive voice is similarly used by Euripides in the lines—

> καὶ ταῦρος ἡμῖν πρόσθεν ἡγεῖσθαι δοκεῖς,
> καὶ σῷ κέρατα κρατὶ προσπεφυκέναι.
> ἀλλ' ἦ ποτ' ἦσθα θήρ; τεταύρωσαι γὰρ οὖν.
> Bacch. 920.

By Aeschylus the meaning is generalized in Cho. 275, *ad tauri ferociam revocari*—

> ἀποχρημάτοισι ζημίαις ταυρούμενον·

but in another passage of Euripides (Med. 92) it is specialised by the accusative ὄμμα, and becomes equivalent to our own *glare*—

> ἤδη γὰρ εἶδον ὄμμα νιν ταυρουμένην.

For ὄμμα ταυρουμένην here, a writer in prose or comedy would have employed ταυρηδὸν βλέπουσαν or δρῶσαν.

The adjective ἀταύρωτος suggests still another signification of ταυροῦν.

The same is true of verbs in -ζω. It depends altogether upon the context whether θερίζω means, *pass the summer* or *mow*; χειμάζω, *pass the winter* or *raise a storm;* and no more fault can be found with ἐαρίζω, in Plato, Ax. 371 C, λειμῶνες ἄνθεσιν ἐαριζόμενοι, than in Xen. An. 3. 5. 15, Ἐκβάτανα, ἔνθα ἐαρίζειν λέγεται βασιλεύς. In the only place in which the verb has been preserved, ξιφίζειν happens to mean, *dance a sword-dance*, Crates (?) in Etym. Mag. 270. 5—

> ξίφιζε καὶ πόδιζε καὶ διαρρίκνου·

but in Aristoph. Eq. 781, διαξιφίζομαι occurs in the sense of *fight with the sword*—

σὲ γάρ, ὃς Μήδοισι διεξιφίσω περὶ τῆς χώρας Μαραθῶνι.

Aristophanes (Eq. 358) uses λαρυγγίζω in the meaning of *throttle*, but in Demosthenes (323. 1) it has that of *bawl*. Many more illustrations of such pliability of signification will meet the student in every Greek author, and it is mere pedantry to restrict γαστρίζω to a single meaning. The lines of Aristophanes, already quoted, establish one signification, and the existence of the substantive γαστρισμός, in the Comic poet Sophilus, implies a similar sense for the verb: Σώφιλος ἐν Φιλάρχῳ—

γαστρισμὸς ἔσται δαψιλὴς κτε.

Athen. 3. 100 A.

From another point of view, γαστρίζω, with the sense of *eat gluttonously*, may be regarded as derived from γάστρις, *a gourmand* (Ar. Av. 1604, Thesm. 816), but the other explanation is preferable. In Eur. Med. 188 the word ταυροῦμαι has been so specialised that it is compounded with ἄπο, just as ὁρῶ or βλέπω might be; and δέργματα ἀποταυροῦται denotes the fixed glare of passionate excitement. Occasionally a preposition serves the same purpose as an accusative in fixing the meaning of a verb, and ἀποσκυθίζω, *scalp*, ἀναχαιτίζω, *rear up*, ὑποσκελίζω, *trip up*, and ἀποτηγανίζω, *eat hot*, convey a very different meaning from that which would attach to the simple verbs if they happened to exist.

LXXVII.

Γαργαλίζειν διὰ τοῦ ρ λέγε, ἀλλὰ μὴ διὰ τῶν δυο γ, γαγγαλίζειν.

'Γαγγαλίζειν vero quam longe a vetustatis consuetudine

absit, vel ex eo patet quod Hemsterhusius, unicus Thomae commentator, omnia expiscatus, nullum nisi ex Hesychio et Glossis Graecolatinis exemplum proferre potuit; adde his δυσγαγγάλιστος ἵππος, Geopon. L. xvi. 2. 1110.' Lobeck.

LXXVIII.

Γήινον λεκτέον διὰ τοῦ η, καὶ μὴ διὰ τοῦ ε, γέϊνον.

'Γέϊνος nusquam locorum vidi, sed γήινος ubique apud antiquissimos pariter ut recentissimos reperitur.' Lobeck. Of Attic writers the word occurs principally in Plato, Polit. 272 D, 288 B, Legg. 6. 778 D, 10. 895 C, Phaedr. 246 C, Tim. 64 C, 65 D, etc. The shortening of the vowel is due to the same tendency that converted πῶμα into πόμα, ἀνάθημα into ἀνάθεμα, πανοικησίᾳ into πανοικεσίᾳ, γλωσσοκομεῖον into γλωσσόκομον, etc.

LXXIX.

Γλωσσόκομον· τὸν μὲν τύπον καὶ τὴν θέσιν ὑπ' ἀρχαίων ἔχει, διεφθαρμένως δὲ λέγεται ὑπὸ τῶν πολλῶν· ἐχρῆν γὰρ γλωττοκομεῖον λέγειν, ὥσπερ ἀμέλει καὶ οἱ ἀρχαῖοι.

The passage is hopelessly corrupt, but in the App. Soph. 32. 28 the genuine words of Phrynichus have survived: Γλωττοκομεῖον· ἐπὶ μόνου τοῦ τῶν αὐλητικῶν γλωττῶν ἀγγείου. ὕστερον δὲ καὶ εἰς ἑτέραν χρῆσιν κατεσκευάζετο, βιβλίων ἢ ἱματίων ἢ ἀργύρου ἢ ὁτουοῦν ἄλλου· καλοῦσι δ' αὐτὸ οἱ ἀμαθεῖς γλωσσόκομον.

LXXX.

Γρυλλίζειν διττὴν ἔχει τὴν ἁμαρτίαν, ἔν τε τῇ προφορᾷ καὶ τῷ σημαινομένῳ, ἐν μὲν τῇ προφορᾷ διὰ τῶν δύο λλ, ἐν δὲ τῷ σημαινομένῳ, ὅτι παρὰ τοῖς ἀρχαίοις τὸ γρυλίζειν ἐστὶ τιθέμενον ἐπὶ τῆς τῶν ὑῶν φωνῆς, οἱ δὲ νῦν τάττουσιν ἐπὶ τῶν φορτικῶς καὶ ἀσχημόνως ὀρχουμένων. ἐρεῖς οὖν γρυλίζειν καὶ γρυλισμὸς ὑῶν, οὐ γρυλλισμός.

Lobeck's conjecture of *ὀδυρομένων* for *ὀρχουμένων* is proved to be wrong by the App. Soph. 33: *γρύλλος δὲ διὰ τῶν δυοῖν λλ ὀρχήματος εἶδός ἐστιν, ἡ μὲν οὖν ὄρχησις ὑπὸ τῶν Αἰγυπτίων γρυλλισμὸς καλεῖται, γρύλλος δὲ ὁ ὀρχούμενος.* The two words are evidently distinct, and it is idle to try to bring them together.

LXXXI.

Γογγύλη· καὶ ἐνταῦθα ἁμάρτημα. οἱ γὰρ παλαιοὶ ἐπὶ τοῦ στρογγύλου τιθέασιν, οἱ δὲ νῦν ἐπὶ τῆς ὑπὸ τῶν Ἑλλήνων γογγυλίδος καλουμένης. λέγε οὖν ἐπὶ τοῦ λαχάνου γογγυλίς, ἀλλὰ μὴ γογγύλη.

The word *γογγύλος* is probably from a reduplicated form of the same root as supplied *γαυλός*, *a milk-pail* (Od. 9. 223), and *γαῦλος*, *a merchant-vessel* (Hdt. 3. 136; 8. 97; Ar. Av. 598; Epicharm. ap. Athen. 7. 320 C). It was replaced in mature Attic by *στρογγύλος*, a word akin to *στράγξ*, *στραγγεύω*, *στραγγάλη*, stringo, strictus, etc., and only by accident having a certain resemblance to *γογγύλος*. The latter word is naturally met with in Ionic, and in Galen's Lexicon to Hippocrates *γογγυλίς* is explained by *στρογγύλη*, a usage which may be paralleled from Herodotus, who employs ἱππάς for ἱππική, Ἰάς for Ἰωνική, etc. As an Ionic word, it was also not out of place in Tragedy, and Strabo (4. p. 183) quotes from Aeschylus γογγύλων πέτρων, and Athenaeus (2. 51 D), γογγύλον μόρον, from Sophocles. Moreover, γογγύλος λίθος ἄθετος appears in an early Attic inscription (Boeckh, 1. 262 a. 22).

The verb γογγύλλω, however, was retained as good Attic, although γογγύλος disappeared, and the older word was also represented in other ways. Its early feminine was crystallized, as Phrynichus shows, in γογγυλίς, *a turnip;* and, although γογγύλη was unknown to Attic in this sense, it was still a good Attic word. As the French influence upon Scotch cookery is still indicated by a term dear to northern children, and 'petit gâteau' survives in '*petticoat* shortbread,' so γογγύλη (Ar. Pax 28), has a meaning for the student of Attic, and proves to him, as plainly as the Apaturian sausages, that the Athenians inherited a sweet tooth from their Ionian ancestors. The old word was further stereotyped as a proper name. Athenaeus (4. 172 F) is wrong when he classes it with names like Νεωκόρος and Ἀρτυσίλεως, and explains its frequency in the island of Delos by the fact that γογγύλαι μᾶζαι were used in the sacred ceremonies of the Delian festival. The first of the Γογγύλοι was an Ionian Falstaff—the prototype of 'the whoreson round man' of Shakespeare. In Thuc. 1. 128 and Xen. Hell. 3. 1. 6 an Eretrian is so called. Had the proper name been Athenian, and originated in Attic times, it would have been Στρογγύλος, not Γογγύλος, but the designation carries us back to old Ionian days.

LXXXII.

Πάντοτε μὴ λέγε, ἀλλ' ἑκάστοτε καὶ διαπαντός.

'Πάντοτε et ἀπάντοτε a nullo classicorum auctorum usurpatum esse, convenit mihi cum Sturzio, de Dial. Mac. p. 87, cujus copiis mantissam adjicere nolo. Zonaras, Lex. p. 1526, τὸ πάντοτε παρ' οὐδενὶ τῶν δοκίμων εὑρίσκεται.' Lobeck. Add Moeris, 319, πάντοτε οὐδεὶς τῶν Ἀττικῶν.

LXXXIII.

Γενέσια· οὐκ ὀρθῶς τίθεται ἐπὶ τῆς γενεθλίου ἡμέρας. Γενέσια γὰρ Ἀθήνησιν ἑορτή. Λέγειν οὖν δεῖ τὰς γενεθλίους ἡμέρας ἢ γενέθλια.

Of course, γενέσια, in the sense of a *birth-day feast*, is not a misuse for γενέθλια, but simply indicates that in other dialects the word had retained its natural meaning, whereas in Attic it had become fixed to the feast in memory of the birth-day of a *deceased* friend, while its place was taken in the ordinary sense by the newer formation, γενέθλια. Ἑορτή would be out of place if the reference was to a mournful occasion. From Herod. 4. 26 it is plain that all the Greeks celebrated γενέσια, but in Athens the fact that it was the birth-day, and not the death-day, of the dead which they were celebrating, was early lost sight of, probably from the circumstance that it was made a national festival, celebrated in the month Boedromion. The significance of the festival in great part disappeared when men reserved their rejoicing for a day fixed by law; and perhaps Ammonius represents the opinion even of Athenians when he states that it was intended to recall the day of a friend's death (de Diff. Voc. p. 36), Γενέθλια τάσσεται ἐπὶ τῶν ζώντων καὶ ἐν ᾗ ἕκαστος ἡμέρᾳ ἐγεννήθη, γενέσια δὲ ἐπὶ τῶν τεθνηκότων ἐν ᾗ ἕκαστος ἡμέρᾳ τετελεύτηκε. To the same effect is one of the λέξεις ῥητορικαί in Bekker's Anecdota (231. 17), Γενέλθια· τὰ ἐπὶ τῇ ἡμέρᾳ τῆς γενέσεως δῶρα καὶ τὴν εὐωχίαν. Γενέσια· ἑορτὴ παρὰ Ἀθηναίοις πενθήμερος, οἱ δὲ τὰ Νεκύσια.

It may be observed, in passing, that even *γενέθλιος* itself is an old word, and in Attic used only in this connection. Like *γένεθλον* and *γενέθλη*, it is otherwise confined in Attic literature to Tragedy.

LXXXIV.

Ἀργὴ ἡμέρα, μὴ λέγε, ἀλλ' ἀργὸς ἡμέρα καὶ ἀργὸς γυνή, καὶ τὰ λοιπὰ ὁμοίως.

This remark holds true of all Attic Greek; and though inferior manuscripts occasionally present the defaulting forms, the better codices retain the genuine termination. In Cyr. 3. 2. 19, however, Xenophon may have written *ἀργὴ γῆ*. The word is really a compound, *ἀεργός*, and follows the rule of compound adjectives. Those who care to have the late usage established will find copious examples in Lobeck.

LXXXV.

Πνῖγος· ἁμαρτάνοντες οἱ βραχύνοντες τὸ ι· ἐκτείνουσι γὰρ τοὔνομα καὶ τὰ ἀπ' αὐτοῦ, οἷον πνιγηρὰ καλύβη.

The example comes from Thucydides (2. 52), and, according to Lobeck, is an addition by a later hand. It does not illustrate the point at issue.

Moeris (312) has the same caution—*πνῖγος, μακρῶς, Ἀττικῶς· βραχέως, Ἑλληνικῶς*: and *πνίγω* is always long in Attic verse, as—

> *καὶ μὴν πάλαι γ' ἐπνιγόμην τὰ σπλάγχνα κἀπεθύμουν.*
>
> Ar. Nub. 1036.

'Idem in centenis aliis accedit, *βρῖθος, μύρον, τῦφος, σκῦλον, σκύτος, κύτος*, ut librarii inscitia recti nunc acutum pro circumflexo ponerent, nunc acuta circumflecterent.' Lobeck.

LXXXVI.

Ἀποκριθῆναι, διττὸν ἁμάρτημα.. ἔδει γὰρ λέγειν ἀποκρίνασθαι, καὶ εἰδέναι ὅτι τὸ διαχωρισθῆναι σημαίνει, ὥσπεροῦν καὶ τὸ ἐναντίον αὐτοῦ, τὸ συγκριθῆναι, καὶ εἰς ἓν καὶ ταὐτὸν ἐλθεῖν. Εἰδὼς οὖν τοῦτο ἐπὶ μὲν τοῦ ἀποδοῦναι τὴν ἐρώτησιν τὸ ἀποκρίνασθαι λέγε, ἐπὶ δὲ τοῦ διαχωρισθῆναι, τὸ ἀποκριθῆναι.

The distinction is just, and is supported by the usage of all Attic writers. The aorist passive is correctly used by Thucydides (4. 72) and Plato (Legg. 961 B). The latter writer also uses the aorist middle in the sense of *separate for oneself*, in one passage, Legg. 966 D, but the signification of *answer* is attached to it far more frequently: Thuc. 1. 28, 1. 90, 1. 144, 1. 145; 3. 61; 4. 139; 5. 42, etc.; Plato, Prot. 311 C, D, 329 B, 331 A, 338 D, 356 C; Gorg. 447 D, 463 D, 465 E; Legg. 901 C, et al.; Arist. Vesp. 964, 1433, Nub. 345, 1244, Plut. 902, Thesm. 740, et al.

The perfect has legitimately the four meanings, *to have separated for oneself*, *to have been separated*, *to have answered*, *to have been answered;* but no other tense of the passive seems to have been used in the sense of *be answered*. This may be set down to accident, and ἀπεκρίνεται τοῦτο, *this answer is made;* ἀπεκρίθη τοῦτο, *this answer was made*, would certainly not have struck an Attic ear as out of place; but such passive usage of deponents was avoided by good writers in the present and imperfect tenses, and was not common in the aorist, although in the perfect it was of frequent occurrence.

Ἀπεκρίθην, in the sense of *I answered,* is encountered in three passages of the post-Attic Comic poet Machon—

τοῦτ' ἀποκριθῆναί φασι τῷ Βηρισάδῃ.
Athen. 8. 349 D.

ἡ δὲ τοῦτ' ἀπεκρίθη.
Id. 13. 577 D.

ἡ δὲ γελάσασ' ἀπεκρίθη.
Id. 13. 582.

In Xenophon's Anab. 2. 1. 22 there are two readings, ἀπεκρίνατο Κλέαρχος and ἀπεκρίθη ὁ Κλέαρχος, the latter being supported by the best codices. To my own mind there is no doubt that Xenophon employed the un-Attic form, and that ἀπεκρίνατο is merely an early emendation. Strong evidence in favour of this view is supplied by another passage of the same book. Ἀποκρίνομαι replaced in Attic the earlier ἀμείβομαι. In fact, Euripides was the first of the Tragic poets to depart from the tradition of the literary guild to which he belonged, and introduce into his verse the usurping verb (ἀπεκρίνω, I. A. 1354; ἀποκρίναιο, Bacch. 1272; ἀπόκριναι, I. A. 1133). On the other hand, ἀμείβομαι, rare in any sense outside poetry, is certainly unknown to Attic in the signification of *answer*. Like very many other words, which, by their existence in Ionic and in Tragedy, are proved to have been used in Attica at an early date, ἀμείβομαι and ἀπαμείβομαι[1] fell completely into disuse. Xenophon, however, not only employs the words, but actually prefers ἀπημείφθη to ἀπημείψατο, An. 2. 5. 15,

[1] Both ἀμείβομαι and ἀπαμείβομαι are familiar to readers of Homer. In Ionic the simple verb is well known: Hdt. 1. 9, 35, 37, 40, 42, 115, 120; 2. 173, etc.; and in Tragedy is the regular word, Aesch. Eum. 442, 586, Supp. 195, 249; Soph. O. C. 991, Aj. 766, Phil. 378, 844; Eur. Supp. 478, Hipp. 85, Hec. 1196, Rhes. 639, Or. 608, Tro. 903, etc. Xenophon does not eschew it, Mem. 3. 11. 12, Cyn. 9. 14. In any sense the word is singularly rare in Attic—ἀμεῖβον, Plat. Parm. 138 D; ἀμείβοντα, Soph. 224 B; ἀμειβόμενος, Apol. 37 D. Demosthenes, 458. 29, has it in a proverb, τοῖς ὁμοίοις ἀμειβόμενοι.

Κλέαρχος μὲν οὖν τοσαῦτα εἶπε. Τισσαφέρνης δ' ὧδε ἀπημείφθη. Pindar had preceded him in this irregularity—

> τὸν δὲ θαρσήσαις ἀγανοῖσι λόγοις
> ὧδ' ἀμείφθη·
>
> Pyth. 4. 102.

but there is no other instance till late Greek. This fact crowns the testimony of the manuscripts in favour of ἀπεκρίθη, and convicts Xenophon once more of a violation of Attic rule. That the true Attic form is met with in other places of his writings, as ἀπεκρίνατο in the paragraph succeeding that in which ἀπεκρίθη occurs, is an argument of no weight to one who is acquainted with Xenophon's work. Moreover, not even Xenophon uses ἀποκριθήσομαι. In the Συναγωγὴ λέξεων χρησίμων occurs the note: ἀποκρινεῖται λέγουσι μᾶλλον ἢ ἀποκριθήσεται. Μένανδρος Κανηφόρῳ—

> ὁ δ' ἀποκρινεῖται, κἂν ἐγὼ λέγοιμί σοι·

Ὑποβολιμαίᾳ—

> ὡς μηδὲν ἀποκρινουμένῳ δ' οὕτω λαλεῖν.

Aristophanes, however, is of more authority than Menander—

> ἐγὼ γὰρ αὐτίκ' ἀποκρινοῦμαί σοι σαφῶς.
>
> Nub. 1245.

The passive future is first met with in this active sense in very late Greek. The number of Greek verbs in which the aorist in -θην occurs, in an active or middle sense, is very small indeed, if those verbs only are considered which justly belong to it. Many verbs are translated into English as actives which in Greek are genuine passives. Such are the following—

ἐναντιοῦμαι,	oppose,	ἠναντιώθην.
ἑστιῶμαι,	feast,	εἱστιάθην.
εὐωχοῦμαι,	feast,	εὐωχήθην.
ὁρμῶμαι,	rush,	ὡρμήθην.
περαιοῦμαι,	cross,	ἐπεραιώθην.

πλανῶμαι,	wander,	ἐπλανήθην.
πορεύομαι,	go,	ἐπορεύθην.
ποτῶμαι,	fly,	ἐποτήθην[1].
φοβοῦμαι,	fear,	ἐφοβήθην.

This apparent change of meaning may be illustrated by the history of the verb διαιτῶ. All dictionaries give a false history to this word. Its primitive meaning is *to regulate*, and διαιτῶμαι, in the sense of *pass life*, is passive and not middle, and has for aorist the passive form ἐδιῃτήθην. In fact, the aorist middle is only found in the compound καταδιαιτῶ in a regular middle sense, as Lys. 172. 38, δίαιταν καταδιαιτησάμενος οὐδενός, *having got an arbitration delivered against no one.*

With these verbs may be classed the three which from the beginning of Greek literature are practically established as passive deponents—

βούλομαι,	wish,	ἐβουλήθην.
δεόμαι,	beseech,	ἐδεήθην.
δύναμαι,	am able,	ἐδυνήθην.

But the fact of ἐδυνησάμην being found in Homer, together with the difficulty of eliciting their signification from an original passive meaning, makes it probable that they are only early instances of the general tendency illustrated in this article.

That all this class have invariably[2] a future in -ήσομαι is not surprising. The form that is generally called future

[1] The present and aorist are in Attic only poetical, their place in Attic being filled by πέτομαι and ἐπτόμην, but πεπότημαι is the regular perfect.

[2] Forms like δυνηθήσομαι, φοβηθήσομαι, βουληθήσομαι must be carefully avoided. They are debased and late, and almost as reprehensible as the aorists ἐδυνησάμην, ἐφοβησάμην, ἐβουλησάμην. In Plat. Rep. 470 A and other passages φοβήσομαι must be preferred, and even Xenophon (Hell. 6. 5. 20) did not write ἐξωρμήσατο, but the well supported ἐξώρμητο. In Ar. Ran. 138, περαιωθήσομαι, *shall be set across*, is intentionally used to give a different meaning from περαιώσομαι—

A. εἶτα πῶς περαιωθήσομαι;
B. ἐν πλοιαρίῳ τυννουτῳί σ' ἀνὴρ γέρων
ναύτης διάξει δύ' ὀβολὼ μισθὸν λαβών.

It is the exception which proves the rule.

middle, and is constantly noted by lexicographers as a peculiarity when in a passive sense, is far the most common future for the passive voice, as will be demonstrated by me in my larger work.

Now it is the group of verbs just discussed that introduced confusion of voice into the Greek aorist. On the false analogy of *πορεύομαι, πλανῶμαι*, and the others, a passive aorist was assigned to verbs which had no right to the form in *-θην*, just as *ἀπεκρίθην* at a later stage was recognized as equivalent to *ἀπεκρινάμην*, and, conversely, *ἐδυνησάμην* replaced *ἐδυνήθην*. The subjoined groups will exhibit the working of this false principle in Attic times.

I. Verbs which employ the perfect in *-μαι* only in an active sense, and use both the aorists in *-άμην* and *-θην* in the same sense—

ἀρνοῦμαι, deny,	*ἀρνήσομαι*,	*ἠρνησάμην*.
	ἤρνημαι,	*ἠρνήθην*.
μεταχειρίζομαι, manage,	*μετακεχείρισμαι*,	*μετεχειρισάμην*.
	μεταχειριοῦμαι,	*μετεχειρίσθην*.
μιμνήσκομαι, remember,	*μνήσομαι*,	*ἐμνησάμην*.
	μέμνημαι,	*ἐμνήσθην*.
	μνησθήσομαι.	
ὁρμίζομαι, lie at anchor,	*ὥρμισμαι*,	*ὡρμισάμην*.
	ὁρμιοῦμαι,	*ὡρμίσθην*.
παύομαι, cease,	*πέπαυμαι*,	*ἐπαυσάμην*.
	παύσομαι,	*ἐπαύθην*.
	παυθήσομαι.	
φράζομαι (poet.), consider,	*πέφρασμαι*,	*ἐφρασάμην*.
	φράσομαι,	*ἐφράσθην*.
προνοοῦμαι, provide for,	*προνενόημαι*,	*προὐνοησάμην*.
	προνοήσομαι,	*προὐνοήθην*.
ὑπισχνοῦμαι, promise,	*ὑπέσχημαι*,	*ὑπεσχόμην*.
	ὑποσχήσομαι,	*ὑπεσχέθην* (?).

II. Verbs which use the perfect in *-μαι*, both in an active and passive sense, and employ the two aorists in an active sense—

ἀπολογοῦμαι, make a defence,	ἀπολελόγημαι, ἀπολογήσομαι,	ἀπελογησάμην. ἀπελογήθην.
πραγματεύομαι, labour at,	πεπραγμάτευμαι, πραγματεύσομαι,	ἐπραγματευσάμην. ἐπραγματεύθην.

III. Verbs which use the perfect in -μαι, both in a middle and a passive sense, and which have both aorists in an active sense, and that in -θην also in a passive sense—

ἁμιλλῶμαι, strive,	ἡμίλλημαι,	ἡμιλλησάμην. ἡμιλλήθην.
κομίζω, carry, mid. return,	κεκόμισμαι,	ἐκομισάμην. ἐκομίσθην.
λοιδοροῦμαι, rail at,	λελοιδόρημαι,	ἐλοιδορησάμην. ἐλοιδορήθην.
πειρῶ, prove, mid. try,	πεπείραμαι,	ἐπειρασάμην. ἐπειράθην.
πολιτεύω, govern, mid., live as a citizen,	πεπολίτευμαι,	ἐπολιτευσάμην. ἐπολιτεύθην.
πονῶ, labour, mid. δια-,	πεπόνημαι,	διεπονησάμην. (δι)επονήθην.

IV. Verbs which have the perfect in -μαι, both as middle and passive, and the aorist in -θην also in both senses, the aorist in -άμην not being used—

ἀποροῦμαι, doubt, pass. be in doubt, be disputed,	ἠπόρημαι,	ἠπορήθην.
δαπανῶμαι, expend,	δεδαπάνημαι,	ἐδαπανήθην.
διανοοῦμαι, purpose,	διανενόημαι,	διενοήθην.

V. Verbs which use the perfect in -μαι, both as active and passive, but have the aorist in -θην always in an active sense—

διαλέγομαι, discuss,	διείλεγμαι,	διελέχθην.
ἐνθυμοῦμαι, consider,	ἐντεθύμημαι,	ἐνεθυμήθην.

Now in the history of many of these verbs there are facts which distinctly prove that the use of the aorist in

-θην, in a middle or active sense, was comparatively late, and originated in false analogy with verbs like δύναμαι and βούλομαι. Thus the aorist of μιμνήσκομαι is in Homer ἐμνησάμην, and the Tragic poets, as usual, retained the old faith, and rarely admitted the modern ἐμνήσθην, which, from Thucydides' time, is the regular Attic form of the aorist.

Of ἀρνοῦμαι Veitch says, 'In Epic poetry and Ionic prose the aorist middle alone is used; in classical Attic, with the exception of one instance in Euripides, two in Aeschines, and one in Hyperides, the aorist passive.'

The tendency was early at work, as is well shown by πειρῶμαι. Even in the Iliad and Odyssey both ἐπειρήθην and ἐπειρησάμην are met with, but the form in -θην gradually became predominant. Veitch thus traces its history in Attic: 'The aorist middle is confined to Thucydides and Plato. In Thucydides it is the prevailing form, occurring six times, and aorist passive thrice. Plato again has aorist middle once only, the aorist passive eleven times. The compounds, except ἀπο- Thuc. 6. 90; 4. 135, etc., and perhaps κατα- Lys. 30. 34, are, in classic authors, not used in the active, and have, we think, always the aorist of the passive form, ἀποπειρηθῇ, Her. 2. 73; διεπειράθην, Antipho, 5. 33; ἐξεπειράθ-, Eur. Supp. 1089.'

It is only verbs of frequent occurrence that can be regarded in such an inquiry, as they only supply a sufficient number of instances to form trustworthy evidence. Thus the aorist of δαπανῶμαι occurs too seldom to tell us much. There can be no question that ἐδαπανησάμην preceded ἐδαπανήθην, but, as far as our records go, there is no trace of it in Classical Greek. In studying the forms of a dead language, it is necessary to exercise reason and tact in the manipulation of materials. The two last classes proclaim the victory of the form in -θην, but not so plainly as the four verbs ἁμιλλῶμαι, διανοοῦμαι, διαπονοῦμαι, and λοιδοροῦ-

μαι. These are peculiarly significant. Thus *λοιδοροῦμαι* belongs to that class of verbs which have a signification to which, for some reason or other, middle inflexions were regarded as especially applicable. Such verbs are *μέμφομαι, μωμῶμαι, αἰτιῶμαι, ἐπιγλωττῶμαι, χαριεντίζομαι, δημοῦμαι, λυμαίνομαι, λωβῶμαι*, while the vacillation of the future between active and middle in *σκώπτω, τωθάζω, ὑβρίζω*, etc., points to the same phenomenon. Perhaps the explanation of this is the same as of the middle form in *ἁμιλλῶμαι*, and the two compounds of *διά*. Whenever *διά* introduces into the verbal notion the idea of pitting one thing against another, it requires for its verb the endings of the middle voice, even although in the simple the deponent form would be absurd. This is true, not only when the imported idea is the unmistakeable one of rivalry or contention, as *ἀκοντίζειν*, *to throw the javelin*, *διακοντίζεσθαι*, *to contend in throwing the javelin*, but also when it assumes an almost intangible form, as in *διανοεῖσθαι*, which, though ultimately acquiring the meaning of *purpose*, primarily represented the process of *meditation* or the balancing of one thought against another. In this way is explained a considerable group of deponents which imply the comparison of oneself with others, either by actually pitting oneself against them or by mentally making oneself a standard by which to measure them. Thus rivalry of hand, word, or wit, is expressed by the verbs *μάχομαι, ἀγωνίζομαι, ἁμιλλῶμαι, ὠστίζομαι, δικαιολογοῦμαι, ἰδιολογοῦμαι, κοινολογοῦμαι, βιάζομαι*.

Accordingly, when even in verbs of this class the aorist in *-θην* became possible in an active sense, its victory over the genuine middle form might be regarded as complete.

LXXXVII.

Γεννηθῆναι παρὰ Ἐπιχάρμῳ καὶ ἔστι Δώριον· ἀλλ' ὁ Ἀττικίζων γενέσθαι λεγέτω.

There are no instances of ἐγενήθην till Macedonian times, when Philemon and Machon certainly used it—

κἂν δοῦλος ᾖ τις, σάρκα τὴν αὐτὴν ἔχει·
φύσει γὰρ οὐδεὶς δοῦλος ἐγενήθη ποτὲ
ἡ δ' αὖ τύχη τὸ σῶμα κατεδουλώσατο.
Philemon.

Θαλλόν· παρεγενήθη γὰρ εἰς τὴν Ἀττικήν.
Machon, Ath. 13. 582 E.

That Lysias employed it no one will believe on the evidence of the Sophist Apsines (Rhet. Graec. 9. p. 591, Waltz.) who cites the sentence Ἀκράτης λύπης γενηθεῖσα αὑτὴν ἀπέκτεινε. In early recensions of Plato it appeared in two passages, in Legg. 840 D, where γεννηθέντες is now read, and in Phil. 62 D, where ἐξεγενήθη ἡμῖν has been replaced by ἐξεγένεθ' ἡμῖν. The future γενηθήσομαι is equally debased, and in Plato, Parmen. 141 E, is simply absurd. It occurs twice in company with γενήσεται and ἔσται. Τὸ ἔσται καὶ τὸ γενήσεται καὶ τὸ γενηθήσεται and οὔτ' ἔστιν, οὔτ' ἔπειτα γενήσεται, οὔτε γενηθήσεται, οὔτ' ἔσται. 'Inter γενήσεται et γενηθήσεται,' Heindorf remarks, 'quid intersit non video,' and every man of sense will be of his opinion. Perhaps the ν should be doubled. Others may prefer Schleiermacher's γεγενήσεται. All that is certain is that Plato did not write γενηθήσεται, any more than he wrote ἐξεγενήθη in the Philebus, or than Lysias penned γενηθεῖσα. Lobeck's note will supply numerous examples of the defaulting form in late authors, and it is from this source that the Attic texts became corrupted. Even metre was not always an effectual safeguard. Thus the extraordinary form ἀχθεσθήσομαι, which violates one of the most consistent of Attic rules, is found in several passages of prose (Andoc. 26. 7; Plato, Gorg. 506 C; Aeschin. 88. 23), but the fact that in Plato, Rep. 10. 603 E, there are the variants ἀχθέσομαι and ἀχθεσθήσομαι, and in Aesch. in l. c. συναχθησόμενος remains in one codex to indicate the original reading, would of itself be sufficient to condemn the longer form even if the evidence of verse was not added. But when ἀχθεσθήσει is actually exhibited by a good manuscript in Ar. Nub. 1441—

καὶ μὴν ἴσως γ' οὐκ ἀχθέσει παθὼν ἃ νῦν πέπονθας,

the case against the longer form is conclusively established.

LXXXVIII.

Πελαργός· οἱ ἀμαθεῖς ἐκτείνουσι τὸ α, δέον συστέλλειν· πελαργὸς γὰρ οὐδὲν ἄλλ' ἢ Ἐρετριακῶς Πελασγός.

These words still require an interpreter. The following, however, may be the true explanation: 'Eorum verborum sensus ab Müllero in libro de Etruscis 2. 357, declaratus hic est—ciconiae nomen πελαργός α brevi esse, Πελαργός vero α longo pronuntiatum nihil aliud esse quam Eretriacam Pelasgorum nominis formam. Quo simul docemur Pelâsgos pronuntiandum esse, non Pelásgos.' W. Dindorf in Steph. Thes. sub voc.

The two methods of writing the proper name afforded Aristophanes an opportunity for a pun on πελαργός, *a stork*—

τίς δαὶ καθέξει τῆς πόλεως τὸ Πελαργικόν;
Av. 832.

To illustrate the line the Scholiast quotes Callimachus, Τυρσηνῶν τείχισμα Πελαργικόν. In Thuc. 2. 17 one manuscript has Πελαργικόν.

LXXXIX.

Ἀσπάραγος· καὶ τοῦτο δυοῖν ἁμαρτήμασιν ἔχεται, ὅτι τε ἐν τῷ π καὶ οὐκ ἐν τῷ φ λέγεται, καὶ ὅτι ἴδιόν τι φυτόν ἐστιν ἄγριον ὁ ἀσφάραγος καὶ οὐκ ἐν τοῖς ἡμέροις καταλεγόμενον· ὁ γοῦν Κρατῖνος ἐν ἄλλοις ἀγρίοις αὐτὸ καταλέγων φησίν·

Αὐτομάτη δὲ φέρει τιθύμαλον καὶ σφάκον πρὸς αὖον,
ἀσφάραγον, κύτισόν τε· νάπαισι δ' ἀνθέρικος ἐνηβᾷ
καὶ φλόμον ἄφθονον ὥστε παρεῖναι πᾶσι τοῖς ἀγροῖσι[1].

ἅπαντα γὰρ τὰ καταλεγόμενα ἄγρια. οἱ δὲ νῦν τιθέασι τὸ ἓν[2] ἐπὶ παντὸς ἀμαθῶς. τῶν γὰρ λαχάνων αἱ ἄνθαι ὅρμενα καλοῦνται καὶ ἐξορμενίζειν τὸ ἐκβλαστάνειν καὶ ἐξανθεῖν. λέγε οὖν ὅρμενα, ἀλλὰ μὴ ἀσπαράγους, ἀδόκιμον γὰρ λίαν.

The same caution is delivered with greater clearness in App. Soph. 24. 8: *Ἀσφάραγος· διὰ τοῦ φ βοτάνης εἶδος ἀσφάραγος, πρὸς τὰς καθάρσεις ἐπιτήδειον. οἱ δὲ πολλοὶ τὰ ὅρμενα τῶν λαχάνων διὰ τοῦ π ἀσπαράγους καλοῦσι, δυσὶ περιπίπτοντες ἁμαρτήμασιν, ὅτι τε διὰ τοῦ π λέγουσι, δέον διὰ τοῦ φ, καὶ ὅτι τὸ ἰδίως καλούμενον ἐπί τινος πόας ἐπὶ πάντων τῶν ἐξορμενιζόντων λαχάνων τίθενται.* Cp. id. 38. 17: *Ἐξορμενίζειν· τὸ ἐξανθεῖν, ὅπερ οἱ πολλοὶ ἐκβάλλειν λέγουσιν. ὅρμενα γὰρ καλεῖται ὑπὸ τῶν Ἀττικῶν τὰ τῶν λαχάνων ἐξανθήματα. οἱ δὲ πολλοὶ καὶ ἀμαθεῖς* (leg. *ἀμαθῶς*) *ταῦτα ἀσπαράγους καλοῦσιν.*

Other instances of Attic aspiration are *θυηχοῦς* for *θυηκόος*, *σχινδαλμός* for *σκινδαλμός*, *λίσφος* for *λίσπος*, *φιδάκνη* for *πιθάκνη*. The subject is discussed by Weckiein in Cur. Epigraph. pp. 42, 43. Athenaeus in 2. 62 cites from Theopompus—

[1] The metre is given as restored by Hermann and Meineke.

[2] Lobeck omits *τὸ α* after *τιθέασι*. He should have remembered its use as *τὸ ἓν* or *τὸ πρῶτον*. It is here evidently intended to represent the initial *ἀσπάραγος* as opposed to the following *ἀσφάραγος*.

κἄπειτ' ἰδὼν ἀσφάραγον ἐν θάμνῳ τινί,

and from Ameipsias—

οὐ σχῖνος, οὐδ' ἀσφάραγος, οὐ δάφνης κλάδοι,

but asserts that Antiphanes and Aristophon employed the form in π. He even seems to say that Diphilus used ἀσφάραγος for ὄρμενον: Δίφιλος δέ φησιν ὡς ὁ τῆς κράμβης ἀσφάραγος, λεγόμενος ἰδίως ὄρμενος, εὐστομαχατώτερός ἐστι καὶ εὐεκκριτώτερος, ὄψεως δὲ βλαπτικός.

XC.

Ἀσβόλη μὴ λέγε, ἀλλὰ ἄσβολος.

The same remark is made by Moeris, p. 11. In App. Soph. p. 17 Phrynichus supplements his present statement: Ἄσβολος θηλυκῶς λέγουσιν, Ἱππῶναξ δὲ ἀρσενικῶς· τινὲς δὲ καὶ τὴν ἀσβόλην.

XCI.

Αἴθαλος λέγε ἀρσενικῶς, ἀλλὰ μὴ αἰθάλη θηλυκῶς.

Heinrich Schmidt in his 'Synonymik,' 2. p. 373, has shown that *αἴθαλος* differs from *ἄσβολος* in connoting the action of fire as productive of a black colour. He quotes *αἰθός* in Ar. Thesm. 246—

φῦ, ἰοῦ τῆς ἀσβόλου·
αἰθὸς γεγένημαι πάντα τὰ περὶ τὴν τράμιν,

and justly ridicules the ordinary explanation of the expression *αἴθοψ καπνός* in Od. 10. 152, as smoke mixed with flame—a meaning which might apply to the smoke from Vulcan's forge, but not to that gently curling from Circe's home. *Αἰθός*, *αἴθοψ*, and *αἰθών*, when meaning *black*, always imply that the colour has been produced by fire. Accordingly, *αἴθοψ οἶνος* is not the same as *μέλας οἶνος*, or even *ἐρυθρὸς οἶνος*, and does not refer to colour at all, but to the effect on the blood of the drinker, 'fiery wine.' The *Αἴθοπες* received the name from early travellers who imagined that their swart colour was produced by exposure to the sun.

XCII.

Θερμότης λέγε, ἀλλὰ μὴ θερμασία.

The one word is formed from *θερμός*, the other from *θερμαίνω*. Phrynichus is right, and no Attic writer could have employed *θερμασία*. The general rule of which it is a violation is simple enough. Whenever there exists an adjective in *-ος* which may be regarded as the primitive of a verb in *-αίνω*, the abstract substantive is in Attic formed in *-της* from the adjective, not in *-ασία* from the verb, as *θερμός, θερμαίνω, θερμότης, λευκός, λευκαίνω, λευκότης, ἐρυθρός, ἐρυθραίνω, ἐρυθρότης, ὑγρός, ὑγραίνω, ὑγρότης, ξηρός, ξηραίνω, ξηρότης*. No such substantives as *ὑγρασία, ξηρασία,* or *θερμασία*, are ever encountered in a genuine Attic writer. They are the spawn of late writers and their badge, and Xenophon was, as usual, anticipating them when he employed *θερμασία* in An. 5. 8. 15. Even when there is no adjective, the substantive is not so formed from the verb. The true form is *φλεγμονή* not *φλεγμασία, ὄσφρησις* not *ὀσφρασία*. Thomas, p. 441, adds to the statement of Phrynichus when he says, *θερμότης καὶ θέρμη Ἀττικοί, θερμασία Ἕλληνες*. There are not many forms like *θέρμη*. Besides it *κάκη* was in common use, and *λεύκη, λεύκαι* was the name applied to a form of leprosy. It is natural to compare the English term 'the blues' and to remark that the old name for jaundice, namely, *the yellows*, lingers in the provincial districts of England.

XCIII.

Ἀτταγήν· καὶ τοῦτο παρανενόμηται καὶ τόνῳ καὶ θέσει. χρὴ γὰρ ἀτταγᾶς λέγειν, ὥσπερ ἀλλᾶς.

A grammarian in the Συναγωγὴ λέξεων χρησίμων is more precise: Ἀτταγᾶς· ὄρνις οὕτω καλεῖται ὑπὸ τῶν Ἀττικῶν. Ἀριστοφάνης Σφηξί—

τὸν πηλὸν ὥσπερ ἀτταγᾶς τυρβάσεις βαδίζων.

καὶ αἱ πλάγιοι ἀτταγᾶν καὶ ἀτταγᾶς πληθυντικῶς.

Ἀλλᾶς is not a real parallel as its genitive is ἀλλᾶντος. It was intended by Phrynichus simply to illustrate the accentuation which in ἀτταγᾶς is peculiar. Athen. 9. 387 F: περισπῶσι δὲ οἱ Ἀττικοὶ παρὰ τὸν ὀρθὸν λόγον τοὔνομα. Τὰ γὰρ εἰς ας λήγοντα ἐκτεταμένον ὑπὲρ δύο συλλαβάς, ὅτε ἔχει τὸ α παραλῆγον, βαρύτονά ἐστιν οἷον ἀκάμας, Σακάδας, ἀθάμας. λεκτέον δὲ καὶ ἀτταγαῖ καὶ οὐχὶ ἀτταγῆνες.

XCIV.

Κολυμβάδες ἐλαῖαι οὐ λέγονται, ἀλλὰ ἁλμάδες ἐλᾶαι χωρὶς τοῦ ι.

This is an apt illustration of the singular purity of Attic Greek. It contents inself with saying no more than is necessary, whereas κολυμβάδες is a weak attempt at a picturesque designation. In describing the different kinds of olives, Athenaeus, 1. 56, quotes two lines of Aristophanes—

οὐ ταὐτόν ἐστιν ἁλμάδες καὶ στέμφυλα,

and—

θλαστὰς γὰρ εἶναι κρεῖττόν ἐστιν ἁλμάδος.

For the orthography of ἐλάα see supra p. 112.

XCV.

Γρηγορῶ, γρηγορεῖ οὐ δεῖ, ἀλλὰ ἐγρήγορα λέγειν καὶ ἐγρήγορεν.

Porson first removed the defaulting present from Attic texts, restoring ἐγρηγόρεσαν for ἐγρηγόρησαν in Xen. An. 4. 6. 22. It is a most debased form and crept into classical manuscripts at a late date.

The perfect tense had originally in Greek a very different meaning from that of the English perfect. Thus the words *the door has been opened*, direct the attention to a process rather than to a fact, but in Greek the converse is true, and ἡ θύρα ἀνέῳκται originally meant *the door is open*, without any reference to the process of opening. There is in fact no means of expressing ἀνέῳκται in English, as *is open* implies too little, and *is opened* implies too much. *Is open* is too absolute and does not convey the notion of agency, and *is opened* is not absolute enough, still referring too much to the process of which it marks the completion. The same is true of the pluperfect and the future perfect, ἀνέῳκτο hitting the mean between *was open* and *was opened*, and ἀνεῴξεται between *shall be open* and *shall be opened*.

But when an attempt is made to express the primitive force of the Greek perfect in the active the English language fails still more signally, and the word has to be turned passively. In other words ἀνέῳχα τὴν θύραν is not *I have opened the door*, but represents an agent at the completion of his action, without any reference to the steps which led to that condition of things.

This is the meaning which the perfect generally has in the Homeric poems, e. g.—

> ἡμεῖς δ' ὅπλα ἕκαστα πονησάμενοι κατὰ νῆα
> ἥμεθα, τὴν δ' ἄνεμός τε κυβερνήτης τ' ἴθυνεν.

τῆς δὲ πανημερίης τέταθ' ἱστία ποντοπορούσης·
δύσετό τ' ἠέλιος, σκιόωντό τε πᾶσαι ἀγυιαί·
Od. 11. 10.

and in an earlier stage of the language the numerous perfects with a so-called present meaning had their origin. ἐγρήγορα, *I am awake*, δέδοικα, *I fear*, εἴωθα, *I am used*, ἄνωγα, *I bid*, δέδορκα, *I see*, τέθηλα, *I flourish*, σέσηπα, *I moulder*, κέχηνα, *I gape*, σέσηρα, *I grin*, etc. The perfect form of many of these words, such as κέχηνα, δέδορκα, σέσηρα, it would be quite impossible to explain on any other hypothesis as to the original force of the perfect.

Although the Greek perfect never lost this meaning, it gradually assumed much of the same force as we associate with the tense and approached our idiom in most respects. Thus even in Homer it had begun to be used for the aorist with the adverbs (χρονικὰ ἐπιρρήματα), ἤδη, πολλάκις, πω, πώποτε, a usage which was quite incompatible with its primitive signification, but which is not rare in Attic.

XCVI.

Αὐθέντης μηδέποτε χρήσῃ ἐπὶ τοῦ δεσπότης, ὡς οἱ περὶ τὰ δικαστήρια ῥήτορες, ἀλλ' ἐπὶ τοῦ αὐτόχειρος φονέως.

There are two ways of accounting for the only exception to this rule, that in Eur. Supp. 442—

καὶ μὴν ὅπου γε δῆμος αὐθέντης χθονός,
ὑποῦσιν ἀστοῖς ἥδεται νεανίαις.

Either *αὐθέντης* is, as Markland conjectured, an error of the copyists for εὐθυντής, or Tragedy has here, as often, preserved an old meaning. The late signification of *master* must have had some origin, and it is more natural to regard it as entering the Common dialect from some of the older ones than as being a perversion of the meaning recommended by Phrynichus, and frequent in early Attic.

Latterly *αὐθέντης* disappeared from Attic, even in its recognized sense, its place being usurped by *αὐτόχειρ*. Appearing in Herodotus, in Tragedy, and in Thucydides and Antiphon, it finally succumbed to the law of parsimony, like many other words which are not found in any but the earliest masters of Attic prose.

XCVII.

Ἀγήοχεν, εἴ τις εἴποι, ὅτι ἐν τῷ συνθέτῳ Λυσίας κέχρηται καταγηόχασι, μὴ πάνυ πείθου· ἦχε μὲν γὰρ λέγουσι καὶ Δημοσθένης ἤχασι λέγει, ἀλλ' οὐκ ἀγηόχασι.

The passage of Lysias here referred to has not been preserved. The form occurs in Aristotle, Polybius, Plutarch, and other late writers, while some authors used both the disyllabic and quadrisyllabic words.

Notwithstanding the general opinion as to the purity of Lysias' diction, there are to be found in his writings many slight divergences from Attic usage, which are to be attributed to the fact that by far the greater part of his life was spent in Magna Graecia. He dwelt, it is true, among Athenians, but Athenians who, as colonists, were dissociated entirely from the peculiar civilization of Athens, and from the intellectual and refining influences of its fascinating city life, while, at the same time, they were necessarily thrown more into contact with men of other Greek races.

XCVIII.

Μεσιδιωθῆναι· τέτριπται καὶ ἐν τοῖς δικαστηρίοις καὶ ἐν τοῖς συμβολαίοις, ἀλλὰ σὺ μεσεγγυηθῆναι λέγε.

'*Μεσίδιος* praeter binos Aristotelis locos (Eth. Nic. 7. 1132.

a23, Pol. 6. 1306. a28) reperitur in Michael. in V. Nicom. p. 66 b. ex ipso Aristotele depromptum; *μέσον δικαστήν* vocat Thucydides, 4. 83, *μεσιδιωθῆναι* autem, sive a nullo scriptorum eorum, quos fortuna nobis reliquos fecit, admissum est, sive adhuc in angulo quodam inaccesso latet, nobis certe invisum inauditumque erat.' Lobeck.

XCIX.

Καλλιγραφεῖν, διαλελυμένως λέγουσιν ἐκεῖνοι εἰς κάλλος γράφειν·

As far as formation goes the word is quite legitimate, as is shown by *καλλιεπῶ* and *καλλιερῶ*. It is only a question of usage, and certainly *καλλιγραφῶ* does not occur before Aristotle. '*Καλλιγραφεῖν* primum mihi occurrit sensu figurato in *subditicia* Aristotelis Epistola ad Alexandrum Rhetoricae praefixa.' Lobeck.

C.

Ἀκμὴν ἀντὶ τοῦ ἔτι· Ξενοφῶντα λέγουσιν ἅπαξ αὐτῷ κεχρῆσθαι· σὺ δὲ φυλάττου, λέγε δὲ ἔτι.

The signification here reprehended used to be required in Isocrates, 1 C, before *σὺ μὲν ἀκμὴν φιλοσοφεῖς* was replaced by *σοὶ μὲν ἀκμὴ φιλοσοφεῖν*. It is an excellent instance of the copyists' habit of importing the usages of their own day into the texts of Classical authors. Xenophon, however, is past praying for; Moeris (p. 79), as well as Phrynichus, states that in this point he departed from Attic usage, and in An. 4. 3. 26 *ἀκμήν* is employed as Polybius, Strabo, Plutarch, Theocritus, and their contemporaries employed the term. There is nothing to choose between Xenophon's *καὶ ὁ ὄχλος ἀκμὴν διέβαινε*, and Polybius, 1. 25. 2, *συνιδόντες τοὺς μὲν ἀκμὴν ἐμβαίνοντας, τοὺς δὲ ἀναγομένους*, or id. 6. 51, *παρὰ μὲν τοῖς Καρχηδονίοις τὴν δύναμιν ὁ δῆμος ἤδη μετειλήφει, παρὰ δὲ Ῥωμαίοις ἀκμὴν εἶχεν ἡ σύγκλητος.*

'Suïdas Sophoclem et Hyperidem testes citat; de Sophocle manifesto errat; Hyperidem testem adhibet in hac causa etiam Antiatticista Bekk. p. 77, sed locum non apposuit, neque fidem fecit judicii sui.' Lobeck.

CI.

Εἶτεν καὶ ἔπειτεν ἐσχάτως βάρβαρα· εἶτα οὖν σὺ καὶ ἔπειτα λέγε.

Aelius Dionysius, whose opinion is always worthy of consideration, is quoted by Eustath. 1158. 38, *ἐν τοῖς Διονυσίου φέρεται ὅτι Ἀττικὰ μὲν τὸ εἶτα καὶ ἔπειτα, τὸ δὲ εἶτεν καὶ ἔπειτεν, Ἰακά. διό, φησί, καὶ παρ' Ἡροδότῳ κεῖνται.* In most manuscripts of Herodotus, however, *εἶτα* and *ἔπειτα*, or *ἐπεί τε*, are now read, e.g. 1. 146; 2. 52; 9. 84, 98. In Arist. Ach. 745, the un-Attic form is put in a Megarian's mouth—

κἤπειτεν ἐς τὸν σάκκον ὧδ' ἐσβαίνετε.

Machon, the late Comic poet, whose name has already occurred in a similar connection, used *ἔπειτεν* (Athen. 13. 582 A), and *ἔπειτεν εἰπεῖν* was justly restored for *ἔπειτ' ἐνεῖπεν* by Porson in another line of the same writer—

ἔπειτεν εἰπεῖν φασι τὴν Γναθαίνιον.

Ath. 13. 581 F.

CII.

Ἀνατέλλει μὲν ἐρεῖς ὁ ἥλιος, ἐπιτέλλει δὲ ὁ κύων, ἢ ὁ Ὠρίων, ἢ ἄλλο τι τῶν μὴ ὡσαύτως τῷ ἡλίῳ καὶ τῇ σελήνῃ πολευόντων.

This distinction between ἀνατέλλω and ἐπιτέλλω, ἀνατολή and ἐπιτολή, is always carefully observed in Attic prose. Plat. Polit. 269 A, Legg. 887 E, Crat. 409 A; Ar. Nub. 754; Thuc. 2. 78. In poetry it is not always regarded, and even the simple verb may be used of either phenomenon. Ἐπιτολή and ἐπιτέλλω, however, are not used of the sun till very late. The meaning of the ἐπί is the same as is found in ἐπέρχομαι in phrases like ἐπήλυθον ὧραι in—

> ἀλλ' ὅτε τέτρατον ἦλθεν ἔτος καὶ ἐπήλυθον ὧραι.
> Od. 2. 107.
>
> ἀλλ' ὅτε δὴ μῆνές τε καὶ ἡμέραι ἐξετελεῦντο
> ἂψ περιτελλομένου ἔτεος καὶ ἐπήλυθον ὧραι.
> 11. 294.

CIII.

Εὐκαιρεῖν οὐ λεκτέον, ἀλλ' εὖ σχολῆς ἔχειν.

The words εὔκαιρος and εὐκαιρία are excellent Attic words, but not in the sense of σχολαῖος and σχολή. Photius: Σχολή. οὐχί ὁ τόπος ἐν ᾧ σχολάζουσι καὶ διατρίβουσι περὶ παιδείαν· οὐδὲ αὐτὴ ἡ ἐν λόγοις (εὐμουσία) καὶ διατριβή, ἀλλὰ ἣν οἱ πολλοὶ ἀκύρως καλοῦσιν εὐκαιρίαν· τὸ δὲ εὐκαιρεῖν βάρβαρον, ἀλλ' ἀντὶ μὲν τούτου σχολὴν ἄγειν λέγουσιν. ἡ δὲ εὐκαιρία βάρβαρον οὐκ ἔστιν ὄνομα, τάττεται δὲ οὐκ ἐπὶ σχολῆς, ἀλλ' ἐπὶ καιροῦ τινὸς εὐφυΐας καὶ ἀρετῆς.

CIV.

Ἐξεπιπολῆς λέγουσί τινες, οἰόμενοι ὅμοιον εἶναι τῷ ἐξαίφνης, οἷον ἐξεπιπολῆς τοῦ παντός. ἀτόπως· οἱ γὰρ ἀρχαῖοι ἄνευ τῆς ἐξ προθέσεως εἶπον ἐπιπολῆς.

In App. Soph. 38. 3 Phrynichus traces this corruption to false analogy: οἱ δὲ ἐξεπιπολῆς λέγοντες ἐπλανήθησαν ἀπὸ τοῦ ἐξαίφνης καὶ ἐξεπίτηδες. It is another instance of the misuse discussed above, pp. 117 ff. Late writers elevated the adverb into a substantive, forming a nominative ἐπιπολή, and declining it throughout. They combined their new creation with other prepositions besides ἐξ. Athenaeus used δι' ἐπιπολῆς, and Strabo actually ἐπ' ἐπιπολῆς. The fact that an elevated quarter of the city of Syracuse was named Ἐπιπολαί (Thuc. 6. 96) does not prove the early existence of the substantive ἐπιπολή. It does not mean *surfaces*, but, derived in the same way as ἐπιπολῆς, adopted the termination αι on the analogy of Ἀθῆναι, Θηβαί, etc., just as the -ῆς in the adverb stands on the same footing as the similar ending of ἐξαίφνης.

CV.

Ἔνδον εἰσέρχομαι, βάρβαρον. ἔνδον γάρ ἐστί, καὶ ἔνδον εἰμί, δόκιμον. δεῖ οὖν εἴσω παρέρχομαι λέγειν. εἴσω δὲ διατρίβω οὐκ ἐρεῖς, ἀλλ' ἔνδον διατρίβω.

The collocation ἔνδον εἰσέρχομαι stands on a different basis from εἴσω διατρίβω, being a distinct violation when used absolutely of the law of parsimony, and, consequently, un-Attic. As a synonym for the simple εἰσέρχομαι, Phrynichus rightly suggests εἴσω παρέρχομαι. But, although ἔνδον as used for εἴσω is as barbarous as εἴσω εἰσέρχομαι would be, the converse is not true, and Attic writers frequently employ εἴσω with verbs of rest, as any dictionary will show.

CVI.

Κληρονομεῖν τόνδε· οὐχ οὕτως ἡ ἀρχαία χρῆσις, ἀλλὰ κληρονομεῖν τοῦδε.

A sentence of Demosthenes illustrates the only usage possible in Attic, 329. 15, *κεκληρονόμηκας μὲν τῶν Φίλωνος τοῦ κηδεστοῦ χρημάτων πλείονων ἢ πεντεταλάντων*, the genitive of the person being dependent upon the genitive of the thing which is governed by the verb. In late Greek the ordinary construction was the accusative in either case—*κληρονομεῖν τί τινος* and *κληρονομεῖν τινά*.

CVII.

Θρίδακα Ἡρόδοτος ἰάζων εἶπεν, ἡμεῖς δὲ θριδακίνην ὡς Ἀττικοί.

This is another instance of the Common dialect preferentially departing from the premier dialect. The lexicography of the word is given in detail by Lobeck.

CVIII.

Ἐπίκλιντρον ῥητέον, οὐκ ἀνάκλιντρον.

Pollux makes the same statement (10. 34): *Μέρη δὲ κλίνης καὶ ἐνήλατα καὶ ἐπίκλιντρον· τὸ μὲν ἐπίκλιντρον ὑπὸ Ἀριστοφάνους εἰρημένον. Σοφοκλῆς δὲ εἶπε ἐνήλατα ξύλα*: id. 6. 9, *τὸ καλούμενον ἀνάκλιντρον ἐπίκλιντρον Ἀριστοφάνης εἶπε, τὸ δὲ ἐνήλατον κλιντήριον.* In 9. 72 he quotes, for a different purpose, two lines from the Anagyrus of Aristophanes—

τοῦτ᾽ αὐτὸ πράττω δύ᾽ ὀβολὼ καὶ σύμβολον
ὑπὸ τῷ ᾽πικλίντρῳ· μῶν τις αὔτ᾽ ἀνείλετο;

The question must rest upon their authority.

CIX.

'Επίδοξον, τὸ προσδοκώμενον καὶ ἐλπιζόμενον ἐρεῖς, οὐχ, ὡς οἱ ἀμαθεῖς, τὸν ἐπίσημον.

Like verbs of hoping and expecting, ἐπίδοξος may be followed by the present and aorist as well as by the regular tense—the future infinitive. Isocr. 397 C, ἐπίδοξος γενήσεσθαι πονηρός: Antipho, 115. 22, τὸν μεγάλα μὲν κακὰ προπεπονθότα, ἔτι δὲ μείζονα ἐπίδοξον ὄντα πάσχειν: Isocr. 117 E, ἐπίδοξος ὢν τυχεῖν τῆς τιμῆς. The preposition seems to have the same force as in the word ἐπίτεξ or ἐπίτοκος.

There is no instance in Attic of the meaning here found fault with by Phrynichus, but that is its prevailing sense in late writers. The signification ἐπίσημος was not, however, a coinage of the Common dialect, but existed outside the precincts of Attic even in Classical times, as is proved by Pindar—

εἰ γὰρ ἅμα κτεάνοις πολλοῖς ἐπίδοξον ἄρηται
κῦδος, κτε.

Nem. 9. 46.

CX.

Μάμμην τὴν τοῦ πατρὸς ἢ μητρὸς μητέρα οὐ λέγουσιν οἱ ἀρχαῖοι ἀλλὰ τήθην, μάμμην δὲ καὶ μαμμίον τὴν μητέρα. ἀμαθὲς οὖν τὸ τὴν μάμμην ἐπὶ τῆς τήθης λέγειν.

'Phrynichi praescriptum plerique recentiorum neglectum reliquere, aviam μάμμην dicentes, Josephus, Plutarchus, Appianus, Herodianus, Artemidorus, Basilius, neque adversari videtur Pollux, 3. 17, ἡ δὲ πατρὸς ἢ μητρὸς μήτηρ τήθη καὶ μάμμη καὶ μάμμα. Sed cum Phrynicho faciunt acriores vitiorum inolescentium animadversores, Aelius Dionysius, Helladius, Moeris, Photius, Suïdas.' Lobeck.

CXI.

Εἰ ποιητὴς εἶπεν ἀμεινότερον, χαιρέτω· οὐδὲ γὰρ καλλιώτερον, οὐδὲ κρεισσότερον ῥητέον. συγκριτικοῦ γὰρ συγκριτικὸν οὐ γίνεται. λέγε οὖν ἄμεινον καὶ κάλλιον καὶ κρεῖσσον.

Stobaeus (Flor. 7. 12. 9) quotes from Mimnermus—

οὐ γάρ τις κείνου δηΐων ἔτ' ἀμεινότερος φὼς
ἔσκεν ἐποίχεσθαι φυλοπίδος κρατερῆς
ἔργον.

The forms *χειρότερος*, *χερειότερος*, are not double comparatives. That *καλλιώτερον* once appeared in Thuc. 4. 118 indicates that this remark of Phrynichus was not uncalled for. 'Recentiores cum similibus *μειζότερος*, *ἐλαχιστότατος*, usi sunt.' Lobeck.

CXII.

Μονόφθαλμον οὐ ῥητέον, ἑτερόφθαλμον δέ. Κρατῖνος δὲ μονόφθαλμον εἶπε τὸν Κύκλωπα.

Lobeck supposes the words *Κρατῖνος δὲ μονόφθαλμον εἶπε τὸν Κύκλωπα* to be a late addition, but they appear in the *Συλλ. Ἀττικ.* of Moschopulus, and may well be genuine, as *μονόφθαλμος* or *μονόμματος* is the natural word for a Cyclops. A writer in the *Λέξεις Ῥητορικαί* (Bekk. 280. 22) has the remark: *Μονόφθαλμος· ἔθνος τι ἀνθρώπων ἕνα ὀφθαλμὸν ἐχόντων· τοὺς γὰρ τὸν ἕτερον ἐκκοπέντας ὀφθαλμὸν ἑτεροφθάλμους καλοῦσιν*, and Strabo, 1. 43, quotes *μονόμματος* from Aeschylus, *Αἰσχύλου κυνοκεφάλους καὶ στερνοφθάλμους καὶ μονομμάτους ἱστοροῦντος.*

Ammonius makes the same distinction: *Ἑτερόφθαλμος καὶ μονόφθαλμος διαφέρουσιν. Ἑτερόφθαλμος μὲν γὰρ ὁ κατὰ περίπ-*

τωσιν πηρωθεὶς τὸν ἕτερον τῶν ὀφθαλμῶν, μονόφθαλμος δὲ ὁ ἕνα μόνον ὀφθαλμὸν ἔχων ὡς ὁ Κύκλωψ.

It is an interesting question how the later notion of the Cyclopes originated. In Homer the Cyclops is *ἑτερόφθαλμος*, not *μονόφθαλμος*, as Aristarchus plainly saw. On Odyss. 9. 383 he has the remark, *ὁ Κύκλωψ κατὰ τὸν Ὅμηρον οὐκ ἦν μονόφθαλμος φύσει, ἀλλὰ κατά τινα συντυχίαν τὸν ἕτερον τῶν ὀφθαλμῶν ἀπεβεβλήκει. δύο γὰρ ὀφρύας εἶχε· φησὶ γάρ*—

πάντα δέ οἱ βλέφαρ' ἀμφὶ καὶ ὀφρύας εὗσεν ἀϋτμή.

By the time of Hesiod the later notion prevailed, as is seen from two lines of the Theogon. 144—

Κύκλωπες δ' ὄνομ' ἦσαν ἐπώνυμον οὕνεκ' ἄρα σφέων
κυκλοτερὴς ὀφθαλμὸς ἕεις ἐνέκειτο μετώπῳ,

and became as firmly established as the similar erroneous notion that the Sirens were three in number, whereas Homer plainly says there were but two. Some mistake of an early potter probably originated both errors, and fictile ware tells the same story as Hesiod, Cratinus, and Theocritus, 11. 31—

ὥνεκά μοι λασία μὲν ὀφρῦς ἐπὶ παντὶ μετώπῳ.

CXIII.

Ἐωνησάμην· εἷς λόγος περὶ τοῦ ἁμαρτήματος. ἔνθα ἂν μὴ δυνήθῃς τὸ πρίασθαι ἢ ἐπριάμην θεῖναι, ἐκεῖ τὰ ἀπὸ τοῦ ὠνοῦμαι[1] τάττε, ἔνθα δ' ἂν τὰ ἀπὸ τοῦ πρίασθαι, φυλάττου θάτερον.

[1] The MSS. and editions have the unmeaning *ἐώνημαι*. After *θάτερον* they add *οἷον ἐώνημαι οἰκίαν· ἐνταῦθα ἐγχωρεῖ τὸ ἐπριάμην οὕτω χρήσῃ ἐπριάμην οἰκίαν. πάλιν ἔτυχον ἐωνημένος οἰκίαν ἢ ἀγρόν· ἐνταῦθα οὐδὲν ἐγχωρεῖ τῶν ἀπὸ τῶν πρίασθαι· μένει τὸ ἐωνημένος δόκιμον. πάλιν δεῖ λέγειν πριάμενος, τὸ γὰρ ὠνησάμενος ἀδόκιμον· οὕτως οὖν κἀπὶ τοῦ ἐωνησάμην· παρὸν γὰρ ἐπριάμην εἰπεῖν, μὴ εἴπῃς ἐωνησάμην· ὁ γὰρ τοῦτο λέγων ληρεῖ.* Lobeck justly says, 'alto hic Phrynichus demersus est luto;' but he fails in trying to extricate him. It is strange that the words following *οἷον* in Phrynichus should so frequently be unintelligible or contradictory to the rule he lays down. They seem frequently to be late additions.

Herodian (453 ed. Piers.) likewise remarks on the way in which the two stems *ὠνε-* and *πρι-* were combined in Attic to make up the verb corresponding to the English 'buy.' His words are these, *πρίασθαι ἐρεῖς, οὐκ ὠνήσασθαι· ὅπου δὲ μὴ δυνατὸν κλῖναι τὸ πρίασθαι ῥῆμα, τότε τῷ ὠνεῖσθαι χρήσῃ, οἷον ἐπριάμην, ἐπρίω, ἐπρίατο· καὶ πρίω τὸ προστατικόν.* Εὔπολις *πρίω μοι σελάχιον φησί. ἐπὶ δὲ τοῦ παρακειμένου ἐώνημαι, οὐ γὰρ ἐνεχώρει ὁ παρακείμενος τὴν τοῦ πρίασθαι χρῆσιν.* These dicta are confirmed by other authorities and by the universal usage of Attic writers. The following passages will put in the clearest light the dovetailing of the two verbs into one another. In the 'Acharnians' Dicaeopolis asks the price of the Boeotian's pigs—

> *πόσου πρίωμαί σοι τὰ χοιρίδια; λέγε·*

and when the answer is satisfactory makes up his mind to buy them—

> *ὠνήσομαί σοι· περίμεν' αὐτοῦ.*

The enormous sums expended upon fish by Athenian epicures is a common-place in the Middle and New Comedy, and a passage of this kind is quoted by Athenaeus (6. 227 A) from the 'Greek Woman' of Alexis—

> *αὐτοί (οἱ ἴχθυες) τ' ἐπὰν ληφθῶσιν ὑπὸ τῶν ἁλιέων*
> *τεθνεῶτες ἐπιτρίβουσι τοὺς ὠνουμένους.*
> *τῆς οὐσίας γάρ εἰσιν ἡμῖν ὤνιοι,*
> *ὁ πριάμενός τε πτωχὸς εὐθὺς ἀποτρέχει:*

Plato, Rep. 563 B, *ὅταν δὲ οἱ ἐωνημένοι μηδὲν ἧττον ἐλεύθεροι ὦσι τῶν πριαμένων*: Lysias, 108. 35, *'Αντικλῆς παρ' αὐτοῦ πριάμενος ἐξεμίσθωσεν· ἐγὼ δὲ παρ' 'Αντικλέους εἰρήνης οὔσης ἐωνούμην*: Dem. 307. 15, *ὁ ὠνούμενος νενίκηκε τὸν λαβόντα ἐὰν πρίηται.*

But the locus classicus is the speech of Lysias against the corn merchants (*Κατὰ τῶν σιτοπωλῶν*): *'Εγὼ τῶν ἀρχόντων κελευόντων συνεπριάμην.*

Ἂν μὲν τοίνυν ἀποδείξῃ, ὦ ἄνδρες δικασταί, ὡς ἔστι νόμος ὃς κελεύει τοὺς σιτοπώλας συνωνεῖσθαι τὸν σῖτον, ἂν οἱ ἄρχοντες κελεύωσιν, ἀποψηφίσασθε. εἰ δὲ μή, δίκαιον ὑμᾶς καταψηφίσασθαι. ἡμεῖς γὰρ ὑμῖν παρεσχόμεθα τὸν νόμον ὃς ἀπαγορεύει μηδένα τῶν ἐν τῇ πόλει πλείω σῖτον πεντήκοντα φορμῶν συνωνεῖσθαι.

Ἄνυτος δ' ἔλεγεν ὡς . . . . συμβουλεύσειεν αὐτοῖς παύσασθαι φιλονικοῦσιν, ἡγούμενος συμφέρειν ὑμῖν τοῖς παρὰ τούτων ὠνουμένοις ὡς ἀξιώτατον τούτους πρίασθαι. δεῖν γὰρ αὐτοὺς ὀβολῷ μόνον πωλεῖν τιμιώτερον. ὡς τοίνυν οὐ συμπριαμένους καταθέσθαι ἐκέλευεν αὐτοὺς ἀλλὰ μὴ ἀλλήλοις ἀντωνεῖσθαι συνεβούλευεν, αὐτὸν ὑμῖν Ἄνυτον μάρτυρα παρέξομαι, καὶ ὡς οὗτος μὲν ἐπὶ τῆς προτέρας βουλῆς τούτους εἶπε τοὺς λόγους, οὗτοι δ' ἐπὶ τήνδε συνωνούμενοι φαίνονται [1].

It may be useful to add a detailed list of the tenses and moods as used by Attic writers. The references are chiefly to Aristophanes:—

ὠνοῦμαι, Arist. Av. 530, Eccl. 1002. *Subjunctive*, Lys. 560, Vesp. 493. *Optative*, Eq. 649. *Participle*, Nub. 1224, Thesm. 504, Eq. 897, Ach. 549.

ἐωνούμην, Fr. Com. (Eupolis), 2. 505, and Orators.

ὠνήσομαι, Arist. Plut. 140, 518, Ach. 815, Eq. 362, Pax 1239, 1252, 1261, Vesp. 304, Lys. 600, Eccl. 1034; Orators.

ἐπριάμην, Arist. Nub. 23, 864, Eq. 44, 676, Thesm. 503, Pax 1200, 1241. 2nd sing. ἐπρίω, Vesp. 1439. *Subjunctive*, Ach. 812, Ran. 1229, Nub. 614. *Optative*, Pax 21, 1223, Vesp. 1405, Ach. 737. *Imperative*, πρίω, Ach. 34, 35; Fr. Com. 2. 743, 883; ἀποπρίω, Ran. 1227 [2]. *Infinitive*, Ach. 691, 749, Vesp. 253, 294, Av. 715. *Participle*, Ach. 901, Eq. 600, 872, Nub. 749, Plut. 883.

[1] Cp. Xen. Vect. 4. 18, πριάσθαι . . . ὠνήθη . . . ὠνοῦνται . . . ὠνηθέντα.

[2] Good MSS. read πρίω for πρίῃ in Nub. 614. The form πρίασο in Ach. 870 is probably Attic. Veitch, however, errs when he puts it on the same footing as πρίω in id. 34 by the remark 'both in trimeter,' for he has not observed that πρίασο is put into the mouth of a Boeotian.

ἐώνημαι, Fr. Com. (Eupolis), 2. 492, (Aristoph.) 2. 1076; Orators; *Partic.*, Arist. Pl. 7.

PASSIVE.

ὠνοῦμαι, Plato, Phaed. 69 B.

ἐωνούμην, Xen. Eq. 8. 2.

ἐωνήθην, Dem. 1124, 1126; Xen. Mem. 2. 7. 12, etc.; Plato, Legg. 850 A, Soph. 224 A.

ἐώνημαι, Pax 1182; Plat. Rep. 563; Orators.

Pollux (3. 124) quotes ἀπωνηθήσεται from the Comic Poet Theopompus. The verbal ὠνητέος occurs in Plato, Legg. 849 C, and ὠνητός in a true verbal sense in Thuc. 3. 40, ἐλπίδα οὔτε λόγῳ πιστὴν οὔτε χρήμασιν ὠνητήν. In Plato, Phaed. l. c., the present is found in the participle ὠνούμενά τε καὶ πιπρασκόμενα. This is the only instance in Classical Greek, although periphrases are used. Such is πρᾶσιν εὑρίσκω in a passage quoted by Pollux (7. 13) from the 'Seasons' of Aristophanes—

κράτιστον ἡμῖν εἰς τὸ Θησεῖον δραμεῖν,
ἐκεῖ δ' ἕως ἂν πρᾶσιν εὕρωμεν μένειν,

till we find a purchaser[1]. In the sense of *to be for sale*, ὤνιος εἶναι was used.

ἐπὶ ταῖς πύλαισιν οὗ τὸ τάριχος ὤνιον.
Arist. Eq. 1247.

Plato, Legg. 848 A, τρίτον μέρος ὤνιον ἐξ ἀνάγκης ἔστω τοῦτο μόνον, τῶν δὲ δύο μερῶν μηδὲν ἐπάναγκες ἔστω πωλεῖν.

πῶς ὁ σῖτος ὤνιος;
Arist. Ach. 758.

'What is the price of wheat?'

πῶς οὖν ὁ τυρὸς ἐν Βοιωτοῖς ὤνιος;
Id. Eq. 480.

To make a purchase was in Greek ὠνὴν ποιεῖσθαι, or, in

[1] The note of Pollux is ridiculous enough and shows how little Classic Greek was understood even by a scholar in the second century A. D., ὁ δὲ οἱ νῦν φασι τοὺς οἰκέτας πρᾶσιν αἰτεῖν ἔστιν εὑρεῖν ἐν ταῖς Ἀριστοφάνους Ὥραις. He must have translated ἕως ἄν = 'while.'

poetry, ὠνὴν τίθεσθαι, as Dem. 894. 27, ὠνὴν ποιοῦμαι τῆς νεώς:

> ὠνὴν ἔθου καὶ πρᾶσιν ὡς Φοῖνιξ ἀνήρ.
>
> Soph. Frag.

The primitive sense of the verb ἀγοράζειν was *to attend the ἀγορά* either for business or pleasure, but it gradually acquired the meaning of *buy*. The former signification is encountered often in Aristophanes—Ach. 625, 720, Vesp. 557, Lys. 556, 633, Eq. 1373, 1374; but the latter only once—

> καὶ ταῖς ἀδελφαῖς ἀγοράσαι χιτώνιον
> ἐκέλευσεν ἄν, τῇ μητρί θ' ἱματίδιον.
>
> Plut. 984.

The term, however, both in the active and the middle voice, became ultimately quite synonymous with ὠνεῖσθαι and πρίασθαι, as Dem. 563, 7, ἧ δ' ἐξὸν αὐτῇ βελτίω πρίασθαι ταύτης τῆς τιμῆς τοῦτον ἠγόρασεν. The verb was doubtless complete in all three voices, but in what remains of Attic literature does not extend beyond the aorist and perfect.

CXIV.

Παρασίτους οὐκ ἔλεγον οἱ ἀρχαῖοι ἐπ' ὀνείδους, ὡς νῦν, ἀλλὰ κόλακας· καὶ δρᾶμα ἔστι Κόλακες τοιούτων ἀνθρώπων.

Athenaeus discusses at great length the word παράσιτος (in 6. 235 seq.). For the existence of the παράσιτος in Homeric times, he quotes—

> ἔσκε δ' ἐνὶ Τρώεσσι Ποδῆς, υἱὸς Ἠετίωνος,
> ἀφνειός τ' ἀγαθός τε· μάλιστα δέ μιν τίεν Ἕκτωρ
> δήμου, ἐπεί οἱ ἑταῖρος ἔην φίλος εἰλαπιναστής·
>
> Il. 17. 575.

and shows that in the time of Epicharmus the character had acquired all its features. It was Araros, however, who first employed the word *παράσιτος* in this dishonourable sense, and Antiphanes, Alexis, and Diphilus had all plays of this name. Accordingly, Phrynichus must not be considered as denying the signification *κόλαξ* throughout Attic, but only as reminding his readers that the term *παράσιτος* had originally an honourable meaning. The words of Athenaeus are on this point very distinct: Τὸ δὲ τοῦ παρασίτου ὄνομα πάλαι μὲν ἦν σεμνὸν καὶ ἱερόν. Πολέμων γοῦν γράψας περὶ παρασίτων φησὶν οὕτως· "Τὸ τοῦ παρασίτου ὄνομα νῦν μὲν ἄδοξόν ἐστι, παρὰ δὲ τοῖς ἀρχαίοις εὑρίσκομεν τὸν παράσιτον ἱερόν τι χρῆμα καὶ τῷ συνθοίνῳ παρόμοιον. Ἐν Κυνοσάργει μὲν οὖν ἐν τῷ Ἡρακλείῳ στήλη τίς ἐστιν ἐν ᾗ ψήφισμα μὲν Ἀλκιβιάδου, γραμματεὺς δὲ Στέφανος Θουκυδίδου, λέγεται δ' ἐν αὐτῷ περὶ τῆς προσηγορίας οὕτως· 'Τὰ δὲ ἐπιμήνια θυέτω ὁ ἱερεὺς μετὰ τῶν παρασίτων. οἱ δὲ παράσιτοι ἔστων ἐκ τῶν νόθων καὶ τῶν τούτων παίδων κατὰ τὰ πάτρια. Ὃς δ' ἂν μὴ θέλῃ παρασιτεῖν, εἰσαγέτω καὶ περὶ τούτων εἰς τὸ δικαστήριον.'" There is much more to the same effect.

CXV.

Εὕρασθαι οὐκ ἐρεῖς προπαροξυτόνως διὰ τοῦ α, ἀλλὰ παροξυτόνως διὰ τοῦ ε, εὑρέσθαι.

CXVI.

Ἀφείλατο ὅσοι διὰ τοῦ λα λέγουσιν ἀσχημονοῦσι, δέον διὰ τοῦ λε λέγειν, ἀφείλετο. καὶ ἀφειλόμην δεῖ λέγειν διὰ τοῦ ο, ἀλλὰ μὴ διὰ τοῦ α.

The second of these articles has been brought from another place in the Ecloga. Εὐράμην for *εὑρόμην*, and *ἀφειλάμην* for *ἀφειλόμην*, represent a common corruption of late Greek. Veitch hesitates, as usual; but on consulting him it will be seen that in both cases the form in alpha has disappeared from all texts, not only of Attic, but of Classical Greek writers. The same is true of the active forms *εὕρησα* and *εἶλα, ἥρησα,* and whatever Aristophanes wrote in Thesm. 761, he certainly did not write *ἐξηρήσατο.* That word crept into the text at a date when *ὠψάμην* might be used for *εἶδον,* and *ἀνεπεσάμην* for *ἀνέπεσον.* The second line of the couplet destroys the force of the first—

> *ταλαντάτη Μίκκα, τίς ἐξεκόρησέ σε;*
> *τίς τὴν ἀγαπητὴν παῖδά σου 'ξηρήσατο;*

Instead of *ἐξηρήσατο,* which cannot have a double meaning, some word that has is required to correspond with *ἐξεκόρησε.* Lobeck proposed *ἐξετρήσατο,* Meineke has adopted *διεχρήσατο.* Neither emendation is of value, and the genuine word still awaits discovery, if the line is not regarded as merely an interpolated extension of *ἐξεκόρησε.* Many forms, equally corrupt, were imported into Attic books by copyists, who were ignorant of Greek syntax of the Classical age. Thus, in Thuc. 8. 10, the historian used the regular construction in object clauses, and made a future indicative follow *ὅπως,* after a verb of preparing, *παρεσκευάζοντο ὅπως μὴ λήσουσιν αὐτούς,* but textual critics had to banish *λήσωσιν* from the received text. They had the best manuscripts on their side, but even against all such authority the change ought to have been made. Veitch (p. 411) has a record of other instances. The case of the Homeric *ἐπέλησα* is very different—

> *ἀλλὰ τὸ μὲν καὶ ἀνεκτὸν ἔχει κακόν, ὁππότε κέν τις*
> *ἤματα μὲν κλαίῃ πυκινῶς ἀκαχήμενος ἦτορ,*
> *νύκτας δ' ὕπνος ἔχῃσιν· ὁ γάρ τ' ἐπέλησεν ἁπάντων*
> *ἐσθλῶν ἠδὲ κακῶν, ἐπεὶ ἂρ βλέφαρ' ἀμφικαλύψῃ.*
>
> Od. 20. 83.

Then the word is causative, the *ἐπί* making possible the active in this sense, just as it helped *ψηφίζομαι* to an active voice. As λανθάνω in the active can only mean *escape notice*, so ψηφίζω had no signification besides that of *use pebbles, calculate*. For the causative of ψηφίζομαι, *to vote*, the compound of ἐπί was employed, just as ἐπιλανθάνω supplied a causative to λανθάνομαι.

The authority of Hesiod used to be advanced for the aorist first of λείπω—

> ὅς κεν τὴν ἐπίορκον ἀπολείψας ἐπομόσσῃ
> ἀθανάτων·
>
> Theogon. 793.

just as ἔφευξα in Aesch. Agam. 1308—

> τί τοῦτ' ἔφευξας; εἴ τι μὴ φρενῶν στύγος,

was regarded as a proof that φεύγω had a weak aorist as well as a strong. In the one case the word comes from ἀπολείβω, in the other from φεύζω.

It is true that there are several verbs which in Classical times used both aorists—the weak and the strong—in the same sense, but in Attic proper, such verbs were singularly rare. Χέζω is an undisputed instance, and with it may go φθάνω, the two aorists of which run parallel, except in the participle, which Attic confined to the weak. The case of κτείνω and πείθω is different, ἔκτανον, ἔκανον, and ἔπιθον, being not found out of poetry. Even ἐπιθόμην gradually retreated before ἐπείσθην, as Attic matured. Xenophon must be left to settle the right of κατέκανον to a place in Attic prose. Certainly, no other writer in that fastidious dialect would have employed the word. The form ἦξα stands on precarious footing, but must be admitted in early Attic. Homer certainly used the weak aorist middle—

> ἀτὰρ καλλίτριχας ἵππους
> λύσαθ' ὑπὲξ ὀχέων, παρὰ δέ σφισι βάλλετ' ἐδωδήν·
> ἐκ πόλιος δ' ἄξασθε βόας καὶ ἴφια μῆλα
> καρπαλίμως, οἶνον δὲ μελίφρονα οἰνίζεσθε.
>
> Il. 8. 505.

ἐκ πόλιος δ' ἄξαντο βόας καὶ ἴφια μῆλα
καρπαλίμως, οἶνον δὲ μελίφρονα οἰνίζοντο.
Id. 545.

for to read ἄξεσθε in the former of these passages is criticism of the most futile and puerile kind. Moreover, Herodotus employed προεσάξαντο (1. 190), ἐσάξαντο (5. 34), and προσέξαντο (8. 20). Accordingly, when the active ἄξαι is encountered in Antiphon, and προσῆξαν in Thucydides, in a sense perfectly natural, and with the support of all manuscripts, they must at once be accepted as genuine, and regarded as fresh indications of a fact more than once referred to already—namely, that in these two writers the Attic dialect had not reached its full development. Antipho, 134. 41, μὴ οὖν ἐξέληται τοῦτο ὑμῶν μηδείς, ὅτι τὸν μηνυτὴν ἀπέκτειναν, καὶ διετείναντο αὐτὸν μὴ εἰσελθεῖν ἐς ὑμᾶς, μηδ' ἐμοὶ ἐγγενέσθαι παρόντι ἄξαι τὸν ἄνδρα καὶ βασανίσαι αὐτόν: Thuc. 2. 97, φόρος τε ἐκ πάσης τῆς βαρβάρου καὶ τῶν Ἑλληνίδων πόλεων, ὅσον προσῆξαν ἐπὶ Σεύθου κτε. Such forms, however, were quite alien to mature Attic, and ἀπῇξας has been justly restored to Aristophanes (Ran. 468), in place of ἀπῆξας, τάξαντες, to Lycurgus (166. 16) in place of κατάξαντες, and perhaps καθέντας even to Xenophon (Hell. 2. 2. 20) in place of κατάξαντες. In all three passages the sense requires an alteration which there is excellent manuscript authority to support.

The history of the weak aorist of ἀποδιδράσκω is singularly instructive. Veitch has traced it with his usual care: 'The first aorist does not *now* occur in Classic Greek; ἀποδράσασα Andoc. 1. 125 (Vulg.), ἀποδρᾶσα (Bekk.), ἀποδράσας Lys. 6. 28 (old edit.), was altered by Reiske to ἀποδράς, which has been adopted by Bekker and every subsequent editor, ἀποδράσῃ Xen. Cyr. 1. 4. 13 (Vulg.) now ἀποδρᾷ (best MSS., Schneid., Popp., Dind.), ἐξέδρασ' Eur. I. T. 194 (MSS., Vulg., Musgr., Seidler), now ἐξ ἕδρας in every edition,' etc. In fact, ἀπέδρασα must be classed with ἔθυηξα, ἔθρωξα, ἔλαμψα, ἔδηξα, ἔφευξα, ἔπεσα, εἶλα, ἥρησα, ἡμάρτησα, ἔβλωξα or ἐμόλησα, ὠλίσθησα, ἔβαλα, ὠσφράμην, et hoc genus omne. Further, there is little question that Aristophanes did not use ἐνέτεξα, or Lysias ὤφλησα. In Ar. Lys. 553 the manuscripts have ἐντέξῃ or ἐντεύξῃ, the latter being also supported by Suïdas, s. v. τέτανος. The true word is lost, as neither ἐντέξῃ nor ἐντεύξῃ provides a suitable meaning. For ὤφλησεν in Lys. 136. 1, συκοφαντίας αὐτοῦ κατέγνωτε καὶ ὤφλησεν ὑμῖν μυρίας δραχμάς, either ὠφείλησεν or ὦφλεν must be substituted.

Some verbs, which originally possessed two aorists of identical meaning, dropped one of them in Attic, just as ἄγω has been shown to have done. Such a word is βλαστάνω, which in Ionic writers had an aorist ἐβλάστησα, Hippocr. 7. 528, 546, and ἀναβλαστήσῃ must be preferred to ἀναβλαστήσει in Hdt. 3. 62, as even Herodotus could hardly have given other than the middle inflexions to the future of such a verb. The Homeric ἔθρεξα survived in Attic poetry by the side of ἔδραμον, but could not have been used in prose. Both ἔλακον and ἐλάκησα appear in Comedy; but the verb is never used by Aristophanes except in para-tragedy, or when he wishes to have a hit at Euripides, who was ridiculously fond of the term. Of the two forms ἔρρευσα and ἐρρύην, late writers selected the poetical active, as in the case of κατέδαρθον they preferred the passive form.

The aorist εἶπα must not be reduced to the same level as εἶλα, ἦλθα, ἔφαγα, etc., nor yet must εἶπον and εἶπα be regarded as rivals. The two accurately supplement one another in Attic Greek, according to the following paradigm—

εἶπον	εἰπάτην		εἰπάτων
εἶπας	εἴπομεν	εἰπέ	
εἶπε	εἴπατε	εἰπάτω	εἴπατε
εἴπατον	εἶπον	εἴπατον	εἰπόντων.

The subjunctive may be referred to either; the optative draws its forms wholly from the second aorist, which also supplies the infinitive and the participle. The case of ἤνεγκον versus ἤνεγκα is somewhat more intricate; but, under the influence of a transitory desire for system, Veitch has demonstrated that, in the indicative and imperative, the forms in alpha were used in Attic, except when the requirements of metre or a wish to avoid hiatus suggested ἤνεγκον and ἔνεγκον. The infinitive was always ἐνεγκεῖν and the participle ἐνεγκών, and the omicron forms were at least preferentially used in the optative, while the subjunctive may be assigned indifferently to either tense.

The rule for the aorists of τίθημι and ἵημι is too well-known to need remark; but it may not be unnecessary to remind my readers, that, although the weak aorist of δίδωμι was occasionally used in the plural, such forms were generally eschewed by Attic writers. Herwerden thus sums up the evidence of Inscriptions: 'Aor. 1 hujus verbi et compositorum in plurali numero perraro reperitur. In T. N. xiii. m. 45, legitur παρεδώκαμεν. Paullo minus rara est 3 pers. pl., sed ne haec quidem reperitur, quod sciam, ante saeculum quartum,' (Lapid. Test. p. 48). The aorist ἔφρηκα probably followed the analogy of ἵημι and τίθημι in the indicative, as it certainly did in the other moods, and the gloss in Hesychius: 'Απέφρησαν, ἀφῆκαν Κρατῖνος Θρᾴτταις, should stand 'Απέφρεσαν, κτε.

As is now acknowledged, the form ἐπεισέφρηκε in Eur. El. 1032—

ἀλλ' ἦλθ' ἔχων μοι μαινάδ' ἔνθεον κόρην
λέκτροις τ' ἐπεισέφρηκε καὶ νύμφα δύο
ἐν τοῖσιν αὐτοῖς δώμασιν κατεῖχ' ὁμοῦ,

is no perfect, but an aorist, which in H. F. 1266 has by some fatality been corrupted to ἐπεισέφρησε—

ἔτ' ἐν γάλακτί τ' ὄντι γοργωποὺς ὄφεις
ἐπεισέφρηκε σπαργάνοισι τοῖς ἐμοῖς·

and is recorded by Hesychius in the glosses—

Εἰσέφρηκεν· εἰσήγαγεν.
Ἐξέφρηκεν· ἀφῆκεν.

Its subjunctive appears in Alc. 1056, ἐπεσφρῶ, Phoen. 264, ἐκφρῶσι, and its participle in a fragment of Eur. Phaethon—

μήτιν' Ἥφαιστος χόλον
δόμοις ἐπεισφρεὶς μέλαθρα συμφλέξῃ πυρί.

Aristophanes, Vesp. 162, used its imperative ἔκφρες, and its infinitive is preserved in the gloss of Hesychius: Εἰσφρῆναι· εἰσάξαι.

CXVII.

Ῥάφανον ἐπὶ τῆς ῥαφανῖδος μὴ θῇς. σημαίνει γὰρ τὴν κράμβην.

'Idem affirmant Hesych., Suïd., Ammon, Schol. ad Aristoph.. Poll., et alii. Addit Hesych. ῥαφανίδας vocari ῥαφάνους parvos Dorice. Ammon. vero et Thom. adjungunt Ionice ῥέφανον nominari τὴν ῥαφανίδα. Aristot. Hist. V. 17. 219 etiam ῥάφανον ait ab aliis κράμβην nominari.' Nuñez.

CXVIII.

Εὔνως ἔχει μοι μὴ λέγε, ἀλλ' εὐνοικῶς.

The same caution is also found in App Soph. 38, εὐνοικῶς δόκιμον, τὸ δὲ εὔνως φεύγειν χρή, and it is in accordance with the usage of Attic Greek. Similarly, ἄνως was not in use, but ἀνοήτως, and for the Xenophontean ὁμονόως, Attic writers employed ὁμονοητικῶς. The adverbs of δύσνους, κακόνους, and ἀγχίνους, do not happen to be found; but as εὐνοικός was confined to the adverb εὐνοικῶς, εὐνοικώτερον, εὐνοικώτατα, there can be no question, that, if used at all, δυσνοικῶς, κακονοικῶς, and ἀγχινοικῶς, were similarly preferred to the regularly-formed δύσνως and ἀγχίνως. There is in fact not a single instance in Attic Greek of an adverb directly formed from adjectives of this class, πρόνους, κουφόνους, εὔρρους, εὔπνους, δύσπλους, etc. It is hardly necessary to point out that words like ἁπλῶς do not belong to the same category, but even ἀθρόως appears to be under a ban.

CXIX.

Εὐθύ· πολλοὶ ἀντὶ τοῦ εὐθύς. διαφέρει δέ. τὸ μὲν γὰρ τόπου ἐστίν, εὐθὺ Ἀθηνῶν, τὸ δὲ χρόνου, καὶ λέγεται σὺν τῷ σ.

This point is proved by the evidence of Aristophanes alone. The form εὐθύ is demanded by the metre in Nub. 162, Pax 77, 301, Av. 1421, Eccl. 835, and gives the more regular verse in Pax 68 and 819, while in no line is εὐθύς found referring to place. On the other hand, εὐθὺς χρονικόν is invariably encountered, being demanded by the metre in Plut. 152, 238, 700, 707, 1121, Nub. 785, 855, 878, 987, 1134, 1215, 1365, 1371, 1373, Ach. 638, Eq. 570, 625, Vesp. 103, 553, 568, Pax 84, 217, 763, 894, Lys. 201, 239, 248, 519, 525, 641, 664, Thesm. 405, 482, 507, Ran. 126, 137, 566, 694, 744, 859, 1029, 1135. Other Attic poets tell the same tale, except that Euripides uses εὐθύς for εὐθύ in one passage—

> τὴν εὐθὺς Ἄργους κἀπιδαυρίας ὁδόν.
>
> Hipp. 1197.

Photius remarks upon the anomaly: Εὐθὺ Λυκείου· τὸ εἰς Λύκειον· ὅθεν Ἐρατοσθένης καὶ διὰ τοῦτο ὑποπτεύει τοὺς Μεταλλεῖς· καὶ Εὐριπίδης οὐκ ὀρθῶς—

τὴν εὐθὺς Ἄργους κἀπιδαυρίας ὁδόν.

The author of this Μεταλλεῖς is not known for certain, and without the rest of the line no reasoning can be based on εὐθὺς Λυκείου, but the words of Euripides doubtless stand as they came from his pen. The distinction between εὐθύ and εὐθύς originated in the desire for precision, which is the predominant characteristic of Attic, and was not observed either by Homer or in other dialects at a period contemporary with the Attic. Ἰθύς is of common occurrence, as applied to place, in the Iliad and Odyssey, while Pindar employed εὐθύς in both senses. Accordingly, in Tragedy εὐθύς (τὸ τόπου) is not out of place, and in Euripides it may well be a conscious imitation of older usage. In Comedy and Prose, however, the rule was carefully observed, and any deviations from it in the texts of Prose authors should be unflinchingly removed.

Like the English *immediately*, εὐθύς is sometimes used of place, as in Thuc. 6. 96, χωρίου ἀποκρήμνου τε καὶ ὑπὲρ τῆς πόλεως εὐθύς κειμένου. In such sentences εὐθύ would naturally be amiss.

CXX.

Ζωρότερον ὁ ποιητής, σὺ δὲ λέγε εὔζωρον κέρασον καὶ εὐζωρότερον, ὡς Ἀριστοφάνης καὶ Κρατῖνος καὶ Εὔπολις.

The poet referred to is Homer, in Il. 9. 203—

ζωρότερον δὲ κέραιε δέπας δ' ἔντυνον ἑκάστῳ,

a line which Ephippus, the Comic poet, had in mind when he wrote—

φιάλην ἑκατέρᾳ
ἔδωκε καράσας ζωρότερον Ὁμηρικῶς·

Antiphanes employed ζωρότερος in the passage preserved by Athenaeus, 10. 423 D—

τοῦτον ἐγὼ κρίνω μετανιπτρίδα τῆς Ὑγιείας
πίνειν ζωροτέρῳ χρώμενον Οἰνοχόῳ·

but without the context it would be rash to regard it as a contravention of the rule laid down by Phrynichus. Herodotus has the simple word (6. 84), and it was probably in use in Tragedy. Its reappearance in the Common dialect is but another instance of what has so often been encountered already—the inability of Attic to hold its own against the other dialects.

The word εὔζωρος is found in Ar. Eccl. 227; Eur. Alc. 757. Like ἄκρατος, it formed its comparative and superlative in -έστερος, -έστατος, Ephipp. ap. Athen. 9. 374 D; Antiphanes, id. 10. 423 E. Eustathius, however, quotes from Diphilus the regular comparative εὐζωρότερον, and he is confirmed by Athen. 10. 423 E—

ἔγχεον σὺ δὴ πιεῖν.
εὐζωρότερόν γε νὴ Δί', ὦ παῖ, δός· τὸ γὰρ
ὕδαρες ἅπαν τοῦτ' ἐστὶ τῇ ψυχῇ κακόν.

CXXI.

Χειρσὶν ἀδοκίμως, χερσὶ δέ.

The same is true of the genitive and dative dual, χειροῖν being never used in these cases.

CXXII.

Εὐέριον μὴ λέγε, ἀλλ' εὔερον ἱμάτιον, τρισυλλάβως καὶ ἄνευ τοῦ ι.

Εἴ τινα πόλιν φράσειας ἡμῖν εὔερον
ὥσπερ σισύραν ἐγκατακλινῆναι μαλθακήν.
Ar. Av. 121.

The Scholiast quotes γλῶσσαν εὐέρων βοτῶν from Cratinus, and from Plato (Comicus), the substantive εὐερία.

On the other hand, there is no occasion to alter εὐείρου in Sophocles—

> ᾧ γὰρ τὸν ἐνδυτῆρα πέπλον ἀρτίως
> ἔχριον, ἀργῆτ' οἰὸς εὐείρου πόκῳ,
>
> Trach. 675.

as is done by Elmsley and Lobeck, for they ought as readily to replace ἐνδυτῆρα and ἀργῆτα by other words. As an old form, εὔειρος is natural in Tragedy. It is employed in Ionic, and supported by the gloss of Photius, Εὔειρον· εὐέριον.

CXXIII.

Νεομηνία μὴ λέγε, τῶν Ἰώνων γάρ, ἀλλὰ νουμηνία.

'Νεομηνία non contractis primoribus syllabis perrarum est etiam in vulgari Graecitate.' Lobeck.

CXXIV.

Ἦς ἐν ἀγορᾷ, σόλοικον. λέγε οὖν ἦσθα. ὀρθότερον δὲ χρῷτο ἂν ὁ λέγων, ἐὰν ᾖς ἐν ἀγορᾷ.

CXXV.

Ἔφης· ἔστι μὲν παρὰ τοῖς ἀρχαίοις, ἀλλ' ὀλίγον. τὸ δὲ πλεῖστον ἔφησθα.

The second of these articles has been brought from a later place. In the case of ἔφησθα, Phrynichus is too lenient; ἔφης was never used by good writers any more than ᾖς, ᾔεις, ᾔδης. It is true that the manuscripts occasionally exhibit the shorter forms, but as the longer are often demanded and always allowed by metre, they should invariably be restored in verse and prose. The argument from seriation is very strong—

ἔφησ-θα οἶσ-θα ᾔδη-σθα ᾖσ-θα ᾔεισ-θα
φα-θί ἴσ-θι ἴσ-θι ἴ-θι.

but the testimony of verse is much more valuable. It is as follows—

A. ἀτὰρ γεγένηται; B. ναὶ μὰ Δί' οὐκ ᾔδησθά με;
Ar. Eccl. 551.

The Ravenna has ᾔδησθα, others ᾔδεισθα.

ἀλλ' οὐκ ἂν ἔτ' ἔχοις· ὅσα γὰρ ᾔδησθ' ἐξέχεας ἅπαντα.
Thesm. 554.

The MSS. ᾔδεις.

ταύτας μέντοι σὺ θεὰς οὔσας οὐκ ᾔδησθ' οὐδ' ἐνόμιζες;
Nub. 329.

Ravenna ᾔδης, others ᾔδεις.

The second person does not occur in Aeschylus. In Euripides it is found only twice—

πῶς; πορθμὸν οὐκ ᾔδησθα πατρῴας χθονός;
Cycl. 108.

MSS. ᾔδεισθα.

ᾔδησθα γὰρ δῆτ' ἀνόσιον γήμας γάμον.
El. 926.

In the two cases in which it occurs in Sophocles the verse admits of the true form—

ἆρ' ἐξῄδησθ' ὅσον ἦν κέρδος.
Trach. 988.

MSS. ἐξῄδης.

ᾔδησθα κηρυχθέντα[1] μὴ πράσσειν τάδε;
Ant. 445.

MSS. ᾔδης τά.

The evidence for ᾖσθα is overpowering. There is no line

[1] Cobetus emendavit. For the plural participle cp. Ant. 576—
δεδογμέν', ὡς ἔοικε, τήνδε κατθανεῖν.

in Attic verse in which ᾖς is required, though it occurs sometimes in the manuscripts. Thus in Eur. I. A. 339—

> ὡς ταπεινὸς ἦσθα πάσης δεξιᾶς προσθιγγάνειν,

all the manuscripts have ᾖς ἁπάσης. The following details are of value. In Sophocles alone ἦσθα occurs fourteen times, and in eight of the fourteen passages the disyllabic form is required by the metre. In Aristophanes, out of nineteen lines in which the word occurs, nine require the longer form. In Aeschylus it is found twice, once doubtful and once required. About ᾔεισθα there is some question, the word not occurring in verse. Aeschines (77. 11) is credited with περιῄεις, and Plato, Tim. 26 C, Euthyph. 4 B, with διῄεισθα. Περιῄεις is certainly wrong, but is διῄεισθα right? The legitimate form would be διῇσθα. While οἶσθα is claimed for mature Attic, it is probable that οἶδας should be acknowledged as old Attic, as it appears in Eur. Alc. 780—

> τὰ θνητὰ πράγματ' οἶδας ἣν ἔχει φύσιν;

and as forms like οἴδατε, οἴδαμεν, were good Ionic, and should be retained when found in Attic as early as that of Antiphon. It is quite natural that at a period of transition he should write οἴδαμεν in one passage and ἴσμεν in another. The same licence must be extended to Xenophon as a Greek cosmopolitan. What in Antiphon was due to the time at which he wrote was in Xenophon caused by the migratory life he led.

In the case of οἶδα a third form has certain claims to notice. In his note upon the dictum of Moeris: Οἶσθα, χωρὶς τοῦ σ, Ἀττικῶς. οἶδας, Ἑλληνικῶς, Pierson quotes the following passage of Eustathius (Od. 1773. 27): Τὸ δὲ οἶσθα γὰρ οἷος θυμὸς ἐλέγχει Ζηνόδοτον καὶ τοὺς κατ' αὐτὸν κακῶς γράφοντας τὸ οἶσθας παρὰ τῷ ποιητῇ. ἐν τέλει μὲν γὰρ στίχου ἢ καὶ ἐπιφορᾷ φωνήεντος εἴη ἂν γενέσθαι συγχωρηθεῖσαν τοιαύτην γραφήν, ἐνταῦθα δὲ οὐκ ἂν γένοιτο διὰ τὸ κακομέτρητον. Αἴλιος μέντοι Διονύσιος γράφει ὅτι καὶ τὸ οἶσθα καὶ τὸ οἶσθας ἄμφω Ἑλληνικὰ καθὰ καὶ ἦσθα καὶ ἦσθας. Any record of an opinion of Dionysius always merits careful consideration, but here the ambiguity of the term Ἑλληνικά robs his words of most of their value. Hesychius, it is true, enfranchises οἶσθας: Οἶσθας· οἶδας, ἑκατέρως Ἀττικῶς, and Photius does the same: Οἶσθα· ἀντὶ τοῦ οἶδας· λέγεται καὶ χωρὶς τοῦ σ· μετὰ δὲ τοῦ σ ποτὲ ἢ διὰ μέτρον ἢ διὰ τὸ μὴ συγκροῦσαι σύμφωνα: but Nauck is rash in the extreme to alter οἶδας to οἶσθας in Alc. 780. The authority of his favourite Grammarian, George Choeroboscus, is advanced in its favour, εὕρηται δὲ καὶ μετὰ τοῦ σ οἶσθας ὡς παρὰ Κρατίνῳ ἐν Μαλθακοῖς: but dependence upon the broken reed of one of the least talented and least critical of the old grammarians is a weak spot in Nauck's work, and has often seriously misguided him. There is, in fine, not one assured instance of the form οἶσθας in Attic of any period. The passages quoted by Veitch in its favour are as evidence quite worthless.

The evidence for ἦσθας is still less, as it does not occur at all in Greek.

On the other hand, the easy remedy which it would apply to—

πῶς οὖν ἂν ἐνθάδ' ἦσθ' ἐν Τροίᾳ θ' ἅμα,
Eur. Hel. 587.

almost justifies Nauck's introduction of the form in that line, and, if it were once established there, his alteration of Eur. Her. 65 and I. T. 814 (οἶσθας for οἶσθ' ἐν) might be adopted at once. But the question of Comedy and Prose is not affected by such lines of Tragedy, and the forms in -θας must be denied in both till more convincing evidence is adduced of their existence in any species of pure Attic writing.

CXXVI.

Ἠκηκόεσαν, ἐγεγράφεσαν, ἐπεποιήκεσαν, ἐνενοήκεσαν ἐρεῖς· ἀλλ᾽ οὐ σὺν τῷ ι, ἠκηκόεισαν.

No error has spread so widely through the texts of Greek authors as the late endings of the pluperfect indicative active. The genuine inflexions of the singular are proved not only by the evidence of verse, but also by the best manuscripts of prose writers, to have been for the singular -η, -ης, and -ει, or before a vowel -ειν. The forms known to late Greek were those which now rule in our texts, and it is to the pestilent habit which late transcribers had of altering texts to suit their own age that this wholesale corruption of the manuscripts is to be ascribed. In regard to the third person plural, however, the corruption is not so great. For example, in Plato the lighter ending predominates in the manuscripts, there being perhaps no example of the heavier suffix undisputed.

Attention was first drawn to the question of the pluperfect endings by a scholar who occupies a high place in that remarkable company of Greek critics who in the last century made the name of England respected for acute and sensible scholarship. Dawes was always willing to accept the lessons which the study of Attic Comedy taught, and had the rare good fortune to have many of his emendations on Aristophanes confirmed when the Ravenna manuscript was subsequently given to the world.

The common reading in Aristophanes, Nub. 1347, was till his time—

> ὡς οὗτος εἰ μή τῳ πέποιθεν οὐκ ἂν ἦν
> οὕτως ἀκόλαστος.

Dawes showed that the pluperfect, equivalent in sense to an imperfect, was required by the context, and altered the unmeaning πέποιθεν to 'πεποίθειν, i. e. ἐπεποίθειν. 'At enim dicet non nemo,' he goes on, 'quid sibi vult prima singularis, cum οὗτος tertiam postulet? Age igitur, attento paulisper fac sis animo.

"Dum veteres avias tibi de pulmone revellam."

Itaque tandem dicas temporis praeteriti perfecti terminationem Atticam -ειν non jam primae singularis, uti omnes didicimus, sed tertiae; primae vero alteram istam -η esse propriam. Id quod ex poetarum Atticorum scriptis ad examen revocatis fidenter assevero. Solutae autem orationis scriptores nihil moror. Nam in his quidem grammaticorum recentiorum insomnia constanter conspicienda sese exhibent. Immo in poetis etiam non raro, sed nusquam nisi ubi veram scripturam versus recipiat.'

Dawes' emendation 'πεποίθειν was afterwards confirmed by the Ravenna. Dawes further proved that the copyists sometimes actually changed the genuine -η of the first person into the late -ειν, not only in violation of the laws of metre, but with a total disregard of common sense. In Aristoph. Av. 511—

τουτὶ τοίνυν οὐκ ᾔδη 'γώ· καὶ δῆτά μ' ἐλάμβανε θαῦμα,

ᾔδειν 'γώ was read in most manuscripts and by all editors, till Kuster restored ᾔδη from the Vatican—a reading subsequently confirmed by the Ravenna. There could hardly be more convincing proof of the futility of trusting manuscripts on this question. A further argument he based upon the fact that -η is the natural contraction from the Ionic -εα, and -ει(ν) from the Ionic -εε(ν), and he demonstrated that the genuine third-person ending -ειν was occasionally preserved because the copyists mistook it for the first person. This is the case in Vesp. 635—

οὐκ, ἀλλ' ἐρήμας ᾤεθ' οὗτος ῥᾳδίως τρυγήσειν·
καλῶς γὰρ ᾔδειν ὡς ἐγὼ ταύτῃ κράτιστός εἰμι.

The second line might just be translated as 'me *tamen noram* quid hic valerem,' instead of the true, 'Probe *enim norat* me hac arte plurimum valere.' To the same mistake is due the preservation of the ancient form in Pax 1182—

τῷ δὲ σιτί' οὐκ ἐώνητ'· οὐ γὰρ ᾔδειν ἐξιών,

and a slight alteration of ὡς for ὅς enabled the transcribers to retain ᾔδειν in Vesp. 558—

ὃς ἔμ' οὐδ' ἂν ζῶντ' ᾔδειν, εἰ μὴ διὰ τὴν προτέραν ἀπόφευξιν.

In fact, passages in which it was just possible to make sense by translating the third person by the first escaped violation. All others were altered, but altered as a rule in a way so puerile as not to disguise the primitive reading. Two instances of this—Nub. 1347, and Av. 511—have already been described as corrected by Dawes, and another, Av. 1298, was similarly emended by him—

ὄρτυξ ἐκαλεῖτο, καὶ γὰρ ᾔκειν ὄρτυγι.

No manuscript has the genuine ᾔκειν. They read ᾔκεν, ἦκεν, ἧκεν. Even the Ravenna has εἶκεν, as if εἴκω could represent ἔοικα, and εἶκεν or ᾔκεν stand for the Ionic ἐῴκειν. All the best editors have now adopted the emendation of Dawes. Photius supports ᾔκειν by the testimony of some unnamed critic. Once between ᾔα and ᾔσμεν occurs, ᾔκειν· ὅμοιος ἦν: and again after ᾔκειν comes, Ἤκειν, τὸ ἐῴκειν ἐπὶ τρίτου προσώπου. οὕτως Ἀριστοφάνης. The two glosses taken together prove the truth of the emendation of Dawes. The ν ἐφελκυστικόν after the diphthong -ει was a constant stumblingblock to the scribes. In Aristophanes, Plut. 696, a few manuscripts read correctly—

A. ὁ δὲ θεὸς ὑμῖν οὐ προσῄειν; B. οὐδέπω·

but even the Ravenna changes προσῄειν into προσῄει γ', the γε possessing no meaning whatever.

How little faith can be put in manuscript authority in cases of this kind is proved by nothing so much as the mistakes made by scribes in reproducing the glosses of ancient critics. In regard to this very question under discussion, a Greek grammarian (Bekk. Anecd. p. 422. 4) has the excellent note: Ἀπέρρωγεν· οὐκ ἀπέρρηκται· καὶ ἀπερρώγει καὶ σὺν τῷ ν ἀπερρώγειν τὸ τρίτον πρόσωπον (quoting the end of an iambic)—

κᾆτ' ἀπερρώγειν ὁ πούς·

but the transcribers have made him say, ἀπερρώγη καὶ σὺν τῷ ν ἀπερρώγην.

As in Aristophanes the late form of the first person led to an elisional absurdity like ᾔδειν 'γώ, so the inability of the copyists to understand the classical ᾔδειν of the third person occasioned an eloquent hiatus in Euripides, Ion 1187—

κοὐδεὶς τάδ' ᾔδει' ἐν χεροῖν ἔχοντι δέ,

where Porson restored ᾔδειν. These two instances would in themselves be sufficient to warrant us in affirming that the first person of the pluperfect active ended in Attic in -η, and the third before a vowel affixed ν; but even in prose good manuscripts occasionally preserve the true forms, and there is no lack of other evidence fully as convincing.

Thus in Homer the first person singular of the pluperfect ended in -εα, and the third in -εε(ν) or -ει(ν):—

ἔνθ' ἤτοι μὲν ἐγὼ διερῷ ποδὶ φευγέμεν ἡμέας
ἠνώγεα, τοὶ δὲ μέγα νήπιοι οὐκ ἐπίθοντο.
Od. 9. 43.

τὸν δ' ἂψ ἠνώγεα αὐτὴν ὁδὸν ἡγήσασθαι.
Id. 10. 263.

Πείραιον δέ μιν ἠνώγεα προτὶ οἶκον ἄγοντα.
Id. 17. 55.

αὐτὰρ ἑταίρους
τρεῖς ἄγον οἷσι μάλιστα πεποίθεα πᾶσαν ἐπ' ἰθύν.
Id. 4. 433.

ἀλλ' ἐν πρώτοισιν ὀΐω
ἔμμεναι, ὄφρ' ἥβη τε πεποίθεα χερσί τ' ἐμῇσιν.
Id. 8. 180.

ὣς δ' αὔτως καὶ κεῖνο ἰδὼν ἐτεθήπεα θυμῷ.
Id. 6. 166.

And for the third person, those passages only being quoted in which a vowel follows the pluperfect:—

Τληπόλεμος δ' ἄρα μηρὸν ἀριστερὸν ἔγχεϊ μακρῷ
βεβλήκειν, αἰχμὴ δὲ διέσσυτο μαιμώωσα.
Il. 5. 660.

καὶ δὲ τόδ' ἠνώγειν εἰπεῖν ἔπος αἴ κ' ἐθέλητε.
Id. 7. 394.

δεῖξαι δ' ἠνώγειν ᾧ πενθερῷ ὄφρ' ἀπόλοιτο.
Id. 6. 170.

στῆθος βεβλήκειν ὑπὲρ ἄντυγος, ἀγχόθι δειρῆς.
Id. 14. 412.

ἑστήκειν ὥς τίς τε λέων περὶ οἷσι τέκεσσιν.
Id. 17. 133.

ἑστήκειν· αὐτοῦ γὰρ ὑπήριπε φαίδιμα γυῖα.
Id. 23. 691.

τῶν νῦν σ' ἠνώγειν ἀποπεμπέμεν ὅττι τάχιστα.
Od. 5. 112.

εὖθ' ὁ δεδειπνήκειν, ὁ δ' ἐπαύετο θεῖος ἀοιδός.
Id. 17. 359.

βεβλήκειν, ἄλλος δὲ θύρην πυκινῶς ἀραρυῖαν.
Id. 22. 275.

οὐδέ τις ἄλλος
ᾔδεεν οὔτε θεῶν οὔτε θνητῶν ἀνθρώπων.
Il. 18. 404.

Τηλέμαχος δ' ἄρα μιν πάλαι ᾔδεεν ἔνδον ἐόντα.
Od. 23. 29.

Now the first-person ending -εα became in Attic -η by the ordinary rule of contraction, just as -ῆες, which in Homer is the nominative plural ending of substantives in -ευς, became in Attic -ης—

σκηπτοῦχοι βασιλῆες· ἐπεσσεύοντο δὲ λαοί.
Il. 2. 86.

οἱ δ' ἀμφ' Ἀτρείωνα διοτρεφέες βασιλῆες.
Id. 445.

πεζοί θ' ἱππῆές τε· πολὺς δ' ὀρυμαγδὸς ὀρώρει.
Od. 24. 70.

Yet even here the -ῆς is often corrupted to -εις, as the -η of the pluperfect to -ειν. But the manuscripts of Thucydides, Plato, Aristophanes, and the Orators, though often exhibiting forms in -εις, yet preserve the old -ῆς sufficiently often to prove that it was the only form known to Attic of the best age. In fact -εις is as depraved for the nominative[1] as it is for the accusative, and in the case of the accusative the verdict of verse in favour of -έᾱς is final.

Eustathius is very clear on the question of the Attic form of the first person pluperfect active. His words are (1946. 22): Παραδίδωσι γὰρ Ἡρακλείδης ὅτε Ἀττικοὶ τοὺς τοιούτους ὑπερσυντελικοὺς ἐν τῷ ἦτα μόνῳ περατοῦσιν, ᾔδη λέγοντες καὶ

[1] 'Non funditus interiit Attica forma in Codd. nostris. Bodleianus γονῆς et βασιλῆς servavit in Sympos. p. 178 B et id. 196 C. In libris de Rep. Parisinus A. fol. 19 v. χαλκῆς, 58 v. βασιλῆς, 83 r. γονῆς, 110 r. δρομῆς, dederat, quae omnia corrector depravavit. Intactum mansit fol. 61 v. ὥσπερ γραφῆς, sed prima manus fol. 41 v. οἱ βραφεῖς scripsit et 62 v. οἷον οἱ γραφεῖς ne unquam librariis certa fides haberi possit.' Cobet, in Mnem. N. S. V. 19.

The rarer the noun the more likely is the old ending to be retained. Thus in Arist. Plut. 807, all the best MSS. have ἀμφορῆς, and of his two Plays the one is more commonly entitled Ἱππεῖς, the other Ἀχαρνῆς.

As to the accusative, ἱππέᾱς occurs six times in Aristophanes, Nub. 120, 554, Eq. 610, Ach. 7, Lys. 676, Ran. 653. So Ἀχαρνέᾱς, Ach. 177, 200, 203, 222. But in late Middle and New Comedy, as also in Euripides, sometimes -εᾰς, and even in the singular -ᾰ, but never -εις. Antiphanes, Stob. Flor. 79. 7—

πρὸς τοὺς ἑαυτοῦ γονέᾰς οὐκ ἔστιν κακός.

Alexis, Athen. 11. 473 D—

κάνθαρον, καταστρέφοντα, πλησίον δὲ κειμένον
στρωματέᾰ καὶ γύλιον αὐτοῦ.

On the other hand, forms like ἰχθύας are certainly un-Attic, and must be replaced by ἰχθῦς, etc. Theocritus even uses ἰχθύα and ὀφρύα for ἰχθύν and ὀφρύν, but Theocritus uses ἰδήσω = ὄψομαι, and μαθεῦμαι = μαθήσομαι!

Wecklein (Curae Epigraphicae, pp. 19–21) states the evidence of Inscriptions. The nom. pl. of nouns in -ευς ended invariably in -ῆς up to Ol. 100 (376 B. C.). From that date till Ol. 113 (about 325 B. C.) -ῆς was still the commoner form, but -εις had begun to be used. After 325 B. C. -εις prevailed.

According to Herwerden (Lapidum de Dialecto Attica Testimonia, p. 49), the earliest examples of -εις for the accusative -εας occur in Inscriptions of a date just before the close of the fourth century B. C., 307–300.

ἐνενοήκη καὶ ἐπεποιήκη· καὶ οὕτω φησὶ Παναίτιος ἔχειν τὰς γραφὰς παρὰ Πλάτωνι, καὶ Θουκυδίδης δὲ κέχρηται τῷ τοιούτῳ Ἀττικῷ ἔθει. The best manuscripts of Plato use both forms, but the better the manuscript is acknowledged to be, the more frequently do the forms in -η occur in its pages. Moreover, in a genuine form like ἀπωλώλη, -ειν is often written over the -η, as in Apol. 31 D, 36 A, etc. In Plato, Rep. 337 A, καὶ τοῦτ' ἐγὼ ᾔδη τε καὶ τούτοις προὔλεγον, the ᾔδη has escaped from being mistaken for the adverb.

The following passages of Photius are probably the authoritative dicta of Aelius Dionysius: Ἑωράκη [1] τὸ πρῶτον πρόσωπον, ὡς ἐπεπόνθη [1] καὶ ἐπεποιήκη [1] καὶ ᾔδη [1] τὸ ᾔδειν. Πλάτων τοῖς τοιούτοις χρῆται σχηματισμοῖς. Again: Καὶ τὸ ᾔδη ἀντὶ τοῦ ᾔδειν καὶ τὸ ἐπεπόνθη ἀντὶ τοῦ ἐπεπόνθειν.

Aristophanes uses the first person of the pluperfect five times, and in every case except one the form in -η has manuscript authority:—

ὅτε δὴ κεχήνη προσδοκῶν τὸν Αἴσχυλον.
Arist. Ach. 10.

MSS. κεχήνη.

ἠκηκόη γὰρ ὡς Ἀθηναῖοί ποτε.
Vesp. 801.

Some MSS. ἠκηκόειν. Ravenna ἠκηκόη.

τουτὶ τοίνυν οὐκ ᾔδη 'γώ κτε.
Av. 511.

Some MSS. ᾔδειν 'γώ. Rav. and Vat. ᾔδη 'γώ.

ἐγὼ δέ γ' ὑμᾶς προσδοκῶσ' ἐγρηγόρη.
Eccl. 32.

MSS. ἐγρηγόρειν and ἐγρηγόρουν. Porsonus emendavit.

δεινὸν μέντοι ἐπεπόνθη.
Eccl. 650.

MSS. ἐπεπόνθειν. Rav. and Suïdas ἐπεπόνθη.

Here it will be observed that, except in the case of Av. 511, the metre affords no assistance. The point is proved by the weight of the documentary evidence.

[1] Even here the transcribers actually write -ει for -η all the four times.

The metrical evidence of Tragedy is even less than that of Comedy, there being in no tragic Poet a single instance of the first person preceding a vowel. But the verdict of the manuscripts is plain enough in the case of the frequently occurring past of *οἶδα*.

Of the two forms *ᾔδη* and *ᾔδειν* the former is found in—

οὐ γάρ τί σ' ᾔδη μῶρα φωνήσοντ', ἐπεί.
Soph. O. R. 433.

Laurentian A has *ᾔδει* with *ν* written above.

ᾔδη δ' ὁθούνεκ' ἄνδρα καὶ πατροκτόνον.
Id. O. C. 944.

All MSS. *ᾔδη*, although three lines infra all read *ξυνῄδειν* for *ξυνῄδη*.

ᾔδη καλῶς καί σ' ἐκτὸς αὐλείων πυλῶν.
Id. Ant. 18.

Laurentian A has *ᾔδειν*, but that the Scholiast read *ᾔδη* is plain from his gloss, *ἀντὶ τοῦ ᾔδεα*.

οἲ 'γὼ τάλαινα· τοῦτ' ἐκεῖν' ᾔδη σαφές.
Id. El. 1115.

The MSS. have *ἤδη*, the true form being preserved by being mistaken for the adverb.

ᾔδη σ' ἀπορριψοῦσαν ἁπηγγελλόμην.
Id. 1018.

Laurentian B indicates the original reading by *ᾔδην*. Other MSS. have *ᾔδειν*.

ᾔδη τάδ'· οὐδὲν μάντεως ἔδει φράσαι.
Eur. Rhes. 952.

One MSS. *ᾔδη*, others *ᾔδειν*.

τὸ δ' ἔργον ᾔδη τὴν νόσον τε δυσκλεᾶ.
Id. Hipp. 434.

MSS. *ᾔδη*, *ἤδη*, and *ᾔδειν*.

On the other hand, *ᾔδειν* without variant is met with in the following passages:—

ᾔδειν· τί δ' οὐκ ἔμελλον; ἐμφανῆ γὰρ ἦν.
Soph. Ant. 448.

ὡς οὐκ ἄρ' ᾔδειν τῶν ἐμῶν οὐδὲν κακῶν.
Id. El. 1185.

ἐγὼ ξυνῄδειν χθόνιον ὄνθ' ὃς οὐκ ἐᾷ.
Id. O. C. 748.

πάλαι μὲν ᾔδειν σ' ὄντα τοιοῦτον φύσει.
Eur. Cycl. 649.

παρεῖχον· ᾔδειν δ' ἁμὲ χρῆν νικᾶν πόσιν.
Id. Tro. 655.

There is no question that ᾔδη must be everywhere restored.

In regard to the second person, the evidence is by no means so complete as that which establishes the true ending of the first and third persons. As a matter of fact, however, no evidence is required; for if the original endings were respectively -εα, -εας, -εε(ν), and it is proved that -εα became -η, and -εε(ν), -ει(ν), then -εας must have been represented in Attic by -ης. The frequently recurring past of οἶδα, which naturally occurs more often than a true pluperfect, is of some service in deciding the genuine ending of the second person, although it has retained the old suffix -θα, ᾔδησθα. The mere fact of its being ᾔδησ-θα, and not ᾔδεισ-θα, is good evidence for -ης in ordinary pluperfects.

To return to the dictum of Phrynichus on the third person plural. On that point the authority of Aristophanes is decisive, and whenever the form with a long penultimate syllable is encountered in Prose it should be replaced by the lighter ending:—

τὸν Πλοῦτον ἠσπάζοντο καὶ τὴν νύχθ' ὅλην
ἐγρηγόρεσαν ἕως διέλαμψεν ἡμέρα.
Arist. Plut. 743.

οἱ δ' ἀνεκρότησαν καὶ πρὸς ἐμ' ἐκεχήνεσαν.
Id. Eq. 648.

ἐκεκράγεσάν τε τοὺς πρυτάνεις ἀφιέναι.
Ib. 674.

In Thucydides, 4. 27, ἐδεδοίκεσαν is supported by the manuscripts, as it is Xenophon, Anab. 3. 5. 18. In Anab. 4. 6. 22 ἐγρηγόρεσαν was restored by Porson, and is now the accepted reading for ἐγρηγόρησαν. The latter, from the late present γρηγορῶ, is a debased aorist form and no pluperfect. (See supra p. 200.)

The other persons had also a short penultimate, and if λύω is taken as a typical verb, the Attic inflexions of the pluperfect are these—

ἐλελύκη		ἐλελύκεμεν
ἐλελύκης	ἐλελύκετον	ἐλελύκετε
ἐλελύκει(ν)	ἐλελυκέτην	ἐλελύκεσαν.

The plural of ᾔδη is in Attic ᾖσμεν, ᾖστε, ᾖσαν, but in Euripides, Bacch. 1345, an older form has survived—

ὄψ' ἐμάθεθ' ἡμᾶς, ὅτε δ' ἐχρῆν, οὐκ ᾔδετε·

as in Sophocles, O. R. 1232—

λείπει μὲν οὐδ' ἃ πρόσθεν ᾔδεμεν[1] τὸ μὴ οὐ κτε.

The line of the Lysistrata (1098)—

ὦ Πολυχαρείδαν δεινά κα 'πεπόνθεμες,

though the words are Laconian, furnishes important confirmatory evidence.

In fact, it is impossible, on philological grounds, to account for the long penultimate in Attic. By rejecting it, forms like ᾖσμεν, ᾖστε, ᾖμεν, ᾖτε, are satisfactorily accounted for; and in two out of the three cases in which the plural of the pluperfect occurs in verse, a short penultimate syllable is demanded by the metre.

CXXVII.

Ὁ ῥύπος ἐρεῖς, οὐ τὸ ῥύπος.

The masculine gender is proved by Aristophanes—

τοὺς ῥύπους ἀνασπάσαι,

Lys. 1200.

and read in all other passages of Attic writers. 'Ὁ ῥύπος

[1] MSS. ᾔδειμεν. Elmsley emend.

Atticum esse Aristophanis et Alexidis, Athen. 4. 161 D, testimoniis constat, eoque genere etiam vulgo usi videntur.' Lobeck.

Of much more importance than the gender of the substantive is the meaning of the verb connected with it. If *ῥύπτω* is really akin to *ῥύπος*, then its signification is anomalous in the extreme. In the lines at the beginning of the Acharnians—

> ἀλλ' οὐδεπώποτ' ἐξ ὅτου γε ῥύπτομαι,
> οὕτως ἐδήχθην ὑπὸ κονίας τὰς ὀφρῦς,
> ὡς νῦν,

the sense of *become dirty* is as agreeable to the context as *wash myself*, and recalls a well-known passage of Sterne's unholy wit; but the meaning *wash* is demanded in Aristotle, Meteor. 2. 3. 359 a22, *ῥύπτειν τὰ ἱμάτια*, and Theophrastus, H. Pl. 9. 9. 3, *τρὺξ ᾗ ῥυπτόμεθα.* If it is said that, as from un-Attic writers, these passages are not of authority, and if the meaning of the word is, from the evidently corrupt state of the text, little helped by the lines of Antiphanes—

> ἔρχεται,
> μετέρχεθ' αὕτη, προσέρχετ', οὐ μετέρχεται,
> ἥκει, πάρεστι, ῥύπτεται, προσέρχεται,
> σμῆται, κτενίζετ', ἐκβέβηκε, τρίβεται,
> λοῦται, σκοπεῖται, στέλλεται, μυρίζεται,
> κοσμεῖτ', ἀλείφετ', ἂν δ' ἔχῃ τι ἀπάγχεται·

nevertheless Plato has the adjective *ῥυπτικός*, in the sense of *cleansing*, in Tim. 65 D, *τὰ δὲ τούτων τε ῥυπτικὰ καὶ πᾶν τὸ περὶ τὴν γλῶτταν ἀποπλύνοντα κτε.*, just as Plutarch, in Symp. 697 A, *καὶ κατακαυθέντος ἡ τέφρα ῥυπτικωτάτην παοέχει κόνιν*, and Aristotle, de Sensibus, 5. 443 a1, *πλυντικὸν ἢ ῥυπτικὸν ἐγχύμου ξηρότητος.*

If the substantive and the verb are related, then there is no reason why the derivation of *lucus* from *luceo* should be treated with ridicule and contempt.

CXXVIII.

Ἀλεῖν ἐρεῖς, οὐκ ἀλ'θειν, καὶ ἤλει, οὐκ ἤληθεν, ἀλοῦσα, οὐχὶ δὲ ἀληθοῦσα.

Ἄιδειν τε πίνουθ' ὡσπερεὶ κάχρυς γυναῖκ' ἀλοῦσαν.
Ar. Nub. 1358.

εἶτα πρὸς τούτοισιν ἤλουν ὄρθριαι τὰ σιτία.
Pherecr. (Athen. vi. 263 B).

For the perfect and aorist passive of this verb see p. 98; and for late forms similar to *ἀλήθω* see pp. 134, 155, 157.

CXXIX.

Μέθυσος ἀνὴρ οὐκ ἐρεῖς, ἀλλὰ μεθυστικός· γυναῖκα δὲ ἐρεῖς μέθυσον καὶ μεθύσην.

Grammarians are in accord upon this point. Pollux, 6. 25, remarks that Menander first used *μέθυσος* of a man: *Μεθυστικός, ἡ γυνὴ δὲ μεθύση, καὶ μεθύστρια παρὰ Θεοπόμπῳ τῷ Κωμικῷ. ὁ γὰρ μέθυσος ἐπὶ ἀνδρῶν Μενάνδρῳ δεδόσθω.* It will be observed that there is some difference of meaning between *μεθυστικός* and *μέθυσος*, the former denoting a habit, the latter not necessarily so. 'The man is a drunkard, and his wife tipples,' *ὁ μὲν ἀνὴρ μεθυστικός ἐστιν, ἡ δὲ γυνὴ μεθύση.* The usage probably originated from some ethical cause.

CXXX.

Ἤμην, εἰ καὶ εὑρίσκεται παρὰ τοῖς ἀρχαίοις, οὐκ ἐρεῖς, ἀλλ' ἦν ἐγώ.

That Phrynichus should allow the possibility of *ἤμην* in Classical Greek is even more surprising than his uncertainty about ἦς and ἦσθα. In two passages of Sophocles ἤμην was once read—

> ἐγὼ γὰρ ἤμην ἐκπεπληγμένη φόβῳ.
> Trach. 24.
>
> ὅ τ᾽ ἐχθρὸς ἡμῖν ἐς τοσόνδ᾽ ἐχθραντέος.
> Aj. 679.

In the former ἤμην has been restored from a correction in the Laurentian, and from the Scholium, ἤμην, δασέως, ἵνα συνᾴδῃ τῷ—'Αλλ᾽ ὅστις ἦν θακῶν ἀταρβὴς τῆς θέας,—εἰ δὲ ψιλῶς, ἀντὶ τοῦ ὑπῆρχον. The corruption arose at a date when such constructions as N. T. Ep. ad Gal. 1. 22 became common, ἤμην δὲ ἀγνοούμενος τῷ προσώπῳ ταῖς ἐκκλησίαις τῆς 'Ιουδαίας. In the Ajax all the manuscripts exhibit ἤμην as well as Suïdas sub voc. ἤμην, but ἡμῖν was restored by Bentley from Suïdas sub voc. ἄημα, and is now the acknowledged reading. In Eur. Hel. 930—

> κλύοντες, εἰσιδόντες, ὡς τέχναις θεῶν
> ὤλοντ᾽ ἐγὼ δὲ προδότις οὐκ ἄρ᾽ ἦν φίλων·

ἤμην was substituted for ἄρ᾽ ἦν from the Etym. Magn. on the authority of George Choeroboscus, the Grammarian, whose vagaries it has already been necessary to reprehend. Ἄρ᾽ ἦν has excellent manuscript authority, and must be retained. Considering the way in which ἤμην originated in these three places, no one will hesitate unreservedly to alter it in the two passages in which it is found in Prose. In Lysias, III. 16, ἕτοιμος ἤμην should become ἕτοιμος εἴην, and even Xenophon, Cyr. 6. 1. 9, cannot have employed such a form. It is one of those words to which false analogy gave birth in late times, and though ἦσθα itself made room for ἦς, it bore ἤμην in time to receive its dying breath.

That Nauck should conjecture ἤμην in Eur. Tro. 474 is another instance of his ignorance of the science of Greek forms, and his unreasonable dependence on Choeroboscus, who, if possible, is more ignorant than himself. The manuscripts present the passage as follows—

ἦμεν τύραννοι κεἰς τύραννʼ ἐγημάμην,
κἀνταῦθʼ ἀριστεύοντʼ ἐγεινάμην τέκνα.

Now the ἦμεν τύραννοι is simply a corruption of ἦ μὲν τύραννος, caused by the misunderstanding of ἦ, the genuine Attic form of the first person singular imperfect of the substantive verb. The Grammarian Porphyrius, in a scholium to Od. 8. 186, which appears also in one codex in Il. 5. 533, distinctly states that in his time ἦν had completely superseded ἦ: Τὸ ἦν ἐπιπολάζει νῦν, τῶν δὲ Ἀττικῶν οἱ μὲν ἀρχαῖοι μονογράμματον αὐτὸ προεφέροντο· and again: Τὸ μονοσύλλαβον τῶν Ἀττικῶν ἐστι παρὰ Κρατίνῳ ἐν Πυτίνῃ—

γυνὴ δʼ ἐκείνου πρότερον ἦ, νῦν δʼ οὐκέτι·

καὶ παρὰ Σοφοκλεῖ ἐν τῇ Νιόβῃ—

ἦ γὰρ φίλη ʼγὼ τῶνδε τοῦ προφερτέρου·

καὶ ἐν Οἰδίποδι Τυράννῳ—

ἦ δοῦλος οὐκ ὠνητός, ἀλλʼ οἴκοι τραφείς·

καὶ παρὰ Πλάτωνι τῷ φιλοσόφῳ· εἰ μὲν γὰρ ἐγὼ ἔτι ἐν δυνάμει ἦ τοῦ ῥᾳδίως (πορεύεσθαι εἰς τὸ ἄστυ) The last passage is from Rep. 328 C. Even in the text of the scholium itself the copyists have substituted ἦν for ἦ in the passages adduced to prove the latter form.

In Soph. O. C. 973 and 1366 ἦ is found in L., but in 1366 ν has been added by a late hand. The ἦν in Trach. 564—

φέρων ἐπʼ ὤμοις, ἡνίκʼ ἦν μέσῳ πόρῳ,

may, as Cobet suggests, be no more than a misreading of ἦ ʼν μέσῳ πόρῳ. In Aesch. Cho. 523—

οἶδʼ, ὦ τέκνον, παρῆ γάρ· ἔκ τʼ ὀνειράτων,

the true reading was restored by Porson from its lurking-place—the manuscript reading πάρει. Neither in Sophocles nor in Aeschylus is there any line where ἦν is required by the metre, but in Euripides and Aristophanes the case is different. On this point Elmsley's opinion was that ἦν in Euripides was a corruption, and in Aristophanes, as occurring only in his last play, was to be explained as a growth, or rather decay, of Attic. Soph. O. R. p. 12, 'ἦ pro ἦν, eram, quater reposui. Ἦν aliquoties ante vocalem legitur apud Euripidem, ut in Hipp. 1012, Alc. 655, I. A. 944, Ion 280. Quamquam haec omnia corrupta esse suspicor. Sic etiam ter Aristophanes, sed in Pluto, novissima omnium fabula, 29, 695, 822. Nihil tale apud Sophoclem reperitur.' As a matter of fact, Euripides in this, as in many other cases, allowed himself a licence of which neither Aeschylus nor Sophocles would have availed themselves, and introduced into the dignified company of *γεγώς, δάμαρ, τέξω, ἐλεύσομαι,* etc. a modern form, which even Aristophanes for long eyed askance. That any Attic poet or prose writer ever used ἦν before a consonant is subject to grave doubt, and probably in prose the biliteral form was unknown even before a vowel. With regard to Aristophanes, the facts are these. In no case is ἦ required by the metre, but in many it is read by the best manuscripts, and in others the scholia prove that it was known in the texts to which they were appended. The Ravenna reads ἦ in Plut. 77, Vesp. 1091, Eq. 1339, Lys. 645, but in Av. 1363 it has ἦν, although the Scholiast annotates ἦ ἀντὶ τοῦ ἦν Ἀττικῶς. On the other hand, ἦν is demanded by the metre in Pl. 29, 695, 822.

In Plato, Cratylus 396 D, the Bodleian has συνῆ, but ν written at the side. This is simply an indication of what has happened in every case. The Attic form became unintelligible to late Greeks, and was either changed at once or explained in the margin, as in this passage of Plato. In Phaed. 61 B, *καὶ αὐτὸς οὐκ ἦ μυθολογικός,* even Stallbaum has been forced to admit the genuine form.

It is worth quoting the scholium on Ar. Plut. 77—

λέγειν ἃ κρύπτειν ἦ παρεσκευασμένος,

if only to show the strange mixture of truth and error

which was the learning of most of the scholars through whose hands the present texts of Classical authors came and suffered; with all its absurdity, it contains an attempt to appreciate the philological argument for ἦ, which is of some value: Τὸ ἦ ἄνευ τοῦ ν ἀντὶ τοῦ ἤμην· οἱ γὰρ Ἀττικοὶ τὸ ἦν καὶ ὑπῆρχον ἐγὼ ἦ φασίν· οὕτως ἀπὸ τοῦ εἰμὶ τὸ ὑπάρχω γίνεται ὁ παρατατικὸς εἶν διὰ διφθόγγου ὡς καὶ ἀπὸ τοῦ εἴδημι ᾔδειν καὶ διαλύσει Ἰωνικῇ τῆς ει διφθόγγου εἰς ε καὶ α γράφεται ἔα, ὡς καὶ τὸ ᾔδεα καὶ τὸ τιθεῖσι τιθέασιν, ἡ χρῆσις δὲ παρ' Ὁμήρῳ ὡς τό—

οὐ γὰρ ἀμενηνὸς ἔα·

εἶτα κιρνῶντες τὸ ε καὶ α εἰς ἦ, ἦ φασίν; ὡς καὶ ἐνταῦθα καὶ ἐν τοῖς ἑξῆς εὑρήσεις.

CXXXI.

Ὤιδηκεν, ᾠκοδόμηκεν διὰ τοῦ ω ἄριστα ἐρεῖς, ἀλλ' οὐ διὰ τοῦ οι, οἴδηκεν, οἰκοδόμηκεν.

A general rule must be elicited from these examples. Manuscript authority is naturally of little value on such a question, and is not to be regarded. On the other hand, stone records are of signal importance, and serve to establish on a sound footing the augmentation in imperfect, aorist, and perfect of Attic verbs which begin in a diphthong. It is true that they undermine any faith in manuscripts with which the inquirer may have started; but to the serious scholar little is lost thereby, and with pleasure he draws his pen through the elaborated records of what are really manuscript corruptions.

One general principle of great importance is clearly demonstrated by stone records, namely, that verbs beginning with diphthongs were in the best age of Attic subject to the same laws of augmentation as verbs beginning with a simple vowel. Thus, ηὕρισκον, ηὗρον, ηὕρηκα, ηὐχόμην, ηὖγμαι, ᾔκαζον, ᾔκασα, must be restored to the Tragic poets, to the writers of the Old and Early Middle Comedy, to Thucydides, Plato, Antiphon, Andocides, Lysias, Isocrates, and Isaeus; but for Dinarchus, Aeschines, and Demosthenes, there is no rule possible. It is true that, up to the archonship of Euclides, the letter E represented the two sounds of η and ε, and accordingly till that date the augmentation is not *visible*; but the inscriptions written in the enlarged alphabet prove that, till the middle of the fourth century B.C., εὐ- by augmentation became ηὐ-, and εἰ- became ῃ-, and by parallelism αὐ- and οἰ- would become ηὐ- and ᾠ- respectively.

This rule, however, is subject to one limitation, which must not be disregarded. It is true in regard to εὐ- and οἰ- only when these syllables immediately precede a consonant; when they are followed by a vowel, that vowel and not the initial diphthong receives the augment. Thus, ηὐδαιμόνουν, ηὐδοκίμουν, ηὐδόξουν, ηὐθάρσουν, ηὐθύμουν, ηὐλαβούμην, ηὐνομούμην, ηὕρισκον, ηὐσέβουν, ηὔφραινον, ηὐχόμην, etc., but εὐηγγελιζόμην, εὐηργέτουν, εὐωδώθην, εὐώρκουν. When the vowel succeeding the εὐ- is already long by nature, the verb has no augment, εὐειμάτουν, εὐηθιζόμην, εὐημέρουν, εὐωχήθην. Similarly with οἰ-, ᾤδησα, ᾠκείουν, ᾤκουν, ᾤκιζον, ᾠκοδόμουν, ᾠκούρουν, ᾤκτειρον, ᾤμωζον, ᾠνάριζον, ᾤστρουν, ᾠχόμην, but οἰωπόλουν, while οἰωνιζόμην, οἰάκιζον, οἰωνοσκόπουν, remain unaugmented. Accordingly, Dindorf is wrong in reading ηὐωχημένος in Aristophanes (Lys. 1224, Vesp. 1305), and Porson in changing οἰᾰκοστρόφουν (Aesch. Pers. 767) to ᾠακοστρόφουν.

CXXXII.

Ἀνίστατο λέγε καὶ μὴ ἠνίστατο.

The form ἠνίστατο is due to the principle which in

pp. 81 ff. has been proved to have been active even in Attic of the best days.

CXXXIII.

Βρῶμος· πάνυ ἐζήτηται, εἰ χρὴ λέγειν ἐπὶ τῆς δυσωδίας. μέχρι οὖν εὑρίσκεται ἐπὶ δυσωδίας ἄχαριν ὀσμὴν λέγε ὥσπερ οἱ κωμῳδοποιοί·

In our existing texts *βρῶμος* certainly does not occur till late. When necessary, *ὀσμή* was defined by an adjective, generally *καλή* or *κακή*.

CXXXIV.

Ἡρακλέα, Περικλέα, Θεμιστοκλέα ἐπεκτείνων τὴν ἐσχάτην λέγε, ἀλλὰ μὴ Ἡρακλῆν καὶ Περικλῆν καὶ Θεμιστοκλῆν.

'Nominum in *-κλῆς* genitivus in *-κλέου* et accusativus in *-κλῆν* maxime recens est, nec fortasse ante Ol. 123 referendus.' Wecklein, Cur. Epigr. p. 23.

CXXXV.

Ἀνέῳγεν ἡ θύρα σολοικισμός. χρὴ γὰρ λέγειν ἀνέῳκται.

CXXXVI.

Διεφθορὸς αἷμα· τῶν ἀμαθῶν τινες ἰατρῶν λέγουσιν οὕτω, σολοικίζοντες, δέον λέγειν διεφθαρμένον αἷμα. τὸ γὰρ διέφθορε, διέφθειρεν.

In the manuscripts the second of these articles follows that on *ἱερόθυτον* (138 infr.).

Veitch makes a signal mistake in quoting ἀνεώγει as a pluperfect active from Pherecrates. That writer used ἀνέῳγε, the only form of the imperfect known to Attic (see p. 85 supra). For the perfect and pluperfect ἀνέῳχα and ἠνεῴχη were alone used.

In the intransitive sense, here reprehended by Phrynichus, Veitch quotes the word from Hippocr. 7. 558 (Lit.); Aristaen. 2. 22; Plut. Mor. 693; Luc. Gall. 30, D. Mort. 4. 1; Herodn. 4. 2. 7; Polyaen. 2. 28, adding the sentence, 'which earlier Attic (sic) writers seem to have avoided, and used ἀνέῳγμαι instead: Dinarchus, the Orator, is said in Cramer's Anecd. 1. 52 to have been the only exception.' The writers first named are not generally regarded as Attic, and even Dinarchus could hardly have employed ἀνέῳγα intransitively, although his Attic was far from pure.

Besides ἀνεῳγότες ὀφθαλμοί in Gall. 30, and τοῦ σκαφιδίου τὰ ἀνεῳγότα in D. Mort. 4. 1, Lucian also used ἀνεῳγυῖα παλαίστρα in Navig. 4, although in De Soloecismo, 8, he ridicules this departure from the rules of Attic.

In De Soloec. 3 it is doubtful whether or not Lucian is of *malice prepense* using διέφθορα as a neuter; but in Plutarch, Josephus, Heliodorus, and other late writers, it has always that sense. If φρένας ἠλεός did not occur in other passages of Homer, as—

> Μέντορ ἀταρτηρέ, φρένας ἠλεέ, ποῖον ἔειπες,
>
> Od. 2. 243.

it would be tempting to separate the two words in—

> μαινόμενε, φρένας ἠλέ, διέφθορας· ἦ νύ τοι αὔτως
> οὔατ' ἀκουέμεν ἔστι, νόος δ' ἀπόλωλε καὶ αἰδώς,
>
> Il. 15. 128.

but there can be no question that the perfect is there neuter, as also in Hippocr. de Morb. Mul. 2. 23, αἷμα διεφθορός, and id. 2. 5, γυναικὶ διεφθορυίῃ.

In Attic, however, διέφθορα had the same signification as

διέφθαρκα—the latter occurring in Plato, Apol. 33 C, Legg. 636 B; Lysias, 93. 15; Aeschin. 22. 38; Demosth. 1109 21; Eur. Med. 226; the former in Soph. El. 306; Eur. Hipp. 1014, I. T. 719, Med. 349; Cratin. 2. 226; Pherecr. 2. 327; Aristoph. 2. 1149, 1173, etc.

CXXXVII.

Οἱ ἥρως οὐ λέγουσιν, ἀλλ' οἱ ἥρωες τρισυλλάβως· ἐπὶ δὲ τῆς αἰτιατικῆς, δισυλλάβως τοὺς ἥρως. ἅπαξ βιασθεὶς Ἀριστοφάνης ὑπὸ τοῦ μέτρου οἱ ἥρως εἶπε. τῷ δ' ἠναγκασμένῳ οὐ χρηστέον.

The passage of Aristophanes is probably that referred to by Choeroboscus (Bekk. An. 3. 1197), who quotes from Herodian a remark similar to this of Phrynichus: *Εὕρηται κατὰ κρᾶσιν παρὰ Ἀριστοφάνει ἐν Ὄρνισιν, οἷον—*

οἱ γὰρ ἥρως ἐγγύς εἰσιν,

ἀντὶ τοῦ οἱ ἥρωες. No such words occur in the *Birds*, and *Ἥρωσιν* has been proposed for *Ὄρνισιν*.

On the other hand, there is no question that Aristophanes never used *ἥρων* for *ἥρωα*, and the Scholiast on Il. 13. 428 must be in error: *Ἥρων τινες Ἀττικῶς—*

Ἀλλ' εἰς ἥρων τι παρήμαρτον,

Ἀριστοφάνης. The Attic form was *ἥρω*. The dative singular was in Attic *ἥρῳ*, not *ἥρωι*, Plato, Com. (Ath. 10. 442 A)—

ἥρῳ Κέλητι δέρμα καὶ θυλήματα.

In the Agamemnon, l. 516, Aeschylus employed *ἥρως* as accusative plural—

ἥρως τε τοὺς πέμψαντας, εὐμενεῖς πάλιν.

CXXXVIII.

Ἱερόθυτον οὐκ ἐρεῖς, ἀλλ' ἀρχαίως θεόθυτον.

In the App. Soph. p. 42, Phrynichus has the words, *Θεόθυτα (ἃ οἱ πολλοὶ ἱερόθυτα καλοῦσι) Κρατῖνος τὰ τοῖς θεοῖς θυόμενα ἱερεῖα.* The defaulting term is encountered in—

> ἀποκεκλήκαμεν διογενεῖς θεοὺς
> μηκέτι τὴν ἐμὴν διαπερᾶν πόλιν,
> μηδέ τιν' ἱερόθυτον ἀνὰ δάπεδον ἄν ἔτι
> τῇδε βροτῶν θεοῖσι πέμπειν καπνόν.
>
> Ar. Av. 1263.

The lines are burlesque, but even so ἱερόθυτον must go with καπνόν, and not with δάπεδον, *the smoke of victims sacrificed.* All Phrynichus reprehends is the use of ἱερόθυτος for θεόθυτος. A late writer said ἱερά or ἱερεῖα ἱερόθυτα, whereas the Classical expression was ἱερά or ἱερεῖα θεόθυτα, *sacrifices offered to god.*

CXXXIX.

Ἀνατοιχεῖν μὴ λέγε ἀλλὰ διατοιχεῖν.

'Convenit Poll. I. 114. In App. p. 34, Phrynichus idem sed paulo copiosius dixit: διατοιχεῖν τὸ εἰς τὸν ἕτερον τοῖχον τῆς νεὼς διαβαίνειν ἐν τῷ πλῷ ὅπερ οἱ ἰδιῶται ἀντιτοιχεῖν λέγουσιν. Sed ἀντιτοιχεῖν veriorem esse scripturam exempla docent quorum praesidio ἀντιτοιχεῖν caret. Quamquam autem neutrum horum verborum, de quibus nostro loco disquiritur crebro usu tritum est, tamen, quid veteres probaverint, non obscurum esse potest. Antiatt. Bekk. p. 89, διατοιχεῖν ἀντὶ τοῦ ἀνατοιχεῖν Εὔβουλος Κατακολλωμένῳ. Aristid. Leuctr. iv. 462 I. I.: καὶ μή, τὸ τῶν πλεόντων, μεταστρέψαι πρὸς τὸν ἐλάττω, διατοιχοῦντας ἀεί.' Lobeck.

CXL.

Ἤνυστρον λέγε, μὴ ἔνυστρον.

Ἐγὼ δέ γ' ἤνυστρον βοὸς καὶ κοιλίαν ὑείαν.
Ar. Eq 356.

καὶ χόλικος ἠνύστρου τε καὶ γαστρὸς τόμον.
Id. 1179.

CXLI.

Ἐλλύχνιον· καὶ τοῦτο τῶν εἰσκωμασάντων ταῖς Ἀθήναις. Θρυαλλίδα οὖν ῥητέον.

A second article to the same effect—*ἐλλύχνιον Ἡρόδοτος κέχρηται, Ἀθηναῖοι δὲ θρυαλλίδα λέγουσιν*—appeared near the end of the codex used by Nuñez, and is also read in the margin near the end of the first Laurentian munuscript in still another form—*ἐλλύχνιον παρὰ Ἡροδότῳ, οἱ δὲ Ἀθηναῖοι θρυαλλίδα.* The word entered the Common dialect from the Ionic, as it is found in Hdt. 2. 62; Hippocr. de Nat. Mul. p. 569. 55, de Morb. Mul. 2. 670. 43.

CXLII.

Θυμέλην· τοῦτο οἱ μὲν ἀρχαῖοι ἀντὶ τοῦ θυσίαν ἐτίθεσαν οἱ δὲ νῦν ἐπὶ τοῦ τόπου ἐν τῷ θεάτρῳ ἐφ' οὗ αὐληταὶ καὶ κιθαρῳδοὶ καὶ ἄλλοι τινὲς ἀγωνίζονται. σὺ μέντοι, ἔνθα μὲν κωμῳδοὶ καὶ τραγῳδοὶ ἀγωνίζονται, λογεῖον ἐρεῖς. ἔνθα δὲ οἱ αὐληταὶ καὶ οἱ χόροι, ὀρχήστραν καὶ μὴ θυμέλην.

'*Θυμέλη* pro orchestra apud veteres non memini me legere praeter quod Pratinas, Athen. 14. 617 C, *Διονυσιάδα πολυπάταγα θυμέλαν* in hunc sensum dixisse videtur. Saepius apud recentiores pro scaena et re scaenica atque musica occurrit, ut Plut. Mor. p. 405 D, τὴν δὲ τῆς Πυθίας φωνὴν καὶ διάλεκτον ὥσπερ ἐκ θυμέλης οὐκ ἀνήδυντον οὐδὲ λιτὴν ἀλλ' ἐν μέτρῳ καὶ ὄγκῳ . . . φθεγγομένην: Lucian. de Salt. 76 (309), ἐπὶ τοῦ παχέος δὲ καὶ πιμελοῦς ὀρχηστοῦ πηδᾶν μεγάλα πειρωμένου, Δεόμεθα, ἔφασαν, πεφεῖσθαι τῆς θυμέλης.' Lobeck. He also cites from Procopius, τῶν τις ἐν θυμέλῃ πεπορνευμένων = *mima;* from Plutarch, μίμοις γυναιξὶ καὶ κιθαρισταῖς καὶ θυμελικοῖς ἀνθρώποις: from Eunapius, ὁ κακοδαίμων τῶν θυμελῶν χόρος = *histriones;* from Josephus, τοῖς ἐν τῇ μουσικῇ διαγομένοις, τοῖς καὶ θυμελικοῖς καλουμένοις: so that there was good reason for the caution of Phrynichus.

The word was, in fact, not Attic at all, being confined to Tragedy: Aesch. Supp. 669; Eur. Supp. 64, Rhes. 235.

Its employment in the sense of *the sacred cake* is at best only doubtful, being dependent upon Hesychius: Θυμέλαι· οἱ βωμοὶ καὶ τὰ ἄλφιτα τὰ ἐπιθυόμενα: and App. Soph. 42. 25: Θυμέλη· Φερεκράτης τὰ θυλήματα, ἅπερ ἐστὶν ἄλφιτα οἴνῳ καὶ ἐλαίῳ μεμαγμένα, οὕτω καλεῖ θυμέλη.

CXLIII.

Θυείαν λέγε, μὴ ἴγδιν.

Pollux, 10. 103, τὴν δὲ θυείαν καὶ θυείδιον εἴποις ἂν κατὰ 'Αριστοφάνην ἐν Πλούτῳ λέγοντα· καὶ ἴγδιν δὲ αὐτὴν κεκλήκασι, Σόλων τε ἐν τοῖς ἰάμβοις λέγων—

σπεύδουσι[1] δ' οἱ μὲν ἴγδιν, οἱ δὲ σίλφιον,
οἱ δ' ὄξος·

καὶ ἔτι σαφέστερον 'Αντιφάνης Κοροπλάθῳ—

γύναι, πρὸς αὐλὸν ἦλθες, ὀρχήσει πάλιν
τὴν ἴγδιν·

[1] Adopting Casaubon's conjecture for the unintelligible πευσίδ'.

ἔστι μὲν οὖν ἴγδις ὀρχήσεως σχῆμα· ὁ δὲ παίζων πρὸς τοὔνομα κωμικὸς ἐπήγαγε—

τὴν θυείαν ἀγνοεῖς;

τουτέστιν ἡ ἴγδις

Phrynichus is here reprehending τοὺς ὑπεραττικίζοντας. The old word ἴγδις meant *a mortar*, and in that sense appears in Ionic, Hipp. 635. 34, Τρῖβε ἐν ἴγδει[1]: and in old Attic, as in the passage of Solon cited. In Attic proper, however, it was replaced by θυεία, but retained, as the name of a certain dance, in which a pestle-like motion was conveyed to the loins: Etym Mag. p. 464. 49, ἔστι δὲ καὶ εἶδος ὀρχήσεως ἴγδισμα, ἐν ᾗ ἐλύγιζον τὴν ὀσφὺν ἐμφερῶς τῷ δοίδυκι.

Unlike many other such terms, ἴγδις did not find its way into the Common dialect in the sense of θυεία, as is demonstrated by a passage of Sextus Empiricus, adv. Gram. p. 265, τὸ αὐτὸ ἀρτοφόριον καὶ πανάριον λέγεται, καὶ πάλιν τὸ αὐτὸ σταμνίον καὶ ἀμίδιον, καὶ ἴγδις καὶ θυΐα. ἀλλὰ στοχαζόμενοι τοῦ καλῶς ἔχοντος καὶ σαφῶς καὶ τοῦ μὴ ἐπιγελασθῆναι ὑπὸ τῶν διακονούντων ἡμῖν παιδαρίων καὶ ἰδιωτῶν, πανάριον ἐροῦμεν καὶ εἰ βάρβαρόν ἐστιν, ἀλλ' οὐκ ἀρτοφορίδα, καὶ σταμνίον, ἀλλ' οὐκ ἀμίδα, καὶ θυΐαν μᾶλλον ἢ ἴγδιν.

CXLIV.

Ἱστῶν λέγε, ἀλλὰ μὴ ἱστεών. ἁμαρτήσει γὰρ τῷ λέγοντι ὁμοίως καλαμεών, ἱππεών, ἀνδρεών, δέον καλαμών, ἱππών, καὶ τὰ ὅμοια.

The longer forms came into the Common dialect from the Ionic. Of this class Lobeck mentions ἀνδρών, γυναικών, παρθενών, ξενών, μυλών, κοπρών, ἱππών, οἰνών, πιθών. The exceptions to the rule of contraction are interesting.

[1] Corrige pro MS ἴγδη.

Nothing fixes the form of a word so effectually as attachment to the soil, and in this way the old Ionic forms κεγχρεών and βολεών remained unchanged through all Attic, the former a *locative* from κέγχρος, *a grain*, being at an early date attached to the place where the grains of metal from the mines at Laurium were purified, the latter signifying the public dust-heap of the city. Both are explained by Harpocration: Κεγχρεών· Δημοσθένης ἐν τῇ πρὸς Πανταίνετον παραγραφῇ, "κᾆπειτ' ἔπεισε τοὺς οἰκέτας τοὺς ἐμοὺς καθέζεσθαι εἰς τὸν κεγχρεῶνα," ἀντὶ τοῦ εἰς τὸ καθαριστήριον, ὅπου τὴν ἐκ τῶν μετάλλων κέγχρον διέψυχον ὡς ὑποσημαίνει Θεόφραστος ἐν τῷ περὶ μετάλλων: Βολεῶνες· ὁ τόπος ὅπου ἡ κόπρος βάλλεται βολεὼν καλεῖται. Νίκανδρος, ἐν γ' Ἀττικῆς διαλέκτου: "Βολεῶνας ἐπὶ τῶν ἀγρῶν εἰς οὓς τὰ κόπρια ἐκφέρει." οὕτω Δείναρχος καὶ Φιλήμων καὶ ἄλλοι. The former word is better explained in the Λέξεις Ῥητορικαί, p. 271. 23: Κεγχρεών· τόπος Ἀθήνῃσιν οὕτω καλούμενος, ὅπου ἐκαθαίρετο ἡ ἀργυρῖτις κέγχρος καὶ ἄμμος ἡ ἀπὸ τῶν ἀργυρείων ἀναφερομένη. The same explanation serves for περιστερεών, which occurs four times in a well-known passage of the Theaetetus, 197 C, D, 198 B, 200 B. The dove-cote was a familiar appendage of the Greek household, and at Athens retained the old form of its name when words less domesticated underwent change.

CXLV.

Αὐταύλης μὴ λέγε, ἀλλὰ ψιλὸς αὐλητὴς ἐπεὶ καὶ ἕτερος κύκλιος αὐλητής.

This use of ψιλός is common in Plato, Legg. 2. 669 D, διασπῶσιν οἱ ποιηταὶ ῥυθμὸν μὲν καὶ σχήματα μέλους χωρίς, λόγους ψιλοὺς εἰς μέτρα τιθέντες, μέλος δ' αὖ καὶ ῥυθμὸν ἄνευ ῥημάτων, ψιλῇ κιθαρίσει τε καὶ αὐλήσει προσχρώμενοι. Cp. Symp. 215 C, Polit 268 B.

CXLVI.

Καταπροΐξεται οὐκ ὀρθῶς διαιροῦσι, δέον καταπροίξεται.

Οὔ τοι καταπροίξει, μὰ τὸν Ἀπόλλω, τοῦτο δρῶν.
Ar. Vesp. 1366.

οὔ τοι, μὰ τὼ θεώ, καταπροίξει Μυρτίας.
Id. 1396.

The word is used also in Ar. Nub. 1240, Eq. 435, Thesm. 566; Herod. 3. 36, Κροίσῳ μὲν συνήδεσθαι, ἔφη, περιεόντι, ἐκείνους μέντοι τοὺς περιποιήσαντας οὐ καταπροΐξεσθαι: id. 156, οὐ γὰρ δὴ ἐμέ γε ὧδε λωβησάμενος καταπροΐξεται. This isolated future, always so used with a preceding negative, and in Attic Greek never found outside of Comedy, is an excellent type of the class of words mentioned on p. 10. To those there given ma be added ἀλφάνειν in the sense of εὑρίσκειν, *fetch a price* (cp. Hom. παρθένοι ἀλφεσίβοιαι), Bekk. Anecd. 382. 8: Ἀλφάνει· εὑρίσκει. Ἀριστοφάνης Θεσμοφοριαζούσαις—

οἴμοι κακοδαίμων τῆς τόθ' ἡμέρας ὅτε
εἶπέν μ' ὁ κῆρυξ, οὗτος ἀλφάνει.

Εὔπολις Ταξιάρχοις—

οὐ θᾶττον αὐτὴν δεῦρό μοι τῶν τοξοτῶν
ἄγων ἀποκηρύξει τις ὅ, τι ἂν ἀλφάνῃ.

CXLVII.

Αἱ νῆες ἐρεῖς, οὐχ αἱ ναῦς. σόλοικον γάρ. ἥμαρτον μέντοι Φαβωρῖνος, Πολέμων, καὶ Σύλλας, αἱ ναῦς εἰπόντες· τὰς νῆας οὐκ ἐρεῖς, ἀλλὰ τὰς ναῦς. Λολλιανὸς δ' ὁ σοφιστὴς ἀκούσας παρά τινος, ὅτι οὐ χρὴ αἱ ναῦς λέγειν, ἀλλὰ αἱ νῆες, ᾠήθη δεῖν λέγειν καὶ τὴν αἰτιατικὴν ὁμοίως τὰς νῆας. οὐκ ἔχει δὲ οὕτως· ἀλλ' ἐπὶ μὲν τῆς εὐθείας δισυλλάβως, ἐπὶ δὲ τῆς αἰτιατικῆς μονοσυλλάβως.

CXLVIII.

Κνημίδα, πινακίδα, καρίδα· βραχέως τούτων τὴν παρατέλευτον. τὴν μέντοι ῥαφανίδα ἐκτείνουσι καὶ συστέλλουσιν.

The passage is either corrupt or contains an erroneous statement.

CXLIX.

Κλᾶν ἀμπέλους φαθί, ἀλλὰ μὴ κλαδεύειν.

The editions have *κλαδᾶν* instead of *κλᾶν*, both here and in Thom. Mag. 535; but it is very probable that Hemsterhuys was right in supposing *κλαδᾶν* to be an early corruption of the text of Phrynichus, ignorantly reproduced by Thomas. Moeris escaped unaltered, p. 229: *Κλάσαι Ἀττικοί, κλαδεῦσαι Ἕλληνες.* Hesychius: *Κλᾶν· τέμνειν ἀμπέλους ὅπερ ἡμεῖς κλαδεύειν.*

> *ἐκ πυκινῆς δ᾽ ὕλης πτόρθον κλάσε χειρὶ παχείῃ.*
> Hom. Od. 6. 128.

Theophr. C. Pl. 3. 14. 1, *τῶν δ᾽ ἀμπέλων τῶν τελέων ἤδη πρῶτον μὲν καὶ μέγιστόν ἐστιν ἡ κλάσις*: id. 3. 14. 2, *κατὰ τὴν κλάσιν καὶ ἀμπελουργίαν.* Hesychius has the two glosses—

> *Κλαστήριον· δρέπανον τὸ τῆς ἀμπέλου.*
> *Κλάστης· ἀμπελουργός.*

CL.

Πολίτης λέγε, ἀλλὰ μὴ συμπολίτης.

To words like *πολίτης*, which imply fellowship, no Attic writer added *σύν*. He left that emphatic weakness to poets and his negligent successors. In late Greek it is the rule to prefix the preposition in such cases, *συμπατριώτης, συμφυλέτης, συνδημότης, συνακόλουθος, συνέταιρος, συγκασίγνητος, συνομαίμων*. But to words like *στρατηγός, χορηγός, πλανήτης*, etc. it was natural and necessary to prefix the *σύν* in order to convey the sense of partnership. Euripides, I. T. 800, has *συγκασιγνήτη*, and if Antiatt. 113. 20 is right in attributing *συμπατριώτης* to the Comic poet Archippus, the word must have occurred outside the iambics, or in paratragedy: Συμπατριώτης Ἄρχιππος. τὸ μέντοι πατριώτης, Ἄλεξις.

CLI.

Τύλην, εἰ καὶ εὕροις που, σὺ κνέφαλον λέγε.

Pollux, 7. 191, 'Υπερείδης δὲ ἐν τῷ ὑπὲρ Μυκάλου ἔφη **ἐμισθώσατο τυλυφάντας**. Σοφοκλῆς δ' ἔφη **λινορραφῆ τυλεῖα**. Εὔπολις δὲ Κόλαξι **κεκρύφαλοί τε καὶ τύλη**. Ἀντιφάνης δὲ ἐν Φάωνι, **στρώματα, κλίνας, τύλας**: id. 10. 39, τὰ μὲν οὖν τυλεῖα καὶ τὰ κνέφαλα οὐ μόνον παρὰ τοῖς κωμῳδοῖς ἐστιν, ἀλλὰ καὶ ἐν Δημιοπράτοις πέπραται, κνέφαλον καινὸν καὶ κνέφαλον παλαιόν. καὶ τυλεῖα δὲ παρ' Εὐπόλιδί ἐστιν ἰάζοντι ἐν τοῖς Κόλαξι, καὶ παρὰ τῷ Σοφοκλεῖ ἐν τῷ Ἰοκλεῖ λέγοντι **ἀλλὰ καὶ λινορραφῆ τυλεῖα**. ὧν καὶ τοὺς τεχνίτας ἔοικεν 'Υπερείδης ἐν τῷ ὑπὲρ Μυκάλου ὀνομάζειν εἰπών, ἐμισθώσατο τυλυφάντας . . . ἐν δὲ τῷ Ἀντιφάνους Φάωνι καὶ κατὰ τὴν κοινὴν χρῆσίν ἐστιν εὑρεῖν **τὰς τύλας, στρώματα, κλίνας**, ὥσπερ καὶ παρὰ Σαπφοῖ.

From the words Εὐπόλιδι ἰάζοντι, and καὶ ἐν Δημιοπράτοις, the history of the word is plain. An old Ionic domestic term, it fought hard for life, and was probably in daily use in the households of Athens, as it was retained in public auctions, and in the Tragic dialect. Hence it naturally cropped up from time to time even in Prose and Comedy.

The other meaning, *knot, hump*, remained good Attic. It is interesting to compare the Latin *torus*, which has the same two meanings, appearing in that of τύλη=τυλεῖον, chiefly, if not only, in poetry, and in the other being common in prose. This marked similarity of signification, the identity of quantity in the υ and ο, and the existence of a side form τύλος, which at first had doubtless no difference of meaning, all point to the fact that τύλη and *torus* sprang from the same root.

CLII.

Τὸ ῥάπισμα οὐκ ἐν χρήσει· χρῶ οὖν τῷ καθαρῷ. τὸ γὰρ τὴν γνάθον πλατείᾳ τῇ χειρὶ πλῆξαι, ἐπὶ κόρρης πατάξαι Ἀθηναῖοί φασιν.

Phrynichus here finds fault with two late usages, the employment of *ῥάπισμα,* and of *πλῆξαι* as the aorist of *τύπτω.* No Attic writer ever used *πλῆξαι,* or any other form but *πατάξαι,* as the aorist equivalent of *τύπτειν,* in the phrase *ἐπὶ κόρρης τύπτειν*: Dem. 562. 9, *Ταυρέαν ἐπάταξε χορηγοῦντα ἐπὶ κόρρης.* No Attic rule is so carefully observed as this. By an unfortunate accident the Attic equivalents of the English term *strike* were for centuries sadly misrepresented. The verb *τύπτω* was selected by unscientific grammarians of the Byzantine school to convey their own crude notions of the Greek verb system. A more unsuitable choice of a typical verb it was impossible to make. It is in all dialects markedly irregular, in no dialect more irregular than in Attic. A very large portion of the forms, which till recently every Greek grammar presented, are not met with in any Greek dialect of the Classical period. A search throughout Greek literature as a whole for forms like *τέτυφα* and *τέτυπα* would end in disappointment, and the words *τύψω, ἐτύφθην, τυφθήσομαι* are quite without Classical authority. When such tenses were required they were supplied in a different way. Yet *τύπτω* has become an institution, and even in an English dictionary place might reasonably be given to the Shandean hybrid τυπτωing.

It is almost reprehensible to destroy such a time-honoured structure, and root up so many fond associations, and it will readily be believed that the following pages were penned in a turbulence of spirit almost equal to Luther's when he nailed his articles on the church door at Wittenberg. Attention must be drawn at starting to a just distinction between two significations of the present τύπτω, namely, *I wound* and *I beat.* In both senses—in that of *ferio*, or πληγὴν δίδωμι, no less than in that of *verbero*, πληγὰς δίδωμι—the present τύπτω, with its passive τύπτομαι, was in general use; but τύπτω was more common in the sense of πληγὰς ἐμβάλλω, and τύπτομαι, though occurring in the nobler sense, was still principally employed as a synonym of πληγὰς λαμβάνω, or *vapulo.* The verb παίω was similarly used, and in reference to present time τύπτω, παίω, πληγὰς ἐμβάλλω, τύπτομαι, παίομαι, πληγὰς λαμβάνω may be regarded as absolutely interchangeable in Classical authors. But the correspondence did not continue throughout the tenses. In the future there was complete divergence—μέγα χάσμα ἐστήρικτο. Τύπτω, *ferio*, had its future πατάξω, whereas τύπτω, *verbero*, made a future τυπτήσω by extending its own stem from τυπτ to τυπτε[1]. The aorists were equally divergent. For *ferii, vulnus injeci,* Classical writers employed ἐπάταξα, and in elevated styles occasionally ἔπαισα. On the other hand, ἐπάταξα was almost unknown in the humbler sense of *verberavi.* The aorist was supplied by a periphrasis like πληγὰς ἐνέβαλον, ἐνέτεινα, or ἐνέτριψα, but Xenophon is not to be imitated in his use of ἔπαισα in this signification. The perfect of both was drawn from a third stem still, and if πληγὰς δεδωκέναι was the ordinary equivalent of

[1] Compare χαίρω, χαιρήσω: παίω, παιήσω: κλαίω, κλαιήσω: βάλλω, βαλλήσω: καθίζομαι, καθιζήσομαι.

cecidisse or *verberibus contudisse*, yet πεπληγέναι had certainly the baser as well as the nobler meaning—

ὃς ἂν πεπλήγῃ τὸν πατέρα νεοττὸς ὤν·

Arist. Av. 1350.

Xen. Anab. 6. 1. 5, ὁ ἕτερος τὸν ἕτερον παίει ὡς πᾶσιν ἐδόκει πεπληγέναι τὸν ἄνδρα.

In the passive voice the presents τύπτομαι and παίομαι were used in all authors in either signification, but the periphrases πληγὰς εἰληφέναι and πληγὰς λαβεῖν were the equivalents of *vapulasse* in its perfect and aorist force. There was no single word to express it. Aristophanes, however, in Nub. 1379,

ἀλλ' αὖθις αὖ τυπτήσομαι[1],

makes τυπτήσομαι as authoritative as πληγὰς λήψομαι.

The perfect of τύπτομαι, *ferior*, was πέπληγμαι, but the periphrastic πληγὴν εἴληφα and πληγὴν ἔχω were sometimes employed. For futures the aorist ἐπλήγην, itself Classical, supplied πληγήσομαι, and the perfect formed πεπλήξομαι.

These results may be thus presented synoptically:—

VERBERO.

τύπτω, παίω, πληγὰς ἐμβάλλω, ἐντείνω, ἐντρίβω, δίδωμι.
τυπτήσω.
πληγὰς ἐνέβαλον (ἔπαισα).
πληγὰς δέδωκα, πέπληγα.

FERIO.

τύπτω, παίω, πληγὴν δίδωμι.
πατάξω, παίσω.
ἐπάταξα, ἔπαισα.
πέπληγα.

[1] The reading τυπήσομαι, found in some texts, is merely a conjecture of Buttmann's, as baseless as it is uncalled for.

VAPULO.

τύπτομαι, παίομαι, πληγὰς λαμβάνω.
τυπτήσομαι, πληγὰς λήψομαι.
πληγὰς ἔλαβον.
πληγὰς εἴληφα.

FERIOR.

τύπτομαι, πληγὴν λαμβάνω.
ἐπλήγην.
πληγήσομαι.
πέπληγμαι, πληγὴν εἴληφα, πληγὴν ἔχω.
πεπλήξομαι.

The habit of Aristophanes in regard to these words is representative of all Attic writers.

In the sense of *verbero*, *caedo* occur τύπτεις, Nub. 1325, 1332; τύπτει, Nub. 542, 1326; τύπτῃ, Nub. 494, Eccl. 643; τύπτοι, Eccl. 638; τύπτοις, Ran. 585; τύπτε, Ran. 622, Nub. 1433, Av. 1364; τύπτειν, Nub. 442, 1333, 1413, 1447; τύπτων, etc., Ran. 624, Av. 1327, Lys. 357, Eccl. 664; ἔτυπτον, Nub. 1332; ἔτυπτες, Nub. 1409; ἐτύπτετε, Pax 643.

Special attention may be called to Eccl. 642—

τότε δ' αὐτοῖς οὐκ ἔμελ' οὐδὲν
τῶν ἀλλοτρίων ὅστις τύπτοι· νῦν δ' ἢν πληγέντος ἀκούσῃ.
μὴ αὐτὸν ἐκεῖνον τύπτῃ δεδιὼς τοῖς δρῶσιν τοῦτο μαχεῖται·

and to Vesp. 1322—

ἔπειτ' ἐπειδὴ 'μέθυεν, οἴκαδ' ἔρχεται
τύπτων ἅπαντας, ἤν τις αὐτῷ συντύχῃ.
ὁδὶ δὲ καὐτὸς σφαλλόμενος προσέρχεται,
ἀλλ' ἐκποδὼν ἄπειμι πρὶν πληγὰς λαβεῖν.

The future τυπτήσω occurs Nub. 1444 and Plut. 20.

Of passive forms are found the following—τύπτομαι, Eq. 257, 266, 730, Nub. 1379; τύπτει, Ran. 636; τύπτου, Ran. 1024; τυπτόμενος etc., Nub. 962, Av. 1031, Thesm. 917,

Ran. 1097, 639, 1407, Nub. 962, Pax 744; ἐτυπτόμην, Plut. 1015.

The future and aorist of τύπτω, *ferio*, are found, πατάξω in Ran. 645, 647; ἐπάταξα, in Eq. 1130, Ran. 645, 647; ἐπάταξε, Ran. 38; πατάξαι, Ran. 741, Vesp. 1254, 1422; πατάξας, in Av. 757—

> εἰ γὰρ ἐνθάδ' ἐστὶν αἰσχρὸν τὸν πατέρα τύπτειν νόμῳ,
> τοῦτ' ἐκεῖ καλὸν παρ' ἡμῖν ἐστιν ἤν τις τῷ πατρὶ
> προσδραμὼν εἴπῃ πατάξας, αἶρε πλῆκτρον εἰ μαχεῖ.

In this passage, as in Ran. 150, 547, Lys. 362, 635, it is used of striking one in the face, and in Ach. 93 of striking in the eye so as to gouge it out.

In Ran. 54 it has a metaphorical meaning—

> ἐξαίφνης πόθος
> τὴν καρδίαν ἐπάταξε, πῶς οἴει σφόδρα;

The present παίω is found in Ach. 686, Av. 497; παίειν in Pax 899; and παίουσα in Eccl. 542: all rather in the nobler sense, as the aorist ἔπαισα in Nub. 549, but παίουσι, in Ran. 1094, in the meaner. It is extremely frequent in the second person singular imperative παῖε, as in a line from the 'Samians' of Crates quoted by Athenaeus (3. 117 B)—

> παῖ' ἐκεῖνον, ἄγχ' ἐκεῖνον· ἐν Κέῳ τίς ἡμέρα;[1]

In this way it occurs about a dozen times in Aristophanes alone, Nub. 1508, Eq. 247, 251, Ach. 282, Vesp. 398, 456, 458, Pax 1119, Av. 365. In several of these places it is repeated more than once and generally in a storm of Comic heroics.

The use of πέπληγμαι in Ran. 1214, Ach. 1218, Eq. 271,

[1] Ἐν Κέῳ τίς ἡμέρα; is thus explained by Hesychius, ἐπὶ τῶν οὐκ εὐγνώστων. οὐδεὶς γὰρ οἶδεν ἐν Κέῳ τίς ἡ ἡμέρα, ὅτι οὐχ ἑστᾶσιν αἱ ἡμέραι, ἀλλ' ὡς ἕκαστοι θέλουσιν ἄγουσιν. It was a sort of slang phrase, like 'What time of day is it?' 'What o'clock is it?' 'Does your mother know you are out?' but seems to have been often used to finish off a riddle or guess, in a sense like 'There's a nut for you to crack;' 'Guess me what's that.' It is probably so used here, for the four lines preceding that quoted are almost unintelligible.

Av. 1299, Thesm. 179; ἐπλήγην, Ran. 1048; πληγείς, Vesp. 399, Pax 613, Av. 1492, Thesm. 694, will be seen to correspond with the paradigm on p. 260; but Eccl. 642, quoted on the same page, proves distinctly that ἐπλήγην was sometimes employed in the baser sense of *vapulavi*, or πληγὰς ἔλαβον. The latter phrase is itself used in Ran. 673, 747, Vesp. 1325; πληγὰς ἔχειν in Nub. 1425; and πληγὰς λήψομαι in Pax 493, and Eccl. 324.

The habit of one Attic writer in regard to these words has been thus carefully analysed that he might serve as a mirror of all, but the following quotations will show still more clearly how these tenses, simple, composite, and derived from different roots dovetail into one another as consistently as φέρω, οἴσω, ἤνεγκα, and ἐνήνοχα, or as the Latin fero, tuli, latum, ferre.

Lysias, 94. 9 and 17, πατάξας καταβάλλω . . . πληγεὶς κατέπεσεν: id. 102. 12, καὶ πότερον πρότερος ἐπλήγην ἢ ἐπάταξα ἐκείνη μᾶλλον ἂν ᾔδειν: id. 136. 23, ὁ μὲν Θρασύβουλος τύπτει τὸν Φρύνιχον καὶ καταβάλλει πατάξας, ὁ δὲ Ἀπολλόδωρος οὐχ ἥψατο.

Antiphon, 127, τύπτειν τὰς πληγὰς . . . ὁ μὲν πατάξας καὶ μὴ ἀποκτείνας τῆς πληγῆς βουλευτὴς ἐγένετο, ὁ δὲ θανασίμως τύπτων τοῦ θανάτου . . . ἔστι δὲ ἡ μὲν ἀτυχία τοῦ πατάξαντος, ἡ δὲ συμφορὰ τοῦ παθόντος.

Thuc. 8. 92, ὁ Φρύνιχος πληγεὶς ἀπέθανεν παραχρῆμα καὶ ὁ πατάξας διέφυγεν.

Demosthenes, 572 fin. σκῦτος ἔχων ἐπόμπευε, καὶ τούτῳ μεθύων ἐπάταξέ τινα ἐχθρὸν ὑπάρχονθ' αὐτῷ· ἐδόκει γὰρ ὕβρει καὶ οὐκ οἴνῳ τύπτειν κτε.: id. 525, 526, τὸν θεσμοθέτην ὃς ἔναγχος ἐπλήγη . . . ὁ τὸν θεσμοθέτην πατάξας: id. 1264 fin. τῷ πατάξαντι τύπτειν παρεκελεύσατο.

Plato, Hipp. Maj. 292 B, ἢ οὐκ ἔνδικος ὑμῖν ἡ πόλις ἐστίν, ἀλλ' ἐᾷ ἀδίκως τύπτειν ἀλλήλους τοὺς πολίτας; ΣΩ. οὐδ' ὁπωστιοῦν ἐᾷ. ʽΙΠ. οὐκοῦν δώσει δίκην ἀδίκως γέ σε τύπτων . . . ΣΩ. οὐκοῦν εἴπω σοι καὶ ᾗ αὐτὸς οἴομαι δικαίως ἂν τύπτεσθαι ταῦτα ἀποκρινόμενος; ἢ καὶ σύ με ἄκριτον τυπτήσεις. . . . εἰπέ μοι, φήσει, ὦ Σώκρατες, οἴει ἂν ἀδίκως πληγὰς λαβεῖν; id. Legg. 879 D, τοῦ τύπτειν δὲ εἰργέσθω ἵνα πόρρω γίγνηται τοῦ τὸν ἐπιχώριον ἂν τολμῆσαί ποτε πατάξαι . . . τύπτειν . . . πατάξῃ.

Xen. Cyr. I. 3. 17, ἐπὶ μιᾷ ποτε δίκῃ πληγὰς ἔλαβον ὡς οὐκ ὀρθῶς δικάσας . . . ἐν τούτῳ αὖ με ἔπαισεν ὁ διδάσκαλος: id. Rep. Lac. 6. 2, ἢν δέ τις παῖς ποτε πληγὰς λαβὼν ὑπ' ἄλλου κατείπῃ πρὸς τὸν πατέρα, αἰσχρόν ἐστι μὴ οὐκ ἄλλας πληγὰς ἐμβάλλειν τῷ υἱεῖ.

Dem. 1261, πολλάκις περὶ ἑταίρας καὶ εἰληφέναι καὶ δεδωκέναι πληγάς.

No Attic writer employs the forms τύψω, ἔτυψα, τέτυφα, τέτυπα, τέτυμμαι, ἐτύφθην, ἐτύπην, τυφθήσομαι, τυπήσομαι, τετύψομαι, or ἐτύπτησα, τετύπτηκα, τετύπτημαι, ἐτυπτήθην. Unknown to Attic, in fact almost unknown to Greek, are the forms πατάσσω, πεπάταγμαι, ἐπατάχθην, παταχθήσομαι, and πέπαικα, πέπαισμαι, ἐπαίσθην, παισθήσομαι. In no Attic author is there a single trace of πλήσσω or πλήττω, πλήξω, ἔπληξα, πέπληχα, πλήττομαι, ἐπληξάμην.

The Ionic dialect supplies the words ἔτυψα, τέτυμμαι, ἐτύπην, ἐτυψάμην, and πλήσσω, πλήξω, ἔπληξα, ἐπληξάμην. These were naturally used in Tragedy as belonging to the early stage of Attic, and in Aeschylus occurs an additional form not otherwise found—

κἀμοὶ προσέστη καρδίας κλυδώνιον
χολῆς, ἐπαίσθην δ' ὡς διανταίῳ βέλει.

Cho. 184.

A. παισθεὶς ἔπαισας.
I. σὺ δ' ἔθανες κατακτανών.

Sept. 961.

As Cobet justly observes, the latter line would in Attic Prose or Comedy assume the form πληγεὶς ἐπάταξας· σὺ δέ γ' ἀπέθανες ἀποκτείνας.

Even in Ionic the simple πατάσσω was irregular. It had the meaning of πάλλομαι, *palpito*, but ἐξεπάταξα, ἐκπεπάταγμαι, and ἐξεπατάχθην were used in the sense of ἐξέπληξα, ἐκπέπληγμαι, and ἐξετινάχθην.

In Nub. 1125 and Lys. 459 the future forms παιήσομεν and παιήσετε are met with. The analogy of κλαιήσω and βαλλήσω makes it probable that παιήσω was a word recognized in Attic Greek.

The middle of τύπτω was not an Attic form. Xenophon has the middle of παίω in Cyr. 7. 3. 6, ἐπαίσατο τὸν μηρόν, 'Smote his own thigh.' There was no middle to πατάξω, ἐπάταξα, and πλήξομαι and ἐπληξάμην were confined to Ionic. In Ionic too τύπτομαι was employed in the sense of *bewail*, for which the Attic term was κόπτομαι, Plato, Rep. 605 D, 619 C, Phaed. 60 A; Ar. Lys. 396—

> ἡ δ' ὑποπεπωκυῖ' ἡ γυνὴ ἐπὶ τοῦ τέγους
> "κόπτεσθ' Ἄδωνιν" φησίν.

The interest of so striking an example of the delicacy and precision of the Athenian mind in its best days has too long diverted the attention from the principal point discussed by Phrynichus. The justice of his dictum as to ῥάπισμα cannot be questioned. It is true that Antiphanes (Ath. 14. 623 F) used the word—

> τευθίς, μεταλλάξασα λευκαυγῆ φύσιν
> σαρκὸς πυρωτοῖς ἀνθράκων ῥαπίσμασιν
> ξάνθαισιν αὔραις σῶμα πᾶν ἀγάλλεται·

but the lines are para-tragoedic and suggest that the word might have been used in Tragedy—a fancy which receives valuable support from the fact that the verb ῥαπίζω was used by Xenophanes (ap. Diog. Laert. 8. 36) and Hipponax (Tzetz. Hist. 5. 746) and occurs in Herodotus. In 7. 35, and 223 it has the sense of lash; in the former, of the lashing of the Hellespont by the order of Xerxes, in the latter of the Persian custom of encouraging troops by the lash. It is encountered in two other passages of Classical

Greek. According to Athenaeus (13. 571 A) Timocles wrote the lines—

> ἀγωνιᾶσαι καὶ ῥαπισθῆναί τε καὶ
> πληγὰς λαβεῖν ἁπαλαῖσι χερσίν, ἡδύ γε·

but the context, if consulted, will show that the meaning of ῥαπίζειν there is very far different from that of ἐπὶ κόρρης τύπτειν. The place of Demosthenes (787. 23) in which it does bear its late meaning belongs to a speech which on good grounds is considered spurious. In another passage (537 extr.) the true term is employed and its meaning clearly marked by the context, ἐπὶ κόρρης τύπτειν being distinguished from κονδύλοις τύπτειν: Οὐδὲ τὸ τύπτεσθαι τοῖς ἐλευθέροις ἐστὶ δεινόν, καίπερ ὂν δεινόν, ἀλλὰ τὸ ἐφ' ὕβρει. πολλὰ γὰρ ἂν ποιήσειεν ὁ τύπτων ὧν ὁ παθὼν ἔνια οὐδ' ἂν ἀπαγγεῖλαι δύναιθ' ἑτέρῳ, τῷ σχήματι, τῷ βλέμματι, τῇ φωνῇ, ὅταν ὡς ὑβρίζων, ὅταν ὡς ἐχθρὸς ὑπάρχων, ὅταν κονδύλοις, ὅταν ἐπὶ κόρρης.

CLIII.

Παροψὶς τὸ ὄψον, οὐχὶ δὲ τὸ ἀγγεῖον· τοῦτο δὲ τρύβλιον ἢ λεκάριον καλοῦσιν.

Phrynichus also insists upon this point in App. Soph. 60. 3, and Moeris, p. 297, is no less strict; but Athenaeus (9. 367 D) quotes from Antiphanes a line in which the word has the signification common in late Greek and seen in N. T. Matth. 23. 25, τὸ ἔξωθεν τοῦ ποτηρίου καὶ τῆς παροψίδος, and in Juvenal, 3. 142—

> 'Quam multa magnaque paropside coenat.'

But this line—

> καλέσας τε παρατίθησιν ἐν παροψίδι,

is the only one of all the passages quoted by him in which

παροψίς has necessarily the meaning of a vessel. In some of the others, as in Sotades—

> *παροψὶς εἶναι φαίνομαι τῷ Κρωβύλῳ·*
> *τοῦτον μασᾶται παρακατεσθίει δ' ἐμέ,*

the word is certainly employed in its true sense, while in others its reference is doubtful. The English word *dish* has the same ambiguity of meaning.

CLIV.

Κροῦσαι τὴν θυράν, ἴσως μέν που παραβεβιάσται ἡ χρῆσις· ἄμεινον δὲ τὸ κόπτειν τὴν θύραν.

Phrynichus is much too fine here. Not only was *κρούειν τὴν θύραν* in constant use, but both *θένω* and *ἀράττω*—words in other respects little used, survived in this connection as is proved by Aristophanes (see pp. 6, 10).

The phrase *κόπτειν τὴν θύραν* occurs in Ar. Pl. 1097, Eccl. 976, Ran. 460, Nub. 132, Ach. 403, cp. Nub. 1144, Av. 56; Andoc. 6. 29; Lys. Fr. 45. 4; Dem. 1156. 18; Xen. Hell. 5. 4. 7, Anab. 7. 1. 15.

Whereas *κρούειν τὴν θύραν* is employed in Ar. Eccl. 316, 990; Plato, Prot. 310 A, 314 D, Symp. 212 C; Xen. Symp. 1. 11.

This forms an excellent illustration of the lines on which Phrynichus worked. Like all true scholars, he disregarded exceptions, and considered the knowledge of anomalies not science but pedantry. Till the rules are known—and every usage which is true in three cases out of four should be elevated into a rule—no attempt need be made to elucidate departures from them.

CLV.

Ἐνήλατα κλίνης ἢ σκίμποδος οὐ χρὴ λέγειν τὸν Ἀττικίζοντα ἀλλὰ κραστήρια.

Euripides thrice uses the word *ἐνήλατον*, in Phoen. 1179 and Supp. 729, of the rungs of a ladder—

> κλίμακος ἀμείβων ξέστ' ἐνηλάτων βάθρα·

and—

> ὃς ἔν τε τοῖς δεινοῖσίν ἐστιν ἄλκιμος
> μισεῖ θ' ὑβριστὴν λαόν, ὃς πράσσων καλῶς
> εἰς ἄκρα βῆναι κλιμάκων ἐνήλατα
> ζητῶν ἀπώλεσ' ὄλβον ᾧ χρῆσθαι παρῆν·

and in Hipp. 1235, of linch-pins (*τὰ ἐμβαλλόμενα πρὸς τῷ ἄξονι ὥστε μὴ ἐξιέναι τὸν τροχόν*, Schol.)—

> σύριγγές τ' ἄνω
> τροχῶν ἐπήδων ἀξόνων τ' ἐνήλατα.

According to Pollux (10. 34), Sophocles had the word in the sense which Phrynichus reprehends: *Σοφοκλῆς δ' ἐν Ἰχνευταῖς Σατύροις ἔφη—Ἐνήλατα ξύλα τρίγομφα διατορεῦσαι δεῖται*, but the words are too corrupt to convey any meaning. On the other hand, *κραστήρια* is not met with elsewhere, although Hesychius has the gloss: *Κρατηρίαι· τῶν ἐνηλάτων αἱ κεφαλαὶ καὶ συμβολαὶ καὶ ἄκρα.* The question must be left unsettled.

CLVI.

Κλίβανος οὐκ ἐρεῖς, ἀλλὰ κρίβανος διὰ τοῦ ρ.

Athenaeus, 3. 110 C, has the instructive remark, *Οἶδα δὲ ὅτι Ἀττικοὶ μὲν διὰ τοῦ ρ στοιχείου λέγουσι καὶ κρίβανον καὶ κριβανίτην· Ἡρόδοτος δ' ἐν δευτέρᾳ τῶν ἱστοριῶν ἔφη* "*κλιβάνῳ δια-*

φανεῖ," καὶ ὁ Σώφρων δὲ ἔφη "*τίς σταιτίτας ἢ κλιβανίτας, ἡμιάρτια πέσσει;*" which indicates from what sources the *κλίβανος* of the Common dialect came, and makes it probable that the form with λ is correctly read in the lines of Aeschylus quoted by Ath. 9. 375 E—

> *ἐγὼ δὲ χοῖρον καὶ μάλ' εὐθηλούμενον*
> *τόνδ' ἐν ῥοθοῦντι κλιβάνῳ θήσω. τί γὰρ*
> *ὄψον γένοιτ' ἂν ἀνδρὶ τοῦδε βέλτερον;*

In parody, choric songs, and some other metres, *κλίβανος* was probably employed even in Comedy; a consideration which may give a value to such remarks as that of the Antiatticista, p. 103. 3: Κλιβανίτης ἄρτος· 'Αμειψίας 'Αποκοτταβίζουσιν. To this article some sciolist has appended the words, *διὰ τὸ τὴν πρώτην τροφὴν τῶν ἀνθρώπων κριθὴν εἶναι.* They cannot be by Phrynichus.

CLVII.

Κυνίδιον λέγε. Θεόπομπος δὲ ὁ Κωμῳδὸς ἅπαξ που κυνάριον εἶπεν.

CLVIII.

Λιθάριον πάνυ φυλάττου λέγειν, λιθίδιον δέ.

The manuscripts assign to the second of these articles a place near the end of the book.

'Hic ut renunciemus Phrynicho cogit nos Plato. Nam *κυνάριον* usurpat bis in Euthydemo 298, cui Xenophontem, Theophrastum, Lucianum, aliosque permultos addunt. Neque perstitit in sententia Phrynichus; nam in App. Soph. p. 49, *Κυνάριον καὶ κυνίδιον δόκιμα*: illud ex Alcaeo Comico affert Antiatt. p. 104. De multis aliis hujus generis diminutivis inter ipsos Atticistas controversia fuisse videtur. Phrynichus, App. Soph. p. 49, Κλινάρια, οὐ μόνον κλινίδια, Ἀριστοφάνης (Poll. 10. 32). Idem, p. 43, Ἱππίδιον, οὐ μόνον ἱππάριον.

'Alterum λιθάριον, Thomae improbatum, nullum auctorem habet Theophrasto antiquiorem (H. Pl. 3. 7. 5) quem sequuntur Philostratus, Alexander Trallianus, Dioscorides, Geoponica, λιθίδιον Plato, Lucianus, Themistius. Lexicis deest λίθιον Paus. 2. 25. 8.' Lobeck.

CLIX.

Ἐδεδίεσαν· καὶ τοῦτο τῆς Λολλιανοῦ μούσης· σὺ δὲ λέγε τετρασυλλάβως ἄνευ τοῦ ε, ἐδέδισαν.

Such forms as δεδίαμεν, δεδίατε, ἐδεδίεσαν are as corrupt as διδόαμεν for δίδομεν, or διδόατε for δίδοτε. The record of Comedy in regard to the legitimate forms of this present perfect is as follows:—

δέδοικα, Ach. 370, Eq. 28, 112, 395, Nub. 493, 508, 1133, Vesp. 427, 630, Pax 173, Lys. 620, (Ran. 1260), Eccl. 338, 585, 870, 1063, Plut. 199, Fr. ap. Photium Τῶν τριῶν.

δέδοικας, Vesp. 628, 629, Thesm. 202, 1186.

δέδοικε(ν), Vesp. 1358, Fr. Babyl. τὴν αὑτοῦ σκιὰν δέδοικεν: Alexis, ap. Athen. 6. 240 C.

δέδια, δέδιας, δέδιε never occur, except δέδιεν in a Fragment of Amphis (Ath. 10. 448 A)—

> διὰ τὸ λεπτῶς καὶ πυκνῶς
> πάντ' ἐξετάζειν δέδιεν ἐπὶ τὰ πράγματα
> ὁρμᾶν προχείρως.

The plural forms are unfortunately rare: δεδοίκατε occurs in Eccl. 181, but δεδίασιν in Eq. 224, 1113.

The only form of the past encountered in Comedy is ἐδεδοίκης in Plut. 684.

Of imperative forms δέδιθι occurs in Eq. 230, Vesp. 373.

The participle is δεδοικώς in Pax 606; Alexis (Athen. 6. 226 A); Antiphanes (Athen. 4. 156 C); Anaxandrides (Athen. 15. 688 B).

But δεδιώς in Eccl. 643, Plut. 448; ὑποδεδιώς, Av. 65. Δεδιότα occurs in a corrupt line of Xenarchus (Ath. 13. 569 A)—

δεδιότα ἐν τῇ χειρὶ τὴν ψυχὴν ἔχοντα,

while δεδιυῖα is quoted from Eubulus by Antiatt. p. 90. 1.

Δεδοικέναι may be found in Plut. 354, Nub. 1461, Vesp. 109, whereas δεδιέναι is not met with in Comedy till Menander's time, ap. Stob. Flor. 73. 43, ap id. 32. 2.

This record demonstrates the inaccuracy of Dindorf's statement in Steph. Thes. 2. 936: 'In Prosa Atticorum vix credam reperiri δέδια, δεδοίκαμεν, δεδοίκασιν, δεδοικέναι, sed dici δέδοικα (Thuc. 1. 81, 6. 38), δέδιμεν, δεδίασιν, δεδιέναι, alia autem promiscue usurpari ut ἐδεδοίκεσαν (Thuc. 4. 27), et ἐδέδισαν.' The facts seem to be that the singular of both present and past tenses was preferentially formed from the longer stem, but the plural from the shorter; in the participle both forms were in use, while in the infinitive both δεδιέναι and δεδοικέναι; in the imperative certainly only δέδιθι, δεδίτω, etc. were legitimate.

The subjunctive δεδίω is well-established by δεδίῃ in Xenoph. Rep. Ath. 1. 11, δεδίωσι Isocr. freq., but the optative depends upon one passage of Plato. In Phaedr. 251 A the books have καὶ εἰ μὴ δεδιείη τὴν τῆς σφόδρα μανίας δόξαν θύοι ἂν ὡς ἀγάλματι καὶ θεῷ τοῖς παιδικοῖς, and even that instance is destroyed by Cobet: 'Prudenter Buttmannus judicat de Platonis loco in Phaedro, p. 251 A, ubi ridiculam formam et prorsus barbaram δεδιείη Bekkerus recepit. Sententia loci postulat εἰ μὴ ἐφοβεῖτο (non φοβοῖτο), itaque scribendum est: εἰ μὴ ἐδεδίει τὴν τῆς σφόδρα μανίας δόξαν θύοι ἂν κτε.' Certainly, the substitution of the irregular for the regular conditional sentence does in this case emend the passage. The narrative both before and after refers to present time, and the meaning required for the sentence in dispute is, *he is afraid of being thought mad or he would sacrifice.*

CLX.

Οὐθείς διὰ τοῦ θ· εἰ καὶ Χρύσιππος καὶ οἱ ἀμφ' αὐτὸν οὕτω λέγουσι, σὺ δὲ ἀποτρέπου λέγειν. οἱ γὰρ ἀρχαῖοι διὰ τοῦ δ λέγουσιν.

The corruption had its beginning long before the time of Chrysippus. Wecklein (Cur. Epigraph. p. 30) shows that in the archonship of Nausinicus B.C. 378–7, *μηθενί* occurs twice in one inscription, and that after that date the spelling with the aspirate gradually made its way: 'Ex titulo a Rang. II. 381 edito, Ol. 100. 3 exarato, in quo bis scribitur *μηθενί*, discimus jam Ol. 100. 3 scripturam *οὐθείς*, *μηθείς* in usu fuisse. Tab. Nav. I. a (Ol. 101. 4) *οὐθέν*, (Ib. III. et XI. rursus *οὐδέν* legitur), etc.'

As Herwerden thinks, (Test. Lapid. p. 61) such a usage can hardly have been found in writers anterior to Aristotle.

Wecklein cites the disjoined form *μηδὲ εἷς* from an inscription earlier than Euclides: 'Rang. I. 271 (ante Euclid.) *μηδὲ ἑνί*; C. I. 73 b (c. Ol. 84) *οὐδὲ ἕνα*. M. H. E. Meier. Com. ep. 2 (post Ol. 114) *μηδὲ εἷς*.

'*Οὐδὲ εἷς, μηδὲ εἷς* (*οὐδεείς, μηδεείς*) frequentat Aristophanes (cf. Ran. 927, Lys. 1044, Plut. 37, 138, 1115, 1182). A Tragicorum usu *οὐδὲ εἷς* (nullo vocabulo interposito ut *οὐδ' ἂν εἷς*, Soph. Trach. 1072) abhorret. Soph. Fragm. 769, *θνητῶν δ' οὐδείς*, non *θνητῶν δ' οὐδὲ εἷς* habetur.'

Herwerden appends several points of great interest: 'Unum tamen addere juvat idque valde memorabile; siquidem unicum, ni fallor, exemplum est hodie formae ἁμοῦ separatim positae in sermone Attica. Videlicet in tit. II. 11 exarato inter Ol. 96. 3 et 98. 2 legitur μηδὲ ἁμοῦ pro μηδαμοῦ. Praeterea notatu dignum videtur in antiquioribus certe titulis paene constanter (si non prorsus constanter, quam in rem diligentius inquirere nunc non vacat) scribi, οὐδὲ πρὸς ἕνα, μηδὲ πρὸς ἕνα, οὐδὲ ὑφ' ἑνός pro πρὸς οὐδένα (μηδένα), ὑπ' οὐδενὸς (μηδενός) similia.'

CLXI.

Λάγνης διὰ τοῦ η, ἀλλὰ μὴ λάγνος.

Pollux recognizes both forms, 6. 188, ὁ μαινόμενος ἐπ' ἀφροδίσια λάγνης ἂν καὶ λάγνος ῥηθείη, whereas Photius supports Phrynichus: Λάγνης οὐ λάγνος ὑπὸ τῶν 'Αττικῶν λέγεται,

τοιαῦτα μέντοι πόλλ' ἀναγκαίως ἔχει
πάσχειν ὅταν λάγνην τὸν ὀφθαλμὸν φορῇς·

ἡ δὲ ἀναλογία, οἶμαι, καὶ λάγνητα, ὡς Κράτητα καὶ Μάγνητα.

Lobeck compares ἀδολέσχης, which gradually gave way to ἀδόλεσχος: 'Sed ἀδόλεσχος jam in Aristotelis scriptis hic ibi emicat, et paucis saeculis post ita divulgatum est ut v. c. Plutarchus in commentatione περὶ ἀδολεσχίας sexies ἀδολέσχης, ἀδόλεσχος autem plus quam vicies usurpaverit, neque Pollux 6. 119 unum prae altero probasse videtur . . . Etiam φιλογύνης a nonnullis magis probatum est quam φιλόγυνος, conjicere licet ex Antiatticista Bekk. p. 115, Φιλόγυνος, οὐ μόνον φιλογύνης, cp. Piers. ad Moer. p. 391, quorum secundum probat Pollux 2. 46, vicissim γυναικοφίλης improbans 6. 168. Idem 2. 47 seq. ἀγύνης, μισογύνης· 'Αριστοφάνης ἄγυνον τὸν ἀγύνην· Φρύνιχος δὲ ἀγύναικος.' Lobeck.

CLXII.

Λαγώς, ὁ 'Αττικός, διὰ τοῦ ο. ὁ Ἴων λαγός.

The Attic form came from the Homeric λαγωός—

ἁρπάξων ἢ ἄρν' ἀμαλὴν ἢ πτῶκα λαγωόν.

Il. 22. 310.

The Ionic λαγός may well have been used by Sophocles; Ath. 9. 400 D: Λέγουσι δὲ καὶ 'Αττικοὶ λαγὸς ὡς ὁ Σοφοκλῆς—

γέρανοι, κορῶναι, γλαῦκες, ἰκτῖνοι, λαγοί·

but only in Tragedy could that form appear in Attic.

CLXIII.

Λίβανον λέγε τὸ δένδρον, τὸ δὲ θυμιώμενον λιβανωτόν· εἰ καὶ διὰ τὴν ποιητικὴν λίβανον καὶ τοῦτο Σοφοκλῆς λέγει. ἄμεινον δὲ Μένανδρος ἐν τῇ Σαμίᾳ φησί·

φέρε τὴν λιβανωτόν, σὺ δ' ἐπίθες τὸ πῦρ, Τρύφη.

'Ammonium (p. 88) quam Phrynichum hic sequi maluit Thomas p. 577 qui, ut λίβανος pariter de arbore quam de lacrima dicatur, concedit, λιβανωτόν nisi de thure dici vetat; cui Theophrastum opponunt λιβανωτόν etiam de arbore dicentem. Sed neque is magnam in hac re auctoritatem habet, neque multum valet ad sententiam Phrynichi oppugnandam, si Eurip. Bacch. 144, Anaxandrid. comicus Athen. 4. 131 D, atque recentiores Diod. Sic. 3. 41, Herodian 4. 8, Galen. Theriac. ad Pamph. p. 964, B. T. 13, aliique, thus, quod Aristophanes et Plato λιβανωτόν dicere solent, arboris nomine vocaverunt. De singulis locis nemo praestet, quum saepe codices inter se dissentiant, Herodo. 4. 75, Joseph. Antiq. 3. 6. 136, sed liberiorem fuisse hujus vocis usum vel ex eo colligi licet, quod similiter χελώνη de supellectile testudinea (τρίκλινα χελώνης Philo de Vit. Contempl.) et σαρδώ pro sardonyche Philostr. Imag. et μέλισσα pro melle usurpatur Soph. O. C. 481, ut notiora praeteream.' Lobeck.

CLXIV.

Τὴν λιμὸν Δωριεῖς, σὺ δὲ ἀρσενικῶς τὸν λιμὸν φάθι.

'Femininum genus recte doriensi dialecto adscribi patet ex eo quod Aristophanes Megarensem hoc genere utentem facit quodque Spartae in Apollinis templo *Λιμός* erat *διὰ γραφῆς ἀπομεμιμημένος ἔχων γυναικὸς μορφήν*, Athen. 10. 452 B.' Lobeck.

CLXV.

Ἐλουόμην, ἐλούου, ἐλούετο, λούομαι, λούεται, ἐλουόμεθα, ἐλούοντο, λούεσθαι· πάντα οὕτω λεγόμενα ἀδόκιμα. Εἰ δὲ δόκιμα βούλει αὐτὰ ποιῆσαι τὸ ε καὶ τὸ ο ἀφαίρει καὶ λέγε λοῦσθαι καὶ λοῦμαι, λοῦται, ἐλούμην, ἐλοῦτο, ἐλούμεθα, ἐλοῦντο· οὕτω γὰρ οἱ ἀρχαῖοι λέγουσιν.

There is only one verb in *-όω* which has its first person singular present indicative active disyllabic. *Χόω*, *heap up*, contracts according to the same rule as its polysyllabic fellows, *χῶ, χοῖς, χοῖ, χοῦτον, χοῦμεν, χοῦτε, χοῦσι(ν)*. Imperfect, *ἔχουν, ἔχους, ἔχου, ἐχοῦτον, ἐχούτην, ἐχοῦμεν, ἐχοῦτε, ἔχουν*. Subjunctive, *χῶ, χοῖς*, etc. Optative, *χοίην, χοίης*, etc. Imperative, *χοῦ*. Participle, *χῶν*. Infinitive, *χοῦν*. Passive, *χοῦμαι, ἐχούμην, χοῦσθαι*, etc.[1]

But in some of its forms *λούω*, *bathe, wash*, behaves as if its first person was *λόω*. It is in fact a mixed form, following both the contracted and the uncontracted conjugation. Those persons in which the ending is preceded by a short connecting vowel, *ε* or *ο*, are supplied as if from

[1] Thuc. 2. 102, *προσχοῖ*: Hdt. 1. 161, *χῶν*: Plat. Legg. 958 E, *χοῦν*, where the late form *χώννυναι* actually occurs in some MSS. Thuc. 2. 75, *ἔχουν* bis.

λόω, and contract the ο of the stem with the connecting vowel. The other persons are formed from λούω, which by some grammarians has been regarded as itself contracted from λοέω, an extended form of λόω.

The modification λόω is encountered in Homer in the imperfect—

> ἔς ῥ' ἀσάμινθον ἕσασα λό', ἐκ τρίποδος μεγάλοιο,
>
> Od. 10. 361.

and in the middle in—

> οὐδ' ἐς βαλανεῖον ἦλθε λουσόμενος· σὺ δὲ
> ὥσπερ τεθνεῶτος καταλόει μου τὸν βίον.
>
> Arist. Nub. 838.

In the latter case, however, all the manuscripts read καταλούει, and possibly Bekker ought to have left that form alone, as it is quite possible to consider the diphthong short, like the οι in ποιῶ and τοιοῦτος. Now, although ποῶ occasionally occurs in inscriptions, ποιῶ is the regular form, and has been retained in verse even when a short penult is demanded by the metre. The fact is, both ποιῶ and λούω were in Attic pronounced in such a way (see p. 113) that there was no difficulty in giving them either an iambic or spondaic value. Other diphthongs were similarly affected according to their position in a word. Thus, θειάζω (from θεῖος), but ἐπιθεάζει[1] in a line of Pherecrates quoted by Suïdas: Ἀρᾶται . . . εὔχεται ἢ καταρᾶται. Φερεκράτης—

> ὕστερον ἀρᾶται κἀπιθεάζει τῷ πατρί.

Similarly, θειῶ, *fumigate*, from θεῖον, *brimstone*, but περιθεασάτωσαν in Menander—

> καὶ περιθεωσάτωσαν ἀπὸ κρουνῶν τριῶν.

[1] In Aesch. Cho. 856—

> Ζεῦ, Ζεῦ, τί λέγω, πόθεν ἄρξωμαι
> τάδ' ἐπευχομένη κἀπιθεάζουσ';

and Eur. Med. 1409—

> θρηνῶ κἀπιθεάζω
> μαρτυρόμενος δαίμονας.

In both cases the MSS. have ἐπιθοάζω.

It is the same tendency which gives Ἀρεοπαγίτης and Ἀρεοπαγιτικός from Ἄρειος πάγος, and τελέως and τελεοῦν from τέλειος.

But whether καταλούει or καταλόει is written in Aristophanes, the general rule remains unaltered, that λούω supplies those forms in which the ending is not preceded by a short connecting vowel, and λόω those in which it is. The testimony of Phrynichus is very distinct (cp. Eustath. Od. 1560. 28: λούμενος· οὕτω γὰρ οἱ Ἀττικοί, οὐ μὴν λουόμενος; Photius, λοῦσθαι λέγουσιν, οὐχὶ λούεσθαι), and it is more than borne out by the test of metre—

εἶτ' αὐτὸν ἀπέλου κἀκάθαιρ' ὁ δ' οὐ μάλα.
Arist. Vesp. 119.

ἔπειτ' ἐλοῦμεν. B. νὴ Δί', εὐδαίμων ἄρ' ἦν.
Plut. 657.

ὅταν διαριθμῶν ἀργυρίδιον τύχῃ
ἄνθρωπος οὗτος ἢ καθῆται λούμενος.
Av. 1622.

τῆς γυναικὸς λουμένης.
Pax 1139.

ἀνὴρ γέρων ψυχρᾷ θαλάττῃ λούμενος.
Plut. 658.

ὅστις σε θερμῷ φησι λοῦσθαι πρῶτον οὐκ ἐάσειν.
Nub. 1044.

ἀλλὰ πάντας χρὴ παραλοῦσθαι καὶ τοὺς σπόγγους ἐᾶν.
Id. 'Anagyrus.'

Aristophon, 'The Pythagorist' (Athen. 6. 238 C)—

ὕδωρ δὲ πίνειν, βάτραχος· ἀπολαῦσαι θύμων
λαχάνων τε, κάμπη· πρὸς τὸ μὴ λοῦσθαι, ῥύπος.

Antiphanes, 'Malthace' (Clem. Alex.)—

σμῆται, κτενίζετ', ἐκβέβηκε, τρίβεται,
λοῦται, σκοπεῖται, στέλλεται, μυρίζεται.

Pherecrates, 'The Oven or Wake' (Pollux, 10. 181)—

ἤδη μὲν ᾤαν λουμένῳ προζώννυται.

Menander, 'Anger'[1] (Athen. 4. 166 A)—

ἀλλ' οὐκ ἐλούμην πεντάκις τῆς ἡμέρας.

Ephippus (Athen. 2. 48 B)—

ὡς ἐγὼ σκιρτῶ πάλαι
ὅπου ῥοδόπνοα στρώματ' ἐστὶ καὶ μύροις
λοῦμαι ψακαστοῖς.

By the rule given above, all the forms of the subjunctive and optative, active and middle, are derived from λούω. The other moods of the present and imperfect tense are inflected as follows, the forms from λόω being printed in spaced type :—

PRESENT INDICATIVE.

	ACTIVE.	MIDDLE.
S. 1.	λούω	λ ο ῦ μ α ι
2.	λούεις	λούει
3.	λούει	λ ο ῦ τ α ι
D. 2.	λ ο ῦ τ ο ν	λ ο ῦ σ θ ο ν
3.	λ ο ῦ τ ο ν	λ ο ῦ σ θ ο ν
P. 1.	λ ο ῦ μ ε ν	λ ο ύ μ ε θ α
2.	λ ο ῦ τ ε	λ ο ῦ σ θ ε
3.	λ ο ύ ο υ σ ι	λ ο ῦ ν τ α ι.

IMPERFECT.

S. 1.	ἔ λ ο υ ν	ἐ λ ο ύ μ η ν
2.	ἔ λ ο υ ς	ἐλούου
3.	ἔ λ ο υ	ἐ λ ο ῦ τ ο
D. 2.	ἐ λ ο ῦ τ ο ν	ἐ λ ο ῦ σ θ ο ν
3.	ἐ λ ο ύ τ η ν	ἐ λ ο ύ σ θ η ν
P. 1.	ἐ λ ο ῦ μ ε ν	ἐ λ ο ύ μ ε θ α
2.	ἐ λ ο ῦ τ ε	ἐ λ ο ῦ σ θ ε
3.	ἔ λ ο υ ν	ἐ λ ο ῦ ν τ ο.

[1] Ὀργή, his first play, B.C. 322.

IMPERATIVE.

	ACTIVE.	MIDDLE.
S. 2.	λοῦ	λούου
3.	λούτω	λούσθω
D. 2.	λοῦτον	λοῦσθον
3.	λούτων	λούσθων
P. 2.	λοῦτε	λοῦσθε
3.	λούντων	λούσθων.

INFINITIVE.

λούειν	λοῦσθαι.

PARTICIPLE.

λούων, λουοῦσα, λοῦν	λούμενος, η, ον.

CLXVI.

Δυσωπεῖσθαι· Πλουτάρχῳ μέν ἐστι περὶ δυσωπίας βιβλίον, τοῦτο ὅπερ οἴεται δηλοῦν τὸ ἐντρέπεσθαι καὶ μὴ ἀντέχειν δι' αἰδῶ. ἀλλὰ σημαίνει ἡ δυσωπία παρὰ τοῖς ἀρχαίοις τὴν ὑφόρασιν καὶ τὸ ὑποπτεύειν.

'Idem pronunciant Moeris p. 125, Suïdas s. v. Zonaras Lex. p. 585, et Thomas p. 255, neque errant. Δυσωπεῖσθαι et ionicum νωπεῖσθαι, quantum ex etymo intelligi potest, proprie de oris confusione dicitur, quae ex variis perturbationibus, metu, suspicione, pudore existit. Sed veteres illi tantum de praesensione instantis periculi vel molestiae usurparunt.' Lobeck. Plato, Polit. 285 B, *μὴ δυνατὸν εἶναι δυσωπούμενον παύεσθαι*: Legg. 11. 933 A, *δυσωπουμένους πρὸς ἀλλήλους*: Phaedr. 242 C, *καί πως ἐδυσωπούμην . . . μή τι . . . ἀμείψω*: Demosth. 127. 25, *καὶ τοὺς εἰς τοῦθ' ὑπάγοντας ὑμᾶς ὁρῶν οὐκ ὀρρωδῶ ἀλλὰ δυσωποῦμαι*: Xen. Mem. 2. 1. 4, *ταῦτα γὰρ (τὰ ζῷα) δήπου τὰ μὲν γαστρὶ δελεαζόμενα, καὶ* μάλα ἔνια δυσωπούμενα, ὅμως τῇ ἐπιθυμίᾳ τοῦ φαγεῖν ἀγόμενα πρὸς τὸ δελέαρ ἁλίσκεται, τὰ δὲ ποτῷ ἐνεδρεύεται.

CLXVII.

Σαλπικτής· τὸ δόκιμον διὰ τοῦ κ, οὐχὶ δὲ διὰ τοῦ σ, καὶ τὸ σαλπίσαι διὰ τοῦ σ παραιτοῦ, διὰ τοῦ ξ δὲ λέγε.

The testimony of inscriptions is given by Herwerden (Test. Lap. p. 64) as follows: '*Σαλπικτής, σαλπιστής*. 2. 444, 44. 445, 18. 446, 40 (qui tituli ad sec. 2. a. C. pertinere putantur) exhibent *σαλπικτάς*. Bis *σαλπικτής* legitur 3. 1284 (37/8, p. C.), bis 3. 1288, praeterea 3. 1284 et 1285. Tertiae quae in codd. nostris reperiri solet *σαλπιγκτής* in titulis Atticis nec vola est nec vestigium.'

This evidence has little bearing upon the Attic period, as the word is not found in Attic inscriptions before the second century, so that Liddell and Scott are in grave error when they say, 'The Inscriptions are in favour of *σαλπιγκτής*.'

No manuscript can be of any value in such a question, and for the present the authority of Phrynichus must be regarded as the guide best to follow. The analogy of *συρικτής* and *φορμικτής* is in favour of his dictum. Accordingly, if *σάλπιγξα* is retained in Homer, Il. 21. 388, yet *ἐσάλπιξα* should be restored to Archippus, ap. Athen. 6. 322 A—

σάλπης δ' ἐσάλπιξ' ἕπτ' ὀβολοὺς μισθὸν φέρων,

and to Xenophon, An. 1. 2. 17, while the more numerous instances of *σαλπιγκτής* should receive a still shorter shrift.

CLXVIII.

'Αφιερῶσαι· καὶ τοῦτο Φαβωρῖνος· σὺ δὲ καθιερῶσαι.

The verb ἀφιερῶ is good Greek, but not as an equivalent of καθιερῶ. In Aesch. Eum. 451—

> πάλαι πρὸς ἄλλοις ταῦτ' ἀφιερώμεθα
> οἴκοισι καὶ βοτοῖσι καὶ ῥυτοῖς πόροις,

it is found in the sense of ἀφοσιοῦν, the force of the preposition being the same as in ἀπολούειν, ἀπομάσσειν, ἀπομοργνύναι, etc. There is no instance in Classical Greek of ἀφιεροῦν in its late sense as equivalent to καθιεροῦν. For the treatise 'de Morbo sacro,' which sometimes goes under the name of Hippocrates, is probably a late work. In it (Hipp. p. 301. 36) ἀφιεροῦν is equivalent to καθιεροῦν: ἐμοὶ δὲ δοκέουσιν οἱ πρῶτοι τοῦτο τὸ νόσημα ἀφιερώσαντες τοιοῦτοι εἶναι ἄνθρωποι οἷοι καὶ νῦν εἰσι μάγοι τε καὶ καθαρταὶ καὶ ἀγύρται.

CLXIX.

Κολλάβους τοὺς ἐν τῇ λύρᾳ ἡ μὲν ἄλλη διάλεκτος λέγει· οὐ φροντὶς Ἱπποκλείδῃ φασί. σὺ δὲ ὡς Ἀθηναῖος λέγε κόλλοπας.

Even in late Greek κόλλαβος for κόλλοψ is very rarely met with. In Attic κόλλαβοι were a kind of loaves: Athen. 3. 96 D; Ar. Ran. 507, Pax 1196.

CLXX.

Νίμμα ὁ πολὺς λέγει, ἡμεῖς ἀπόνιπτρον λέγομεν, ὡς Ἀριστοφάνης καὶ οἱ ἀμφ' αὐτόν.

> Ὥσπερ ἀπόνιπτρον ἐκχέοντες ἑσπέρας.
>
> Ar. Ach. 616.

''Ἀπόνιμμα pro sordibus elutis Clem. Alex Paed. 2. 3.

Hoeschel. Simplex *νίμμα* ne in recentiori quidem Graecitate frequentatum v. ad Thom. p. 100. Veteribus autem plane ignotum fuisse videtur.' Lobeck.

CLXXI.

Νὴ τὼ θεώ· ὅρκος γυναικός, οὐ μὴ ἀνὴρ ὀμεῖται εἰ μὴ γυναικίζοιτο.

Photius, *μὰ τὼ θεώ, γυναικεῖος ὅρκος· δυικῶς δὲ ὀμνύουσι τὴν Κόρην καὶ τὴν Δήμητραν. ἀνδράσι δὲ οὐ πρέπει τοῦτον ὀμνύναι.*

In Ar. Eccl. 155 a woman dressed as a man betrays herself by this expression—

A. *ἐμοὶ μὲν οὐ δοκεῖ μὰ τὼ θεώ.*
B. *μὰ τὼ θεώ; τάλαινα ποῦ τὸν νοῦν ἔχεις;*
A. *τί δ' ἔστιν; οὐ γὰρ δὴ πιεῖν γ' ᾔτησά σε.*
B. *μὰ Δί', ἀλλ' ἀνὴρ ὢν τὼ θεὼ κατώμοσας,*
καίτοι τά γ' ἄλλ' εἰποῦσα δεξιώτατα.

Among the Spartans, however, *ναὶ τὼ σίω* referred to the Dioscuri, and might be used by men as well as women: Ar. Lys. 81; Xen. Anab. 6. 6. 34, etc. In the mouth of a Boeotian, in Ach. 905, *ναὶ τὼ σιώ* probably refers to Amphion and Zethus.

CLXXII.

Μεσοδάκτυλα· ἐναυτίασα τοῦτο ἀκούσας τοὔνομα. λέγομεν οὖν, τὰ μέσα τῶν δακτύλων.

'Vellem narrasset nobis nauseator Phrynichus fabricatorem vocabuli, cujus tanta est raritas ut lexicographis plane non innotuerit. Reperimus tamen apud Dioscoridem 4. 188, *ῥαγάδες ἐν μεσοδακτύλοις.*' Lobeck.

CLXXIII.

Λάσταυρος οἱ μὲν νῦν χρῶνται ἐπὶ τῶν πονηρῶν καὶ ἀξίων σταυροῦ· οἱ δὲ ἀρχαῖοι ἐπὶ τοῦ καταπύγονος.

'*Λάσταυρος* pro homine improbo generaliori sensu usurpasse videntur Theopompus (Athen. 4. 167 B) et Alciphro, Ep. 1. 37 extr.' Lobeck.

CLXXIV.

Μάλη οὐκ ἐρεῖς, ὑπὸ μάλης μέντοι.

The accusative *ὑπὸ μάλην*, which some read in this place, is not found till very late writers like Anna Comnena (9. p. 254), and was not written by Phrynichus. No Classical writer uses *μάλη*, except in the phrase *ὑπὸ μάλης*, but that occurs with frequency.

> *κἄπειτα δόρυ δῆθ' ὑπὸ μάλης ἥκεις ἔχων;*
>
> Ar. Lys. 985.

Plato, Gorg. 469 D, *λαβὼν ὑπὸ μάλης ἐγχειρίδιον*: Legg. 7. 789 C, *λαβόντες ὑπὸ μάλης ἕκαστος, τοὺς μὲν ἐλάττονας (ὄρνιθας) εἰς τὰς χεῖρας, μείζους δ' ὑπὸ τὴν ἀγκάλην ἐντός*—a sentence which indicates how fixed the phrase had become: Xen. Hell. 2. 3. 23, *ξιφίδια ὑπὸ μάλης ἔχοντες*:

> *ὥστ' ἐξελὼν ἐκ τοῦ λυχνούχου τὸν λύχνον*
> *μικροῦ κατακαύσας ἔλαθ' ἑαυτόν, ὑπὸ μάλης*
> *τῇ γαστρὶ μᾶλλον τοῦ δέοντος προσαγαγών·*
>
> Alexis, ap. Athen. 15. 698 F.

Diphilus, ap. Athen. 11. 499 D.

Demosthenes has the phrase metaphorically, 848. 12, *ἀλλὰ μὴν οὐδ' εἷς οὐδὲ δύο ταῦτ' ἴσασιν, οὐδ' ὑπὸ μάλης ἡ πρόκλησις γέγονεν ἀλλ' ἐν τῇ ἀγορᾷ μέσῃ, πολλῶν παρόντων.*

CLXXV.

Μεγιστᾶνες· Ἀντίοχος ὁ σοφιστὴς βιβλίον τι ὑπέγραφεν Ἀγορὰν ἐπιγραφόμενον, ἔνθα τοὔνομα ἔθηκεν ἴσως Μενάνδρῳ ἀκολουθήσας, οὐ γὰρ δή τινι τῶν ἀρχαίων· ἡμεῖς δὲ οὐ μεγιστᾶνες ἑπόμενοι τοῖς ἀρχαίοις ἀνδράσιν, ἀλλὰ μέγα δυναμένους λέγομεν.

The passage, or passages, of Menander have not come down to us. Sturtz, in Dial. Maced. p. 182, has shown that this and other words date from Macedonian times.

The collocation *μέγα δύναμαι* is met with in the following places, Hom. Od. 1. 276—

ἂψ ἴτω ἐς μέγαρον πατρὸς μέγα δυναμένοιο·

Herod. 2. 143, *ἀνὴρ μέγα δυνάμενος*, (cp. 7. 5, *δυνάμενος ἐν Λακεδαίμονι μέγιστα ξείνων*): Aesch. Eum. 950—

μέγα γὰρ δύναται
πότνι' Ἐρινὺς παρά τ' ἀθανάτοις·

Eur. Hel. 1358 (ch.)—

μέγα τοι δύναται νεβρῶν
παμποίκιλοι στολίδες·

Ar. Ran. 141—

ὡς μέγα δύνασθον πανταχοῦ τὼ δύ' ὀβολώ·

Thuc. 2. 29, *δυνάμενον παρ' αὐτῷ μέγα κτε.*: id. 6. 105, *αἰσθανόμενος αὐτοὺς μέγα παρὰ βασιλεῖ δύνασθαι*: Plato, Rep. 2. 366 A, *αἱ τελεταὶ μέγα δύνανται.* Xenophon has it very frequently. So *μᾶλλον, πλέον, μεῖζον, μέγιστα, μάλιστα δύνασθαι.* This use of *μέγα* must be carefully distinguished from its use with adjectives, which is unknown to Attic Prose or Comedy, though found in Ionic, Tragedy, and Xenophon (see p. 28).

CLXXVI.

Λόγιος· ὡς οἱ πολλοὶ λέγουσιν ἐπὶ τοῦ δεινοῦ εἰπεῖν καὶ ὑψηλοῦ οὐ τιθέασιν οἱ ἀρχαῖοι, ἀλλ' ἐπὶ τοῦ τὰ ἐν ἑκάστῳ ἔθνει ἐπιχώρια ἐξηγουμένου ἐμπείρως.

'Recte Thomas et Moeris ab Atticis *λογίους* dici *τοὺς πολυίστορας* contendunt, a vulgo scribentium *τοὺς λεκτικούς*.' Lobeck.

CLXXVII.

Ἐξιδιάζονται· καὶ τοῦτο Φαβωρῖνος λέγει κακῶς. ἰδιοῦσθαι γὰρ τὸ τοιοῦτον λέγουσιν οἱ ἀρχαῖοι.

According to Antiatt. p. 96, Diphilus used the defaulting word, *Ἐξιδιάσασθαι· Δίφιλος Ἐπιτροπῇ* : but there is no other instance till writers like Diodorus, Strabo, etc. *Ἰδιοῦσθαι*, on the other hand, is common enough, and *ἐξιδιοῦμαι* also is met with, as in Xen. Hell. 2. 4. 8 ; Isocr. 241 D.

Certainly the form in -*όω* was the natural one for a Classical Greek to use. Verbs in -*άζω* from adjectives in -*ος* are rare at the best, and though *ἀτιμάζω*, *διπλασιάζω*, and one or two more bear a transitive meaning, the majority of such words are neuter—*ἀντιάζω*, *ἰσάζω*, *ἠλιθιάζω*, *ἡσυχάζω*, *μετριάζω*, *νεάζω*, *ῥοθιάζω*, *σκυθρωπάζω*, *ἐλευθεριάζω*, and others.

CLXXVIII.

Μύκας μὴ λέγε, ἀλλὰ μύκητας.

Ἔπεισι γοῦν τοῖσιν λύχνοις οὑτοιὶ μύκητες,
φιλεῖ δ' ὅταν τοῦτ' ᾖ ποιεῖν ὑετὸν μάλιστα.

Ar. Vesp. 262.

In 2. 60 Athenaeus quotes from Antiphanes and Ephippus. The former poet supplies the lines—

μύκητας ὠμοὺς ἂν φαγεῖν ἐμοὶ δοκῶ,

and—

ὄπτα μύκητας πρινίνους τουσδὶ δύο·

while the latter has the words—

ἵν' ὥσπερ οἱ μύκητες ἀποπνίξαιμί σε.

Even in late writers the correct form often appears, and with the passage of Aristophanes may be compared the line of Agathias—

μήποτε, λύχνε, μύκητα φέροις, μηδ' ὄμβρον ἐγείροις ;

and with Ephippus another of Strato—

τίς κάλυκας συνέκρινε βάτῳ ; τίς σῦκα μύκησιν ;

The form *μύκη* was, however, not merely late (Theophrast. Fr. de Sig. 3. 5 ; Aristias, Nicander, ap. Ath. 9. 372 F, etc.), but entered the Common dialect from the Doric, as Athenaeus quotes from Epicharmus the words—

οἰοναὶ μύκαις ἄρ' ἐπισκληκότες πνιξεῖσθε.

CLXXIX.

Αὐτότροφος μὴ λέγε, ἀλλ' οἰκόσιτος, ὡς 'Αθηναῖοι· μηδὲ οἰκογενῆ, ἀλλ' οἰκότριβα.

The words that follow in the manuscripts and editions—*μήποτε δὲ καὶ τῷ οἰκογενὴς ὡς δοκίμῳ χρηστέον*—cannot be by Phrynichus, even if the clause preceding them is assigned to him. As it is, they are an idle iteration of the erroneous part of his article. The words *οἰκότριψ* and *οἰκογενής* are both excellent Attic terms.

Athenaeus discusses *οἰκόσιτος* in 6. 247, quoting from Anaxandrides, 'The Hunters'—

υἱὸς γὰρ οἰκόσιτος ἡδὺ γίγνεται.

Antiphanes, 'The Scythian'—

ταχὺ γὰρ γίγνεται
κἀκκλησιαστὴς οἰκόσιτος.

Menander, 'The Ring'—

οἰκόσιτον νυμφίον
οὐδὲν δεόμενον προικὸς ἐξευρήκαμεν.

Id. 'The Harper'—

οὐκ οἰκοσίτους τοὺς ἀκροατὰς λαμβάνεις.

These passages show the meaning of the word to have been *self-supporting*, *with an income of one's own.*

Suidas: Οἰκόσιτος· ὁ ἑαυτὸν τρέφων.

CLXXX.

Τὸ ὁλοσφύρατον ἔκβαλλε καὶ ἤτοι σφυρήλατον λέγε.

The editions add ἢ ὁλόσφυρον, which cannot have come from the hand of Phrynichus, although Photius has the gloss, Ὁλόσφυρον· τὸ ὁλοσφύρατον: and Hesychius, Ὁλόσφυροι· ὁλοσφύρατοι. Lobeck is wrong in considering the α in ὁλοσφύρατος as in any way a departure from ordinary usage. If there had been an Attic verb σφυρᾶν, its verbal would have been σφύρατος, not σφύρητος. Σφυρήλατος stands on quite a different footing.

CLXXXI.

Ὀπωροπώλης· τοῦθ' οἱ ἀγοραῖοι λέγουσιν, οἱ δὲ πεπαιδευμένοι ὀπωρώνης ὡς καὶ Δημοσθένης.

The passage referred to is De Cor. 314. 13, σῦκα καὶ βότρυς καὶ ἐλαίας συλλέγων, ὥσπερ ὀπωρώνης ἐκ τῶν ἀλλοτρίων χωρίων. As ὀπώρα and even ὀπῶραι were good Attic for the 'fruits of autumn,' it seems ultra-purism to find fault with *ὀπωροπώλης*. Plato, Legg. 8. 844 D, *ὃς ἂν ἀγροίκου ὀπώρας γεύσηται, βοτρύων εἴτε καὶ σύκων*: Isaeus, 88. 27, *κατέλιπεν ἔπιπλα, πρόβατα, κριθάς, οἶνον, ὀπώρας, ἐξ ὧν ἐνεπώλησαν τετρακισχιλίας ἐννακοσίας.*

'Thomas *ὀπωρῶν ὠνήτωρ οἱ ἀγοραῖοι, σὺ δὲ ὀπωρώνης*, qui cum cetera e Phrynicho hauserit, mirum mihi est, unde illud *ὀπωροπώλης* omiserit, vocabulumque nunquam lectum, neque plebeii coloris, *ὠνήτωρ ὀπωρῶν* sublegerit. Photius *ὀπωρώνας ὠνητὰς ὀπώρας* interpretatur . . . . Pollux vi. 128 *ὀπωρώνης* et *ὀπωροπώλης* eodem loco habet, neque *θεατρώνης* et *θεατροπώλης*, *ἐλαώνης* et *ἐλαοπώλης* differunt: quod valet de omnibus, qui coëmunt aut conducunt per aversionem, quae singulis divendant.' Lobeck.

CLXXXII.

Νοσσός, νοσσίον· ἀμφοῖν λείπει τὸ ε. διὰ τοῦτο ἀδόκιμα· λέγε οὖν νεοττός, νεοττίον ἵνα ἀρχαῖος φαίνῃ. νοσσάριον ἐκβλητέον τελέως.

'Nihil eorum quae hic a Phrynicho reprehenduntur in Attici sermonis monimentis cernitur.' Even in Menander, quoted by Photius and Suïdas s. v., there is no necessity to read *τὸν νοττόν* for *τὸν νεοττόν* as *τὸ νεοττίον* better serves the purpose—

> *καὶ τεττάρων ᾠῶν μετὰ τοῦτο, φιλτάτη,*
> *τὸ νεοττίον.*

CLXXXIII.

Χρύσεα, ἀργύρεα, χάλκεα, κυάνεα, ταῦτα Ἰακὰ διαιρούμενα. χρὴ οὖν λέγειν χρυσᾶ, ἀργυρᾶ, κυανᾶ τὸν ἀττικίζοντα.

Χρυσοῦς λέγε. τὸ γὰρ χρύσεος Ἰακόν. ὡσαύτως καὶ ἀργυροῦς ἀλλὰ μὴ ἀργύρεος· χαλκοῦς, κυανοῦς καὶ τὰ ὅμοια.

'Ex scriptoribus qui aetatem tulerunt prope nullus reperitur tam antiquus tamque incorruptus quin vel sua vel librariorum culpa eo declinarit.' Lobeck. The open forms are quite alien to Attic proper. For *σιδάρεος* in Comedy see p. 49.

CLXXXIV.

Ἐκτρῶσαι καὶ ἔκτρωμα· ταῦτα φεῦγε, λέγε δὲ ἐξαμβλῶσαι καὶ ἄμβλωμα καὶ ἀμβλίσκει.

Ἐξέτρωσεν ἡ γυνὴ μὴ λέγε· ἐξήμβλωσε δέ.

Ἔκτρωμα· μηδὲ τοῦτο λέγε. ἐξάμβλωμα δὲ καὶ ἀμβλωθρίδιον.

Of these three sentences the two second have been brought from a later place in the manuscripts, where they are in juxtaposition.

Lobeck's note on these words is peculiarly apt, but vitiated by his inability to draw the just inference from his facts. They are these:—

Ἐκτιτρώσκω, Herod. 3. 32, *καί μιν ἐκτρωσάσαν ἀποθανεῖν*: Hippocr. de Steril. 686. 27, *ἢν γυνὴ ἐκτιτρώσκῃ ἀέκουσα*: id. de Aer. 287. 28, *πρὸς τῷ ἦρι ἐκτιτρώσκεσθαι*. Τρωσμός= *ἐκτρωσμός*, Hipp. 206 D et freq.; *τιτρωσμός*, id. 601. 30; Aristotle, H. A. 7. 4, p. 585. 22, *καὶ ἐκτιτρώσκουσαί τινες συνέλαβον ἅμα*: id. 9. 3, p. 610. 35, *ἐκτιτρώσκει ἐὰν τύχῃ κύουσα*: id. De Gener. An. 4. 5, p. 773. 18, *κυήματα ἐκπίπτει παραπλήσια τοῖς καλουμένοις ἐκτρώμασιν*: Dioscorides, 3. 147, *φασὶ δὲ ὅτι κἂν ἔγκυος ὑπερβῇ τὴν πόαν ἐκτιτρώσκει*: Plut. Mor. 974 D, *καταμαθεῖν ταῖς ἐγκύοις τὴν βοτάνην παρεῖχον* ἐκτρωτικὴν δύναμιν ἔχουσαν. Add Diodorus, Apollonius Dyscolus, 'et recentiores medicos.'

Ἐξαμβλίσκω, Ar. Nub. 137—

A. ἀπεριμερίμνως τὴν θύραν λελάκτικας
καὶ φροντίδ' ἐξήμβλωκας ἐξηυρημένην.
B. ἀλλ' εἰπέ μοι τὸ πρᾶγμα τοὐξημβλωμένον.

Plato, Theaet. 150 E, πολλοὶ ἀπῆλθον πρῳαίτερον τοῦ δέοντος, ἀπελθόντες δὲ τά τε λοιπὰ ἐξήμβλωσαν καὶ τὰ ὑπ' ἐμοῦ μαιευθέντα κακῶς τρέφοντες ἀπώλεσαν: id. 149 D, τίκτειν τε καὶ ἀμβλίσκειν. The existence of ἀμβλωθρίδιον in the Orators is proved by Harpocration's gloss: Ἀμβλωθρίδιον· τὸ ἀμβλωθὲν βρέφος, and ἄμβλωσις Pollux quotes from Lysias, and ἄμβλωμα from Antiphon. (Pollux, 2. 7.)

Moreover in Tragedy either word might be used—

ἡμεῖς γὰρ εἰ σὴν παῖδα φαρμακεύομεν
καὶ νηδὺν ἐξαμβλοῦμεν.

Eur. Andr. 356.

Hesychius preserves ἐκτιτρώσκω in Sophocles: Ἀμβλύσκει· ἐξαμβλοῖ· κυρίως δὲ ἐπὶ ἀμπέλου· καὶ ἐκτιτρώσκει, Σοφοκλῆς Ἀνδρομέδῃ.

The words are a type of many others. Τιτρώσκω or ἐκτιτρώσκω—the older word in this connection—was ousted in Attic by ἐξαμβλίσκω, but reappeared in the Common dialect with its early meaning—a meaning which it had never lost in the dialect of tragedy, the representative of Early Attic.

CLXXXV.

Δυσὶ μὴ λέγε, ἀλλὰ δυοῖν. δυεῖν δ' ἔστι μὲν δόκιμον, τῷ δὲ ἀλλοκότως αὐτῷ χρῆσθαί τινας ἐπιταράττεται· ἐπὶ γὰρ μόνης γενικῆς τίθεται, οὐχὶ δὲ δοτικῆς.

All of this article, except the first five words, is quite erroneous, and probably the error is to be explained as in

Art. 179. In Attic Greek the only forms of the second cardinal number are δύο and δυοῖν—the former being employed for the nominative, vocative, and accusative, and in earlier writers like Thucydides even for all the cases, while the latter is confined to the genitive and dative. The dual number is of very frequent occurrence in Attic Greek, and as a general rule δύο or δυοῖν is added, as τὼ δύο θεώ, τὼ δύο νεάνιδε, τοῖν δυοῖν θεοῖν, τοῖν δυοῖν νεανίδοιν. The form δύο, however, may be attached to substantives in the plural, whereas if δυοῖν is used the substantive must always have the inflexion of the dual number, except it be an abstract noun. This rule was first formulated by Elmsley, and the exception first perceived by Wecklein: 'Comprobatur igitur quod statuit Elmsleius ad Eur. Med. 798 Not., δυοῖν apud Atticos duali semper jungi, δύο vero interdum plurali, dummodo *veteres* Atticos intellegamus. Corrigit Elmsleius Aesch. Eum. 600, δυοῖν γὰρ εἶχε προσβολὰς μιασμάτοιν, ubi libri μαισμάτων, Ag. 1384, κἂν δυοῖν οἰμωγμάτοιν, ubi libri οἰμώγμασι. Pers. 720 dualem M. cum aliis libris exhibet (δυοῖν στρατευμάτοιν) cfr. Ch. 304, δυοῖν γυναικοῖν, 944 δυοῖν μιαστόροιν, 1047 δυοῖν δρακόντοιν. Elmsleium secutus est G. Hermannus, Dindorfius, libros Weilius. Vide ne apud Tragicos alia ratio sit in nominibus abstractis. Sophoclem quidem video in *hominibus* etiam δύο semper cum duali jungere (cfr. Phil. 539, ἄνδρε δύο, O. R. 1505, O. C. 532, Ant. 533, δύο δ' ἄτα—hoc enim eandem vim habet—Ant. 55, ἀδελφὼ δύο, 989, δύ' ἐξ ἑνὸς βλέποντε)—ut uno loco Trach. 539, δύ' οὖσαι, vel in δύ' οὖσα, vel in δύ' ὄντε corrigi debeat, contra dicere Phil. 117, δύο δωρήματα. Itaque valde dubito an Aeschylus in abstracto μιάσματα, οἰμώγματα duali usus non sit, et ut velis Eum. 600, δυοῖν μιασμάτοιν scribere Ag. 1383 *dativum* dual. nom. abstracti nullo modo probaverim. Cho. 931, autem τῶνδε mutari debet in τοῖνδε.' (Wecklein, Curae Epigraph. pp. 16, 17.)

CLXXXVI.

῎Ωτοις μὴ λέγε, ὥς τινες τῶν γραμματικῶν ἀλλ' ὠσί.

Phrynichus is here reprehending those grammarians who suggested that, because *ὦτα*, the nominative, and *ὥτων*, the genitive plural, might be regarded as belonging either to the second or third declension, therefore the dative could be *ὥτοις* as well as *ὠσί*. They were led astray by the anomalous accentuation of the genitive plural *ὥτων*, and the genitive-dative dual *ὥτοιν*, these cases being accented as if from *ὦτον*.

CLXXXVII.

Μείρακες καὶ μεῖραξ· ἡ μὲν κωμῳδία παίζει τὰ τοιαῦτα· τὸ γὰρ μεῖραξ καὶ μείρακες ἐπὶ θηλειῶν τάττουσιν, τὸ δὲ μειρακίσκος καὶ μειράκιον καὶ μειρακύλλιον ἐπὶ ἀνδρῶν.

The *παίζει* refers to places like that in Cratinus—

ποδαπὰς ὑμᾶς εἶναι φάσκων, ὦ μείρακες, οὐκ ἂν ἁμαρτεῖν,

where *εἰκὸς αὐτοὺς θηλυκῇ προσηγορίᾳ σκώπτειν τοὺς πασχητιῶντας*. Otherwise the distinction is carefully observed by Attic writers.

Μεῖραξ, of a girl, in Ar. Eccl. 611, 696, 1138, Plut. 1071, 1079, Thesm. 410; Xenarchus, Ath. 13. 569 A; Cratinus, Ath. 2. 49 A.

Μειράκιον, of a boy, in Ar. Eq. 556, 1375, Nub. 917, 928, 990, 1000, 1071, Vesp. 687, Av. 1440, Ran. 1071, Eccl. 702, Pl. 88. 975, 1038, 1096; Theopompus, Ath. 14. 649 B; Philyllius, Ath. 11. 485 B; Epicrates, Ath. 2. 59 C etc.; Plato, Prot. 315 D, Parm. 126 C, Conv. 215 D, Apol. 18 C, 34 C; Charm. 154 B, Theaet. 142 C, 144 C, 168 E, 173 B, Gorg. 485 A, C, D, 499 B, Rep. 468 B, 497 E, 498 B, Lach. 179 D, 200 D, Legg. 658 D, etc.; Aeschines, 6. 14, 25. 3, 50. 26; Isaeus, 55. 7; Lysias, 96. 24, 97. 18; Xenophon, Mem. 1. 2. 42, etc.

Μειρακύλλιον, of a boy, Ar. Ran. 89; Anaxandrides, Athen. 6. 227 C; Epicrates, id. 262 D; Demosthenes, 539, 23.

On the other hand, either *μειρακίσκος* or *μειρακίσκη* may be used—the former occurring in Alexis, Ath. 12. 544 E, id. 10. 421 D; Plato, Phaedr. 237 B, Rep. 7. 539 B, Theag. 122 C; the latter in Ar. Ran. 409, Pl. 964.

The words are not known to Tragedy. The Attic rule is thus just the converse of the Latin, which gave *puella* for the feminine, but for the masculine the unqualified *puer*. In late Greek the above distinction is not observed.

CLXXXVIII.

'Αναθέσθαι κακῶς οἱ ἰδιῶται· σὺ δὲ ἀναβάλλομαι φαθί. οἱ γὰρ ἐπὶ τούτου τάττοντες τὸ ἀναθέσθαι ἁμαρτάνουσι. λέγουσι γὰρ ἀνατίθεμαι εἰσαῦθις τὸ πρᾶγμα, ἀγνοοῦντες, ὡς τὸ ἀνατιθέναι δύο σημαίνει, ἓν μὲν τὸ μεταγιγνώσκειν ἐφ' οἷς εἴρηκε, καὶ ἄρρητα ποιεῖν, ἕτερον δ' ἀνατιθέναι τὸ φορτίον.

The word *ἰδιώτης* has its usual sense of *an untrained man, one who does not know*. Phrynichus finds fault with the use of *ἀνατίθεμαι* in the sense of *ἀναβάλλομαι*, *put off*, which it bears in late writers, as in Themist. de Anima, 3, *τοῦτο γὰρ ἀνεθέμεθα ἐπισκέψασθαι*, *we put off discussing this point*, and in his own example, *ἀνατίθεμαι εἰσαῦθις τὸ πρᾶγμα*, *I put off the business for another time* (lit. *to again*). He recognizes as Attic only two significations, the one, *to retract what one has said and do what one has not suggested*, the other, *to put on one's shoulders*. The former meaning is found in Plato, Gorg. 461 D, *καὶ ἔγωγε ἐθέλω τῶν ὡμολογημένων ἀναθέσθαι ὅ τι ἂν σὺ βούλῃ*: id. 462 A, Prot. 354 E, Phaed. 87 A; Xen. Mem. 1. 2. 44, etc., the latter in Lys. 110. 7, *ἀναθέμενος δ' ὁ βοηλάτης ᾤχετο ἀπάγων τὰ ξύλα*.

This second sense is, with the necessary modification, also found in the active. That of retract is a metaphor from draughts, as is shown by a note in Harpocration's lexicon: Ἀναθέσθαι· Ἀντιφῶν ἐν τῷ Περὶ ὁμονοίας, 'ἀναθέσθαι δὲ ὥσπερ πεττὸν τὸν βίον οὐκ ἔστιν.' ἀντὶ τοῦ ἄνωθεν βιῶναι μετανοήσαντας ἐπὶ τῷ προτέρῳ βίῳ· εἴρηται δὲ ἐκ μεταφορᾶς τῶν πεττευομένων· Πλάτων ἐν Ἱππάρχῳ ἢ Φιλοκέρδει. The passage of Plato is 229 E, ἀλλὰ μὴν καὶ ὥσπερ πεττεύων ἐθέλω σοι ἐν τοῖς λόγοις ἀναθέσθαι ὅ, τι βούλει τῶν εἰρημένων.

CLXXXIX.

Σταθερὸς ἄνθρωπος· οὕτως οὐ χρῶνται οἱ ἀρχαῖοι, ἀλλὰ σταθερὰ μὲν μεσημβρία λέγουσι καὶ σταθερὰ γαλήνη, σταθερὸς δὲ ἄνθρωπος οὐδαμῶς, ἀλλ' ἐμβριθής· οὐ καλῶς οὖν Φαβωρῖνος σταθερὸς ἄνθρωπος εἶπεν.

The phrase σταθερὰ μεσημβρία is referred to by Plato, Phaedr. 242 A, μήπω γε, ὦ Σώκρατες, πρὶν ἂν τὸ καῦμα παρέλθῃ· ἢ οὐχ ὁρᾷς ὡς σχεδὸν ἤδη μεσημβρία ἵσταται ἡ δὴ καλουμένη σταθερά· and Photius, in addition to this passage, quotes the adjective from Aeschylus and Aristophanes, τινὲς καὶ ἐπὶ τοῦ στασίμου ὡς Αἴσχυλος ἐν Ψυχαγωγοῖς, **σταθεροῦ χεύματος**, καὶ Ἀριστοφάνης ἐν Προάγωνι, **σταθερὰ δὲ κάλυξ νεαρᾶς ἥβης**. The word, as a whole, is much more frequent in late than in Classical Greek.

CXC.

Ἀναπεσεῖν οὐ καλῶς ἐπὶ τοῦ ἀνακλιθῆναι τάττεται, ἐὰν δ' ἐπὶ τοῦ τὴν ψυχὴν ἀδημονῆσαι, καλῶς· οἷον ἀνέπεσεν ἄνθρωπος ἀντὶ τοῦ τὴν ψυχὴν ἠθύμησεν.

Besides its primitive signification of *fall back*, ἀναπίπτειν, was employed as a technical term for throwing oneself back in rowing, as is well shown by Polybius, 1. 21. 2, ἅμα πάντας ἀναπίπτειν ἐφ' αὑτοὺς ἄγοντας τὰς χεῖρας καὶ πάλιν προνεύειν ἐξωθοῦντας ταῦτας. In this sense the word is met with in (Xen.) Oec. 8. 8, ἐν τάξει μὲν κάθηνται, ἐν τάξει δὲ προνεύουσιν, ἐν τάξει δ' ἀναπίπτουσιν, and in Cratinus (Ath. 1. 23 B), ῥοθίαζε κἀνάπιπτε.

In the metaphorical sense Thucydides (1. 70) has νικώμενοι ἐπ' ἐλάχιστον ἀναπίπτουσι· and Demosthenes (411. 3), δέδοικα μὴ ἀναπεπτωκότες ἦτε. In the last writer it is also applied to things (567. 12), ἀνεπεπτώκει τὰ τῆς ἐξόδου. There is no instance in Attic Greek of the meaning *recline*, as in the passage of Alexis, quoted by Athenaeus in 1. 23 E, the verb has a special reference.

CXCI.

Ἀνακεῖται· καὶ τοῦτο ἄλλο μὲν παρ' αὐτοῖς σημαίνει, ἀντ' ἄλλου δὲ ὑπὸ τῶν πολλῶν τίθεται. Ἀνάκειται μὲν γὰρ ἀνδριὰς καὶ ἀναθήματα καλῶς ἐρεῖς, ἀνάκειται δ' ἐπὶ τῆς κλίνης οὐκέτι, ἀλλὰ κεῖται.

As is well-known, κεῖμαι is always used in Attic Greek as the perfect passive of τίθημι, the perfect τέθειμαι being always middle in meaning. Accordingly, ἀνάκειμαι as naturally refers to ἀναθήματα and ἀνδριάντες, as it supplies a perfect passive to ἀνατίθημι in phrases like ἀνατιθέναι τὰ πράγματα, s. τὴν αἰτίαν τινί. Herodian represents some comic poet as ridiculing that use of the verb which Phrynichus here reprehends, Pierson's ed. p. 441: Κατακεῖσθαι· ἐπὶ τῶν ἑστιωμένων, ἀνακεῖσθαι δ' ἐπὶ εἰκόνων καὶ ἀνδριάντων· εἰπόντος γοῦν τινὸς Ἀνάκεισο[1], ὁ Κωμικὸς παίζων ἀνδριάντας ἑστιᾷς ἔφη.

[1] Ἀνάπιπτε, the reading of the editions, cannot be right.

CXCII.

Ἀντιβαλεῖν· καὶ τοῦθ' ἕτερόν τι σημαίνει καὶ ἑτέρως ὑπὸ τῶν πολλῶν λέγεται· σημαίνει γὰρ τοιοῦτόν τι, ὁποῖον τὸ ἀντιτιθέναι· λέγεται δὲ νῦν ἀντὶ τοῦ ἀνταναγνῶναι.

The manuscripts have *ἀνατιθέναι*, which sprang from *ἀντιθέναι*, produced by the accidental omission of one of the two adjacent syllables. Phrynichus, in App. Soph. p. 27. 10, again remarks upon this late use of *ἀντιβάλλειν*: *Ἀνταναγνῶναι· χρήσιμον, οὐκ ἀντιβαλεῖν, οὐδ' ἀντεξετάσαι*, and a writer in the *Λέξεις χρήσιμοι*, p. 410. 31, refers to Cratinus for this use of *ἀνταναγιγνώσκειν*, *to read in order to compare.* The practice is well exemplified by Lobeck: 'Lexicon *περὶ πνευμάτων* a Valckenario editum: *ἀντιγράφοις διαφόροις* (*alternis lectionibus*) *ἀντιβληθὲν καὶ ὀρθωθέν*, p. 207, *ἵνα ἀντιβάλῃς ὃ μετεγράψω καὶ κατορθώσῃς πρὸς τὸ ἀντίγραφον* . . . Neque id solum in comparatione librorum in exemplaria transcriptorum dicitur, sed etiam si quis quaelibet alia *παράλληλα ἐξετάζει*, ut v. c. *ἕνα πρὸς ἕνα ἀντιβαλεῖν* Damasc. Suïd. s. *Ἐπίκτητος*, quod qui integre et sincere loquuntur, *ἀντιπαραβάλλειν* dicere solent. Isocr. 111 B, Plato. Apol. 41 B.'

CXCIII.

Σκορπίζεται· Ἑκαταῖος μὲν τοῦτο λέγει Ἴων ὤν, ὁ Ἀττικὸς δὲ σκεδάννυται φασί.

The word is of frequent occurrence in the Common dialect, but the passage referred to by Phrynichus is the only instance known in Classical Greek.

CXCIV.

Κατασχάσαι· ἰατροὶ μὲν τοῦτο λέγουσιν ἔχοντες ἀπολογίαν, ὡς ὄντος παρὰ τοῖς ἀρχαίοις τοῦ ἔσχων καὶ ἔσχαζον καὶ ἐκέντουν, ἀλλὰ κατανύξαι ἡμεῖς λέγομεν.

The evidence of literature does not support Phrynichus in his preference for *κατανύξαι* over *κατασχάσαι*. Xenophon employs *σχάζω* in Hell. 5. 4. 58, *ἰατρὸς σχάζει τὴν παρὰ τῷ σφυρῷ φλέβα αὐτοῦ*, and the word is also found with the same meaning in Hippocrates and Aristotle. Hipp. 552. 40, *σχάσαι αὐτοῦ τοὺς ἀγκῶνας καὶ ἀφαιρέειν τοῦ αἵματος*: Aph. 6. 5. 21, *σχάζειν τὰς ἐν τοῖς ὠσὶν ὄπισθεν φλέβας*: Arist. H. A. 21, 603. [b]15, *βοηθεῖ τὸ λουτρὸν καὶ ἐάν τις σχάσῃ ὑπὸ τὴν γλῶτταν*. On the other hand, no Classical writer employs *κατανύσσω* is any sense, whether lay or medical. There is practically nothing in his dictum. *Σχάζω* and *νύσσω* were both good Classical words, and the one might well be used of opening a vein by cutting, the other by pricking; but in *κατανύσσω*, no less than in *κατασχάζω*, there is an attempt at that false emphasis which vitiates all late Greek.

CXCV.

Ῥέει, ζέει, πλέει. Ἰακὰ ταῦτα διαιρούμενα. λέγε οὖν ῥεῖ, ζεῖ, πλεῖ.

CXCVI.

Ἐδέετο, ἐπλέετο. Ἰωνικὰ ταῦτα· ἡ δὲ Ἀττικὴ συνήθεια συναιρεῖ, ἐδεῖτο, ἐπλεῖτο, ἐρρεῖτο.

CXCVII.

Προσδεῖσθαι λέγε, ἀλλὰ μὴ προσδέεσθαι διαιρῶν, ὡς Φαβωρῖνος λέγων ἁμαρτάνει.

These articles were brought together by Lobeck. The third is not found in the Laurentian manuscripts, or in the editions of Callierges and Vascosan. The middle *ἐρρεῖτο* actually does occur in Eur. Hel. 1602—

φόνῳ δὲ ναῦς ἐρρεῖτο· παρακέλευσμα δ' ἦν κτε.

being either a natural outcome of the same feeling which prompted *ῥεύσομαι*, or an artificial imitation of the same.

If the first person singular present indicative active is in its uncontracted form disyllabic, this fact influences the contraction of verbs in *-έω*[1], but leaves those in *-άω* unaffected. Thus, while *δράω* was contracted to *δρῶ*, just as *τιμάω* to *τιμῶ*, and as *δράοιμι* was in Attic replaced by *δρῴην*, just as *τιμάοιμι* was replaced by *τιμῴην*, yet *χέω* was retained by the side of the contracted *ποιῶ*, and *χέοιμι* was not modified like *ποιοίην*. On the other hand, *χέεις* contracted to *χεῖς*, just as *ποιέεις* to *ποιεῖς*, and *χέει* to *χεῖ*, like *ποιέει* to *ποιεῖ*.

The rule for the contraction of verbs like *χέω* is, however, extremely simple.

They contract only when the vowel *ε* is followed by another simple *ε*, or by the diphthongal endings *-εις* and *-ει* of the active. In all other cases their inflexion is identical with that of *λύω*. Their subjunctive and optative are consequently regular, *χέω*, *χέῃς*, *χέῃ*, etc., *χέοιμι*, *χέοις*, *χέοι*, etc., and in the optative they do not, as polysyllabic verbs like *ποιέω*, assume the Attic singular forms in *-ιην*, *-ιης*, *-ιη* :—

[1] For verbs in *-όω*, see p. 274.

Present Indicative.

		Active.	Middle and Passive.
S.	1.	χέω	χέομαι
	2.	χεῖς	χέει
	3.	χεῖ	χεῖται
D.	2.	χεῖτον	χεῖσθον
	3.	χεῖτον	χεῖσθον
P.	1.	χέομεν	χεόμεθα
	2.	χεῖτε	χεῖσθε
	3.	χέουσι	χέονται.

Imperfect.

S.	1.	ἔχεον	ἐχεόμην
	2.	ἔχεις	ἐχέου
	3.	ἔχει	ἐχεῖτο
D.	2.	ἐχεῖτον	ἐχεῖσθον
	3.	ἐχείτην	ἐχείσθην
P.	1.	ἐχέομεν	ἐχεόμεθα
	2.	ἐχεῖτε	ἐχεῖσθε
	3.	ἔχεον	ἐχέοντο.

Imperative.

S.	2.	χεῖ	χέου
	3.	χείτω	χείσθω
D.	2.	χεῖτον	χεῖσθον
	3.	χείτων	χείσθων
P.	2.	χεῖτε	χεῖσθε
	3.	χεόντων	χείσθων

Infinitive.

χεῖν	χεῖσθαι.

Participle.

χέων, χέουσα, χέον	χεόμενος, η, ον.
χέοντος, χεούσης	

The evidence of verse is conclusive—

> ὥστ' ἐπειδὴ 'ξῃρέθη, ῥεῖ μου τὸ δάκρυον πολύ.
> Arist. Lys. 1034.
>
> κατάχει σὺ τῆς χορδῆς τὸ μέλι· τὰς σηπίας στάθευε.
> Id. Ach. 1040.
>
> ἐν γῇ πένεσθαι μᾶλλον ἢ πλουτοῦντα πλεῖν.
> Antiphanes (Fr. Com. 3. 53).
>
> γέρων ὢν καὶ σαπρὸς
> κέρδους ἕκατι κἂν ἐπὶ ῥιπὸς πλέοι.
> Arist. Pax 699.
>
> εἴποιμ' ἂν ἄλλους εἰ μὴ μηκύνειν δέοι.
> Id. Lys. 1132.
>
> ἀλλὰ πλείτω χωρὶς αὐτὸς ἐς κόρακας, εἰ βούλεται.
> Id. Eq. 1314.
>
> ποταμοὶ μὲν ἀθάρης καὶ μέλανος ζωμοῦ πλέῳ
> διὰ τῶν στενωπῶν τονθολγοῦντες ἔρρεον.
> Pherecrates, 'The Miners' (Ath. 6. 268 E.).

In fact to this rule, that verbs which have their first person singular present indicative disyllabic, and ending in -εω, only contract in those cases in which the ε of their stem is followed by another ε, or in the active by -ει or -εις, there is no exception in Attic verse, except in conjectural *emendations*. Thus Dindorf alone is responsible for such forms as δῇ for δέῃ in Arist. Ran. 265, etc. In Arist. Plut. 216 the Ravenna, it is true, and other manuscripts, read κἂν δεῖ, but it is the conjunction and not the verb that is amiss, just as the Ravenna also exhibits κἂν βούλει for κεἰ βούλει in the next line—

> A. ἐγὼ γάρ, εὖ τοῦτ' ἴσθι κἂν δεῖ μ' ἀποθανεῖν
> αὐτὸς διαπράξω ταῦτα.
> B. κἂν βούλει γ' ἐγώ[1].

Like Dindorf, Westphal and Veitch go very far wrong in making exceptions for themselves. True, ἔχεε(ν) is not

[1] Cobet reads κἂν χρῇ and κἂν βούλῃ, emendations adopted by Meineke.

uncommon in Greek, but it is not an imperfect form, as they imagine, but an aorist, and, as such, not subject to the rules of contraction. This is conclusively proved, first, by the meaning of the passages in which it occurs, and, secondly, by the fact that the forms ἔρρεε(ν) and ἔπλεε(ν) are never found, because the aorists of ῥέω and πλέω are ἔρρευσα and ἔπλευσα.

That ἔχει is imperfect, ἔχεε(ν) aorist, is seen from the following examples—

οὐδέποτ' ἐγὼ Πόλεμον οἴκαδ' ὑποδέξομαι,
οὐδὲ παρ' ἐμοί ποτε τὸν 'Αρμόδιον ᾄσεται
συγκατακλινεὶς ὅτι παροινικὸς ἀνὴρ ἔφυ,
ὅστις ἐπὶ πάντ' ἀγάθ' ἔχοντας ἐπικωμάσας
εἰργάσατο πάντα κακά, κἀνέτρεπε κἀξέχει
κἀμάχετο καὶ προσέτι πολλὰ προκαλουμένου
'πῖνε, κατάκεισο, λαβὲ τήνδε φιλοτησίαν,'
τὰς χάρακας ἧπτε πολὺ μᾶλλον ἐν τῷ πυρί,
ἐξέχει θ' ἡμων βίᾳ τὸν οἶνον ἐκ τῶν ἀμπέλων.

Arist. Ach. 979-987.

ἐπεὶ δὲ θᾶττον ἧμεν ἠριστηκότες
ὁ παῖς περιεῖλε τὰς τραπέζας, νίμματα
ἐπέχει τις, ἀπενιζόμεθα, τοὺς στεφάνους πάλιν
τοὺς ἰρίνους λαβόντες ἐστεφανούμεθα.

Dromo, 'The Music Girl' (Athen. 9. 409 E).

Here κἀξέχει, ἐξέχει, ἐπέχει are, by their place in a series of imperfects, as conclusively proved to be themselves imperfects as the context of the following shows κατέχεεν and ἐνέχεεν to be aorists —

ἀλλ' οὐκ ἐπίθετο τοῖς ἐμοῖς οὐδὲν λόγοις,
ἀλλ' ἵππερών μου κατέχεεν τῶν χρημάτων.

Arist. Nub. 74.

Pherecrates, 'Corianno' (Athen. 10. 430 E), in a conversation between Corianno, Glycé, and Syriscus—

Co. ἄποτ' ἔστ', ὦ Γλύκη.
Gl. ὑδαρῆ 'νέχεέν σοι; Co. παντάπασι μὲν οὖν ὕδωρ.

Gl. τί εἰργάσω; πῶς, ὦ κατάρατε, δ' ἐνέχεας;
Syr. δύ' ὕδατος, ὦ μάμμη. Gl. τί δ' οἴνου; Syr. τέτταρας.
Co. ἔρρ' ἐς κόρακας· βατράχοισιν οἰνοχοεῖν σε δεῖ.

Such passages of prose writers as copyists have corrupted from ignorance of this natural and simple distinction ought at once to be corrected. Thus, in Plato, Rep. 379, συνέχεεν is right because the aorist is wanted, but in Antiphon, 113. 29, ἐνέχεε should be substituted for ἐνέχει, though a few lines above the imperfect ἐνέχει must be retained.

There are two verbs, however, of this class which follow the analogy of polysyllables and contract throughout—the frequently occurring δεῖν, *to bind*, and the rare ξεῖν, *to polish*.

There is no undisputed instance of the imperfect or any mood of the present of ξέω in Attic writers as the 'Theages,' in which (124 B) the participle τῶν ξεόντων is found is certainly not a genuine Platonic dialogue. But in Inscriptions the participle occurs twice, and both times contracted—ἀναξῶν and καταξοῦντι[1].

The following lines prove the case with regard to δῶ—

λήροις ἀναδῶν τοὺς νικῶντας τὸν πλοῦτον ἐᾷ παρ' ἑαυτῷ.
Arist. Plut. 589.

ἴθι δὴ σὺ περιδοῦ καὶ ταχέως ἀνὴρ γενοῦ.
Id. Eccl. 121.

τῶν δ' ἀκοντίων
συνδοῦντες ὀρθὰ τρία λυχνείῳ χρώμεθα.
Antiphanes, 'The Knights' (Athen. 15. 700 C.).

In—

ἄγε νυν ὑπολύου τὰς καταράτους ἐμβάδας
τασδὶ δ' ἀνύσας ὑποδοῦ τι τὰς λακωνικάς,
Arist. Vesp. 1158.

the word ὑποδοῦ is merely a conjecture of Hirschig's for ὑπόδυθι, as ὑπολύου in the preceding line for ἀποδύου or ὑποδύου. The reading ὑπολύου is probably right, as ὑποδύου

[1] See Wecklein, Curae Epigraphicae, p. 32; Herwerden, Lapidum Testimonia, p. 43.

is certainly wrong, and ἀποδύου merely an attempt to correct it, but there is more doubt about ὑπόδυθι. It is true that ὑποδεῖσθαι is the ordinary word for 'putting on shoes' in every age of Greek, as in the well-known ὑπὸ ποσσὶν ἐδήσατο καλὰ πέδιλα, and in another passage of Aristophanes—

ὑποδεῖσθε δ' ὡς τάχιστα τὰς Λακωνικάς.
Eccl. 269.

but the commonly received ὑποδήσασθαι in Vesp. 1159—

ἐγὼ γὰρ ἂν τλαίην ὑποδήσασθαί ποτε·

and ὑποδησάμενος in id. 1168—

ἄνυσόν ποθ' ὑποδησάμενος κτε.

are in themselves merely conjectures of Scaliger's for the manuscript ὑποδύσασθαι and ὑποδυσάμενος.

In a passage of 'The Dolon' of Eubulus (Athen. 3. 100 A) there is the same difficulty—

ἐγὼ κεχόρτασμαι μέν, ἄνδρες, οὐ κακῶς,
ἀλλ' εἰμὶ πλήρης, ὥστε καὶ μόλις πάνυ
ὑπεδυσάμην ἅπαντα δρῶν τὰς ἐμβάδας·

but in a line from 'The Sirens' of Theopompus (quoted by the Scholiast on Arist. Lys. 45)—

ὑποδοῦ λαβὼν τὰς περιβαρίδας,

the ordinary expression is unquestioned.

It may well be that ὑποδύομαι and ὑπέδυν were used as slang to express the same thing as ὑποδοῦμαι, and, as slang, were not out of place in Comedy, just as the middle of σχάζω, 'cut,' is used in the sense of our English slang term 'cut,' 'have done with'—

τούτων γενοῦ μοι σχασάμενος τὴν ἱππικήν,
Ar. Nub. 107.

'cut the turf and take to books:' Plato, Com. (Schol. Ach. 351)—

καὶ τὰς ὀφρῦς σχάσασθε καὶ τὰς ὄμφακας,

'have done with your temper and your gibes.'

This question, however, does not affect the rule of contraction for δῶ. The texts of prose writers generally exhibit the true forms, but not in every case. Thus Plato is credited with δέον in Phaed. 99, but δοῦν must be restored. In late Greek the uncontracted forms prevailed, and it was probably from want of familiarity with the shorter and earlier ὑποδῶν for their own ὑποδέων[1] that led the scribes to replace it by ὑπὸ ποδῶν in one passage of Plato, Prot. 321 A, ἐπειδὴ δὲ αὐτοῖς ἀλληλλοφθοριῶν διαφυγὰς ἐπήρκεσε, πρὸς τὰς ἐκ Διὸς ὥρας εὐμάρειαν ἐμηχανᾶτο ἀμφιεννὺς αὐτὰ πυκναῖς τε θριξὶ καὶ στερέοις δέρμασιν, ἱκανοῖς μὲν ἀμῦναι χειμῶνα, δυνατοῖς δὲ καὶ καύματα καὶ εἰς εὐνὰς ἰοῦσιν ὅπως ὑπάρχοι τὰ αὐτὰ ταῦτα στρωμνὴ οἰκεία τε καὶ αὐτοφυὴς ἑκάστῳ· καὶ ὑποδῶν τὰ μὲν ὁπλαῖς τὰ δὲ θριξὶ καὶ δέρμασι στερέοις καὶ ἀναίμοις, where ὑποδῶν corresponds to ἀμφιεννύς above. The true reading was extracted by Badham from the ὑπὸ ποδῶν of the manuscripts.

CXCVIII.

Ἀρτοκόπος, ἀδόκιμον. χρὴ δὲ ἀρτοπόπος ἢ ἀρτοποιὸς λέγειν.

Lobeck considers that in this article the words ἀρτοκόπος and ἀρτοποιός have changed places, and that Phrynichus finds fault only with the latter. At all events ἀρτοκόπος rests on excellent authority, being quoted from Attic Inscriptions (C. I. vol. 1. p. 548, n. 1018), and occurring in Plato, Gorg. 518 B; Xen. Hell. 7. 1. 38; Hdt. 1. 51, 9. 82; whereas ἀρτοποιός has at best no better warrant than Xenophon (Cyr. 5. 5. 39), and even that weakened by the fact that in the passages of Plato and Xenophon already

[1] δῶ seems to have been for the most part replaced by δεσμεύω in late Greek. Pollux 8. 71, δεῖν . . . Δείναρχος δὲ καὶ δοῦσαν τὴν δεσμεύουσαν: Moeris, p. 130, δοῦσιν Ἀττικῶς, δεσμεύουσιν Ἑλληνικῶς: Hesych. δοῦσι, δεσμεύουσι.

cited inferior manuscripts present *ἀρτοποιός*. In another place (App. Soph. 22. 23) Phrynichus has the note: *Ἀρτοποπεῖν· οὕτως Ἀττικοὶ διὰ τοῦ π*, and to the same effect are the words in the *Συναγωγὴ λέξεων χρησίμων· Ἀρτοπόπον καὶ Ἀττικοὶ καὶ Ἴωνες τὸν ἀρτοποιόν· ἔστι δὲ τὸ ἀρτοποπεῖν ἐν Μονοτρόπῳ Ψρυνίχου.*

The form *ἀρτοπόπος* comes from *πέπ-τω* (cp. *πόπ-ανον*, a cake), and there can be no question that *ἀρτοκόπος* is also from that root (Lat. coquo), and not from *κόπτω* at all.

CXCIX.

Ἐνθήκη· τὸ μὲν παρενθήκη ὅπως ὑπὸ Ἡροδότου εἴρηται ὕστερον ὀψόμεθα. τὸ δὲ ἐνθήκη, ὡς οἱ πολλοὶ λέγουσιν, ἄτοπον. ἀφορμὴν γὰρ λέγουσιν οἱ ἀρχαῖοι.

In the sense of 'something put in besides,' Herodotus employs *παρενθήκη* several times (1. 186, 6. 19, 7. 5, 171), but the words of Phrynichus in regard to it have been lost. A hint like this occasionally conveyed indicates how careless and perfunctory have been the transcribers of his work.

Harpocration thus explains *ἀφορμή*: *Ἀφορμή· ὅταν τις ἀργύριον δῷ ἐνθήκην, ἀφορμὴ καλεῖται ἰδίως παρὰ τοῖς Ἀττικοῖς*: and the following passages will put in a clear light the sense of the word under discussion: Lycurg. 151. 20, *οἰκῶν ἐν Μεγάροις, οἷς παρ' ὑμῶν ἐξεκομίσατο χρήμασιν ἀφορμῇ χρώμενος, ἐκ τῆς ἠπείρου παρὰ Κλεοπάτρας εἰς Λευκάδα ἐσιτήγει καὶ ἐκεῖθεν εἰς Κόρινθον*: Demosth. 947. 22, *εἰ ἦν ἰδία τις ἀφορμὴ τούτῳ πρὸς τῇ τραπέζῃ*: 958. 3, *πίστις ἀφορμὴ πασῶν ἐστὶ μεγίστη πρὸς χρηματισμόν*: Lysias, Fr. ap. Athen. 13. 611 E, *οὗτος γὰρ ὀφείλων ἀργύριον ἐπὶ τρισὶ δραχμαῖς Σωσινόμῳ τῷ τραπεζίτῃ καὶ Ἀριστογείτονι προσελθὼν πρὸς ἐμὲ ἐδεῖτο μὴ περιδεῖν αὐτὸν διὰ τοὺς τόκους ἐκ τῶν ὄντων ἐκπεσόντα.*

"κατασκευάζομαι δέ," ἔφη, "τέχνην μυρεψικήν, ἀφορμῆς δὲ δέομαι, καὶ οἴσω δέ σοι ἐννέ' ὀβολοὺς τῆς μνᾶς τόκους."

CC.

Ἐξυπνισθῆναι οὐ χρὴ λέγειν, ἀλλ' ἀφυπνισθῆναι.

'Ἐξυπνίσαι uno ore damnant Herodianus Philet. p. 448, Moeris, p. 61, Thomas, 134.' Lobeck. It certainly is not employed by any pre-Macedonian writer, whereas ἀφυπνίζω is met with in the following passages:—

Aristides (Orat. 49. vol. 2. p. 521, Dind.) cites it from Cratinus, καί τις αὐτῶν ἐν ἀρχῇ τοῦ δράματος μεγαλαυχούμενος ὡς προφήτης προαγορεύει τοιάδε·

> ἀφυπνίζεσθαι χρὴ πάντα θεατήν,
> ἀπὸ μὲν βλεφάρων αὐθημερινῶν ποιητῶν λῆρον ἀφέντα.

ὥσπερ ἐν ἐκείνῃ τῇ ἡμέρᾳ μέλλων ἅπαντας σοφούς τε καὶ σπουδαίους ποιήσειν· διδάξας δὲ τοὺς Χείρωνας κτε. In the Συναγωγὴ λέξεων χρησίμων, p. 473. 8, the word is quoted from Pherecrates: Ἀφυπνισθῆναι· τὸ ἐξ ὕπνου ἐγερθῆναι. Φερεκράτης·

> ἵν' ἀφυπνισθῆτ' οὖν ἀκροᾶσθ', ἤδη γὰρ καὶ λέξομεν,

and it is found in the Rhesus (of Euripides) l. 25—

> ὄτρυνον ἔγχος ἀείρειν, ἀφύπνισον.

CCI.

Βαλαντοκλέπτης μὴ λέγε, ἀλλὰ βαλαντιοκλέπτης.

Thomas has the same sensible dictum, p. 140, βαλαντιοκλέπτης, οὐ βαλαντοκλέπτης, καὶ βαλαντιοτόμος, οὐ βαλαντοτόμος. The editions, which on this passage all exhibit βαλανοκλέπτης μὴ λέγε ἀλλὰ βαλανειοκλέπτης, were justly ridiculed by Scaliger: 'Βαλαντιοκλέπτης legendum esse in Ed. Paris. anno praeterito notabamus, et βαλαντοκλέπτης. Nam quam ridiculum esset βαλανειοκλέπτης? id enim non esset qui in balneis furatur sed qui balneas furaretur.'

CCII.

Βασίλισσα· οὐδεὶς τῶν ἀρχαίων εἶπεν, ἀλλὰ βασίλεια ἢ βασιλίς.

CCIII.

Βασίλισσαν Ἀλκαῖόν φασι τὸν κωμῳδοποιὸν καὶ Ἀριστοτέλην ἐν τοῖς Ὁμήρου ἀπορήμασιν εἰρηκέναι· σὺ δὲ βασιλικὸς ἐπιστολεὺς ἀποφανθεὶς ἀνάλογον τῇ σαυτοῦ παρασκευῇ γεννικώτατον ἡμῖν ἐκόμισας μάρτυρα τὸν συγγράψαντα τὸν κατὰ Νεαίρας· ὃς διά τε τὰ ἄλλα ὑπωπτεύθη μὴ εἶναι Δημοσθένους καὶ διὰ τὰ τοιαῦτα τῶν ἀδοκίμων ὀνομάτων. τοῖς πλείοσιν οὖν πειθόμενοι βασίλειαν ἢ βασιλίδα λέγωμεν. οὕτω γὰρ διακρίνειν δόξαιμεν ἂν τό τε καλὸν καὶ τὸ αἰσχρόν.

The latter of these articles is in the manuscripts the second of the second part of the Ecloga. From this it is natural to infer that the Imperial Secretary, to whom the book is dedicated, was not so strict an Atticist as its author. It would almost seem as if Cornelianus had found fault with the stringency of the earlier dictum. Phrynichus humorously turns upon his friend: 'In your authoritative position, and from your great learning, you ought to know better than you do. Though I omitted to mention them, I knew of better examples than yours, which does you little credit. Even Aristotle, whom I care not to follow, is better than the author of the speech you cite, and my instance from Alcaeus is more authoritative still. Moreover, you know how little I allow one exception or two to affect my rules.' The article next but two is probably a similar addendum.

CCIV.

Σικχαίνομαι, τῷ ὄντι ναυτίας ἄξιον τοὔνομα. ἀλλ' ἐρεῖς βδελύττομαι ὡς Ἀθηναῖος.

'Verbi *σικχαίνομαι* nulla antiquior memoria quam in Callimachi epigrammate; huic accedunt Arrianus et M. Antoninus V. 9. 87. Neque plus auctoritatis habet primitivum *σικχός*, Plut. 2. 87 B, Athen. 962 A; *σικχασία*, Moschio de Aff. Mul. 28; *σικχότης*, Eust. 972. 35.' Lobeck.

CCV.

Γελάσιμον μὴ λέγε, ἀλλὰ γελοῖον.

CCVI.

Γελάσιμον· Στράττιν μέν φασι τὸν κωμῳδοποιὸν εἰρηκέναι τοὔνομα, ἀλλ' ἡμεῖς οὐ τοῖς ἅπαξ εἰρημένοις προσέχομεν τὸν νοῦν, ἀλλὰ τοῖς πολλάκις κεχρημένοις· κέχρηται δὲ τὸ γελοῖον.

The principle of Phrynichus' work is here lucidly stated, and there can be no question about the genuineness of the second article, although it is not found in the Laurentian manuscripts. No hand but his could have presented so clear a statement of his position as an Atticist.

CCVII.

Ἀλεκτορὶς εὑρίσκεται ἐν τραγῳδίᾳ που καὶ κωμῳδίᾳ, λέγε δὲ ἀλεκτρυὼν καὶ ἐπὶ θήλεος καὶ ἐπὶ ἄρρενος ὡς οἱ παλαιοί.

No Comic poet could have used *ἀλέκτωρ* or *ἀλεκτορίς* except outside the iambics, as Cratinus, ap. Ath. 9. 374 D—

ὥσπερ ὁ Περσικὸς ὥραν πᾶσαν καναχῶν ὀλόφωνος ἀλέκτωρ,

Plato (Eust. ad Odyss. p. 1479. 47)—

σὲ δὲ κοκκύζων ὄρθρι' ἀλέκτωρ προκαλεῖται,

or of *malice prepense*, as Aristophanes in the *Clouds*, and parodying the Tragic poet Phrynichus in Vesp. 1490—

πτήσσει Φρύνιχος ὥς τις ἀλέκτωρ.

The words of Phrynichus have been preserved by Plutarch (Amat. 762 F)—

ἔπτηξ' ἀλέκτωρ δοῦλον ὡς κλίνας πτέρον,

and as an old term ἀλέκτωρ was naturally common in Tragedy, Aesch. Ag. 1671, Eum. 861. Athenaeus cites ἁμερόφων' ἀλέκτωρ from Simonides, and from Epicharmus—

ὤεα χανὸς κἀλεκτορίδων πετεηνῶν.

Both old words, ἀλέκτωρ and ἀλεκτορίς, were in Attic superseded by ἀλεκτρυών, one form for both genders, but reappeared in the Common dialect. The orator Demades, as ὀνοματοθήρας, used ἀλέκτωρ in a pompous metaphor, speaking of a trumpeter (Ath. 3. 99 D) as κοινὸς 'Αθηναίων ἀλέκτωρ.

CCVIII.

Γλωσσίδας αὐλῶν ἢ ὑποδημάτων μὴ λέγε, ἀλλ' ὡς οἱ δόκιμοι γλώττας αὐλῶν, γλώττας ὑποδημάτων.

There is the same caution in App. Soph. p. 32, γλῶτται αὐλῶν καὶ γλῶτται ὑποδημάτων ἃ γλωττίδας λέγουσιν οἱ ἀμαθεῖς.

Athenaeus (15. 677 A) cites a passage of Plato, in which there is a play upon the different senses of γλῶττα—

καίτοι φορεῖτε γλῶτταν ἐν ὑποδήμασιν
στεφανοῦσθ' ὑπογλωττίσιν ὅταν πίνητέ που,
κἂν καλλιερῆτε, γλῶτταν ἀγαθὴν πέμπετε·

and Aeschinus makes a point by the same means (86. 27), ὅταν δ' ἐξ ὀνομάτων συγκείμενος ἄνθρωπος, καὶ τούτων πικρῶν καὶ περιέργων, ἔπειτα ἐπὶ τὴν ἁπλότητα καὶ τὰ ἔργα καταφεύγῃ τίς ἂν ἀνάσχοιτο; οὗ τὴν γλῶτταν, ὥσπερ τῶν αὐλῶν, ἐάν τις ἀφέλῃ, τὸ λοιπὸν οὐδέν ἐστιν.

CCIX.

Γρύτη· καὶ τοῦτο τῶν παραπεποιημένων. τὸ γὰρ τοιοῦτον ἅπαν γρυμέαν συμβέβηκε καλεῖσθαι.

The words are explained in App. Soph. 33. 32, Γρυμεία, ἣν οἱ πολλοὶ γρύτην. Δίφιλος ἄνευ τοῦ ι, γρυμέαν· ἔστι δὲ παρ' Ἀθηναίοις πήρα τις γρυμέα καλουμένη, ἐν ᾗ παντοῖα σκεύη ἐστί. Σαπφὼ δὲ γρύτην καλεῖ τὴν μύρων καὶ γυναικείων τινῶν θήκην. The Attic form is also found in a passage of Sotades, quoted by Athenaeus (7. 293 A)—

Καρῖδας ἔλαβον πρῶτον, ἀπεταγήνισα
ταύτας ἁπάσας· γαλεὸς εἴληπται μέγας,
ὤπτησα τὰ μέσα, τὴν δὲ λοιπὴν γρυμέαν
ἕψω ποιήσας τρίμμα συκαμίνινον.

Its existence in Sappho indicates the source from which γρύτη entered the Common dialect. In Geopon. 20. 1 it is used as γρυμέα is in Sotades, τὴν λεπτὴν γρύτην θαλασσίαν.

CCX.

Διώρυγος, διώρυγι, διώρυγα, οὔ. οἱ γὰρ ἀρχαῖοι ταῦτα διὰ τοῦ χ λέγουσι, διώρυχος, διώρυχι, διώρυχα.

'Διῶρυξ, διώρυχος per χ semper apud Herodotum (uno loco excepto) et Platonem scribi monuit Valckenarius in Notis Posth. ad Thom. p. 157, itemque scribitur ap. Thucyd. I. 109, II. 109, Xenoph. An. 1. 7. 11, Theophr. H. Pl. 4. 8, Plut. Vit. Ages. 39, Caes. 49, Arrian. Alex. 3. 6, 7. 18, Dion. Cass. 42, 41, Heliod. 9. 5, etc. Altera forma διώρυγες (Hippocr. de Aer. et Loc. 5. 83) in Atticorum scriptis non deprehenditur; sed recentiores, Polybium, Diodorum, Strabonem, Pausaniam, partim ea sola, partim utraque communiter uti Hemsterhusius ad Thom. et Tzchuckius ad Pomp. Mel. vol. 2. 3. 292 docuerunt. Sic etiam κατῶρυξ ab Aeschylo et Sophocle per χ flectitur.' Lobeck.

CCXI.

Δίκρανον· τοῦτο οἱ ἀρχαῖοι δίκρουν καλοῦσιν.

In Attic δίκρουν ξύλον means *a forked stick, a fork*, as in Timocles, ap. Athen. 6. 243 B—

τὸν παραμασήτην λαμβάνει δίκρουν ξύλον·

and Aristophanes substituted κεκράγμασιν in Pax 637, παρὰ προσδοκίαν, for ξύλοις—

τήνδε μὲν δικροῖς ἐώθουν τὴν θεὸν κεκράγμασιν.

Plato has δίκρους=*with two branches*, of the throat, Tim. 78 B.

In Lucian the later form occurs in Timon. 12. 120, καὶ μονονουχὶ δικράνοις ἐξεώθει με τῆς οἰκίας καθάπερ οἱ τὸ πῦρ ἐκ τῶν χειρῶν ἀπορριπτοῦντες.

CCXII.

Διόσκουροι, ὀρθότερον Διόσκοροι. γελάσει οὖν τοὺς σὺν τῷ υ λέγοντας.

Lobeck's note on this article is in his best style: 'Nimirum natura ita comparatum est ut dualis numeri longe major sit usus, apud veteres praesertim, quam plurativi nominis. Διοσκόρω Eur. Or. 465, Arist. Pax 285, Eccl. 1069, Amphis ap. Athen. 14. 642 A . . . Atque haec ipsa causa fuit cur atticismus in hac formula in qua fixus et fundatus erat, diutissime retineretur; certe Themistius inter delicias Atticionum numerat τὸ δήπουθεν καὶ τὸ κἄπειτα καὶ τὼ Διοσκόρω, Or. 21. 253 D. Genetivus est in illo Menandri versu a Grammaticis decantato, ὁ θάτερος μὲν τοῖν δυοῖν Διοσκόροιν. Τῶν Διοσκόρων, Plato, Legg. 796 B, sed Διοσκούρω, Plat. Euthyd. 293 A, Διοσκούρων, Thucyd. 3. 75, unico codice germanam scripturam servante . . . In recentiorum scriptis exempla hujus generis ita spissantur ut Attica forma ne tum quidem satis tuta reponatur, ubi ex uno aut altero chirographo emerserit. Ac perrarum est ut in ea libri editi et scripti conspirent. Verum ista scripturae discrepantia ab ipsis vocabuli stirpibus progenerata est: κόρη in pedestri sermone tritissimum hac una forma gaudet; κόρος et κοῦρος tantum in certa formula usurpatur; κούρῳ καὶ κόρῃ, Plato, Legg. 6. 785 A, cui statim succedit rectius κόρῳ· κόρου καὶ κόρης, 7. 793 D, κόρους καὶ κόρας, p. 796 B . . . In Tragicorum diverbiis Attica forma tantam habet constantiam ut Valckenarius non dubitaverit in Eur. Frag. Meleagri, 6, pro κοῦροι reponere κόροι. Mansit veteris dialecti nota in vocc. Κουρεῶτις, κουρεῖον, κουροτρόφος.' Lobeck. Like that of Comedy, the evidence of Tragedy is in favour of the short penult—

δισσοὶ δέ σε
Διόσκοροι καλοῦμεν.
Eur. Hel. 1643.

καλοῦσι μητρὸς σύγγονοι Διόσκοροι.
Id. El. 1239.

In I. A. 769, Διοσκούρων Ἑλέναν corresponds to ῥίπτειν ξανθοὺς πλοκάμους: but in a choric passage the older form is quite in keeping.

CCXIII.

Ὑστερίζειν τῷ καιρῷ οὐ λέγεται, ἀλλ' ὑστερίζειν τοῦ καιροῦ. Φαβωρῖνος δὲ οὐχ ὑγιῶς κατὰ δοτικὴν συντάττει.

Dem. 260. 13, ὑστερίζουσαν τὴν πόλιν τῶν καιρῶν: id. 51. 12, ὑστερίζειν τῶν ἔργων: 730. 19, τοῖς τοῦ πολέμου καιροῖς *ἀκολουθεῖν καὶ μηδένος ὑστερίζειν*: Isocr. 30 D, *ὑστερίζουσι τῶν πραγμάτων*: 204 A, *ὑστερίζω τῆς ἀκμῆς τῆς ἐμαυτοῦ*.

The meaning is different with the dative, as with *ὑστερεῖν* in Plato, Rep. 539 E, *ἵνα μηδ' ἐμπειρίᾳ ὑστερῶσι τῶν ἄλλων*.

CCXIV.

Παραβόλιον· ἀδόκιμον τοῦτο. τῷ μὲν οὖν ὀνόματι οὐ κέχρηνται οἱ παλαιοί, τῷ δὲ ῥήματι. φασὶ γὰρ οὕτω, παραβάλλομαι τῇ ἐμαυτοῦ κεφαλῇ. ἐχρῆν οὖν κἀπὶ τούτων λέγειν, παραβάλλομαι ἀργυρίῳ.

Παραβάλλομαι was occasionally used for *παρατίθεμαι* in the sense of *make a deposit:* Hdt. 7. 10, *ἡμέων ἀμφοτέρων παραβαλλομένων τὰ τέκνα*: Thuc. 5. 113, *Λακεδαιμονίοις πλεῖστον δὴ παραβεβλημένοι*. The substantive, however, is unknown in the Classical age, *παραθήκη* or *παρακαταθήκη* being used instead, the former by Ionic, the latter by Attic writers.

CCXV.

Στατός· ὁ τῶν αὐλητῶν χιτὼν οὐ λέγεται, ὡς Φαβωρῖνος, ἀλλ' ὀρθοστάδιος χιτών.

Pollux, 7. 48, explains the *χιτὼν ὀρθοστάδιος* as *ὁ οὐ ζωννύμενος*, i. e. falling straight down without being drawn in at the waist.

CCXVI.

Παιδίσκη· τοῦτο ἐπὶ τῆς θεραπαίνης οἱ νῦν τιθέασιν, οἱ δ' ἀρχαῖοι ἐπὶ τῆς νεάνιδος.

Moeris is more precise, p. 319, Παιδίσκην, *καὶ τὴν ἐλευθέραν καὶ τὴν δούλην*, Ἀττικῶς· *τὴν δούλην μόνον*, Ἑλληνικῶς. Neither Grammarian asserts more than this, that in an

Attic writer the term refers to age, not to condition, and that no such usage as N. T. Ep. ad Galat. 4. 31, *οὐκ ἐσμὲν παιδίσκης τέκνα, ἀλλὰ τῆς ἐλευθέρας*, is possible in Attic Greek. Accordingly, the dictum is not refuted by such passages as Lysias, 92. 41, 136. 8 ; Isaeus, 58. 13, in which the English word *girl* naturally translates the Greek term. The women there referred to were in a humble or debased position, but labour is not incompatible with tender years and immorality, but too frequently accompanies them.

CCXVII.

Παῖξαι· Δωριεῖς διὰ τοῦ ξ, ὁ δὲ Ἀττικὸς παῖσαι. καὶ παίσατε καὶ συμπαίστης διὰ τοῦ σ ἐρεῖς.

Moeris, Thomas Magister, Timaeus, Hesychius, Suïdas, and Eustathius, all insist upon the forms in sigma. The words of the latter are very precise (ad Odyss. p. 1594), *τὸ δὲ παίσατε ἀντὶ τοῦ παίξατε ἀπὸ τοῦ παίζω, παίσω, ὅθεν καὶ ἡ συμπαίστρια καὶ ὁ συμπαίστωρ Ἀττικῶς*. The line of the Odyssey to which this note is attached is 8. 251—

> *παίσατε, ὥς χ' ὁ ξεῖνος ἐνίσπῃ οἷσι φίλοισι,*

and there can be no doubt that in id. 23. 134, *φιλοπαίσμων* should be substituted for *φιλοπαίγμων*—

> *αὐτὰρ θεῖος ἀοιδὸς ἔχων φόρμιγγα λίγειαν*
> *ἡμῖν ἡγείσθω φιλοπαίγμονος ὀρχηθμοῖο.*

Certainly in Attic such a form was impossible, and yet it is occasionally exhibited by manuscripts. Till Bekker restored the form in *σ* from the best codices in Plato, Cratyl. 406 C, *φιλοπαίσμονες γὰρ καὶ οἱ θεοί*, the un-Attic form disfigured the text, and in Plat. Rep. 452 F, *εἴτε τις φιλοπαίσμων εἴτε σπουδαστικός*, the genuine reading has still less numerical support, but is attested by Paris A. In Ar.

Ran. 335 is read *φιλοπαίγμονα* and in 411 *συμπαιστρίας*, but neither in the senarii, and as yet too little is known of the literary use of the dialects in Greece to warrant the change of *φιλοπαίγμων* into *φιλοπαίσμων*.

That Xenophon should write *συμπαίκτωρ* in Cyr. 1. 3. 14, *καὶ παῖδας δέ σοι συμπαίκτορας παρέξω*, is as natural as that he should use the form in *-τωρ* for the Attic form in *-της*, (see supra p. 59), and the reading *συμπέστορας* should have no weight. The future *παιξοῦμαι*, in his Conv. 9. 2, stands on a different footing still, and has already been considered (see p. 91). A glance at Veitch will show that the Attic rule is now generally recognized in Attic texts; but in Lysias, as cited by Pollux, in 7. 200, *ψηφοπαικτοῦσι* must give way to *ψηφοπαιστοῦσι· Εἰ δὲ Λυσίου ὁ κατ' Αὐτοκλέους λόγος ἐν ᾧ γέγραπται* ψηφοπαιστοῦσι τὸ δίκαιον κτε., *play fast and loose with right.*

CCXVIII.

Παλαιστρικός· Ἄλεξιν φασὶν εἰρηκέναι, ὁ δὲ ἀρχαῖος παλαιστικὸν λέγει.

The words were in Attic distinct—*παλαιστικός*, 'expert in wrestling,' 'a wrestler;' *παλαιστρικός*, 'connected with the *παλαίστρα*'—but it is not surprising that the latter should have filled the part of both in an age when nice distinctions, either in meaning or pronunciation, were disregarded. It must also be remembered that *παλαιστρικός* was a natural formation from *παλαιστήρ*, which was probably used in late Greek (see p. 59). In some cases it is quite impossible to decide upon the correct mode of spelling an adjective in *-κός* belonging to this class. Thus the manuscripts support *ληστικώτερον παρεσκευασμένους* in Thuc. 6. 104, but *ἐκ ληστρικῆς Μεσσηνίων τριακοντόρου* in id. 4. 9. Both were probably good forms at this stage of Attic, the one from *ληστής*, the other from *ληστήρ*.

CCXIX.

Ἐπαοιδὴ ἰδιώτης λέγων ἁμαρτάνει. λέγε οὖν ὀρθῶς ἐπῳδή, ἐπεὶ τὸ διαιρούμενον ποιητικόν.

'Phrynichus App. Soph. p. 38, τῷ ἐπαοιδῇ καὶ ἀοιδῇ οὐ χρηστέον, κἂν Ὅμηρος εἶπεν. Ionica forma in omni genere et parte sermonis poetici locum habet, neque iambum scenicum, si paullo altius exsurgit, dedecet. Ion ap. Athen. παλαιθέτων ὕμνων ἀοιδοί, et Phrynichus eodem loco ψαλμοῖσιν ἀντίσπαστ' ἀείδοντες μέλη. Sed ultra non egreditur.' Lobeck. See supra, p. 5.

CCXX.

Διδοῦσιν· ἐν τῷ περὶ Εὐχῆς Φαβωρῖνος οὕτω λέγει, δέον διδόασι, τὸ γὰρ διδοῦσιν ἄλλο τι σημαίνει.

The words τὸ δεῖν which follow σημαίνει in the manuscripts did not come from the hand of Phrynichus, but are the senseless addition of some transcriber who was not acquainted with the dative plural of the participle, and yet recalled some rule about the anomalous contraction of the verb δῶ, *I bind*.

It is only by accident that διδοῦσι, the Ionic form of the third person plural διδόασι, presents the appearance of that of a regularly contracted verb, and διδοῦσι is no more connected with διδῶ than διδοίην, διδοῖτον, or διδῶμεν. This is proved by the existence of τιθεῖσι, the Ionic form of τιθέασι. There are in fact only four forms of δίδωμι which come from the imaginary διδῶ, just as there are only four forms of τίθημι which come from the imaginary τιθῶ. For δίδωμι there are the three singular persons of the imperfect and the second person singular of the imperative, while for τίθημι they are the second and third persons singular of the imperfect and the second person singular of both present indicative and imperative. Besides ἐδίδουν, ἐδίδους, ἐδίδου, and δίδου, the regular διδῶ is inactive, and similarly τιθῶ exists only in τιθεῖς, ἐτίθεις, ἐτίθει, and τίθει. This is the Attic rule. There is no τιθεῖν, τιθεῖτον, ἐτίθουν, ἐτιθοῦμεν, τιθοίην, τιθῶν, no διδοῖς, ἐδιδοῦτον, διδούτω, διδῶν, ἔδωσα, δεδίδωκα, or ἐδιδώθην. The middle imperative τίθου is for τίθεσο, and that the optative forms τιθοίμην, τιθοῖτο, etc., if Attic at all, are not from τιθεῖσθαι is proved by the existence of similar forms in the aorist θοίμην, θοῖτο, θοῖο, etc. Διδῷς and διδῷ, δῷς and δῷ similarly demonstrate that it is only by accident that the subjunctive τιθῶ, τιθῇς, τιθῇ may be ascribed to τιθεῖν. Many scholars refuse to acknowledge even the Atticicity of τιθεῖς as second person singular of the present indicative, and consequently disfranchise ἱεῖς as well, since ἵημι corresponds throughout with τίθημι, except that εἶμαι has a passive no less than a middle signification, whereas τέθειμαι has none but a middle sense.

All scholars recognize the fact that ἐτίθεις, ἐτίθει, ἵεις, ἵει were used preferentially to ἐτίθης, ἐτίθη, ἵης, ἵη, and that τίθει and ἵει were the only forms by which the meaning of the second person imperative present could be conveyed; but the authority of Porson (ad Eur. Or. 141) has induced many scholars to prefer ἵης and τίθης to ἱεῖς and τιθεῖς. Brunck, on Arist. Lys. 895 and Soph. Phil. 992, took the opposite view to that of Porson, and in this case the verdict of the great English critic must be reversed. The authority of the manuscripts is wholly on the side of Brunck. Thus in Ar. Lys. 895 the Ravenna exhibits διατιθεῖς, and on Eq. 717 ἐντιθεῖς. Further proof is supplied by the mistakes of copyists. They often substitute the participle for the indicative, as in Euripides—

> ἕπου νυν· ἴχνος δ' ἐκφύλασσ' ὅπου τιθεῖς,
>
> Ion 741.

ἔπειτα τῷ θεῷ προστιθεῖς τὴν αἰτίαν,

Id. 1525.

where good manuscripts read τιθείς and προστιθείς, exactly as in Ar. Lys. 895, διατιθεῖσ' is a variant from διατιθεῖς. In Soph. O. R. 628—

εἰ δὲ ξυνιεὶς μηδέν;

all the best manuscripts read ξυνίεις, or, in other words, substitute the imperfect for the present in accordance with the extraordinary remark of Eustathius, 1500. 52, that ἵεις, μεθίεις were used of present time, κατὰ ἐναλλαγὴν χρόνου. In Soph. El. 596 for the true ἱεῖς the manuscripts present ἵῃς or ἵεις, as in id. 1347 they divide between ξυνίεις and ξυνίῃς. The plain inference to be drawn from the above facts is that the contracted second person singular, being unknown to late Greeks, was altered when possible into the participle, otherwise was converted into the imperfect or late ἵῃς.

CCXXI.

Προαλῶς· τοῦτο δοκεῖ μοι γυναικῶν εἶναι τοὔνομα. ἀνιῶμαι δὲ ὅτι ἀνὴρ λόγου ἄξιος κέχρηται αὐτῷ Φαβωρῖνος. τοῦτο μὲν οὖν ἀποδιοπομπώμεθα, ἀντ' αὐτοῦ δὲ λέγωμεν προπετῶς.

The article is absent from the best Laurentian Manuscript, and from the editions of Callierges and Vascosan.

Neither adverb nor adjective is found in Attic writers. They were, however, probably both old words, as Homer employed the adjective in Il. 21. 262—

τὸ δέ (sc. ὕδωρ) τ' ὦκα κατειβόμενον κελαρύζει
χώρῳ ἔνι προαλεῖ, φθάνει δέ τε καὶ τὸν ἄγοντα.

A fact of this kind throws considerable light upon the constitution of the Common dialect.

CCXXII.

Πηχῶν, πήχως· δεινῶς ἑκάτερον ἀνάττικον, δέον πηχέων καὶ πήχεος.

Verse does not afford any help on this point, as *πηχέων*, *πήχεος* might, if necessary, be pronounced as dissyllables by synizesis—

σκύφος τε κισσοῦ παρέθετ' εἰς εὖρος τριῶν
πηχέων, βάθος δὲ τεσσάρων ἐφαίνετο,

Eur. Cycl. 390.

but there can be no question about the correctness of Phrynichus' rule.

CCXXIII.

Σύμπτωμα πολλάκις εὗρον κείμενον παρὰ Φαβωρίνῳ ἐν τῷ περὶ Ἰδεῶν λόγῳ. πόθεν δὲ λαβὼν ἔθηκεν οὐκ οἶδα. χρὴ οὖν συντυχίαν λέγειν ἢ λύσαντας οὕτω, συνέπεσεν αὐτῷ τόδε γενέσθαι.

Δημοσθένης μέντοι ἐν τῷ κατὰ Διονυσοδώρου ἅπαξ εἴρηκε τοὔνομα.

The last sentence probably belongs to a second edition of the Ecloga, but compare art. 203 supra. Perhaps the exception was, in this case correctly, discovered by Cornelianus himself. The place of Demosthenes is 1295. 20, *εἰ γὰρ ὡς ἀληθῶς ἀκούσιον τὸ συμβὰν ἐγένετο καὶ ἡ ναῦς ἐρράγη, τὸ μετὰ τοῦτ', ἐπειδὴ ἐπεσκεύασαν τὴν ναῦν οὐκ ἂν εἰς ἕτερα δήπου ἐμπόρια ἐμίσθουν αὐτὴν ἀλλ' ὡς ὑμᾶς ἀπέστελλον ἐπανορθούμενοι τὸ ἀκούσιον σύμπτωμα.* The term is also found in Thucydides, 4. 36, *καὶ οἱ Λακεδαιμόνιοι βαλλόμενοί τε ἀμφοτέρωθεν ἤδη καὶ γιγνόμενοι ἐν τῷ αὐτῷ συμπτώματι, ὡς μικρὸν μεγάλῳ εἰκάσαι, τῷ ἐν Θερμοπύλαις κτε.* Plato uses *περίπτωμα* in Prot. 345 B, *ὑπὸ νόσου ἢ ὑπὸ ἄλλου* τινὸς περιπτώματος, and μετάπτωσις in Legg. 10. 895 B, μηδεμίας γε ἐν αὐτοῖς οὔσης ἔμπροσθεν μεταπτώσεως: these words are eschewed by Attic writers. In late Greek they are used without restraint, and παράπτωμα, ἀπόπτωμα, παράπτωσις, περίπτωσις, ἀπόπτωσις, ἔκπτωμα, ἔκπτωσις, ἔμπτωσις, ἐπίπτωσις, κατάπτωμα, κατάπτωσις, ὑπόπτωσις, ἀνάπτωσις are encountered in different authors.

CCXXIV.

Ἔκθεμα βάρβαρον· σὺ δὲ λέγε πρόγραμμα.

The verb ἐκτιθέναι, in the sense of προγράφειν, *publish*, is also late, but the low estate of the substantive may be inferred from its make. Moeris is only giving one example out of many when he says, p. 28, Ἀνάθημα Ἀττικῶς, ἀνάθεμα Ἑλληνικῶς. Similarly πῶμα became πόμα, εὕρημα εὕρεμα, ἄρωμα ἄρομα, ἔνδῦμα ἔνδυμα, κλῖμα κλἵμα, while the formation of a word like δόμα (= δῶρον) became possible. It is to the same tendency that the insertion of the sigma in χρῖμα is to be ascribed. The Attic form was χρῖμα; in late Greek it became χρίσμα.

CCXXV.

Κατορθώματα· ἁμαρτάνουσι κἀνταῦθα οἱ ῥήτορες, οὐκ εἰδότες ὅτι τὸ μὲν ῥῆμα δόκιμον, τὸ κατορθῶσαι, τὸ δ' ἀπὸ τούτου ὄνομα ἀδόκιμον, τὸ κατόρθωμα· λέγειν οὖν χρὴ ἀνδραγαθήματα.

It is the philosophical sense of the late κατόρθωμα which Phrynichus is here especially reprehending, as the substituted term ἀνδραγάθημα shows; Cicero, de Fin. 3. 7, 'Quae autem nos aut recta aut recte facta dicamus, si placet, illi autem appellant κατορθώματα omnes numeros virtutis continent, id 4, 'illud enim rectum quod κατόρθωμα dicebas contingit sapienti soli;' id. de Off. 1. 3, 'Perfectum autem officium *rectum*, opinor, vocemus, quod Graeci κατόρθωμα; hoc autem *commune*, quod ii καθῆκον vocant.' As a matter of fact ἀνδραγάθημα is as late as κατόρθωμα. At all events neither ἀνδραγαθεῖν nor its substantive appears in Attic books. Thucydides has ἀνδραγαθίζομαι in rather a contemptuous sense in 2. 63; 3. 40, but ἀνδραγαθία had a good sense and was used by good writers.

In the other meaning of *a success*, κατόρθωμα is equally un-Attic. Demosthenes employs the neuter participle of the intransitive active, 23. 28, νῦν μὲν ἐπισκοτεῖ τούτοις τὸ κατορθοῦν· αἱ γὰρ εὐπραξίαι δειναὶ συγκρύψαι τὰ τοιαῦτα ὀνείδη, but τὸ ὀρθούμενον was more often used, as ὀρθούμενος was equivalent to *successful*, Thuc. 4. 18, καὶ ἐλάχιστ' ἂν οἱ τοιοῦτοι πταίοντες διὰ τὸ μὴ τῷ ὀρθουμένῳ αὐτοῦ πιστεύοντες ἐπαίρεσθαι: Antiphon, 130. 7, ὁρῶ γὰρ τοὺς πάνυ ἐμπείρους μᾶλλον ὀρθουμένους:

τῶν δ' ὀρθουμένων
σώζει τὰ πολλὰ σώμαθ' ἡ πειθαρχία.
Soph. Ant. 675.

On the other hand, κατόρθωσις has the authority of Aeschines in 51. 5, ἀπαγγείλας τοίνυν πρῶτος τὴν τῆς πόλεως νίκην ὑμῖν καὶ τὴν τῶν παιδῶν ὑμετέρων κατόρθωσιν, and of Demades in 179. 28, προσελθὼν δὲ τοῖς κοινοῖς οὐκ εἰς δίκας καὶ τὴν ἀπὸ τῆς λογοραφίας ἐργασίαν ἔθηκα τὸν πόνον, ἀλλ' εἰς τὴν ἀπὸ τοῦ βήματος παρρησίαν, ἣ τοῖς μὲν λέγουσιν ἐπισφαλῆ παρέχεται τὸν βίον, τοῖς δ' εὐλαβουμένοις μεγίστην δίδωσιν ἀφορμὴν πρὸς κατόρθωσιν. Both ἐπανόρθωσις and ἐπανόρθωμα were excellent Attic, the former occurring in Plato, Prot. 340 A, D, Theaet. 183 A; Dem. 774. 20, and the latter in Dem. 707. 7, while διόρθωσις, with the meaning *right arrangement*, has the sanction of Plato, Legg. 1. 642 A.

CCXXVI.

Ὕπαιθρον μὴ λέγε, τὸ δὲ ὑπαίθριον τετρασυλλάβως.

To this rule there is no exception in Attic Greek except the use of *ὕπαιθρος* in the phrase *ἐν ὑπαίθρῳ, sub dio,* is to be so regarded, Antiphon. 130. 29; Xen. Mem. 2. 1, 6. In that phrase *ὑπαίθριος* is unknown.

CCXXVII.

Τὸ μὲν κοιτὼν ἀδόκιμον, τὸ δὲ προκοιτὼν οὐ δόκιμον. ἡμῖν δὲ καλὸν χρῆσθαι τῷ Ἀττικῷ ὀνόματι· προδωμάτιον γὰρ λέγουσιν ἐπεὶ καὶ δωμάτιον τὸν κοιτῶνα.

According to Pollux 1. 79, Aristophanes used the defaulting term, *κοιτών· εἰ γὰρ καὶ Μένανδρος αὐτὸ βαρβαρικὸν οἴεται, ἀλλ' Ἀριστοφάνης τὰ τοιαῦτα πιστότερος αὐτοῦ ἐν Αἰολοσίκωνι*

κοιτὼν ἁπάσαις εἷς, πύελος δὲ μί' ἀρκέσει,

but little can be proved by a single line in a case of this kind, especially in a play like the Aeolosicon, which must have teemed with para-tragedy. On the other hand, *δωμάτιον* has the sanction of Aristophanes in Lys. 160, Eccl. 8; Lysias in 93. 18; 94. 7; Plato in Rep. 390 C.

CCXXVIII.

Σμῆγμα καὶ σμῆξαι καὶ τὰ τοιαῦτα ἀναττικά· τὸ γὰρ ἀττικὸν σμῆμα καὶ σμῆσαι, τὸ μὲν ἄνευ τοῦ γ, τὸ δὲ διὰ τοῦ σ.

The tendency of transcribers to introduce the late *σμήχω* is strikingly illustrated by a line of Antiphanes cited by

Clemens Alex. (Paed. 3. 2), in which *σμήχεται* actually stands in open violation of the metre—

σμῆται, κτενίζετ', ἐκβέβηκε, τρίβεται.

Accordingly, the genuine *διασμηθείς* should be substituted for the debased *διασμηχθείς* in Ar. Nub. 1237—

ἁλσὶν διασμηθεὶς ὄναιτ' ἂν οὑτοσί.

Even a transcriber was forced to leave *σμωμένην* alone in another place of the Comic poet—

ἀλλ' ἀρτίως κατέλιπον αὐτὴν σμωμένην
ἐν τῇ πυέλῳ·

and *σμήσας* seems to have escaped in Alexis ap. Ath. 7. 324 B—

σμήσας τε λεπτοῖς ἁλσί, δειπνούντων ἅμα,

but *σμῆμα* was less fortunate in Antiphanes ap. Ath. 9. 409 C—

ἐν ὅσῳ δ' ἀκροῶμαί σου, κέλευσόν μοί τινα
φέρειν ἀπονίψασθαι. B. *δότω τις δεῦρ' ὕδωρ*
καὶ σμῆμα.

Some manuscripts however, even here preserved *σμῆμα*, which is also vouched for by Eustath. 1401. 6. In two passages Pollux mentions *γῆ σμητρίς*, 7. 40, *τὴν* (lege *γῆν*) *δὲ σμητρίδα Κηφισόδωρος ἐν Τροφωνίῳ εἴρηκεν*: 10. 35, *τὰ δὲ περὶ τὴν θεραπείαν τῶν ἐσθήτων σκεύη, πλυνοὶ καὶ πλυντήρια καὶ γῆ σμητρὶς κατὰ Νικόχαριν.* The reading *σμικρίδα* in the one case and *σμητίς* in the other indicate the original hand.

Σμήχω was, however, not merely an invention of the Common dialect, like *ἀροτριῶ* and others, but came from an ancient source—

ἐκ κεφαλῆς δ' ἔσμηχεν ἁλὸς χνόον ἀτρυγέτοιο,
Hom. Od. 6. 226.

θωρήκων τε νεοσμήκτων σακέων τε φαεινῶν,
Il. 13. 342.

and in Tragedy, or in a writer like Xenophon, would doubtless have been as little amiss as in Homer or Hippocrates.

Accordingly, it is not surprising to encounter its neighbour *καταψήχειν* in Euripides, Hipp. 110—

τράπεζα πλήρης· καὶ καταψήχειν χρέων

and *ψήχω* in Xenophon (Eq. 6. 1; 4. 4), while *ἔψηγμαι* should be retained in Sophocles, Trach. 698—

ῥεῖ πᾶν ἄδηλον καὶ κατέψηκται χθονί.

By the side of *ψῇ* in id. 678 it is simply another illustration of the conventional character of the Tragic dialect in which forms that had long dropped out of use in Attic were retained side by side with those before which they had given way.

CCXXIX.

Σάκκος· Δωριεῖς διὰ τῶν δύο κκ, οἱ δὲ Ἀττικοὶ δι' ἑνός.

κλάων μεγαριεῖς· οὐκ ἀφήσεις τὸν σάκον;
Ar. Ach. 822.

ἅπασα καὶ μίσει σάκον πρὸς τοῖν γνάθοιν ἔχουσα.
Eccl. 502.

But in Ach. 745 *σάκκος* is used as a Megarian is speaking—

κἤπειτεν ἐς τὸν σάκκον ὧδ' ἐσβαίνετε.

Accordingly, in Dem. 1170. 27, *σακχυφάντης* should be replaced by *σαχυφάντης*, as there can have been no reason why *σαχυφάντης* should not have been said. Our method of pronouncing Greek is apt to mislead us on such points.

CCXXX.

Πέπων· τοῦτο καθ' αὑτὸ οὐκ ὀρθῶς τιθέμενον ὁρῶ. σημαίνει γὰρ τὸ ὄνομα πᾶν τὸ ἐν πεπάνσει ὄν. τιθέασι δ' αὐτὸ οἰκείως ἐπὶ τῶν σικύων. χρὴ οὖν οὕτω λέγειν, ὡς ὁ Κρατῖνος, σίκυον σπερματίαν ἢ εἰ 'θέλεις πέπονα σίκυον, καθ' αὑτὸ δὲ τὸ πέπων ἐπὶ τοῦ αὐτοῦ μὴ τίθει.

There is the same caution in Soph. App. p. 63, Σίκυος σπερματίας, ὃν οἱ πολλοὶ πέπονα οὐκ ὀρθῶς λέγουσι. τὸ γὰρ πέπων κατὰ πάντων φέρεται τῶν εἰς πέψιν φθασάντων. It is only late writers who employ πέπων as a substantive. Lobeck quotes from Galen, ἢ πέπονος ἢ σικύου, and from Nicetas Choniates, τῶν σικύων καὶ τῶν πεπόνων.

CCXXXI.

Ἐπαρίστερον οὐ χρὴ λέγειν, ἀλλὰ σκαιόν.

The prepositional phrases, ἐπὶ δεξιά (cp. πρὸς δεξιά, χειρὸς εἰς τὰ δεξιά), and ἐπ' ἀριστερά (cp. πρὸς τὰ ἀριστερὰ εἰς ἀριστερά), gave rise respectively to the adjectives ἐπιδέξιος and ἐπαρίστερος, with a meaning practically the same as the simple δεξιός and ἀριστερός. However, while ἐπιδέξιος acquired even the metaphorical meaning of δεξιός, ἐπαριστέρος did not win its way in Attic even to the physical sense of ἀριστερός, and σκαιός, which had practically been driven from the field of physical relations by ἀριστερός, kept a firm hold of the signification *awkward*, *uncouth*. It is this sense of ἐπαρίστερος which Phrynichus is here reprehending, a sense which gradually made way as the language degenerated, being first found in the Comic poets of the early Macedonian period.

ἐπαρίστερ' ἔμαθες, ὦ πόνηρε, γράμματα.
Theognetus.

A. πρὸς τὸ πρᾶγμ' ἔχω
κακῶς. B. ἐπαριστέρως γὰρ αὐτὸ λαμβάνεις.
Menander.

CCXXXII.

Πλόκιον· ἐπὶ ὑποθέσεως πεπλεγμένης οἱ εἰκαῖοι τιθέασιν. θαυμάζω οὖν πῶς ὁ πρῶτος δόξας τῶν Ἑλλήνων εἶναι

Φαβωρῖνος ἐχρῆτο ἐν συγγράμματι ἐπιγραφομένῳ περὶ τῆς Δημάδους σωφροσύνης.

The words *ὑπόθεσις πεπλεγμένη* here signify an involved or intricate argument. It is doubtful whether Phaborinus used *πλόκιον* as a substantive or adjective; but it is of no moment, as neither use is possible in Greek.

CCXXXIII.

Στυππεϊνὸν τετρασυλλάβως οὐ χρὴ λέγειν, ἀλλὰ ἄνευ τοῦ ε τρισυλλάβως, στυππινόν.

There is no means of deciding which is the true spelling of this word—*στυππινός* or *στυπινός*—and the same doubt attaches to *στυππεῖον* and *στυππειοπώλης*. All that verse can tell us is that the *υ* is long, but whether by nature or position is uncertain. The tetrasyllabic form of the adjective entered the Common dialect from the Ionic.

Τέλος τοῦ πρώτου τμήματος.

Τοῦ αὐτοῦ τμῆμα δεύτερον.

CCXXXIV.

Ἀντίρρησιν μὴ λέγε, ἀντιλογίαν δέ.

Veitch and Cobet are alike actuated by an elevated devotion to genuine learning, but while the Dutch scholar relies upon an intellect of striking natural vigour, trained by long and wide experience in textual criticism, the Scots student trusts too implicitly in the authority of codices and editions. Cobet's bold and unflinching manner rather courts such attack, and too frequently supplies Veitch with an occasion for criticism. Such an occasion was given him by the too absolute statements of Cobet (in Var. Lect. p. 36) in regard to the forms of *ἀγορεύω* used in Attic. Cobet's rule was unquestionably right, but he erred in denying all exceptions. These Veitch proved, and the Dutch scholar subsequently revised this question in some critical remarks on the Second Oration of Isaeus, *περὶ τοῦ Μενεκλέους κλήρου*, which appeared in the New Series of Mnemosyne (vol. 2, p. 127 ff). The following is a modified transcript of the results there stated.

The rule followed by Attic writers was indisputably this:—Whether as a simple verb, or when compounded with a preposition, *ἀγορεύω* had for its future *ἐρῶ*, its aorist *εἶπον*, its perfect *εἴρηκα*; and in the passive voice it employed the aorist *ἐρρήθην*, the perfect *εἴρημαι*, and the futures *ῥηθήσομαι* and *εἰρήσομαι*. Every schoolboy knows that *εἴρηκα* was the perfect of *λέγω*, and that the aorist was as often *εἶπον* as *ἔλεξα*, the future as often *ἐρῶ* as *λέξω*. According to our rule, therefore, λέγω must have had a rival in ἀγορεύω. As a matter of fact this was so, as Arist. Plut. 102—

οὐκ ἠγόρευον ὅτι παρέξειν πράγματα
ἐμελλέτην μοι;

and in the ancient formula, τίς ἀγορεύειν βούλεται; but such a use was rare. The true sphere of ἀγορεύω was in compounds, to supply the place of λέγω, which was never compounded with any preposition except ἀντί, πρό, and ἐπί. Ἐπαγορεύειν never took the place of ἐπιλέγειν, or ἐπίρρησις of ἐπίλογος; but προαγορεύειν and ἀνταγορεύειν were sometimes used for προλέγειν and ἀντιλέγειν. As a religious term προαγορεύειν was constant in the formula excluding the profane from participation in religious ceremonies. Similarly προαγορεύειν τινὶ εἴργεσθαι ἱερῶν καὶ ἀγορᾶς was 'to give notice to one accused of murder that he was deprived of religious and civil privileges.' Such notice of exclusion was termed πρόρρησις[1], as is seen from Antiphon, *de Caede Herodis*, § 88, and *de Choreut.* § 6.

But, except with ἐπί, ἀντί, and πρό, λέγω was never compounded; its place was taken by ἀγορεύω in the present and imperfect, while -λέξω and -έλεξα completely disappeared before -ερῶ and -εῖπον, and -ελέχθην and λέλεγμαι before -ερρήθην and -είρημαι. In this way ἀπερῶ, ἀπεῖπον, and ἀπείρηκα, etc., are to be rèferred to ἀπαγορεύω, just as οἴσω, ἤνεγκα, and ἐνήνοχα are ascribed to φέρω. A Greek naturally used οἴσω as the future of φέρω, as Socrates in Xenophon (Sympos. 8. 6) says to Antisthenes—τὴν δ' ἄλλην χαλεπότητα ἐγώ σου καὶ φέρω καὶ οἴσω φιλικῶς, and the case was not different with ἀγορεύω. Any one wishing to use the future or aorist of ἀπαγορεύω, προσαγορεύω, προαγορεύω, ὑπαγορεύω, καταγορεύω, ἀναγορεύω, συναγορεύω, διαγορεύω, made use of

[1] Pollux says it was termed προαγόρευσις,—Εἴργεσθαι δὲ ἱερῶν καὶ ἀγορᾶς οἱ ἐν κατηγορίᾳ φόνου ἄχρι κρίσεως, καὶ τοῦτο προαγόρευσις ἐκαλεῖτο—and he may be right, for Inscriptions prove that ἀναγόρευσις was as good as ἀνάρρησις, although ἀνάρρησις is preferred by writers.

ἀπερῶ, προσερῶ, etc., of *ἀπεῖπον, προσεῖπον*, etc.; and so *ἀπείρηκα, ἀπείρηται, ἀπερρήθη, ἀπορρηθήσεται*, are to be referred to *ἀπαγορεύω*, and *προσείρηκα, προσείρημαι, προσερρήθην* to *προσαγορεύω*; and in a phrase like *προσειπὼν οὐκ ἀντιπροσερρήθην* the forms are to be referred to *προσαγορεύω* and *ἀντιπροσαγορεύω* respectively. Thrown into present time, *ὑπερῶ τὸν ὅρκον* becomes *ὑπαγορεύω τὸν ὅρκον*, and *συνείρηκα* is the perfect of *συναγορεύω*, *κατεῖπον* the aorist of *καταγορεύω*, *διείρηκα* and *διείρηται* perfects of *διαγορεύω*, and the same method of tense formation was maintained in all the compounds without exception. Only very rarely did good writers draw upon the stem *ἀγορευ* for tenses other than the present and imperfect, using *προσαγορεύσας* for *προσειπών*, and *ἀπηγόρευται* for *ἀπείρηται*. Later writers did so with frequency, and employed even nouns and adverbs derived from *ἀγορευ*. In Classical Greek the noun corresponding to *προσαγορεύω* was *πρόσρησις*, and similarly *πρόρρησις, ἀπόρρησις*, and *ἀνάρρησις* answered to the verbs *προαγορεύω, ἀπαγορεύω*, and *ἀναγορεύω*, while the adjective *ἀπόρρητος* corresponded to *ἀπαγορεύω*.

The verb *ἀναγορεύειν* was commonly used of proclamations by herald, and was sometimes replaced by the periphrasis *ποιεῖσθαι τὴν ἀνάρρησιν*, as its passive might be turned by phrases like *ἡ ἀνάρρησις γίγνεται*. In the speech of Aeschines against Ctesiphon, in which the orator enlarges on the mode of presenting the golden crown to Demosthenes, the Attic usage is very clearly demonstrated. In § 122 is read, *ὁ κῆρυξ ἀνηγόρευεν*, and shortly after, *ὁ κῆρυξ ἀνεῖπεν*: in § 155, *προελθὼν ὁ κῆρυξ τί ποτ' ἀνερεῖ*: in § 45, *ἀναρρηθῆναι*: and in § 189, *δεῖ γὰρ τὸν κήρυκα ἀψευδεῖν ὅταν τὴν ἀνάρρησιν ἐν τῷ θεάτρῳ ποιῆται πρὸς τοὺς Ἕλληνας*: and again in § 153, *νομίσαθ' ὁρᾶν προϊόντα τὸν κήρυκα καὶ τὴν ἐκ τοῦ ψηφίσματος ἀνάρρησιν μέλλουσαν γίγνεσθαι*. A similar testimony is more succinctly conveyed by Plato in Rep. 580 B, *μισθωσώμεθα οὖν κήρυκα . . . ἢ αὐτὸς ἀνείπω ὅτι κτε. . . .*

ἀνειρρήσθω σοί, ἔφη. ἡ οὖν προσαναγόρευσις . . . ; προσαναγόρευε, ἔφη. So Plato, Legg. 730 D, ὁ μέγας ἀνὴρ ἐν πόλει ἀναγορευέσθω: id. 946 B, πᾶσιν ἀνειπεῖν ὅτι Μαγνήτων ἡ πόλις κτε. The phrases ἀνεῖπεν ὁ κῆρυξ, and πρόσθε τῶν ἐπωνύμων ἀνειπεῖν, are in fact of constant occurrence, and hardly call for the explanation of Hesychius—ἀνεῖπεν· ἐκήρυξεν, διὰ κήρυκος εἶπεν.

As κηρύττειν was compounded with the prepositions πρό, ἐπί, and πρός, so προαναγορεύειν, ἐπαναγορεύειν, and προσαναγορεύειν were good Attic words. The expression ἀργύριον or χρήματα ἐπικηρύττειν τινί is well known in the sense of 'setting a price on a man's head.' It is thus used in Dem. de Fals. Legat. 347. 25, διὰ ταῦτα χρήμαθ' ἑαυτῷ τοὺς Θηβαίους ἐπικεκηρυχέναι, and slightly varied in Lysias 104. 44 (vi. 18), τοὺς δὲ φεύγοντας ζητεῖτε συλλαμβάνειν, ἐπικηρύττοντες τάλαντον ἀργυρίου δώσειν τῷ ἀγαγόντι (MSS. ἀπάγοντι, corr. Cobet) ἢ ἀποκτείναντι. The same meaning attaches to ἐπαναγορεύω in Aristophanes, Av. 1071—

> τῇδε μέντοι θἠμέρᾳ μάλιστ' ἐπαναγορεύεται
> ἢν ἀποκτείνῃ τις ὑμῶν Διαγόραν τὸν Μήλιον
> λαμβάνειν τάλαντον:
>
> Av. 1071.

and to ἐπανειπεῖν in Thucydides 6. 60, τῶν δὲ διαφυγόντων θάνατον καταγνόντες ἐπανεῖπον ἀργύριον τῷ ἀποκτείναντι. It is probably to this passage that Pollux refers in 2. 128, ἐπανειπὼν ἀργύριον οἷον ἐπικηρύξας, and Hesychius in the similar note, ἐπανεῖπον, ἐπεκήρυξαν.

The meaning of διαγορεύω was often expressed by a periphrasis with the adverb διαρρήδην. It was possible to say either διαγορεύει ὁ νόμος, or ὁ νόμος διαρρήδην λέγει. The adverb is formed like τμήδην (τμηθείς), ἀνέδην (ἀνεθείς), κλήδην (κληθείς), σύδην (συθείς), φύρδην (φυρθείς), etc., and may be at once pressed into service. In Plato, Legg. 6. 757, διαγορευόμενοι is quite unintelligible—δοῦλοι γὰρ ἂν καὶ δεσπόται οὐκ ἄν ποτε γένοιντο φίλοι οὐδὲ ἐν ἴσαις τιμαῖς διαγορευόμενοι φαῦλοι καὶ σπουδαῖοι. The meaning required is certainly not that of διαρρήδην λεγόμενοι. The genuine reading has been preserved in Photius in a learned note on φαῦλος, from the pen of Boethius—τάττοιτο δ' ἂν καὶ ἐπὶ τοῦ μοχθηροῦ· ὅτ' ἂν διαστέλληται πρὸς τὸ σπουδαῖον, ὡς Πλάτων· δοῦλοι γὰρ καὶ δεσπόται οὐδέ ποτ' ἂν γένοιντο φίλοι, οὐδ' ἐν ἴσαις τιμαῖς διαγενόμενοι φαῦλοι καὶ σπουδαῖοι. The question is thus settled not only by the authority of a true scholar, but also by the inherent excellence of the reading διαγενομένοι. There is no mistaking the meaning in Plato, Polit. 275 A, συμπάσης τῆς πόλεως ἄρχοντα αὐτὸν ἀπεφήναμεν, ὅντινα δὲ τρόπον οὐ διείπομεν, that is, οὐ διαρρήδην (explicitly) εἴπομεν. In the same sense it is used in id. Phaedrus 253 D, ἀρετὴ δὲ τίς τοῦ ἀγαθοῦ ἢ κακοῦ κακία οὐ διείπομεν. Hesychius is therefore not accurate when he explains διειπεῖν by διηγήσασθαι, διαλεχθῆναι, and goes still further wrong in another place—Διαγορεύει· θεσπίζει, διαγγέλλει, and again in Διείρηται· διήγγελται. The true meaning of the word was in fact lost in late Greek, as is proved beyond question by the corrupt variants which have taken its place in the manuscripts of Classical authors.

Herodotus employed the word in its true sense in 7. 38. Pythias has addressed Xerxes in the obscure terms—ὦ δέσποτα, χρηΐσας ἄν τευ βουλοίμην τυχεῖν τὸ σοὶ μὲν ἐλαφρὸν τυγχάνει ὑπουργῆσαι, ἐμοὶ δὲ μέγα γενόμενον, and the king will have him speak to the point (διαρρήδην λέγειν)—ἔφη τε ὑπουργήσειν καὶ διαγορεύειν ἐκέλευε ὅτου δέοιτο. The manuscripts have δὴ ἀγορεύειν.

But it is the perfect forms which have suffered most. They are constantly confused with the similar forms from διαίρω—διείρηκεν ὁ νόμος, διείρηται, τὰ διειρημένα, being frequently altered to διήρηκεν, διήρηται, and διηρημένα. It is never difficult to restore the text, as a moment's consideration is sufficient to decide which word best adapts itself to the context. A passage of Plato (Legg. 932) provides an unequalled illustration of the Attic usage in regard to διαγορεύειν—Τὰ μὲν θανάσιμα αὐτῶν διείρηται, τῶν δὲ ἄλλων οὐδέν πω διερρήθη· διτταὶ γὰρ δὴ φαρμακεῖαι κατὰ τὸ τῶν ἀνθρώπων οὖσαι γένος ἐπίσχουσι τὴν διάρρησιν, ἣν μὲν γὰρ ταννῦν διαρρήδην εἴπομεν κτε. Yet even here the noxious διῄρηται has manuscript authority in its favour. Ast has noticed this confusion on Legg. 809 E, ταῦτα οὕτω σοι πάντα ἱκανῶς παρὰ τοῦ νομοθέτου διείρηται . . . . ὡς οὔπω διείρηκέ σοι. Here also most manuscripts read διῄρηται. Among other instances he quotes Legg. 813 A, καὶ ταῦτα ἡμῖν ἐν τοῖς πρόσθεν διείρηται πάντα . . . . ἀληθῆ καὶ ταῦτα διείρηκας, but he makes a grave mistake in adding to his list Legg. 647 B, ἄφοβον ἡμῶν ἄρα δεῖ γενέσθαι καὶ φοβερὸν ἕκαστον· ὧν δ' ἑκάτερον ἕνεκα, διῃρήμεθα. The Middle διῄρημαι is unquestionably required. He would have done better in restoring διείρηκεν for δὴ εἴρηκεν in Legg. 809 A, νῦν μὲν γὰρ δὴ εἴρηκεν οὐδέν πω σαφὲς οὐδὲ ἱκανὸν ἀλλὰ τὰ μὲν τὰ δ' οὔ.

The Orators have fared as badly as the Philosopher. The text of Demosthenes supplies the following variants—465. 20, ὁρᾶθ' ὡς σαφῶς μηδένα εἶναι τριηραρχίας ἀτελῆ διείρηκεν (διῄρηκεν) ὁ νόμος: 644. 4, καὶ ἄλλ' ἄττα διείρηκεν (διῄρηκεν) ἃ χρὴ ποιῆσαι . . . . ὁ νόμος: 976. 28, σαφῶς ὁ νόμος διείρηκεν (διῄρηκεν) ὧν εἶναι δίκας προσήκει μεταλλικάς: 666. 13, διείρηται (διῄρηται) τί πρακτέον ἢ μή. In all these passages Dindorf, following Dobree, has edited διῄρηκεν and διῄρηται, but a careful examination of the passages will show that the perfects are all to be referred to διαγορεύειν, i. e. διαρρήδην λέγειν. It is easy to understand what is meant by the sentence ὁ νόμος διαγορεύει μηδένα εἶναι τριηραρχίας ἀτελῆ, but substitute διαιρεῖ for διαγορεύει and the words become unintelligible. The verb διαιρεῖν is found in combination with ὁ νόμος—ὁ νόμος διαιρεῖ, διεῖλεν ὁ νόμος,—but only when the law distinguishes between two distinct things. Dem. 115. 10, τίς γὰρ ἁλώσεται ἔτι ποτε ψευδομαρτυριῶν εἰ μαρτυρήσει τε ἃ βούλεται καὶ λόγον ὧν βούλεται δώσει; ἀλλ' οὐχ οὕτω ταῦτα ὁ νόμος διεῖλεν. 'The law,' he says, 'makes no such distinction, but requires that everything stated as evidence should be taken into account.'

There is only one passage of Demosthenes in which the perfect passive occurs without a variant, namely, 212. 13, ᾤοντο ἅμα τε ναυπηγήσεσθαι ἐνταῦθα καὶ πληρώσεσθαι ἐν ταῖς κοιναῖς ὁμολογίαις διειρημένον μηδὲν τοιοῦτον εἰσδέχεσθαι. Yet even here the accusative διειρημένον is demanded by the rules of Greek syntax.

In Isaeus, 86. 10 (11. 22), the primitive reading must have been διείρηται, although it is not represented in the manuscripts—ἀλλ' ὅτι διείρηται καθ' ἕκαστον περὶ αὐτῶν, ἐκ τοῦ νόμου γνῶναι ῥᾴδιον. Immediately after follows, ὁ νόμος . . . διαρρήδην κελεύων τοῦ μέρους ἕκαστον λαγχάνειν.

In a preceding paragraph, 84. 37 (11. 12), ἀλλ' ἀπέδωκε . . . τὴν κληρονομίαν κατὰ ταὐτὰ καθάπερ καὶ ἐξ ἀρχῆς ἦν ὑπειρημένον, the perfect ὑπειρημένον is to be referred to ὑπαγορεύω, as throughout Isaeus the correspondence between ἀγορεύω, ἐρῶ, εἶπον, εἴρηκα, etc., is consistently maintained.

'Απαγορεύω corresponds with ἀπόρρησις in Isaeus, 2. 28, ἀπηγόρευε τοῖς ὠνουμένοις μὴ ὠνεῖσθαι . . . τούτῳ δὲ λαγχάνει δίκην τῆς ἀπορρήσεως. The series is completed by Demosthenes, 902. 20, ἀπηγόρευεν ὁ Παρμένων . . . μὴ γιγνώσκειν ἄνευ τῶν συνδιαιτητῶν . . . ὅταν δὴ ἄνευ συνδιαιτητῶν παρὰ τὴν ἀπόρρησιν φῇ δεδιῃτηκέναι: and about the same thing in 899. 10, οὐ μόνον ἀμφισβητηθεὶς ἀλλὰ καὶ ἀπορρηθὲν αὐτῷ οὐδὲν ἧττον τὴν ἀπόφασιν ἐποιήσατο . . . : 903. 20, ἀπεῖπε δὲ αὐτῷ μὴ διαιτᾶν. A common meaning of ἀπαγορεύω was *to disinherit a son*, and because this was generally done by a crier, there occur phrases like ὑπὸ κήρυκος ἀπαγορεύειν, ἀπειπεῖν, and ἀπορρηθῆναι, in the sense of ἀποκηρύττειν, ἐκκηρύττειν, etc., all which terms are used as interchangeable in the Eleventh Book of the Laws, as 928 D, τὸν υἱὸν ὑπὸ κήρυκος ἀπειπεῖν: and 929 A, ὑπὸ τοῦ γένους ἀπορρηθῆναι παντός. Hence ἀπόρρησις was used for ἀποκήρυξις *disinheriting*, a fact expressly mentioned by a Grammarian in Bekker, Anecd. 1. 216, 10, ἀπόρρησις· καὶ τὸ ἀποκηρύσσειν. In fact, ἀπόρρησις is used in all the senses of ἀπαγορεύω, whether *forbid, disinherit*, or *become weary*. It has already been quoted in the sense of *forbidding*, corresponding to ἀπαγορεύω as a synonym of ἀπαυδῶ and the Homeric ἀπεμυθεόμην, and with the meaning of *giving in*, the word is found in Plato, Rep. 357 A, τοῦ Θρασυμάχου τὴν ἀπόρρησιν οὐκ ἀπεδέξατο. Such is the common usage in the Orators with regard to ἀπαγορεύω; but in Dem. 1021. 20, ἀπηγόρευσεν is used where the rule calls for ἀπεῖπεν, namely, ἀπηγόρευσεν αὐτῷ μὴ διαιτᾶν, and a few other aberrations from ordinary usage are encountered here and there in Classical Greek. After the time of Alexander these exceptions became the rule, and the verb formed its tenses regularly, -αγορεύσω, -ηγόρευσα, -ηγόρευκα, -ηγορεύθην, -ηγόρευμαι, while substantives like προσαγόρευσις, ἀπαγόρευσις, took the place of πρόσρησις and ἀπόρρησις.

In Attic writers use was occasionally made of -ηγόρευσα, -αγορεύσω, etc., by the side of -εῖπον and -ερῶ, etc., to emphasize distinction of meaning. Thus, ἀπαγορεύω, when it signified ἀποκάμνω, had always ἀπερῶ, ἀπεῖπον, and ἀπείρηκα, and the compound with πρό always προαπερῶ, προαπεῖπον, προαπείρηκα; but when it had the meaning of *forbid*, its aorist might be ἀπηγόρευσα, and its perfect passive ἀπηγόρευμαι. Similarly προσαγορεύω in the sense of ἀσπάζομαι had προσερῶ, προσεῖπον, and προσερρήθην, but in the sense of *call* sometimes employed προσηγόρευσα and προσηγορεύθην: Xen. Mem. 3. 2, 1, τοῦ ἕνεκεν Ὅμηρον οἴει τὸν Ἀγαμέμνονα προσαγορεῦσαι ποιμένα λαῶν; By itself the authority of Xenophon would go for nothing, but Plato uses προσαγορευτέα (Phaed. 104 A), and Demosthenes—if the speech is not ascribed to Dinarchus—προσηγορεύθην, 1008. 5, ὅταν τις ὀνόματι μὲν ἀδελφὸς προσαγορευθῇ τινῶν. Προαγορεύω formed *προερῶ, προεῖπον, προείρηκα,* but as *τὰ προειρημένα* meant *ante dicta*, for *edicta τὰ προηγορευμένα* was used.

It is in a similar way that Cobet explains *ἀπηγόρευσεν* in Dem. 1021. 20. It was possible in the sense of *forbade,* but could not be used with the meaning *gave in.* Accordingly, for the aorist *ἀπαγορεύσῃς*, the present *ἀπαγορεύῃς* should be substituted in Plato, Theaet. 200 D, when Socrates having said *οὐ γάρ που ἀπεροῦμεν γέ πω*, Theaetetus replies *ἥκιστα, ἐάνπερ μὴ σύ γε ἀπαγορεύσῃς.* The change is easily made, and perhaps restores the text, but few scholars will listen to Cobet's proposal to alter *προσαγορεύσομεν* to *προσεροῦμεν* in Theaet. 147 D, *ἡμῖν οὖν εἰσῆλθέ τι τοιοῦτον . . . πειραθῆναι συλλαβεῖν εἰς ἓν ὅτῳ πάσας ταύτας προσαγορεύσομεν τὰς δυνάμεις.* If *προσαγορευτέα* was, as he admits, used in the Phaedo, and *προσαγορεύθῃ* by Demosthenes, without any essential difference of meaning from *προσαγορεύσομεν* in the present passage, then it is not only perilous but inconsistent to demand *προσεροῦμεν.* The rule once established, such rare exceptions should be regarded as anomalies, and relegated to the obscurity which they merit. No purpose is served by burdening the memory with unquestioned anomalies in language, and no intellect is safe from degeneration which occupies itself in finding a metaphysical explanation for every irregularity of syntax. Irregularities in construction, and still more so anomalies in form, are generally due to the desperately corrupt condition of the manuscripts. To rise by the help of broad generalisations and careful inductions to a knowlege of the Greek language as used by the Greeks themselves should be the aim of every true scholar, as it is certainly the only course which a man of sense can follow.

CCXXXV.

Εὐαγγελίζομαί σε· καὶ περὶ ταύτης τῆς συντάξεως διασκεπτόμενος ἐπὶ συχνὸν δὴ χρόνον εἴτε αἰτιατικῇ συντακτέον αὐτὸ πτώσει εἴτε δοτικῇ, εὑρίσκω κατὰ δοτικὴν ἡρμοσμένον· Ἀριστοφάνους μὲν οὕτω λέγοντος ἐν τοῖς Ἱππεῦσιν,

Εὐαγγελίσασθαι πρῶτος ὑμῖν βούλομαι.

Φρυνίχου δὲ τοῦ κωμῳδοῦ ἐν τοῖς Σατύροις οὕτως.

The rest of the article is corrupt—*Ὅτι πρὶν ἐλθεῖν αὐτὸν εἰς βουλὴν ἔδει καὶ ταῦτ᾽ ἀπαγγείλαντα πάλιν πρὸς τὸν θεὸν ἥκειν, ἐγὼ δ᾽ ἀπέδραν ἐκεῖνον δευριανὸν δεῖ. Καὶ οὕτω λέγουσιν εὐαγγελίζομαι ἢ εὐαγγελῶ· οὗ ὁ Πλάτων τὸ δεύτερον πρόσωπον λέγει εὐαγγελεῖς.* William Dindorf imagines that two distinct articles have been confused, and that the mutilated lines from *ὅτι* to *δεῖ* are a quotation intended to establish the true forms of the aorist of *ἀποδιδράσκω*—a supposition which is supported by App. Soph. 11. 1, *Ἀπέδραμεν τετρασυλλάβως, καὶ ἀπέδρατε καὶ ἀπέδραν, βραχείας τῆς τοῦ ἀπέδραν ἐσχάτης συλλαβῆς· ἀλλὰ καὶ τὸ ἑνικὸν πρῶτον πρόσωπον ἀπέδραν, ἐκτεταμένου τοῦ ἐπὶ τέλους α, καὶ ἀπέδρας καὶ ἀπέδρα, οὐχ ὡς οἱ ῥήτορες ἀπεδράσαμεν· τὸ δὲ ἀπέδραν τινὲς τῶν ῥητόρων διὰ τοῦ ω εἶπον, ἀπέδρων, ἀλλ᾽ ἄμεινον διὰ τοῦ α· ὁμοίως καὶ ἐξέδραν.*

The passage of Plato referred to as containing the form *εὐαγγελεῖς* must be either Rep. 432 D or Theaet. 144 B. In both of these places *εὖ ἀγγέλλεις* is the received reading, and in neither do manuscripts exhibit the compound verb. There is the same difficulty with *κάκ᾽ ἀγγέλλω* versus *κακαγγελῶ*. Photius has preserved the dictum—*Εὐεγγελεῖν ὑφ᾽ ἓν λέγουσι καὶ κακαγγελεῖν*, and if *εὐαγγελεῖς* is assigned to Plato, then *κακαγγελῶν* and *κακαγγελεῖν* may respectively replace *κάκ᾽ ἀγγέλλων*, and *κάκ᾽ ἀγγελεῖν* in a line of Euripides—

τί φῄς; τί δράσας; ὦ κακαγγελῶν πάτερ—
H. F. 1136.

and in a tragic senarius, ap. Dem. 315. 24—

κακαγγελεῖν μὲν ἴσθι μὴ θέλοντ᾽ ἐμέ.

In Lobeck's edition will be found the various unsuccessful attempts to restore the passage from the Comic poet, and a Greek dictionary will supply proof of the classical construction of the verb εὐαγγελίζομαι.

CCXXXVI.

Ἐκαθέσθη, καθεσθείς, καθεσθήσομαι καὶ τὰ πληθυντικὰ καθεσθήσονται, ἔκφυλα. λέγε οὖν καθέζομαι, καθεδοῦμαι, καθεδοῦνται, καθεδούμενος.

Probably ἐκαθεζόμην should be here substituted for καθέζομαι as ἐκαθέσθην suggests. Moreover, the form καθέζομαι is by some scholars denied to Attic Greek, and when exhibited by manuscripts is replaced by καθίζομαι. As is well known, ἐκαθεζόμην has generally the force of an aorist, and would naturally correspond to the late ἐκαθέσθην.

The three verbs, καθίζω, καθέζομαι, and κάθημαι, supplement one another. Καθίζω has both a transitive and an intransitive meaning. It is possible to say either καθίζω Σωκράτην κριτήν, *I make Socrates sit as a judge*, or ὁ Σωκράτης κριτὴς καθίζει, *Socrates sits as a judge*. Notwithstanding this intransitive use of the active voice, the passive—it is passive and not middle—is also in use with the signification of *sit*. The aorist, however, is not found, its place being filled by καθῖσα or ἐκάθῖσα and καθεζόμην. Κάθημαι may be considered as the perfect passive of the transitive καθίζω, but a perfect which must necessarily have much of a present force. Lucian, in his Pseudosophist, well brings out the difference between κάθιζε and κάθησο—

A. τὸ καθέσθητι ἤκουόν σου λέγοντος ὡς ἔστιν ἔκφυλον.

B. καὶ ὀρθῶς γε ἤκουσας, ἀλλὰ τὸ κάθισον τοῦ κάθησο διαφέρειν φημί.

A. καὶ τῷ ποτ' ἂν εἴη διάφερον;

B. τῷ τὸ μὲν πρὸς τὸν ἑστῶτα λέγεσθαι τὸ κάθισον, τὸ

δὲ πρὸς τὸν καθεζόμενον·
ἧσ', ὦ ξεῖν', ἡμεῖς δὲ καὶ ἄλλοθι δήομεν ἕδρην
ἀντὶ τοῦ μένε καθεζόμενος.

Attic writers observe the distinction.

κάθημαι may be used intransitively of everything of which καθίζω is used transitively, as Thuc. 6. 66, οἱ Ἀθηναῖοι καθῖσαν τὸ στράτευμα ἐς χωρίον ἐπιτήδειον· id. 2. 20, περὶ τὰς Ἀχαρνὰς καθήμενος εἰ ἐπεξίασιν· ἅμα γὰρ αὐτῷ ὁ χῶρος ἐπιτήδειος ἐφαίνετο ἐνστρατοπεδεῦσαι κτε. Similarly, καθίζειν ἀνδριάντα, but ὁ ἀνδριὰς κάθηται, and τοὺς δικαστὰς or τὸ δικαστήριον καθίζειν, but οἱ δικασταὶ κάθηνται. 'To bring one in weeping,' as an actor would present a character, is in Greek καθίζειν τινὰ κλάοντα, and the character so presented may be said κλάων καθῆσθαι.

The Attic forms of these three alternating and mutually supplementary verbs are confined to the following :—

TRANSITIVE.	MIDDLE.
καθίζω, set, make to sit.	καθίζομαι, set for myself.
καθῖζον, ἐκάθιζον.	καθιζόμην, ἐκαθιζόμην.
καθιῶ.	καθιοῦμαι.
καθῖσα, ἐκάθῖσα.	καθῑσάμην, ἐκαθισάμην.

INTRANSITIVE.	PASSIVE.
καθίζω, sit, take my seat.	καθίζομαι, [καθέζομαι].
καθῖζον, ἐκάθιζον.	ἐκαθιζόμην
καθῖσα, ἐκάθισα.	καθιζήσομαι, καθεδοῦμαι.
κάθημαι, am seated.	ἐκαθεζόμην.
καθήμην, ἐκαθήμην.	κάθημαι
	καθήμην, ἐκαθήμην.

Though not met with till late, the perfect κεκάθικα was certainly in use in Attic, at all events in its transitive signification. Καθιῶ, however, was not used intransitively Moeris 212, καθεδεῖ Ἀττικοί, καθίσεις Ἕλληνες. Καθιζήσομαι and *καθεδοῦμαι* were sufficient. The corrupt *προσκαθεσθήσει* has manuscript authority in Aeschin 77. 34, but has justly succumbed to *προσκαθιζήσει*.

'Participio aoristi Josephum, Apollodorum, Lucianum et horum similes alios usos esse demonstravit Graevius. Indicativo, *ἐκαθέσθη*, Longus, 3. 5, *περιεκαθέσθη* Eunapius, *ἐπικαθεσθείη* Geoponica, *καθεσθῇ* Pausanias, *καθεσθῆναι* Libanius, *ἐπικαθεσθῆναι* Eusebius.' Lobeck.

CCXXXVII.

Ἀνέκαθεν· φυλακτέον ἐπὶ χρόνου λέγειν, οἷον ἀ ν έ κ α θ έ ν μ ο ι ἐ σ τ ὶ φ ί λ ο ς. ἐπὶ γὰρ τόπου τάττουσιν αὐτὸ οἱ Ἀθηναῖοι, λέγοντες ἀ ν έ κ α θ ε ν κ α τ έ π ε σ ε. λέγειν οὖν χρή, ἄ ν ω θ έ ν σ ο ι φ ί λ ο ς ε ἰ μ ί. εἰ δέ τις φαίη ἐπὶ χρόνου παρ' Ἡροδότῳ εἰρῆσθαι τοὔνομα, ἀληθῆ μὲν φήσει· εἴρηται γάρ. οὐ μὴν τῷ ὑφ' Ἡροδότου εἰρῆσθαι τὸ δόκιμον τῆς χρήσεως παρέχεται. οὐ γὰρ Ἰωνικῶν καὶ Δωρικῶν ἐξέτασίς ἐστιν ὀνομάτων ἀλλ' Ἀττικῶν.

The word *ἀνέκαθεν* is not Attic in either signification. It is one of those old words which lived on in Tragedy from Ionic times, and with the meaning 'from above' it occurs in Aesch. Eum. 369—

> *μάλα γὰρ οὖν ἁλομένα ἀνέκαθεν βαρυπεσῆ*
> *καταφέρω ποδὸς ἀκμάν.*

In Herodotus it is frequent, and from Ionic it passed into the Common dialect. Herod. 4. 57, of place, *ποταμός, ὃς ῥέει τἀνέκαθεν ἐκ λίμνης μεγάλης ὁρμεόμενος*: but more frequently of time, 1. 170, *ἀνδρὸς τὸ ἀνέκαθεν ἐόντος Φοίνικος*: 6. 125, *ἔσαν τὰ ἀνέκαθεν λαμπροί.*

Plut. Num. 13, *ἡ ἀνέκαθεν φορά*: Lucian, Jud. Voc. 7 (91), *Βοιώτιος τὸ γένος ἀνέκαθεν*: Polyb. 16. 12. 2, *εὔχονται τὸ ἀνέκαθεν Ἀργείων ἄποικα γεγονέναι*: et frequentissime.

CCXXXVIII.

Κεφαλαιωδέστατον· τοῦτο τοὔνομα εὗρον ἐν ἀρχῇ τῶν Πολέμωνος τοῦ Ἰωνικοῦ σοφιστοῦ Ἱστοριῶν κατὰ προοίμιον, καὶ θαυμάζω Σεκούνδου τοῦ συγγενομένου αὐτῷ γραμματικοῦ, πῶς ὢν τὰ ἄλλα δεξιὸς ἐπὶ λέξιν καὶ ἐπανορθῶν τὰ συγγράμματα τοῦ σοφιστοῦ, τοῦτο παρεῖδεν ἀδόκιμον ὄν.

The Polemo here referred to flourished in the first half of the second century A.D. That he should have kept a grammarian to correct his work shows no less clearly than the work of Phrynichus himself the state to which literature had fallen in the second century.

The defaulting form is cited by Lobeck from Lucian, Diogenes Laertius, Eusebius, and others, and the comparative from writers equally debased. Such *ἐπίτασις ὑπερθέσεως* has already been considered (p. 144).

CCXXXIX.

Ἔσθ' ὅπη· τί πάσχουσιν οἱ οὕτω λέγοντες, δέον ἔστιν ὅτε λέγειν, οὐκ ἄν τις εἰκάσειεν, ἀλλ' ἢ τοῦτο μόνον ὅτι ἠμελημένοι εἰσὶν οἱ τούτῳ τῷ ὀνόματι χρώμενοι.

Examples of this transference of *ἔσθ' ὅπη* from its legitimate meaning, 'in some way,' to the absurd sense of 'sometimes,' are cited by Lobeck from Herodian, Galen, Aristaenetus, Nicetas Choniates, etc.

CCXL.

Βάκηλος· ἁμαρτάνουσιν οἱ τάττοντες τοῦτο κατὰ τοῦ βλακός. σημαίνει γὰρ ὁ βάκηλος τὸν ἀποτετμημένον τὰ αἰδοῖα, ὃν Βιθυνοί τε καὶ Ἀσιανοὶ Γάλλον καλοῦσι. λέγε οὖν βλάξ καὶ βλακικόν, ὡς οἱ ἀρχαῖοι.

The correction, *βλακικόν* for *βλάκιον*, restores the hand of Phrynichus. Both *βλάξ* and *βλᾰκικός* are of the best authority in Attic.

CCXLI.

Ἑκὼν εἶναι· καὶ περὶ τοῦτο ἰδιώτης μὲν οὐκ ἂν πταίσειε· τῶν δὲ σφόδρα προσποιουμένων ἀρχαίᾳ φωνῇ κεκριμένῃ χρῆσθαι, τόδε ἁμάρτημα τοιοῦτόν ἐστιν. οἱ μὲν παλαιοὶ οὕτω συντάττουσι τὸ ἑκὼν εἶναι, ὥστε πάντως ἀπαγόρευσιν ἢ ἄρνησιν ἐπιφέρειν ἢ προστιθέναι, οἷον, ἑκὼν εἶναι οὐ μὴ ποιήσω. οὕτω καὶ οἱ νῦν εὖ φρονοῦντες. ὅσοι δὲ ἐπὶ καταφάσεως τιθέασι τὸ ἑκὼν εἶναι, οἷον, ἑκὼν εἶναι ἔπραξα, ἑκὼν εἶναι ἐπεβουλευσάμην, μέγιστα ἁμαρτάνουσιν.

The rule is absolute in Attic. Plato, Phaed. 61 C, *οὐδ' ὁπωστιοῦν σοι ἑκὼν εἶναι πείσεται*: Phaedr. 252 A, *ὅθεν δὴ ἑκοῦσα εἶναι οὐκ ἀπολείπεται*: Gorg. 499 C, *καίτοι οὐκ ᾤμην γε κατ' ἀρχὰς ὑπὸ σοῦ ἑκόντος εἶναι ἐξαπατηθήσεσθαι ὡς ὄντος φίλου*: Apol. 37 A, *πέπεισμαι ἐγὼ ἑκὼν εἶναι μηδένα ἀδικεῖν ἀνθρώπων*: Thuc. 2. 89, *τὸν δὲ ἀγῶνα οὐκ ἐν τῷ κόλπῳ ἑκὼν εἶναι ποιήσομαι*: 4. 98, *νῦν δέ, ἐν ᾧ μέρει εἰσίν, ἑκόντες εἶναι ὡς ἐκ σφετέρου οὐκ ἀπιέναι*: 7. 81, *θᾶσσόν τε γὰρ ὁ Νικίας ἦγε, νομίζων οὐ τὸ ὑπομένειν ἐν τῷ τοιούτῳ ἑκόντας εἶναι καὶ μάχεσθαι σωτηρίαν.* Thomas, p. 290, adds that the phrase could stand in interrogative sentences which are virtually negative, as *τί τις ἂν ἑκὼν εἶναι ποιήσειεν*, and there can be no question that he is right, as such a usage is in accordance with the facts of language. To extend the phrase to conditional sentences, as L. Dindorf would do (in Thes. Steph. 3. 653) on the strength of Plato, Legg. 646 C, *θαυμάζοιμεν ἂν εἴ ποτέ τις ἑκὼν εἶναι ἐπὶ τὸ τοιοῦτον ἀφικνεῖται*, is quite erroneous, as in this case *εἶναι* is not found in the best manuscripts, being merely a late interpolation, and, moreover, the sentence is not a conditional one, but illustrates the well-known use of *εἰ* after *θαυμάζω*. The same scholar errs still more grossly in denying that the negative influences *ἑκόντας εἶναι* in the third passage of Thucydides cited above. No one, however, questions its use in affirmative sentences in Herodotus, as 7. 164, *ὁ δὲ Κάδμος οὗτος . . . ἑκών τε εἶναι καὶ δεινοῦ ἐπιόντος οὐδενὸς ἀλλὰ ἀπὸ δικαιοσύνης ἐς μέσον Κῴοισι καταθεὶς τὴν ἀρχήν*, and it was this looser use which was followed in the Common dialect.

CCXLII.

Ὄρθρος νῦν ἀκούω τῶν πολλῶν τιθέντων ἐπὶ τοῦ πρὸ ἡλίου ἀνίσχοντος χρόνου. οἱ δὲ ἀρχαῖοι ὄρθρον καὶ ὀρθρεύεσθαι τὸ πρὸ ἀρχομένης ἡμέρας, ἐν ᾧ ἔτι λύχνῳ δύναταί τις χρῆσθαι. ὃ τοίνυν ἁμαρτάνοντες οἱ πολλοὶ λέγουσιν ὄρθρον, τοῦθ' οἱ ἀρχαῖοι ἕω λέγουσιν.

The usage of Attic writers is distinctly in favour of this view. In his App. Soph. p. 54, Phrynichus places *ὄρθρος* after *μέσαι νύκτες*, and explains it as *ἡ ὥρα τῆς νυκτὸς καθ' ἣν ἀλεκτρυόνες ᾄδουσιν*. The expression *ὄρθρος βαθύς* is well-known.

CCXLIII.

Μαγειρεῖον· τὸ μὲν μάγειρος δόκιμον, τὸ δὲ μαγειρεῖον οὐκέτι, ἀντὶ δὲ τούτου ὀπτάνιον λέγουσι.

The words *τῆς μὲν δευτέρας συλλαβῆς ὀξυτονουμένης τῆς δὲ τρίτης συστελλομένης* appended by some editors to this article are merely a gloss, but a correct gloss as is proved by verse—

ἐκφοιτῶν τ' ἐς τοὐπτάνιον λήσει σε κυνηδόν.

Ar. Eq. 1033.

τουτὶ δ' ὁρᾶτ' ὀπτάνιον ἡμῖν ὡς καλόν.

Pax 891.

A. ὀπτάνιον ἔστιν; B. ἔστι. A. καὶ κάπνην ἔχει.

Alexis (Athen. 9. 386 A).

Pollux, however, quotes *μαγειρεῖα* from Antiphanes 9. 48, *καὶ μαγειρεῖα τῶν πόλεως μερῶν οὐχ ἧπερ τὰ λοιπὰ τῶν ὑπὸ ταῖς τέχναις ἐργαστηρίων, ἀλλ' ὁ τόπος ὅθεν μισθοῦνται τοὺς μαγείρους ὡς Ἀντιφάνης ἐν Στρατιώτῃ ὑποδηλοῦν ἔοικεν*—

Ἐκ τῶν μαγειρείων βαδίζων ἐμβαλῶν
εἰς τοὔψον.

The passage does not traverse the dictum of Phrynichus. The lexicography of the two words is given by Lobeck with his usual elaboration.

CCXLIV.

Τυγχάνω· καὶ τούτῳ προσεκτέον· οἱ γὰρ ἀμελεῖς οὕτω λέγουσι, φίλος σοι τυγχάνω, ἐχθρός μοι τυγχάνεις. δεῖ δὲ τῷ ῥήματι τὸ ὢν προστιθέναι, φίλος μοι τυγχάνεις ὤν, ἐχθρός μοι τυγχάνεις ὤν.

Even in the best age the participle of the substantive verb was sometimes carelessly omitted after *τυγχάνω*. If the Prose instances are set aside as of no importance in such an inquiry, there is a line of Aristophanes to confute such scholars as would correct the texts of prose writers by the dictum of Phrynichus—

καὶ τῶν θεατῶν εἴ τις εὔνους τυγχάνει.

Eccl. 1141.

There are, however, seven lines in which the correct construction is unquestioned—

τὸν δ' υἱὸν ὅσπερ ὢν μόνος μοι τυγχάνει.

Pl. 35.

εἰ τυγχάνοι γ' ὁ δακτύλιος ὢν τηλίας.
Pl. 1037.

μὴ καί τις ὢν ἀνὴρ ὁ προσιὼν τυγχάνει.
Eccl. 29.

μὰ τὸν Δί', οὐ γὰρ ἔνδον οὖσα τυγχάνει.
Id. 336.

ἐτύγχανεν γὰρ οὐ τρίβων ὢν ἱππικῆς.
Vesp. 1429.

ὅτι τυγχάνει λυχνοποιὸς ὤν· πρὸ τοῦ μὲν οὖν
Pax 690.

εἰ δὲ τυγχάνει τις ὢν Φρὺξ μηδὲν ἧττον Σπινθάρου.
Av. 762.

These at once elevate the construction with the participle into a rule, and shew that the omission of the substantive verb is quite exceptional. Such exceptions are sometimes unfairly multiplied by such lines as—

εἰ δὲ τυγχάνει τις ὑμῶν δραπέτης ἐστιγμένος
Ar. Av. 760.

on the one hand, and

σωτὴρ γένοιτ' ἂν Ζεὺς ἐπ' ἀσπίδος τυχών
Aesch. Sept. 520.

on the other. In the former of these lines *ἐστιγμένος* is participial, not adjectival, and in the latter the participle is naturally supplied from *γένοιτο*. Aeschylus does not elsewhere employ this construction, but in Sophocles it occurs five times—

ἔνδον γὰρ ἀνὴρ ἄρτι τυγχάνει, κάρα
Aj. 9.

μέγιστος αὐτοῖς τυγχάνει δορυξένων.
El. 46.

θυραῖον οἰχνεῖν· νῦν δ' ἀγροῖσι τυγχάνει.
Id. 313.

χαίροις ἂν εἴ σοι χαρτὰ τυγχάνοι τάδε.
Id. 1457.

μένοιμ' ἄν· ἤθελον δ' ἂν ἐκτὸς ὢν τυχεῖν.
Aj. 88.

It will be observed that in four of these five lines is found the construction which the evidence of Aristophanes proves to be exceptional in pure Attic, but on such a point the testimony of a Tragic poet is as little to be regarded as that of an un-Attic, or late writer, or even of Homer.

ἔνθ' ἐπεὶ ἐς λιμένα κλυτὸν ἤλθομεν ὃν πέρι πέτρη
ἠλίβατος τετύχηκε διαμπερὲς ἀμφοτέρωθεν.

Od. 10. 87.

CCXLV.

Σύγκρισις· Πλούταρχος ἐπέγραψε σύγγραμμά τι τῶν αὑτοῦ—

Σύγκρισις Ἀριστοφάνους καὶ Μενάνδρου.

καὶ θαυμάζω πῶς φιλοσοφίας ἐπ' ἄκρον ἀφιγμένος καὶ σαφῶς εἰδὼς ὅ τι ποτέ ἐστιν ἡ σύγκρισις, καὶ ὅ τι διάκρισις ἐχρήσατο ἀδοκίμῳ φωνῇ. ὁμοίως δὲ καὶ τὸ συγκρίνειν καὶ συνέκρινεν ἡμάρτηται. χρὴ οὖν ἀντεξετάζειν καὶ παραβάλλειν λέγειν.

'Haec quoque labes temporibus Alexandri Magni nata est. Primus, quod constet, Aristoteles Rhet. 1. 9, 1368 a 21, *συγκρίνειν τι πρός τι* pro *ἀντιπαραβάλλειν* usurpavit: Polit. 4. 11, 1295 a 27, *πρὸς ἀρετὴν συγκρίνουσι τὴν ὑπὲρ τοὺς ἰδιώτας*: H. A. 9. 38, 622 b 20, *ὡς πρὸς τἆλλα συγκρίνεσθαι.* Hinc verbi usum accepit Theophrastus, C. Pl. 4. 2, cujus aequalem, Philemonem, *σύγκρισις* usurpasse contra Phrynichi mentem notat Berglerus. Nihil jam in scriptis Graecorum frequentius quam hoc vocabulum. . . . In librorum elogiis id fuit unum celebratissimum; sic olim legebatur Chrysippi, *Σύγκρισις τῶν τροπικῶν ἀξιωμάτων* Diog. La. 7. 194; Caeciliani Siculi *Σύγκρισις Δημοσθένους καὶ Αἰσχίνου,* Suïd.; Meleagri Gadareni *λεκίθου καὶ φακῆς*, Athen. 4. 157; Plutarchus ipse comparationem Graecorum et Romanorum imperatorum *σύγκρισιν* vocat, Vit. Flamin. c. 21.' Lobeck.

CCXLVI.

Κατ' ἐκεῖνο καιροῦ· καὶ ἐγὼ μὲν φυλάττεσθαι παραινῶ οὕτω χρῆσθαι. εἰ δ', ὅτι Θουκυδίδης εἴρηκε, θαρροίη τις χρῆσθαι, χρήσθω μὲν σὺν δὲ τῷ ἄρθρῳ. παρὰ μὲν γὰρ ἄλλῳ τῶν δοκίμων οὐχ εὗρον. ἡγοῦμαι δὲ καὶ Θουκυδίδην ἐν τῇ ἡ μετὰ τοῦ ἄρθρου εἰρηκέναι κατ' ἐκεῖνο τοῦ καιροῦ.

The phrase is not met with in Thucydides, but in the seventh book, not the eighth, are encountered the corresponding words, *κατὰ τοῦτο καιροῦ* (ch. 2). Lobeck quotes Thuc. 7. 69, *ἄλλα τε λέγων ὅσα ἐν τῷ τοιούτῳ ἤδη τοῦ καιροῦ ὄντες ἄνθρωποι εἴποιεν ἄν*: Demosth. 20. 13, *καιροῦ μὲν δὴ πρὸς τοῦτο πάρεστι Φιλίππῳ τὰ πράγματα*: Aristoph. Pax 1171, *τηνικαῦτα τοῦ θέρους*: Eq. 944, *οὐδείς πω χρόνου*: Plato, Rep. 9. 588 A, *ἐπειδὴ ἐνταῦθα λόγου γεγόναμεν*: Theaet. 177 C, *οὐκοῦν ἐνταῦθά που ἦμεν τοῦ λόγου.* Similarly in Rep. I. 328 E occurs *ἐπειδὴ ἐνταῦθα ἤδη εἶ τῆς ἡλικίας*, but in 329 B, *ὅσοι ἐνταῦθα ἦλθον ἡλικίας.* Of course no such rule as Phrynichus would fain lay down was known to Attic authors, the article being employed or omitted according to the whim of the writer or as the meaning required.

CCXLVII.

'Επέστησε καὶ ἐπιστάσεως ἄξιον τὸ πρᾶγμα, ἀντὶ τοῦ ἠπόρησε καὶ ἀπορίας ἄξιον τὸ πρᾶγμα. οὕτω χρωμένων τῶν Στωικῶν φιλοσόφων πολλάκις ἀκήκοα, εἰ δὲ καὶ ἀρχαίως ἢ δοκίμως, ἄξιον ἐπισκέψεως.

Two passages of Classical Greek will show how this meaning was acquired by *ἐπίστασις* and *ἐφιστάναι.* The one is the well-known speech of the Guard in the Antigone of Sophocles—

ἄναξ, ἐρῶ μὲν οὐχ ὅπως τάχους ὕπο
δύσπνους ἱκάνω, κοῦφον ἐξάρας πόδα.
πολλὰς γὰρ ἔσχον φροντίδων ἐπιστάσεις,
ὁδοῖς κυκλῶν ἐμαυτὸν εἰς ἀναστροφήν·
ψυχὴ γὰρ ηὔδα πολλά μοι μυθουμένη,
τάλας, τί χωρεῖς οἷ μολὼν δώσεις δίκην;
τλήμων, μενεῖς αὖ; κτε.

The third line precisely expresses the state of mind described at greater length in what follows—resolves suddenly adopted and as suddenly cast aside, the current of the man's thoughts receiving a check (ἐπίστασις), as a horse is quickly pulled up by its rider.

In the second passage Isocrates says that the benefits which Evagoras had conferred upon the state were severally so important that refusing to appraise them the mind adjudged the palm in succession to each, according as it was forced to consider it in particular: 203 A, εἴ τις ἔροιτό με τί νομίζω μέγιστον εἶναι τῶν Εὐαγόρᾳ πεπραγμένων . . . εἰς πολλὴν ἀπορίαν ἂν καταστταίην· ἀεὶ γάρ μοι δοκεῖ μέγιστον εἶναι καὶ θαυμαστότατον καθ' ὅτι ἂν αὐτῶν ἐπιστήσω τὴν διάνοιαν.

Good writers also use the second aorist as the intransitive equivalent of the active with διάνοιαν, as Dem. 245. 10, ἀφ' ἧς ἡμέρας ἐπὶ ταῦτα ἐπέστην: Isocr. 213 d, ἐπιστὰς ἐπὶ τὰ Θησέως ἔργα: Epicrates ap. Athen. 2. 59—

πρώτιστα μὲν οὖν πάντες ἀναυδεῖς
τότ' ἐπέστησαν καὶ κύψαντες
χρόνον οὐκ ὀλίγον διεφρόντιζον—

but the use of ἐφίστημι, ἐπιστήσω, ἐπέστησα, without νοῦν, γνώμην, or διάνοιαν, is unknown to Attic, and even with these accusatives it is rare. In Epicrates as cited the metaphor is still crisp, ἐπέστησαν meaning 'were pulled up sharp,' rather than 'were at a loss' (ἠπόρησαν). As it is, the Attic of the lines is not high, as a pure Attic writer would have employed διεφροντίζοντο rather than διεφρόντιζον.

CCXLVIII.

Εὐστάθεια, εὐσταθής, πόθεν καὶ ταῦτα εἰς τὴν τῶν Ἑλλήνων φωνὴν εἰσερρύη, ἀδοκιμώτατα ὄντα, φροντίδος ἄξιον. ἀλλὰ σὺ ἐμβρίθεια λέγε καὶ ἐμβριθής.

The defaulting terms are both of great antiquity, although unknown to Attic. Homer and Hippocrates use the adjective, the former applying it to buildings in the sense of 'firmly built,' the latter to diseases and to the weather, with the meaning 'equable.' Il. 18. 374, *ἑστάμεναι περὶ τοῖχον ἐϋσταθέος μεγάροιο*: Hippocr. Aph. 1247, Epid. 1. 938, *εὐσταθέες νοῦσοι*: Epid. 3. 1091, *θέρος οὐκ εὐσταθές*. In the form *εὐσταθίη* the substantive is met with in Hippocr. 24. 45, *πρὸς τοὺς ὄχλους τοὺς ἐπιγινομένους εὐσταθίης (μεμνῆσθαι) τῆς ἐν ἑαυτῷ*.

Epicurus re-introduced the words, and his example was followed by subsequent writers, Plutarch, Josephus, Appian, Arrian, Philo, and others. Cleomedes, Cycl. Theor. 2, p. 112, ed. Bak., expressly mentions *εὐσταθής* among the corrupt terms employed by Epicurus, *ἐπεὶ πρὸς τοῖς ἄλλοις καὶ τὰ κατὰ τὴν ἑρμηνείαν αὐτῷ* (sc. Ἐπικούρῳ) *διεφθορότα ἐστί, σαρκὸς εὐσταθῆ καταστήματα* (equable temperament of body) *λέγοντι κτε.* Phrynichus ought to have suggested *στάσιμος* rather than *ἐμβριθής* as the authorised equivalent, the latter word being properly applied only to men of solid and dignified behaviour.

CCXLIX.

Πάλι· οὕτω λέγουσιν οἱ νῦν ῥήτορες καὶ ποιηταί, δέον μετὰ τοῦ ν πάλιν, ὡς οἱ ἀρχαῖοι λέγουσιν.

This article is not found in the Laurentian manuscript, or in the edition of Callierges, and is not given by Phavorinus.

It is of no intrinsic importance, and if it really came from the hand of Phrynichus subsequent grammarians had the sense not to repeat it.

CCL.

Ὑπόστασις ἔργων· καὶ τοῦτο τῶν ἠμελημένων, ἐπὶ πολὺ δὲ παρὰ τοῖς ἐργολάβοις τῶν ἔργων. ζητοῦντες δὲ τί ἂν ἀντ᾽ αὐτῶν ἀρχαῖον θείημεν ὄνομα, οὐ ῥᾳδίως ἄχρι νῦν εὑρίσκομεν, εἰ δ᾽ εὑρεθείη, ἀναγεγράψεται.

The reading *ἀπόστασις* is due to Nuñez, whose manuscript had the first letter omitted for subsequent illumination. *Ὑπόστασις* is undoubtedly right, and must have meant the 'plan' of the work submitted to contractors.

CCLI.

Γεννήματα· πολλαχοῦ ἀκούω τὴν λέξιν τιθεμένην ἐπὶ τῶν καρπῶν, ἐγὼ δὲ οὐκ οἶδα ἀρχαίαν καὶ δόκιμον οὖσαν. χρὴ οὖν ἀντὶ τοῦ γεννήματα καρποὺς λέγειν ξηροὺς καὶ ὑγρούς.

This late use of *γεννήματα* supplies an excellent illustration of the tendency of debased Greek to adopt poetical modes of expression, and neglect simple terms, and such as commend themselves to common sense. Of the authors who used *γεννήματα* as a synonym of *καρποί*, Lobeck enumerates Diodorus, Polybius, Zosimus, Gregory Nazianzene, Apollonius Dyscolus, while the word is also found in the Septuagint, the New Testament, and the Geoponica.

CCLII.

Ἵνα ἄξωσιν οὐ χρὴ λέγειν, ἀλλ᾽ ἵνα ἀγάγωσιν.

CCLIII.

Ἐὰν ἄξῃς οὐδεὶς ἂν φαίη, ἀλλ' ἐὰν ἀγάγῃς.

The second article has been brought from a later place in the manuscripts.

The question has already been discussed in an earlier article, see p. 217.

CCLIV.

Συνήντετο καὶ ἀπήντετο ποιητικά. χρὴ οὖν ἀπήντησε λέγειν καὶ συνήντησε.

The middle *ἄντομαι* is common in the Homeric poems in the sense of 'meet,' and in Attic Tragedy governed the accusative of a person with the meaning 'approach as a suppliant,' but to pure Attic the deponent form is unknown. It is confined only to the present and imperfect tenses, but in *συναντήσωνται* (Il. 17. 134) Homer transferred to the aorist of the cognate *ἀντάω* the middle inflexions, which, if used at all, an Attic writer would have attached only to the future.

'*Ἄντομαι, to meet, entreat,* Poet. Emped. 14 (Stein); Soph. O. C. 250; Eur. Alc. 1098; Ar. Thesm. 977 (Chor.); Ap. Rh. 2. 1123; *-εσθαι*, Il. 15. 698; *-όμενος*, 11. 237; Pind. P. 2. 71; *imp. ἤντεο*, Callim. Epigr. 31; *ἤντετο*, Il. 22. 203.' '*συνάντομαι, pres.*, Od. 15. 538; Hes. Th. 877; Pind. Ol. 2. 96; and *imp. συνήντετο*, Il. 21. 34; Archil. 89; Eur. Ion 831; Theocr. 8. 1, but dual unaugm. *συναντέσθην*, Il. 7. 22.' Veitch.

CCLV.

Σίναπι οὐ λεκτέον, νᾶπυ δέ.

In Attic Greek there are no substantives ending in iota

as *ἄστυ* ends in upsilon, but foreign words were naturally represented in the Greek characters which corresponded to the original sounds, as *κίκι* in Plato, Tim. 60 A, and *νᾶπυ* frequently in Aristophanes. In the same way *πέπερι*, *κόμμι*, and *κιννάβαρι* must have been in common use. They were, however, not declined in Attic, although Eubulus seems once to have used *πεπέριδος* as the genitive of *πέπερι*—

> *κόκκον λαβοῦσα Κνίδιον ἢ τοῦ πεπέριδος*
> *τρίψασ' ὁμοῦ σμύρνῃ διάπαττε τὴν ὁδόν.*
>
> Athen. 2. 66 D.

Un-Attic and late writers generally attached the inflexions of vowel stems. Accordingly *νᾶπυ* was replaced not only by *σίναπι*, *σίνηπι*, or *σίναπυ*, but by forms like *σινάπεως*, *σίνηπυν*, *σινάπει*, and *σινάπυος*.

CCLVI.

Ὀνυχίζειν καὶ ἐξονυχίζειν· ταὐτὸ σημαίνει ἑκάτερα καὶ τίθεται ἐπὶ τοῦ ἀκριβολογεῖσθαι. τὸ δ' ἀπονυχίζειν τὸ τὰς αὐξήσεις τῶν ὀνύχων ἀφαιρεῖν σημαίνει. Ἐπειδὴ δ' ὁ πολὺς συρφετὸς λέγουσιν ὀνύχισόν με καὶ ὠνυχισάμην, διὰ τοῦτο σημαινόμεθα τὰ ὀνόματα καί φαμεν, ὅτι εἰ μὲν ἐπὶ τοῦ τοὺς ὄνυχας ἀφαιρεῖν τίθησί τις, χρήσαιτο ἂν τῷ ἀπονυχίζειν, εἰ δὲ ἐπὶ τοῦ ἀκριβολογεῖσθαι καὶ ἐξετάζειν ἀκριβῶς, τῷ ὀνυχίζειν χρήσαιτ' ἄν.

There is a sad irony in reading authoritative dicta upon Attic usage expressed in language so slovenly and incorrect. What would an Athenian have thought of *ὅτι* following *φαμέν*, or of *σημαινόμεθα* as used here? The credit of Phrynichus may be saved by a supposition of some credibility, namely, that few of the articles are now worded as they came from his pen. Thus, the Paris manuscript here presents the concise sentence: *Ὀνυχίζειν καὶ ἐξονυχίζειν ταὐτόν, τίθεται δὲ ἐπὶ τοῦ ἀκριβολογεῖσθαι· τὸ δὲ ἀπονυχίζειν, τὸ τὰς αὐξήσεις τῶν ὀνύχων ἀφαιρεῖν.* The distinction is also clearly drawn in App. Soph. 13. 13, and 55. 9, and is natural and convenient, although there is practically no authority for it beyond the statements of grammarians. Photius and Suïdas assert that Aristophanes employed *ὀνυχίζεται* in the sense of *ἀκριβολογεῖται*, and Hippocrates used *ἀπονυχίζεσθαι* as a term of the toilet, 618. 38, *τὰς χεῖρας χρὴ ἀπονυχίσασθαι.*

CCLVII.

Ὁ νῶτος ἀρσενικῶς λεγόμενος ἁμαρτάνεται. οὐδετέρως δὲ τὸ νῶτον καὶ τὰ νῶτα δοκίμως ἂν λέγοιτο.

The truth of this statement is established not only by the unimpeachable evidence of Attic Comedy but also by other kinds of verse—

κυνοκοπήσω σου τὸ νῶτον.
Ar. Eq. 289.

ἐς τὰς πλευρὰς πολλῇ στρατιᾷ κἀδενδροτόμησε τὸ νῶτον.
Pax 747.

ἔξω τείχους καὶ λωποδύτης παίει ῥοπάλῳ με τὸ νῶτον.
Av. 497.

ὀτιὴ τὸ νῶτον τὴν ῥάχιν τ' οἰκτείρομεν.
Eur. Cycl. 643.

τὰ δ' ἕσπερα νῶτ' ἐλαύνει.
El. 731.

ἀστεροειδέα νῶτα διφρεύουσ'.
Ar. Thesm. 1067 (parody of Eur. Andromeda).

It is, however, still possible to regard *τὸν νῶτον* in Xen. Eq. 3. 3 as the genuine reading, as the word was certainly often masculine in the Common dialect, and a writer like Xenophon may well have used that gender.

CCLVIII.

Βρέχειν ἐπὶ τοῦ ὕειν ἔν τινι κωμῳδίᾳ ἀρχαίᾳ προστιθεμένῃ Τηλεκλείδῃ τῷ κωμῳδῷ ἐστὶν οὕτως εἰρημένον. ὅπερ εἰ καὶ γνήσιον ἦν τὸ δρᾶμα, τὸ ἅπαξ εἰρῆσθαι ἐφυλαξάμεθ' ἄν. ὁπότε δὲ καὶ νόθον ἐστί, παντελῶς ἀποδοκιμαστέον τοὔνομα.

'Quamdiu Graecia in fastigio eloquentiae stetit, verbum *βρέχειν* a communi usu sejunctum poetisque aptum fuit, (unde est Pindaricum *βρέχε χρυσέαις νιφάδεσσι* pro *ὗσε χρυσόν*,) postea autem eviluit proletarii sermonis commerciis. Sic primum Polyb. 16. 12. 3, *οὔτε νίφεται οὔτε βρέχεται*: Arrian. Epictet. 1. 6. 26, *οὐ καταβρέχεσθε, ὅταν βρέχῃ*, et pluribus versionis Alexandrinae et Novi Testamenti locis. In eadem culpa sunt substantiva *βροχή pluvia* et *ἀβροχία* pro *ἀνομβρία*.' Lobeck.

CCLIX.

Λάμυρος· οἱ νῦν μὲν τὸν ἐπίχαριν τῷ ὀνόματι σημαίνουσιν, οἱ δ' ἀρχαῖοι τὸν ἰταμὸν καὶ ἀναιδῆ.

The adjective is very rare in pre-Macedonian Greek, occurring only in Xenophon and the Comic poet Epicrates. Xen. Symp. 8. 24, *εἰ δὲ λαμυρώτερον λέγω, μὴ θαυμάζετε· ὁ γὰρ οἶνος συνεπαίρει*: Epicr. ap. Athen. 6. 262 D—

> *γάστριν καλοῦσι καὶ λάμυρον ὃς ἂν φάγῃ*
> *ἡμῶν τι τούτων.*

In both places the Latin *improbus* would supply a correct rendering. In the Common dialect it occurs frequently, but can hardly be said to exist in literature as an exact synonym of *ἐπίχαρις*, although it approaches that signification in Plutarch, Mar. Vit. 38, *ὄνος προσβλέψας τῷ Μαρίῳ* λάμυρόν τι καὶ γεγηθός: and in Eunapius, 58. 3, τοῦ παιδίου τῷ περιττῶς καλῷ καὶ λαμύρῳ δηχθέντες καὶ ἀλόντες.

CCLX.

Ἐπίδεσμος καὶ ἐπίδεσμοι ἀρσενικῶς μὴ λέγε, οὐδετέρως δὲ τὸ ἐπίδεσμον καὶ τὰ ἐπίδεσμα, ὡς ἀρχαῖοι.

The word only occurs once in Attic Greek, namely, in Ar. Vesp. 1439, and then the gender is indeterminate—

εἰ ναὶ τὰν κόραν
τὴν μαρτυρίαν ταύτην ἐάσας ἐν τάχει
ἐπίδεσμον ἐπρίω, νοῦν ἂν εἶχες πλείονα.

There can be little question, however, that Phrynichus is wrong in claiming the neuter gender for the singular. Certainly *σύνδεσμος* and not *σύνδεσμον* was the true form of the compound with *σύν*, and there is no reason why the compound with *ἐπί* should differ in gender from the simple word and the other compounds. The distinction between the plural forms *δεσμοί* and *δεσμά* is worthy of mention. The masculine and neuter inflexions are not interchangeable, and though *δεσμοί* is occasionally used for *δεσμά*, no Attic writer ever employed *δεσμά* for *δεσμοί*. As Cobet well puts it (in Mnem. 7. 74), '*δεσμά* sunt *vincula* quibus quis constringitur, sed *δεσμός* est *in carcerem conjectio et captivitas in vinculis*. Sic Athenis *δεσμὸν καταγιγνώσκειν* dicuntur judices, quorum sententiis aliquis in custodiam publicam conjicitur, et *δεσμός* significat fere *τὸ δεδέσθαι*, ut *θάνατος* est *τὸ τεθνάναι*. Itaque ut de pluribus *θάνατοι* dici solet, sic *δεσμοί* a Xenophonte est positum de pluribus qui in carcerem a tyranno olim conjecti fuissent . . . . Utraque forma et caeteri Graeci omnes et Attici utuntur, sed non promiscue, ut inter se permutari possint, veluti in Platonis Rep. 2. 378 D, Ἥρας δὲ δεσμοὺς ὑπὸ υἱέος καὶ Ἡφαίστου ῥίψεις ὑπὸ πατρός, id est, τὸ δεδέσθαι Ἥραν ὑπὸ υἱέος καὶ ὑπὸ πατρὸς Ἥφαιστον ἐρρῖφθαι, ita dictum est ut δεσμά pro δεσμούς suppositum risum moveret.' Accordingly, it is very natural that δεσμά should be met with far more frequently than δεσμοί or δεσμούς.

Putting aside the genitive and dative cases as identical, in Euripides the masculine occurs in Bacch. 518, 634, the neuter in Andr. 578, 724, I. T. 1204, 1205, 1329, 1333, 1411, Rh. 567, Bacch. 447, 647, H. F. 1009, 1055, 1123, 1342. Similarly, Aeschylus has the masculine once, P. V. 525, the neuter thrice, P. V. 52, 513, 991, while Aristophanes employs only the neuter, Pax 1073, Thesm. 1013; cp. Pollux, 4. 181, εἴποις δ' ἂν καὶ δεσμὰ . . . ἐν Γηρυτάδῃ.

As remarked above, ἐπίδεσμος is not found in the plural, and κατάδεσμος is equally unfortunate; but σύνδεσμα is encountered in Eur. Med. 1193, Hipp. 199, Bacch. 696. Evidence such as this permits the scholar to claim masculine inflexions for the singular number of δεσμός and its compounds, and, with the reservation stated above, neuter endings for the plural.

Forms like δέσμα, δέσματος, δέσματα, ἐπιδέσματα, ἐπιδεσμίδος are allowedly un-Attic.

CCLXI.

Τὸ σκάτος· καὶ τοῦτο ἐπ' εὐθείας τιθέμενον ἀμαθές· γενικῆς γάρ ἐστι πτώσεως, τοῦ σκατός, ἡ δὲ εὐθεῖα τὸ σκώρ. ἁμαρτάνοντες δὲ οἱ πολλοὶ τὴν μὲν ὀρθὴν τὸ σκάτος ποιοῦσι, τὴν δὲ γενικὴν σὺν τῷ υ, τοῦ σκάτους.

No writer of the Classical age can have used σκάτους, and Athenaeus, 8. 362 C, or his transcribers, must be in error in fathering so manifestly late a form upon Sophron—

βαλλίζοντες τὸν θάλαμον σκάτους ἐνέπλησαν.

His mimes would have excited more laughter than he reckoned upon if they had contained debased inflexions of this kind.

CCLXII.

Φλοῦς· καὶ τοῦτο ἡμάρτηται· οἱ γὰρ Ἀθηναῖοι φλέως λέγουσι. καὶ τὰ ἀπὸ τούτου πλεκόμενα φλέϊνα καλεῖται.

The Attic forms were *φλέως, φλέων, φλέω, φλέῳ.* The genitive *φλέω* is read by most manuscripts in Ar. Ran. 243, and should replace *φλέως* in Pherecrates, ap. Athen. 6. 228 E—

ἐπὶ τηγάνοις καθίσανθ' ὑφάπτειν τοῦ φλέω.

The Scholiast on Ran. 243 quotes the accusative from the Amphiaraus—

πόθεν ἂν λάβοιμι βύσμα τῷ πρωκτῷ φλέων;

The monosyllabic *φλοῦς* entered the Common dialect from the Ionic, as is seen from Hdt. 3. 98. Pollux (10. 178), in discussing the adjective, records that *φλόϊνος* was not only used by Herodotus (3. 98), but also survived in the Tragic dialect: *Εὐριπίδου ἐν Αὐτολύκῳ Σατυρικῷ εἰπόντος*—

σχοινίνας γὰρ ἵπποισι φλοΐνας ἡνίας πλέκει·

ἡ δὲ ὕλη ὅθεν ἐπλέκετο φλοῦς μὲν κατὰ τοὺς Ἴωνας, φλέως δὲ κατὰ τοὺς Ἀττικούς.

CCLXIII.

Πεποίθησις οὐκ εἴρηται, ἀλλ' ἤτοι πιστεύειν ἢ πεποιθέναι.

Such formations as *πεποίθησις, ἀντιπεπόνθησις,* and *ἐγρήγορσις* have a certain resemblance to the Homeric *ὀπωπή,* but have really no kinship with it or with the Attic *ἀγωγή, ἐδωδή,* or *ἀνοκωχή.* Substantives in *-σις,* from the perfect stem, were not used by Attic writers.

CCLXIV.

Παλαστὴ τὸ μέτρον καὶ θηλυκῶς λέγεται καὶ ἄνευ τοῦ ι· ἀμαθεῖς δ' οἱ λέγοντες σὺν τῷ ι καὶ σὺν τῷ σ, παλαιστής, ὁμωνύμως τῷ ἀθλητῇ· ὁ μέντοι ἀθλητὴς παλαιστὴς ἀρσενικῶς καλεῖται.

Inscriptions establish the forms preferred by Phrynichus. 'Παλαστή, τριπάλαστος: has formas unice Atticas esse pro παλαιστή, τριπάλαιστος cett. . . . . confirmant tituli I 321, II 167.' (Herwerden, Test. Lap. p. 61.) Accordingly, the spelling with iota is wrong in the words of Cratinus and Philemon, quoted by Photius: Παλαστή· θηλυκῶς, Κρατῖνος Νόμοις—

> μεῖζον τὸ δέος[1] παλαιστής.

Φιλήμων Ἐφεδρίταις—

> σκιμπόδιον ἓν καὶ κώδιον καὶ ψιάθιον
> ἴσως παλαιστῆς.

'Alterius formae, quam Phrynichus praefert, vestigia ita obliterata sunt, ut Perizonius ad Aelian. V. H. 13. 3, neminem reperiret ei obsecundantem. Sed translucet adhuc in Homerico παλαστήσασα, ut nonnullis scribere placuit Od. 1. 252, et in scriptura Medicei Herodot. 1. 50, ἑξαπάλαστα, τριπάλαστα, καὶ παλαστιαῖα, quae et hic in ceteris codd. et 2. 149 in omnibus iota destituuntur.' Lobeck.

CCLXV.

Ἔγγιον ἐπὶ τοῦ ἐγγύτερον μὴ λέγε, ἀλλ' ἐγγύτερον· ἐπὶ δὲ τοῦ ἐν τῇ γῇ, οἷον ἔγγειον κτῆμα, εἴ τις χρῷτο, ἄριστα ἂν χρήσαιτο, ὡς καὶ Δημοσθένης ἔγγειον τόκον λέγει.

[1] Rhunkenius πέος non inepte corrigit. Fortasse pro τό est οὐ etiam scribendum.

The Attic comparative and superlative of ἐγγύς are ἐγγύτερος and ἐγγύτατος, even if an early writer like Antiphon once employs ἔγγιστα, 129. 14, τὸν δὲ μιαρὸν τοῖς ἔγγιστα τιμωρεῖσθαι ὑπολείπετε. Liddell and Scott err here, as they do frequently in such cases, by quoting ἔγγιστα from Demosthenes when the word is really from a spurious decree. Ionic writers used ἔγγιον and ἔγγιστα just as they used even ἀγχοτάτω and ἄγχιστα. Hippocrates has ἔγγιον in De Vict. Rat. 2. 356. 32, ἔγγιον τοῦ πυρὸς καὶ τῆς ἐργασίης εἰσί, and ἔγγιστα in id. 353. 32, τὰ ἔγγιστα ἑκατέρων, while Herodotus uses ἀγχοτάτω in 2. 24, and ἄγχιστα in 1. 134; 4. 81; 5. 79. The Ionic words linger in Tragic poetry and early Attic prose, ἀγχοτάτω being met with in Eur. Fr. 623 (chor.), and ἄγχιστα in Aesch. Supp. 1036, as also in Antiphon, 115. 25, τὰ δ' ἄγχιστα ἱερῶν κλοπῆς δυοῖν ταλάντοιν γεγραμμένος, 'and most recently having been indicted of sacrilege.'

The question as to the orthography of the compounds of γῆ is again referred to in App. Soph. 47. 14, κατάγειον· οὐχὶ κατάγαιον διὰ τῆς αι διφθόγγου. The verdict of Phrynichus is right. In Doric and Ionic, the forms in -αιος were regular, but in Attic the diphthong ει replaced αι. Thus, ἔγγειος in the original spelling in Plato, Rep. 491 D, 546 A, Tim. 90 A; Dem. 872. 12, 914. 10; Lys. Fr. 59; ἐπίγειος in Plato, Rep. 546 A (Axioch. 368 B); and κατάγειος in id. Rep. 514 A, 532 B, Protag. 320 E. On the other hand, Xenophon may have written κατάγαιος in An. 4. 5. 19, as Herodotus used that form in 2. 150, and manuscript authority is in favour of ἔγγαιος in Xen. Symp. 4. 31. The spelling with αι is no more out of place in Xenophon's style than in that of late authors like Aristotle, Plutarch, and Polybius, or in Ionic prose writers and Attic tragedians of his own century. It would be rash also to alter ἐγγαίου to ἐγγείου in Dem. 893. 15, ἄλλου δὲ συμβολαίου οὐκ ὄντος ἐμοὶ περὶ τούτου, οὔτε ναυτικοῦ οὔτε ἐγγαίου, as old pronunciation survives for generations in legal phrases.

There is, however, no excuse for μεσόγαια in Thuc. 6. 88. 4, when μεσόγεια has the support of the best codices in 1. 100, 120; 2. 102; 3. 95; 7. 80; and μεσόγεια should be retained in Plato, Phaed. 111 A, and μεσογείων in Legg. 909 A. In Xenophon, An. 6. 2. 19; 3. 10; 4. 5; Hell. 4. 7. 1; 7. 1. 8, the spelling must remain undetermined.

The form λεπτογέως is unquestioned in Thuc. 1. 2, but it stands alone in Attic Greek, as the substantive ἀνώγεων, so familiar to juvenile Grecians, is really a word of no authority. In the only passage in which it is found, An. 5. 4. 29, the true reading has been restored, from the corruption ἀνοκαίων, by Dindorf, who reads κάρυα δὲ ἐπὶ τῶν ἀνακείων ἦν πολλά. Akin to ἄναξ, ἀνάσσω, and ἀνακῶς, the word ἀνακεῖον is naturally used in the sense of 'store-cupboard;' ἀνακῶς ἔχειν τι having the meaning of 'keep securely;' Moeris, Attic. 43, ἀνακῶς ὡς Πλάτων ὁ κωμικός—

καὶ τὰς θύρας ἀνακῶς ἔχων

ἀντὶ τοῦ ἀσφαλῶς ἢ φυλακτικῶς. The question is discussed in detail by L. Dindorf in Steph. Thesaurus, I. ii. col. 1067, 1068, and the same facts are presented, with slight variations, by Zacher, 'De Nomin. Graecis in -αιος,' pp. 119–121.

CCLXVI.

Ξύστραν μὴ λέγε, ἀλλὰ στλεγγίδα.

This question must rest upon the authority of Phrynichus, as, in the sense of 'scraper,' neither word is encountered in Attic writers.

CCLXVII.

Μαμμόθρεπτον μὴ λέγε, τηθελαδοῦν δέ.

'Μαμμόθρεπτος tantum in Schol. Arist. Ran. 1021, Acharn. 49 et Poll. 3. 20, legere me memini. Quo accidit Atticos cum μάμμη de avia dicere subterfugerent, non potuisse facile μαμμόθρεπτον denominare eum, qui ab avia educatur. Τηθαλλαδοῦς quod ex comici versu citat Eustathius, p. 971. 40—

Ὀκνεῖς λαλεῖν; οὕτω σφόδρ' εἶ τηθαλλαδοῦς;

varie scribitur in glossis grammaticorum, quas Steph. collegit. Ego illam scripturam tenendam puto, quae et plurimis testimoniis et ipsius Phrynichi loco App. Soph. p. 65. 30, nititur.' Lobeck.

The article is probably not by Phrynichus at all, being absent from several authorities.

CCLXVIII.

Σίλφην· καὶ τοῦτο διεφθαρμένον, τίφην γὰρ οἱ παλαιοὶ λέγουσιν.

This article is not found in several other authorities, and in the first Laurentian manuscript only in the margin.

'Triplex reperitur hujus nominis scriptura; una usitatissima σίλφη Aristot. H. A. 9. 17. 601. [a]3, Aelian, H. A. 1. 37, Lucian, Gall. c. 31 (749); Dioscor. 1. 38. 77, tum Galenus, Aetius, Paullus; τίλφη Lucian, adv. Indoct. C. 17 (114); tertia τίφη Ar. Ach. 920, 925, Pollux 7. 20, quae et Phrynicho restituenda videtur[1].' Lobeck.

CCLXIX.

Ψύα· οἱ μὲν ἁπλῶς ἁμαρτάνοντες διὰ τοῦ υ, οἱ δὲ διπλῇ ἁμαρτάνοντες διὰ τοῦ οι, οἷον ψοία. ἔστι δὲ καὶ τὸ ὄνομα πολὺ κίβδηλον. νεφρὸν οὖν λέγε.

[1] The Laurentian has confirmed this conjecture.

Photius supports Phrynichus, *ψόας ἢ ψοίας ἢ ὅπῃ χρὴ καλεῖν παρ' οὐδενὶ ἀττικῶν εὗρον, οἱ δὲ παλαιοὶ γυμνασταὶ ἀλώπεκα προσαγορεύουσιν.* Hippocrates uses the word in de Artic. 810 C, and de Nat. Hum. 229. 31 (cp. 279. 41; 304. 14), and in H. A. 3. 3, 512.[b]21, Aristotle quotes it from Polybius. In Euphron, a poet of the New Comedy, it is found in company with *λοβός*—

> *λοβός τίς ἐστι καὶ ψύαι καλούμεναι.*
>
> Athen. 9. 399 B.

On the other hand, *νεφρός* has excellent authority, the singular being used by Aristophanes in Lys. 962, the dual in Ran. 475, 1280, and the plural by Plato in Tim. 91 A.

CCLXX.

Ὑλιστήρ· τρύγοιπον τοῦτο καλοῦσιν οἱ δοκίμως διαλεγόμενοι.

Χρέμυλος.

ὅμως δ' ἐπειδὴ καὶ τὸν οἶνον ἠξίους
πίνειν, συνεκποτέ' ἐστί σοι καὶ τὴν τρύγα.

Νεανίας.

ἀλλ' ἔστι κομιδῇ τρὺξ παλαιὰ καὶ σαπρά.

Χρέμυλος.

οὐκοῦν τρύγοιπος ταῦτα πάντ' ἰάσεται.

Aristophanes, Plut. 1084.

The word occurs again in Pax 535. *Ὑλιστήρ*, on the contrary, has but a poor record: Dioscor. 2. 123; Oribasius, p. 54. ed. Matth.; Geopon. 7. 37, 20. 46; Tzetz. Hist. 13. 420.

CCLXXI.

Πάπυρος· τοπάσειεν ἄν τις Αἰγύπτιον εἶναι τοὔνομα· πολὺ γὰρ κατ' Αἴγυπτον πλάζεται. ἡμεῖς δὲ βίβλον ἐροῦμεν.

The word found fault with is quoted only from late writers, Plutarch, Strabo, Dioscorides, Achilles Tatius, Nemesius, and the Geoponica.

CCLXXII.

Ἀφρόνιτρον· τελέως ἐξίτηλον καὶ ἀδόκιμον. χρὴ οὖν λίτρον λέγειν ἢ λίτρου ἀφρόν.

Lobeck proves that such compounds as *ἀφρόνιτρον, ἁλόσανθος, χάλκανθος, κυνοκαύματα, θηριοδήγματα, μητράδελφος* for *ἀφρὸς νίτρου, ἁλὸς ἄνθος*, etc., are very late. He quotes the expression from Hippocrates, 621. 46, and Dioscorides, 5. 131, and the word from Galen, vol. 2. p. 320 (1. p. 168 L), Julius Africanus, *Cesti*, 3. 290, and the Geoponica, 2. 28.

CCLXXIII.

Νίτρον· τοῦτο Αἰολεὺς μὲν ἂν εἴποι, ὥσπερ οὖν καὶ ἡ Σαπφὼ διὰ τοῦ ν, Ἀθηναῖος δὲ διὰ τοῦ λ, λίτρον.

Perhaps the spelling with nu may be permitted to Alexis—

τἀκπώματ' εἰς τὸ φανερὸν ἐκνενιτρωμένα·

Athen. 11. 502 F.

but the testimony of Moeris (p. 246), Photius, and Phrynichus is too authoritative to allow of any form but *λίτρον* in Attic writers of an earlier date.

CCLXXIV.

Ἐξάδελφος ἀποδιοπομπητέον, ἀνεψιὸς δὲ ῥητέον.

The late word supplants *ἀνεψιός* in the Septuagint and in Christian writers. Lobeck's note gives minute details.

CCLXXV.

Ὑπάλλαγμα ἀμαθῶς τινες ἀντὶ τοῦ ἐνέχυρον λέγουσι.

This use of *ὑπάλλαγμα* is only known to us from Grammarians, as Bekk. Anecd. 423. 12: *εἰώθασιν οἱ τῇ γυναικὶ γαμουμένῃ προῖκα διδόντες αἰτεῖν παρὰ τοῦ ἀνδρὸς ὥσπερ ἐνέχυρόν τι τῆς προικὸς ἀντάξιον ὃ νῦν ὑπάλλαγμα λέγεται.*

CCLXXVI.

Πανδοχεῖον οἱ διὰ τοῦ χ λέγοντες ἁμαρτάνουσι· διὰ γὰρ τοῦ κ χρὴ λέγειν πανδοκεῖον καὶ πανδοκεὺς καὶ πανδοκεύτρια.

There can be no question that Attic writers invariably spelt this and similar words with kappa, *πανδόκος, ἱεροδόκος, ξενοδόκος, δορυδόκη, δωροδοκῶ*, etc., but, even if the Oeconomicus was written by Xenophon, it is still possible that *ξενοδοχία* in 9. 10 came from the author's hand. *Δωροδόκος* and its derivatives retained the kappa even in late writers.

CCLXXVII.

Τὴν φθεῖρα λέγουσί τινες καὶ τὴν κόριν· σὺ δὲ ἀρσενικῶς τὸν κόριν λέγε καὶ τὸν φθεῖρα, ὡς οἱ ἀρχαῖοι.

'Feminina positione quemquam usum esse ad hunc usque diem tam inauditum fuit ut ne in lexicis quidem ejus generis mentio facta sit.' Lobeck, who discovered several instances of the missing gender in late authors.

CCLXXVIII.

Μόκλον μὴ λέγε διὰ τοῦ κ, ἀλλὰ διὰ τοῦ χ.

'Vocabulum hoc adeo omni auctoritate destitutum est, ut in summa copia et varietate Graecorum monimentorum, praeter illud Anacreonteum (Fr. 88) a grammaticis in lucem evocatum, ne unum quidem exemplum proferre possim, ἢ μὲν νέον ἠὲ παλαιόν.' Lobeck. The article has little textual authority.

CCLXXIX.

Κατὰ κοιλίας ποιεῖν οἱ γυμναστικοὶ λέγουσιν· ὁπόθεν δὲ λαβόντες φασίν, ἄδηλον. οἱ γὰρ παλαιοὶ ὑπάγειν τὴν γαστέρα λέγουσιν.

Ὑπάγειν is used in medical writers both transitively with *γαστέρα* or *κοιλίαν* and intransitively in a similar sense, as *ὑπάγειν τὴν κοιλίην* in Aretaeus, Cur. M. Ac. I. 10, and *κοιλία ὑπάγουσα* in Galen, Comm. 4. ad Hippocr. De Rat. Vict. in Morb. Ac. p. 396. 27. The expression reprehended does not occur at all in written Greek.

CCLXXX.

Ἐφιόρκους· τοῦτο διὰ τοῦ π λέγε.

'Unicum simile novi Hesychii: *Ἐφιορκήσαντες, ψευσάμενοι*, fortasse ex Doricis monimentis ductum.' Lobeck.

CCLXXXI.

Ψίεθος, μιερός, ὕελος, ἁμαρτάνουσιν οἱ δια τοῦ ε λέγοντες. ἀδόκιμον γάρ. καὶ Κορίννα—

τὸν ὑάλινον παῖδα θήσεις.

This article is not found in any of the manuscripts, in the editions of Callierges or Vascosan, or in Phavorinus; but the first Laurentian manuscript and the first editor include *ὕελος* in the next article. Much of this part of the book is undeniably spurious.

CCLXXXII.

Ὁ πύελος διὰ τοῦ ε, καὶ μυελὸς ῥητέον.

'*Ψίεθος*, quod etiam Moeris p. 418 Atticis abjudicat, apud Antigonum Carum et fortasse apud plures recentiorum occurrit; namque ad hanc partem non satis attentus fui; neque *μιερός* nunc dicere possum *ποῦ κεῖται*. *Ὕαλος*, non *ὕελος*, dicendum esse, uno ore tradunt Phrynichus App. Soph. p. 68, Aelius Dionysius, Photius, alii. Neque Theophrasti auctoritas tanta videri debet ut grammaticorum sententiae, Aristophanis et Platonis testimonio communitae, idcirco abrogemus. . . . Ad postrema quod attinet, *πύαλος* Hemsterhusius ex Hesychio, *μεμυαλωμένος* Hoeschelius ex Ps. 65, idem *τὸ μύελον* e Greg. Naz. Apol. p. 26, profert.' Lobeck.

CCLXXXIII.

Οἱ χόλικες ἀμαθές· οἱ γὰρ δόκιμοι θηλυκῶς αἱ χόλικες φασίν.

Moeris, 404, *χολάδας οἱ πρῶτοι Ἀττικοί, χόλικας οἱ μέσοι θηλυκῶς, χόλικας ἑφθάς, τοὺς χόλικας, ἀρσενικῶς Ἕλληνες*: Phrynichus, App. Soph. 72. 5, *χόλικες οἱ πολλοὶ ἀρσενικῶς, οἱ δ' ἀρχαῖοι θηλυκῶς*. The quotation in Moeris comes from Aristophanes, Pax 717—

ὅσας δὲ κατέδει χόλικας ἑφθὰς καὶ κρέα.

Ammonius, p. 142, wrongly tries to distinguish between *χολάδες* and *χόλικες*. *χολάδες καὶ χόλικες διαφέρει· χολάδες μὲν γὰρ τὰ ἔντερα*—

χύντο χαμαὶ χολάδες· Il. 4. 526.

χόλικες δὲ αἱ τῶν βοῶν κοιλίαι, Ἀριστοφάνης Βαβυλωνίοις—

ἢ βοιδαρίων τις ἀπέκτεινε ζεῦγος χολίκων ἐπιθυμῶν.

On the other hand, the statement of Moeris is supported by the lexicography of the words. Χολάδες, Hom. Il. 4. 526, 21. 181, Hymn. Merc. 123, and with two lambdas, Pherecrates, ap. Bachmann, Anecd. 1. 418; χόλικες αἱ, Ar. Ran. 576, Babyl. cited, Pax 717; Fr. ap. Poll. 6. 56; Pherecrates, ap. Athen. 6. 268 E; Eubulus, ap. Athen. 7. 330 C; Anaxandrides, ap. Athen. 4. 131.

CCLXXXIV.

Χονδροκώνειον· ἀμαθὲς τὸ σύνθετον τοῦτο καὶ ἀλλόκοτον.

This article is not in the manuscripts or the edition of Callierges. If it is really genuine, then χονδροκώνειον, the reading of Nuñez, ought to be retained, whatever its meaning may be. Suppose it to signify *the cone-shaped vessel* through which the groats are shot into the mill, then such a compound of χόνδρος and κῶνος would merit the remark of Phrynichus. Χονδροκοπεῖον, on the contrary, the conjecture of Pauw, is a perfectly legitimate form mentioned by Pollux 3. 78, and supported by ἀργυροκοπεῖον, quoted by the same writer (7. 103) from Phrynichus (Com.), by Harpocration from Antiphon, and from Andocides by the Schol. ap. Arist. Vesp. 1007.

CCLXXXV.

Ἐκτενῶς μή, ἀλλ' ἀντ' αὐτοῦ δαψιλῶς λέγε.

Adjective, adverb, and substantive, ἐκτενής, ἐκτενῶς, and ἐκτένεια all occur with frequency in late writers, but are unknown in Attic Greek. Even in Aeschylus—

καί μου τὰ μὲν πραχθέντα πρὸς τοὺς ἐκτενεῖς
φίλους πικρῶς ἤκουσαν αὐτανεψίους,

Suppl. 983.

the word has been justly called in question, and by Hermann altered to ἐγγενεῖς. It is true that Phrynichus may be said to find fault only with the signification 'profuse,' but the evidence is also against its being Attic in that of 'earnest.' Of the Comic poets Machon first used the term.—

λήθη θ' ὑπ' αὐτῆς ἐκτενῶς ἀγαπώμενος.

Athen. 13. 579 E.

CCLXXXVI.

Πρώτως Ἀριστοτέλης καὶ Χρύσιππος λέγει. ἔστι δὲ διεφθαρμένον πάνυ τοὔνομα· λέγε οὖν πρῶτον.

Phrynichus is right in absolutely denying these forms to Attic. Moeris, p. 298, and Thom., p. 764, allow them when they denote quality, not number. As a matter of fact, they do not exist at all before Aristotle's time. In Ar. Lys. 316 there is a variant πρώτως, but evidently a correction to restore the metre, which halts in the best manuscripts, the Ravenna presenting πρῶτον, others πρῶτος. Enger has replaced the original πρώτιστ'—

τὴν λαμπάδ' ἡμμένην ὅπως πρώτιστ' ἐμοὶ προσοίσεις.

CCLXXXVII.

Παραθήκην Ἱππίαν καὶ Ἴωνα τινὰ συγγραφέα φασὶν εἰρηκέναι, ἡμεῖς δὲ τοῦτο παρακαταθήκην ἐροῦμεν, ὡς Πλάτων καὶ Θουκυδίδης καὶ Δημοσθένης.

The Ἴων τις συγγραφεύς is evidently Herodotus, who has

the word in 6. 73, *παραθήκην αὐτοὺς παρατίθενται ἐς τοὺς ἐχθίστους*, and 9. 45, *παραθήκην ὑμῖν ἔπεα τάδε τίθεμαι*. The authority for *παρακαταθήκη* and *παρακατατίθεμαι*, however, is so overwhelming—Plato, Thucydides, Lysias, Aeschines, Isocrates, and others—that the note of Photius, *Παραθήκην· Πλάτων Συμμαχίᾳ*, even if credited, may be disregarded. Certainly, the use of *παρατίθεμαι* for *παρακατατίθεμαι* in Xen. Rep. Ath. 2. 16, *τὴν οὐσίαν ταῖς νήσοις παρατίθενται*, is to be considered an anticipation of the Common dialect. It is in place in Herodotus, as 6. 86, *τοῦ παραθεμένου τὰ χρήματα οἱ παῖδες*, and in Polybius, as 33. 12. 3, *φάσκοντες οὐδενὶ προήσεσθαι τὰ χρήματα . . . πλὴν αὐτῷ τῷ παραθεμένῳ*, but not in an Attic writer.

CCLXXXVIII.

Ἀπαράβατον παραιτοῦ λέγειν, ἀλλ' ἀπαραίτητον.

In this case, as in so many others, the diction of late prose meets that of Attic poetry—Aeschylus has *παράβατος* in the sense of *παραίτητος* in a lyric passage of the Supplices—

> *Διὸς οὐ παρβατός ἐστιν μεγάλα φρὴν ἀπέραντος*,

but the word is as alien to prose as *φρήν* or *ἀπέραντος*, its companions in the poet.

CCLXXXIX.

Λυχνίαν· ἀντὶ τούτου λυχνίον λέγε, ὡς ἡ κωμῳδία.

> *Τονδὶ λέγω, σὺ δ' οὐ συνιεῖς· κότταβος*
> *τὸ λυχνίον ἐστί· πρόσεχε τὸν νοῦν· ᾠὰ μέν*
>
> Antiphanes, ap. Ath. 15. 666 F.

It is a shortened form of *λυχνεῖον*, already considered on p. 132 supra. "Ἡ *λυχνία* praeter scriptores sacros, Philonem

p. 425 B, et Josephum, etiam Lucianus, Asin. C. 40 (608), Galenus de Comp. Med. p. locc. I. 2, 326. D, Artemidorus 1. 74. 103, Hero *Spiritualia*, p. 212.' Lobeck.

CCXC.

Ἀγωγόν· τοῦτο τοὔνομα τάττουσιν οἱ παλαιοὶ ἐπὶ τοῦ τινὰ ὁδὸν ἡγουμένου. οὕτω καὶ Θουκυδίδης κέχρηται. νῦν δὲ οἱ περὶ τὰ δικαστήρια ῥήτορες ἀγωγοὺς καλοῦσι τοὺς ὀχετοὺς τῶν ὑδάτων.

The late meaning is cited from Herodian, 7. 12, *ἐκκόψαι πάντας τοὺς εἰσρέοντας εἰς τὸ στρατόπεδον ἀγωγοὺς ὕδατος*: Geopon. 2. 7, *ξυλίνοις δὲ ἀγωγοῖς καθαρὸν τὸ ὕδωρ εἰς τὰ φρέατα συνάγειν*: Galen, de Us. Part. 16. 1. 673 A; Procopius, and others.

CCXCI.

Κρύβεται φεῦγε διὰ τοῦ β λέγειν καὶ κρύβεσθαι, ἀλλὰ διὰ πτ κρύπτεται καὶ κρύπτεσθαι φάθι.

CCXCII.

Καρῆναι καὶ ἐκάρην φασί, καὶ εἶναι τούτου πρὸς τὸ κείρασθαι διαφοράν. Τὸ μὲν γὰρ ἐπὶ προβάτων τιθέασι, κείρασθαι δὲ ἐπὶ ἀνθρώπων.

The distinction is just. Verbs which have a reference to the care or embellishment of the person have naturally what is called the direct middle, that is, a voice purely reflexive. In other cases the reflexive meaning is conveyed by the active voice and a reflexive pronoun.

When Veitch says, 'Neither of the aorists passive seem

to be of Attic usage,' he can only mean that by accident neither occurs in our texts. If occasion had demanded, *ἐκάρην, καρῆναι* would certainly have been used as a matter of course.

Lobeck quotes violations of the Attic rule, Plutarch, V. Lys. 1, *τῶν Ἀργείων ἐπὶ πένθει καρέντων*: Julian Antic. Anth. Pal. 11. 369—

τῷ σε χρὴ δρεπάνοισι καὶ οὐ ψαλίδεσσι καρῆναι.

CCXCIII.

Κοχλιάριον· τοῦτο λίστρον Ἀριστοφάνης ὁ κωμῳδοποιὸς λέγει, καὶ σὺ δὲ οὕτω λέγε

Though this article is absent from the extant manuscripts and the edition of Callierges, and is not in Phavorinus, yet it is possibly by Phrynichus, as in App. Soph. p. 51, the same caution appears again, *Λιστρίον· τὸ ὑπὸ τῶν πολλῶν καλούμενον κοχλιάριον.* The late word is used by Galen, de Medic. Simpl. 11. 1, 8, 23, de Pond. et Mens. vol. 13, p. 976 seqq., by Dioscorides, and in the Geoponica, 7. 13, p. 491.

CCXCIV.

Δεξαμενή φασὶ Πλάτωνα ἐπὶ τῆς κολυμβήθρας εἰρηκέναι. ἐγὼ δὲ οὔ φημι· ἀλλὰ δεξαμένη τῷ τόνῳ εἶπεν ὡς ποιουμένη. χρὴ οὖν καὶ ἡμᾶς κολυμβήθρα λέγειν.

The Grammarian is here in error. Not only did Herodotus employ the despised synonym of *κολυμβήθρα* in 3. 9, and 6. 119, but Plato also in Crit. 117 A, *ταῖς δὲ δὴ κρήναις, τῇ τοῦ ψυχροῦ καὶ τῇ τοῦ θερμοῦ νάματος, πλῆθος μὲν ἄφθονον ἐχούσαις, ἡδονῇ δὲ καὶ ἀρετῇ τῶν ὑδάτων πρὸς ἑκατέρου τὴν χρῆσιν θαυμαστοῦ πεφυκότος, ἐχρῶντο περιστήσαντες οἰκοδομήσεις καὶ δένδρων φυτεύσεις πρεπούσας ὕδασι, δεξαμένας τε αὖ τὰς μὲν ὑπαιθρίους, τὰς δὲ χειμερινὰς τοῖς θερμοῖς λουτροῖς ὑποστέγους περιτιθέντες, χωρὶς μὲν βασιλικάς, χωρὶς δὲ ἰδιωτικάς, ἔτι δὲ γυναιξὶν ἄλλας καὶ ἑτέρας ἵπποις καὶ τοῖς ἄλλοις ὑποζυγίοις, τὸ πρόσφορον τῆς κοσμήσεως ἑκάστοις ἀπονέμοντες.*

CCXCV.

Χθιζὸν ἀποσοβητέον ὅτι ποιητικόν, ἀντὶ δὲ τοῦ χθιζὸν ἐροῦμεν χθεσινόν, πρὸς τὸ πολιτικὸν ἀποτορνεύοντες τὸν λόγον, ὡς καὶ Ἀριστοφάνης.

There is no means of ascertaining which form Phrynichus preferred, as the apparatus criticus will show. The adjective occurs twice in Aristophanes (Ran. 987 and Vesp. 282), but in metres too irregular to control the form, some editors preferring the tribrach, others the dactyl, although in both places the manuscripts exhibit only *χθεσινόν*. Neither form is found elsewhere in Attic Greek, although the repudiated *χθιζός* is very common in Homer, and is found in Herodotus. The reason why the adjective appears so seldom in Attic is that the premier dialect preferred instead to use the adverb with the article. Here a difficult question suggests itself: Which was the recognised form, the monosyllabic *χθές*, or the disyllabic *ἐχθές*? Grammarians contradict each other, and the inquirer is thrown back upon his trusty guides, Attic Comedy and common sense. The verdict of metre is conclusive. The monosyllable is encountered in the following lines—

χθὲς οὖν Κλεὼν ὁ κηδεμὼν ἡμῖν ἐφεῖτ' ἐν ὥρᾳ,
Vesp. 242.

κἀμέ γ' ἡ πόρνη χθὲς εἰσελθόντα τῆς μεσημβρίας,
Id. 500.

ταῦτ' ἄρα ταῦτα Κλεώνυμον αὗται τὸν ῥίψασπιν χθὲς ἰδοῦσαι,
Nub. 353.

ἐς Ὀρσιλόχου χθὲς τῶν τριχῶν κατέσπασα,
Lys. 725.

χθές τε καὶ πρῴην κοπεῖσι τῷ κακίστῳ κόμματι,
Ran. 725.

οὐκ ᾔδησθά με
φράσαντά σοι χθές;
Eccl. 552.

ὦ Βλεψίδημ' ἄμεινον ἢ χθὲς πράττομεν,
Plut. 344.

ποῖον χρόνου ταλάνταθ', ὃς παρ' ἐμοὶ χθὲς ἦν.
Id. 1046.

Much more numerous are the examples of ἐχθές—

ἐχθὲς δέ γ' ἡμῖν δεῖπνον οὐκ ἦν ἑσπέρας,
Nub. 175.

ἐχθὲς δὲ μετὰ ταῦτ' ἐκφθαρεὶς οὐκ οἶδ' ὅποι,
Pax 72.

φροῦδοι γὰρ ἐχθές εἰσιν ἐξῳκισμένοι,
Id. 197.

οὐκ ἔστιν ἡμῖν· ἐχθὲς εἰσῳκίσμεθα,
Id. 260.

A. ἀλλ' οὐκ ἐκύεις σύ γ' ἐχθές; B. ἀλλὰ τήμερον,
Lys. 745.

στραγγουριῶ γάρ· ἐχθὲς ἔφαγον κάρδαμα,
Thesm. 616.

ἐχθὲς δ' ἔχοντ' εἶδόν σ' ἐγὼ τριβώνιον,
Plut. 882.

ἐχθὲς μετὰ ταῦτ' ἔπινον ἡμέραν τρίτην,
Antiphanes, Zonar. Lex. 2. 1745.

ἐχθὲς ὑπέπινες, εἶτα νυνὶ κραιπαλᾷς,
Alexis, Athen. 2. 34 D.

ἐχθὲς Μελανώπῳ πολυτελοῦς Αἰγυπτίου,
Anaxandrides, Athen. 12. 553 D.

ταπιδόσιμ' ἡμῖν ἐστὶν ἧς ἐχθὲς πιεῖν,
Crobylus, Athen. 8. 365 A.

δύ' ἐχθὲς ὤμοὺς εἰς τὸ πῦρ ἀποσβέσας,
Euphron, Athen. 9. 379 E.

ἐχθὲς κεκινδύνευκας· οὐδεὶς εἶχέ σοι,
Id. Athen. 9. 377 D.

The word is found only once in Tragedy—

οὐ γάρ τι νῦν γε κἀχθὲς ἀλλ' ἀεί ποτε
ζῇ ταῦτα. Soph. Ant. 456.

'Εχθές, therefore, was the regular Attic form, the old Ionic *χθές* being naturally retained in phrases like *χθές τε καὶ πρῴην*, and occasionally, as in Nub. 353, and Vesp. 242, to help the metre. After a word ending in a vowel *ἐχθές* yielded to its older rival even in prose, as *ἐκεῖνος* also seems sometimes to have done. Editors may please themselves as to using the apostrophe or not, *πρῴην τε καὶ 'χθές*, or *πρῴην τε καὶ χθές*, but to a seeing eye the principal fact is placed beyond dispute by the evidence given.

CCXCVI.

Βαθμὸς ἰακὸν διὰ τοῦ θ, διὰ τοῦ σ ἀττικόν, βασμός.

So Moeris 97, *βασμὸς 'Αττικῶς, βαθμὸς 'Ελληνικῶς.*

CCXCVII.

Πυρία· τοῦτο τάττουσιν οἱ πολλοὶ ἐπὶ τῆς ἐν τῷ βαλανείῳ πυέλου, καὶ ἔχει μὲν το ἔτυμον ἀπὸ τοῦ πυροῦσθαι, οὐ μὴν τὸ ἀκριβὲς καὶ δόκιμον. πυέλους γὰρ οἱ ἀρχαῖοι καλοῦσιν, ἀλλ' οὐ πυρίας.

The rejected word does not appear at all in Attic Greek. It is, however, classical, though not in the sense of *πύελος*. Herodotus has it of a vapour-bath, 4. 75, *οἱ Σκύθαι τῆς καννάβιος τὸ σπέρμα ἐπεὰν λάβωσι, ὑποδύνουσι ὑπὸ τοὺς πίλους, καὶ ἔπειτα ἐπιβάλλουσι τὸ σπέρμα ἐπὶ τοὺς διαφανέας λίθους τῷ πυρί· τὸ δὲ θυμιᾶται ἐπιβαλλόμενον καὶ ἀτμίδα παρέχεται τοσαύτην ὥστε 'Ελληνικὴ οὐδεμία ἂν μιν πυρίη ἀποκρατήσειε· οἱ δὲ Σκύθαι ἀγάμενοι τῇ πυρίῃ ὠρύονται.*

It is used for *πύελος* by Moschion as quoted by Athenaeus in 5. 207 F, *ἦν δὲ καὶ βαλανεῖον τρίκλινον, πυρίας χαλκᾶς ἔχον τρεῖς, καὶ λουτῆρα, πέντε μετρητὰς δεχόμενον*: and by Nicarchus in Anth. Pal. 11. 243, *οἱ βαλανεῖς γὰρ εἰς τότε τάσσονται τὴν πυρίαν καθελεῖν*. Both Moschion and Nicarchus probably wrote in the same century as Phrynichus.

CCXCVIII.

Ἵπτασθαι παραιτητέον, εἰ καὶ ἅπαξ που εἴη κείμενον ἢ δίς. πέτεσθαι δὲ λέγε.

The Attic verb corresponding to the English 'fly' derives its tenses from one or other of the three stems, *ἱπτα*, *πετ*, and *ποτα*. The reduplicated *ἱπτα*, which belongs to the same group as *ἱστα*, *τιθε*, and *ἱε*, supplied the future and its moods—

ἵπτημι	ἵστημι	τίθημι	ἵημι
πτήσομαι[1]	στήσω	θήσω	ἥσω,

From *πετ* came the present *πέτομαι*, the imperfect *ἐπετόμην*, and the syncopated aorist *ἐπτόμην*, while *ποτα* furnished the perfect *πεπότημαι*. No Attic writer uses *ἵπτημι* or *ἵπταμαι*, *ἔπτην* or *ἐπτάμην*, *ποτῶμαι*, *ἐποτώμην*, or *ἐποτήθην*, but the future *πετήσομαι* is found by the side of *πτήσομαι*. In Homer and the Tragic poets are encountered forms from *ἔπτην* and *ἐπτάμην*, as *πταίην*, *πτῆναι*, *πτάς*, *πτάσθαι*, *πτάμενος*, and from *ποτῶμαι* forms like *ποτᾶται* and *ἐποτήθην*, but in Attic prose and Comedy they were unknown. In the Common dialect any form from any of the three stems passed muster, and even new tenses were manufactured which could be referred neither to *ἱπτα*, *πετ*, or *ποτα*. Such were *ἐπετάσθην* and *πέπταμαι*, which in Attic belong not

[1] For the middle, see infra, p. 399.

to πέτομαι, but to πετάννυμι. By others ποτῶμαι was lengthened to πωτῶμαι, and used as a regular verb.

It is therefore not surprising if Attic texts have suffered at the hands of transcribers. The principal risk naturally fell to the aorist ἐπτόμην, so apt to be confounded with the un-Attic ἐπτάμην. Thus in Ar. Av. 788—

ἐκπτόμενος ἂν οὗτος ἠρίστησεν ἐλθὼν οἴκαδε
κᾆτ' ἂν ἐμπλησθεὶς ἐφ' ἡμᾶς αὖθις αὖ κατέπτετο—

the Ravenna preserves the true forms, but other manuscripts have inconsistently ἐκπτόμενος and κατέπτατο, or still worse, ἐκπετάμενος and κατέπτετο. The Ravenna is equally invaluable in Av. 48, where it confirms the conjectures of Dawes and Brunck—

εἴ που τοιαύτην εἶδε πόλιν ᾗ 'πέπτετο—

against the vulgate—

εἴ που τοιαύτην οἶδε πόλιν ᾗ πέπταται.

In Av. 90 ἀπέπτετο, 278 εἰσέπτετο, 789, 792 κατέπτετο, 791, 795 ἀνέπτετο, 1173 εἰσέπτετο, the Ravenna retains the original spelling when most other manuscripts replace omicron by alpha. But in 1206 ἀναπτάμενος, and 1613 προσπτάμενος, even the Ravenna slips, although it supports the true form of the participle in 1384 ἀναπτόμενος, and in 1624 καταπτόμενος.

As in the case of ἠρόμην, the subjunctive and optative, ἔρωμαι and ἐροίμην, might as far as form goes belong to the present tense; so the subjunctive πτῶμαι may be a mood of either ἐπτάμην or ἐπτόμην, but in Attic it certainly belongs to the latter.

The longer form of the future is met with in two lines of Aristophanes—

ὅπως πετήσει μ' εὐθὺ τοῦ Διὸς λαβών,
Pax 77.

οὐκ ἀποπετήσει θᾶττον εἰς 'Ελύμνιον,
Id. 1126.

but the shorter has good authority—

> οἴμοι κακοδαίμων, στροῦθος ἀνὴρ γίγνεται·
> ἐκπτήσεται, ποῦ, ποῦ 'στί μοι τὸ δίκτυον;
> Vesp. 208.

The perfect *πεπότημαι* rests upon prose instances, and upon Aristophanes—

> ταῦτ' ἄρ' ἀκούσασ' αὐτῶν τὸ φθέγμ' ἡ ψυχή μου πεπότηται·
> Nub. 319.

> ἀνεπτερῶσθαι καὶ πεποτῆσθαι τὰς φρένας.
> Av. 1445.

This verb admirably illustrates the refined eclecticism of the Attic dialect, and the record of its corruption tells only too plainly how the intellectual refinement from which it sprang decayed and passed away.

CCXCIX.

Νήστης βάρβαρον, τὸ δ' ἀρχαῖον νῆστις διὰ τοῦ ι.

The form may well have been used by the Parody-writer Matron, Athen. 4. 134 F—

> νήστης, ἀλλοτρίων εὖ εἰδὼς δειπνοσυνάων—

but there is only the questionable authority of Grammarians to support its occurrence in Simonides. Bekk. Anecd. 1402.

It is cited from late writers, as Apollon. Hist. Mir. c. 51, *ὅτε νήστης ὑπῆρχεν.*

CCC.

Κατὰ χειρῶν δεινῶς ἀνελλήνιστον, καὶ τὸ ἐπὶ χειρῶν δέ· μεστὴ γὰρ ἡ κωμῳδία τοῦ κατὰ χειρός.

The edition of Nuñez, and the margin of the first

Laurentian manuscript, are the only warrants for this article, but it is correct as a statement of usage. Athenaeus 9. 408 E, *ἡ πλείων δὲ χρῆσις κατὰ χειρὸς ὕδωρ εἴωθε λέγειν, ὡς Εὔπολις ἐν Χρυσῷ Γένει, καὶ Ἀμειψίας Σφενδόνῃ, Ἀλκαῖός τε ἐν Ἱερῷ Γάμῳ. Πλεῖστον δ' ἐστὶ τοῦτο. Φιλύλλιος δὲ ἐν Αὔγῃ κατὰ χειρῶν εἴρηκεν οὕτως—*

καὶ δὴ δεδειπνήκασιν αἱ γυναῖκες ἀλλ' ἀφαιρεῖν
ὥρα 'στὶν ἤδη τὰς τραπέζας, εἶτα παρακορῆσαι,
ἔπειτα κατὰ χειρῶν ἑκάστῃ καὶ μύρον τι δοῦναι.

Μένανδρος Ὑδρίᾳ—

οἱ δὲ κατὰ χειρῶν λαβόντες, περιμένουσι φίλτατοι.

CCCI.

Φάγομαι βάρβαρον. λέγε οὖν ἔδομαι καὶ κατέδομαι. τοῦτο γὰρ Ἀττικόν.

CCCII.

Βρώσομαι, κακῶς ὁ Φαβωρῖνος. οἱ γὰρ Ἀττικοὶ ἀντ' αὐτοῦ ἔδομαι χρῶνται καὶ κατέδομαι.

The former of these articles has little better footing than 300, and in the edition of Nuñez the latter, which comes from a later position in the manuscripts, is augmented by the sentence, *ἄκριτον οὖν καὶ ἀπόβλητον τῶν ἀττικῶν φωνῶν τὸ βρώσομαι ῥῆμα.*

The marvellous rule by which middle inflexions were necessarily attached to the future of a verb like *ἐσθίω* was mentioned on article 45, and I shall here carefully and fully redeem the promise there made.

An important instance of a very common manuscript error is to be found in the lines of Aristophanes in which

Trugaeus asks the son of Cleonymus to sing him a stave that will not suggest war and arms—

ᾆσον πρὶν εἰσιέναι τι· σὺ γὰρ εὖ οἶδ' ὅτι
οὐ πράγματ' ᾄσει· σώφρονος γὰρ εἶ πατρός.

All the manuscripts read ᾄσεις for ᾄσει, but Dawes was right beyond question in replacing the active by the middle future. Not only in Attic, but throughout Greek literature till a late period, the middle ᾄσομαι was the only future of the verb ᾄδω. But in debased Greek the active ᾄσω was the more usual form[1], and it is no wonder that a copyist should insert its second person singular in Aristophanes when it had the same metrical value as the classical ᾄσει, and was suggested by the fact of the following word beginning with a sigma. It is true that ᾄσουσιν is actually read in Plato, Legg. 666 D, ποίαν δὲ ᾄσουσιν οἱ ἄνδρες φωνήν; but the expression is unintelligible till we restore ἥσουσιν, the word which Plato wrote, and which he was fond of using in this connexion: Legg. 890 D, πᾶσαν φωνὴν ἱέντα: Legg. 934 D, πολλὴν φωνὴν ἱέντες: Theaet. 194 A, Σειρῆνα φωνὴν μίαν ἱεῖσαν: Legg. 812 D, ἄλλα μέλη τῶν χορδῶν ἱεισῶν: Phil. 51 D, τὰς ἕν τι καθαρὸν ἱείσας μέλος: Phaedr. 259 D, αἳ ἵασι καλλίστην φωνήν.

The same lesson is taught by the consideration of the future forms of διώκω.

The active is supported by the manuscripts in—

χρυσοῦ διώξεις σμικύθην καὶ κύριον.
Arist. Eq. 969.

οὐ πάλιν
τηδὶ διώξεις; τοὔμπαλιν τρέχεις σύ γε.
Thesm. 1224.

οὐκ ἀποδιώξεις σαυτὸν ἀπὸ τῆς οἰκίας.
Nub. 1296.

[1] 'Babr. F. 12. 18; late prose, Himer. Or. 1. 6; Menand. Rhet. 617; Nicol. Rhet. 11, 14; Aeneae Epist. 18, προσ- Ael. H. A. 6 .1, Dor. ᾀσῶ, Theocr. 1. 145.' ''Αείσω, Callim. Apol. 30; Dian. 186, Del. 1; Anth. (Mnas.) 7. 192; Q. Sm. 3. 646; Opp. Cyn. 1. 80, 3. 83.' Veitch.

Xen. Cyr. 6. 3. 13, διώξεις δὲ : id. An. 1. 4. 8, διώξω : Dem. 989. 11, διώξετε.

The middle is read in Ar. Eq. 368—

διώξομαί σε δειλίας·

Thuc. 7. 85, διωξομένους,
Plat. Prot. 810 C, διωξοίμην,
Theaet. 168 A, διώξονται,
Clit. 407 A, διώξομαι,
Xen. Cyr. 1. 3. 14, διώξει,
4. 1. 19, διωξόμεθα,
4. 3. 18, διώξομαι.

These facts distinctly prove that in Attic Greek διώκω had invariably a future middle. In our texts it is occasionally active, but the texts were altered by the copyists of an age in which Dionysius of Halicarnassus could use διώξομαι in a passive sense. Excepting διώξω in Xen. Cyr. 6. 3. 13, and διώξετε in Demosthenes, the active is confined to the second person singular, which, except in one letter and that a finial one, is identical with the middle. Add to this, that in three cases out of the five the following word began with the same letter sigma. It is well known that this is no unfrequent source of error, as in Eur. Or. 383—

ἱκέτης ἀφύλλους στόματος ἐξάπτων λίτας—

the manuscripts have the absurd reading ἀφύλλου. In Thesm. 1224 the active is due simply to erroneous division of the words, διώξει' 's τοὔμπαλιν being, as Cobet shows, what Aristophanes really wrote. The διώξετε of Demosthenes must be altered to διώξεσθε, and perhaps Cobet is right in restoring διώξομαι in Xen. Cyr. 6. 3. 13; but Xenophon is too uncertain a writer to take any account of, and whether he wrote διώξω or διώξομαι does not affect Attic usage in the least degree.

The history of these two futures, ᾄσομαι and διώξομαι,

teaches the valuable lesson that manuscripts are of no authority in establishing the true form of a future when it has survived only in the second person singular.

In other cases in which two forms were nearly alike, the copyists have blundered by using the one for the other. In Arist. Plut. 932, the Informer addresses his witness, calling upon him to bear testimony to the conduct of Cariôn—

ὁρᾷς ἃ ποιεῖ; ταῦτ᾽ ἐγὼ μαρτύρομαι—

but the manuscripts read ποιεῖς. Budaeus was the first to make the necessary correction, and Brunck and others have confirmed it.

When the middle φυλάξει is unquestionably demanded in Arist. Pax 176—

κεἰ μὴ φυλάξει, χορτάσω τὸν κάνθαρον—

the copyists have nothing to offer but the meaningless active φυλάξεις.

In Arist. Av. 1568, on approaching Nephelococcugia, Poseidon turns to his fellow-ambassador Triballus, and tries to get him to arrange his dress more gracefully—

οὗτος τί δρᾷς; ἐπ᾽ ἀριστέρ᾽ οὕτως ἀμπέχει;
οὐ μεταβαλεῖ θοἰμάτιον ὧδ᾽ ἐπὶ δεξιά.

the middle is required, and yet the manuscripts read μεταβαλεῖς.

The verb ἡλιάζομαι is not rare, but it is never found in the active voice except in Arist. Lys. 380, ἡλιάζεις, where no manuscript has the true reading ἡλιάζει.

Another type of manuscript blunder is presented by optatives like μεθείμην and μεθείην becoming interchanged as in Ran. 830—

οὐκ ἂν μεθείμην τοῦ θρόνου, μὴ νουθέτει,

and Soph. El. 1306—

ὑπηρετοίην τῷ παρόντι δαίμονι.

Now in both these cases the manuscripts present the wrong voice; in the line of Aristophanes μεθείην, in Sophocles ὑπηρετοίμην. Dawes corrected the former and Elmsley the latter[1].'

The same verb μεθίημι affords an excellent example of the other kind of manuscript error already shown in διώξετε for διώξεσθε. In the lines—

κόκκυ, μέθεσθε· καὶ πολύ γε κατωτέρω,
Arist. Ran. 1384.

μέθεσθε, μέθεσθε· καὶ τὸ τοῦδέ γ' αὖ ῥέπει,
Id. 1393.

the manuscripts read μεθεῖτε in all three cases. The active voice may thus be used intransitively, but the second person plural imperative active has its penultimate syllable short, μέθετε. The way in which the blunder arose is shown by l. 1380—

καὶ μὴ μεθῆσθον, πρὶν ἂν ἐγὼ σφῷν κοκκύσω.

The Ravenna has the true reading μεθῆσθον, but other manuscripts have only μεθεῖσθον, a form half-way to μεθεῖτον, as διώξετε sprang from διώξεσθε.

Take another type still from the same play. In l. 1235—

ὁρᾷς, προσῆψεν αὖθις αὖ τὴν λήκυθον.
ἀλλ' ὦγάθ' ἔτι καὶ νῦν ἀπόδου πάσῃ τέχνῃ,
λήψει γὰρ ὀβολοῦ πάνυ καλήν τε κἀγαθήν—

many good manuscripts have ἀπόδος, 'give back,' instead of the genuine middle ἀπόδου, 'sell,' required by the sense.

The facts just enumerated have a peculiarly apt application to the class of Greek verbs now under discussion, which have a future tense, middle in form, but in no other respect differing from the other tenses which use the inflexions of the active voice. The verbs of this group employ the middle form consistently throughout the moods of the future, but the active in all other tenses. So thoroughly

[1] Another instance is παρασταίμην for παρασταίην in Soph. O. C. 491.

had they become active in all but the inflexional ending, that expressions such as οὐκ ἀποδιώξει σαυτόν (Arist. Nub. 1296) did not appear strange to an Attic ear.

This external peculiarity corresponds to a very marked peculiarity of meaning. The verbs which reject the active endings of the future in favour of the middle endings, at the same time that they retain the active inflexions in their other tenses, are all words expressing the exercise of the senses or denoting some functional state or process. In fact, within the limits of this class are embraced most verbs which express the action of what Shakespeare calls in one place 'the mortal instruments,' and in another 'the corporal agents.'

The reason for this anomaly in form it is useless to discuss, as it is impossible to discover. If the meaning was originally felt to be most fitly expressed by the middle voice, as undoubtedly it was, what was there in the future tense to make it acquire this signification when the others rejected it? It is possible to collect isolated instances of verbs of this class using other tenses besides the future in the middle voice. Thus, in a beautiful passage of the Δαναΐδες, Aeschylus[1] puts τίκτομαι into the mouth of Aphroditê—

> ἐρᾷ μὲν ἁγνὸς οὐρανὸς τρῶσαι χθόνα,
> ἔρως δὲ γαῖαν λαμβάνει γάμου τυχεῖν·
> ὄμβρος δ' ἀπ' εὐνάεντος οὐρανοῦ πεσὼν
> ἔκυσε γαῖαν· ἡ δὲ τίκτεται βροτοῖς
> μήλων τε βοσκὰς καὶ βίον Δημήτριον·
> δενδρῶτις ὥρα δ' ἐκ νοτίζοντος γάμου
> τέλειός ἐστι· τῶν δ' ἐγὼ παραίτιος.

And a good many examples of λαμβάνομαι might be found to keep λήψομαι in countenance. It is even possible that the passage quoted by Athenaeus (10. 426 F) from the 'Gods' of Hermippus has come down to us as he wrote

[1] Quoted by Athenaeus, 13. 600 B.

it, although πίνομαι and διψῶμαι are found nowhere else in the sense of their actives, πίνω and διψῶ—

> ἔπειθ' ὅταν πινώμεθ' ἢ διψώμεθα,
> εὐχόμεθα,

especially when Suïdas (s. v.) affirms that Cratinus used βαδίζου in the sense of βάδιζε[1]. It is difficult to understand that βαδίζομαι should be distasteful to an Athenian ear when βαδιοῦμαι was not only not displeasing but even demanded. But it is also difficult to see why τραυλίζω, *I lisp*, should be active when ψελλίζομαι, *I stammer*, is middle. As a matter of fact, neither τραυλίζομαι nor ψελλίζω would have offended an Athenian of the best age, and that the middle of the one verb and the active of the other have the best authority is merely due to accident[2]. But, notwithstanding, the future in each case was in Attic middle. Here the active ψελλιῶ and τραυλιῶ would undoubtedly never have been used by a writer of Attic, but ψελλιοῦμαι and τραυλιοῦμαι were the only forms possible. It is to elucidating this marvellous caprice of Attic Greek that the present inquiry is directed, and the critical remarks with which it was opened will be often referred to in restoring to Attic books the genuine future middle forms which copyists in their ignorance of so eccentric a rule have repeatedly marred.

An interesting point of this inquiry is that a very large proportion of the verbs which by signification belong to this class, are deponents to begin with, and accordingly do not attract so much attention as their strikingly irregular fellows, which are deponents only in the future tense. These deponents, however, merit a place by the side of

[1] βάδιζε· καὶ βαδίζου ἀντὶ τοῦ βάδιζε. Κρατῖνος. Other instances are ἀλαλάζομενη, Soph. Fr. 489 (ch.); γηρύομαι, Aesch. P. V. 78, etc.; ἐπωλολύξατο, Aesch. Agam. 1236; κλαίομαι, ἐκλαυσάμην, freq.; διώκεται, Aesch. Cho. 289; Hom.

[2] τραυλίζω occurs Arist. Vesp. 44, Nub. 862, 1381; τραυλίζομαι in Archippus ap. Plutarch, Alc. cap. 1; ψελλίζω, Aristotle, etc.; ψελλίζομαι, Plat. Gorg. 485 C.

the others, if for no other reason than that the juxtaposition may put some future inquirer on the track of the true elucidation of the marvellous phenomenon which is here to be established, not explained.

All verbs, then, which refer primarily to a physical process, and do not merely state the fact that such and such an action is going on, are either deponent throughout or deponents in the future tense. In other words, if the primary reference of a verb is to any physical action, functional or organic, that verb has the inflexions of the middle voice, either in all its tenses or in one, the future.

It will be advantageous to subdivide the great class of verbs to which this rule applies, and a large subordinate group at once suggests itself, composed of verbs which denote the exertion of the vocal organs in man or other animals.

Poetical and un-Attic words are printed in spaced type.

Deponents.

βληχῶμαι,	bleat.	ὠ ρ ύ ο μ α ι,	howl.
β ρ υ χ ῶ μ α ι,	roar.	ψελλίζομαι,	stammer.
γ ο ῶ μ α ι,	wail.	μινύρομαι,	hum.
κνυζῶμαι,	whimper.	κινύρομαι,	wail.
μυκῶμαι,	bellow.	φθέγγομαι,	speak.

Deponents in the Future Tense.

ᾄδω,	sing,	ᾄσομαι.
βοῶ,	shout,	βοήσομαι.
γ η ρ ύ ω,	speak out,	γ η ρ ύ σ ο μ α ι.
κωκύω,	wail,	κωκύσομαι.
λ ά σ κ ω,	scream,	λ α κ ή σ ο μ α ι.
κ ε λ α δ ῶ,	sound,	κ ε λ α δ ή σ ο μ α ι.
ἀλαλάζω,	raise the war-cry,	ἀλαλάξομαι.
γρύζω,	grunt,	γρύξομαι.
οἰμώζω,	groan,	οἰμώξομαι.

ὀλολύζω,	scream,	ὀλολύξομαι.
ὀτοτύζω,	lament,	ὀτοτύξομαι.
κέκλαγγα,	scream,	κεκλάγξομαι.
κέκραγα,	cry out,	κεκράξομαι.

That the tendency of language represented by these forms was active at a very early date is known to every reader of Homer, and is also proved by the existence of the deponents. Moreover, the fact that though γοῶ, and not γοῶμαι, was the present form used by Homer, yet the future employed by him was γοήσομαι, shows how soon the future tense was especially associated with the middle inflexions. Still, in Ionic there are many indications of a laxity in usage with regard to the middle future. Accordingly, if the relationship between Tragedy and Ionic be remembered, it is not surprising that Aeschylus should use κωκύσειν even in senarii (Agam. 1313), but the testimony of Aristophanes distinctly proves that in this direction also there was a strong tendency towards uniformity at work in Attic. It is the law of parsimony under another aspect.

οὐκ ἄπιτε; κωκύσεσθε τὰς τρίχας μακρά.
Ar. Lys. 1222.

If Athenaeus (8. 396 C) had not happened to preserve two lines from the 'Palaestra' of Alcaeus—

ὁδὶ γὰρ αὐτός ἐστιν· εἴ τι γρύξομαι
ὧν σοι λέγω πλέον τι γαλαθηνοῦ μυός—

the verb γρύζω would have been dependent upon the law of uniformity for the true form of its future, for in Arist. Eq. 294—

διαφορήσω σ' εἴ τι γρύξει—

the manuscripts read γρύξεις.

On the other hand, οἰμώξομαι is more than usually secure, as it occurs in Aristophanes alone some ten times—

ὡς σεμνὸς ὁ κατάρατος· οὐκ οἰμώξεται;
Ran. 178.

τὰ δεῖν' ἔφασκ' ἐκεῖνος. Β. ὡς οἰμώξεται.
Ran. 279.

ἀλλ' οὐχ οἷόν τε. Β. νὴ Δί' οἰμώξεσθ' ἄρα.
Nub. 217.

So οἰμώξει, Plut. 111, Av. 1207; οἰμώξεται, Thesm. 248, Ran. 706; οἰμώξεσθε, Pax 466; οἰμωξόμενος, Vesp. 1033, Pax 756. In Plut. 111 some manuscripts have οἰμώξεις, but as in Av. 1207 the true form has been preserved probably by being mistaken for the third person. In Plutus 876—

εἰπεῖν ἃ πεπανούργηκας. Β. οἰμώξἄρα σύ,

the Ravenna has οἰμώξ' ἆρα, but most other manuscripts οἴμωζ' ἆρα.

A fragment of Eupolis, quoted by Zonaras (Lex. p. 605), shows how apt copyists were to replace the middle by the active [1]—

τίς οὐξεγείρας μ' ἐστίν; οἰμώξει μακρά
ὁτιή μ' ἀνίστησ' ὠμόϋπνον.

The true reading is of course ἀνίστης.

The verbs κράζω and κλάζω have as futures κεκράξομαι and κεκλάγξομαι, as coming from κέκραγα and κέκλαγγα, which in Attic bear a present signification. Perhaps this fact has something to do with the old way of regarding such perfects as perfects middle.

οὐδέποτε· κεκράξομαι γάρ,
Ran. 264.

τριπλάσιον κεκράξομαί σου,
Eq. 285.

κατακεκράξομαί σε κράζων.
Eq. 287.

ἵνα μὴ κεκλάγγω διὰ κενῆς ἄλλως ἐγώ·
ἐὰν δὲ μή, τὸ λοιπὸν οὐ κελάγξομαι.
Arist. Vesp. 929-30.

εἰ μὴ τετορήσω ταῦτα καὶ λακήσομαι·
ὦ πονηροί, μὴ σιωπᾶτ'· εἰ δὲ μή, λακήσεται.
Pax 381, 384.

[1] In Eur. Alc. 635, τόνδ' ἀποιμώξει νεκρόν, not a few codices read ἀποιμώξεις νεκρόν.

Besides the verbs already mentioned there are many others, the futures of which do not happen to occur in those portions of the works of Attic writers which have been preserved. But the case is so strong in favour of a future middle in verbs of this class, that it may be confidently assigned them even in cases in which dialectic or late Greek supplies a future in the active. For by the side of the Attic futures deponent of βοῶ, γελῶ, ᾄδω, and the rest, βοήσω, γελάσω, ᾄσω, etc., are met with in late authors. The group of verbs denoting the exercise of the vocal organs will therefore be enlarged by the following—

συρίττω,	whisper,	συρίξομαι.
σίζω,	hiss,	σίξομαι.
σαλπίζω,	trumpet,	σαλπίξομαι.
μινυρίζω,	whine,	μινυρίξομαι.
πιππίζω,	cheep,	πιππίξομαι.
κέκριγα,	squeak,	κεκρίξομαι.
τέτριγα,	chirp,	τετρίξομαι.
αἰάζω,	wail,	αἰάξομαι.
πυππάζω,	cry bravo,	πυππάξομαι.
στενάζω,	groan,	στενάξομαι.
βαΰζω,	yelp,	βαΰξομαι.
(ἀνα)βορβορύζω,	grumble,	(ἀνα)βορβορύξομαι.
ἰΰζω,	yell,	ἰΰξομαι.
κοκκύζω,	cry like a cuckoo,	κοκκύξομαι.
λύζω,	sob, hiccup,	λύγξομαι.
μύζω,	moan,	μύξομαι.
ῥύζω,	snarl,	ῥύγξομαι.
τονθορύζω,	babble,	τονθορύξομαι.
κλώζω,	hoot,	κλώξομαι.
κρώζω,	croak,	κρώξομαι.
βομβῶ,	hum,	βομβήσομαι.
ῥοιζῶ,	hiss,	ῥοιζήσομαι.
καχάζω,	laugh aloud,	καχάσομαι.
κραυγάζω,	screech,	κραυγάσομαι.

κελαρύζω,	babble,	κελαρύσομαι.
ποππύζω,	whistle,	ποππύσομαι.
κιχλίζω,	giggle,	κιχλιοῦμαι.
τραυλίζω,	lisp,	τραυλιοῦμαι.
χρεμετίζω,	neigh,	χρεμετιοῦμαι.
ψιθυρίζω,	whisper,	ψιθυριοῦμαι.

This rule has considerable critical interest, as in several cases various readings occur or emendations have been made which violate its precepts. Thus, in Aeschines 90. 30 (3. 260), the position of ἂν before οἴεσθε, the usual one in Attic, has, as in many other cases, induced the scribes to alter an aorist infinitive into a future, and omit the particle. Θεμιστοκλέα δὲ καὶ τοὺς ἐν Μαραθῶνι τελευτήσαντας καὶ τοὺς ἐν Πλαταιαῖς καὶ αὐτοὺς τοὺς τάφους τοὺς τῶν προγόνων οὐκ ἂν οἴεσθε στενάξαι εἰ ὁ μετὰ τῶν βαρβάρων ὁμολογῶν τοῖς Ἕλλησιν ἀντιπράττειν στεφανωθήσεται; The other reading, οὐκ οἴεσθε στενάξειν, is certainly to be rejected. The only form possible to a writer of Attic was στενάξομαι. But in Tragedy[1] the active inflexion would not have been impossible even in the Senarii, as ἐκβάξω occurs in Aesch. Agam. 498—

ἀλλ' ἢ τὸ χαίρειν μᾶλλον ἐκβάξει λέγων,

and, accordingly, critics may please themselves in altering στενάζετε of the manuscripts in Eur. H. F. 243, and αἰάζετε in line 1054 of the same play, to στενάξετε and αἰάξετε respectively.

Accident has made συρίττω an important word. Its future, though not occurring in Attic, is in Lucian συρίξομαι. Now, though himself an Atticist, Lucian wrote at a time when most of the verbs of this class no longer followed the Attic usage. There is, therefore, no doubt that συρίξομαι

[1] Thus although Veitch is wrong in making the aorist subjunctive ἰαχήσω a future in Eur. Phoen. 1295, 1523, and αὔσω future in Ion 1446, yet ἰαχήσω is almost certainly future in Eur. Tro. 516 (ch.), and ἐπιθωΰξω occurs in Eur. I. T. 1127 (ch.).

was the acknowledged Attic form. Similiar evidence is afforded by Hesychius in the gloss, *κελαρύσεται· μετὰ φωνῆς ἠχήσει*. It is the only occasion on which the future of *κελαρύζω* is found, and the lexicographer had some passage in view when he explained the term.

Care must be taken accurately to draw the line between this class of verbs and the other, which is represented by words like λέγω and λαλῶ, in which the physical act does not form the principal part of the signification. Otherwise there would be some danger of giving φληναφῶ, *chatter*, a future φληναφήσομαι, or παταγῶ, *clash*, a future παταγήσομαι. This whole class, ληρῶ, φλυαρῶ, ὑθλῶ, λαλῶ, στομφάζω, κτυπῶ, etc., have really no reference to any physical process, and accordingly follow the ordinary laws of inflexion. And, although ὀλοφύρομαι, ὀδύρομαι, στωμύλλομαι may owe their deponent form to having originally had a physical reference, their meaning has been so much modified that they can no longer be classed with verbs like μυκῶμαι and κινύρομαι.

In σιωπῶ and σιγῶ are encountered the negations of the whole class, and both verbs follow their more numerous opposites in employing middle inflexions to express future meaning—

σιωπῶ	σιωπήσομαι
σιγῶ	σιγήσομαι.

The next class is a much smaller one, as the modifications possible in the action of the organs of sight are very few in number.

DEPONENTS.

δέρκομαι,	look.
θεῶμαι,	gaze at.
σκέπτομαι,	spy.
αὐγάζομαι,	see distinctly.

DEPONENTS IN THE FUTURE TENSE.

[ὁρῶ],	see,	ὄψομαι.
βλέπω,	see,	βλέψομαι.

But if, they are few in number, verbs of this class are in more cases than the others peculiarly significant. How naturally the middle inflexions were applied to such verbs is demonstrated by the use in all poetry from Homer downwards of the middle ὁρῶμαι and εἰδόμην, while the survival of ὄψομαι, and its use as the future of ὁρῶ, shows that this tendency was especially active in reference to future time. This latter fact is also signally manifested in the case of σκοπῶ. Although σκοπῶ has almost driven σκέπτομαι from the field in the present and imperfect tenses, yet not one instance of σκοπήσω could be discovered in good Greek, σκέψομαι being invariably employed.

Of other verbs[1], λεύσσω from its formation is denied a future tense, and, as a matter of fact, no part of the future of ἀθρῶ[2] has survived. If it had it would doubtless have been middle, as σκαρδαμύττω, *blink*, which of the rest is the nearest approach to a negative which the language supplies, would have formed σκαρδαμύξομαι.

The third of the types of manuscript errors detailed in the beginning of this discussion is well exemplified in Demosth. 799. 17: Ἓν δ' εἰπὼν ἔτι παύσασθαι βούλομαι· ἔξιτε αὐτίκα δὴ μάλα ἐκ τοῦ δικαστηρίου, θεωρήσουσι δὲ ὑμᾶς οἱ περιεστηκότες καὶ ξένοι καὶ πολῖται καὶ κατ' ἄνδρα εἰς ἕκαστον τὸν παριόντα βλέψονται καὶ φυσιογνωμονήσουσι τοὺς ἀποψηφισαμένους· τί οὖν ἐρεῖτε ὦ ἄνδρες Ἀθηναῖοι εἰ προέμενοι τοὺς νόμους ἔξιτε; ποίοις προσώποις ἢ τίσιν ὀφθαλμοῖς πρὸς ἕκαστον τούτων ἀντιβλέψεσθε; Here Bekker and Dindorf actually shut their eyes and read ἀντιβλέψετε, although

[1] ὀπτεύω, ὀπιπτεύω, παπταίνω, σκοπιάζω, hardly merit attention. The future of none of them occurs in Greek except διοπτεύσων, in Il. 10. 451.

[2] ἀθρήσω, in Nub. 731, is aorist subjunctive.

βλέψονται precedes, and there is absolutely no possibility of the preposition *ἀντι-* regulating the voice of the verb. The middle has as good manuscript authority as the active, and the scribe would have altered *βλέψονται* also if the change could have been as easily made. The passage also affords, in *θεωρήσουσι*, an example of a verb of sight, which, like *λέγω* and *λαλῶ*, had no special reference to the physical fact. It is a derived verb, and originally meant *to act as a spectator* (*θεωρός*).

Verbs of hearing, like verbs of seeing, are few in number, and for the same reason, namely, the want of capacity for modification in the organ the exertion of which they express. In fact there are only two verbs which affect the enquiry, *ἀκροῶμαι* and *ἀκούω*, for *πυνθάνομαι* does not strictly belong to this class, and *κλύω* and *αἴω* form no future while *ὠτακουστῶ* is, like *θεωρῶ*, a derived verb, formed from *ὠτακουστής*, *a listener*.

In Hyperides, Fun. Orat. col. 13. 3, the active *ἀκουσόντων* is unquestionably an error for *ἀκουόντων*: *εἰ δ' ὠφελείας ἕνεκεν ἡ τοιαύτη μελέτη γίγνεται, τίς ἂν λόγος ὠφελήσειε μᾶλλον τὰς τῶν ἀκουσόντων ψυχὰς τοῦ τὴν ἀρετὴν ἐγκωμιάζοντος.* The innumerable well-authenticated instances of the future middle, to say nothing of the cogent rule under discussion, give authority sufficient to alter this one passage even without the sensible though metaphysical remark of Cobet: 'Nulla unquam fuit oratio neque erit, quae prodesse possit animis eorum qui eam *sint audituri*, id est quae prosit etiam *priusquam* audita sit.'

The verbs denoting the action of the senses of smell and touch will not occupy the attention long. Of the former there are only two, and both deponents—

ὀσφραίνομαι	*ὀσφρήσομαι*
ὀσμῶμαι	*ὀσμήσομαι*,

as the general verb *αἰσθάνομαι*, which can replace most verbs of this great class, is itself deponent. The verbs of touch present a singular difficulty. The place of ἅπτομαι is assured. It is the word, which in obedience to the law of parsimony in the development of the Attic dialect, was selected to express the process which had been before expressed by the three verbs, ἅπτομαι, θιγγάνω[1], and ψαύω[2]. Accordingly, there are no Attic instances of the future of either ψαύω or θιγγάνω, and in Tragedy either form might probably have been used. The middle θίξομαι occurs in Eur. Hipp. 1086—

κλαίων τις αὐτῶν ἆρ' ἐμοῦ γε θίξεται,

and doubtless Elmsley was right in substituting προσθίξει for προσθίξεις in Eur. Heracl. 647—

εἰ δὲ τῶνδε προσθίξει χερὶ
δυοῖν γερόντοιν οὐ καλῶς ἀγωνιεῖ,

but little more reliance can be placed upon the usage of Tragedians than upon the readings of manuscripts. Certainly, there is one undoubted[3] instance of the active future of ψαύω—

χώρει· τίς ὑμῶν ἅψεται; κλαίων ἄρα
ψαύσει· θεῶν γὰρ οὕνεχ' ἱππικοῦ τ' ὄχλου κτε.
Eur. Andr. 759.

[1] Hippocrates, 5. 184; 6. 90, 300; 8. 88, 350, etc.; Aesch. Sept. 44, 258, Agam. 663; Soph. O. C. 329, Phil. 761, 1398, etc.; Eur. Bacch. 1317, Hec. 605, etc. In Antiphanes, Athen. 15. 667 A, θίγῃ is a useless conjecture for τύχῃ, and in Pherecrates, Athen. 6. 263 B, θιγγανουσῶν τὰς μύλας, evidently in a domestic phrase which has preserved the word. (Xen. Cyr. 1. 3. 5; 5. 1. 16, see p. 169).

[2] Hdt. 2. 90, 93; 3. 30; Hippocr. 2. 411; 6. 640; 7. 556; 8. 356, etc.; Aesch. Pers. 202, Cho. 182, Supp. 925; Soph. O. R. 1467, O. C. 1639, Trach. 565, etc., Eur. very frequently. Antiphon, in 123. 2, and Xenophon, in Mem. 1. 4, 12, are co-partners in sinning against Attic usage.

[3] Dictionaries occasionally quote as futures what are really aorists subjunctive Soph. O. C. 1131, like Eur. Phoen. 1693—

προσάγαγέ νύν με μητρὸς ὡς ψαύσω σέθεν.

In Soph. O. C. 863—

ὦ φθέγμ' ἀναιδές, ἦ σὺ γὰρ ψαύεις ἐμοῦ,

the Laurentian has the present, others the future. So in Aesch. Cho. 181, ψαύει might well be read for ψαύσει, and in Eur. Med. 1320 ψαύσεις changed to ψαύσει, but either form may be read in Tragedy.

But the whole verb is really as un-Attic as the Ionic and Tragic ἐπαφῶ[1], which, like ψαύω itself and θιγγάνω, gave place to ἅπτομαι, the only word which concerns the present inquiry.

The next group, consisting of verbs which express the action of the throat, mouth, or lips, is a significantly large one—

DEPONENTS.

λιχμῶμαι,	lick.
μασῶμαι,	chew.
σκορδινῶμαι,	yawn.
χασμῶμαι,	yawn.
λαφύττομαι,	gorge.
χρέμπτομαι,	clear the throat.
ἐ ρ έ π τ ο μ α ι,	*feed upon* (Epic).
π α τ έ ο μ α ι,	*eat* (Epic).

It is worth remarking that, as in the first group, a very large proportion of these deponents are verbs contracted from *αο*.

DEPONENTS IN THE FUTURE TENSE.

δάκνω,	bite,	δήξομαι.
πίνω,	drink,	πίομαι.
λάπτω,	lap with the tongue,	λάψομαι.
ῥοφῶ,	gulp down,	ῥοφήσομαι.
τρώγω,	gnaw,	τρώξομαι.
χάσκω,	yawn,	χανοῦμαι.
ἔδω, ἐσθίω,	eat,	ἔδομαι.

It is true that in Arist. Ach. 278—

ἕωθεν εἰρήνης ῥοφήσει τρύβλιον,

[1] Plato, Crat. 404 D, uses the word for a philological purpose. Hippocr. 621. 25, has the *middle* aorist ἐπαφήσῃ, and Hesychius quotes both active and middle. Aesch. P. V. 849 has the active, which shows the irregularity of Greek till a strong formative and regulative force arose, like that which made the Attic dialect.

and in Eq. 360—

τῶν πραγμάτων ὁτιὴ μόνος τὸν ζωμὸν ἐκροφήσει

the manuscripts read ῥοφήσεις and ἐκροφήσεις, but in Vesp. 814—

αὐτοῦ μένων γὰρ τὴν φακῆν ῥοφήσομαι

the true form has been perforce preserved, and the middle must be restored, not only in Ach. 278 and Eq. 360, but also in Pax 716—

ὅσον ῥοφήσει ζωμὸν ἡμερῶν τριῶν,

where the same blunder has been made[1].

The middle future of λάπτω is put beyond doubt by a line of Aristophanes—

τὸν ζωμὸν αὐτῆς προσπεσὼν ἐκλάψεται,
Pax 885.

but in Nub. 811, there occurs ἀπολάψεις before a vowel—

σὺ δ' ἀνδρὸς ἐκπεπληγμένου καὶ φανερῶς ἐπηρμένου
γνοὺς ἀπολάψεις ὅ τι πλεῖστον δύνασαι.

The chorus are congratulating Socrates on the conquest he has made of Strepsiades. 'But you, while the man is overwhelmed and elated beyond question, knowing your time, will . . . him as much as you can.' The meaning required is, 'will make as much out of him as you can;' and that is easily obtained by reading ἀπολέψεις, 'you will skin,' a reading found in the Scholiast[2], and in all early editions, and approved by Bentley. Bentley himself proposed ἀπολόψεις, 'quod ipsum est quod Schol. hic suggerit ἀπολεπίσεις, aut melius ἀποτιλεῖς *evelles*. 'Ολόπτειν enim

[1] In addition to the instances already given on p. 379, may be added the following. In Nub. 824 a good MS. has actually διδάξῃ (i. e. -ει) for διδάξεις. In id. 1035, τὸν ἄνδρ' ὑπερβαλεῖ καὶ ὀφλήσεις, some MSS. have ὑπερβαλεῖς.

[2] The words of the Scholiast are, **ἀπολέψεις**· ἀπολεπίσεις. ἐὰν δέ, ὡς τοῖς πολλοῖς, ἀπολάψεις, ἐκπιεῖ. ἀπὸ τῶν κυνῶν ἡ μεταφορὰ ἢ ὅσα λάπτοντα πίνει. καταστρέφει δὲ εἰς τὸ ἀποκερδανεῖς ἢ ἀφαρπάσεις. ἀποσπάσεις.

est τίλλειν, *vellere*. Hesych. 'Ολόπτειν· λεπίζειν, τίλλειν, κολάπτειν.'

These suggestions were made without any reference to the form of ἀπολάψεις. It was its meaning only that made the word difficult. If that difficulty is surmounted—the difficulty of making 'you will lap up' mean 'you will fleece'—and if ἀπολάψεις is retained, it does not follow that the active future was Attic, as it is put in the mouth of the chorus.

To these verbs must be added many more of which no future has survived in Attic books.

βρύκω,	grind the teeth,	βρύξομαι.
κυνῶ,	kiss,	κυνήσομαι.
λείχω,	lick,	λείξομαι.
βήσσω,	cough,	βήξομαι.
πτύω,	spit,	πτύσομαι.
κάπτω,	gulp down,	κάψομαι.
κατα]βροχθίζω,	gulp down,	κατα]βροχθιοῦμαι.
χναύω,	nibble,	χναύσομαι.
νωγαλίζω,	munch,	νωγαλιοῦμαι.
ἐρυγγάνω,	disgorge,	ἐρεύξομαι.
πτάρνυμαι,	sneeze,	πταροῦμαι.
πυτίζω,	spit violently,	πυτιοῦμαι

The only instance of a future to κυνέω is in Eur. Cycl. 172—

εἶτ' ἐγὼ οὐ κυνήσομαι
τοιόνδε πῶμα,

and there most editors prefer the variant ὠνήσομαι. Προσκυνήσω occurs, it is true, but the preposition has so altered the meaning that a future middle is not only not demanded but would have been plainly out of place. The Ionic of Hippocrates supplies both πτύσομαι and ἀποβήξομαι, and if the middle inflexions occur in a writer who in such cases often preferred the active, they were certainly the only ones recognized in Attic Greek. As a matter of fact, ἐρεύξομαι is really the future of ἐρεύγομαι and πταροῦμαι presupposes a present πταίρω; but ἐρεύγομαι is Ionic and poetical, and πταίρω does not occur till late, πτάρνυμαι being used even in Hippocrates, who employs πταρῶ for future. For ἐρεύγομαι Attic writers used ἐρυγγάνω[1], but the future was beyond question still derived from the rejected present, a fact curiously confirmed by the following series—

ἁμαρτάνω	ἁμαρτήσομαι	ἥμαρτον
ἐρυγγάνω	ἐρεύξομαι	ἤρυγον
θιγγάνω	θίξομαι	ἔθιγον
κιγχάνω	κιχήσομαι	ἔκιχον
λαγχάνω	λήξομαι	ἔλαχον
λαμβάνω	λήψομαι	ἔλαβον
μανθάνω	μαθήσομαι	ἔμαθον
τυγχάνω	τεύξομαι	ἔτυχον
φθάνω	φθήσομαι	ἔφθην.

In fact all verbs which form their present by inserting the syllable αν before the person-endings, employ middle inflexions to express future meaning, except αὐξάνω, λανθάνω, and ὀφλισκάνω, of which all three are separated by meaning and one by formation from the rest of the group. A future middle would have been quite incongruous with the signification of αὐξάνω and λανθάνω, while ὀφλι-σκ-άν-ω has an additional element of formation in its present. Accordingly, there is good reason for supplying a future middle to βλαστάνω and ὀλισθάνω, though in these verbs that tense has accidentally not survived.

βλαστάνω	βλαστήσομαι	ἔβλαστον
ὀλισθάνω	ὀλισθήσομαι	ὤλισθον.

Compare the deponents—

αἰσθάνομαι	αἰσθήσομαι	ᾐσθόμην.
πυνθάνομαι	πεύσομαι	ἐπυθόμην

[1] See p. 138.

Moreover to assign due weight to the series it should be remembered that a strong aorist active is an extraordinarily rare tense in the Greek language, although from the frequency with which any of the verbs possessing it occur, it is comparatively familiar to every student.

The English word *gargle* has two equivalents in Greek. Plato uses the term ἀνακογχυλιάζω, and Hippocrates ἀναγαργαρίζω. The latter word is onomatopoetic, and occurs also in the middle, so that if recognized in Attic its future would certainly have the inflexions of the middle. The other word comes from κογχύλιον, 'a little seal,' and primarily means 'to open a seal,' as in Arist. Vesp. 589. It is, therefore strongly metaphorical in its secondary sense, and being a derived word probably retained the active forms throughout.

To this group may conveniently be added the deponent βριμῶμαι, *snort with passion.* Its synonym μυχθίζω occurs twice in Aeschylus, the active in a fragment (D. 337), and the middle compounded with ἀνά in P. V. 743, so that the future μυχθιοῦμαι can in no case be wrong. With these may also be classed ῥέγκω, *snore.*

ῥέγκω ῥέγξομαι.

Another very large group is composed of verbs which denote bodily activity generally, the action of the muscles, whether voluntary or involuntary. To take those which express voluntary activity first, there are the following :—

DEPONENTS.

ἀλῶμαι,	wander.	ἅλλομαι,	leap.
ἀναρριχῶμαι,	scramble.	ἰλυσπῶμαι,	wriggle.
ὀρχοῦμαι,	dance.	οἴχομαι,	am gone.
βρενθύομαι,	swagger.	ἔρχομαι,	go.
ὀριγνῶμαι,	strain.	ὀρέγομαι,	stretch.

Deponents in the Future Tense.

βαδίζω,	walk,	*βαδιοῦμαι.*
χωρῶ,	proceed,	*χωρήσομαι.*
-βαίνω,	go,	*-βήσομαι.*
βλώσκω,	*come,*	*μολοῦμαι.*
ἀπαντῶ,	meet,	*ἀπαντήσομαι.*
θέω,	run,	*θεύσομαι.*
(τρέχω),	run,	*δραμοῦμαι.*
φεύγω,	flee,	*φεύξομαι.*
ἀποδιδράσκω,	run away,	*ἀποδράσομαι.*
σπουδάζω,	make haste,	*σπουδάσομαι.*
διώκω,	pursue,	*διώξομαι.*
πηδῶ,	leap,	*πηδήσομαι.*
θρώσκω,	*leap,*	*θοροῦμαι.*
νέω,	swim,	*νεύσομαι.*
νήχω,	swim,	*νήξομαι.*
κύπτω,	stoop,	*κύψομαι.*
κωμάζω	go revelling,	*κωμάσομαι.*
παίζω,	play,	*παίσομαι.*
φθάνω,	get before,	*φθήσομαι.*

And the negations of these—

πίπτω,	fall,	*πεσοῦμαι.*
κάμνω,	am weary,	*καμοῦμαι.*

The future of *χωρῶ* was occasionally active, although chiefly in early writers and in the compound *ἐγχωρῶ*, which by composition had acquired a sense far removed from the simple. In fact there is only one instance (Thuc. I. 92) of the future active in the simple verb. It is impossible to decide with confidence as to the future of *πατῶ*, for although *ἀποπατησόμενοι* is certainly found in Aristophanes (Plut. 1184)—

πλὴν ἀποπατησόμενοί γε πλεῖν ἢ μύριοι,

the peculiar meaning of that compound has to be taken into account. Xenophon is never of any authority in settling points of Attic usage, and consequently *περιπατήσοντες* in Conv. 9. 7 must be disregarded, and the testimony of Comedy is vitiated by the circumstance that only the second person singular is encountered in its verse—

> *βουλὴν πατήσεις καὶ στρατηγοὺς κλαστάσεις,*
> Ar. Eq. 166.

Antiphanes, in Athen. 9. 409 D—

> *καὶ τότε περιπατήσεις κἀπονίψει κατὰ τρόπον.*

In Fr. Com. 2. 868, *ἐναποπατήσεις* is a reckless conjecture, though soberly quoted by Veitch, and *συμπεριπατήσεις* quoted from Menander by Diogenes Laert. 6. 93—

> *συμπεριπατήσεις γὰρ τρίβων᾽ ἔχουσ᾽ ἐμοὶ*
> *ὥσπερ Κράτητι τῷ Κυνικῷ ποθ᾽ ἡ γυνή,*

is not only subject to the same objection as the others but has no authority in a writer so late as Menander. Doubtless *ἀποπατήσομαι* was invariably used, and though *πατήσω*, *περιπάτησω* were, like *χωρήσω*, recognized forms, yet *πατήσομαι* and *περιπατήσομαι* were most commonly used.

The future of *κύπτω* does not occur except in late Greek, but compounded with *ἀνά* is met with in Aristophanes,—

> *ἡμῖν γε παρὰ θάλατταν ἵν᾽ ἀνακύψεται,*
> Av. 146.

and in Plato (Euthyd. 302 A), where Bekker and Stallbaum read *ἀνακύψοι* there is a variant, *ἀνακύψοιτο*, which must be preferred. *Ἆρ᾽ ἂν ἡγοῖο ταῦτα σὰ εἶναι ἅ σοι ἐξείη καὶ ἀποδόσθαι καὶ δοῦναι καὶ θῦσαι ὅτῳ βούλοιο θεῶν; ἃ δ᾽ ἂν μὴ οὕτως ἔχῃ οὐ σά; Κἀγώ, ᾔδη γὰρ ὅτι ἐξ αὐτῶν καλόν τι ἀνακύψοιτο τὸ τῶν ἐρωτημάτων καὶ ἅμα βουλόμενος ὅτι τάχιστ᾽ ἀκοῦσαι. Πανὺ μὲν οὖν, ἔφην, οὕτως ἔχει.* The late form *κύψω* would suggest to copyists an alteration which the *τό* following made only too easy.

An active future of *φθάνω* is found in Ionic and read in two places of Xenophon. The position of *φθήσομαι* in

Attic Greek is too well assured to be shaken by a writer so capriciously irregular, but even in those two cases the active *φθάσω* is not beyond question. In Cyr. 7. 1. 19, *νῦν γὰρ εἰ φθάσομεν τοὺς πολεμίους κατακανόντες οὐδεὶς ἡμῶν ἀποθανεῖται,* a manuscript D, which has many good qualities, reads *ἢν φθάσωμεν,* and in the other instance (Cyr. 5. 4. 38) it would not be reckless to alter *φθάσεις* to *φθήσει*: *βούλομαι γάρ τοι, ἔφη, καὶ τὴν μητέρα ἄγειν μετ' ἐμαυτοῦ. Ναὶ μὰ Δί', ἔφη, φθάσεις μέντοι.* There is, however, little room for doubt that the active form should be retained, as one of the Ionicisms or un-Attic words which are to be found in every page, almost in every line of that prolific writer.

It is worthy of remark, that *πτήσομαι* is not actually the future of the deponent *πέτομαι,* but itself a deponent tense of an active verb not in use. Its legitimate present is *ἵπτημι,* as is shown by the series—

ἵπτημι	*πτήσομαι.*	
ἵστημι	*στήσομαι*	*στήσω*
ἵημι	*ἥσομαι*	*ἥσω.*

The limits of this group include the two verbs *ῥέω* and *πλέω,* which strictly hardly belong to it; and with these may be classified the poetical deponent *ναυτίλλομαι.*

πλέω,	sail,	*πλεύσομαι.*
ῥέω,	flow,	*ῥεύσομαι.*

They belong to the same well-marked series as *νέω, swim,* and *θέω, run,* and are all derived from digammated stems—

θέω,	run,	*θεύσομαι,*	*θεϝ.*
νέω,	swim,	*νεύσομαι,*	*νεϝ.*
πλέω,	sail,	*πλεύσομαι,*	*πλεϝ.*
πνέω,	blow,	*πνεύσομαι,*	*πνεϝ.*
ῥέω,	flow,	*ῥεύσομαι,*	*ῥεϝ.*
χέω,	pour,		*χεϝ.*

Probably *πνέω* should be classed with *θέω, νέω, πλέω,* and *ῥέω*, and not with words like *τίκτω*, as it primarily refers to the motion of a natural force—the wind, as *ῥέω* of water, and not to the breathing of man. It is a curious fact that *χέω*, the only member of this group which is transitive and does not involve motion in its subject, employs its present, *χέω*, both in a present and a future sense, and that even in the middle voice *χεύσομαι* is not used, but *χέομαι*.

There are several other verbs which properly belong to this class, but the future of which has not been preserved. In Attic Greek they were unquestionably deponents in the future tense—

κολυμβῶ,	dive,	*κολυμβήσομαι*.
κυβιστῶ,	tumble,	*κυβιστήσομαι*.
λακτίζω,	kick,	*λακτιοῦμαι*.
νεύω,	nod,	*νεύσομαι*.
ὀκλάζω,	crouch,	*ὀκλάσομαι*.
πτήσσω,	cower,	*πτήξομαι*.
σκιρτῶ,	bound,	*σκιρτήσομαι*.
φοιτῶ,	go to and fro,	*φοιτήσομαι*.

It is true that *φοιτάσω* occurs in Sappho and Callimachus, and *φοιτήσω* in late Greek, but the authority of Thomas Magister, combined with the incontestible law of Attic which has now been distinctly established, puts *φοιτήσομαι* beyond dispute. The words of Thomas Magister (p. 106), *ἀποφοιτήσομαι κάλλιον ἢ ἀποφοιτήσω*, are, like the testimony of Hesychius as to the future of *κελαρύζω*, a valuable confirmation of the legitimacy of the present method of reconstructing verbs accidentally incomplete by a judicious use of the principle of seriation.

Στείχω is one of those words which were in use in Attica at a time when the language still retained in a great degree the features of Ionic Greek, and consequently is found in Tragedy as in Ionic, but by the law of parsimony it was rejected in mature Attic. Even its future does not happen to occur, and may be disregarded. The same is true of ἕρπω (see p. 50), and accordingly the active ending of ἐφέρψω in a chorus of Aeschylus (Eum. 500) is of no moment in regard to the question of Attic usage.

Less definite in signification, but still belonging to the same natural class, are those verbs which it was decided to treat separately, namely those expressing involuntary action of the muscles or functional movement.

DEPONENTS.

κυίσκομαι,	conceive.
γλίχομαι,	yearn.
λίπτομαι,	*yearn.*

DEPONENTS IN THE FUTURE TENSE.

ἐμῶ,	vomit,	ἐμοῦμαι.
οὐρῶ,	make water,	οὐρήσομαι.
τίκτω,	bear,	τέξομαι.
χέζω,	ease oneself,	χεσοῦμαι.
λαικάζω,	relieve oneself,	λαικάσομαι.
θηλάζω,	suckle,	θηλάσομαι.
πνέω,	breathe,	πνεύσομαι.

As mentioned above it is questionable whether πνέω properly belongs to this class. However, the middle endings of its future are undisputed, and the only exception is one which proves the rule. Demosthenes is credited with συμπνευσόντων in 284. 17, τὴν Ἐλάτειαν κατέλαβεν ὡς οὐδ' ἂν εἴ τι γένοιτο ἔτι συμπνευσόντων ἂν ἡμῶν καὶ τῶν Θηβαίων, but the future participle with ἄν is as absurd in Attic syntax as would be the future indicative, infinitive, or optative with ἄν, and the aorist συμπνευσάντων must be restored as satisfying the demands both of syntax and accidence.

Another syntactical rule constantly violated by transcribers is exemplified in the case of θηλάζω. Attic usage does not allow the subjunctive mood to be used after ὅπως or ὅπως μή in object clauses, but it repeatedly happens that the future indicative, which in these cases is the normal sequel to ὅπως, is altered into the aorist subjunctive even when the aorist is not from the same voice as the future. A singularly apt example occurs in Lucian, Cron. 11 (394), παρασκευάζομενοι ὅπως θύσωσι καὶ εὐωχήσωνται. Now verbs like εὐωχοῦμαι are invariably passive, with the so-called future middle—

ἑστιῶμαι	ἑστιάσομαι	εἱστιάθην
θοινῶμαι	θοινήσομαι	ἐθοινήθην
εὐωχοῦμαι	εὐωχήσομαι	εὐωχήθην,

and εὐωχήσονται and θύσουσι[1] should be restored as Cobet insists on grounds both of syntax and accidence.

Similarly in Plato (Rep. 460 D), αὐτῶν τούτων ἐπιμελήσονται ὅπως μέτριον χρόνον θηλάσονται, the reading θηλάσωνται must be rejected, and the deponent future θηλάσομαι assured to the active present θηλάζω. No attention is to be paid to the active ἐνεξεμῶ, quoted by Veitch from Fr. Com. 2. 868, a passage it has already been necessary to characterise as desperately corrupt and plainly mangled by Providence to give critics the opportunity of working their wicked will on what was left.

A Fragment of Cephisodorus preserved by Athenaeus (15. 689 F)—

ὦ λακκόπρωκτε, βάκχαριν τοῖς σοῖς ποσὶν
ἐγὼ πρίωμαι; λαικάσομ' ἄρα· βάκχαριν;

establishes the future of λαικάζω, and at the same time affords to the moralist a saddening proof of the use to which it was put. In Arist. Eq. 167—

δήσεις, φυλάξεις, ἐν πρυτανείῳ λαικάσει

[1] In a similar construction the same verb has been equally unfortunate in Arist. Nub. 258—

ὥσπερ με τὸν 'Αθάμανθ' ὅπως μὴ θύσετε,

where *every* manuscript, the Rav. and Ven. among the rest, reads θύσητε, in open violation of the metre.

the Ven. manuscript has not seized the opportunity of reading λαικάσεις, and in Stratto (Athen. 9. 383 A)—

'πηγὸς πάρεστι;' πηγός; οὐχὶ λαικάσει;

the true form was safely concealed in λεκὰς εἶ till Coray made sense by restoring λαικάσει.

In regard to τίκτω, critics have been too bold in substituting τέξομαι for τέξω in every passage of Aristophanes in which the active forms are found. In the Tragic dialect both are legitimate, τέξω occurring by the side of τέξομαι, in much the same way as στείχω, and βαίνω survived in Tragedy when ἔρχομαι or εἶμι had usurped their place in Prose. Consequently Aristophanes employs τέξω in a passage (Thesm. 466 ff.) which he distinctly intended to suggest reminiscences of Tragedy, as in the *form* περιήρχετο for περιῄειν, the metaphor ἐπιζεῖν τὴν χολήν (see p. 17), and the parody—

κᾆτ' Εὐριπίδῃ θυμούμεθα
οὐδὲν παθοῦσαι μεῖζον ἢ δεδράκαμεν,

which is only slightly altered from the Telephus of Euripides—

εἶτα δὴ θυμούμεθα
παθόντες οὐδὲν μᾶλλον ἢ δεδρακότες.

Cobet has a humorously serious defence of Hirschig's conjecture, τίκτειν [1], but in this case, as in that of περιήρχετο (l. 504), he has been reduced to conjecture, because his point of view was misplaced (see p. 108 supra).

In Lys. 744, however, when τέξομαι is demanded τέξομαι is found,

A. τί ταῦτα ληρεῖς; B. αὐτίκα μάλα τέξομαι,

[1] Sibylla ita loquebatur in oraculis et Dii immortales et heroes; mulierculae Atticae τέξομαι solebant dicere. Rectissime igitur Hirschigius τίκτειν emendavit, quod et Graecum est et rei, quae agitur, unice convenit. Non *parituram* sese sed *parere* clamat, ut virum sine mora extrudat foras.' Cobet.

whereas in a pseudo-oracle in Eq. 1037, the active is again intentionally used,

ἔστι γυνή, τέξει δὲ λέονθ' ἱεραῖς ἐν 'Αθήναις.

The middle κλαύσομαι is the only form of the future of κλαίω found in Attic Comedy and Tragedy, with the exception of κλαυσοῦμαι (see p. 91 extr.) in Aristophanic hexameters (Pax 1081). Demosthenes uses κλαιήσω or κλαήσω, an instance of that tendency towards bringing all verbs to uniformity which δοκήσω in Aristophanes proves to have begun at an early date, and which, in some cases like κεκέρδηκα and ἠσέλγημαι, was calculated to enrich the language. But there is no doubt that κλαύσομαι ought to be considered the better Attic.

The middle δακρύομαι occurs in Aesch. Sept. 814—

τοιαῦτα χαίρειν καὶ δακρύεσθαι πάρα,

where the present is certainly demanded, though there is a variant δακρύσεσθαι. In either case it makes sufficient evidence for a deponent future. But in Eur. El. 658—

ναί· καὶ δακρύσει γ' ἀξίωμ' ἐμῶν τόκων

the active is equally well supported, and neither Comedy nor Prose supplies examples to settle the difficulty. Either form may be safely employed, but in Attic of the best age δακρύσομαι was probably preferred. The same result is obtained with regard to ποθῶ. There is no authority better than Xenophon's for the active ποθήσω, but ποθέσομαι occurs in authors of irreproachable purity. It must be placed as a future deponent by the side of the entire deponent γλίχομαι.

Neither κυῶ nor ὠδίνω (with its tenses formed from ὠδινῶ) have a future extant in Attic, but in Hippocrates both κυήσω and κυήσομαι occur. The Attics no doubt used κυήσομαι and ὠδινήσομαι, but as the futures of derived verbs, δυστοκήσω and εὐτοκήσω.

A form of no ordinary import has been preserved by Hesychius in *βρυάσομαι.* It affords the necessary authority to supply deponent futures to a group of verbs which belong to the series under discussion, but of which by a singular fatality no future form has been preserved. The verb *βρυάζω* signifies *to teem*, and is a good representative of its class, *κιττῶ, σφριγῶ, ὀργῶ, σφυδῶ, σφύζω, ἱδρῶ, ἀσθμαίνω, ἀσπαίρω, οἰδῶ, σπλεκῶ.* As having primarily no physical reference, *ἐπιθυμῶ* on the contrary has its future active, *ἐπιθυμήσω.*

All verbs connected with drinking, and answering to our words *soak*, etc., are passive, like *βρέχομαι* and *ἐξοινοῦμαι*, except *μεθύσκομαι*, which is deponent, and a member of this series.

The verb *ἀμβλίσκω*, as the negative of *τίκτω*, must go with these, and have confidently restored to it the deponent future which it undoubtedly possessed in Attic Greek.

Deponent.

μεθύσκομαι,	am drunk.

Deponents in the Future Tense.

κλάω,	weep,	κλαύσομαι.
δακρύω,	weep,	δακρύσομαι.
κυῶ,	conceive,	κυήσομαι.
ὠδίνω,	travail,	ὠδινήσομαι.
ποθῶ,	yearn,	ποθέσομαι.
βρυάζω,	*teem*,	βρυάσομαι.
κιττῶ,	yearn,	κιττήσομαι.
σφριγῶ,	am lusty,	σφριγήσομαι.
σφυδῶ,	*am lusty*,	σφυδήσομαι.
ὀργῶ,	am rampant,	ὀργήσομαι.
οἰδῶ,	swell,	οἰδήσομαι.
ἀσπαίρω,	*pant*,	ἀσπαροῦμαι.
ἀσθμαίνω,	*pant*,	ἀσθμανοῦμαι.

σφύζω,	*throb,*	*σφύξομαι.*
σπλεκῶ,	coeo,	*σπλεκώσομαι.*
ἱδρῶ,	sweat,	*ἱδρώσομαι.*
ἀμβλίσκω,	miscarry,	*ἀμβλώσομαι.*

Of far more general signification than any of the groups already classified is the last in the large series which in the preceding pages has been subjected to analysis. The verbs now to be enumerated express some one or other of the more general facts relating to the physical side of the human organism.

εἰμί,	am,	*ἔσομαι.*
(*βιῶ*),	live,	*βιώσομαι.*
γηράσκω,	become old,	*γηράσομαι.*
-θνήσκω,	die,	*-θανοῦμαι.*
φθίνω,	waste away,	*φθίσομαι.*
πάσχω,	suffer,	*πείσομαι.*
τλάω,	*endure,*	*τλήσομαι.*

The future of *γηράσκω* has in good Attic active inflexions as well as middle, and it is likely that by the side of *ἡβήσω* we should also place *ἡβήσομαι*. Moreover, it is natural to connect *γηράσομαι* and *ἡβήσομαι* with the older formations, *ἡβάσκω* and *γηράσκω*, while *ἡβήσω* and *γηράσω* are considered the futures of the modern *ἡβῶ* and *γηρῶ*.

γηρῶ	*γηράσω*
ἡβῶ	*ἡβήσω*
γηράσκω	*γεράσομαι*
ἡβάσκω	*ἡβήσομαι.*

To these must be added *βλαστάνω*, already referred to as one of the series which in the present tense extend their stem with the syllable *αν*. Its future does not exist even in Ionic, for in Herodotus (3. 62) *ἀναβλάστῃ* is now read in place of *ἀναβλαστήσει*. Of course its fellow, *αὐξήσομαι*, is really passive.

It is probably from a community of meaning with *λαμ-*

βάνω, λαγχάνω, κιγχάνω, τυγχάνω, verbs of the same series, that ἁρπάζω, κλέπτω, and πλεονεκτῶ use either active or middle person-endings to express future meaning. The middle predominates in the case of ἁρπάζω, the active in that of κλέπτω. In fact the evidence for the Atticicity of ἁρπάσω is by no means convincing. It is found in Euripides and Xenophon, both poor authorities; the former from writing in what was really an artificial dialect, the latter from the general character of his style.

σὺ τῶν ἀτέκνων δῆτ' ἀναρπάσεις δόμους;
Eur. Ion 1303.

συναρπάσουσι καὶ κατασκάψουσι γῆν.
I. A. 535.

Xen. Hipp. 4. 17, ἁρπάσοντας. In the first of these three places ἀναρπάσεις is practically of no more authority than ἀναρπάσει, and Xenophon has ἁρπασόμενοι in another passage (Cyr. 7. 2. 9). The verdict of Aristophanes is very decided, for although in Nub. 490—

ἄγε νυν ὅπως ὅταν τι προβάλλω σοι σοφὸν
περὶ τῶν μετεώρων εὐθέως ὑφαρπάσει,

even the Ravenna reads ὑφαρπάσεις, other lines plainly prove that the middle must be substituted.

ἐξαρπάσομαί σου τοῖς ὄνυξι τἄντερα.
Eq. 708.

ἀλλ' ἁρπάσομαι σφῷν αὐτά· κεῖται δ' ἐν μέσῳ.
Pax 1118.

ἁρπασόμενος τὰ χρήματ' αὐτοῦ.
Av. 1460.

ἔδεισας οὗτος; οὐ ξυναρπάσει μέσην;
Lys. 437.

τῶν ἐσφερόντων ἁρπάσομαι τὰ σιτία.
Eccl. 866.

ἀνίσταθ' ὡς ἁρπασόμενος τῶν ἰσχάδων.
Plut. 801.

It is true that in Arist. Eccl. 667 κλέψει is only a correction of Brunck for κλέψαι—

A. οὐδ' αὖ κλέπτης οὐδεὶς ἔσται;
B. πῶς γὰρ κλέψει μετὸν αὐτῷ;

but κλέψαι is so intolerable, both as regards form and construction, that the correction is certainly necessary. Πλεονεκτῶ must be added with confidence to this class. It certainly is active in Plato, Rep. 349 C, πλεονεκτήσει: Thuc. 4. 62, πλεονεκτήσειν: but in Plato, Lach. 192 E, οἷον εἴ τις καρτερεῖ ἀναλίσκων ἀργύριον φρονίμως εἰδὼς ὅτι ἀναλώσας πλέον ἐκτήσεται, τοῦτον ἀνδρεῖον καλοίης ἄν; the future exact is quite out of place, and πλεονεκτήσεται must be preferred. It is also very doubtful if Plato refined so much as to use κέκτημαι, κεκτήσομαι only after vowels, ἔκτημαι and ἐκτήσομαι always after consonants.

It is natural to consider καύσομαι as springing from the same feeling of language as ἁρπάσομαι, κλέψομαι, and πλεονεκτήσομαι. Really, all four futures have much of a true middle force, and in Aristophanes (Plut. 1053)—

ἐὰν γὰρ αὐτὴν εἷς μόνος σπινθὴρ λάβῃ
ὥσπερ παλαιὰν εἰρεσιώνην καύσεται

the force of the middle voice may well be transferred to English. Wakefield denied the possibility of καύσομαι here (Silv. Crit. 3. p. 74), and found fault with λάβῃ as 'nec (l. neque) elegans nec (l. neque) usitatum,' but his method of emending the lines is weak in the extreme—

ἐὰν γὰρ αὐτὴν εἷς μόνος σπινθὴρ βάλῃ
ὥσπερ παλαιά γ' εἰρεσιώνη καύσεται.

The Greeks did not use γε merely to avoid the loss of a final vowel by elision, and καύσομαι, like λάβῃ, is not only defensible but elegant.

A few more Greek verbs have the peculiarity of employing the inflexions of the middle voice in their future tense, but to bind them together there is no general principle like that which runs through the preceding series.

Γιγνώσκω may be placed by the side of the early formations, ἁμαρτάνω and μανθάνω—

ἁμαρτάνω	ἁμαρτήσομαι
μανθάνω	μαθήσομαι
γιγνώσκω	γνώσομαι,

and φροντιοῦμαι may, on the analogy of these, be readily left unaltered in Euripides (I. T. 343)—

τὰ δ' ἐνθάδ' ἡμεῖς οἷα φροντιούμεθα.

It may be that in the three verbs, δείδω (?), θαυμάζω, and ἀπολαύω, as certainly was the case in τλάω, the physical side of the state expressed by them was primarily uppermost, but, however that may be, δείσομαι, θαυμάσομαι, and ἀπολαύσομαι have no active rivals in Attic Greek. In late writers δείσω, θαυμάσω, and ἀπολαύσω took their place, and have accordingly repeatedly crept into the texts of the Classical age. Thus in Plato, Charmides 172 B, one manuscript (Par. E.) reads ἀπολαύσομεν for ἀπολαυσόμεθα, the reading supported by all the others, and in our only manuscript of Hyperides ἀπολαύσομεν is read (Orat. Fun. col. 11. 142), but must be corrected to ἀπολαυσόμεθα as in id. col. 13. 3, ἀκουσόντων has already been replaced by ἀκουόντων. Errors like θαυμάσεις or θαυμάσῃς for θαυμάσει in Eur. Alc. 157—

ἃ δ' ἐν δόμοις ἔδρασε θαυμάσει κλύων

by this time hardly need remark, and other instances of the active have all been corrected by the best editors and with the sanction of manuscripts.

It is difficult to give a reason for the deponent future of ὄμνυμι, *swear*, but ἐπιορκήσομαι by the side of ἐπιορκήσω may well be explained as due to analogy with it.

Although there is no example of εἰκάσομαι, the form

ἀπεικάσομαι and ἀντεικάσομαι demonstrate its existence, as the prepositions which are prefixed to these compounds can in no way have influenced their form. The three verbs indicate the indisputable adaptability of a middle meaning to the future tense.

Before this inquiry is brought to a conclusion, a small compact group of verbs possessing the peculiarity under discussion deserves serious attention. Probably all of them had also an active future, but in no case would it be wrong to assign a middle future to an active verb denoting praise or blame.

Λωβῶμαι and λυμαίνομαι, μέμφομαι and αἰτιῶμαι, are entirely deponents, while λοιδορῶ or λοιδορῦμαι are used indifferently, although, as might be expected, the active is in the future tense of extraordinary rarity. All verbs corresponding to our *scoff*, *flout*, *jeer*, belong to this class, and while there is no unquestioned instance of the active of σκώπτω or τωθάζω, yet both verbs occur so rarely in the future tense that the analogy of ὑβριῶ by the side of ὑβριοῦμαι, as well as of λοιδορῶ by the side of λοιδοροῦμαι, must be regarded as indicating that neither form of the future would be displeasing to Attic ears.

Παίζω has been considered in another class; ἐπιγλωττῶμαι, *abuse*, *jest*, χαριεντίζομαι and δημοῦμαι, *jest*, are deponents throughout, and ἐπηρεάζω, *banter*, σκιμαλίζω, *insult*, and χλευάζω, *scoff*, do not happen to occur in the future tense. If it is easy to suggest προπηλακιεῖται τάχα for προπηλακιεῖ τάχα in Plat. Gorg. 527 A, yet Thucydides in προπηλακιῶν (6. 54) supplies an indisputable instance of the active. Κολάζω, like λοιδορῶ, oscillates between the middle and the active voice, and in Thucydides δικαιῶ has at one time an active, at another a middle future.

'Επαινέσω and ἐπαινέσομαι, ἐγκωμιάζω and ἐγκωμιάσομαι, are about equally well supported, and strongly confirm the view taken of the others.

These three classes, consisting of verbs altogether deponent, verbs either active or deponent, and verbs which though otherwise active are occasionally middle in the future tense, may be thus presented:—

μέμφομαι,	blame.	χαριεντίζομαι,	jest.
μωμῶμαι,	blame.	δημοῦμαι,	jest.
αἰτιῶμαι,	blame.	λυμαίνομαι,	outrage.
ἐπιγλωττῶμαι,	abuse.	λωβῶμαι,	outrage.

λοιδορῶ,	λοιδοροῦμαι,	insult.
κολάζω,	κολάζομαι	punish.

σκώπτω,	jeer,	σκώψω or σκώψομαι.
τωθάζω,	flout,	τωθάσω or τωθάσομαι.
ὑβρίζω,	insult,	ὑβριῶ or ὑβριοῦμαι.
ἐπηρεάζω,	banter,	ἐπηρεάσω or ἐπηρεάσομαι.
χλευάζω,	scoff,	χλευάσω or χλευάσομαι.
προπηλακίζω,	abuse,	προπηλακιῶ or προπηλακιοῦμαι.
σκιμαλίζω,	insult,	σκιμαλιῶ or σκιμαλιοῦμαι.
δικαιῶ,	punish,	δικαιώσω or δικαιώσομαι.
ἐπαινῶ,	praise,	ἐπαινέσω or ἐπαινέσομαι.
ἐγκωμιάζω,	panegyrise,	ἐγκωμιάσω or ἐγκωμιάσομαι.

The relationship between future tense and middle meaning, which is so clearly proved by the numerous examples considered above, must originally have arisen from some refined sense of language. It was helped by analogy at the later period which is called classical; but even at that early date had begun to decay, as is indicated by such forms as ἑστήξω and τεθνήξω by the side of στήσομαι and θανοῦμαι. These verbs belong to a group in which the idiosyncrasy of meaning is not very clearly marked, and though the analogy of κεκράξομαι, and κεκλάγξομαι gave the forms birth, the analogy of θανοῦμαι and στήσομαι proved incapable of assigning to them the middle form. They acquired it in late Greek, and in that way middle forms have crept into the texts even of Classical authors, but only in the case of the easily altered second person singular. The authority for the active is conclusive.

A. ὡς τεθνήξων ἴσθι νυνί·
B. δήξομἄρ' ὑμᾶς ἐγώ.
Arist. Ach. 325.

οὐ μὴν ἄτιμοί γ' ἐκ θεῶν τεθνήξομεν.
Aesch. Agam. 1279.

ὡδέ θ' ἑστήξω παρ' αὐτόν· αὐτὸ γάρ μοι γίγνεται.
Arist. Lys. 634.

Accordingly the following passages must be all altered, as has already been done by good editors—

εἴσει σύ, χερνίβων γὰρ ἑστήξει πέλας.
Eur. I. A. 675.

A. οἴμ' ὡς τεθνήξει.
B. μηδαμῶς, ὦ Λάμαχε.
Arist. Ach. 590.

μάτην ἐμοὶ κεκλαύσεται, σὺ δ' ἐγχανὼν τεθνήξει.
Nub. 1436.

οὐκ ἔστιν ὅπως οὐχὶ τεθνήξει, κἂν κτε.
Vesp. 654.

In two of these places the Ravenna manuscript, our best authority, not only blunders in the termination, but even in the body of the word, giving τεθνήσει for τεθνήξεις. No faith can be put in such authorities, no reliance at a pinch.

CCCIII.

Ἡμικεφάλαιον μὴ λέγε, ἀλλὰ ἡμίκρανον.

Either Phrynichus has fallen into error, or he did not write ἡμίκρανον. The Attic word is ἡμίκραιρα[1], as is seen from Aristophanes—

οὔκουν καταγέλαστος δῆτ' ἔσει
τὴν ἡμίκραιραν τὴν ἑτέραν ψιλὴν ἔχων;
Thesm. 227.

[1] Schol. in Hom. Il. Σ. 3—
οἱ Ἀττικοὶ τὸ τῆς κεφαλῆς ἥμισυ ἡμίκραιραν λέγουσι.

and from other passages quoted by Athenaeus as in 9. 368 E—

κωλῆ, τὸ πλευρόν, ἡμίκραιρ' ἀριστερά—
Ameipsias.

and 9. 384 D—

εἰσῆλθεν ἡμίκραιρα τακερὰ δέλφακος.
Crobylus.

CCCIV.

'Ενάρετος· πολὺ παρὰ τοῖς Στωικοῖς κυκλεῖται τοὔνομα, ουκ ὂν ἀρχαῖον.

Plutarch (Mor. 116 F) or his copyists have substituted this late formation for ἐνδίκων in two lines which Plutarch assigns to Aeschylus, but Stobaeus (Flor. 108. 43) with greater probability to Euripides—

ἀνδρῶν τάδ' ἐστὶν ἐνδίκων τε καὶ σοφῶν
κἂν τοῖσι δεινοῖς μὴ τεθυμῶσθαι θεοῖς.

The word is common in late writers.

CCCV.

Γαστροκνημίαν μὴ λέγε, ἀλλὰ κνήμην.

'Neque γαστροκνημία, neque ἀντεκνήμιον oratorium est. Haec sunt scholae vocabula, quae sermo vulgaris forte arrepta volvit, sed nemo cultior in rerum civilium expositione ad popularem sensum accommodata immiscet. Verum putidae in verborum delectu subtilitatis exemplum praebuit Nicetas Ann. 4. 5. 78 D, γαστροκνημίδας (leg. γαστροκνημίας) καὶ χεῖρας, καὶ ὅσα τοῦ σώματος ὀστώδη διαθρυβεὶς ἦν. Artis medicae scriptoribus ista non solum permissa, etiam necessaria sunt.' Lobeck.

CCCVI.

Θέρμα· οὕτως ὁ Μένανδρος διὰ τοῦ α, ἀλλ' οὔτε Θουκυδίδης, οὔθ' ἡ ἀρχαῖα κωμῳδία, οὔτε Πλάτων, θέρμη δέ.

This article, like the last, may well be spurious, as neither has much textual authority. The statement is also made by Zonaras (Lex. 1030), by the Etymologicum Magnum (206. 57) and by Suïdas, sub voc. *βουβών*. The word occurred in the *Γεωργός*—

> *βουβὼν ἐπήρθη τῷ γέροντι θέρμα τε*
> *ἐπέλαβεν αὐτόν.*

As a matter of fact, too much has been made of this form. The grammarians have followed their usual practice of using one another's writings in a way which in literature proper would be called plagiarism, and have given an undue emphasis to what was originally an erroneous dictum. *Θέρμη*, as has been said already, is a very peculiar formation, and stands upon quite a different footing from *τόλμα* (*τόλμη*), *εὔθυνα*, and *πρύμνα* (*πρύμνη*). There is no reason in the world why *θέρμα*, a substantive legitimately formed from *θέρομαι*, should not be regarded as distinct from *θέρμη* connected with *θερμός*. The verb *θέρομαι* is a primitive passive (not middle), of which no active exists in Classical Greek, and which was itself an excellent though rare Attic word—

> *ἐς τὸ βαλανεῖον τρέχε·*
> *ἔπειτ' ἐκεῖ κορυφαῖος ἑστηκὼς θέρου.*
> Ar. Plut. 953.

Plato, Phileb. 46 C, *ὁπόταν τις τἀνάντια ἅμα πάθη πάσχῃ, ῥιγῶν ποτε θέρηται καὶ θερμαινόμενος ἐνίοτε ψύχηται.* In Menander, therefore, *θέρμα* is to be considered as a neuter with genitive *θέρματος*, and the remarks of the grammarians are to be attributed to the fact that the line of Menander happened to recall the strikingly memorable account of the symptoms which first marked the victims of the Great Plague, Thuc. 2. 49, ἀλλ' ἐξαίφνης ὑγιεῖς ὄντας πρῶτον μὲν τῆς κεφαλῆς θέρμαι ἰσχυραὶ καὶ τῶν ὀφθαλμῶν ἐρυθήματα καὶ φλόγωσις ἐλάμβανε κτε. It is doubtless for the same absurd reason that Timaeus (139) altered θέρμα in Plato's Theaet. 178 C to θέρμαι. Plato, like Menander, wrote θέρμα, and Aristophanes also used the neuter substantive. Pollux 4. 116 θέρμα καὶ πῦρ Ἀριστοφάνης ἔφη—

ὁ δ' ἔχων θέρμα καὶ
πῦρ ἧκε.

CCCVII.

Τεθεληκέναι· Ἀλεξανδρεωτικὸν τοὔνομα. διὸ ἀφετέον Ἀλεξανδρεῦσιν καὶ Αἰγυπτίοις αὐτό, ἡμῖν δὲ ῥητέον ἠθεληκέναι.

The Attic verb was ἐθέλω, with perfect ἠθέληκα, whereas in the Common dialect it was θέλω with perfect τεθέληκα.[1] The word has suffered grievously from the want of pliability in Tragic trimeter verse, and from the careless habits of transcribers. Homer, Hesiod, Theognis, and Pindar knew no form but the trisyllabic. The tragic senarius, however, admitted of its present only under limited conditions, and the form θέλω was necessarily used, especially as βούλομαι[2]

[1] 'Ἠθέληκα, Aeschin. 2. 139; Xen. Cyr. 5. 2. 9; Dem. 47. 5; *plp.* ἠθελήκει, Xen. Hell. 6. 5. 21.' 'τεθέληκα, Mosch. παθ. γυν. P. 14. 19; Sext. Emp. 682 (Bekk.); Orig. Ref. Haeres.' 4. 15 (Miller); *plp.* ἐτεθελήκεσαν, Dio Cass. 44. 26.' Veitch.

[2] "Βούλομαι ist bei Homer und in den Hymnen zwar bei weitem seltner als ἐθέλω, aber doch den eben gültig. Dann aber verswindet es fast aus der Dichtersprache: Hesiod (Op. 647), Simonides Ceus (fr. 92. 3. epigr.), Pindar (fr. 83), die Batrachom. (72) haben ganz vereinzelt stehende Beispiele. Aeschylus hat es ebenfalls sehr selten (Pers. 215; Prom. 867, 929) und, wie auch Sophokles, *nicht in Chorliedern.* Sonst aber haben die jüngeren Dramatiker es

was for some reason or other eschewed by the early tragedians. Ἤθελον and ἠθέλησα, however, were much more convenient for an Iambic line than ἔθελον and ἔθελησα, forms probably unknown to Classical Greek, although the tragic subjunctive and other moods, θελήσω, θελήσαιμι, θέλησον etc., naturally suggest them.

Aristophanes always uses ἐθέλω, except in the phrases ἢν θεὸς θέλῃ, εἰ θεὸς θέλοι, in which the attrition of constant use is manifest. Thus ἐθέλω is demanded by the metre in Eq. 791, Pax 852, Av. 581, Plut. 512, 524, etc., while θέλω occurs in one or other of the phrases mentioned above, in Plut. 347, 1188, Pax 939, 1187, Ran. 533, Eq. 713. In Thesm. 908 θέλω is from Eur. Hel. 562, and in l. 412 of the same play θέλει is used for tragic effect, the next line being taken from the Phoenix of Euripides.

In prose the trisyllabic form must be restored, except after a vowel, and in the phrases just mentioned, and in similar expressions like θεοῦ θέλοντος.

CCCVIII.

Ψύλλος βάρβαρον, ἡ δὲ ψύλλα δόκιμον ὅτι καὶ ἀρχαῖον.

'Feminina positio inde ab Aristophane et Xenophontis Symp. 6. 8 (πόσους ψύλλης πόδας ἐμοῦ ἀπέχεις) omnibus viguit aetatibus . . . Masculinum genus, quod Moeris p.

oft, *namentlich Euripides*. Verbindet man hiermit das die ältesten Attischen Prosaiker, besonders Thucydides, βούλομαι en grosser Fülle, dagegen nur sparsam ἐθέλω (θέλω ganz selten) haben, so kommen wir wohl auf die rechte Spur. Es muss in βούλομαι eben so sehr etwas gelegen haben, was es von der hohen Poesie fern hielt, wie en ἐθέλω, was es ihr besonders lieb machte. War der unterschied zunächst der zwischen Poesie und Prosa, so war es naturlich schwer einen *begrifflichen* unterschied zu finden, der, wenigstens für die Zeit zwischen Homer und den jüngeren Tragikern vielleicht gar nicht vorhander war. Letztere, wenn sie des Wort zu gleichem richten mit ἐθέλω aufnahmen, hiengen wohl darin von den neueren Philosophen ab. u. s. w." Tycho Mommsen, Σύν und Μετά bei Euripides, p. 2.

418 in numerum communium aggregat, in versione Alexandrina 1 Reg. 24. 14, Anon. Antiqq. Constantinopol. 2. p. 26 A, 37 A, et ap. Aristot. H. A. 4. 10, 537. a6, Dioscorid. 4. 70, et Galenum de Administr. Anat. 6. 1. 130, multo saepius legitima forma utentem.' Lobeck.

CCCIX.

Εὐσχήμων· τοῦτο μὲν οἱ ἀμαθεῖς ἐπὶ τοῦ πλουσίου καὶ ἐν ἀξιώματι ὄντος τάττουσιν· οἱ δ' ἀρχαῖοι ἐπὶ τοῦ καλοῦ καὶ συμμέτρου.

The rejected signification seems confined to Christian writers. Thus, in Mark 15. 43, *εὐσχήμων βουλευτής* corresponds to *πλούσιος* in Matth. 27. 57. The word bears the same meaning in Luke, Acts 13. 50, *γυναῖκας τὰς εὐσχήμονας*.

CCCX.

Ἐπίτοκος ἡ γυνὴ ἀδοκίμως εἶπεν Ἀντιφάνης ὁ κωμῳδός, δέον ἐπίτεξ εἰπεῖν.

The word reprehended is met with in Hippocrates, 1201 H, *ἡ κοῦρος ἐπίτοκος ἐοῦσα τοῦ ἔμπροσθεν χρόνου*: Aristot. H. A. 6. 18, 573. a2, *καὶ οὕτω γινώσκουσιν ὅτι ἐπίτοκα εἰσὶν οἱ ποιμένες* etc., the word recommended, in Hdt. 1. 108, *τὴν θυγατέρα ἐπίτεκα ἐοῦσαν*: id. 111, *ἡ γυνὴ ἐπίτεξ ἐοῦσα πᾶσαν ἡμέρην*: Hipp. 603. 4, etc. There is no means of deciding between the words. The force of *ἐπί* has been explained above, p. 208.

CCCXI.

Ἐγκάθετος· οὕτως Ὑπερείδης ἀπερριμμένως, δέον δοκιμώτερον χρήσασθαι τῷ θετὸς ἢ εἰσποίητος ἢ ὑπόβλητος.

Antiatt. Bekk. 96. 30, also refers the word to Hyperides, but says nothing of the meaning: *Ἐγκάθετος· Ὑπερείδης κατὰ Αὐτοκλέους.* If correctly cited this is the only instance in Attic Greek, as neither the letters of Demosthenes nor the Axiochus are genuine, Plat. Ax. 368 E, *οἱ δὲ περὶ Θηραμένην καὶ Καλλίξενον τῇ ὑστεραίᾳ προέδρους ἐγκαθέτους* (suborned) *ὑφέντες*: Epist. Demosth. 1483. 1, *ὑπ' ἀνθρώπων ἐγκαθέτων διαβληθέντες.* In late Greek it is not uncommon, as Polyb. 13. 5. 1, Joseph. B. J. 2. 2. 5, Luke 20. 20.

'Adoptatos *θετούς* vocari, *ποιητούς* et *εἰσποιήτους*, ignorat nemo; illud praetermittunt, *τὸν θέμενον* vocari *θέτην* apud Photium: *Θέτης, ὁ εἰσποιησάμενος θετούς τινας.* hoc ultimum vereor ne germanam lectionem specie non dissimilem expulerit *υἷας*; tali abundantia *θετὸν υἱὸν ποιῆσαι* dicitur, Suïd. s. *υἱῶσαι, θετὸν υἱὸν ποιεῖσθαι* Hdt. 6. 57.' Lobeck.

CCCXII.

Ἐνδυμενία· ἀμαθῶς, δέον διττῶς λέγειν, ὡς Εὔπολις Κόλαξι, σκεύη τὰ κατὰ τὴν οἰκίαν καὶ ἔπιπλα.

This article has little authority, being absent from Laurentian A and the editions of Vascosan and Callierges, and from Phavorinus.

The derivation and orthography of *ἐνδυμενία* are both uncertain, some preferring to spell it with an omicron, others with an upsilon, while it is connected severally with *ἔνδον, δόμος*, and *ἔνδυμα*. Even Pollux rejects the term, 10. 12, *τὴν δὲ τοιαύτην κατασκευὴν ἐνδομενίαν οἱ πολλοὶ καλοῦσιν· ἐγὼ δὲ οὐκ ἐπαινῶ τοὔνομα . . . κάλλιον δὲ τὴν ἐνδομενίαν παγκτησίαν ἢ παμπησίαν ὀνομάσαι, ὡς ἐν Ἐκκλησιαζούσαις Ἀριστοφάνης· τραγικώτερον γὰρ ἡ παγκληρία. τὰ δὲ σκεύη καὶ σκευάρια φίλον τοῖς κωμῳδοῖς καλεῖν κτε.* The passage of Eupolis is cited in an earlier paragraph (10. 10) but in a corrupt state, *αὐτὰ δὲ τὰ σκεύη καλοῖτ' ἂν ἔπιπλα, ἤγουν ἡ κουφὴ κτῆσις, τὰ ἐπιπολῆς ὄντα τῶν κτημάτων. ὁ γοῦν Εὔπολις ἐν τοῖς Κόλαξιν προειπών*—

> *ἄκουε δὴ σκεύη τὰ κατὰ τὴν οἰκίαν*

ἐπήγαγε παραπλήσιον,

> *τεσσυγέγραπται τοῖς τὰ ἔπιπλα.*

CCCXIII.

Ἐμπυρισμός· οὕτως Ὑπερείδης ἠμελημένως, δέον ἐμπρησμὸς λέγειν.

Pollux, 9. 156, *Ἐν μέντοι τῷ Ὑπερείδου ὑπὲρ Λυκόφρονος εὗρον γεγραμμένον 'ἢ νεωρίων προδοσίαν ἢ ἀρχείων ἐμπυρισμὸν ἢ κατάληψιν ἄκρας,' καὶ οὕτω γέγραπται ἐν πλείοσι βιβλίοις.* Both words occur only in late writers.

CCCXIV.

Ἡμίκακον, οὐχ οὕτως ἀλλ' ημιμόχθηρον φάθι.

This article if by Phrynichus is certainly unworthy of him. The adjectives are equally good—

ἡμίκακος—

> *τέως μὲν οὖν ἀλλ' ἡμικακῶς ἐβοσκόμην.*
>
> Ar. Thesm. 449.

Cp. Pollux, 6. 162, *ἡμίκακον δὲ Εὐκλείδης λέγει καὶ Σοφοκλῆς, Ἀριστοφάνης δὲ καὶ ἡμικάκως*: Antiatticista, 98. 13, *ἡμίκακον. Ἄλεξις Αἰχμαλωτῷ.*

ἡμιμόχθηρος—

Plato, Rep. 1. 352 C, *ὥρμησαν δὲ ἐπὶ τὰ ἄδικα ἀδικίᾳ ἡμιμόχθηροι ὄντες.*

CCCXV.

Ἔμελλον ποιῆσαι, ἔμελλον θεῖναι, ἁμαρτήματα τῶν ἐσχάτων εἴ τις οὕτω συντάττει, τετήρηται γὰρ ἢ τῷ ἐνεστῶτι συνταττόμενον ἢ τῷ μέλλοντι, οἷον ἔμελλον ποιεῖν, ἔμελλον ποιήσειν, τὰ δὲ συντελικὰ οὐδένα τρόπον ἁρμόσει τῷ ἔμελλον.

CCCXVI.

Ἔμελλον γράψαι· ἐσχάτως βάρβαρος ἡ σύνταξις αὕτη· ἀορίστῳ γὰρ χρόνῳ τὸ ἔμελλον οὐ συντάττουσιν οἱ Ἀθηναῖοι, ἀλλ' ἤτοι ἐνεστῶτι, οἷον ἔμελλον γράφειν, ἢ μέλλοντι, οἷον ἔμελλον γράψειν.

In the manuscripts and the edition of Nuñez the second of these articles comes much later, while the two are necessarily in juxtaposition in Callierges.

It may be too subtle to regard the scholarly addition of *θεῖναι*, the poetical equivalent of *ποιῆσαι*, not only as an indication that the former of the two edicts certainly originated with Phrynichus, but also as intended to make the rule apply to poetry as well as prose. As it is, the edicts themselves are disputed, while some scholars would make them absolute by the ridiculous device of asserting that the remarks refer only to the imperfect of *μέλλω*. The following analysis of the usage of Attic poetry will demonstrate the justice of the general rule laid down by Phrynichus. It need hardly be added that only those passages are recorded in which *μέλλω* has the signification of 'intend' or 'am going to.'

To begin with Comedy, the present infinitive follows *μέλλω* in the following passages:—

μέλλων ὑπὲρ Λακεδαιμονίων ἀνδρῶν λέγειν.
Ar. Ach. 482.

ἅπασι μέλλεις εἷς λέγειν τἀνάντια.
Id. 493.

εἰ πτωχὸς ὢν ἔπειτ' ἐν Ἀθηναίοις λέγειν
μέλλω περὶ τῆς πόλεως.
Id. 498.

οὗτος τί δράσεις; τῷ πτίλῳ μέλλεις ἐμεῖν;
Id. 588.

ἄνεστιν, ἡδονῶν θ' ὅσων μέλλεις ἀποστερεῖσθαι.
Nub. 1072.

τὰ μέλλοντ' εὖ λέγεσθαι.
Vesp. 1011 (Chor.).

μῦς καὶ γαλᾶς μέλλεις λέγειν ἐν ἀνδράσιν;
Id. 1185.

ἆ, ἆ, τί μέλλεις δρᾶν; B. ἄγειν ταύτην λαβών.
Id. 1379.

ὅτ' οὐδ' ἔμελλες ἐγγὺς εἶναι τῶν θεῶν.
Pax 196.

ἀλλ' εἶμι· καὶ γὰρ ἐξιέναι γνώμην ἐμὴν
μέλλει.
Id. 232.

λουσάμενα πρῴ· μέλλω γὰρ ἑστιᾶν γάμους.
Av. 132.

κἀγὼ πίπτω μέλλω τε βοᾶν, ὁ δ' ἀπέβλισε θοἰμάτιόν μου.
Id. 498.

ἑστιᾶν δὲ μέλλομεν ξένους.
Lys. 1058 (Chor.).

A. οὐ δεῖ μ' ἀκούειν; B. οὐχ ἅ γ' ἂν μέλλῃς δρᾶν.
Thesm. 7.

A. μέλλει γὰρ ὁ καλλιεπὴς Ἀγάθων
πράμος ἡμέτερος, B. μῶν βινεῖσθαι;
A. δρυόχους τιθέναι δράματος ἀρχάς.
Id. 50.

μέλλει δικάζειν οὔτε βουλῆς ἔσθ' ἕδρα,
Id. 79.

κὰν θεσμοφόροιν μέλλουσι περί μου τήμερον
ἐκκλησιάζειν ἐπ' ὀλέθρῳ.
Id. 83.

A. ἀτὰρ τί μέλλεις δρᾶν μ'; B. ἀποξυρεῖν τάδε.
Ar. Thesm. 215.

ἵν' ἄττα βουλεύοισθε καὶ μέλλοιτε δρᾶν.
Id. 587.

μὴ δῆθ' ἱκετεύω πλήν γ' ὅταν μέλλω 'ξεμεῖν.
Ran. 11.

μέλλεις ἀνάγειν εἴπερ γ' ἐκεῖθεν δεῖ σ' ἄγειν.
Id. 77.

τί ποτ' ἄρα δρᾶν μέλλουσιν ἀλλ' ἁπλῷ τρόπῳ.
Eccl. 231.

μέλλοι βαδίζειν ἢ θύραζ' ἑκάστοτε.
Id. 271.

μὰ Δί' ἀλλ' ἀποφέρειν αὐτὰ μέλλω τῇ πόλει.
Id. 758.

ὦ φίλαι γυναῖκες εἴπερ μέλλομεν τὸ χρῆμα δρᾶν.
Id. 1164.

εἰ τοῦτο δρᾶν μέλλοντες ἐπιλαθοίμεθα.
Pl. 466.

μέλλω στρατηγὸν χειροτονεῖν 'Αγύρριον[1].
Id. ap. Plut. de rep. gerend. 801 B.

ἀλλ' εἰ μέλλεις εὖ κἀνδρείως
φῴζειν ὥσπερ μύστακα σαυτόν.
Strattis, in Etym. Mag. 803. 47.

Πότερ' ὅταν μέλλω λέγειν σοι τὴν χύτραν, χύτραν λέγω;
Antiphanes, ap. Athen. 10. 449 B.

συσσίτιον μέλλεις νοσηλεύειν; ὅσον
ἀκροκώλι' ἕψειν – ᴗ – ῥύγχη, πόδας.
Anaxilas, ap. Athen. 3. 95 A.

μέλλοντα δειπνίζειν γὰρ ἄνδρα Θετταλόν.
Alexis, ap. Athen. 4. 137 C.

[1] The following lines are too uncertain to be used in settling this question:—
Ar. ap. Hesychius s. ἀφορμή—
μέλλει δὲ πέμπειν τοὺς εἰς ἀφορμήν:
Pherecrates, ap. Athen. 9. 396 C—
οὐ γαλαθηνὸν ἄρ' ὗν θύειν μέλλεις:
Plato, ap. Athen. 15. 667 B—
μὴ σκληρὰν ἔχε
τὴν χεῖρα μέλλων κοτταβίζειν.

To complete the list may be added the Boeotian's patois in Ar. Ach. 947—

μέλλω γέ τοι θερίδδεν.

The future infinitive is in Comedy much more rare, occurring only in the following places:—

σὲ δὲ
γνώμην ἐρεῖν μέλλοντα περὶ
Μιλησίων καὶ κερδανεῖν
τάλαντον.

Ar. Eq. 931.

μέλλων ὀφλήσειν μὴ παρόντων μαρτύρων.

Nub. 777.

αἰσχρὸν ποιεῖν, ὅ τι τῆς αἰδοῦς μέλλει τἄγαλμ' ἀναπλήσειν.

Id. 995.

φεύγεις; ἔμελλον σ' ἆρα κινήσειν ἐγώ.

Id. 1301.

μέλλεις ἀναπείσειν ὡς δίκαιον καὶ καλόν.

Id. 1340.

οὐ ξυλλήψεσθ' ὁπόσοισι δίκαι τῆτες μέλλουσιν ἔσεσθαι.

Vesp. 400.

ἀλλ' ὦ περὶ τῆς πάσης μέλλων βασιλείας ἀντιλογήσειν.

Id. 546.

μέλλουσαν ἤδη λεσβιεῖν τοὺς ξυμπότας.

Id. 1346.

κατὰ χειρὸς ὕδωρ φερέτω ταχύ τις. B. δειπνήσειν μέλλομεν
ἢ τί;

Av. 464.

εἴπερ μέλλομεν
ἀναγκάσειν τοὺς ἄνδρας εἰρήνην ἄγειν.

Lys. 120.

μέλλουσί μ' αἱ γυναῖκες ἀπολεῖν τήμερον.

Thesm. 181.

In one passage the governed verb may be regarded either as present or future—

ἄνευ δρυφάκτου τὴν δίκην μέλλεις καλεῖν.

Vesp. 830.

Against these forty-eight examples of the present or future—thirty-five of the present, twelve of the future, and one doubtful—there are only three, or more correctly only two, instances of the aorist, to set; for the Laconic in Lys. 117—

ἐγὼ δὲ καί κα ποττὸ Ταΰγετον ἄνω
ἔλσοιμ' ὄρος αἰ μέλλοιμί γ' εἰράναν ἰδῆν,

may be set against the Boeotian in Ach. 947. These two instances are, Av. 366—

εἰπέ μοι τί μέλλετ' ὦ πάντων κάκιστα θηρίων
ἀπολέσαι παθόντες οὐδὲν ἄνδρε καὶ διασπάσαι;

and Ach. 1159 (Chor.)—

κᾆτα μέλ-
λοντος λαβεῖν αὐτοῦ κύων
ἁρπάσασα φεύγοι.

They are unquestioned violations of the rule, and do not admit of reasonable emendation. It would be easy to change *ἀπολέσαι* and *διασπάσαι* into *ἀπολέσειν* and *διασπάσειν*, but the cure would be almost worse than the disease, as the Attic future of *ἀπόλλυμι* is *ἀπολῶ*, not *ἀπολέσω*. In Comedy, therefore, of the Attic period, the exceptions to the rule of Phrynichus are four per cent. of the instances.

As to tragedy, full statistics of the usage of Euripides are not yet in my hands, but the following notes on Aeschylus and Sophocles may be of service. Aeschylus prefers the future after *μέλλω*, that tense occurring four times, P. V. 638, 835, Cho. 859, 867, and the present only once, Suppl. 1058, while *τελεῖν* in Agam. 974 may be either present or future—

μέλοι δέ τοι σοὶ τῶνπερ ἂν μέλλῃς τελεῖν.

This writer also supplies an undoubted example of the aorist in P. V. 625—

μήτοι με κρύψῃς τοῦθ' ὅπερ μέλλω παθεῖν.

In Sophocles, on the other hand, the future and the present are evenly balanced, the former occurring nine times, El. 359, 379, 538, Aj. 925, 1027, 1287, Ant. 458, Phil. 483, 1084, and the latter nine, El. 305, 1486, Aj. 443, O. R. 678, 1385, O. C. 1773, Tr. 79, 756, Phil. 409. There is one possible instance of the aorist. The manuscripts present *κτανεῖν* in

> *κτανεῖν ἔμελλον πατέρα τὸν ἐμόν· ὁ δὲ θανών,*
> O. R. 967.

but it is quite possible that Sophocles wrote *κτενεῖν*. If *κτανεῖν* is right, it will be observed that the percentage of aorists is much the same as in Comedy. So small a percentage of exceptions may easily be due to negligent and ungrammatical writing.

CCCXVII.

Κραυγασμός· παρακειμένου τοῦ κεκραγμὸς εἰπεῖν ἐρεῖ τις ἀμαθῶς κραυγασμός.

There is little evidence, but as far as it goes it is in favour of *κεκραγμός*, that form occurring in Eur. I. A. 1357, and *κέκραγμα* in Ar. Pax 637, whereas there is no instance of *κραυγασμός* in a pre-Macedonian writer, although Antiatticista, 101, has the note, *Κραυγασμὸς ἀντὶ τοῦ κραυγή· Δίφιλος Ἀποβάτῃ*. The fact that *κραυγάζω* was hardly an Attic word cannot decide this point, as many substantives remained in use after the verbs which gave them birth had been replaced by more useful synonyms. That *κραυγάζω* was really an old formation, although principally used in late Greek, is proved by the old lines quoted by Plato, Rep. 10. 607 B, *ἡ λακέρυζα πρὸς δεσπόταν κύων κραυγάζουσα κτε.*

CCCXVIII.

Κορυδαλός· Εὐβούλου τοῦ κωμῳδοποιοῦ δρᾶμα ἐπιγράφεται οὕτως· σὺ δὲ τοῖς περὶ Ἀριστοφάνην πειθόμενος κόρυδον λέγε τὸ ζῷον.

This, like the preceding article and the following, has little authority but that of Nuñez.

The words of Thomas are worth quoting, if only to show that *κορυδαλός* must at one time have been used on Attic soil; (p. 549) *Κόρυδος καὶ κορυδαλὸς καὶ κορυδαλὶς τὸ στρουθίον τὸ ἔχον ἐπὶ τῆς κεφαλῆς ἀνεστηκότα πτέρα ὥσπερ λόφον. ἔστι δὲ τὸ μὲν κόρυδος Ἀττικόν· Πλουτάρχος ἐν τῷ περὶ ἀδολεσχίας,* (p. 507 E) **κόρυδος ὦπται πετόμενος.** *τὸ δὲ κορυδαλὸς κοινὸν εἰ καὶ Εὔβουλος χρῆται· ἔστι δὲ καὶ κορυδαλὸς δῆμος Ἀθήνησι, τὸ δὲ κορυδαλὶς ποιητικὸν ὡς Θεόκριτος,* (7. 23) **Ἐπιτυμβίδιοι κορυδαλίδες.**

The Attic form occurs in Ar. Av. 302, 472, 476, 1295; Plato, Euthyd. 291 B; Anaxandrides, ap. Ath. 4. 131 (l. 64), and in late writers, as Theocr. 7. 741. Of *κορυδαλός* Lobeck says, 'rejectitiae formae nullus antiquior auctor proferri potest Aristotele, qui in Histor. Anim. saepissime *κόρυδος*, semel *κορυδαλός* (9. 25) usurpavit. Sed si aliquot ab hoc gradus descendimus, larga exemplorum sylva insurgit, Aelian, H. An. 4. 5. 6. 46, Galen, vol. 4, p. 158, vol. 13, p. 943; Dioscor. 2. 59, Aesop. Fab. 46.'

CCCXIX.

Καμμύει· τοσαύτη κακοδαιμονία περί τινας ἐστὶ τῆς βαρβαρίας ὥστ᾽, ἐπειδὴ Ἄλεξις κέχρηται τῷ καμμύειν ἠμελημένως ἐσχάτως, αἱρεῖσθαι καὶ αὐτοὺς οὕτω λέγειν, δέον ὡς οἱ ἄριστοι τῶν ἀρχαίων καταμύειν.

The passage of Alexis has not been preserved, but there is no reason why he should not have employed such a syncopated form in the lyric, anapaestic, or hexameter metres, or in representing dialectical pronunciation. Thus, Aristophanes puts ἄμβατε into the mouth of a Boeotian in Ach. 732, and ἀμπτάμενος of a Laconian in Lys. 106. Similarly, ἀμπάλλετε occurs naturally in the parody of the choruses of Aeschylus in Ran. 1358 (cp. ἀμπάλλοντι, Lys. 1310). In Tragedy these forms were in place even in the senarii, as οὐκ ἐς ἀμβολάς, Eur. Heracl. 270; ἀμβάτης, Bacch. 1107.

In this respect as in others Xenophon approximates to the usage of the Common dialect, employing ἀμβάτης in De Re Eq. 3. 12; 5. 7; Mem. 3. 3. 2, and perhaps at Hell. 5. 3. 1, ἀνάμβατος in Cyr. 4. 5. 46, and ἀμβολὰς γῇ in id. 7. 5. 12.

The form καμμύω seems most frequent in the sacred writers, as Esai. 29, καμμύσει τοὺς ὀφθαλμούς; Luke, Acts 28. 27, ἐκάμμυσαν τοὺς ὀφθαλμούς.

CCCXX.

Κεφαλοτομεῖν· ἀπόρριπτε τοὔνομα καὶ Θεόφραστον κεχρημένον αὐτῷ· λέγε δὲ καρατομεῖν.

This appears a mere matter of opinion. Euripides (?) uses καρατομεῖν in Rhes. 586—

Πάριν μολόντε χρὴ καρατομεῖν ξίφει,

and Theophrastus, κεφαλοτομεῖν; Antiatticista, 104. 31; Κεφαλοτομεῖν· Θεόφραστος περὶ Εὐδαιμονίας. There is not much basis for choice, as either word is a legitimate formation.

CCCXXI.

Λάκαιναν μὲν γυναῖκα ἐρεῖς, Λάκαιναν δὲ τὴν χώραν οὐδαμῶς, ἀλλὰ Λακωνικήν, εἰ καὶ Εὐριπίδης παραλόγως,—

ὡς ἡ Λάκαινα τῶν Φρυγῶν μείων πόλις [1].

[1] Androm. 194. So id. 151, 209, Tro. 1110, Hel. 1473, etc.

Such adjectival use of substantives has been discussed already on p. 21. It is common in Tragedy and in Ionic prose, but is practically unknown in genuine Attic. The exceptions enumerated by Lobeck are not to the point, as both *Λάκαινα κύων*[1], or *σκύλαξ*[2], and *Λάκαινα*[3], a sort of cup, are mere remnants of old usage, or to be regarded in the same way as an English expression like *Swedes* for *Swedish turnips*. Accordingly when Xenophon, in Hellen. 7. 1. 29, writes *εἰς τὴν Λάκαιναν*, he is not writing Attic, but approximating to the *Λάκαινα χώρη* of Herodotus or the Tragedians.

CCCXXII.

Μὲν οὖν τοῦτο πράξω· τίς ἀνάσχοιτο οὕτω συντάττοντός τινος ἐν ἀρχῇ λόγου τὸ μὲν οὖν; οἱ γὰρ δόκιμοι ὑποτάσσουσιν, ἐγὼ μὲν οὖν λέγοντες, τὰ καλὰ μὲν οὖν καὶ τὰ μὲν οὖν πράγματα.

'Satis exemplorum nobis praebent scriptores sacri, a *μενοῦν* et *μενοῦνγε* saepe periodos exorsi, ne quis admonitionem illam inutilem fuisse credat.' Lobeck.

CCCXXIII.

Μιαρία ἀδόκιμον, τὸ δὲ μιαρὸς ἀρχαῖον.

Phrynichus is in error, the substantive being used by Demosthenes, 845. 23, *περὶ μὲν οὖν τῆς αἰσχροκερδίας τῆς τούτου καὶ μιαρίας ὕστερόν μοι δοκεῖ διεξελθεῖν*, by Isaeus, 51. 32, *εἰς τοῦτο ὕβρεως καὶ μιαρίας ἀφίκετο*, and in the early

[1] Soph. Aj. 8; Xen. Cyr. 10. 1, 4.

[2] Plat. Parm. 128 C.

[3] Athenaeus 11. 484 F, *Λάκαιναι· κυλίκων εἶδος οὕτως λεγόμενον ἢ ἀπὸ τοῦ κεράμου, ὡς τὰ Ἀττικὰ σκεύη, ἢ ἀπὸ τοῦ σχήματος ἐπιχωριάσαντος ἐκεῖ, ὥσπερ αἱ Θηρίκλειαι λέγονται. Ἀριστοφάνης, Δαιταλεῦσι·*

Συβαρίτιδάς τ' εὐωχίας καὶ Χῖον ἐκ Λακαινᾶν.

sense of 'bloodguiltiness,' by Antiphon 118. 2; 119. 3; 124. 2. It is also found in Xen. Hell. 7. 3. 6.

Thomas blindly follows Phrynichus, p. 615, *μιαρός, οὐ μιαρία δὲ ἀλλὰ βδελυρία*, and so Antiatt. p. 108.

CCCXXIV.

Γαμῴη μὴ λέγε, ἀλλὰ γαμοίη διὰ τῆς οι, ὡς νοοίη, φιλοίη· τὰ γὰρ τῆς πρώτης συζυγίας καὶ τρίτης τῶν περισπωμένων ῥημάτων εὐκτικὰ διὰ τῆς οι διφθόγγου λέγεται, οἷον τελοίη· τὰ δὲ τῆς δευτέρας διὰ τοῦ ω, οἷον νικῴη, γελῴη.

CCCXXV.

Διδῴη καὶ διδῴης· τούτου τὸ εὐκτικὸν οὐδεὶς τῶν Ἀττικῶν εἶπε διὰ τοῦ ω, ἀλλὰ διὰ τῆς οι διφθόγγου. τεκμηριοῖ δὲ Ὅμηρος ἐὰν μὲν ὑποτακτικῶς χρῆται διὰ τοῦ ω λέγων—

εἰ δέ κεν αὖ τοι
δώῃ κῦδος ἀρέσθαι·

ἔστι δέ, ἐὰν δέ σοι δῷ ὁ Ζεύς, εἰ δὲ εὐκτικῶς, οὕτως—

σοὶ δὲ θεοὶ τόσα δοῖεν, ὅσα φρεσὶ σῇσι μενοινᾷς

ἐθαύμασα οὖν Ἀλεξάνδρου τοῦ Σύρου σοφιστοῦ δῴη καὶ διδῴη λέγοντος ἐπὶ τοῦ εὐκτικοῦ.

The second of these articles is in the manuscripts separated from the first by the articles numbered in this edition 326 and 327. Their juxtaposition will enable me to discuss with more conciseness the true forms of the optative mood in Attic Greek. It will be my aim to establish by the authority of Attic Comedy the true forms of the optative mood in those cases in which a longer and a shorter form occur side by side in our prose texts of Attic writers. It may be observed, that the possibility in prose of a form like τελοῖ by the side of τελοίη, or γελῷ by the side of γελῴη, does not seem to have presented itself to Phrynichus, and it will be demonstrated that such corruptions have still more no place in Classical writing.

If it can be proved by the impartial laws of metre that in Comedy only one set of forms was in each case used, a strong argument is obtained for considering as spurious the unsupported prose inflexions. The argument becomes still stronger when by the ignorance or negligence of scribes the defaulting forms have in some manuscripts been foisted into verse, to the detriment of the metre, or, by causing the expulsion of some other word, to the detriment of the sense.

Moreover, it is easy to prove that Aristophanes never scrupled to use two forms when he might do so without violating Attic usage. Up to the Archonship of Euclides (B.C. 402) the longer forms of the dative plural of the first and second declensions, appear constantly in inscriptions, and were certainly used in the intercourse of daily life. In the Comic poets they occur side by side with the shorter, and were for the sake of convenience never rejected, although in prose they are found only in some of the more elevated passages of Plato.

ὁ Ζεύς με ταῦτ' ἔδρασεν ἀνθρώποις φθονῶν.
Ar. Plut. 87.

εἴ τί γ' ἔστι λαμπρὸν καὶ καλὸν
ἢ χάριεν ἀνθρώποισι, διά σε γίγνεται.
Id. 145.

Similarly, the Comic poet, no less than the Epic poet or the tragedian, employs indifferently both the lighter and heavier forms of the first person plural, middle or passive.

οἱ γὰρ βλέποντες τοῖς τυφλοῖς ἡγούμεθα.
Plut. 15.

ἀλλὰ τόν γ' Ἀγύρριον
πονηρὸν ἡγούμεσθα· νῦν δὲ χρωμένων.
Eccl. 185.

A. ἀλλ' ὡς τάχιστ' εὐχώμεθ'.
B. εὐχώμεσθα δή.
Pax 973.

He uses as he requires the two forms of the third person plural optative, middle, or passive, namely the longer in -οίατο[1], and the shorter in -οιντο.

αἱ τριχίδες εἰ γενοίαθ' ἕκατον τοὐβολοῦ.
Eq. 662.

ἵν' αἱ θέσεις γίγνοιντο τῇ νουμηνίᾳ.
Nub. 1191.

πρότερον διαλλάτοινθ' ἑκόντες, εἰ δὲ μή.
Id. 1194.

ὅπως τάχιστα τὰ πρυτανεῖ' ὑφελοίατο.
Id. 1199.

The Attic dialect recognised ἑστηκώς and ἑστηκέναι as legitimate forms by the side of the syncopated ἑστώς and ἑστάναι, and accordingly the usage is reflected in Comedy—

ἔπειτ' ἐκεῖ κορυφαῖος ἑστηκὼς θέρον.
Plut. 953[2].

[1] Besides the instances quoted in the text we find, Pax 209, αἰσθάνοιατο: Ar. 1147, ἐργασαίατο: Lys. 42, id. Fr. Com. 2. 1106 (Aristoph.), ὑφελοίατο. Homer probably never uses -οιντο, as the hiatus in Il. 1. 344—

ὅππως οἱ παρὰ νηυσὶ σόοι μαχέοιντο Ἀχαιοί

makes μαχεοίατ' almost a certain emendation. Other instances are, Il. 2. 340, γενοίατο: 418, λαζοίατο: 282, ἐπιφρασαίατο: 492, μνησαίαθ': Il. 11. 467, βιῴατο: Od. 1. 157, πευθοίατο: 9. 554, ἀπολοίατο. In Aeschylus we have, Pers. 360, 451, ἐκσωζοίατο: 369, φευξοίαθ': Supp. 695 (ch.), θείατ': 754, ἐχθαιροίατο: Cho. 484, κτιζοίαθ': Sept. 552, ὀλοίατο. In Sophocles, Aj. 842, ὀλοίατο: O. R. 1274, ὀψοίαθ' γνωσοίατο: O. C. 44, δεξαίατο: 602, πεμψαίαθ': 921, πυθοίατο: 945, δεξοίατ': El. 211 (ch.), ἀποναίατο. In Euripides, Hel. 159, ἀντιδωρησαίατο: H. F. 547, ἐκτισαίατο: I. T. 1341, οἰχοίατο.

[2] Pax 375, Ran. 613, τεθνηκέναι: Ran. 1012, τεθνάναι: Ran. 67, τεθνηκότος: Av. 1075, τεθνηκύτων: Ran. 171, 1476, τεθνηκύτα: 1175, τεθνηκόσι: *but* Av. 476, τεθνεώς: Nub. 782, 838; Ran. 1028, 1140, τεθνεῶτος. So in Antiphon, 112. 3, τεθνηκότι, followed in id. 5 by τεθνεῶτος, may perhaps be right.

ἀλλὰ βυρσίνην ἔχων
δειπνοῦντος ἑστὼς ἀποσοβεῖ τοὺς ῥήτορας.
Eq. 60.

Both the uncontracted and the contracted forms of comparative adjectives in -ων were good Attic, as inscriptions prove, and both are found in Aristophanes—

ἰὼ στρατηγοὶ πλείονες ἢ βελτίονες.
Ach. 1078.

A. καὶ τῶν θεατῶν ὁπότεροι
πλείους σκόπει.
B. καὶ δὴ σκοπῶ.
Nub. 1097.

αὐτὸς δ' ἑαυτῷ παρετίθει τὰ μείζονα.
Eq. 1223.

στόμωσον οἵαν ἐς τὰ μείζω πράγματα.
Nub. 1110.

The same is true of many other forms, such as ἐς and εἰς[1], οἴομαι and οἶμαι, ᾠόμην and ᾤμην[2], ἑαυτόν and αὑτόν[3], δέρω and δείρω[4], and if this principle is established that

[1] ἐς is the older form, and is the only one found in inscriptions till close upon the Archonship of Euclides, after which time εἰς supersedes ἐς almost entirely. Aristophanes avoided ἐς before a vowel, a fact curiously supported by his invariably using εἴσω, never ἔσω. The tragedians employed ἐς when the metre required it, and so Arist. Thesm. 1122—

πεσεῖν ἐς εὐνὴν καὶ γαμήλιον λέχος.

Pax. 140—

τί δ' ἢν ἐς ὑγρὸν πόντιον πέσῃ βάθος;

are lines from Euripides. For elision, whether before a vowel or a consonant, ἐς was used in Comedy. Ar. Ran. 186—

ἢ 's ὄνου πλοκάς
ἢ 'ς Κερβερίους:

Thesm. 1224—

τῃδὶ διώξει; 's τοὔμπαλιν τρέχεις σύ γε.

Thucydides always used ἐς.

[2] οἴομαι, Nub. 1342; Eq. 414; Vesp. 515. οἶμαι, Nub 1112, 1113, and more than twenty times elsewhere. ᾠόμην, Nub. 1473; Vesp. 791, 1138; Eccl. 168; ᾤμην, Plut. 834.

[3] ἑαυτόν, Nub. 407, 585, 980; Eq. 513; Pax 546: αὑτόν, Pax 735, 1184: ἑαυτοῦ, Vesp. 692, 1026, 1534, etc.: αὑτοῦ, Vesp. 76; Av. 1414: ἑαυτούς, Vesp. 1517; Lys. 577: ἑαυτῷ, Pl. 589; Eq. 544, 1223, etc.: αὑτῷ, Vesp. 130, 804; Pl. 1165.

[4] δέρω occurs Ran. 619, but δείρω Nub. 442 (anapaest); Vesp. 1286 (ἀπεδειρόμην); Av. 365 (troch.)

Aristophanes and the other Comic poets, representing as they did the cultured voice of Athens, readily availed themselves of double forms when such existed, it is not too much to consider the occurrence of only one form in Comic verse as distinct evidence that no other form was in use.

The inflexions which will be placed beyond question by a careful application of this rule are the second and third persons singular of the weak aorist indicative active, and the singular and plural forms of the active optative present of contracted verbs, as well as the corresponding inflexions of the Attic contracted future.

In the texts of prose writers two forms of the second and third persons singular weak aorist optative active are encountered side by side, often in the same paragraph and sometimes in the same line—for the second person a shorter form in *-αις* and a longer in *-ειας*, for the third a shorter in *-αι* and a longer in *-ειε(ν)*. Thus in Dem. 13. 26, *τὸ μὲν οὖν ἐπιτιμᾶν ἴσως φῆσαι τις ἂν ῥᾴδιον καὶ παντὸς εἶναι κτε.*: and just below, 15. 9, *καὶ φήσειε τις ἂν μὴ σκοπῶν ἀκριβῶς κτε.* In Lys. 122. 25 (12. 26) Bekker (in addend.), Cobet, and Scheibe all read *εἶτ', ὦ σχετλιώτατε πάντων, ἀντέλεγες μὲν ἵνα σώσειας, συνελάμβανες δὲ ἵνα ἀποκτείναις.* That *φήσαι* was in Attic impossible, and *ἀποκτείναις* an improbable form, will be proved by the following evidence.

As to third person, the evidence of Aristophanes alone is quite conclusive—

εἰ πάλιν ἀναβλέψειεν ἐξ ἀρχῆς; ὁ δέ.
Plut. 866.

ἀναβαλλομένη δείξειε τὸν φορμίσιον.
Eccl. 91.

ἥπερ διαλλάξειεν ἡμᾶς ἂν μόνη.
Lys. 1104.

ἢ πῦρ ἀπότροπον ἢ διᾴξειεν γαλῆ.
Eccl. 792.

δράσειε τοῦθ᾽. Β. ὅπου; τὸ τοῦ Πανὸς καλόν.
Lys. 911.

τὸν βασιλέως ὀφθαλμόν. Β. ἐκκόψειέ γε.
Ach. 92.

ὄναιο μένταν, εἴ τις ἐκπλύνειέ σε.
Plut. 1062.

αὕτη γὰρ ἐμπρήσειεν ἂν τὸ νεώριον.
Ach. 918.

τίς τῆς τεκούσης θᾶττον ἐπιπέμψειεν ἄν;
Eccl. 235.

ὁ Ζεύς σέ γ᾽ ἐπιτρίψειεν. Β. ἐπιτρίψουσι γάρ.
Id. 776.

πύθοιτ᾽ ἂν ἐπιτρίψειε. Β. νῦν δ᾽ οὐ τοῦτο δρᾷ.
Plut. 120.

κἂν ξυναποδρᾶναι δεῦρ᾽ ἐπιχειρήσειέ μοι.
Ran. 81.

ἅψας ἂν ἐσπέμψειεν ἐς τὸ νεώριον.
Ach. 921.

ὅτι οὐδ᾽ ἂν εἷς θύσειεν ἀνθρώπων ἔτι.
Plut. 137.

ὅστις καλέσειε κάρδοπον τὴν καρδόπην.
Nub. 1251.

κοὐδείς γέ μ᾽ ἂν πείσειεν ἀνθρώπων τὸ μὴ οὐκ.
Ran. 68.

πώγωνα περιδήσειεν ἐσταθευμέναις.
Eccl. 127.

πῶς οὖν τις ἂν σώσειε τοιαύτην πόλιν;
Ran. 1458.

νὴ τοὺς θεοὺς ἔγωγε μὴ φθάσειέ με.
Plut. 685.

τίς ἂν φράσειε ποῦ 'στι Χρεμύλος μοι σαφῶς;
Id. 1171.

τίς ἂν φράσειε ποῦ 'στιν ἡ Λυσιστράτη;
Lys. 1086.

τί δῆτα τοῦτ᾽ ἂν ὠφελήσειέν σ᾽; Β. ὅ τι;
Nub. 753.

The Lacedaemonian Lampito's words in Lys. 171, *πᾷ κά τις ἀμπείσειεν αὖ μὴ πλαδδιῆν*; may be mentioned along with these instances from the senarii, but Plut. 136, where Dindorf reads—

παύσει' ἂν, εἰ βούλοιτο ταῦθ'; Β. ὁτιὴ τί δή;

must be reserved for further discussion. Besides these twenty-two instances in iambic trimeters we have in other regular metres, iambic, trochaic, and anapaestic, the following:—Pax 568, ἀπαλλάξειεν: Plut. 510, βλέψειε: Thesm. 842, δανίσειεν: Plut. 510, διανέμειεν: Plut. 592, ἐξολέσειεν: Ach. 639, καλέσειε: Nub. 969, κάμψειεν: Ran. 923, ληρήσειε: Plut. 506, πορίσειεν: Eccl. 647, φιλήσειεν: and in choric measures—Ach. 1151, Thesm. 1051, ἐξολέσειεν: Pax 1035, ἐπαινέσειεν: Ach. 1171, ἐπάξειεν: Thesm. 328, ἰαχήσειεν: Ach. 1166, πατάξειε. Against these numerous examples of the longer ending there are no instances of the shorter to bring.

The evidence drawn from other Comic writers is equally convincing. The references are to the pages of Meineke's volumes of the 'Fragmenta Comicorum.'

ἀπὸ τοῦ πότου παύσειε, τοῦ λίαν πότου.
2. 122.

εἰ μὴ κόρη δεύσειε τὸ σταῖς ἤθεος.
561.

πῶς ἂν κομίσειέ μοί τις;
786.

ἀλλ' Ἡγέλοχος οὗτός με μηνύσειεν ἄν.
874.

τίς ἂν φράσειε ποῦ 'στι τὸ Διονύσιον;
1001.

In 2. 947, a fragment of Aristophanes, occurs ἐπιθυμήσειε in what seems to be a pseudo-oracle (cp. p. 44), and from other metres are derived, 2. 673, παίσειε: 981, πορίσειεν: 1051, συναρπάσειεν. There is in fact not a single instance of the shorter ending which till now holds the place of honour in all grammars. All examples of it occurring in prose ought once and for all to be altered to the longer. The evidence is simply overwhelming, and proves to certainty that optative forms ending in *-αι* were quite unknown to the Athenians. They do not occur once in Sophocles or Euripides, and in Aeschylus they occur only four times, and in all cases in the chorus—

> *μήποτε λοιμὸς ἀνδρῶν*
> *τῶνδε πόλιν κενῶσαι·*
> *μήδ' ἐπιχωρίοις*
> *πτώμασιν αἱματίσαι πέδον γᾶς.*
>
> Supp. 662 (bis).
>
> *ὁ μέγας Ζεὺς ἀπαλέξαι*
> *γάμον Αἰγυπτογενῆ μοι.*
>
> Id. 1052.
>
> *μηδὲ πιοῦσα κόνις μέλαν αἷμα πολιτᾶν.*
> *δι' ὀργὰν ποινᾶς ἀντιφόνους ἄτας*
> *ἁρπαλίσαι πόλεως* [1].
>
> Eum. 982.

[1] In Supp. 624, *Ζεὺς δ' ἐπικράναι τέλος*, the form is simply a useless conjecture of Dindorf's for *ἐπικράνει*, and in Ag. 170 (ch.) *λέξαι* is only conjectural. The longer form is found in Aesch. P. V. 202, *ἄρξειεν*: 396, *κάμψειεν*: 503, *φήσειεν*: 1049 (ch.), *συγχώσειεν*: 1051 (ch.), *ῥίψειε*: Sept. 739 (ch.), *λούσειεν*: Supp. 281, *θρέψειε*: 487, *ἐχθήρειεν*: Agam. 38, *λέξειεν*: 366 (ch.), *σκήψειεν*: 552, *λέξειεν*: 884, *καταρρίψειεν*: 1328, {π τρέψειεν: 1376, *φάρξειεν*: Cho. 344 (ch.), *κομίσειεν*: 854, *κλέψειεν*. In Sophocles we find O. R. 502 (ch.), *παραμείψειεν*: 1302, *μαρτυρήσειεν*: O. C. 391, *πράξειεν*: 1657, *φράσειε*: Ant. 666, *στήσειε*: Aj. 1149, *κατασβέσειε*: 1176, *ἀποσπάσειε*: El. 572, *ἐκθύσειε*: 1103, *φράσειεν*: Γr. 355, *θέλξειεν*: 388, *λέξειεν*: 433, *πέρσειεν*: 458, *ἀλγύνειεν*: 657 (ch.), *ἀνύσειε*: 729, *λέξειεν*: 906, *ψαύσειεν*: 908, *βλέψειεν*: 933, *ἐφάψειεν*: 935, *ἕρξειεν*: 955 (ch.), *ἀποικίσειεν*: Phil. 281, *ἀρκέσειεν*: 463, *μεταστήσειεν*: 695 (ch.) *ἀποκλαύσειεν*: 698 (ch.), *κατευνάσειεν*: 711, *ἀνύσειε*: 1062, *νείμειεν*. In Euripides, Or. 508, *ἀποκτείνειεν*: 783, *οἰκτίσειε*: Phoen. 152, *ὀλέσειεν*: 517, *δράσειεν*: 948, *ἐκσώσειεν*: 104 (ch.), *ἀφανίσειεν*: Med. 95, *δράσειε*: 760 (ch.), *πελάσειε*: 1389 (ch.), *ὀλέσειε*: Hipp. 684, *ἐκτρέψειεν*: 985, *διαπτύξειεν*: 1253, *πλήσειε*: 1387 (ch.), *κοίμισειε*: I. A. 802, *φάσειε*: 1597, *πλήξειεν*: I. T. 577, *φράσειεν*: 590, *πέμψειε*: 627, *περιστείλειεν*: 740, *ἀγγείλειεν*: Rhes. 217, *πέμψειεν*: 235 (ch.), *κάμψειε*: Tro. 478, *κομπάσειεν*: 719, *νικήσειε*: 928, *κρίνειεν*: 1014, *δράσειεν*: 1161, *ὀρθώσειεν*: 1189, *γράψειεν*: Cycl. 146, *πλήσειε*: 535, *ψαύσειε*: Bacch. 1072, *ἀναχαιτίσειε*: 1259, *καλέσειεν*: Heracl. 179, *κρίνειεν*: 537, *λέξειε*: 538, *δράσειεν*: Hel. 40, *κουφίσειε*: 175 (ch.), *πέμψειε*: 436, *διαγγέλειε*: 522 (ch.), *ψαύσειεν*: 699, *ἀρκέσειεν*: 1045, *σιγήσειεν*: Ion. 372, *δράσειεν*: 529, *σημήνειεν*: 787, *συναντήσειεν*: 1127, *δεύσειε*: H. F. 186, *ἐπαινέσειεν*: 719, *ἀναστήσειε*: 929, *βάψειεν*: 1217, *κρύψειεν*. Eighty-nine instances in all from the three Tragedians.

Accordingly, Dobree's arrangement of the initial words of a fragment of the Tarentini of Alexis (quoted by Athenaeus in 11. 463) is certainly wrong—

οὐδὲ εἷς ἂν εὐλόγως
ἡμῖν φθονῆσαι νοῦν ἔχων, οἳ τῶν πέλας
οὐδέν' ἀδικοῦμεν οὐδέν[1]· ἆρ' οὐκ οἶσθ' ὅτι κτε.

All we can affirm is that οὐδείς and εὐλόγως, without ἄν, were in the first line, and that the second went on—

ἡμῖν φθονήσει νοῦν ἔχων κτε.

Critics have had the same advantage of a broken line in a fragment of the Second Thesmophoriazusae of Aristophanes, and have used it with equal skill. One thing is certain, that Aristophanes did not write—

οὐδ' ἂν λέγων λέξαι[2] τις.

Antiphanes is credited with ἐγχέαι in a passage quoted by Athenaeus (14. 641)—

A. Οἶνον Θάσιον πίνοις ἄν; B. εἴ τις ἐγχέαι.
A. πρὸς ἀμυγδάλας δὲ πῶς ἔχεις; B. εἰρηνικῶς.
μαλακὰς σφόδρα, δι' ἃς μέλιτι προσπαίζειν βία.
A. μελίπηκτα δ' εἴ σοι προσφέροι; B. τρώγοιμι καὶ
ᾠὸν δὲ καταπίνοιμ' ἄν. A. ἄλλου δεῖ τινός;

but πίνοις, προσφέροι, τρώγοιμι, and καταπίνοιμι, all suggest the true reading ἐγχέοι.

The passage of the Plutus which was reserved above for further discussion reads in the manuscripts as follows—

οὔκουν ὅδ' ἐστὶν αἴτιος, καὶ ῥᾳδίως
παύσειεν, εἰ βούλοιτο, ταῦτ' ἄν;
B. ὅτι τί δή;

[1] Naber's correction for οὐδὲν ἀδ. οὐδέν'.

[2] The λῆξαι of Fritsche is out of the question. The form of expression occurs again in the Ion of Eubulus (Athen. 4. 169) in the same connexion—the end of a long enumeration—

Τρύβλια δὲ καὶ βατάνια καὶ κακκάβια καὶ
λοπάδια καὶ πατάνια πυκνὰ ταρφέα
κοὐδ' ἂν λέγων λέξαιμι.

and it must be retained in that shape in whatever way ὅτι τί δή; is translated. Dindorf, in his conjecture, παύσει' ἄν, εἰ κτε., which Meineke has adopted, has fallen into an error which other emendators besides him have committed. Although nearly 150 instances of the optative forms in -ειεν have already been registered, it will be observed that in no single instance is the final syllable elided. The temptation to a writer of verse to elide the final epsilon before ἄν must have been very strong indeed, and that it was never done proves convincingly that Attic usage was absolutely opposed to such elision. Accordingly the metrical fault of the line—

ἴσως ἂν ἐκπνεύσειεν· ὅταν δ' ἀνῇ πνοάς—
Eur. Or. 700.

must not be corrected by docking the ἐκπνεύσειεν[1], but either by reading ἣν δ' ἀνῃ with Nauck, or ὅτε δ' ἀνῃ with Kirchhoff.

Thus, by the incontrovertible testimony of Attic verse, the true ending of the third person singular of the weak aorist optative active is proved to be -ειε before a consonant and -ειεν before a vowel. The two cases of divergence from this law, as occurring in lyrical passages of the earliest of the three Tragedians, and as opposed by more than one hundred and fifty examples, may be regarded as corrupt, or, at all events, are to be treated as antiquated and anomalous.

[1] As most of the instances of the optative ending -αι are due to the ingenuity of critics, so a long list of exceptions to the rule against eliding the final syllable of -ειεν may be drawn up from the emendations of scholars. In Aesch. Choeph. 854, κλέψει' ἄν is read by Heath and Monk. In Agam. 1376, Schutz, without warrant, altered πημονῆς ἀρκύστατ' ἂν | φάρξειεν to πημονῆς ἀρκύστατον φάρξει' ἄν. In Eur. Hipp. 469, for καλῶς ἀκριβώσειαν Valckenaer wrote κανὼν ἀκριβώσει' ἄν, and our rule also invalidates Schneidewin's γυνὴ τεκοῦσα κομπάσει' οἷ' ἄν ποτε in Tro. 478, and Porson's πράξει' ἂν ἐκ θεῶν κακῶς in Andr. 1283. Meineke's attempt, in his 'Curae Criticae,' p. 55, to arrange a fragment of the Comic poet Archippus, quoted by Plutarch, Alcib. 1, is vitiated by the same fault, δόξει' for δόξειεν, and that he should adopt Cobet's φράσει' ὅπου in Ar. Plut. 1171 and leave φράσειέ που in Lys. 1016, is as careless as it is incorrect.

In regard to the second person singular no such absolute rule can be formulated, but the Attic usage is nevertheless distinctly indicated. Aristophanes supplies the following evidence—

> εἰ πάλιν ἀναβλέψειας ὥσπερ καὶ πρὸ τοῦ.
> Plut. 95.
>
> ὅπως ἂν αὐτὴν ἀφανίσειας εἰπέ μοι.
> Nub. 760.
>
> ἵν' αὐτὸν ἐκπέμψειας. B. ἀλλ' οὐκ ἔστασεν.
> Vesp. 175.
>
> πῶς ἂν καλέσειας ἐντυχὼν 'Αμυνίᾳ;
> Nub. 689.
>
> πῶς ἂν σύ μοι λέξειας ἁμὲ χρὴ λέγειν;
> Eq. 15.
>
> μόνος γὰρ ἂν λέξειας ἀξίως ἐμοῦ.
> Thesm. 187.
>
> πῶς δῆτ' ἂν αὐτοὺς ξυγκαλέσειας; B. ῥᾳδίως.
> Av. 201.
>
> ἄνδρα πτερώσειας σύ; B. πάντες τοῖς λόγοις.
> Id. 1438.
>
> εἴ τινα πόλιν φράσειας ἡμῖν εὔερον.
> Id. 121.
>
> τοὺς σοὺς φράσειας, εἰ δεοίμην, οἷσι σύ.
> Ran. 110.

Besides these from the senarii, there are found in other metres three additional instances. In iambic tetrameter catalectic—

> ὥστ' εἰ σὺ βριμήσαιο καὶ βλέψειας ὀστρακίνδα—
> Eq. 855.

in anapaestic dimeters—

> ἀλλ' ἴθι χαίρων καὶ πράξειας
> Eq. 498.

and in a chorus, Thesm. 368, κυρώσειας.

Against these thirteen unquestioned instances of the longer ending there are four equally well-established of the shorter, two in the senarii, and two in anapaestic tetrameter catalectic—

διὰ δακτυλίου μὲν οὖν ἐμέ γ' ἂν διελκύσαις.
Plut. 1036.

ἆρ' ὠφελήσαις ἄν τι τὸν σαυτοῦ φίλον;
Id. 1134.

εἰ μὲν χαίρεις ἀρνὸς φωνῇ, παιδὸς φωνὴν ἐλεήσαις.
Vesp. 572.

οὐκ ἂν δικάσαις. σὺ γὰρ οὖν νῦν μοι νικᾶν πολλῷ δεδόκησαι.
Id. 726.

Now it has been proved (p. 51) that un-Attic forms are of frequent occurrence in anapaestic verse, and accordingly *ἐλεήσαις* and *δικάσαις* must not be regarded as satisfactory evidence for the shorter ending. Besides *ἐλεήσαις* may well be a stately antiquated form used for effect if we consider the preceding line—

ὥσπερ θεὸν ἀντιβολεῖ με τρέμων τῆς εὐθύνης ἀπολῦσαι.

Of the two instances from the senarii, *διελκύσαις* forms part of a proverbial phrase, and *ὠφελήσαις* is put into the mouth of Hermes.

Four other passages demand discussion. In Pax 405, where the manuscripts give—

ἴθι δὴ κάτειπ'· ἴσως γὰρ ἂν πείσαις ἐμε,

Hirschig, followed by Meineke, now reads *ἀναπείσεις*, but even if the text is right it would not support Attic usage, as a few lines before, Hermes, who speaks the line in question, utters the para-tragœdic words—

ἀλλ', ὦ μέλ', ὑπὸ τοῦ Διὸς ἀμαλδυνθήσομαι,
εἰ μὴ τετορήσω ταῦτα καὶ λακήσομαι.

Long ago, the omission of *ἂν* in one manuscript of Nub. 776—

ὅπως ἀποστρέψαις ἂν ἀντιδικῶν δίκην,

led Brunck to conjecture—

ὅπως ἂν ἀποστρέψειας ἀντιδικῶν δίκην,

but Meineke's conjecture of ἀποστρέψαι' ἂν is so manifest an improvement to the sense as to be almost convincing. For the manuscript reading of Vesp. 819—

θήρῳον εἴ πως ἐκκομίσαις τὸ τοῦ Λύκου

the same scholar substitutes—

θήρῳον οὔπω 'ξεκόμισας τὸ τοῦ Λύκου,

and Brunck proposed to omit *τό* as tautological—

θήρῳον εἴ πως ἐκκομίσειας τοῦ Λύκου.

The only remaining instance need not detain us long. Τοῦτο σαυτῇ κρώξαις, in Lys. 506, is a proverbial expression, and loses by Meineke's change of the optative *κρώξαις* to the indicative *'κρωξας*. According to Suïdas the proverb was derived from inauspicious birds, *ἀπ' ὀρνέων τῶν δυσοιωνίστων*, as the similar one in Plut. 369—

σὺ μὲν οἶδ' ὃ κρώζεις· ὡς ἐμοῦ τι κεκλοφότος,
ζητεῖς μεταλαβεῖν,

refers to *τοὺς μάτην θρυλοῦντας ὡς αἱ κορῶναι.*

There are no instances of the second person in the fragments of the other Comic poets of a good age, but the evidence derived from Tragic verse in support of the longer form is curiously even stronger that that from Comedy. In the three tragedians there are over twenty lines which require the dissyllabic inflexion[1], but only two lines of Euripides in which the monosyllabic ending is necessary.

If the testimony thus presented by verse is candidly accepted, it will be seen that although the ending *-αις* was not so carefully avoided as that of the third person *-αι*, yet

[1] Aesch. Supp. 925, *ψαύσειας*: Eum. 645, *λύσειας*: Soph. Ant. 244, *εἰκάσειας*: Aj. 1122, *κομπάσειας*: 1137, *κλέψειας*: El. 348, *ἐκδείξειας*: 801, *πράξειας*: Tr. 700, *βλέψειας*: Phil. 1222, *φράσειας*. Eur. Med. 761 (ch.), *πράξειας*: 1135, *τέρψειας*: Hipp. 345, *λέξειας*: 472, *πράξειας*: Andr. 462, *πράξειας*: I. A. 464, *γήμειας*: I. T. 505, *φράσειας*: 513, *φράσειας*: 1024, *κρύψειας*: Hell. 1039, *πείσειας*: El. 620, *μηνύσειας*. The shorter form does not occur in Aeschylus or Sophocles, for *λέξαις* in Ag. 97, is merely a conjecture for *λέξασ'*. In Euripides occur, Med. 325, *πείσαις*: I. T. 1184, *σώσαις*.

it savoured of antiquity, and ought, when it occurs in Attic, to be regarded as an anomaly allowable only in verse, and in the case of Comedy probably always either an intentional aberration from ordinary usage, or due to the introduction of a crystallized expression, proverbial or otherwise.

In regard to the third person plural, the true form cannot be decided by the dictates of verse, for *-αιεν* has the same metrical value as *-ειᾰν*. But if the form in *-ειε(ν)* was for the singular the only one in use, there can be no doubt that *-ειαν* was the genuine plural ending. The manuscript authority is consistently in its favour, and when that fails it must be restored in our texts.

The next point to be considered is of almost equal importance. Contracted verbs are by far the most numerous class in Greek, and, in number at all events, equal those of all other classes taken together. It is accordingly of some moment to establish the true endings of so frequently occurring a mood as the present optative active. The following facts will be demonstrated. All verbs in *-έω* or *-όω* contracting to *-ῶ* have their present optative singular ending in *-οίην, -οίης, -οίη*, and all verbs in *-αω* contracting to *-ῶ* have the corresponding forms in *-ῴην, -ῴης, -ῴη*. In the dual and plural, on the contrary, Attic requires the shorter forms, namely, *-οῖτον, -οίτην, -οῖμεν, -οῖτε, -οῖεν* for verbs in *-όω* and *-έω*, and *-ῷτον, -ῴτην, -ῷμεν, -ῷτε, -ῷεν* for verbs in *-άω*. Thus the optative of τηρῶ (*-έω*) had from Athenian lips the forms:—

τηροίην		τηροῖμεν
τηροίης	τηροῖτον	τηροῖτε
τηροίη	τηροίτην	τηροῖεν,

while δηλῶ (*-όω*) was inflected as follows—

δηλοίην		δηλοῖμεν
δηλοίης	δηλοῖτον	δηλοῖτε
δηλοίη	δηλοίτην	δηλοῖεν,

and δρῶ (-άω) in a similar way—

δρῴην		δρῷμεν
δρῴης	δρῷτον	δρῷτε
δρῴη	δρῴτην	δρῷεν.

The instances of Singular forms are in Aristophanes peculiarly numerous, and quite sufficient to put their true inflexions beyond question—

ἵνα μὴ στρατεύοιτ' ἀλλὰ βινοίη μένων.
Ach. 1052.

ἵνα μὴ βοῴη κηρίῳ βεβυσμένον.
Thesm. 506.

εὐδαιμονοίης[1], Τηλέφῳ δ' ἁγὼ φρονῶ.
Ach. 446.

εὐδαιμονοίης, ὥσπερ ἡ μήτηρ ποτέ.
Id. 457.

θήσω πρυτανεῖ' ἢ μηκέτι ζῴην ἐγώ.
Nub. 1255.

εἰ ξυνδοκοίη τοῖσιν ἄλλοις ὀρνέοις.
Av. 197.

ὥσπερ κάτοπτρον, κᾆτα τηροίην ἔχων.
Nub. 752.

Besides these, derived from iambic trimeters, there are three in iambic tetrameter catalectic verse, one in trochaic tetrameter, six in anapaestic systems, and four from other metres—

οὐ ταὐτὸν ὦ τᾶν ἐστίν, οὐδ' ἂν Σωκράτει δοκοίη.
Nub. 1432.

ἤδη μεσοίη, ῥήματ' ἂν βόεια δώδεκ' εἶπεν.
Ran. 924.

αἰσθανόμενος σου πάντα τραυλίζοντος ὅ τι νοοίης.
Nub. 1381.

ἐπὶ τί γάρ μ' ἐκεῖθεν ἦγες; B. *ἵν' ἀκολουθοίης ἐμοί.*
Av. 340.

[1] So all the MSS., but Meineke adopts *εὖ σοι γένοιτο* from Athenaeus 5. 186, who quotes the line as from Eur. 'Telephus.' The Scholiast in loco has *καλῶς ἔχοιμι Τηλέφῳ κτε.*

καὶ βασανίζειν πῶς οὐχὶ πάλαι χορὸν αἰτοίη καθ' ἑαυτόν.
Eq. 513.

ἐπὶ τῶν σκήπτρων ἐκάθητ' ὄρνις μετέχων ὅ τι δωροδοκοίη.
Av. 510.

ὁ δ' ἄρ' εἱστήκει τὸν Λυσικράτη τηρῶν ὅ τι δωροδοκοίη.
Id. 513.

οὔτε τέχνην ἂν τῶν ἀνθρώπων οὔτ' ἂν σοφίαν μελετῴη.
Plut. 511.

τίς ἂν οὖν εἴη; ζητεῖθ' ὑμεῖς, ὡς πᾶν ἂν ἔγωγε ποιοίην.
Vesp. 348.

περὶ τὴν κεφαλήν; μή νυν ζῴην.
Lys. 531.

Vesp. 278, ἀντιβολοίη: id. 276, βουβωνιῴη: Thesm. 681, δρῴη: Nub. 1387, χεζητιῴην.

Now, opposed to these twenty-one unquestioned examples of the dissyllabic ending, stands a solitary instance of the monosyllabic—

χοὔτω μὲν ἂν εὖ ποιοῖς
εἴ σοι πυκνότης ἔνεστ'
ἐν τῷ τρόπῳ, ὡς λέγεις,
Eq. 1131.

which Meineke formerly altered to εὖ ποιοίης εἰ πυκνότης, but he now prefers χοὔτω μὲν ἄρ' εὖ ποιεῖς· ᾗ σοι πυκνότης. No conjecture is required, for a single instance of a form that was certainly possible in Tragedy occurring in Comedy out of the regular metres does not enfranchise that form as genuine Attic, or diminish the validity of our argument against it. Wecklein's emendation, however, deserves remark. He considers χοὔτω as a corruption for καὶ τοῦτο, and ἂν subsequently added to restore the syllable so lost, the original line being—

καὶ τοῦτο μὲν εὖ ποιεῖς[1].

[1] It is strange that Veitch should have missed this solitary good instance in his favour as completely as he has missed the point of the general question. The following note to κλαίω, in his 'Greek Verbs Irregular and Defective,' proves how little can be said for the shorter forms. '"Recte Cobetus," says

There are some corruptions of the text of Aristophanes which throw so much light upon the question how our prose texts so frequently present such optatives with monosyllabic singular endings, that they cannot well be passed over without remark. In Av. 204, Pisthetaerus, discussing with Epops the best means of summoning the birds to a conference, asks him the question—

> πῶς δῆτ' ἂν αὐτοὺς ξυγκαλέσειας;

to which Epops replies—

> ῥᾳδίως.
> δευρὶ γὰρ ἐσβὰς αὐτίκα μάλ' ἐς τὴν λόχμην,
> ἔπειτ' ἀναγείρας τὴν ἐμὴν ἀηδόνα,
> καλοῦμεν αὐτούς· οἱ δὲ νῷν τοῦ φθέγματος
> ἐάνπερ ἐπακούσωσι θεύσονται δρόμῳ.

Even in a good manuscript like the Vatican καλοῖμ' ἄν [1]

Franke, "Tragicis νοσοῖμι et δοκοῖμι et similia concessit, non concessit Comicis et Scriptoribus Atticis." Aristophanes uses, to be sure, βοῴη, Thesm. 506; ἀναβιῴην, Ran. 178; δρῴη, Thesm. 681; and βινοίη, Ach. 1052; νοοίης, Nub. 1381; αἰτοίη, Eq. 513; ἀκολουθοίης, Av. 340; but κλάοιμι, 341; ἀπέλθοιμι, Ach. 403; πλέοι, Pax 699; δέοι, Lys. 1132; ἀπο-δοίην, Nub. 118, 755, etc.; but ἐπί-δοιμι, Ach. 1156, etc., etc. Prose, δοκοίη, Thuc. 6. 34; 8. 54, but δοκοῖ, 2. 79, 100; 3. 16; ἐγχειροῖμ' ἄν, Pl. Tim. 48; κοσμοῖ, Lach. 196; νοοῖ, Euthyd. 287; κατηγοροίη, Menex. 244 (Bekk., Stallb.), but κατηγοροῖ, Gorg. 251; ζητοίην, Epist. 318; ζητοῖς, Prot. 327, etc., etc.' The note proves nothing at all, and no one would once think of advocating a form like κλῴην, which Veitch takes the trouble to deny. For κλᾴω never contracts or could contract to κλῶ, and is consequently removed from our rule. His other examples are equally erroneous. ἀπέλθοιμι does not come from a contracted verb, nor does πλέω contract to πλῶ, or δέω (lack) to δῶ. ἀποδοίην and ἀναβιῴην (leg. ἀναβιοίην) belong at worst to a different category from contracted verbs, and we hope that the juxtaposition of ἀποδοίην and ἐπίδοιμι does not prove that Veitch derives ἐπίδοιμι in Ach. 1156 from ἐπιδίδωμι, a hope which his careful hyphening makes dangerously small.

[1] Of course such a form as καλοῖμ' ἄν copyists were constantly meeting in Tragedy, though even there it is the rarer of the two, as the following statistics prove. The longer forms are found — *First person:* Soph. O. C. 764, ἀλγοίην: Ant. 668, θαρσοίην: El. 1306, ὑπηρετοίην: Eur. Hec. 1166, κινοίην: Or. 778, δρᾴην: 1147, ζῴην: Med. 565, εὐδαιμονοίην: Hipp. 1117 (ch.), συνευτυχοίην: Alc. 354, ἀπαντλοίην, Supp. 454, ζῴην: Heracl. 996, συνοικοίην: Hel. 770, ἀλγοίην: 1010, ἀδικοίην.—13 instances. *Second person:* Aesch. Agam. 1049, ἀπειθοίης: Cho. 1063 (ch.), εὐτυχοίης: Soph. O. R. 1478, εὐτυχοίης: O. C. 362, κατοικοίης: Ant. 70, δρῴης: Aj. 526, αἰνοίης: El. 1090 (ch.), ζῴης:

is found, though the correct plural form remains in the Ravenna and others. The source of the error was the inability of a copyist to reconcile the plural *καλοῦμεν* with the preceding *ἐσβάς* and *ἀναγείρας*. Such ignorance, both of syntax and accidence, produced many similar errors. Thus, in Vesp. 1404, the last word of the amusing lines—

> Αἴσωπον ἀπὸ δείπνου βαδίζονθ' ἑσπέρας
> θρασεῖα καὶ μεθύση τις ὑλάκτει κύων.
> κἄπειτ' ἐκεῖνος εἶπεν, ὦ κύον, κύον,
> εἰ νὴ Δί' ἀντὶ τῆς κακῆς γλώττης ποθὲν
> πυροὺς πρίαιο σωφρονεῖν ἄν μοι δοκεῖς,

is altered in some manuscripts to *δοκοῖς*, in others to *δοκῇς*, both errors arising from ignorance of a well-known rule of Attic syntax. According to that rule, *δοκῶ*, *νομίζω*, *οἶμαι*, *ἡγοῦμαι*, *προσδοκῶ*, and similar verbs, may be followed by an infinitive and *ἄν*. Thus, Demosthenes begins his second Olynthiac with the words, Ἐπὶ πολλῶν μὲν ἄν τις ἰδεῖν ὦ ἄνδρες Ἀθηναῖοι δοκεῖ μοι τὴν παρὰ τῶν θεῶν γιγνομένην τῇ πόλει, οὐχ ἥκιστα δ' ἐν τοῖς παροῦσι πράγμασι. There too *δοκοῖ* is not left unrepresented in the manuscripts. In Plato, Lys. 206 A, we have an instance of the corrupt form

Eur. Phoen. 1086, *εὐδαιμονοίης*: Med. 688, *εὐτυχοίης*: Hipp. 105, *εὐδαιμονοίης*: Alc. 713, *ζῴης*: 1037, *εὐδαιμονοίης*: 1153, *εὐτυχοίης*: I. T. 750, *ἀδικοίης*: Hel. 619, *φοροίης*: El. 231, *εὐδαιμονοίης*.—16 instances. *Third person:* Aesch. Supp. 1064 (ch.), *ἀποστεροίη*: Agam. 349, *κρατοίη*: Soph. O. R. 829, *ὀρθοίη*: O. C. 1435, *εὐοδοίη*: El. 258, *δρῴη*: Trach. 902, *ἀντῴη*: Phil. 444, *ἐῴη*: Eur. Andr. 237, *ξυνοικοίη*: I. A. 63, *ἀπωθοίη*.—9 instances. The shorter endings occur—*First person:* Aesch. P. V. 978, *νοσοῖμ' ἄν*: Soph. O. C. 507, *χωροῖμ' ἄν*: Ant. 552, *ὠφελοῖμ' ἐγώ*: Aj. 537, *ὠφελοῖμί σε*: Phil. 895, *δρῷμ' ἐγώ*: 1044, *δοκοῖμ' ἄν*: Eur. Or. 1517, *εὐορκοῖμ' ἐγώ*: Hipp. 336, *σιγῷμ' ἄν*: Hel. 157, *ὠφελοῖμί σε*.—9 instances. *Second person:* Soph. El. 1491, *χωροῖς*: Phil. 674, *χωροῖς*: Eur. Andr. 679, *ὠφελοῖς*.—3 instances. *Third person:* Soph. O. C. 1769 (ch.) *ἀπαρκοῖ*: Eur. Or. 514, *κυροῖ*: Supp. 608, *αἱροῖ*: 897, *δυστυχοῖ*: El. 1077, *εὐτυχοῖ*: *δυστυχοῖ* in Aesch. Agam. 1328 is only a conjecture of Blomfield's.—5 instances. In all, there are in Tragedy 37 instances of the longer forms against 17 of the shorter; in Comedy 21 of the longer against one of the shorter, that one being not in the regular metres. *ὑμεναιοῖ*, which Curtius, 'Das Verbum,' 2. 110, quotes as an optative form from Ar. Pax 1076, is certainly a subjunctive, and in the succeeding line a humorous epicism.

replacing the true even in the best manuscripts. The true reading undoubtedly is ποῖός τις οὖν ἄν σοι δοκεῖ θηρευτὴς εἶναι; After changes of this kind were once made, and forms like δοκοῖ recognized as legitimate, the ulcer went on spreading, and copyists considered one form as good as another, until even undoubted forms in -ίην, like the optative of verbs in -μι, were sometimes corrupted. In this way ἐπιδιδοῖμ' ἄν and ἐπιδιδοῖ ἄν are variants for the true ἐπιδιδοίην ἄν in Plat. Legg. 913 B. The fact that all the best manuscripts support ἐπιδιδοῖ ἄν in this passage indicates how untrustworthy all manuscript authority is, whenever two similar sounds come together, or when one letter or one set of letters is followed by another not readily to be distinguished from it. Accordingly, it will be observed that in very many of the prose instances of the shorter form in the third person singular, the word succeeding the optative begins with Η, Ν, Π, or Κ, as Plato, Phaedr. 276 B, ποιοῖ ἐφ' οἷς: id. 275 C, ἀγνοιοῖ πλέον: Rep. 394, ἐπιχιχειροῖ πολλῶν: Conv. 196 C, ἂν σωφρονοῖ καί: Thuc. 4. 105, προσχωροῖ καί.

It is still more interesting to trace the genuine ending in the more considerable corruptions of the texts. Cases like the substitution of ὑπηρετοίμην for ὑπηρετοίην in Soph. El. 1306, need not detain us long, but there is a very interesting and typical case in Plato's Phaedo, 87 B. There εἴ τις ἀπιστοίη αὐτῷ has been altered in every manuscript to εἴ τις ἀπιστῶν αὐτῷ, though the optative is so necessary that ἀπιστοίη is one of the few emendations which Stallbaum makes. The same transcriber's error disfigures a passage of Lysias, where there is a sentence without a finite verb. Lys. 916. 6 (33. 9), τίς γὰρ οὐκ ἂν ἐνορῶν ἐν τῷ πρὸς ἀλλήλους πολέμῳ μεγάλους αὐτοὺς γεγενημένους; Reisk conjectured ἐντρέποιτο ὁρῶν, but Cobet is beyond question right in reading ἐνορῴη, i. e. ΩΙΗ for ΩΝ.

In Antiphon, 112. 31. (1. 10) ἵνα μὴ ἀναγκαζόμενοι ἃ

ἐγὼ ἐπερωτῶ μὴ λέγοιεν, the manuscripts give *ἐπερωτῶ μή* which Reisk altered to *ἐπερωτῷμι*. Of course the true reading is *ἐπερωτῴην*, i.e. ΩΙΗΝ for ΩΙΜΗ. Plato, Gorg 510 D, supplies us with another type, *εἰ ἄρα τις ἐννοήσειεν ἐν ταύτῃ τῇ πόλει τῶν νέων, Τίνα ἂν τρόπον ἐγὼ μέγα δυναίμην καὶ μηδείς με ἀδικοίη, αὕτη, ὡς ἔοικεν, αὐτῷ ὁδὸς ἔστιν κτε.* Most manuscripts have *ἀδικοῖ ἡ αὕτη*, one *ἀδικοῖ αὐτή*, and only one the genuine *ἀδικοίη, αὕτη*. This separation of the final letter from the rest of the word is likewise exemplified in Xen. Cyrop. 5. 3. 52, *Κῦρος δ' εἰπὼν ὅτι ἐπὶ τῇ ὁδῷ ὑπομενοίη.* Along with *ἑπόμενοι* and *ἐπιμένοι* the manuscripts also present us with *ἐπιμένοι δή*. The Attic future optative ending *-οίη* is concealed in the *οι δή* of a copyist who, ignorant of the genuine ending, severed its last letter from the optative and made a new word out of the tag.

The results arrived at up to this point of the discussion are these. While the shorter endings were in the singular not altogether avoided by the antiquated dialect of Tragedy, the longer were the only forms used in Comedy and prose, and even in Tragedy were decidedly preferred. The manuscripts of prose writers are on this question quite untrustworthy, and must be consistently corrected.

The future optative is a rare tense in Greek, being used only in two constructions, namely, either as representing in indirect discourse a future indicative of direct discourse, or with *ὅπως* or *ὅπως μή* after verbs of striving, etc., and with *μή* or *ὅπως μή* after verbs of fearing. Moreover in both these cases the future indicative is much more common. Accordingly, it is not surprising that there is in use only a single instance of the optative of a contracted future—

ἔπειτ' ἐμοὶ τὰ δείν' ἐπηπείλησ' ἔπη
εἰ μὴ φανοίην πᾶν τὸ ξυντυχὸν πάθος.

Soph. Aj. 312.

But the parallelism between contracted presents and contracted futures is so complete in every respect that there can be no doubt as to the Attic inflexions of the latter. The passage of Xenophon (Cyrop. 5. 3. 52) quoted above is by itself valuable confirmatory evidence. Consequently the futures of στέλλω and βιβάζω, namely, στελῶ and βιβῶ, must have had for singular optative forms the following:—

στελοίην	βιβῴην
στελοίης	βιβῴης
στελοίη	βιβῴη,

and in the same way all similar verbs must have made the mood in question.

Further, the perfect active used these same endings for the singular of its optative mood in those comparatively rare cases in which the analytic form of the perfect participle and εἴην was not preferred. Whenever the unresolved mood appears in verse it has the endings -οίην, -οίης, -οίη. The only instance in Tragedy is Soph. O. R. 840—

> ἐγὼ διδάξω σ'· ἢν γὰρ εὑρεθῇ λέγων
> σοὶ ταὔτ', ἔγωγ' ἂν ἐκπεφευγοίην πάθος.

In Aristoph. Ach. 940, πεποιθοίην is found. Athenaeus (7. 305 B) quotes from Cratinus the line—

> τρίγλη δ' εἰ μὲν ἐδηδοκοίη[1] τένθου τινὸς ἀνδρός.

In Xenophon, Cyrop. 2. 4. 17, προεληλυθοίης is found. The scholiast to Hom. Il. 14. 241 quotes πεπαγοίην from Eupolis, which Ahrens (Dial. Dor. 330) ingeniously supposes to have been spoken by a Lacedaemonian in the Εἵλωτες of that comic poet.

From Plat. Parm. 140 A, εἴ τι πέπονθε χωρὶς τοῦ ἓν εἶναι τὸ ἕν, πλείω ἂν εἶναι πεπόνθοι ἢ ἕν, we see how πεπονθοίη was lost. Even in the line from Cratinus the η had got separated from the ἐδεδήκοι till Porson attached it. In Lys. 166. 39 (23. 4), ὠφλήκοι παρὰ κτε., the old confusion of Π with H

[1] The shortening of the penultimate syllable is worth remarking, but considering the frequency with which οι is short in ποιῶ, τοιοῦτος, etc., this presents no difficulty.

comes in, as in Plat. Legg. 679 B, *καθεστήκοι καταστατέον*, that of K with H.

But if the forms in *-ην*, *-ης*, *-η* are the true Attic optative endings for contracted presents and futures, they are certainly un-Attic in all tenses of uncontracted verbs except the perfect. Not a single instance occurs either in Attic prose or verse[1], and forms like *τρέφοιν*, *ἁμάρτοιν*, and *λάβοιν*, which are occasionally quoted as confirming their existence, are themselves liable to grave question. For *τρέφοιν* our only authority is the Grammarian George Choeroboscus[2], who was also the first to recognize the existence of the extraordinary perfect *τέτυφα*. Quoting, as from Euripides, the line—

ἄφρων ἂν εἴην εἰ τρέφοιν τὰ τῶν πέλας,

he adds the absurd remark, *κατὰ συγκοπὴν τοῦ η ἀπὸ τοῦ τρεφοίην*. *Τρεφοίην* does not exist, and, if it did, it could not become *τρέφοιν* either *κατὰ συγκοπήν* or *κατὰ ἄλλο τι*. As Euripides wrote it, the line must have run—

ἄφρων ἂν εἴην ἐκτρέφων τὰ τῶν πέλας.

The testimony of Suïdas, I. p. 144, is almost as worthless as that of Choeroboscus. His words are, 'Αμάρτοιν εἴρηκε τὸ ἁμάρτοιμι Κρατῖνος Δραπέτισι—

Ποδαπὰς ὑμᾶς εἶναι φάσκων, ὦ μείρακες, οὐκ ἂν ἁμάρτοιν;

καὶ ὅλως σύνηθες αὐτοῖς ('Αττικοῖς?) *τὸ τοιοῦτο.* No one can be asked to believe in the existence of such forms on evidence so weak. If they never occur in the books which

[1] In Plat. Epist. 339 D, *διαβαλοίην* is the true optative of a contracted future and not aorist, though even in this case the corrupt *διαβαλοῖμι* is found.

[2] One learns to distrust a man whose name is chiefly associated with introducing rare and late forms into Classical texts. Thus it is Choeroboscus who, in Eur. Hec. 374, reads—

φύλλοις ἔβαλλον, οἱ δ' ἐπληροῦσαν πυράν,

when all MSS. give *δὲ πληροῦσιν*. The change of tense presents no difficulty, as it is extraordinarily frequent in Eur. (cp. Hec. 21 ff. and 1133–35), and forms like *ἐπληροῦσαν* never occur till post-Macedonian times, when we actually encounter *εἴχοσαν*, *ἔσχοσαν*, *ἤλθοσαν*, etc.

we possess they are not worth unearthing from the crude and fanciful compilations of grammarians. Still a modern scholar now and again lays himself open to the Athenian taunt, *οἴνου παρόντος, ὄξος ἠράσθη πιεῖν*. Dindorf has introduced *τέμνοιν* into Aesch. Supp. 807, and *λάβοιν* into a passage of the Erechtheus of Euripides, quoted by the orator Lycurgus in his speech *κατὰ Λεωκράτους*, 160. 28 (102), and Nauck, in Eurip. Orest. 504, substituted *ἔλθοιν χἠλίου* for *ἔλθοιμ' ἡλίου*.

So much for the optative inflexions of the singular. In the plural it will be necessary to take a wider range and to discuss the optative forms, not only of contracted presents and futures, but also of the aorists passive and of verbs in -*μι*. But principally from the fact that in the Greek drama more than two persons seldom take part in the dialogue at the same time, the evidence to be derived from verse is limited to comparatively few forms.

Dawes, a scholar of great nerve and refinement, observed, long since, in his Miscellanea Critica (ed. Kidd, p. 453), the bearing of the testimony of verse on this question. In Arist. Ran. 1450—

εἰ τῶν πολιτῶν οἷσι νῦν πιστεύομεν
τούτοις ἀπιστήσαιμεν, οἷς δ' οὐ χρώμεθα
τούτοισι χρησαίμεσθ', ἴσως σωθεῖμεν ἄν·

some manuscripts read *σωθείημεν ἄν* with *ἴσως*, others *σωθείημεν ἄν* without *ἴσως*, and others again *σωθῶμεν*. The copyists were evidently at a loss to understand the Attic *σωθεῖμεν*, and, in replacing it by the late form familiar to themselves, injured either the metre or the syntax. When such things happen in verse, the laws of which might keep transcribers to the point, it is not difficult to understand how the texts of prose writers became disfigured by forms which could be foisted into metre only by a scribe of some ingenuity.

In remarking upon *σωθεῖμεν ἄν* Dawes says, 'Ut evitetur deinceps soloecismus, legendum statuo *ἴσως σωθεῖμεν ἄν* (a reading since found in two manuscripts). Librarius, opinor, qui ista grammaticorum insomnia τυφθείητον, τυφθειήτην, τυφθείημεν, τυφθείητε, τυφθείησαν, imberbis didicerat, vera, quam ignorabat, scriptura offensus in ejus locum alterum istud suffecit; nescius interim primo terminationes optativas, είητον, ειήτην, etc. αίητον, etc. οίητον, etc. scriptoribus vere Graecis ignotas fuisse; ac deinde voculam ἄν cum forma subjunctiva, nisi cum certis itidem comitibus nusquam construi.'

The testimony of Comedy is meagre in the extreme, consisting only of the following forms:—

For contracted verbs—

> στύοιντο δ' ἄνδρες κἀπιθυμοῖεν σπλεκοῦν.
> Ar. Lys. 152.
>
> τί ἂν οὖν ποιοῖμεν[1];
> B. οἰκίσατε μίαν πόλιν.
> Av. 172.
>
> ἵνα τἀργύριον σῶν παρέχοιμεν καὶ μὴ πολεμοῖτε δι' αὐτό.
> Lys. 488.
>
> εἰ ναυμαχοῖεν κᾆτ' ἔχοντες ὀξίδας.
> Ran. 1440.
>
> ποίαν τιν' οὖν ἥδιστ' ἂν οἰκοίτην[2] πόλιν;
> Av. 127.
>
> εἴ τι φιλοῖεν τὰς λευκοτάτας, οἱ δ' ἰχθύες οἴκαδ' ἰόντες.
> Fr. Com. 2. 361 (Teleclides).

For aorists passive—

> τούτοισι χρησαίμεσθ', ἴσως σωθεῖμεν ἄν.
> Ran. 1450.
>
> ἆρ' ἂν ὦ πρὸς τῶν θεῶν ὑμεῖς ἀπαλλαχθεῖτέ μου;
> Vesp. 484.
>
> πόσον δίδως δῆτ';
> B. εἰ διαπρισθεῖεν δίχα.
> Pax 1262.

[1] Cobet reads τί οὖν ποιῶμεν; but τί occurs before a short syllable again in Plut. 1161, καὶ τί ἔτ' ἐρεῖς; and Nub. 21, τί ὀφείλω;

[2] The MSS. have οἰκοῖτ' ἄν, which Cobet has emended. The copyists not unfrequently altered dual forms to plural. However, either reading serves our purpose.

And for verbs in -*μι*—

τούτων χάριν ἀνταποδοίτην.

Thesm. 1230.

καὶ τίνες ἂν εἶεν;

B. *πρῶτα μὲν Σαννυρίων.*

Fr. Com. 2. 1008 (Aristoph.).

Tragedy supplies us with a few more—

τἄλλ' εὐτυχοῖμεν πρὸς θεῶν Ὀλυμπικῶν.

Aesch. Supp. 1014.

οὐ γὰρ ἂν κακῶς
οὐδ' ὧδ' ἔχοντες ζῷμεν, εἰ τερποίμεθα.

Soph. O. C. 799.

τί δῆτα τοῦδ' ἐπεγγελῷεν ἂν κάτα;

Id. Aj. 969.

τί δῆτ' ἂν ἡμεῖς δρῷμεν, εἰ σέ γ' ἐν λόγοις;

Id. Phil. 1393.

εἴ μ' ἐκφοβοῖεν μανιάσιν λυσσήμασιν.

Eur. Or. 270.

ἑνὸς γὰρ εἰ λαβοίμεθ' εὐτυχοῖμεν ἄν.

Ib. 1172.

θανάτους τ' ἔθηκαν ὡς ἀπαντλοῖεν χθονός.

Ib. 1641.

ἀλλ' ὡς, τὸ μὲν μέγιστον, οἰκοῖμεν καλῶς.

Id. Med. 559.

εὐδαιμονοῖτον ἀλλ' ἐκεῖ· τὰ δ' ἐνθάδε.

Ib. 1073.

παρρησίᾳ θάλλοντες οἰκοῖεν πόλιν.

Id. Hipp. 422.

ἀλλ' εὐτυχοίτην, τίνι δ' ἐν ἡμέρᾳ γαμεῖ;

Id. I. A. 716.

καὶ τοὐπ' ἔμ' εὐτυχοῖτε καὶ νικηφόρου.

Ib. 1557.

τὸ λοιπὸν εὐτυχοῖμεν ἀλλήλων μέτα.

Id. I. T. 841.

ἐν δόμοις μίμνειν ἅπαντας.

B. *μὴ συναντῷεν φόνῳ.*

Ib. 1209.

εἰ δ' εὐτυχοῖεν Τρῶες, οὐδὲν ἦν ὅδε.

Id. Tro. 1007.

ὅποι νοσοῖεν ξύμμαχοι κατασκοπῶν.
Id. Hel. 1607.

εὐδαιμονοῖμεν, ὡς τὰ πρόσθε δυστυχῆ.
Id. Ion 1457.

εὐδαιμονοῖτ' ἂν σύμμαχον κεκτημένοι.
Id. Bacch. 1343.

εὐδαιμονοῖτε, καὶ γένοιθ' ὑμῖν ὅσων.
Id. Heracl. 582.

ἡμῖν δ' ἂν εἶεν, εἰ κρατοῖμεν, εὐμενεῖς;
Id. El. 632.

Aorists passive—

μακροὶ παλαιοί τ' ἂν μετρηθεῖεν χρόνοι.
Soph. O. R. 561.

ὡς δὴ σκότον λαβόντες ἐκσωθεῖμεν ἄν;
Eur. I. T. 1025.

οἴμοι, διεφθάρμεσθα· πῶς σωθεῖμεν ἄν;
Ib. 1028.

ἀφανεῖς ἂν ὄντες οὐκ ἂν ὑμνηθεῖμεν ἄν.
Id. Tro. 1244.

ἐν ᾧ διεργασθεῖτ' ἄν, ἀλλ' ἐμοὶ πιθοῦ.
Id. Heracl. 174.

πάσχων τ' ἔκαμνον· δὶς δὲ λυπηθεῖμεν ἄν.
Id. Hel. 771.

μί' ἐστὶν ἐλπὶς ᾗ μόνῃ σωθεῖμεν ἄν.
Ib. 815.

ἀλλ' οὐδὲ μὴν ναῦς ἔστιν ᾗ σωθεῖμεν ἄν.
Ib. 1047.

Verbs in -μι—

ὀπτῆρες εἶεν ἀγγέλων πεπυσμένοι.
Aesch. Supp. 185.

τούτῳ μὲν οὕτως εὐτυχεῖν δοῖεν θεοί.
Id. Sept. 421.

οὔ τἂν ἑλόντες αὖθις ἀνθαλοῖεν ἄν.
Id. Agam. 340.

ἄριστα δοῖεν· κεἰ παρ' Ἑλλήνων τινές.
Id. Eum. 31.

οἱ πάντες εὖ ξυνεῖεν εἰσαεὶ θεοί.
Soph. O. R. 275.

ὑμεῖς γ' ἄριστ' εἰδεῖτ' ἂν οὑπιχώριοι.
Ib. 1046.

θεῖέν μ' ἄφωνον τῆσδε τῆς ἀρᾶς ἔτι.
Id. O. C. 865.

παθόντες ἂν ξυγγνοῖμεν ἡμαρτηκότες.
Id. Ant. 926.

ποῦ δῆτ' ἂν εἶεν οἱ ξένοι; δίδασκέ με.
Id. El. 1450.

δοῖέν ποτ' αὐτοῖς ἀντίποιν' ἐμοῦ παθεῖν.
Id. Phil. 316.

ἵν' αἱ Μυκῆναι γνοῖεν ἡ Σπάρτη θ' ὅτι.
Ib. 325.

σοὶ πάντες εἶεν οἱ νεναυστοληκότες.
Ib. 550.

ἡμεῖς ἂν εἶμεν θατέρῳ κεχρημένοι.
Eur. Hipp. 349.

ὦ πρέσβυ, θεοί σοι δοῖεν εὖ καὶ τοῖσι σοῖς.
Id. Andr. 750.

ὡς οὔτε γαίας ὅρι' ἂν ἐκβαῖμεν λάθρα.
Id. H. F. 82.

ἡμῖν δ' ἂν εἶεν εἰ κρατοῖμεν εὐμενεῖς.
Id. El. 632.

οὐ γὰρ ἂν ξυμβαῖμεν ἄλλως ἢ 'πὶ τοῖς εἰρημένοις.
Id. Phoen. 590.

And in lyrical passages *δοῖεν*, Aesch. Supp. 418, and *διδοῖεν*, id. 703, *ἀντιδιδοῖεν*, Eum. 983.

Now, against these fifty or sixty forms there are only two of the longer endings to bring, namely—

οὐκ οἶδ' Ὀδυσσεῦ· πᾶν δέ σοι δρῴημεν ἄν.
Eur. Cycl. 132.

οὐκ οἶδ'· ἀληθῆ δ' εἰ λέγεις φαίημεν ἄν.
Id. Ion 943.

but if the transcribers' errors in the case of *σωθεῖμεν* in Ar. Ran. 1450 are considered, Dawes was certainly right in reading *συνδρῷμεν ἄν* in the former of these lines, and Dindorf in altering *φαίημεν* to *συμφαῖμεν* in the latter. In both cases the compound verb is demanded by the context. The form *ἀδικοίημεν*, read by some in Eur. Hel. 1010, is merely a variant for *ἀδικοίην νιν*, and cannot for one moment stand against evidence so overwhelming, especially when the following ἀποδώσω is considered—

> ἃ δ' ἀμφὶ τίμβῳ τῷδ' ὀνειδίζεις πατρί,
> ἡμῖν ὅδ' αὐτὸς μῦθος· ἀδικοίην νιν ἂν
> εἰ μὴ ἀποδώσω· καὶ γὰρ ἂν κεῖνος βλέπων,
> ἀπέδωκεν ἄν σοι τῆνδ' ἔχειν, ταύτῃ δὲ σέ.

One word as to the absurdity διδῴη. In Eur. Andr. 225 some manuscripts read ἐνδῴην for ἐνδοίην; in Xen. Cyr. 3. 1. 35, δῴης for δοίης; in Plato, Gorg. 481 A, δῴη for δῷ. In Lysias, 105. 5, all manuscripts read δῴη, though a few lines further down μεταδοίη has been preserved. All these are of course wrong, and have been replaced by the forms in -οι by all editors who know their business. The same error sometimes affects the optative of the aorists ἔγνων, ἑάλων, and ἐβίων. Thus, in Aesch. Supp. 215, συγγνῴη occurs instead of συγγνοίη, and in Dem. 736 there is good authority for ἁλῴην, while the optative βιοίην, βιοίης, βιοίη is always misspelt in the same utterly ridiculous way, ἀναβιῴην for ἀναβιοίην, appearing in Ar. Ran. 177, βιῴη for βιοίη, in Plato, Phaed. 87 D, Gorg. 512 E, Tim. 89 C, Legg. 730 C.

CCCXXVI.

Ἐργοδότης οὐ κεῖται, τὸ δὲ ἐργοδοτεῖν παρά τινι τῶν νεωτέρων κωμῳδῶν, οἷς καὶ αὐτοῖς οὐ πειστέον.

This is an instructive article. The word ἐργοδοτεῖν occurs in un-Attic Inscriptions, as Inscr. Aphrodis. ap. Boeckh, vol. 2. n. 2826. 5. Antiatticista, p. 94. 5, cites it from Apollodorus, to whom Phrynichus also probably refers here, and the substantive ἐργοδότης is encountered in Xenophon (Cyr. 8. 2. 5). The inference is plain. Xenophon picked ἐργοδότης up abroad, and ἐργοδοτεῖν in Apollodorus is an early indication of the fusion of Greek dialects to which the Macedonian conquests gave rise.

CCCXXVII.

Ἐντέχνως· πάνυ αἰτιῶνται τὸ ὄνομα καί φασι τεχνικῶς δεῖν λέγειν. ἀλλὰ καὶ Λυσίαν, εἰρηκότα ἐντεχνῶς, παραιτοῦνται.

The adjective is of good authority in this sense, Plato, Legg. 10. 903 C, and there is no reason for finding fault with the adverb.

CCCXXVIII.

Ἄγαγον· καὶ τοῦτο εἰ μὲν τὴν μετοχὴν εἶχεν ὁ ἀγάγας ἐν λόγῳ ἄν τινι ἦν. λεκτέον οὖν ἄγαγε, καὶ γὰρ ἡ μετοχὴ ἀγαγών, ὡς ἄνελε, ἀνελών.

See supra p. 215 ff.

CCCXXIX.

Ἀναισθητεύομαι, τὸ μὲν ὄνομα ἀναίσθητος δοκιμώτερον, τὸ δὲ ῥῆμα οὐκέτι. λέγε οὖν, οὐκ αἰσθάνομαι.

The equivalent proposed by Phrynichus would not mean the same thing as *ἀναισθητεύομαι*, although *ἀναίσθητός εἰμι* would. There is nothing outlandish in the rejected word, it only does not occur. Demosthenes, however, employed *ἀναισθητεῖν* in 302. 3, *ἐπεπείσμην δ' ὑπὲρ ἐμαυτοῦ, τυχὸν μὲν ἀναισθητῶν, ὅμως δ' ἐπεπείσμην.*

CCCXXX.

Αὐθεκαστότης, ἀλλόκοτον. τὸ μὲν οὖν αὐθέκαστος κάλλιστον ὄνομα, τὸ δὲ παρὰ τοῦτο πεποιημένον αὐθεκαστότης κίβδηλον.

The first instance, even of the adjective, is after the Attic period; Arist. Eth. Nic. 4. 7. 4, where *αὐθέκαστος* is said to be the mean between *ἀλαζών* and *εἴρων*. There is no example of the substantive. The formation even of the adjective is peculiar. A similar compound might have been formed if the Sophoclean *πάντ' ἐπιστήμη* had ever coalesced—

φῦναι τὸν ἄνδρα πάντ' ἐπιστήμης πλέων.
Ant. 721.

τούτων ἔχω γὰρ πάντ' ἐπιστήμην ἐγώ.
Trach. 338.

CCCXXXI.

Τὸν παῖδα τὸν ἀκολουθοῦντα μετ' αὐτοῦ. Λυσίας ἐν τῷ κατ' Αὐτοκράτους οὕτω τῇ συντάξει χρῆται· ἐχρῆν δὲ οὕτως εἰπεῖν, τὸν ἀκολουθοῦντα αὐτῷ. Τί ἂν οὖν φαίη τις ἁμαρτεῖν τὸν Λυσίαν ἢ νοθεύειν καινοῦ σχήματος χρῆσιν; ἀλλ' ἐπεὶ ξενικὴ ἡ σύνθεσις, πάντη παραιτητέα, ῥητέον δὲ ἀκολουθεῖν αὐτῷ.

The apparatus criticus will show on how slight authority this article is assigned to Phrynichus. At all events it is erroneous. However remarkable and inexplicable the construction with *μετά* must appear to any one who has once learned to appreciate the unequalled precision of Attic modes of expression, certainly its existence cannot be challenged. Plato, Lach. 187 E, *μετὰ τοῦ πατρὸς ἀκολουθῶν*: Menex. 249 D, *ἀκολούθει μετ' ἐμοῦ*: Isocr. 299 C, *τοῖς μὲν σώμασι μετ' ἐκείνων ἀκολουθεῖν ἠναγκάζοντο, ταῖς δὲ εὐνοίαις μεθ' ἡμῶν ἦσαν*: 168 C, *οἷς ὁπόταν τις διδῷ πλείω μίσθον, μετ' ἐκείνου ἐφ' ἡμᾶς ἀκολουθήσουσιν*: 91. E, *ἅπαντας τοὺς πρότερον μεθ' αὐτῶν ἐπὶ τοὺς ἄλλους ἀκολουθοῦντας*: Lys. 193. 18, *τὰ ἔθνη τὰ μετ' αὐτοῦ ἀκολουθήσαντα*: Xenophon has *σύν*, An. 7. 5. 3, *τοῖς στρατηγοῖς δωροῦ οἳ σὺν ἐμοὶ ἠκολούθησαν*. The speech of Lysias referred to in the article has not come down to us, but the same words are cited by Antiatticista, p. 82. 21.

In the *Συναγ. λεξ. χρησ.* 308. 3 there is an excellent note on this point: *'Ακολουθεῖν μετ' αὐτοῦ· οὕτω συντάσσουσιν οἱ 'Αττικοὶ ἀντὶ τοῦ ἀκολουθεῖν αὐτῷ. καὶ γὰρ Λυσίας οὕτω κέχρηται καὶ Πλάτων· ἀλλὰ καὶ 'Αριστοφάνης ἐν Πλούτῳ ἕπου, φησί, μετ' ἐμοῦ, παιδάριον· καὶ Μένανδρος—*

νίκη μεθ' ἡμῶν εὐμενὴς ἕποιτ' ἀεί·

κἀν τῇ Παρακαταθήκῃ—

συνακολούθει μεθ' ἡμῶν,

φησίν.

CCCXXXII.

Βιωτικόν· ἀηδὴς ἡ λέξις. λέγε οὖν χρήσιμον ἐν τῷ βίῳ

'*Βιωτικός* primum offenditur apud Aristot. H. A. 10. 16, hoc est in ea parte libri, quae plurima continet affectata et inusitate posita, non illa vulgari significatione, sed pro *βιομήχανος* s. *εὐβίοτος*; tum saepissime apud Philonem, Diodorum, Polybium, et Plutarchum. Vulgatissimum est *χρεῖαι βιωτικαί*, Philo de V. M. 3. 677 A; Diod. 2. 29, Artemid. 1. 31, quas elegantius Strabo, 4. 14. 35, *τὰς τοῦ βίου χρείας* dixit.' Lobeck.

CCCXXXIII.

Βουνός· ὀθνεία ἡ φωνὴ τῆς 'Αττικῆς· καὶ γὰρ αὐτὸς ὁ

χρησάμενος τῷ ὀνόματι, συνεὶς ξένως κεχρημένος, σημαίνεται ὡς ἀσαφῶς διαλεγόμενος. εἰπόντος γὰρ τινος—

βουνὸν ἐπὶ ταύτῃ καταλαβὼν ἄνω τινά.

ὁ προσδιαλεγόμενος, οὐ συνεὶς τὸ ξένον τοῦ ὀνόματος, φησί—

τίς ἐσθ' ὁ βουνός; ἵνα σαφῶς σου μανθάνω.

ἐν δὲ τῇ Συρακουσίᾳ ποιήσει καθωμίληται. ἀλλ' οὐ προσίεται ὁ Ἀθηναῖος τὴν ἀλλοδαπὴν διάλεξιν. ὅπου γὰρ ἀνεπίμικτος καὶ ἄχραντος βούλεται μένειν τῆς ἄλλης Ἑλλάδος, Αἰολέων λέγω καὶ Δωριέων καὶ Ἰώνων, τούτων μὲν καὶ συγγενῶν ὄντων, σχολῇ γ' ἂν ἀδόκιμον μιξοβάρβαρον πρόσειτο φωνήν· ὁ δ' οὖν κεχρημένος τῷ βουνὸς ὀνόματι Φιλήμων ἐστίν, εἷς τῶν τῆς νέας κωμῳδίας.

It is strange that this article, one of the most carefully written of the whole book, is not found at all in the manuscripts, in the edition of Callierges, or in Phavorinus. A fact like this proves the impossibility of settling the text of Phrynichus with even approximate accuracy.

Eustathius, on Il. 11. 710, has preserved a valuable testimony: *Αἴλιος Διονύσιος λέγει ὅτι Φιλήμων ἐπισκώπτει τὸ ὄνομα ὡς βάρβαρον.* The additional words, *ἕτεροι δέ, ὅτι βουνὸν ἐν Νόθῳ ὡς σύνηθες τίθησιν, ἄλλοτε δὲ ὡς ξενικὸν ἐπισκώπτει*, may possibly rest upon a misunderstanding of the passage referred to by Phrynichus, although in that case there should be another *ἄλλοτε* before *ὡς σύνηθες*. Herodotus, in 4. 199, states that a portion of the territory of Cyrene went by the name of *βουνοί*, and they say that the term is still used in that district. The name of the favoured region, which produced the *σίλφιον* and *ὀπὸς Κυρηναϊκός*, would naturally become known at an early date in the wealthy commercial city of Syracuse, and *βουνός* may have been naturalised there sooner than in other places, especially as the people of Cyrene were, like the Syracusans, of Dorian race. Its presence in the Common dialect may, however, be most easily accounted for by the proximity of Alexandria to Cyrene.

The word must have been at least intelligible to the Athenians or Aeschylus would not have ventured to employ *βοῦνις* as an adjective in Supp. 117, 129. 176. He had himself become familiarised with the noun in his Sicilian sojourn.

CCCXXXIV.

Μονθυλεύω· οὕτω τινὲς τὸ μολύνοντα ταράττειν λέγουσι. καὶ ἔστι δυσχερές. ἀπόρριπτε οὖν καὶ τοῦτο.

There is a *μονθυλεύω* or *ὀνθυλεύω* in Greek, but it is not used in this sense. The edition of Nuñez is the only authority for this article, and perhaps it has not preserved the original hand. Probably *σάττειν* should replace *ταράττειν*.

Athenaeus, 2. 49 F, quotes from Alexis—

ἢ σπλῆν' ὀπτὸν μεμονθολευμένον,

but *ὀνθυλεύω* is much more common.

νάρκην μὲν οὖν, ὥς φασιν, ὠνθυλευμένην
ὀπτᾶν ὅλην.

Alexis, ap. Ath. 7. 314 D.

ἀλλὰ τὰς μὲν τευθίδας
τὰ πτερύγι' αὐτῶν συντεμὼν στεατίου
μικρὸν παραμίξας, περιπάσας ἡδύσμασιν
λεπτοῖσι χλωροῖς, ὠνθύλευσα.

Id. ap. id. 326 D.

ἀστεῖον ἑφθὴ τευθὶς ὠνθυλευμένη.

Sotades, ap. Ath. 7. 293 B.

μετὰ ταῦτα γαστρίον τις ὠνθυλευμένον.

Athenio, ap. Ath. 14. 661 B.

παρατίθημ' ὁλοσχερῆ
ἄρν' ἐς μέσον σύμπτυκτον, ὠνθυλευμένον.
Diphilus, ap. Ath. 383 F.

παχὺς ὠνθυλευμένος στέατι Σικελικῷ.
Id. ap. Plut. Vit. Nic. 1.

Perhaps, even in the first passage, Dobree was right in restoring ὠνθυλευμένον—

ἑόρακας ἤδη πώποτ' ἐσκευασμένον
ἤνυστρον ἢ σπλῆν' ὀπτὸν ὠνθυλευμένον.

If connected at all with ὄνθος, the Homeric synonym of κόπρος, it is certainly not formed directly from it (see p. 128). The meaning is evidently '*to stuff*.' Is Phrynichus (if it was he who wrote the article) finding fault with some signification different from this, or is τὸ μολύνοντα ταράττειν corrupt, and the initial mu alone reprehended?

CCCXXXV.

Βόλβιτον ὀλίγοι τινὲς λέγουσι τῶν 'Αττικῶν, ἀλλὰ τούτου δοκιμώτερον τὸ βόλιτον ἄνευ τοῦ δευτέρου β.

The tribrach is the only form known in Attic poetry—

ἐν πᾶσι βολίτοις· εἶτα νυνὶ τοῦ δέει;
Ar. Ach. 1026.

κἄγωγ' ὅτε δὴ 'γνων τοῖς βολίτοις ἡττημένος.
Eq. 658.

νὴ τὸν Ποσειδῶ, καὶ βολίτινον θάτερον.
Ran. 295.

In none of these lines could the dactylic spelling stand any more than in the line of Cratinus—

οὐκ ἀλλὰ βόλιτα χλωρὰ κῴσπώτην πατεῖν·

into which the Schol. on Ar. Lys. 575 introduces βόλβιτα.

CCCXXXVI.

Γογγυσμὸς καὶ γογγύζειν· ταῦτα ἀδόκιμα μὲν οὐκ ἔστιν, Ἰακὰ δέ. Φωκυλίδην γὰρ οἶδα κεχρημένον αὐτῷ τὸν Μιλήσιον, ἄνδρα παλαιὸν σφόδρα—

καὶ τόδε Φωκυλιδέω· χρή τοι τὸν ἑταῖρον ἑταίρῳ
φροντίζειν ἅσσ᾽ ἂν περιγογγύζωσι πολῖται.

ἀλλὰ τοῦτο μὲν Ἴωσιν ἀφείσθω, ἡμεῖς δὲ τονθρυσμὸν καὶ τονθρύζειν λέγωμεν, ἢ νὴ Δία σὺν τῷ ο, τονθορυσμὸν καὶ τονθορύζειν.

The rejected words are found chiefly in the Septuagint and the New Testament: John 7. 12; Luke, Acts 6. 1; 1 Peter 4. 10; Matt. 22. 11, etc. Antiatticista, however, quotes the substantive from the New Comedy, p. 87, *Γογγυσμὸς ἀντὶ τοῦ τονθορυσμοῦ Ἀναξανδρίδης Νηρεῖ.*

CCCXXXVII.

Δύνῃ· ἐὰν μὲν τοῦτο ὑποτακτικὸν ᾖ, ἐὰν δύνωμαι, ἐὰν δύνῃ, ὀρθῶς λέγεται· ἐὰν δὲ ὁριστικῶς τιθῇ τις, δύνῃ τοῦτο πρᾶξαι, οὐχ ὑγιῶς ἂν τιθείη· χρὴ γὰρ λέγειν δύνασαι τοῦτο πρᾶξαι.

It is impossible that *δύνασαι* should ever contract to *δύνῃ*, although *δύνᾳ* would be a natural and legitimate form. The latter, however, is not mentioned by Phrynichus, who here contents himself with giving the more frequent *δύνασαι*. There is, however, no question that *δύνασαι* and *δύνᾳ* were both in use in Attic Greek, just as *ἐπίστασαι* and *ἐπίστᾳ*, *ἐπίστασο* and *ἐπίστω*, *ἀνίστασο* and *ἀνίστω*, *ἠπίστασο* and *ἠπίστω* were employed indifferently. It is a singular fact that if alpha was the former of the two vowels between which a sigma came, the rule by which such an intervocal sigma was dropped and contraction took place at once ceased to be absolute. Thus, *βιβάσω* and *βιβῶ*, *βιάσομαι* and *βιῶμαι*, *κολάσομαι* and *κολῶμαι* were equally pure Attic, although forms like *ἀπολέσω* for *ἀπολῶ*, *ὀμόσομαι* for *ὀμοῦμαι* were quite unknown. This fact explains the existence of two sets of forms for the second person singular of the present and imperfect indicative, and the present imperative of deponent verbs, and middle or passive voices in *-αμαι*. This class of verbs is small, being made up in the Attic dialect of *δύναμαι*, *ἐμπίπλαμαι*, *ἐμπίπραμαι*, *κρέμαμαι*, the aoristic *ἐπριάμην*, *ἐπίσταμαι*, and the simple *ἵσταμαι* with its compounds, for neither *μάρναμαι* nor *σκίδναμαι* was in use among Athenians. The testimony of verse with regard to these words is as follows:—

Δύνασαι, Ar. Ach. 291 (chor.), Nub. 811 (chor.), Plut. 574; Soph. Aj. 1164 (chor.).

δύνᾳ, Soph. Phil. 849 (chor.).

ἠδύνω, Philippides, ap. Ath. 15. 700 E.

Ἐπίστασαι, Ar. Eq. 689 (chor.); Aesch. P. V. 374, 982, Supp. 917; Soph. El. 629, Trach. 484, Ant. 402; Eur. Med. 400, 406, 537, Alc. 62, H. F. 346; Alexis, ap. Ath. 7. 322 D, id. ap. Ath. 9. 386 A.

ἐπίστᾳ, Aesch. Eum. 86, 581.

ἐπίστασο, Aesch. P. V. 840, 967; Soph. O. R. 848, Ant. 305, Aj. 979, 1080, 1370, 1379, O. C. 1584; Eur. Andr. 431, Ion 650.

ἐπίστω, Soph. Phil. 419, 567, 1240, 1325, O. R. 658, Trach. 182, 616, 1035.

ἠπίστασο, El. 394, Aj. 1134.

ἠπίστω, Eur. H. F. 344.

ἵστω, Ar. Eccl. 737; Soph. Phil. 893, Aj. 775; Cratinus, Fr. Com. 2. 151.

ἀνίστασο, Ar. Vesp. 286 (chor.), 998, Thesm. 236, 643, Lys. 929; Eur. Hec. 499.

ἀνίστω, Aesch. Eum. 133, 141.
ἐπρίω, Ar. Vesp. 1431; Fr. Com. 2. 1030 (12).
πρίω, Ar. Ach. 34. 35; Hegemon, ap. Ath. 3. 108 C.

These instances are all undisputed, but there is some question about the form of *δύναμαι* to be read in one passage of Aeschylus, two of Sophocles, and two of Euripides. In Aesch. Cho. 374 the Medicean manuscript exhibits the unintelligible line—

μείζονα φωνεῖ· ὁ δυνᾶσαι γάρ,

which Hermann corrected to—

μείζονα φωνεῖς· δύνασαι γάρ·

others prefer *ὀδυνᾷ γάρ*.

As to Soph. O. R. 696, *δύναι*, the reading of the Laurentian, is nothing more nor less than *δύνᾳ*, and the line should be printed—

τανῦν δ᾽ εὔπομπος, εἰ δύνᾳ, γενοῦ.

The other three lines prove that the caution of Phrynichus, presupposing as it does that in his time *δύνῃ* was regarded as an indicative second person singular, was not uncalled for—

οὕτω κατ᾽ ἦμαρ οὐ δύνᾳ μολεῖν ποτε;
Soph. Phil. 798.

δρᾷς δ᾽ οὐδὲν ἡμᾶς εὖ, κακῶς ὅσον δύνᾳ;
Eur. Hec. 253.

σὺ δ᾽ οὐ λέγεις γε, δρᾷς δέ μ᾽ εἰς ὅσον δύνᾳ.
Andr. 239.

The manuscripts have only *δύνῃ* to offer.

The case of *ἐπριάμην* is difficult, as there is no instance of *ἐπρίασο* or *πρίασο* in Attic verse, as the imperative in Ar. Ach. 870 comes from the lips of a Boeotian—

ἀλλ᾽ εἴ τι βούλει πρίασο τῶν ἐγὼ φέρω,

but *κρέμαμαι*, *ἐμπίπραμαι*, and *ἐμπίπλαμαι* are all in like straits, and the futures of many verbs are equally uncertain.

The above facts, however, warrant us in asserting that

the uncontracted forms of these three inflexions were far more numerous than the contracted. In verse indeed they are in the ratio of three to two, and if manuscripts are to be trusted they are still more numerous in prose.

The case is parallel to that of syncopated perfects active like *δεδειπνηκέναι*, and *δεδειπνάναι*, *τεθνεώς* and *τεθνηκώς*, and of adjectives comparative like *πλείονες* and *πλείους*, *μείζονα* and *μείζω*. Neither the contracted nor the full form would have been resented by an Athenian audience, but usage made prominent sometimes the one, sometimes the other, in a way often difficult to determine. For us it is sufficient to ascertain the general rule, and to disregard the niceties of detail as facts which no ingenuity can with certainty extort from a dead language, so delicately organized as Attic was, and so mutilated as it has been by time and unholy hands.

In Homer three sets of forms occur, full like *ἵστασαι*, intermediate like *ἵσταο*, and contracted like *ἐκρέμω*.

CCCXXXVIII.

Ὥρκωσε καὶ ὁρκώτης δ' ἐγώ· οὕτω Κρατῖνός φησι. μᾶλλον δὲ διὰ τοῦ ω λέγε ἢ διὰ τοῦ ι, ὥρκισεν.

As a statement of usage this is meritorious, but *ὁρκίζω* was naturally good Attic, even if more rare than *ὁρκῶ*. The study of Greek would become absurd if prosecuted in such a slavish manner. The point at which every true scholar must aim is to be able to identify himself with the Athenians of the best age, and acquire, as far as may be, the same fine sense of language which they possessed.

Demosthenes employs both words in one passage, 430. 21 ff. *οὐ τὸ μὲν ψήφισμα τοὺς ἄρχοντας ὁρκοῦν τοὺς ἐν ταῖς πόλεσιν, οὗτοι δέ, οὓς Φίλιππος αὐτοῖς προσέπεμψε, τούτους ὥρκισαν*; It is of course open to anyone to say that *ὥρκισαν* is a corruption of *ὤρκωσαν*, the aorist being selected for remark by Phrynichus as the most easily altered tense; but there is no doubt about Dem. 235 fin. *οὐκ ἂν ὡρκίζομεν αὐτόν*, even if *ὁρκίσαι πάλιν αὐτόν* in 678. 5 is, like *ὥρκισαν*, corrupt.

CCCXXXIX.

Εὐκερματεῖν ἀηδὲς πάνυ. ἥδιστα δ' ἂν εἴποις εὐπορεῖν κερμάτων.

On the other hand, Photius cites it from Eubulus: *Εὐκερματεῖν· Εὔβουλός που κέχρηται τῷ ὀνόματι.*

CCCXL.

Ἐνιαυσιαῖον καὶ τοῦθ' ὅμοιόν ἐστι τῷ Διονυσιαῖον, κίβδηλον. λέγε οὖν πεντεσυλλάβως ἐνιαύσιον, ὡς Διονύσιον.

In late writers the extended form occurs with some frequency, but to Attic it is of course unknown.

CCCXLI.

Ἐξαλλάξαι, τὸ τέρψαι καὶ παραγαγεῖν εἰς εὐφροσύνην, φυλαττόμενον χρὴ οὕτω λέγειν· οἱ γὰρ χρῶνται οἱ δόκιμοι, Φιλιππίδης δὲ καὶ Μένανδρος αὐτῷ χρῶνται.

There is a good note on this use of *ἐξαλάττω* in Antiatt. Bekk. 96. 1: Ἐξαλλάξαι· ὡς Ἀλεξανδρεῖς ἀντὶ τοῦ τέρψαι. Μένανδρος—

ἄνθρωπον ἐξαλλάξομεν [1].

Ἐξαλλάγματα· Ἀναξανδρίδης Θησεῖ—

παρθένοι παίζουσι πρὸς ἐλάφρ' ἐξαλλάγματα.

[1] Cp. Suïdas—Ἐξαλλάξαι· ἀντὶ τοῦ τέρψαι. Μένανδρος—
ἄνθρωπον ἐξαλλάξομεν
κακόν τί σοι δώσοντα.

Heraclitus, the late writer Περὶ ἀπίστων, seems also to have used the verb in this sense, p. 70, οὔτε δώροις ἐξαλλαγῆναι, and Parthenius the substantive, 24. 1, τοῦτον ἐξαλλάγμασι πολλοῖς ὑπαγόμενος.

CCCXLII.

Ἐνεχυριμαῖα οὐδεὶς τῶν δοκίμων εἶπεν (εἰ δὲ τῶν ἠμελημένων, οὐ φροντὶς Ἱπποκλείδῃ), ἐνέχυρα δέ.

As in Article 169, Phrynichus uses the proverb *οὐ φροντὶς Ἱπποκλείδῃ* to sum up his scholarly disregard of any accidental exception to a general rule, but Thomas ludicrously misconstrues his meaning (p. 309), *τὸ δὲ ἐνεχυριμαῖον λέγειν, ὡς Ἱπποκλείδης, ἀδόκιμον.* It is but one proof out of many that, as an independent authority, Thomas is of little value.

CCCXLIII.

Ἐκλείψας ἀδόκιμον, ἀλλὰ τὸ ἐκλιπών.

This question has already been discussed on p. 217.

CCCXLIV.

Χρηστὸς τὰ ἤθη πληθυντικῶς φυλάττου. οἱ γὰρ δόκιμοι ἑνικῶς φασὶ χρηστὸς τὸ ἦθος.

By the side of this general rule may be set the other, that when the adjective is in the plural, that is, when such and such a quality is predicated of more than one person, the plural of *ἦθος* is regularly used, as Isocr. 147 fin. *τοὺς γὰρ πολλοὺς τοῖς ἤθεσιν ἀποβαίνειν ὁμοίους ἀνάγκη, ἐν οἷς ἂν ἕκαστοι παιδευθῶσιν*: Plato, Rep. 7. 535 B, *γενναίους τε καὶ βλοσυροὺς τὰ ἤθη.* These rules apply, of course, only to *ἦθος* in the sense of *character*, *natural disposition*, Latin *indoles*. Of *ἤθη* in the sense of *manners*, Latin *mores*, the use is unfettered.

In the case of *τρόπος* no such distinction is made, Attic writers employing not only *χρηστὸς τὸν τρόπον* and *χρηστοὶ τοὺς τρόπους*, but also *χρηστὸς τοὺς τρόπους* and *χρηστοὶ τὸν τρόπον*.

CCCXLV.

Θυρεός· τοῦθ' Ὅμηρος ἐπὶ λίθου τίθησιν ἀντὶ θύρας τὴν χρείαν παρέχοντος, οἱ δὲ πολλοὶ ἀντὶ τῆς ἀσπίδος τιθέασιν, οὐδένος τῶν δοκίμων καὶ ἀρχαίων χρησαμένου. χρὴ οὖν ἀσπίδα λέγειν.

Od. 9. 240, of the door-stone of the Cyclops' cave—

αὐτὰρ ἔπειτ' ἐπέθηκε θυρεὸν μέγαν ὕψοσ' ἀείρας,
ὄβριμον.

So 313, 340. Dionysius, Arch. Rom. 4. 16, translates *clypeus* by *ἄσπις*, *scutum* by *θυρεός*, and Polybius uses the latter word of the national shield of the Romans in 6. 23. 2; 10. 13. 2, but also of the Gauls in 2. 30. 3; cp. Athen. 6. 273 F, *οἱ Ῥωμαῖοι παρὰ Σαυνιτῶν ἔμαθον θυρεοῦ χρῆσιν, παρὰ δὲ Ἰβήρων γαίσων*. There is no instance of the meaning of *shield* before Polybius, as in Callixenus, ap. Ath. 5. 196 F, the signification of the word is uncertain.

CCCXLVI.

Διονυσεῖον· ἀπαίδευτον οὕτω λέγειν, δέον βραχύνειν τὴν σι συλλαβήν· οἱ γὰρ ἐκτείνοντες παρὰ τὴν τῶν Ἀττικῶν διάλεκτον λέγουσι. χρὴ οὖν Ἀριστοφάνει ἀκολουθοῦντας λέγειν, ἐν γὰρ τῷ Γήρᾳ φησί—

A. τίς ἂν φράσειε, ποῦ 'στι τὸ Διονύσιον;
B. ὅπου τὰ μορμολυκεῖα προσκρεμάννυται.

The edition of Nuñez is the only authority for this article, and I have not scrupled to correct the unmeaning *Διονύσιον* to *Διονυσεῖον*. Suïdas gives the general canon: *Ἀθήναιον*[1] *ὅτι Ἀπολλώνιον βραχέως, τὸ ἱερὸν τοῦ Ἀπόλλωνος. οὕτω καὶ παρὰ Θουκυδίδῃ ἀναγνωστέον· καὶ Ποσειδώνιον τὸ τοῦ Ποσειδῶνος, ὡς Ἀθήναιον, τὸ τῆς Ἀθηνᾶς, καὶ Διονύσιον, καὶ Δημήτριον, καὶ πάντα τὰ τοιαῦτα ὁμωνύμως τοῖς ἀνδρωνυμικοῖς· τὸ δὲ Ποσειδανεῖον δῆλον ὅτι Δωριέων ἐστίν.*

CCCXLVII.

Οὐχ οἷον ὀργίζομαι, κίβδηλον ἐσχάτως. μάλιστα ἁμαρτάνεται ἐν τῇ ἡμεδαπῇ, οὐχ οἷον καὶ μὴ οἷον λεγόντων, ὅπερ οὐ μόνον τῷ ἀδοκίμῳ ἀπόβλητον ἀλλὰ καὶ τῷ ἤχῳ ἀηδές, λέγειν δὲ χρή, οὐ δήπου, μὴ δήπου.

Nuñez, quoted apparently with approbation by Lobeck, errs in considering the phrase *ἐν τῇ ἡμεδαπῇ* to refer to the native country of Phrynichus, Bithynia, or, in larger sense, Asia. As in Herodian, 1. 11, it signifies the Roman Empire. There seems to be no example of this use of *οὐχ οἷον* in Greek literature. Even the Antiatticist, who evidently wrote with a copy of Phrynichus before him (if this article is by Phrynichus), does not venture directly to contradict him here, but suggests another equivalent for the rejected expression: *Οὐχ οἷον ὁρίζομαι* (lege *ὀργίζομαι*), *οὐχ οἷον ἁλίσκω* (sic) *καὶ τὰ ὅμοια, σὺ δὲ πολὺ ἀπέχω τοῦ ὁρίζεσθαι* (lege *ὀργίζεσθαι*).

CCCXLVIII.

Οἰκίας δεσπότης λεκτέον, οὐχ ὡς Ἄλεξις, οἰκοδεσπότης.

Pollux, who is by no means a purist, agrees with Phrynichus, 10. 21, *ἀλλὰ μὴν τὸ κοινότατον τουτὶ καὶ μᾶλλον τε-*

[1] i. e. *οὐκ Ἀθηναῖον*.

θρυλλημένον τὸν οἰκοδεσπότην, καὶ τὴν οἰκοδέσποιναν οὐκ ἀποδέχομαι μὲν τοὔνομα. ὡς δὲ ἔχεις εἰδέναι μηνύω σοι ὅτι καὶ ταῦτα ἄμφω εὗρον ἐν Θεανοῦς τῆς Πυθαγόρου γυναικὸς ἐπιστολῇ πρὸς Τιμαρέταν γραφείσῃ. ὁ δὲ οἰκοδεσπότης ἔστι καὶ Ἀλέξιδος ἐν Ταραντίνοις.

CCCXLIX.

Ὁνδηποτοῦν μὴ λέγε, ἀλλὰ δοκίμως ὁντινοῦν.

Lobeck, however, cites from Demosthenes a form of words comparable with that reprehended here, 1010. 15, *τῇ δὲ τούτων μητρὶ Πλαγγόνι ἐπλησίαζεν ὅντινα δήποτ' οὖν τρόπον. οὐ γὰρ ἐμὸν τοῦτο λέγειν ἐστί*, and in Aeschines, 23. 29, *ὁσδηποτοῦν* itself is exhibited by one manuscript, *λεγέτω δὲ παρελθὼν ὁ σοφὸς Βάταλος ὑπὲρ αὐτοῦ, ἵν' εἰδῶμεν τί ποτ' ἐρεῖ· "ἄνδρες δικασταί, ἐμισθώσατό με ἑταιρεῖν αὐτῷ ἀργυρίου ὁστισδηποτοῦν" (οὐδὲν γὰρ διαφέρει οὕτως εἰρῆσθαι)*. For such exceptions Phrynichus would have had his favourite answer—*οὐ φροντὶς Ἱπποκλείδῃ*, as he would have treated with even more contempt those from late writers.

CCCL.

Πρόσφατον· καὶ περὶ τούτου πολλὴν διατριβὴν ἐποιησάμην ἐπισκοπούμενος εἰ μόνον λέγεται πρόσφατος νεκρὸς καὶ μὴ πρόσφατον πρᾶγμα. εὑρίσκετο δὲ Σοφοκλῆς ἐν τῇ Ἀνδρομέδᾳ τιθεὶς οὕτω—

μηδὲν φοβεῖσθε προσφάτους ἐπιστολάς.

In the line of Sophocles I have preferred *φοβεῖσθε*, the reading of Callierges, to the infinitive *φοβεῖσθαι* of Nuñez. The meaning, of which it took Phrynichus so long to discover a solitary instance, is after all not uncommon even in prose, as Dem. 551. 13, *τὰ ἀδικήματα ἕωλα τὰ τούτων ὡς* ὑμᾶς καὶ ψυχρὰ ἀφικνεῖται, τῶν δ' ἄλλων ἡμῶν ἕκαστος . . . πρόσφατος κρίνεται: Lysias, 151. 5, ἔτι τῆς ὀργῆς οὔσης προσφάτου. Perhaps in both these passages, and certainly in the former, the metaphor is still crisp. Alexis applies the word to fish—

οὐ δεινόν ἐστι, προσφάτους μὲν ἂν τύχῃ
πωλῶν τις ἰχθῦς κτε.;

Ap. Ath. 6. 225 F.

CCCLI.

Πτῶμα ἐπὶ νεκροῦ τιθέασιν οἱ νῦν, οἱ δὲ ἀρχαῖοι οὐχ οὕτως, ἀλλὰ πτώματα νεκρῶν ἢ οἴκων.

In Attic literature πτῶμα, with the signification of 'carcase,' seems to be confined to poetry, and in that of 'ruins,' does not happen to occur at all. The rule of Phrynichus is absolute—

Ἑλένης πτῶμ' ἰδὼν ἐν αἵματι.

Eur. Or. 1196.

Ἐτεοκλέους πτῶμα.

Phoeniss. 1697.

πτώματα νεκρῶν τρισσῶν.

Heracl. 1490.

In Aesch. Supp. 662—

μήδ' ἐπιχωρίοις ⏑ ⏑
πτώμασιν αἱματίσαι πέδον γᾶς,

the lost word may be a genitive dependent upon πτώμασιν, and if it is a nominative, like ἔρις or στάσις, and the subject of αἱματίσαι, there is still no necessity to render πτῶμα, 'carcase,' but it may be translated 'downfall,' the plural being used as of many. In any case, a single exception in a lyrical passage is of little moment.

According to Harpocration, the expression πτώματα ἐλαῶν occurred in Lysias, but the lexicographer leaves the meaning doubtful: Πτώματα ἐλαιῶν· Λυσίας ἐν τῷ κατὰ

Νικίδου· λέγοι ἂν ἤτοι τὸν καρπὸν τὸν ἀποπεπτωκότα τῶν φυτῶν ἢ αὐτὰ τὰ δένδρα κατά τινα τύχην πεπτωκότα.

In late Greek *πτῶμα* is frequently met with in the sense of 'dead body,' as Plut. Alexandr. ch. 33, *οἵ τε τροχοὶ τῶν ἁρμάτων διελαύνοντο, συνείχοντο, πτώμασιν πεφυρμένοι τοσούτοις, οἵ τε ἵπποι καταλαμβανόμενοι καὶ ἀποκρυπτόμενοι τῷ πλήθει τῶν νεκρῶν.* In that of 'ruins' it is less frequent, but still found—Polyb. 16. 31. 8; Aristid. I. 546, etc.

CCCLII.

Περίστασις ἀντὶ τοῦ συμφορὰ τιθέασιν οἱ στωικοὶ φιλόσοφοι, οἱ δ' ἀρχαῖοι περίστασιν λέγουσι τὴν διά τινα ταραχὸν παρουσίαν πλήθους, καὶ ἡ τραγῳδία καὶ ἡ κωμῳδία. μάθοις δ' ἂν Τηλεκλείδου λέγοντος ὧδε—

τίς ἥδε κραυγὴ καὶ δόμων περίστασις;

This line of Teleclides is the only passage of Attic Greek preserved in which *περίστασις* has the meaning commended by Phrynichus, in fact the only passage in which the word occurs, although it is extraordinarily common in late Greek. The meaning, however, is natural and forcible, and is supported by certain uses of the corresponding verbal adjective, Isocr. 135 E, *ἀντὶ μὲν τοῦ τιμᾶσθαι καταφρονηθησόμενος, ἀντὶ δὲ τοῦ περίστατος ὑπὸ πάντων δι' ἀρετὴν εἶναι περίβλεπτος ὑπὸ τῶν αὐτῶν ἐπὶ κακίᾳ γενησόμενος*: id. 288, *ταῖς θαυματοποιίαις ταῖς οὐδὲν μὲν ὠφελούσαις, ὑπὸ δὲ τῶν ἀνοήτων περιστάτοις γιγνομένοις.*

CCCLIII.

Παρεμβολὴ δεινῶς Μακεδονικόν· καίτοι ἐνῆν τῷ στρατοπέδῳ χρῆσθαι, πλείστῳ καὶ δοκίμῳ ὄντι.

CCCLIV.

Σαπρὰν οἱ πολλοὶ ἀντὶ τοῦ αἰσχράν. Θέων φησὶν ὁ γραμματικὸς εὑρηκέναι παρὰ Φερεκράτει, ληρῶν, ἅπαντα γὰρ ἃ φέρει μαρτύρια ἐπὶ τοῦ παλαιοῦ καὶ σεσηπότος εὕρηται κείμενα.

'Vitii a Phrynicho reprehensi exemplum apertissimum est in Compar. Philist. et Menand. p. 363—

σαπρὰς γυναῖκας ὁ τρόπος εὐμόρφους ποιεῖ
πολύ γε διαφέρει σεμνότης εὐμορφίας.'

Lobeck.

CCCLV.

Σώματα ἐπὶ τῶν ὠνίων ἀνδραπόδων, οἷον σώματα πωλεῖται οὐ χρῶνται οἱ ἀρχαῖοι.

Pollux will show how this statement has to be taken, 3. 78, *σώματα δ' ἁπλῶς οὐκ ἂν εἴποις, ἀλλὰ δοῦλα σώματα.* Thus limited the rule holds true of Attic, Dem. 480. 10, *τρισχίλια δ' αἰχμάλωτα σώματα δεῦρ' ἤγαγε*: Aeschin. 14. 18, *οὗτος δ' εἰ μή φησι πεπρακέναι, τὰ σώματα τῶν οἰκετῶν ἐμφανῆ παρασχέσθω.* It should be compared with that in article 351.

The late use may be exemplified by Polyb. 3. 17. 10, *κύριος γενόμενος χρημάτων πολλῶν καὶ σωμάτων καὶ κατασκευῆς.*

CCCLVI.

Τὰ πρόσωπα παρῆν ἀμφότερα· οἱ ἀμφὶ τὰς δίκας ῥήτορες οὕτω λέγουσι παραπαίοντες. ἀλλὰ σὺ καθαρὸς καὶ ἀρχαῖος ὢν ῥήτωρ καὶ μόνος μετά γ' ἐκείνους, τοὺς ἀμφὶ τὸν Δημοσθένην λέγω, ἐπανάγων εἰς τὸ ἀρχαῖον σχῆμα καὶ δόκιμον τὴν ῥητορικήν, οὐ μόνον αὐτὸς δυσχεραίνων οὐδεπώποτε ἐχρήσω τῷ ὀνόματι, ἀλλὰ καὶ τοὺς ἄλλους ἐκώλυσας χρήσασθαι, ἐξελληνίζων καὶ ἀττικίζων τὸ βασιλικὸν δικαστήριον καὶ διδάσκαλος καθιστάμενος οὐ μόνον αὐτῶν τῶν λόγων, οἷον χρὴ λέγειν, σχήματος καὶ βλέμματος καὶ φωνῆς καὶ στάσεως. Τοιγαροῦν σε τῶν μεγίστων ἀξιώσαντες οἱ Ῥωμαίων βασιλεῖς, ἀνέθεσαν τὰ Ἑλλήνων ἅπαντα πράγματα διοικεῖν, παριδρυσάμενοι φύλακα ἑαυτοῖς, λόγῳ μὲν ἐπιστολέα ἀποφήναντες, ἔργῳ δὲ συνεργὸν ἑλόμενοι τῆς βασιλείας, ἀλλὰ ταῦτα μὲν καὶ αὖθις.

Τὰ δὲ πρόσωπα, ὡς πρόκειται, οὐκ ἐροῦμεν, ἀλλὰ καθάπερ οἱ παλαιοί, οἷον, καλὸν ἔχει πρόσωπον.

This article, though unquestionably genuine, has little extrinsic authority.

'Hanc vitiosam loquendi consuetudinem quodammodo praeparaverunt poeticae circumlocutiones. Ἀρετᾶς πρόσωπον, Eur. I. A. 1090, ἡσυχίας πρόσωπον, Ar. Av. 1322, dehinc pro homine ipso, quatenus aliquam personam sustinet Aristot. Rhet. 2. 517, et Epicur. Stob. Ecl. 1. 218, et innumeris Polybii, Dionysii, aliorumque locis. *ἐκεῖνα τὰ πρόσωπα, illi*, Longin. 14. 56. *θηλυκὸν πρόσωπον*, Artem. 2. 36, et saepissime apud jurisconsultos Graecos.' Lobeck.

CCCLVII.

Στρηνιᾶν. τούτῳ ἐχρήσαντο οἱ τῆς νέας κωμῳδίας ποιηταί, ᾧ οὐδ' ἂν μανείς τις χρήσαιτο, παρὸν λέγειν τρυφᾶν.

The verb is first met with in the middle Comedy—

ἀπέλαυσα πολλῶν καὶ καλῶν ἐδεσμάτων
πιών τε προπόσεις τρεῖς ἴσως ἢ τέτταρας
ἐστρηνίων πως, καταβεβρωκὼς σίτια
ἴσως ἐλεφάντων τεττάρων.

Antiphanes, ap. Ath. 3. 127 D.

χορτασθήσομαι.
νὴ τὸν Διόνυσον, ἄνδρες, ἤδη στρηνιῶ.

Sophilus, ap. Ath. 3. 100 A.

In neither of these passages is it a synonym of *τρυφῶ*, but expresses the fighting-cock feeling of a man who has just risen from a hearty meal. Στρηνιῶ is from the same root as the Latin 'strenuus;' and if the statement of Pollux may be trusted (2. 112), that Callias used the compound *στρηνόφωνος*, 'loud-voiced,' the root was known in Classical Greek at an early date.

CCCLVIII.

Σύαγρος οὐ ῥητέον· σῦν ἄγριον οἱ ἀρχαῖοι λέγουσι.

Athenaeus (9. 401) gives the history of *σύαγρος*. Sophocles used it in the legitimate sense of 'boar-hunter'—

σὺ δ', ὦ σύαγρε, Πηλιωτικὸν τρέφος·

but Antiphanes is the first writer cited as attaching to it the signification 'wild boar'—

λαβὼν ἐπανάξω σύαγρον εἰς τὴν οἰκίαν
τῆς νυκτὸς αὐτῆς, καὶ λέοντα, καὶ λύκον.

In Sicily it went by the name of *ἀσχέδωρος*, and that was one of the Sicilian words which appeared in the works of Aeschylus after his Sicilian sojourn: Αἴσχυλος γοῦν ἐν Φορκίσι, παρεικάζων τὸν Περσέα τῷ ἀγρίῳ τούτῳ συί, φησίν—

ἔδυ δ' ἐς ἄντρον ἀσχέδωρος ὥς.

Similar compounds, as absurd as *σύαγρος* for *σῦς ἄγριος*, are instanced by Lobeck, *αἴγαγρος*, *βόαγρος*, *ἵππαγρος*, *ὄναγρος*, and others a little more natural, *ἀγριόχοιρος*, *ἀγριόρνιθες*, and *ἀγριοχηνάρια*.

CCCLIX.

Συγγνωμονῆσαι οὐ χρὴ λέγειν ἀλλὰ συγγνῶναι.

Ὁμογνωμονεῖν is the only verb from an adjective in -γνώμων which has any authority: Thuc. 2. 97; Dem. 281. 21. Xenophon, as the first writer in the Common dialect, employed αὐτογνωμονεῖν, Hell. 7. 3. 6, and διχογνωμονεῖν, Mem. 2. 6. 21, and might have employed μεγαλογνωμονεῖν, ὀρθογνωμονεῖν, or any other such form. It is another proof of the spuriousness of the speech Κατὰ Ἀριστογείτονος that φυσιογνωμονεῖν occurs in its pages, Dem. 799. 21, καὶ κατ' ἄνδρα εἰς ἕκαστον τὸν παριόντα βλέψονται, καὶ φυσιογνωμονήσουσι τοὺς ἀποψηφισαμένους.

CCCLX.

Σιτομετρεῖσθαι μὴ λέγε. λύων δ' ἐρεῖς σῖτον μετρεῖσθαι.

In Attic Greek σιτομετρεῖν could bear only one meaning, viz. 'to hold the office of σιτομέτρης.' Such a use as is seen in Polyb. 6. 39. 13 was quite impossible, σιτομετροῦνται δ' οἱ μὲν πεζοὶ, πυρῶν Ἀττικοῦ μεδίμνου δύο μέρη μάλιστά πως.

CCCLXI.

Στηθύνιον ὀρνιθίου λέγουσί τινες οὐχ ὑγιῶς. εἰ γὰρ χρὴ ὑποκοριστικῶς λέγειν, λέγε στηθίδιον· εἰ δ' οὐκ ἔστιν ὑποκοριστικόν, πόθεν εἰσεκώμασε καὶ τοῦτο τὸ κακὸν τῇ τῶν Ἑλλήνων φωνῇ;

Phrynichus, if the article is his, is no doubt right, but στηθίδιον does not happen to occur in Greek literature, whereas στηθύνιον does—

> πνίγειν τε παχέων ἀρνίων στηθύνια.
>
> Eubulus[1], ap. Ath. 2. 65 C.

Diminutives in -ύνιον are a late formation. It is notorious that, as Greek aged, many words were altogether replaced by diminutives formed from them in more or less legitimate ways.

[1] Also attributed to Ephippus in Ath. 9. 370 C.

CCCLXII.

Ὑπέρδριμυς· ἐπεὶ ὑπέρσοφος καὶ ὑπέρδριμυς ἀξιοῦσί τινες λέγειν. λεγόντων δ' εἰ καὶ οἱ ἀρχαῖοι καὶ οἱ δόκιμοι λέγουσιν, εἰ δὲ μή, ἐώντων χαίρειν τὸ ὑπέρδριμυς.

There is no reason why one should not use *ὑπέρδριμυς*. If Greek were to be studied on the principle which underlies this article, it would be impossible to learn it, and the attempt to acquire any knowledge of the language would bring little profit to the student. The edition of Nuñez is almost the only authority for the remark.

CCCLXIII.

Φυγαδεῦσαι καὶ φυγαδευθῆναι· ἐπισκέψεως πολλῆς δεῖται, εἰ ἐγκριτέον τοὔνομα τοῖς δοκίμοις. εἰ τοίνυν εὕροις, βεβαιώσεις τὸ ἀμφισβητούμενον.

The verb is used not only by Xenophon, but also by more trustworthy writers: Xen. Hell. 2. 3. 42, 2. 4. 14, 5. 4. 19; Isocr. 179 B, *Χίων δὲ τοὺς μὲν πρώτους τῶν πολιτῶν ἐφυγάδευσαν*: Dem. 1018. 10, *εἰς Ἄρειον πάγον με προσεκαλέσατο, ὡς φυγαδεύσων ἐκ τῆς πόλεως*: Aristophon, ap. Ath. 13. 563 B—

δεῦρ' αὐτὸν ἐφυγάδευσαν ὡς ἡμᾶς κάτω.

It does no credit to the styles in which it occurs, being a gross violation of the law of parsimony, but its existence in Attic is beyond question. This article is exhibited only by Nuñez.

CCCLXIV.

Φρονιμεύεσθαι μὴ λέγε, φρονεῖν δὲ τὰ ὄντα.

Callierges confuses this article with 367, neither 365 nor 366 appearing in his alphabetical arrangement: *Φρονιμεύεσθαι μὴ λέγε, ἀλλὰ χρήσιμον γενέσθαι.*

The verb only occurs here.

CCCLXV.

Χήμη· πόθεν ἀνεμίχθη τῇ τῶν Ἑλλήνων φωνῇ, ἄδηλον. οἱ γὰρ ἀρχαῖοι κογχύλην λέγουσι τοῦτο.

The word is probably good enough. 'In quaestionibus naturalibus usus ejus multiplex est neque inconcessus: Aelian, H. An. 14. 22, 15. 12: Artemid. 2. 14: Xenocr. de Aquat. 18. 31: Ionem, Philyllium, Apollodorum, Hicesium testatur Athenaeus, 3. 86 C. F., 90. A. E., 93 A.' Lobeck.

CCCLXVI.

Ἐπιχειμάζεις σαυτὸν Μένανδρος εἴρηκεν ἐπὶ τοῦ λυπεῖν, καὶ Ἀλεξανδρεῖς ὁμοίως. πειστέον δὲ τοῖς δοκίμοις, τοῖς μὴ εἰδόσι τοὔνομα.

In English we can say, 'do not distress yourself,' as well as 'a ship in distress;' but perhaps the metaphor is the converse of the Greek one, and 'distress' used of ships to be compared with Caesar's employment of *contumelia* in describing the serviceable sea-going qualities of the Armorican navy, B. G. 3. 13, 'naves totae factae ex robore ad quamvis vim et contumeliam (rough usage) perferendam.' Be this as it may, of all the changes which the Greek language underwent after the Macedonian conquests, few are more observable than the growing freedom in the use of metaphors. Metaphors, which to an Attic ear were out of place except in Tragedy, and even in Tragedy were often strangely condensed, assumed, in writers like Menander, an easy and natural expression, befitting the Comic sock. Anaxandrides will supply an example of the natural freshness which Comedy could bring to a faded Tragic metaphor. Euripides had said in El. 1076—

> μόνην δὲ πασῶν οἶδ' ἐγώ σ' Ἑλληνίδων,
> εἰ μὲν τὰ Τρώων εὐτυχοῖ, κεχαρμένην,
> εἰ δ' ἧσσον εἴη, συννεφοῦσαν ὄμματα.

In Anaxandrides, Ath. 1. 34 D, the metaphor has a modern freedom of movement—

> ἐὰν λούσησθε νῦν
> ῥάφανόν τε πολλὴν ἐντράγητε, παύσετε
> τὸ βάρος, διασκεδᾶτε τὸ προσὸν νῦν νέφος
> ἐπὶ τοῦ προσώπου.

By comparing Latin of the silver age with that of the Republican or Augustan times it will be seen that a similar change in the genius of the language has taken place, and that the enlargement of view which was produced by the consolidation of the Roman world-empire changed the Roman language from an ancient into a modern tongue.

The expression *ἐπιχειμάζεις σαυτόν* is merely an everyday equivalent of many phrases of tragedy in which *χειμάζω* takes part, and which any lexicon will supply.

CCCLXVII.

Χρησιμεῦσαι μὴ λέγε, ἀλλὰ χρήσιμον γενέσθαι.

The veto is just. The addition of *χρησιμεύω* to verbs in -*εύω* (see art. 3) is even more uncalled for than *φυγαδεύω*, and is not sanctioned by any good writer.

CCCLXVIII.

Ἐσχάτως ἔχει ἐπὶ τοῦ μοχθηρῶς ἔχει καὶ σφαλερῶς τάττουσιν οἱ σύρφακες, ἡ δὲ τοῦ ἐσχάτως χρῆσις, οἶσθα, ἐπὶ τοῦ ἄκρου παρὰ τοῖς ἀρχαίοις νομίζεται, ἐσχάτως πονηρός, ἐσχάτως φιλόσοφος. διαγραπτέον οὖν καὶ τοῦτο.

The phrase *ἐσχάτως ἔχειν* is rightly cancelled. It does not appear till late. Good writers avoid the adverb, even in the sense permitted by Phrynichus; no instance of which is known except in Xenophon, An. 2. 6. 1, *ἐσχάτως φιλοπόλεμος*. As we found him employing even the superlative *ἐσχατώτατα* (see p. 144), his authority will not count against the absence of the adverb from Plato, and the Orators, and all Comedy except Menander. Photius, *Ἐσχάτως· ἄκρως, Μένανδρος 'φοβοῦμαι δ' ἐσχάτως.'*

CCCLXIX.

Χρεωλυτῆσαι λέγει ὁ πολύς, ὁ δὲ Ἀττικὸς τὰ χρέα διαλύσασθαι.

Χρεολυτεῖν and all similar compounds of *χρέος*, are late: *χρεοδοτεῖν, χρεοκοπεῖν, χρεωφειλέτης, χρεωστεῖν*, etc.

As late formations they naturally were spelt with omicron, not omega, except when the second part of the compound began with a vowel. The coalescing of *ο*+*ο* into *ω* may be compared with that of *ε*+*ο* into *ω* in *πεντώρυφος, πεντώρυγος*, etc. Herodn. Epim. p. 207, *τὰ παρὰ τοῦ χρέος συγκείμενα διὰ τοῦ ο μικροῦ γράφονται, μέσον ἔχοντα τὸ ο μικρὸν οἷον χρεοκοπῶ, χρεολυτῶ, χρεοδοτῶ, χρεοκοπία, χρεολυσία, χρεοδοσία, καὶ τὰ ὅμοια.*

It is, however, possible that Phrynichus wrote *χρεωλυτεῖν*, as a naïf hit at would-be Atticists.

CCCLXX.

Χρέωϲ· Ἀττικὸϲ ἂν φαίνοιο καὶ ἐπιμελὴϲ εἰ διὰ τοῦ ω μεγάλου χρέωϲ λέγειϲ. σὺ μὲν οὖν τῇ σεαυτοῦ πολυμαθίᾳ τὸν Ἀριστοφάνην διὰ τοῦ ο ἐδείκνυεϲ τὸ χρέοϲ ἐν ταῖϲ ἑτέραιϲ Νεφέλαιϲ εἰπόντα—

ἀτὰρ τί χρέοϲ ἔβα με μετὰ τὸν Πασίαν;

ἔοικε δὲ παρῳδηκὼϲ εἰρηκέναι· διοπερ οὐ χρηστέον αὐτῷ.

The address to Cornelianus in this article is to be compared with that in article 203, as both show that the two scholars were in the habit of discussing together doubtful points of Atticism. The line of the Clouds has been already considered on p. 48.

On the authority of Phrynichus and Moeris (p. 403) *χρέος* ought probably to be regarded as due to a copyist's error when encountered in Attic texts, as in Plato, Polit. 267 A, Legg. 12. 958 B, Isocr. 402 C, and Dem. 791. 2. In Demosthenes the best manuscripts generally exhibit the form in omega, as 900. 14; 988. 24; 1019. 23; 1040. 19; although in the last instance even Paris S has fallen to the level of the worst codices and presents *χρέος*. The genitive and dative must shift for themselves, as there is really no evidence as to the Attic form of either. In Dem. 1189. 25 the best manuscripts read *χρέως* as genitive, but the speech is spurious, and in Lys. 148. 31, *χρέους* seems to be best supported. As for the dative it does not occur once. Similarly in the plural, only two forms are known, but, unlike those of the singular, they are undisputed, *χρέᾱ* being used for the nominative, accusative, and vocative, and *χρεῶν* for the genitive—

σὺ δ' οὖν κάθευδε· τὰ δὲ χρέᾱ ταῦτ' ἴσθ' ὅτι.

Ar. Nub. 39.

ἃ νῦν ὀφείλω διὰ σέ, τούτων τῶν χρεῶν.

Id. 117.

CCCLXXI.

Φιλόλογος ὁ φιλῶν λόγους καὶ σπουδάζων περὶ παιδείαν· οἱ δὲ νῦν ἐπὶ τοῦ ἐμπείρου τιθέασιν οὐκ ὀρθῶς. τὰ μέντοι ἐφιλολόγησα καὶ φιλολογῶ καὶ πάντα τὰ ῥήματα τὰ μετοχικὰ ἀδόκιμα.

Whether intentionally or by mistake Callierges printed *φιλόσοφος* for *φιλόλογος*, and placed Τὰ *μέντοι κτε.* under the letter T. The Paris manuscript omits the whole article.

CCCLXXII.

Τίνι διαφέρει τόδε καὶ τόδε; οὐ χρὴ οὕτω λέγειν κατὰ δοτικὴν πτῶσιν, ἀλλὰ τί διαφέρει, καθὰ καὶ Δημοσθένης φησί· τί δοῦλον ἢ ἐλεύθερον εἶναι διαφέρει;

This rule holds without exception in Attic, but apart from this one phrase the dative was quite legitimate. Plato, Euth. 4 E, *οὐδέ τῳ ἂν διαφέροι Εὐθύφρων τῶν πολλῶν ἀνθρώπων*: Rep. 5. 469 C, *ὅλῳ καὶ παντὶ διαφέρει τὸ φείδεσθαι.* From Aristotle onwards the dative encroached upon the accusative in *τί διαφέρει*; as Arist. Part. An. 4. 8 fin., *τίνι διαφέρει τὰ ἄρρενα τῶν θηλειῶν*;

CCCLXXIII.

Τέτευχε τιμῆς, τέτευχε τοῦ σκοποῦ μὴ λέγε, ἀλλ' ἀντ' αὐτοῦ τῷ δοκίμῳ χρῶ τετύχηκε.

The instance of the trisyllabic form cited by Veitch from Dem. 21. 150 (563. 11) is only a variant foolishly preferred by Bekker to the genuine *τετευχηκώς*. It occurs, however, unquestioned in Menander, Monostich. 44—

ἀρχῆς τετευχὼς ἴσθι ταύτης ἄξιος,

in Macho ap. Ath. 13. 581 (35)—

αὐτὸν μὲν ἀξιοῦντα μὴ τετευχέναι,

and in late writers generally.

CCCLXXIV.

Στρόβιλον οἱ μὲν πολλοὶ τὸ ἐδώδιμον λέγουσι καὶ αὐτὸ τὸ δένδρον. οἱ δ' ἀρχαῖοι τὴν βίαιον τοῦ ἀνέμου εἴλησιν καὶ συστροφὴν στρόβιλον καλοῦσι καὶ στροβιλῆσαι τὸ συστρέψαι. οὕτως οὖν καὶ ἡμῖν ῥητέον, τὸ δὲ ἐδώδιμον πιτύων καρπός, καὶ τὸ δένδρον πίτυς. καὶ γὰρ πίτυος τὸ ἐκκεκοκισμένον ἔτι καὶ νῦν κόκκωνα λέγουσιν οἱ πολλοὶ ὀρθῶς, καὶ γὰρ Σόλων ἐν τοῖς ποιήμασιν οὕτω χρῆται.

Κόκκωνας ἄλλος, ἅτερος δὲ σήσαμα.

There are many variations in the different manuscripts and editions, Laurentian A *συστροβῆσαι τὸ συστρέψαι*, and B and Nuñez *συστροβιλῆσαι τὸ στρέψαι*. Moreover for *καὶ γὰρ πίτυος τὸ ἐκκεκοκισμένον ἔτι κτε.* all have *καὶ γάρ ἐστι πίτυς τὸ ἐκκεκοκισμένον· ἔτι κτε.*

The same caution reappears in App. Soph. 63. 27, *Στρόβιλος· τὴν τοῦ ἀνέμου συστροφήν, οὐχ ὡς οἱ νῦν τὸν καρπὸν τῶν πιτύων. Πλάτων καὶ μεταφορικῶς κέχρηται ἐπὶ ᾠδῆς κιθαρῳδικῆς, πολὺν ἐχούσης τὸν τάραχον*: cp. Galen, vol. 11. 158 D, *Κόκκαλος ὑπ' αὐτοῦ* (Hippocrates) *λελεγμένος οὐχ οὕτως, ἀλλὰ κῶνος μᾶλλον ὑπὸ τῶν παλαιῶν Ἑλλήνων ὠνομάζετο, καθάπερ ὑπὸ τῶν νεωτέρων ἰατρῶν σχέδον ἁπάντων στρόβιλος*: id. 13. 527 C, *οὓς νῦν ἅπαντες Ἕλληνες ὀνομάζουσι στροβίλους, τὸ πάλαι δὲ παρὰ τοῖς Ἀττικοῖς ἐκαλοῦντο κῶνοι.* With the replacement of *κῶνος* by the picturesque *στρόβιλος* may be compared that of *ἁλμάδες* by *κολυμβάδες* discussed in art. 94. The words from *καὶ γάρ* to the end may well be a spurious addition made by some one who happened to have heard *κόκκων* so used by the vulgar. The remark is awkwardly introduced, and contradicts *τὸ δὲ ἐδώδιμον πιτύων καρπός*. There is no reason for assigning to *κόκκων* in Solon's iambics the meaning of *στρόβιλος*, 'the edible kernel of a pine-cone.'

CCCLXXV.

Συγκαταβαίνειν εἰς τὰς σκέψεις, συγκαταβαίνειν εἰς διδασκαλίας μὴ εἴπῃς, ἀλλὰ συγκαθιέναι καὶ συγκαθῆκεν εἰς τὸ παίζειν ἢ εἰς ἄλλο τι.

The use of the Latin *descendere*, almost in the sense of 'condescend,' is well-known. In Attic that meaning was represented by *συγκαθιέναι*, either transitively with *ἐμαυτόν*, *ἑαυτόν*, etc., or intransitively and in late Greek by *συγκαταβαίνειν*. The original notion as suggested by *συγκαταβαίνειν εἰς διδασκαλίας* was of course 'to descend with one's adversary on to the ground selected for a trial of strength.' The following passages will illustrate the usage: Plato, Theaet. 168 B, *ἐὰν οὖν ἐμοὶ πείθῃ, οὐ δυσμενῶς οὐδὲ μαχητικῶς, ἀλλ' ἵλεῳ τῇ διανοίᾳ συγκαθιεὶς ὡς ἀληθῶς σκέψει τί ποτε λέγομεν*: Rep. 8. 563 A, *καὶ ὅλως οἱ μὲν νέοι πρεσβυτέροις ἀπεικάζονται καὶ διαμιλλῶνται καὶ ἐν λόγοις καὶ ἐν ἔργοις, οἱ δὲ γέροντες συγκαθιέντες τοῖς νέοις εὐτραπελίας τε καὶ χαριεντισμοῦ ἐμπίπλανται, μιμούμενοι τοὺς νέους*. In his dictionary to Polybius, Schweighaeuser cites *Συγκαταβαίνειν εἰς πᾶν*, 3. 10. 1; 7. 4. 3: *εἰς τὸν ὑπὲρ τῶν ὅλων κίνδυνον*, 3. 89. 8; 5. 66. 7: *εἰς ὁλοσχερῆ κρίσιν*, 3. 90. 5; 3. 108. 7: *εἰς τὰ τῶν πολεμίων προτερήματα*, 4. 11. 9: *εἰς τοὺς κατὰ μέρος ὑπὲρ τῆς διαλύσεως λόγους*,

5. 67. 3: *εἰς πάντα τὰ φιλάνθρωπα*, 5. 66. 2: *εἰς φόρους καὶ συνθήκας*, 4. 45. 4.

CCCLXXVI.

Σκνιφὸς κατὰ διαφθορὰν οἱ πολλοὶ λέγουσι τὸν γλίσχρον καὶ μικροπρεπῆ περὶ τὰ ἀναλώματα, οἱ δ' ἀρχαῖοι σκνῖπα καλοῦσιν ἀπὸ τοῦ θηριδίου τοῦ ἐν τοῖς ξύλοις τοῦ κατὰ βραχὺ αὐτὰ κατεσθίοντος.

Moeris 387 implies that not only the form but the mean- of *σκνιφός* was un-Attic, *φειδωλοὶ Ἀττικῶς, σκνιφοὶ κοινόν.* As a matter of fact the word occurs in Attic only in the proverb *σκνῖψ ἐν χώρᾳ*; which Zenobius, 5. 35, thus explains, *ἐπὶ τῶν ταχέως μεταπηδώντων ἡ παροιμία εἴρηται· σκνῖψ γάρ ἐστι θηρίδιον ξυλοφάγον, ἀπὸ τόπου εἰς τόπον μεταπηδῶν· μέμνηται ταύτης Στράττις.*

CCCLXXVII.

Σταμνία οἱ μὲν ἀμαθεῖς ἐπὶ τῶν ἀμίδων τάττουσιν, οἱ δ' ἀρχαῖοι ἐπὶ τῶν οἰνηρῶν ἀγγείων.

'Praeter Hesychium: *Ἀμίς, σταμνίον*, Gloss. *matula σταμνίον* exponentes, et Lex. Rhet. Bekk. p. 217: *Ἀμνίδας* (*ἀμίδας* s. Attice *ἁμίδας*) *τὰ σταμνία Δημοσθένης* (c. Conon. 1257), nullum novimus hujus vitii consortem.' Lobeck.

CCCLXXVIII.

Συσχολαστὰς ἐσχάτως ἀνάττικον. χρὴ δὲ συμφοιτητὰς λέγειν.

Xenophon might perhaps have used *συσχολαστής*, as he actually anticipates the late application of *σχολάζω* in Symp. 4. 43, *Σωκράτει σχολάζων διημέρευον.*

CCCLXXIX.

Στρωματεὺς ἀδόκιμον· στρωματόδεσμος ἀρχαῖον καὶ δόκιμον. λέγε οὖν καὶ ἀρσενικῶς καὶ οὐδετέρως.

The name *στρωματεύς* came to be applied to the *στρωματόδεσμος*, the bag into which *στρώματα* and *στρωματεύς* were packed. In Attic *στρωματεύς* means a 'coverlet' or 'counterpane,' in late Greek 'a bag for *στρώματα* or blankets.' This strange perversion of meaning is also noted by Pollux, 7. 19, in enumerating *ἀγγεῖα, εἰς ἃ κατέθεντο τὰς ἐσθῆτας. στρωμάτοδεσμα, ταῦθ' οἱ νεώτεροι στρωματεῖς ἔλεγον, ἐν οἷς ὡς μὲν τὸ ὄνομα δηλοῖ τὰ στρώματα ἀπετίθεντο.*

CCCLXXX.

Εὐχρηστεῖν ἀπόρριψον λέγε δὲ κιχράναι.

There seems to be no instance of this euphemism in Greek literature, 'to be of service to,' instead of 'to lend to.' Even in its ordinary meaning the verb is unknown to Classical Greek.

CCCLXXXI.

Ῥᾳότερον μὴ λέγε ἀλλὰ ῥᾷον· συγκριτικὸν γὰρ συγκριτικοῦ οὐκ ἔστιν, οἷον εἴ τις λέγοι κρεισσότερον.

As the correct *ὤτων* (see art. 186) gave rise to the absurdity *ὤτοις*, so from the neuter comparative *ῥᾷον* sprang the nonsensical *ῥᾷος, ῥᾴως*, and *ῥᾳότερον.*

CCCLXXXII.

Ῥύμη· καὶ τοῦτο οἱ μὲν Ἀθηναῖοι ἐπὶ τῆς ὁρμῆς ἐτίθεσαν,

οἱ δὲ νῦν ἀμαθεῖς ἐπὶ τοῦ στενωποῦ. δοκεῖ δέ μοι καὶ τοῦτο μακεδονικὸν εἶναι. ἀλλὰ στενωπὸν καλεῖν χρή, ῥύμην δὲ τὴν ὁρμήν.

Instances of the Attic use are these: Thuc. 2. 76, *ἡ δὲ δοκὸς ῥύμῃ ἐμπίπτουσα*: Dem. 546 fin., *τῇ ῥύμῃ τῆς ὀργῆς καὶ τῆς ὕβρεως τοῦ Μειδίου*: Ar. Eccl. 4, *τροχῷ γὰρ ἐλαθεὶς κεραμικῆς ῥύμης ἄπο*: Thuc. 7. 70, *τῇ μὲν πρώτῃ ῥύμῃ ἐπιπλέοντες ἐκράτουν τῶν τεταγμένων νεῶν.* The late meaning is well-known from the New Test., e.g. Luke, Acts 9. 11, *ἀναστὰς πορεύθητι ἐπὶ τὴν ῥύμην τὴν καλουμένην Εὐθεῖαν.* The former meaning strengthens the explanation of *ῥύσεσθαι* given on p. 11, while that of 'street' or 'lane' must have existed long before the Common dialect in many a corner of Greece, where *ῥύεσθαι* also may have retained much of its early sense of *draw*. Cp. Lat. *ducere murum*, *ducere sulcum.*

CCCLXXXIII.

Δρωπακίζειν ἀδόκιμον, ἀρχαῖον δὲ τὸ παρατίλλεσθαι ἢ πιττοῦσθαι.

Perhaps the Atticist goes too far here. A new art, even if it be of the toilet, often necessitates a new name, and it is conceivable that there was a measurable difference between *δρωπακισμός* and *πίττωσις*, as there certainly was between *δρωπακισμός* and *παρατιλμός*, the latter being applicable to any depilation, the other only to that in which some sort of paste was used. Galen, however, seems to have considered *δρωπακισμός* and *πίττωσις* interchangeable terms, but he was a Jenner, not a Rimmel: vol. 12. 103, *ὅσα δέ τινά ποτέ εἰσι πιττωτὰ φάρμακα ἢ δρωπακιστὰ νοήσεις ἀκούσας πίτταν καὶ δρώπακα καί σοι λέγειν ἐξέστω καθότιπερ ἂν βουληθῇς; οὐ γὰρ ἀττικίζειν διδάσκειν πρόκειταί μοι τοὺς νέους.*

As a matter of fact πιττοῦσθαι is as unknown to Attic as δρωπακίζειν, but the compound καταπιττοῦν is employed, both in its direct sense of *cover with pitch*, and metaphorically as the opposite of καταχρυσοῦν.

CCCLXXXIV.

Στέμφυλα· οἱ μὲν πολλοὶ τὰ τῶν βοτρύων ἐκπιέσματα ἀμαθῶς· οἱ δ' Ἀττικοὶ στέμφυλα ἐλαῶν.

Athenaeus makes the same statement, 2. 56, Ἀθηναῖοι δὲ τὰς τετριμμένας ἐλάας στέμφυλα ἐκάλουν, βρύτεα δὲ τὰ ὑφ' ἡμῖν στέμφυλα, τὰ ἐκπιέσματα τῆς σταφυλῆς.

CCCLXXXV.

Πενταετηρικὸς ἀγὼν καὶ πενταετηρὶς μὴ λέγε, ἀλλ' ἀφαιρῶν τὸ α πεντετηρὶς καὶ πεντετηρικὸς ἀγών.

The evidence, both of metre and Inscriptions, supports Phrynichus in this article, which, like many more, establishes a particular point upon which a general rule may be fairly based. As false analogy with ἑπταδάκτυλος and δεκαδάκτυλος corrupted the corresponding compound of ὀκτώ from ὀκτωδάκτυλος to ὀκταδάκτυλος, so false analogy with the late ἑπταέτης and δεκαέτης produced the extraordinary forms πενταέτης, πενταετηρίς, etc. It is true that in the only line of Comedy in which πεντέτης occurs the metre allows of it being spelt as a quadrisyllable—

αὗται μέν εἰσι πεντέτεις· γεῦσαι λαβών.
Ar. Ach. 188.

but the following lines, which establish the shorter forms of similar compounds of δέκα and πέντε, establish *a fortiori* that spelling of the compounds of *πέντε* which Phrynichus commands—

> *ὅσπερ με διεκόρησεν οὖσαν ἑπτέτιν.*
> Ar. Thesm. 480.
>
> *σὺ δ' ἀλλὰ τασδὶ τὰς δεκέτεις γεῦσαι λαβών.*
> Ach. 191.
>
> *τὸ γνῶμα γοῦν βέβληκεν ὡς οὖσ' ἑπτέτης.*
> Comic. Anon. ap. Eustathium, 1404. 61.

To the same effect is the testimony of stone records: 'Πέντε in compositione servatur, non mutatur in *πέντα*: vide v. c. I. 322, ubi est *πεντέπους, πεντεπάλαστα.*' 'Ὀκτωδάκτυλος, similia constanter, non *ὀκταδάκτυλος*, v. c. T. N. XIV. e. 104, 185, C. I. A. I. 321. 28. 322.' Herwerden.

In prose texts the longer forms of compounds of *πέντε, ἕπτα,* and *δέκα,* and the shorter of *ὀκτώ* must unflinchingly be removed in favour of those which the genius of the Attic language or, in other words, common sense, the evidence of verse, and the record of stone monuments, prove to have been the only forms known to the Athenians. The general principle thus established, namely that in compounds of cardinal numerals the original form of the numeral is as far as possible retained, is further illustrated in the two articles which follow next, which call for no remark.

CCCLXXXVI.

Πεντάμηνον, πεντάπηχυ· μετάθες τὸ α εἰς τὸ ε, πεντέμηνον λέγων καὶ πεντέπηχυ.

CCCLXXXVII.

Ἑξάπηχυ καὶ ἑξαέτης· καὶ ἐντεῦθεν ἀφαιρήσεις τὸ α, ἕξπηχυ καὶ ἑξέτης καὶ ἕκπλευρον. τοῦτο γὰρ καὶ ἰατροὶ ἐπανορθοῦνται, ἕκπλεθρον λέγοντες καὶ οὐκ ἑξάπλεθρον.

In Laurentian A, the Paris manuscript, and in Callierges, these two articles appear condensed into one. It seems impossible to formulate a reasonable canon as to when ἐξ or ἐκ should be used in the compounds of ἐξ.

CCCLXXXVIII.

Περιεσπάσθην λέγουσί τινες ἐπὶ τοῦ ἐν ἀσχολίᾳ γενέσθαι, τιθέντες πάνυ κιβδήλως· τὸ γὰρ περισπᾶν καὶ περισπᾶσθαι ἐπὶ τοῦ παραιρεῖν καὶ παραιρεῖσθαι τάττουσιν οἱ ἀρχαῖοι. δέον οὖν ἄσχολος ἦν λέγειν.

This markedly late use of *περισπᾶσθαι* occurs in a well-known passage of St. Luke, 10. 40, *ἡ δὲ Μάρθα περιεσπᾶτο περὶ πολλὴν διακονίαν.*

CCCLXXXIX.

Πορνοκόπος· οὕτω Μένανδρος, οἱ δ' ἀρχαῖοι πορνότριψ λέγουσιν.

CCCXC.

Λήθαργος· οὕτω Μένανδρος, οἱ δ' ἀρχαῖοι Ἀθηναῖοι ἐπιλήσμονα καλοῦσιν, οἷς καὶ πειστέον.

CCCXCI.

Μεσοπορεῖν· καὶ τοῦτο Μένανδρος, οὐδὲν ἐπιβάλλων γνώμης τοῖς ὀνόμασιν, ἀλλὰ πάντα φύρων.

Though resting on the authority only of Nuñez' edition there can be little question about the genuineness of this article: 'Inter reliqua composita *εὐθυπορεῖν, βραδυπορεῖν, μακροπορεῖν, ὠκυπορεῖν*, etc. sunt quaedam satis antiqua, sed totum genus ab oratoribus atticis non admodum probatum videtur.' Lobeck.

CCCXCII.

Γῦρος· καὶ τοῦτο Μένανδρος τὴν καλλίστην τῶν κωμῳδιῶν τῶν ἑαυτοῦ, τὸν Μισογύνην, κατεκηλίδωσεν εἰπών. τί γὰρ δὴ γῦρός ἐστιν οὐ συνίημι.

Lobeck thinks that the words of Menander were quoted, but Nuñez, who alone has preserved this remark, has failed to preserve the passage. Though the substantive first appears in Menander, the Homeric adjective *γυρός*, 'round,' indicates as the source from which *γῦρος* entered the Common dialect one or other of the Greek dialects less prominent in literature. Even the adjective, though freely used in late Greek, has for classical authority only one passage of Homer—

γυρὸς ἐν ὤμοισιν, μελανόχροος, οὐλοκάρηνος.
Od. 19. 246.

The Latin 'gyrus' bears testimony to the prevalence of the substantive in post-Macedonian times.

CCCXCIII.

Σύσσημον· οὐχ ὁρῶ μὰ τὸν Ἡρακλέα τί πάσχουσιν οἱ τὸν Μένανδρον μέγαν ἄγοντες καὶ αἴροντες ὑπὲρ τὸ Ἑλληνικὸν ἅπαν. διὰ τί δὲ θαυμάσας ἔχω; ὅτι τὰ ἄκρα τῶν Ἑλλήνων ὁρῶ μανικῶς περὶ τὸν κωμῳδοποιὸν τοῦτον σπουδάζοντα—πρώτιστον μὲν ἐν παιδείᾳ μέγιστον ἀξίωμα ἁπάντων ἔχοντά σε καὶ διὰ τοῦτο ἐκ προκρίτων ἀποφανθέντα ὑπὸ τῶν βασιλέων ἐπιστολέα αὐτῶν, ἔπειτα δευτέρᾳ τιμῇ λειπόμενον πολὺ τῆς σῆς παρασκευῆς, ἐξεταζόμενον δ' ἐν τοῖς Ἕλλησι, Βάλβον τὸν ἀπὸ Τράλλεων, ὃς εἰς τοῦτο προθυμίας καὶ θαύματος ἥκει Μενάνδρου, ὥστε καὶ Δημοσθένους ἀμείνω ἐγχειρεῖν ἀποφαίνειν τὸν λέγοντα μεσοπορεῖν καὶ γῦρος καὶ λήθαργος καὶ σύσσημον καὶ πορνοκόπος καὶ ὀψωνιασμὸς καὶ ὀψώνιον καὶ δύσριγος καὶ ἄλλα κίβδηλα ἀναρίθμητα ἀμαθῆ. τὰ αὐτὰ δὲ σοὶ καὶ Βάλβῳ πεπονθότα καὶ Γαγιανὸν τὸν Σμυρναῖον ῥήτορα, ἄνδρα ζηλωτὴν καὶ ἐραστὴν τῆς σῆς ἐν παιδείᾳ φυλοκαλίας. ἄγε οὖν ὅπως λύσῃς μου τὴν ἐν τῇ τοιᾷδε δυσχερείᾳ τῶν ὤτων ἀπορίαν. οὐ γὰρ περιόψεσθαί σε ἡγοῦμαι ἐρήμως ὀφλόντα σου τὰ παιδικὰ Μένανδρον.

This, the longest continuous piece of writing from the pen of Phrynichus, proves that in his time the writing of Greek was a lost art. Granted that Menander used words and constructions unknown to Attic, yet his Greek was his own, easy, graceful, and elegant, not like that of his critic, a cumbrous and clumsy imitation of good models. In short, the one is Greek and the other is not.

The late origin of *σύσσημον*, *ὀψώνιον*, and *ὀψωνιασμός* is unquestioned, but Pollux, 4. 186, states that *δύσριγος* was used by Aristophanes. Perhaps in the original article which discussed *δύσριγος*, Phrynichus was able to show that Menander used the word incorrectly. As it is, there are no data to go upon. In Hdt. 5. 10, and Aristot. H. An. 8. 25, 605^a. 20 it bears the meaning, 'unable to bear cold.'

CCCXCIV.

Οἰκοδομὴ οὐ λέγεται, ἀντ' αὐτοῦ δὲ οἰκοδόμημα.

The rejected word is for Attic, and indeed for all Classical

Greek, an impossible formation. The subjoined table will recall the normal family relationships of words like *οἰκοδόμος*.

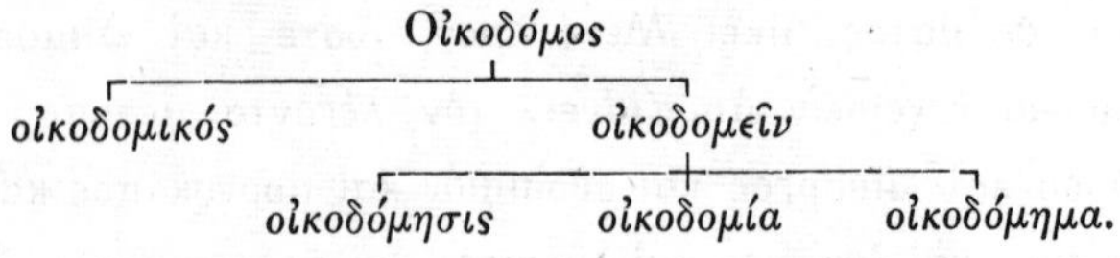

CCCXCV.

Κατ' ὄναρ· Πολέμων ὁ Ἰωνικὸς σοφιστὴς Δημοσθένους τοῦ ῥήτορος εἰκόνα χαλκῆν ἐν Ἀσκληπιοῦ τοῦ ἐν Περγάμῳ τῇ Μυσίᾳ ἀναθείς, ἐπέγραψεν ἐπίγραμμα τοιόνδε Δημοσθένη Παιανιέα Πολέμων κατ' ὄναρ, ἀδοκιμωτάτῳ τῷ κατ' ὄναρ χρησάμενος. ὥσπερ γὰρ καθ' ὕπαρ οὐ λέγεται, ἀλλ' ὕπαρ, οὕτως οὐδὲ κατ' ὄναρ, ἀλλ' ἤτοι ὄναρ ἰδὼν ἢ ἐξ ὀνείρου ὄψεως. οὕτως ἄρα μέγιστόν ἐστιν ὀνομάτων γνῶσις· ὅπου γε δὴ καὶ τὰ ἄκρα τῶν Ἑλλήνων πταίοντα ὁρᾶται.

A similar mistake has already been considered on Art. 104.

CCCXCVI.

Μετριάζειν τοῦτο οἱ μὲν ἀρχαῖοι ἐπὶ τοῦ τὰ συμβαίνοντα μετρίως φέρειν τιθέασι, Μένανδρος δ' ἐπὶ τοῦ ἀσθενεῖν παρα τὴν τῶν δοκίμων χρῆσιν.

The Paris manuscript here differs from the others and from the editions, not only substituting *τὰ συμφέροντα γενναίως* for *τὰ συμβαίνοντα μετρίως*, but in a way unusual with it, appending a whole clause, *σὺ δὲ ἐπὶ τοῦ ἴσον εἶναι καὶ μὴ ὑπερβάλλειν μήτε τῇ ἀλαζονείᾳ μήτε τῇ ταπεινώσει.* Late medical writers sometimes assign to *μετριάζω* the sense of 'am fairly well,' as Aelian H. An. 9. 15, *ὁ μετριάσαι δοκῶν πάλιν ἐξάπτεται εἰς ὀδύνην*, but the signification 'am unwell' is very rare indeed, e.g. as var. lect. in LXX. Nehem. 2. 2. Lexicons supply no instances of a corresponding use of the adjective *μέτριος*.

CCCXCVII.

Καθώς· Γάϊός τις Ἀρεθούσιος γραμματικὸς ἔφασκε δόκιμον εἶναι τοὔνομα· κεχρῆσθαι γὰρ αὐτῷ Φύλαρχον· ὢ τοῦ μάρτυρος ὡς οἴκοθεν ἐπαγομένου ὃς οὐδὲ Θουκυδίδου ἤκουσε λέγοντος καθὸ δεῖ εἰς Σικελίαν πλεῖν ἀλλ' οὐ καθώς· καὶ τὸ καθὰ δόκιμον.

The reading *ὡς οἴκοθεν ἐπαγομένου* is due to Scaliger, who saw that in the meaningless *ὡς ἔοικε τοῦ ἐπαγομένου* lay concealed a reference to the proverb *οἴκοθεν ὁ μάρτυς*, used of those who bear witness against themselves (*ἐπὶ τῶν καθ' ἑαυτῶν μάρτυρας φερόντων*, Diogenian, 7. 29). 'The authority of Gaius,' says Phrynichus, 'was of little value, and his voucher is no better.' *Καθώς* (see art. 32) is now banished from the few passages of Attic into which it had crept with the help of late copyists, such as Aeschin. 16. 23, *καὶ τῶν συνθηκῶν ἀνάγνωθι τὰ ἀντίγραφα καθ' ἃς τὴν πρᾶσιν ἐποιήσατο τοῦ ἀγῶνος*, where two manuscripts have *καθώς*, one *καθῶς*: Xen. Cyrop. 1. 4. 22, *καὶ ἰσχυρὰν τὴν φυγὴν τοῖς πολεμίοις κατέχων ἐποίει*, where *κατέχων* is represented in some codices as *καθὼς εἶχεν*. Editors, however, have wanted nerve to banish the absurdity from Herod. 9. 82, *κελεῦσαι τούς τε ἀρτοκόπους καὶ τοὺς ὀψοποιοὺς κατὰ ταὐτὰ καθὼς Μαρδονίῳ δεῖπνον παρασκευάζειν*. It is true that in citing the passage Athenaeus (4. 138 C) reproduces the error, but ere his time *καθώς* had come into constant use, and the text used by him may well have been already corrupt. Stein suggests *ὡς καί*, others *καθά* or simply *καί*.

CCCXCVIII.

Κάκκαβον· διὰ τοῦ η κακκάβην λέγε· τὸ γὰρ διὰ τοῦ ο ἀμαθές· καὶ γὰρ Ἀριστοφάνης ἐν Δαιδάλῳ χρῆται διὰ τοῦ η.

Athenaeus, 4. 169 C, quotes from the *Δαιταλῆς* the words *κἄγειν ἐκεῖθεν κακκάβην*, and Brunck would for that reason substitute *Δαιταλεῦσι* for *Δαιδάλῳ* here. In the same chapter he cites, without remark, one place of Antiphanes with *κακκάβην* and another with *κάκκαβον*, the metre in neither instance affording any help. In the absence of proof the gender must rest on the authoritative dictum of Phrynichus. Antiphanes certainly did not use both forms.

CCCXCIX.

Κυνηγός· τοῦτο τοὔνομα οὕτω πως μεταχειρίζονται, οἱ μὲν τραγικοὶ ποιηταὶ τρισυλλάβως λέγουσι καὶ δωρίζουσι τὸ η εἰς α μετατιθέντες, κυναγός, οἱ δ' Ἀθηναῖοι τετρασυλλάβως τε προφέρουσι καὶ τὸ η φυλάττουσιν, οἷον κυνηγέτης.

From a comparison of *κυναγός* and *κυνηγέτης* on the one hand, and of *χοραγός* and *χορηγός* on the other, it will be seen how the Athenians at first accepted, without modification, Doric forms relating to the arts of which the Dorians were the acknowledged masters, but subsequently brought these forms into harmony with the laws of their own language. *Κυναγός* is the acknowledged form in Tragedy (Aesch. Ag. 695; Soph. El. 563; Eur. Phoen. 1106, 1169, I. T. 284, Hipp. 1397, Supp. 888 *κυναγία*, Hipp. 109; Soph. Aj. 37 LA), but in ordinary Attic of the same period *κυνηγέτης* was employed—a word which by the mixing of old and new in the Tragic dialect occurs frequently also in Euripides. But in Prose or Comedy *κυναγός* was impossible; it had been altogether replaced by *κυνηγέτης*, as *χοραγός* by *χορηγός*.

This article well illustrates the fact that Phrynichus distinctly recognized that the diction of Tragedy, like that of all poetry, was emphatically a survival.

CCCC.

Καταφαγᾶς· πόθεν, Μένανδρε, συσσύρας τὸν τοσούτων ὀνομάτων συρφετὸν αἰσχύνεις τὴν πάτριον φωνήν; τίς γὰρ δὴ τῶν πρὸ σοῦ τῷ καταφαγᾶς κέχρηται; ὁ μὲν γὰρ Ἀριστοφάνης οὕτω φησίν—

ἔστι γὰρ κατωφαγᾶς τις ἄλλος ἢ Κλεώνυμος;

ἐχρῆν οὖν Κρατίνῳ πειθόμενον φαγᾶς εἰπεῖν. ἴσως δ' ἂν εἴποις ὅτι Ἠκολούθησα Μυρτίλῳ λέγοντι—

Ὡς ὁ μὲν κλέπτης, ὁ δ' ἅρπαξ,
ὁ δ' ἀνάπηρος πορνοβοσκός
καταφαγᾶς·

ἀλλ' οὐκ ἐχρῆν τὰς ἅπαξ εἰρημένας λέξεις ἁρπάζειν·

For this article, which is undoubtedly by Phrynichus, Nuñez is alone responsible. The anti-Atticist (p. 105. 20) refers the defaulting term to the Πωλούμενοι of Menander, and Pollux, in reprehending its use by Myrtilus, implies its occurrence in Aeschylus (Poll. 6. 40), *παμπόνηρος ὁ παρὰ τῷ Μυρτίλῳ καταφαγᾶς εἰ καὶ Αἴσχυλος ἐχρήσατο.* As for the Aristophanic *κατωφαγᾶς* (Av. 288) it has nothing to do with the question, the Scholiast rightly annotating *κωμῳδεῖσθαι τὸν Κλεώνυμον ὅτι κάτω νεύων ἔτρωγε.* The vice of *καταφαγᾶς* is well explained by Lobeck: 'Quaerenti igitur, cur Phrynichus *φαγᾶς* receperit, *καταφαγᾶς* excluserit, sic respondebimus, haec verbalia, in quorum numero est φαγᾶς, propterea quod habitum quendam communem significant, natura sua cum praepositionibus componi non posse, itaque *edacem* quidem et *voracem* dici, sed neque *comedacem* neque *devoracem*. Verumtamen quia voracitatis notio in composito καταφαγεῖν proprie insignita est, poetae illi, καταφαγᾶς (*deglutator*) significantius fore rati quam simplex φαγᾶς, illam universalem rationem aut inscientes aut etiam praesenti animo et meditate reliquerunt.'

CCCCI.

Κολόκυνθα· ἡμάρτηται ἡ ἐσχάτη συλλαβὴ διὰ τοῦ θα λεγομένη, δέον διὰ τοῦ τη, ὡς Ἀθηναῖοι.

CCCCII.

Καταφερής· ἐπὶ τῶν πρὸς ἀφροδίσια ἀκολάστων λέγουσιν οἱ πολλοί, οὐδαμῶς οὕτω τῶν δοκίμων χρωμένων.

Even in its natural signification of *declivis* the adjective is hardly Attic, though it is Classical, being found in Herodotus and Xenophon: Hdt. 3. 63, εὖτ' ἂν δὲ γένηται καταφερὴς ὁ ἥλιος: Xen. de Ven. 10. 9, ἐὰν μὲν ᾖ τὸ χωρίον καταφερές, . . . ἐὰν δὲ ἄπεδον. In the secondary sense of *proclivis* it is certainly late.

CCCCIII.

Καταλογὴν οἱ σύρφακες λέγουσι τὴν πρός τινα αἰδῶ, οὐκ ὀρθῶς.

The rejected meaning is very rare, being cited only from

Polybius, 23. 12. 10, *καταλογὴν ποιεῖσθαι τὴν ἁρμόζουσαν, καθάπερ καὶ Ῥωμαῖοι ποιοῦνται τῶν παραγιγνομένων πρὸς αὐτοὺς πρεσβευτῶν.*

CCCCIV.

Κολλυβιστὴς οὐκ ὀρθῶς· πάλιν οὐδὲν ἡμᾶς μολύνων τι διαπαύεται ὁ Μένανδρος τὸν ἀργυραμοιβὸν κολλυβιστὴν λέγων· τὸ μὲν γὰρ νόμισμα κόλλυβος δόκιμον, τὸ δὲ κολλυβιστὴς παρασεσημασμένον.

Pollux (7. 170) cites *κολλυβιστής* from Lysias: *ἀργυραμοιβός, ἀργυραμοιβική, ἀργυρογνώμων, δοκιμαστής, κολλυβιστής, ὡς Λυσίας ἐν τῷ περὶ τοῦ χρυσοῦ τρίποδος. καὶ ὁ νῦν κόλλυβος ἀλλαγή.* No Attic writer, however, can have used *κολλυβιστής* as equivalent to *ἀργυραμοιβός*, for *κόλλυβος*, though Attic in the sense of 'small coin,' was in that of 'exchange,' as Pollux implies, unknown to Greek of a good age.

CCCCV.

Τὰ ἴδια πράττω καὶ τὰ ἴδια πράττει οἱ πολλοὶ λέγουσιν εἰκῆ, δέον τὰ ἐμαυτοῦ πράττω καὶ τὰ σαυτοῦ πράττεις λέγειν ὡς οἱ παλαιοὶ ἢ τὰ ἴδια ἐμαυτοῦ πράττω καὶ τὰ ἴδια σαυτοῦ πράττεις.

'Hoc sensu *τὰ ἴδια πράττειν* veteres nunquam, recentiores raro dixisse invenio. Plurimum abest *ἴδια πράσσων ἢ στρατοῦ ταχθεὶς ὕπο*; Eur. Iph. A. 1363, i.e. *ἰδίᾳ*, *privatim*, quomodo etiam *τὰ οἰκεῖα πράσσειν* Thuc. 1. 141, opponitur *τῷ τὰ κοινά.* Verum auctor Ep. I. ad Thess. 4. 11, et Hesychius s. v. *ἰδιοπραγεῖν* exemplum vitiosi usus prodiderunt.' Lobeck.

CCCCVI.

Ἀκρατεύεσθαι· ἀδοκίμῳ ὄντι οἵ γε πολλοὶ χρῶνται τούτῳ τῷ ὀνόματι, καὶ Μένανδρος. λέγε οὖν οὐκ ἐγκρατεύεσθαι.

Judging from the books which remain to us, *ἀκρατεύομαι* and *ἐγκρατεύομαι* are equally late, both appearing for the first time in Aristotle.

CCCCVII.

Αἰχμαλωτισθῆναι· τοῦθ' οὕτως ἀδόκιμον ὡς μηδὲ Μένανδρον αὐτῷ χρήσασθαι. διαλύων οὖν λέγε αἰχμάλωτον γενέσθαι.

Thomas rightly characterises the whole verb as *ἀδόκιμον*: (p. 23) *αἰχμαλωτίζω καὶ πάντες οἱ ἀπὸ τούτου χρόνοι ἀδόκιμοι.*

CCCCVIII.

Ἀντικρύ· τοῦτο τοπικὸν καὶ ἐπιεικῶς ποιητικὸν ἄνευ τοῦ σ λεγόμενον. ὅθεν οἱ ἐπὶ τοῦ ἄντικρυς τιθέντες ἁμαρτάνουσιν. εἰ μέντοι τις προθείη τὴν πρόθεσιν τῷ ἀντικρὺ καὶ εἴποι καταντικρὺ ὀρθῶς ἐρεῖ.

Ἄντικρυς, like *εὐθύς* (see p. 222), may, even in Attic be regarded as an *ἐπίρρημα τοπικόν* in certain constructions, as Thuc. 2. 4, *οἰόμενοι πύλας τὰς θύρας τοῦ οἰκήματος εἶναι καὶ ἄντικρυς* (right through) *δίοδον ἐς τὸ ἔξω.* Ar. Lys. 1070—

> *ἀλλὰ χωρεῖν ἄντικρυς* (straight)
> *ὥσπερ οἴκαδ' εἰς ἑαυτῶν,*

but no Attic writer ever employed *ἄντικρυς* for *καταντικρύ* in the sense of 'right opposite,' or ἀντῑκρύ for ἄντῐκρυς in the sense of 'straight,' 'right through.' In Homer, however, ἀντῑκρύ bears the meaning of the Attic ἄντικρυς (Il. 4. 481; 16. 285; Od. 10. 162, etc.); and Xenophon, in this case also, sins against his native tongue, Cyr. 7. 1. 30, ὁ δὲ Ἀβραδάτας ἀντικρὺ δι' αὐτῶν εἰς τὴν τῶν Αἰγυπτίων φάλαγγα ἐμβάλλει. As from εὐθύ and εὐθύς, so from ἀντικρύ and ἄντικρυς, is to be learned the striking lesson that no refinement in form or meaning was too subtle for the Athenian mind as long as the masculine instincts of the language were not violated.

CCCCIX.

Ἀνυπόδετος ἐρεῖς ἐν τῷ η· τὸ γὰρ ἐν τῷ ε ἁμάρτημα. καὶ γὰρ ὑποδήσασθαι λέγεται καὶ οὐχ ὑποδέσασθαι.

'Idem decernitur ac non varie sed prope conjunctis sententiis a Phrynicho App. p. 17. Gramm. Bekk. p. 412, Moeride, p. 29: Thoma, p. 76, et Suïda, non addita ea ratione, quae hoc loco, dubium an ab ipso Phrynicho, subponitur. Ἀνυπόδητος apud Atticos persaepe legitur, ἀνυπόδετος numquam, quin genuina forma aut in Codd. appareat, áut ex alio quodam recessu emergat.' Lobeck.

CCCCX.

Εὕρημα χρὴ λέγειν διὰ τοῦ η, οὐχ εὕρεμα.

Lobeck's notes will supply materials for the history of this corruption, as also the converse one of εὕρησις and δῆσις for εὕρεσις and δέσις, etc. The fact of both is now a commonplace of grammarians, and no one would question the late origin of forms like εὕρεμα on the one hand, or εὕρησις on the other (see Art. 224).

CCCCXI.

'Απηρτισμένον, ἀπήρτικα, καὶ τὰ ἀπὸ τούτων ἅπαντα σόλοικα. ἀποτετέλεσται δὲ καὶ ἀποτετελεσμένον χρὴ λέγειν.

The rejected verb is Ionic and late: Hippocr.Epidem. 2. p.180 B, *ἀπαρτιζούσης τῆς ὀκταμήνου*: de Morb.4.11.p.608 A, *ἀπηρτισμένης τῆς περιόδου*: Polyb. 31. 20. 10, *τἄλλα πρὸς τὸν πλοῦν ἀπαρτιεῖν*. In Aesch. Sept. 374—

σπουδῇ δὲ καὶ τοὐδ' οὐκ ἀπαρτίζει πόδα

most editors doubt *ἀπαρτίζει*. As far as form goes there is no reason why Aeschylus should not have employed it, but it certainly does not bear its ordinary meaning.

Τέλος τῆς Φρυνίχου ἐκλογῆς 'Αττικῶν ῥημάτων καὶ ὀνομάτων.

APPENDIX A.

SINCE the revival of learning there has been no lack of editions of Phrynichus. The first issued from the press of Zacharias Callierges, a Cretan who had settled in Rome. It bears date July 1, 1517. *Ἡ τοῦ Φρυνίχου αὕτη ἐκλογὴ ἐν Ῥώμῃ παρὰ Ζαχαρίᾳ τῷ Καλλιέργῃ σὺν Θεῷ ἁγίῳ ἐτυπώθη χιλιοστῷ πεντακοσιοστῷ ιζ´ Μηνὸς Ἰουλίου πρώτῃ, Λέοντος δὲ κα´ τοῦ μεγίστου ἀρχιερέως Ῥώμην ὁσίως κε καὶ εὐτυχῶς ἡνιοχοῦντος.* It has the title *Φρυνίχου ἐκλογὴ Ἀττικῶν ῥημάτων καὶ ὀνομάτων*, and the articles are arranged alphabetically (*ἥτις παρ' ἡμῶν ἐνταῦθα, κατὰ στοιχεῖον ἐξετέθη*). It is generally met with bound up with an edition of Thomas Magister published four months previously (March 4, 1517). A few years later Callierges published the great dictionary of Phavorinus[1] which contained the Ecloga of Phrynichus, — Magnum et perutile dictionarium, quod quidem Varinus Phavorinus, Nucerinus Episcopus, ex multis variisque auctoribus in ordinem alphabeti collegit. Romae per Zachariam Calliergi, 1523, fol. There followed an edition by Franciscus Asulanus, forming part of a Lexicon containing Thomas Magister, Moschopulus, and Ammonius, and published by Aldus at Venice in 1524. Next came the edition of Vascosan, the great Paris printer,—*Θωμᾶ τοῦ μαγίστρου ὀνομάτων ἀττικῶν ἐκλογαί, Φρυνίχου ἐκλογὴ ἀττικῶν ῥημάτων καὶ ὀνομάτων, Μανουῆλος τοῦ μοσχοπούλου ἀττικῶν ὀνομάτων ἐκλογὴ ἀπὸ τῆς τεχνολογίας τῆς τοῦ Φιλοστράτου εἰκόνων καὶ βιβλίων τῶν ποιητῶν*—

Πάντα κατὰ ἀλφάβητον.

Τάξις παλαιὰ καὶ ὀνομασίαι τῶν ἀρχόντων ἐκ τοῦ Αἰλιανοῦ.

Ὀρβικίου τῶν περὶ τὸ στράτευμα τάξεων.

The date of this edition was Nov. 1532,—Lutetiae apud Michaelem Vascosanum mense Novembri, MDXXXII.

None of these editions differed much from one another, but towards the close of the century there was published in Spain an edition

[1] Phavorinus or Favorinus (Varinus or Guarino), born at Favora, near Camerino, in 1460, was a disciple of Lascaris and Politian, and himself the preceptor of Leo X. He was also director of the Library of the Medici at Florence, and became bishop of Nocera.

which seems to have been based upon a manuscript differing very widely from those used by Callierges, Phavorinus, and Vascosan. The editor was Pedro Juan Nuñez, a prolific writer, and the author of an interesting little Greek Grammar[1], which differs marvellously little from those now used in schools. He employed only one manuscript, and professes to have followed it faithfully. In that manuscript the Ecloga was divided into three books, the beginning of the second book being headed τοῦ αὐτοῦ ἐπιτομή, and of the third ἀρχὴ τοῦ τρίτου, but of these the third book contains only a few articles, and these mostly repeated from the other two. The edition bears date Barcinone, A.D. iii. Kal. Ian. Anni Salutis MDLXXXVI., and is dedicated to Andreas Schottus of Antwerp.

Subsequent editions were little more than reprints of this, with more notes added; one edition by Hoeschel appearing in the seventeenth century, a second by Pauw in the eighteenth, and Lobeck's well-known work in the nineteenth. The title-page of Hoeschel's edition is as follows: 'Phrynichi Epitomae Dictionum Atticarum Libri iii, sive Ecloga, a Petro Io. Nunnesio Valentino integritati restituta, Latine conversa, ejusdemque et Davidis Hoeschelii Aug. Notis, in quîs et aliorum auctorum loca partim emendantur, partim illustrantur, aucta. Augustae Vindelicorum typis Michaelis Mangeri, cum S. Caes. Majest. privilegio MDCI.' After the text, with a Latin rendering, follow the Notes of Nuñez, then the Notes of Hoeschel, then certain Notes of Scaliger with a fresh title-page: 'Ad Phrynichum et ejus interpretem viri illustris Notae, a Davide Hoeschelio Augustano editae.' Appended is a letter of Scaliger[2].

Pauw's edition is entitled 'Phrynichi Eclogae nominum et verborum Atticorum, cum versione Latina Petri Ioannis Nunnesii et ejusdem ac Davidis Hoeschelii Notis ut et Notis Iosephi Scaligeri in Phrynichum et Nunnesii notas; Curante Ioanne Cornelio de Pauw, qui notas quoque suas addidit. Trajecti ad Rhenum apud Ioannem Evelt. MDCCXXXIX,' while the title-page of Lobeck's edition runs on the same lines, 'Phrynichi Eclogae Nominum et Verborum Atticorum

[1] Institutiones Grammaticae Linguae Graecae, auctore Petro Johanne Nunnesio Valentino. Barcinone, cum licentia ex typographia viduae Huberti Gotardi, anno 1590.

[2] ὁ δεῖνα

Davidi Hoeschelio.

Notas tuas in Phrynichum (jam incipiebam legere, quum haec scriberem) valde laudo: diligentiam admiror. Quid dicam praeterea? Multum disco. Doctissimus et accuratissimus est Hispanus ille, qui illustravit. Sed ad quaedam libenter responderem, quod alius temporis et operae est. Nimis certo fidit Phrynicho, quem anno praeterito inter legendum deprehendi in multis falli. Id quoque a Thoma Magistro animadversum et laetatus sum, et admiratus. Sed de his alias.

cum Notis P. I. Nunnesii, D. Hoeschelii, I. Scaligeri et Cornelii de Pauw partim integris partim contractis edidit, explicuit Chr. August. Lobeck. Accedunt Fragmentum Herodiani et notae praefationes Nunnesii et Pauwii et Parerga de Vocabulorum terminatione et compositione, de aoristis verborum authypotactorum, etc. Lipsiae MDCCCXX.'

The manuscript used by Nuñez contained many articles unquestionably by Phrynichus which are wanting in the other editions and in the manuscripts now known, but the absurd name given by it to the Second Part of the Ecloga, and the existence of a Third Part of so poor a quality, as well as the paltry character of not a few of the articles which are found only in it, make it very probable that much of its apparent completeness is really interpolation.

Before considering this question it will be well to give an account of the manuscripts known to me.

Two of these are in the Mediceo-Laurentian Library at Florence, and a beautiful transcript of the more important of them, with a full collation of the other, was with great kindness procured for me by the present sub-praefect of the Bibliotheca Laurentiana. The press-mark of the one is Pluteus vi. 22, and in the following pages it will be designated Laurentian A, or simply A, while the press-mark of the other is Pluteus lvii. 24, and it will be referred to as Laurentian B, or simply as B[1].

Laurentian A bears date 1491. The scribe's name is given, and he wrote it at Venice. *Μετεγράφησαν καὶ τὰ παρόντα τῆς Φρυνίχου ἐκλογῆς διὰ χειρὸς ἐμοῦ Ἰωάννου πρεσβυτέρου Ῥώσου Κρητὸς τὸ γένος, χιλιοστῷ τετρακοσιοστῷ ἐνενηκοστῷ πρώτῳ Ἰουνίου πρώτῃ, Οὐενετίαις.*

Laurentian B, though in many respects much inferior to A, still contains in the second part of the Ecloga many articles which are absent from all other authorities except the edition of Nuñez.

The third manuscript, referred to as P, is at Paris, and a collation of it is printed in Bachmann's 'Anecdota Graeca' (Leipsic, 1828). It is headed, *Ἐκ τῶν τοῦ Φρυνίχου*, and occupies twelve folios of a codex thus described by Bachmann: 'Codex est bombycinus, forma quadrata, totus ab eadem manu non ineleganter scriptus, haud raro tamen praesertim in locis ex aliis scriptoribus efferendis lacunosus. Erat olim in Bibliotheca Petri Danielis Huetii, Episcopi, videtur esse saec. xv. It is without very many of the articles usually attributed to Phrynichus, but is of value as implying an original differing in many respects from the other manuscripts and editions. It is only in P that the true reading of Article 201 has been preserved, and it is no mean praise to bestow upon any manuscript that it confirms a conjecture of a scholar like Scaliger.

[1] There is also a third manuscript in the Laurentian Library, with press-mark Pluteus lvii. 34, which contains selections from the Ecloga. A transcript of it is printed as Appendix B.

On the other hand, A shows a general correspondence with the earlier editions of Callierges, Phavorinus, and Vascosan, but many of its readings prove conclusively that it was not used by any of them, not even by Phavorinus, who was at one time the praefect of the Library in which it now lies.

The text of B has many affinities to that given to the world by Nuñez, and both manuscripts may have sprung from the same original. It has even a sort of Third Part, only of greater length than that of Nuñez. After the article on *αἰχμαλωτισθῆναι* are found the following sentences: *ἐγρήγορα χρή, καὶ ἐγρήγορεν. ἀλλ' οὐκ ἠγρηγόρει καὶ γρηγορῶ: δίαιτα ἡ χωρὶς δικαστηρίου κρίσις καὶ διαιτητής· καὶ διαιτῶ ἐπὶ τούτου· δίκη δὲ ἡ ἐν τῷ δικαστηρίῳ, καὶ δικαστής· καταχρηστικῶς δὲ καὶ χωρὶς δικαστηρίου ταῦτα λέγεται: πομπὴ ἡ πρόπεμψις· λέγεται καὶ ἡ πέμψις παρὰ Θουκυδίδῃ· ξύλων ναυπηγησίμων πομπήν: καταπροίξεται ἀδιαιρέτως γράφεται: ἀντικρὺ τοπικὸν καὶ ποιητικόν· γράφεται δὲ μετὰ τῆς προθέσεως καταντικρύ: ἀνυπόδυτος μετὰ τοῦ ι* (sic) *ἐρεῖς καὶ ὑποδήσασθαι: εὕρημα οὐχ εὕρεμα: ἀπηρτισμένον· ἀπήρτικα· καὶ τὰ ἀπὸ τούτων ἅπαντα σόλοικα· ἀποτετέλεσται δὲ καὶ ἀποτετελεσμένον χρὴ λέγειν: κεφαλαιωδέστατον οὐ γράφεται.* Moreover, in a later and less skilled hand are appended,—*ἀνατοιχεῖν μὴ λέγε, ἀλλὰ διατοιχεῖν. ἔνυστρον μὴ λέγε ἀλλὰ ἤνυστρον· ὅτι καὶ ἀρχαῖον. καταπροίζεται οὐκ ὀρθῶς διαιροῦσι, δέον καταπροίζεται ἀδιαιρέτως· ξενιτεῦσαι ἀδόκιμον.*

As a matter of fact the text of Phrynichus has been terribly tampered with, and although I believe most of the articles in the First Part came from the hand of the Grammarian much in the shape in which they appear in the present edition, it would be rash in the extreme to make the same assertion with regard to the Second Part. Nuñez may be said hardly to have described the manuscript on which he based his edition, but without that manuscript, corrupt as it certainly was, several of the most important articles would have been lost to us. Until more manuscripts are unearthed an authoritative text of Phrynichus is out of the question.

The reasons for regarding the manuscript of Nuñez as interpolated are as follows. It abounds in what are unquestionable marks of the interpolator's hand, feeble and meaningless additions like *δόκιμον γάρ* and *ἀδόκιμον γάρ.* To many of the articles are appended sentences couched in unworthy Greek, and plainly at variance with the statement which precedes them. The so-called 'Third Part' is an attempt, and an unsuccessful attempt, to increase the work by another chapter, and suggests only too readily a similar origin for many of the articles in the Second Part, if not in the First.

Moreover, if the Ecloga as at present known to us contains much that Phrynichus never wrote, it probably also is without a good deal that came from his pen. Thus Stephen of Byzantium, who wrote an 'Ethnica,' probably about 500 A.D., mentions a dictum of Phrynichus which is now read neither in the Ecloga nor in the 'Sophisticus Apparatus:' ἡ δὲ θεὸς Ἀθηναία λέγεται μονογενῶς. λέγεται δὲ καὶ ἐπὶ γυναικὸς ὡς ἄλλοι μὲν πολλοί. Φιλήμων δὲ οὕτως ἐν Πτερυγίῳ—

> νυνὶ δ' ὅταν λάβῃ τις εἰς τὴν οἰκίαν
> τὰς Ἱππονίκας τάσδε καὶ Ναυσιστράτας
> καὶ Ναυσινίκας, τὰς Ἀθηναίας λέγω.

Δίδυμος δέ φησιν ὅτι Ἀθηναίας λέγουσιν ἀντὶ τοῦ Ἀττικάς, ὁ δὲ Φρυνίχος ἀνάττικόν φησιν εἶναι τὴν φωνὴν καὶ θαυμάζει πῶς ὁ Φερεκράτης ἀττικώτατος ὢν χρῆται. (Ed. Meineke, p. 33.)

Finally, it has become with me almost a conviction that the Ecloga was originally written in two parts published at different times, and that the Second Part was written by Phrynichus as supplementary to the First—his earlier work. In this way may be explained such articles as that numbered 203 in this edition. The Grammarian seized the opportunity afforded him by his Supplement to modify or confirm statements made by him in the Ecloga itself. A striking argument in favour of this view is supplied by the following fact. Between the Epistle to Cornelianus and the first article the manuscript used by Nuñez contained the words ὅστις ἀρχαίως καὶ δοκίμως ἐθέλει διαλέγεσθαι, τάδ' αὐτῷ φυλακτέα, and at the end of the First Book ταῦτα φυλαττόμενός τις βελτίων καὶ δοκιμώτατος εἴη ἄν. The latter sentence also appears in the same place in A. There is no similar colophon at the end of the Second Book, or in the case of Nuñez at the end of the Third, nothing but the conventional τέλος τῆς Φρυνίχου ἐκλογῆς.

The following are the more important variations of reading in the different manuscripts and editions. They will demonstrate how precarious a thing a text of Phrynichus must be. The manuscripts are designated by single letters, the editions by two:—Laurentian MS. 1. = A. Laurentian MS. 2. = B. Paris MS. = P. Callierges = Ca. Phavorinus = Ph. Vascosan = Va. Nuñez = Nu.

Epistle, om. B. P. θαυμάζω] θαυμάζων MSS. Edd. οἷός τε] οἷος A. Ca. Va. ἀποπεπτωκότες] ἀποπλανηθέντες Ca. Va. καταφεύγοντες] καταπεφευγότες Nu. τὰ δοκιμώτατα] τὰ δοκιμώτερα A. Ca.

3. om. P. ἱκετεία] ἱκεσεία B. 4. λέγε] δέ A, Ca. Va. 5. ὅταν] om. A, Ca. Va. Ph. 6. μέχρι δὲ καὶ ἄχρι λέγε] om. Ca. Va. λέγε] om. A. 7. om. P. Ἀπίναι, προσίναι, ἐξίναι, κατίναι] Ἐπίναι, κατίναι, προσίναι, ἐξίναι Ca. Va. ἀπιέναι, ἐξιέναι λέγειν] ἀπιέναι, ἐξιέναι, κατιέναι λέγειν Ca. Va. add. καὶ τὰ λοιπὰ ὁμοίως Nu, B. 8. P. om. 9. μηδαμῶς] μηδαμοῦ Nu. καὶ κατέπτυσα αὐτοῦ] om. P. add. λέγε B, Nu. 10. om. P. 12. ἐπὶ τοῦ μέλλοντος] om. τοῦ Nu. τοῦ ἐνεστηκότος καὶ τοῦ] τοῦ ἐνεστῶτος καὶ B, Nu. ἥκω ἄρτι] ἥκω καὶ ἄρτι B, Nu. 13. ἐπὶ ἰχθύος] add. λέγεται B, Nu. 14. τὰ τοῦ ῥήματος] πάντα γὰρ τὰ ῥήματα A, vulg. εὐδόκιμα] δόκιμα B.

add. ἀμύνομαι. τὸ δὲ ὄνομα ἀδόκιμον B, Nu. Corripuit P. ἄμυναν οὐκ εἴποις ἀλλὰ διὰ ῥήματος, ἀμύνομαι, ἀμύνασθαι, ἀμυνοῦμαι. 15. om. P. χρὴ λέγειν] χρὴ γὰρ λέγειν B, Nu. σε] σοι A, B, vulg. ἀπαλλάττωνται] ἀπαλλάχθωνται Ph. 16. om. P. 17. om. P. ἐφλέγμανε] Ἀφλέγμαναι A. καὶ ταῦτα διὰ τοῦ η] διὰ τοῦ η καὶ ταῦτα λέγεται B, Nu. καὶ ταῦτα διὰ τοῦ η λέγεται Ca. 18. προθεσμίαν] A, B, Ca. Va. Ph. προθεσμία vulg. 19. δεῖ γὰρ] δέον ὂν B. 20. ἀλλοκότως] A, B, Ca. Ph. ἀλλοκοτέρως vulg. ἐχρῆν] χρῆν B. 22. διὰ τοῦ ἑτέρου λ κάκιστον] διὰ τοῦ ἑτέρου ἐστὶ κάκιστα B, idem literula λ addita Nu. δι' ἑνὸς λ κάκιστον Va. ἀνείλλειν] Nu. ἀνειλλεῖν A, Va. ἀνειλεῖν B. 23. ἐρεῖτε] ἐρεῖς B, vulg. 24. om. Ca. ἤλειπται] εἴλειπται A. εἴληπται Ph. κατώρυκται] καὶ κατώρυκται vulg. τὴν φωνὴν] τὴν πρώτην conj. Lobeck. ἀλήλειπται] ἀλήλιπται B. 26. ὁμοειδέσιν] ὁμοιειδέσιν Va. ὁμοιοειδέσιν Nu. Articulum corripuit P. ἀπελεύσομαι οὐκ εἴποις ἀλλ' ἄπειμι. 27. ἐπεξελευσόμενος ὁ Φαβωρῖνός φησι, σὺ δὲ ἐπεξιὼν καὶ ἐπέξειμι] P. ἐπεξελευσόμενος ἀδόκιμον· σὺ δὲ ἐπεξιών· καὶ γὰρ ἐπέξειμι λέγεται ἀλλ' οὐκ ἐπεξελεύσομαι B. οὗτος] οὗτος ἦν Nu. Va. χρὴ γὰρ] χρὴ μέν Va. 28. δι' ἑνὸς ι] om. A, Ca. ἀλκαιικόν, τροχαιικόν] A, B. ἀλκαιικόν, ὡς τροχαιικόν Ca. ἀλκαιικόν, τροχαιικὸν καὶ ἀρχαιικόν Nu. 29. μηδαμῶς] μὴ εἴπῃς al. 30. εἰ δὲ ἐν τῷ υ] εἰ δὲ ἐκ τοῦ υ B. ἐν δὲ τῷ υ A, Ca. 32. ἀπόπαλαι καὶ] om. καὶ B, al. δυσχεραίνω] A, B, Ca. δυσχέραινε al. 33. ἕωθεν] om. Ca. Va. 34. χωρὶς τοῦ ν] om. Nu. 35. καὶ τοῦτο] om. καὶ B, Nu. τοῦ ν, ὄψιος] τοῦ ν λέγειν ὄψιος ὡς ὄρθριος Nu. τοῦ ν ὄψιος λέγειν ὡς ὄρθριος. 38. λέγοντες ἁμαρτάνουσιν] λέγουσιν ἁμαρτάνοντες B, Nu. 39. ποταπὸς δέ ἐστιν εἰ εἴποις ποταπός] τὸ ποταπὸς δέ, ἔστι ποταπός Nu. τὸ ποταπὸς δέ ἐστιν εἰ εἴποις, ποταπός B. Φρύνιχος; ἐπιεικής] Φρύνιχος; φρόνιμος, ἐπιεικής al. 40. λυχνοῦχον λέγε] om. λέγε B, Nu. 43. ἐρεῖς τὸ] ἐρεῖς θηλυκῶς τὸ B, Nu. οὐ κατὰ τὸ ἀρρενικόν] om. B. 44. κράββατος] addit B μιαρὸν γάρ. 46. φάρυγξ] φάρυξ B. 47. ἀναιδίζεσθαι] αὐθαδίζεσθαι MSS. Edd. 48. om. P. 49. om. P. τοῦ σοφιστοῦ om. B. τοὔνομα om. B. υἱέος] υἱέως A, B, Ph. ἐν τοῖς ε] ἐν τοῖς πέντε Ca. Ph. τοῦτο δὲ καὶ Φιλόξενος ad fin.] om. B. 50. om. P. τευτάζειν] σπουδάζειν B, sed in margine τευτάζειν. δεῖν λέγειν] λέγειν om. A. 51. παρέχει] παρέχοι B. εἰ καὶ μάρτυρα παρέχοι τις om. P. 52. om. P. 54. ὕσπληγξ] ὕσπληξ B. λέγεται οὐχ] λέγε ἀλλ' οὐχ A, Ca. 56. λέγουσι] om. A, Ca. κοράσιον οὔ] κοράσιον παράλογον B, Nu. 58. om. P, bis scribit B diversis autem locis, alio recte ut editur, alio cum spurio additamento μᾶλλον μὲν οὖν Ἕλληνες τὸ τάχιον, θᾶττον δὲ Ἀττικοί. 59. δόκιμοι] δοκιμώτεροι A, Ca. 60. om. P. 61. θαυμάσειεν ἄν] Phrynicho reddidi. θαυμάσαι δ' ἂν Nu. θαυμάσεται δ' ἂν B. θαυμάσαι ἂν A, Ca. Ph. 64. λέγουσιν ἁμαρτάνοντες] λέγοντες ἁμαρτάνουσιν B, Nu. λέγουσιν A. τῆς ἐν νόμῳ] τῆς ἐννόμου Nu. Lo. 65. om P. τῶν ἀρχαίων φανερῶς] φανερῶς τῶν ἀρχαίων A, Ca, Ph. 66. παρ' αὐτοῖς οὐκ ἔστι] οὐκ ἔστι παρ' αὐτοῖς B, Nu. 68. om. P. προβασκάνιον μετὰ τῆς πρό] προσβασκάνιον μετὰ τῆς πρός MSS. Edd. Hoeschelius correxit. addit ἀδόκιμον γάρ B, Nu. 69. om. P. νοίδιον καὶ βοίδιον] βοίδιον καὶ βοΐδιον Nu. νούδιον καὶ βούδιον] βούδιον καὶ βοῦδιον Nu. 70. om. P. διαιροῦντες λέγουσιν] om. B. 71. γοῦν] οὖν B. εἰς τὴν πάτριον διάλεκτον, ὀδμή λέγων] om. Ca. 73. ἀκεστῆς λεγ. οἱ παλ. οὐκ ἠπ.] om. Va. ἔστι μὲν ἠπήσασθαι] ἠπήσασθαι ἔστι μὲν A, Va. Ph. ὑποθήκας] συνθήκας Va. 76. Verba certo spuria addunt B, Va. Nu. viz. haec, μήποτε δὲ καὶ ὡς οἱ πολλοὶ λέγουσιν χρῶνται οἱ ἀρχαῖοι καὶ ἐπὶ τοῦ τὴν γαστέρα τύπτειν. 77. διὰ τοῦ ρ λέγε] διὰ τοῦ γ λέγε A. διὰ τοῦ γ Ph. 78. P. om. καὶ μὴ] ἀλλὰ μὴ B. Nu. 79. P. om. τὸ γρυλίζειν] τὸ γρυλλίζειν A. καὶ ἀσχημόνως] om. Ca. γρυλίζειν καὶ γρυλισμὸς] γρυλλίζειν καὶ γρυλλισμὸς A. 84. ἡμέρα, μὴ] ἡμέρα, ἀργὴ γυνή, μὴ B, Nu. ἡμέρα καὶ ἀργὸς γυνὴ ad fin.] om. P. 85. ἁμαρτάνοντες] ἁμαρτάνουσιν B, Edd. οἷον] om. B. 86. καὶ εἰς ἓν] εἰς ἓν B, Va. Nu. 87. om. A, P, Ca; in B articulo praeeunti adjungitur παρὰ Ἐπιχάρμῳ κτε. nisi γενέσθω pro γενέσθαι. Ne in Nunnesii quidem exemplo γενηθῆναι apparet, sed ab Oudendorpio ad Thom. p. 189 conjectaneum addebatur. 88. om. A, P. οὐδὲν ἄλλ'] οὐκ ἄλλο B. 89. ἄγριον] om. A. ὁ ἀσφάραγος] ὁ ἀσπάραγος A. ἀσπάραγος B. αὖον] αὐτό A, Nu. αὐτῷ B. νάπαισι δ'] ἐν ἅπασιν A, B, Nu. ἐνηβᾷ] ἅνηβᾷ B. φλόμον] φλόον A, Nu. φλοίον B. ἀγροῖσι] ἀγρίοις A, B, Nu. καταλεγόμενα] καταλελεγμένα B. τὸ ἓν] om. A, B, Nu. τὸ α. Ca. Va. ἄνθαι] ἄκανθαι B, Nu. Articulus hunc in modum apud P legitur, ὅρμενα αἱ τῶν λαχάνων ἄνθαι, καὶ ἐξορμενίζειν τὸ ἐκ βλαστάνειν καὶ ἐξανθεῖν. λέγε οὖν ὅρμενα καὶ μὴ ἀσπαράγους. 91. λέγε] λέγεται καὶ Nu. λέγεται B. 93. om. P. 96. μηδέποτε χρήσῃ] μήποτε εἴπῃς A, Ca. Va. 97. οὐκ ἀγηόχασι] οὐ καταγηόχασι A, Ca. 98. om. P. ἐκεῖνοι εἰς] ἐκεῖνοι, σὺ δὲ εἰς A, Ca. Va. φυλάττου] φυλάττου χρῆσθαι B, Nu. 101. om. P. 104. τοῦ παντός] ἐξαίφνης B, Nu. εἶπον] om. A, Ca. Va. 106. In A solum est κληρονομεῖν τοῦδε. Sic quoque Ca. et Va. qui tamen οὐ τόδε adjungunt. 107. εἶπεν] om. A, Ca. Va. 109. τὸ προσδοκ] τὸν προσδοκ. B, Nu. τὸν ἐπίσημον] τὸ ἐπίσημον Ca. 110. τήθην] sic B. τίθην A. τίτθην Ca. Nu. Va. τήθης] sic A, B. 111. οὐδὲ γὰρ] οὐδὲ A, Ca. καὶ κάλλιον καὶ κρεῖσσον] om. A, Ca. 112. μονόφθαλμον] μονόμματον Nu. 113. πρίασθαι] πρίαμαι A, B, Ca. 114. om. P. ὡς νῦν] ὡς οἱ νῦν Ca. 116. om. P. ἀλλὰ μὴ] καὶ μὴ A. 120. om. P. 121. om. P. 122. om. P. ἄνευ] χωρὶς Ca. Nu. Ph. 130. εἰ καὶ] οὐχ Ph. οὐκ ἐρεῖς] om. Ph. 132. ἀνίστατο] ἐνίστατο Nu. cujus exemplari literae initiales semper defuisse videntur. 133. ἐζήτηται] ἐξίτηλον A. Ca. Va. λέγειν] λέγεσθαι A. ἐπὶ δυσωδίας] om. B, Nu. ἐπὶ τῆς δυσωδιάς Ca. Va. λέγε] εἰ χρὴ λέγειν B, Nu. 134. addit B post Θεμιστοκλῆν verba haec, συναίρεσις γὰρ συναιρέσεων οὐκ ἔστιν. 136. διεφθορὸς] φθορός

A, Ca. λέγουσιν] om. B, Nu. 138. om. P. ἀρχαίως] ἀρχαῖον Nu. 139. om. P. 140. om. P. μὴ] ἀλλὰ μὴ A, Ca. Va. Ph. 142. ἐτίθεσαν] ἐτίθουν Nu. ἐφ' οὗ] B. ἀφ' οὗ A, Ca. ἐν ᾧ Nu. καὶ μὴ θυμέλην] μὴ λέγε δὲ θυμέλην B, Nu. 143. ἴγδιν] ἴγδην Nu. 144. om. P. ἁμαρτήσει] ἁμαρτήσεις MSS. Edd. καὶ τὰ ὅμοια] om. A, Ca. Ph. 145. om. P. αὐταύλης] αὐθαύλης A. πυθαύλης B. 146. om. P. καταπροίξεται] καταπροίζεται A, B, Ca. 147. ἥμαρτον] ἥμαρτε Nu. ἥμαρται A, B. Λολλιανὸς] λολλισμὸς A, Ca. Va. Ph. Hoc verbum et cetera om. B. Ex P desunt cuncta praeter αἱ νῆες ἐρεῖς, οὐχ αἱ ναῦς. σόλοικον γάρ. τὰς νῆας οὐκ ἐρεῖς, ἀλλὰ τὰς ναῦς. 148. om. P. ῥαφανίδα] ῥαφίδα Nu. 149. κλᾶν] κλαδᾶν MSS. Edd. 150. ἀλλὰ] om. B, Nu. 152. καθαρῷ B. κρείττονι Nu. χρῶ οὖν τῷ καθαρῷ. τὸ γὰρ τὴν] χρῶ οὖν τῷ γὰρ τὴν A. χρῶ οὖν τῷ τὴν Ca. Va. 153. ἀγγεῖον] ἀγγεῖον ὥς τινες B, Nu. 155. om. P. λέγειν om. A. 157. κυνίδιον λέγε] adjungit οὐ κυνάριον B cetera omittens. 158. λέγειν] om. B, Nu. λέγε post δὲ adjecto. 159. in angustum contraxit B. ἐδέδισαν οὐκ ἐδεδίεσαν. 160. οὐθεὶς] οὐθεὶς ἀποτρέπου B. εἰ καὶ Χρ. . . . . λέγειν om. B. οἱ γὰρ . . . οὐδεὶς] οὐδεὶς γὰρ οἱ ἀρχαῖοι B. In P desunt cuncta praeter οὐδεὶς δόκιμον, οὐχὶ δὲ οὐθείς. 161. λάγνος] λάγνος φάθι B, Nu. 162. διὰ τοῦ ο ὁ Ἴων, λαγός] διὰ δὲ τοῦ ο λαγοὸς ὁ Ἴων B. διὰ δὲ τοῦ ο λαγὸς ὁ Ἴων Nu. Addunt Nu. et B τὸ λαγωὸς οὐκ ἔστιν. 163. εἰ καὶ διὰ τὴν . . . . Τρύφη] om. B, P. Τρύφη] τρυφῇ Nu. τρυφᾶν Ca. Va. τρυφεῖν A. 166. δι' αἰδῶ] μὴ αἰδῶ A, Va. 169. ἡ μὲν] εἰ μὲν Va. Ca. 170. ὡς Ἀριστοφάνης κτε.] om. B. 171. οὐ μὴ] οὐ μὴν MSS. Edd. ὀμεῖται] τοῦτ' ὀμεῖται B. 172. μεσοδάκτυλα μηδαμῶς εἴποις ἀλλὰ τὰ μέσα τῶν δακτύλων P. 174. μάλης] A, P. μάλην B, Nu. 175. In angustum contraxerunt B et P, viz. μεγιστᾶνας οὐ χρὴ λέγειν ἀλλὰ μέγα δυναμένους B. μεγιστᾶνες ἀδόκιμον· σὺ δὲ μέγα δυναμένους λέγε P. 176. om. P. 177. τὸ τοιοῦτον om. B. 178. post μύκητας addunt τὰ μανιτάρια A, Ca. 179. Pessime A, Ca. εὔτροφος μὴ λέγε μήποτε ὡς Ἀθηναῖοι, μηδὲ οἰκογενῆ, ἀλλ' οἰκότριβα μήποτε κτε. 180. om. P. 182. ἀρχαῖος φαίνῃ] ἀρχαῖος Ἀττικὸς φαίνοιο A. νοσσάριον] νεοσσάκιον Ca. Va. ὀσσάκιον A. Brevissime B, νεοττὸς καὶ νεόττιον Ἀττικοὶ γράφουσι. 183. χρυσοῦς λέγε om. Nu. 184. καὶ ἔκτρωμα] om. A. ταῦτα φεῦγε] τοῦτο φεῦγον A. τοῦτο φευκτὸν Ca. ἀδόκιμα B. καὶ ἄμβλωμα om. A, Ca. ἀμβλίσκει] ἀμβλώσκει A, Ca. 185. δυεῖν δ' ἔστι μὲν . . . . ἐπιταράττεται] om. B. ἐπὶ γὰρ μ. γ. τ.] τίθεται δὲ ἐπὶ μόνης γενικῆς B. 186. ὥς τινες τῶν γραμματικῶν] om. B. 187. τὸ γὰρ μεῖραξ κτε.] οἷον ἡ γυνὴ ὅταν οὖν εἴπωσιν ὁ μεῖραξ ἐπὶ γυναικὸς λέγουσι τὸ δὲ μειράκιον ἐπὶ ἀρσενικῶν A. Brevissime Ca, μείρακες καὶ μεῖραξ ἐπὶ γυναικὸς λέγουσι, τὸ δὲ μειράκιον ἐπὶ ἀρσενικῶν. 188. om. P. κακῶς] καλῶς A, B, Nu. οἱ ἰδιῶται] ὁ ἰδιώτης B. ἰδιώτης Nu. σὺ δὲ ἀναβάλλομαι φαθὶ] ἀναβάλλομαι φησὶν A, B, Nu. 189. οὐ καλῶς ad extr.] om. B. Breviter P, σταθερὸς ἐπὶ τοῦ ἀνθρώπου οὐδαμῶς λέγεται ἀλλ' ἐμβριθής. 190. τάττεται] τάττουσιν A, Ca. ἀδημονῆσαι] ἀθυμῆσαι Nu. 191. om. P. 193. Ἴων ὤν] Ἰώνων MSS. 194. om. P. τοῦτο λέγουσιν ἔχοντες] χρώμενοι ἔχουσιν B, Nu. 198. ἀρτοπόπος] ἀρτοπόλης A. 199. om. P. 201. βαλαντοκλέπτης] P. βαλαντιοκλέπτης] P. 202. βασίλισσα οὐδεὶς εἶπεν ἀλλὰ βασιλὶς Ἑλληνικὸν ἢ βασίλεια ποιητικόν P. 203. Brevissime B, βασίλισσαν μὴ λέγε ἀλλὰ βασίλειαν ἢ βασιλίδα. ἀποφανθεὶς] ἐπιφανεὶς Nu. ἀπορήμασιν] ἀπομνημονεύμασι Ca. 204. ὡς Ἀθηναῖος] om. P. 205. om. P. 206. om. A, B, Ca. ἀλλ' ἡμεῖς οὐ κτε.] ἡμεῖς δὲ γελόποιόν φαμεν οὐ τοῖς ἅπαξ ῥηθεῖσι προσέχοντες ἀλλὰ τοῖς πολλάκις κεκριμένοις P. 209. om. P. 212. ὀρθότερον] ὀρθώτεροι A. γελάσει] γελάσεις MSS. Edd. 213. om. P. 214. om. P. κέχρηνται] χρῶνται Nu. ῥήματι] πράγματι A, Ca. 215. om. A, P. Ca. Ph. 216. θεραπαίνης] θεραπαινίδος A. Adjungit B οἷς ἀκολουθητέον post νεάνιδος. 219. ἁμαρτάνει] οὐχ ἁμαρτάνει MSS. Edd. 221. om. A, Ca. Va. 223. om. P. πολλάκις εὗρον κείμενον .... οἶδα] om. B. Δημοσθένης μέντοι κτε.] om. B. 225. om. P. 227. οὐ δόκιμον] εὐδόκιμον A, B, Ca. Va. 228. τὸ μὲν . . . τοῦ σ.] om. A, Ca. Va. 230. om. P. ὡς ὁ Κρατῖνος om. B. -τιαν ἢ εἰ ἐθέλεις .... τίθει] om. B. τίθει] τιθῆς Nu. 232. om. B, P. ἐχρῆτο ἐν συγγράμμασι κτε.] ἐχρήσατο ἐν ἐπιγράμμασι περὶ τῆς δημώδους σωφροσύνης Ca. ἐπιγραφομένῳ] ἐπιφερομένῳ A. 233. Στυππέϊνον] στυπτέϊνον A, B, Ca. Ph. στύπινον] στύπτινον A, B, Ca. Ph. Huic articulo adjungit A τάδε φυλαττόμενός τις βελτίων καὶ δοκιμώτερος εἴη ἄν, eadem Nu. nisi quod pro δοκιμώτερος legat δοκιμώτατος. Sequitur in Nu. τοῦ αὐτοῦ ἐπιτομή, in A τοῦ αὐτοῦ τμῆμα δεύτερον οὗ ἀρχή. 235. Brevissime B et P, εὐαγγελίζομαί σε μὴ λέγε ἀλλὰ δοτικῇ B. εὐαγγελίζομαι αἰτιατικῇ συντάσσουσιν, οἱ πλείους δὲ δοτικῇ. γράφεται δὲ καὶ εὐαγγελῶ, οὗ τὸ δεύτερον εὐαγγελεῖς P. 236. τὰ πληθυντικά] ὅσα ἀπὸ τούτων P. 237. aliter P, ἄνωθέν σε φίλος εἰμί, ἀλλ' οὐκ ἀνέκαθεν ἐρεῖς· τὸ γὰρ ἀνέκαθεν κατέπεσεν ἐπὶ τόπου λαμβάνουσιν Ἀθηναῖοι, εἰ δὲ ὑπὸ Ἡροδότου φήσει τις καὶ ἐπὶ χρόνου λαμβάνεσθαι, ἀληθῆ μὲν φήσει. οὐ μὴν τὸ ὑπὸ Ἡροδότου ἅπαξ εἰρῆσθαι τὸ δόκιμον τῆς κρίσεως αὐτῷ παρέχεται. οὐ γὰρ Ἰωνικῶν . . . . Ἀττικῶν] om. B, Nu. 238. om. P. καὶ θαυμάζω .... ἀδόκιμον ὄν] om. B. 239. om. A, B, Ca. 240. βλακικόν] βλάκιον MSS. Edd. 241. ὥστε πάντως . . . . τιθέασι τὸ ἑκὼν εἶναι] om. B, adnotantur vero in margine alia manu. Articulus hic in P sic legitur, τὸ ἑκὼν εἶναι οἱ παλαιοὶ ἐπὶ ἀπαγορεύσεως τιθέασιν, ἑκὼν εἶναι μὴ ποιήσῃς ἢ ποιήσω, καὶ ἑκόντες ὄντες μὴ ποιήσητε ἢ ποιήσομεν· ὅσοι δὲ ἐπὶ καταφάσεως τιθέασιν οἷον ἑκὼν εἶναι ἐποίησα, ἁμαρτάνουσιν. μέγιστα ἁμαρτάνουσιν] οὗτοι δὲ μάλιστα ἁμαρτάνουσιν Nu. οὗτοι δὲ μέγιστα ἁμαρτάνουσιν B. 242. aliter B et P, viz. ὄρθρον καὶ ὀρθρεύεσθαι οἱ παλαιοὶ τὸν πρὸ ἡλίου καιρὸν ἐν ᾧ λύχνον τις χρῆται· οἱ δὲ νῦν τὸ γλυκαυγὲς ὃ καὶ ἕω φασί. 243. ὀπτάνιον] ὀπτανεῖον A, Ca. Ph. ὀπτάνιον συστελλόμενον B. Breviter P, μάγειρος δόκιμον, μαγειρεῖον δὲ οὔ, ἀλλ' ὀπτάνιον διὰ τοῦ ι. 244. *οἱ γὰρ ἀμελεῖς .... προστιθέναι*] om. P. 245. *καὶ ὅ τι διάκρισις*] om. B. Nu. Aliter brevissime P, συγκρίνειν τόνδε τῷδε οὐ χρὴ λέγειν ἀλλὰ παραβάλλειν καὶ ἀντεξετάζειν. 246. *καὶ ἐγὼ μὲν φυλάττεσθαι κτε.*] παρὰ μὲν ἄλλῳ τῶν δοκίμων οὐχ εὗρον· ἡγοῦμαι δὲ καὶ Θουκυδίδην ἐν τῇ η μετὰ τοῦ ἄρθρου εἰρηκέναι κατ' ἐκεῖνο τοῦ καιροῦ, καὶ ἐγὼ μὲν φυλάττεσθαι παραινῶ οὕτω χρῆσθαι· εἰ δ' ὅτι Θουκυδίδης εἴρηκε θαρροίη τις χρῆσθαι, χρήσθω μὲν σὺν δὲ τῷ ἄρθρῳ B, Nu. Breviter P, κατ' ἐκεῖνο τοῦ καιροῦ Θουκυδίδης ἐν τῇ η εἴρηκε μετὰ τοῦ ἄρθρου ἀλλ' οὐ χωρὶς ἄρθρου. οὕτως οὖν καὶ αὐτὸς ἐρεῖς. 247. om. P. 248. *πόθεν καὶ ταῦτα .... φροντίδος ἄξιον· ἀλλά*] om. B. idem P nisi quod ἀλλὰ retineat, verbo ἀδόκιμα post εὐσταθὴς posito. *ἐμβρίθεια*] ἐπιείκεια A, Ca. Ph. ἐμβρίθεια, ἐπιείκεια B. 249. om. B, P. Ca. Ph. Brevissime et in margine A, πάλιν μετὰ τοῦ ν. 250. om. P. *ἐπὶ πολὺ δὲ .... ἀναγεγράψεται*] om. B. 251. breviter B P, γεννήματα ἐπὶ καρπῶν μὴ λέγε ἀλλὰ καρποὺς ξηροὺς ἢ ὑγρούς B. γεννήματα ἐπὶ καρπῶν τινες ἀδοκίμως τιθέασι· σὺ δὲ καρποὺς ξηροὺς καὶ ὑγροὺς λέγε P. 254. om. P. *χρὴ οὖν ἀπήντησε λέγειν καὶ συνήντησε*] συνήντησε δὲ καὶ ἀπήντησε λέγε B. 255. adjungunt verba ὅτι ἀττικὸν καὶ δόκιμον B, Nu. 256. *αὐξήσεις*] ὑπεραιξήσεις B, Nu. *σημαινόμεθα*] σημαίνομεν Nu. Brevissime P, ὀνυχίζειν καὶ ἐξονυχίζειν ταὐτόν. τίθεται δὲ ἐπὶ τοῦ ἀκριβολογεῖσθαι, τὸ δὲ ἀπονυχίζειν τὸ τὰς αὐξήσεις τῶν ὀνύχων ἀφαιρεῖν. 257. *καὶ τὰ νῶτα δοκίμως ἂν λέγοιτο*] om. A, Ca. καὶ τὰ νῶτα δόκιμον B. Breviter P, ὁ νῶτος ἀδοκίμως ἀρσενικῶς, οὐδετέρως δὲ τὸ νῶτον καὶ τὰ νῶτα. 258. Brevissime A, B, Ca. P. βρέχει ἐπὶ (ἀντὶ Ca.) τοῦ ὕει ἔν τινι κωμῳδίᾳ A, Ca. βρέχει ἐπὶ τοῦ ὕει οὐ τῶν δοκίμων πάνυ B. βρέχειν ἐπὶ τοῦ ὕειν τινὲς τιθέασιν ἐν κωμῳδίᾳ, ἔστι δὲ ἀδόκιμον P. 259. om. P. 260. *μὴ λέγε*] add. ἀλλὰ κατάδεσμος Nu. Aliter P, ἐπίδεσμος ἀρσενικῶς μὴ λέγε ἀλλὰ κατάδεσμος, καὶ ἐπίδεσμον οὐδετέρως καὶ ἐπίδεσμα οἱ ἀρχαῖοι. 261. *τιθέμενον*] ταττόμενον P. 262. *φλέως*] φλέος Nu. *πλεκόμενα*] A, P. λεγόμενα Nu. γινόμενα Ca. Breviter B, φλοῦς οὐ λέγεται ἀλλὰ φλεώς, καὶ τὰ ἀπὸ τούτου φλεΐνα. 264. *ἀμαθεῖς δὲ οἱ λέγοντες σὺν κτε.*] λέγουσι σὺν τῷ ι καὶ σ ὡς παλαιστὴς καὶ ἀθλητής B. ἀμαθὲς τὸ λέγειν παλαιστής, παλαιστὴς γὰρ ὁ ἀθλητής P. 265. *ἐπὶ δὲ τοῦ κτε.*] ἔγγειον δὲ ἐπὶ τοῦ ἐν τῇ γῇ ἄριστον, καὶ Δημοσθένης ἔγγειον τόκον φησίν P. 267. om. A, Ca. Ph. 268. om. A, P, Ca. Ph. Aliter P, ψύα καὶ ψόα, οἱ ἁπλῶς ἁμαρτάνοντες, οἱ δὲ διπλῶς, ψοιά, σὺ δὲ νεφρὸν λέγε. 270. om. A. ὑλιστὴρ ἀδόκιμον, σὺ δὲ τρύγοιπον λέγε P. 271. omit A, Ca. *πάπυρος*] πάπειρος Nu. πάπυρον οὐκ ἐρεῖς ἀλλὰ βίβλον, Αἰγύπτιον γὰρ τὸ πάπυρον P. 272. om. P. 273. Brevius B et P, Νίτρον αἰολικῶς, ἀθηναῖος δὲ διὰ τοῦ λ. B. νίτρον αἰολικόν, οἱ δὲ 'Αθηναῖοι λίτρον P. 274. *ἀνεψιὸς ὁ ἐξάδελφος*, ἐξάδελφος δὲ οὔ P. 275. om. P. 276. *πανδοχεῖον οὐκ ἐρεῖς ἀλλὰ διὰ τοῦ κ*, πανδοκεῖον καὶ πανδοκεύτρια καὶ πανδοκεύς P. 277. *τὸν κύριν λέγε κτε.*] ἀμφότερον P. 278. om. A. μόχλος γράφε B. 279. *ὁπόθεν δὲ .... ἄδηλον*] om. A, B, Ca. Va. Ph. 281. om. A,

B, P, Ca, &c. 282. πύελος, μύελος, ὕελος· ἁμαρτάνουσιν οἱ μὴ διὰ τοῦ ε λέγοντες, ἀλλὰ διὰ τοῦ α. πύελος διὰ τοῦ ε καὶ μύελος ῥητέον A, om. B, P. 283. om. A. αἱ χόλικες θηλυκῶς γράφε B. 284. om. A, B, P, Ca. 285. ἀλλ' ἀντ' κτε.] ἀλλὰ δαψιλῶς B. 287. om. P. Brevius A, B. παρακαταθήκην καὶ μὴ παραθήκην λέγε A. παραθήκην μή, παρακαταθήκην δέ B. 290. Brevius P, ἀγωγὸν οἱ παλαιοὶ ἐπὶ τοῦ ἡγουμένου ὁδόν τινα, οἱ δὲ νῦν ἐπὶ τῶν ὀχετῶν. 291. om. P. κρύπτεται καὶ κρύπτεσθαι φάθι, μὴ διὰ τοῦ β. B. 292. τιθέασι] τιθεάσι καὶ ἐπὶ ἀτίμου κουρᾶς B. ἀνθρώπων] ὃ δεῖ φυλάττειν adj. B. Non male P, καρῆναι καὶ ἐκάρη ἐπὶ ἀτίμου κουρᾶς, ἐπὶ δὲ ἐντίμου κουρᾶς, κείρασθαι. 293. om. A, P, Ca. 294. om. P. 295. om. P. ἀποσοβητέον] ἀποβλητέον Nu. χθεσινόν] χθειζόν A, Ca. Va. Brevissime B, χθιζὸν ποιητικόν· σὺ δὲ χθειζὸν γράφε. 296. om. B. 297. om. P. 298. om. P. 299. om. P. 300. om. A, P, Ca. Va. Ph. 301. om. Ca. Va. Ph. 302. om. B. 303. om. P. 304. om. P. 305. om. A, P, Ca. Va. Ph. 306. om. A, P, Ca. Va. Ph. 307. Brevissime B, P. τεθεληκέναι μὴ εἴποις, ἠθεληκέναι δέ B. τεθεληκέναι Ἀλεξανδρεωτικόν, τὸ δὲ Ἀττικὸν ἠθεληκέναι P. 308. om. P. ἡ δὲ ψύλλα κτε.] δόκιμον δὲ ἡ ψύλλα B. 309. om. P. 310. Brevius B, P, οὐκ ἐπίτοκος ἀλλ' ἐπίτεξ γυνή P. ἐπίτοκος γυνὴ ἀδόκιμον, ἐπίτεξ δὲ φάθι B. 311. om. P. 312. om. A, Ca. Va. Ph. ἐνδυμενία μὴ λέγε, σκεύη δὲ κατὰ τὴν οἰκίαν καὶ ἔπιπλα B. 313. om. P. ἐμπυρισμὸς μὴ λέγε ἀλλ' ἐμπρησμός B. 314. ἡμιμόχθηρον] ἡμεληνμένον A, Ca. Va. Ph. 315. ἔμελλον θεῖναι] om. P. εἴ τις οὕτω συντάττει] om. P. 316. om. P. 317. om. A, Ca. Va. Ph. 318. om. A, Ca. Ph. 319. Brevissime καταμύειν οὐ καμμύειν A, Ca. Va. καμμύειν ἐσχάτως ἀδόκιμον, καταμύειν γάρ B. 320. καὶ Θεόφραστον κεχρημέν. αὐτῷ] om. B. 321. εἰ καὶ κτε.] om. B. 322. om. A, P, Ca. 323. τὸ δὲ μιαρὸς ἀρχαῖον] μιαρὸς δὲ B. 326. om. P. 327. ἀλλὰ καὶ Λυσίαν κτε.] om. A, B, Ca. Va. 328. om. B, P. 329. om. P. 330. τὸ δὲ παρὰ τοῦτο κτε.] om. B. 331. om. A, P, Ca. Va. τί ἂν οὖν φαίη κτε.] om. B. 332. om. A, P, Ca. Va. Ph. 333, 334. Nunnesii codex unicus hos articulos conservavit. 335. om. A, Ca. Va. Ph. 336. om. A, Ca. Va. Ph. Brevissime B, γογγυσμὸς καὶ γογγύζειν, ταῦτα ἰακά, σὺ δὲ τονθρυσμὸν καὶ τονθρύζω λέγε ἢ νὴ δία κτε. 338. οὕτω . . . διὰ τοῦ ι.] om. B. 339. om. P. 341. om. A, P, Ca. Va. Ph. Φιλιππίδης δὲ καὶ κτε.] om. B. 342. om. A, Ca. Va. Ph. Brevissime B, ἐνεχυριμαῖα μὴ λέγε ἐνέχυρα δέ. 343. om. A, Ca. Va. Ph. 344. οἱ γὰρ δόκ. κτε.] χρηστὸς δὲ τὸ ἦθος καὶ οὐ τὰ ἤθη B. 345. addit P audacia inepta, καὶ τὴν μεγάλην πέτραν Συνέσιος θυρεὸν καλεῖ. θυρεὸν οὐκ ἐρεῖς, ἀλλ' ἀσπίδα. 346. hunc articulum Nunnesii codex unicus servavit. 347. om. A, B, Ca. Va. Ph. οὐχ οἷον καὶ μὴ οἷον κίβδηλον, οἷον, οὐχ οἷον ὀργίζομαι· οὐ δήπου τοίνυν ἐρεῖς καὶ μὴ δήπου. 348. ὡς Ἄλεξις] om. B. 349. ὁνδηποτοῦν] A, οὐδηποτοῦν P. ὀντινοῦν] οὑτινοῦν B. οὑτινοσοῦν P. 350. om. P. Brevissime B πρόσφατος νεκρὸς καὶ πρᾶγμα. 352. ἀντὶ τοῦ συμφορὰ] ἡ συμφορὰ A, Ca. Va. 353. om. P. 354. om. A, Ca. Brevissime B, σαπρὰν οἱ πολλοὶ ἀντὶ τοῦ αἰσχράν, σὺ δὲ ἐπὶ τοῦ σεσηπότος. 355. om. A, P, Ca. Va. Ph. 356. om. A, P, Ca. *ἀλλὰ σὺ καθαρὸς* ad fin.] σὺ δὲ καλὸν ἔχει πρόσωπον ἐρεῖς. 357. om. A, Ca. Va. Ph. Brevissime B, στρηνιᾶν· ἀντὶ τούτου λέγε τρυφᾶν. 360. om. A, Ca. Va. Ph. 361. om. A, Ca. Va. Ph. στηθίδιον ὑποκοριστικῶς μὴ λέγε ἀλλὰ στῆθος B. στηθύνιον ὀρνιθίου λέγουσι, σὺ δὲ στηθίδιον εἰ ὑποκοριστικῶς βούλῃ λέγειν, εἰ δ' οὐ, στῆθος P. 362. om. A, P, Ca. Va. Ph. ὑπέρσοφος ῥητέον οὐ μὴν δὲ ὑπέρδριμυς B. *ἑώντων*] emendavit Scaligerus, ἑκόντων in Nu. codice apparente. 363. Nunnesius solus servavit. 364. *φρονεῖν δὲ τὰ ὄντα*] ἀλλὰ τὰ ὄντα φρονεῖν B. 365. om. A, Ca. Va. Ph. 366. om. A, B, P, Ca. 368. *ἔχει καὶ σφαλερῶς τάττουσιν* om. B. *ἡ δὲ τοῦ ἐσχάτως κτε.*] σὺ δὲ ἐπὶ τοῦ ἄκρου τίθει· ἐσχάτως πονηρός, ἐσχάτως φιλόσοφος. 369. *πολύς, ὁ δὲ ἀττικός*] πολὺς λεώς, ἀλλ' οἱ ὀλίγοι καὶ Ἀττικοὶ Nu. οἱ πολλοί, σὺ δὲ B. 370. Brevissime B, χρέως ἀττικῶς διὰ τοῦ ω μεγάλου λέγε. *ἑτέραις*] δευτέραις Ca., om. Nu. 371. om. P. οἱ δὲ νῦν . . . ὀρθῶς om. B. 372. καθὰ καὶ Δημοσθένης ad extr. om. A, Ca. Va. *λέγε οὖν τί διάφερει*] om. Ph. 373. *χρῶ*] χρηστέον A, Ca. Va. Brevissime B, τέτευχε τιμῆς μὴ λέγε, ἀλλὰ τετύχηκε· 374. *στροβιλῆσαι τὸ συστρέψαι*] συστροβῆσαι τὸ συστρέψαι A. συστροβιλῆσαι τὸ στρέψαι B, Nu. συστροβῆσαι τὸ συστρέψαι Ca. *οὕτως . . . ῥητέον*] om. B. *καρπός*] καρπόν MSS. edd. *πίτυς*] πίτυν MSS. edd. *ἔτι νῦν κτε.*] om. B. *καὶ γὰρ Σόλων κτε.*] om. A. 375. *σκέψεις*] ὄψεις Ca. *συγκαταβαίνειν εἰς διδασκαλίας*] om. P. 376. *κατὰ διαφθορὰν*] om. B. 379. om. P. *λέγε οὖν κτε.*] λέγεται οὖν καὶ ἐπὶ τῶν τριῶν ὀνομάτων A, Ca. Va. 380. om. P. 381. om. P. 382. *δοκεῖ δέ μοι κτε.*] om. B. Breviter P, ῥύμην· οὐ τὴν στενωπὸν ἀμαθῶς κατὰ Μακεδόνας ἀλλὰ τὴν ὁρμὴν Ἀττικῶς. 386, 387. in unum redegerunt A, Ca. 386. om. P. 387. *τοῦτο γὰρ καὶ ἰατροὶ κτε.*] om. A. Breviter P, ἔξπηχυ καὶ ἑξέτης· οὕτω γὰρ οἱ ἰατροὶ λέγουσιν ἔξπλεθρον καὶ ἑξάπλεθρον. 388. *γενέσθαι*] om. Nu. 391. om. omnes codd. et edd. praeter Nunnesium. 392. Brevissime B, γῦρος οὐ γράφεται. om. al. praeter Nu. 393. σύσσημον οὐ χρῶ B. om. al. praeter Nu. 395. Brevius B et P. κατ' ὄναρ οὐ γράφεται, ὡς οὐδὲ τὸ καθ' ὕπαρ, ἀλλ' ἤτοι ὄναρ ἰδὼν ἢ ἐξ ὀνείρου ὄψεως B. οὐ χρὴ κατ' ὄναρ λέγειν, ὥσπερ οὐδὲ καθ' ὕπαρ· ἀλλ' ἤτοι ὄναρ ἰδὼν ἢ ἐξ ὀνείρου ὄψεως οὕτω καὶ ὕπαρ P. 396. *παρὰ . . . χρῆσιν*] ἀδοκίμως B. 397. aliter B, τὸ καθὼς οὐ γράφεται· ἀλλὰ τὸ καθό· καὶ Θουκυδίδης· καθὸ δεῖ εἰς Σικ. πλ. καὶ τὸ καθὰ δόκιμον. 398. om. A. μὴ κάκκαβον ἀλλὰ κακκάβην διὰ τοῦ η B. 399. Breviter omnes praeter Nu. κυνηγὸς οὕτως οἱ τραγικοὶ ποιηταὶ δωρικῶς τρισυλλάβως· οἱ δ' Ἀττικοὶ κυνηγέτης λέγουσι B. κυνηγέτης οἱ Ἀττικοί, ἀλλ' οὐ κυνηγός, τραγικὸν γὰρ τοῦτο P. κυνηγέτης λέγε τετρασυλλάβως A, Ca. Va. Ph. 400. Nunnesius servavit. 401. om. A, B, Ca. Va. 402. *πολλοί*] παλαιοί A, Ca. Va. Ph. Breviter B, πρὸς ἀφροδίσια ἀκόλαστος, οὐ καταφερής. 403. om. A, B, P, Ca. Va. Ph. 404. *οὐκ* ὀρθῶς ἐπὶ τοῦ ἀργυραμοιβοῦ Nu. διαπαύεται] ἀναπαύεται Nu. παρασεσημασμένον] inepte Nu. ἀδόκιμον. Brevius B, κολλυβιστὴς οὐ γράφεται· κόλλυβος δὲ νόμισμα δόκιμον. 405. ἢ τὰ ἴδια ἐμαυτοῦ κτε.] om. A, Ca. Va. 406. om. Ca. Va. Aliter A, ἀλέγειν ὡς οἱ παλαιοί· ἐγκρατεύεσθαι καὶ μὴ ἀκρατεύεσθαι. Brevissime B, οὐκ ἐγκρατεύεται γράφεται. 407. μηδὲ] οὐδὲ Ca. καὶ μὴ Nu. Huic articulo adjungit A, τέλος τῆς Φρυνίχου ἐκλογῆς ἀττικῶν ῥημάτων καὶ ὀνομάτων, sed Nunnesii codex τέλος τοῦ δευτέρου, ἀρχὴ τοῦ γ., vide p. 504 supra. Articulos, quos in tertio libro edidit Nu., illos adjeci qui non in alio loco jam nobis obviam ierunt. 411. In Nu. codice accessit ἄμεινον γάρ· ἐκτὸς εἰ μή ποθεν τοῦτο εἰς Φαβωρῖνον ἦλθεν, ὅθεν οὐδεὶς οἶδεν. ἀρχαῖοι μὲν γὰρ οὕτως οὐ λέγουσιν, ἐκεῖνος δέ. πλὴν εἴη εἶς· ἡμεῖς οὖν ὡς οἱ ἀρχαῖοι, ἀλλὰ μὴ ὡς Φαβωρῖνος.

APPENDIX B.

Cod. Med. Laurent. Plut. lvii. Cod. 34.

Ἀπὸ τῶν τοῦ φροινίχου (sic).

Ἐπίτοκος ἡ γυνή· οὐ δοκίμως εἶπεν ἀντιφάνης ὁ κωμικός· δέον ἐπίτεξ ἡ γυνή.—ἐμπυρισμὸς οὕτως ὑπερείδης ἠμελημένως· δέον ἐμπρησμὸς λέγειν.—ἡμίκακον οὐχ οὕτως· ἀλλ' ἡμιμόχθηρον φᾶθι.—κεφαλοτομεῖν ἀπόρριπτε τοὔνομα καὶ θεόφραστον κεχρημένον αὐτῷ· λέγε δὲ καρατομεῖν.—λάκαιναν μὲν γυναῖκα ἐρεῖς· λάκαιναν δὲ τὴν χώραν οὐδαμῶς· ἀλλὰ λακωνικήν· εἰ καὶ εὐριπίδης παραλόγως φησίν.—μιαρία οὐ δόκιμον· τὸ δὲ μιαρός, ἀρχαῖον.—ἐργοδότης οὐ κεῖται· τὸ δὲ ἐργοδοτεῖν παρά τινι τῶν νεωτέρων κωμῳδῶν· οἷς οὐ πιστέον (sic).—ἐντέχνως πάνυ αἰτιῶνται τοὔνομα· καὶ φασὶ τεχνικῶς δεῖ λέγειν· ἀλλὰ καὶ λυσίαν εἰρηκότα ἐντέχνως παραιτοῦνται.—γαμῴη μὴ λέγε· ἀλλὰ γαμοίη διὰ τῆς οι· ὡς νοοίη φιλοίη· τὸ (sic) γὰρ τῆς πρώτης συζυγίας καὶ τρίτης τῶν περισπωμένων ῥημάτων εὐκτικὰ διὰ τῆς οι διφθόγγου λέγεται· οἷον τελοίη. τὰ δὲ τῆς δευτέρας διὰ τῆς ῳ· οἷον νικῴην· γελῴην· γελῴης· γελῴη. διδῴης· διδῴης διδῴη τοῦτο τὸ εὐκτικόν, οὐδεὶς τῶν ἀττικῶν διὰ τῆς ῳ εἶπεν· ἀλλὰ διὰ τῆς οι διφθόγγου· τεκμηριοῖ δὲ ὅμηρος· ἐὰν μὲν γὰρ ὑποτακτικῶς χρῆται, διὰ τοῦ ῳ λέγει· εἰ δέ κεν αὐτῷ δῴη κῦδος ἀρέσθαι· ἔστι γὰρ ὑποτακτικόν· εἰ δ' εὐκτικῶς οὕτως· σοὶ δὲ θεοὶ τόσα δοῖεν, ὅσα φρεσὶ σῇσιν· ἐθαύμασαν γοῦν ἀλεξάνδρου τοῦ σύρου σοφιστοῦ δῴη καὶ διδῴη λέγοντος.—ἀναισθητεύομαι· τὸ μὲν ἀναίσθητος ὄνομα, δοκιμώτατον· τὸ δὲ ῥῆμα, οὐκέτι· λέγε οὖν οὐκ αἰσθάνομαι.—αὐθεκαστότης, ἀλλόκοτον· τὸ μὲν γὰρ αὐθέκαστος κάλλιστον ὄνομα· τὸ δὲ παρὰ τοῦτο πεποιημένον ἡ αὐθεκαστότης κίβδηλον.—τὸν παῖδα τὸν ἀκολουθοῦντα μετ' αὐτοῦ λυσίας ἐν τῷ κατὰ αὐτοκράτην οὕτω τῇ συντάξει χρῆται· ἐχρῆν δὲ οὕτως εἰπεῖν· τὸν ἀκολουθοῦντα αὐτῷ· τί γοῦν ἄν τις φαίη. ἁμαρτεῖν τὸν λυσίαν, ἢ νοθεύειν καινὴν σχήματος χρῆσιν· ἀλλ' ἐπεὶ ξένη πάντη ἡ σύνθεσις παραιτῆται. ῥητέον δ' ἀκολουθεῖν αὐτῷ.—βιωτικὸν ἀηδὴς ἡ λέξις· λέγε δὲ χρήσιμον ἐν τῷ βίῳ.—γογγισμὸς καὶ γογγίζειν, ταῦτα δόκιμα μὲν οὐκ ἔστιν· ἰακὰ δέ· ἡμεῖς δὲ τονθρυσμὸν καὶ τονθρύζω λέγομεν· ἢ σὺν τῷ ο τονθορύζω καὶ τονθορυσμόν.—δύνῃ· ἐὰν μέντοι τὸ ὑποτακτικὸν ᾖ ἐὰν δύνωμαι ἐὰν δύνῃ, ὀρθῶς λέγεται. ἐὰν δὲ ὁριστικῶς τιθῇ τις δύνῃ τοῦτο πράξαι, οὐχ ὑγιῶς ἄν, τιθείη χρὴ γὰρ λέγειν οὐ δύνασαι τοῦτο πράξαι.—ὥρκισε· καὶ ὁρκώτης ἐγώ· οὕτω κρατῖνος φησί· μᾶλλον δὲ διὰ τοῦ ω̄ λέγε· ἢ διὰ τοῦ ῑ ὥρκισεν.—ἐδέετο· ἐπλέετο· ἰακὰ ταῦτα· ἡ δὲ ἀττικὴ συνήθεια συναιρεῖ· ἐπλεῖτο ἐδεῖτο.—ἐξαλλάξαι τὸ τρέψαι καὶ παραγαγεῖν· εἰς δ' εὐφροσύνην, χρὴ φυλάττεσθαι οὕτω λέγειν.—θυρεὸς τοῦτο ὅμηρος ἐπὶ λίθου τίθησιν· ἀντὶ θύρας τὴν χρείαν παρέχοντος· ἐπι τῆς ἀσπίδος δὲ οἱ πολλοὶ τιθέασιν οὐτινὸς τῶν ἀρχαίων καὶ δοκίμων χρησαμένων· χρὴ οὖν ἀσπίδα λέγειν.—ὁνδηποτοῦν μὴ λέγε· ἀλλὰ δοκίμως ὁντινοῦν.—πτῶμα ἐπὶ νεκροῦ τιθέασιν οἱ νῦν· οἱ δὲ ἀρχαῖοι, οὐχ οὕτως· ἀλλὰ πτῶμα νεκρῶν ἢ οἴκων.—περίστασις ἀντὶ τοῦ συμφορά· οἱ στωϊκοὶ χρῶνται φιλόσοφοι· οἱ δὲ ἀρχαῖοι περίστασιν λέγουσι τὴν διά τινα τάραχον παρουσίαν πλήθους· μάθοις δ' ἄν, τηλεκλείδου λέγοντος ὧδε τις (sic) ἧδε (sic) κραυγή· καὶ δώμων περίστασις.—παρεμβολὴ δεινῶς μακεδονικόν· καίτοι ἐνῆν τῷ στρατοπέδῳ χρῆσθαι πλείστῳ τὲ καὶ δοκίμῳ ὄντι.—σιτομετρεῖσθαι μὴ λέγε· διαλύων δὲ ἐρεῖς σῖτον μετρεῖσθαι.—φρονιμεύεσθαι μὴ λέγε· φρονεῖν δὲ τὰ ὄντα.—χρησιμεῦσαι μὴ λέγε· ἀλλὰ χρήσιμον γενέσθαι.—ἐσχάτως ἔχειν ἐπὶ τοῦ μοχθηρῶς ἔχειν καὶ σφαλερῶς τάττουσιν οἱ σύρφακες· ἡ δὲ τοῦ ἐσχάτως χρῆσις, οἶσθα ὅτι ἐπὶ τοῦ ἄκρου παρὰ τοῖς ἀρχαίοις νομίζεται· ἐσχάτως πονηρῶς (sic) φιλόσοφος· διαγραπτέον οὖν καὶ τοῦτο.—χρεολυτῆσαι λέγει ὁ πολὺς λεώς· ἀλλ' οἱ ὀλίγοι καὶ ἀττικοί, τὰ χρέα διαλύσασθαι.—φιλολόγος ὁ φιλῶν λόγους· καὶ σπουδάζων περὶ παιδείαν· οἱ δὲ νῦν, ἐπὶ τοῦ ἐμπύρου τιθέασι τοὔνομα, οὐκ ὀρθῶς· τὸ μέντοι ἐφιλολόγησα καὶ φιλολογῶ καὶ πάντα ῥήματα καὶ τὰ μετοχικά, εὐδόκιμα.—τίνι διαφέρει τόδε καὶ τόδε, οὐ χρὴ οὕτω λέγειν κατὰ δοτικὴν πτῶσιν· ἀλλὰ τί διαφέρει· καθὰ καὶ δημοσθένης φησί· τί δοῦλον ἢ ἐλεύθερον εἶναι διαφέρει· λέγε γοῦν τί διαφέρει.—τέτευχε τιμῆς· τέτευχε τοῦ σκόπου μὴ λέγῃς· ποιητικὸν γάρ· ἀλλ' ἀντ' αὐτοῦ τῷ δοκίμῳ χρῶ τετύχηκεν.—στρόβιλον οἱ μὲν πολλοί, τὸ ἐδώδιμον λέγουσι καὶ αὐτὸ τὸ δένδρον. οἱ δὲ ἀρχαῖοι, τὴν βιαίαν τοῦ ἀνέμου εἴλησιν καὶ συστροφήν, στρόβιλον φασί· καὶ συστροβιλῆσαι τὸ συστρέψαι· οὕτως οὖν καὶ ἡμῖν ῥητέον· τὸ δὲ ἐδώδιμον, πιτύων καρπῶν καὶ τὸ δένδρον, πίτυν.—συγκαταβαίνειν εἰς τὰς σκέψεις· συγκαταβαίνειν εἰς διδασκαλίαν μὴ εἴπῃς· ἀλλὰ συγκαθιέναι· καὶ συγκαθῆκεν εἰς τὸ παίζειν· ἢ ἄλλό τι.—συσχολαστὰς ἐσχάτως ἀνάττικον· σὺ δὲ συμφοιτητὰς λέγε.—ῥαότερον μή· ῥᾷον δέ· συγκριτικὸν γὰρ συγκριτικοῦ οὐκ ἔστιν. οἷον εἴ τις λέγει κρεισσότερον.—ῥύμην καὶ τοῦτο οἱ μὲν ἀθηναῖοι, ἐπὶ τῆς ὁρμῆς ἐτίθεσαν· οἱ δὲ νῦν ἀμαθῶς ἐπὶ τοῦ στενωποῦ· δοκεῖ δέ μοι καὶ τοῦτο μακεδονικὸν εἶναι. ἀλλὰ στενωπὸν καλεῖν χρή· ῥύμη δὲ τὴν ὁρμήν.—πεντάμηνον· πεντάπηχυ· μετάθες τὸ ᾱ εἰς ε̄· πεντέμηνον· λέγων καὶ πεντέπηχυ.—περιεσπάσθην λέγουσι τινὲς ἐπὶ τοῦ ἐν ἀσχολίᾳ γενέσθαι· τιθέντες πάνυ κιβδήλως· τὸ γὰρ περισπᾶν καὶ περισπᾶσθαι, ἐπὶ τοῦ παραιρεῖν καὶ παραιρεῖσθαι τάττουσιν οἱ ἀρχαῖοι· δέον οὖν ἄσχολος ἦν λέγειν.—πορνοκόπος. οὕτω μένανδρος· οἱ ἀρχαῖοι ἀθηναῖοι, πορνότριψ λέγουσιν.—οἰκοδομή, οὐ λέγεται· ἀντ' αὐτοῦ δέ, οἰκοδόμημα λέγεται.—κατ' ὄναρ οὐ λέγεται· ἀδοκιμώτατον γάρ· ὥσπερ γὰρ καθ' ὕπαρ οὐ λέγεται· ἀλλ' ὕπαρ, οὕτως οὐδὲ κατ' ὄναρ· ἀλλ' ἤτοι ὄναρ ἰδών, ἢ ἐξ ὀνείρου ὄψεως.—κυνηγός· τοῦτο τοὔνομα, οὕτω πως μεταχειρίζονται οἱ μὲν τραγικοὶ ποιηταί, τρισυλλάβως, καὶ δωρίζουσι τὸ η̄ εἰς ᾱ μετατιθέντες· κυναγός· οἱ δ' ἀθηναῖοι, τετρασυλλάβως, κυνηγέτης λέγοντες.—

κολόκυνθα, ἡμάρτηται ἡ ἐσχάτη συλλαβὴ διὰ τῆς θα λεγομένη· δέον διὰ τῆς τη· κολοκύντη, ὡς ἀθηναῖοι.—κατωφερὴς ἐπὶ τῶν πρὸς ἀφροδίσια ἀκολάστων λέγουσιν οἱ πολλοί· οὐδαμῶς οὕτω τῶν δοκίμων χρωμένων.—τὰ ἴδια πράττω· καὶ τὰ ἴδια πρᾶττε (sic) λέγουσιν οἱ πολλοὶ εἰκῇ· δέον τὰ ἐμαυτοῦ πράττω· καὶ τὰ σαυτοῦ πράττε λέγειν· ὡς οἱ παλαιοί.—ἴδιον ἐμαυτοῦ. ἴδιον σαυτοῦ· ἴδιον ἑαυτοῦ.—ἐγκρατεύεσθαι μὴ λέγε· ἀλλὰ λέγε οὐκ ἐγκρατεύεται· οὕτω καὶ εἰρηναῖος· ὃς καὶ τὸ ἐγκρατεύεσθαι ἐσχάτως βάρβαρον καλεῖ.—αἰχμαλωτισθῆναι συνθέτως οὐ λέγεται· διαλελυμένως δὲ λέγε, αἰχμάλωτον γενέσθαι.—ἀνυπόδητος ἐρεῖς διὰ τοῦ η· τὸ γὰρ ἐν τῷ ε ἁμάρτημα· καὶ γὰρ ὑποδήσασθαι λέγεται· οὐχ ὑποδέσασθαι.—εὕρημα χρὴ λέγειν διὰ τοῦ η. οὐχ εὕρεμα.—ἀπηρτημένον ἀπήρτηκα· καὶ τὰ ἀπὸ τούτων ἅπαντα σόλοικα· ἀποτετέλεσθαι δὲ καὶ ἀποτετελεσμένον χρὴ λέγειν. ἄμεινον γάρ.

INDEX I.

The words printed in **black type** *occur in the Ecloga itself; the others are found in the Introductions and Commentary.*

A.

ἄγαγον, an un-Attic imperative, 457.
ἀγαθός, comparative and superlative of, 176.
ἄγγος, 23.
ἄγειν, aorists of, 217, 218.
ἀγήοχα, un-Attic, 202.
ἀγλαΐα, 165.
ἀγνύναι for *καταγνύναι*, 6.
ἀγοράζειν, 214.
ἀγορᾶσθαι, 14.
ἀγορεύειν and compounds, 326 ff.
ἀγρεύειν, 165.
ἀγχέμαχα, 165.
ἄγχιστα, 21.
ἀγχιτέρμων, 165.
ἀγχοῦ, 21.
ἀγωγός, 368.
ἀγωνίζεσθαι, 193.
ἀδαής, 165.
ᾄδειν, future of, 377.
ἀείδειν, Tragic for *ᾄδειν*, 5.
ἀείρειν, Tragic for *αἴρειν*, 5.
ἄελπτος, 26.
Ἀθάνα, Tragic for *Ἀθηνᾶ*, 112.
Ἀθηνᾶ, forms of the name, 112.
Ἀθηνάα, 112.
Ἀθηναία, forms of the name, 112.
ἀθροίζειν, orthography of, 160.
αἰγυπιός, 19.
αἰεί, old Attic and Tragic for **ἀεί**, 112.
αἰετός, old Attic and Tragic for **ἀετός**, 112.
αἴθαλος, gender of, 197.
αἴθοψ, meaning of, 197, 198.
αἰθριοκοιτεῖν, 69.
-αίνειν, verbs in, have no perfect active, 96; aorists of, 76 ff.
αἰνεῖν, for *ἐπαινεῖν*, 5.
αἰνός, 26.
-αίρειν, verbs in, aorists of, 76 ff.
ἀΐσσειν, Tragic for *ᾄσσειν*, 5.
αἰσχύνη, 74.
αἰτιᾶσθαι, 193.
αἰχμαλωτίζεσθαι, 500.
αἰχμάλωτος, 13.
αἰχμή, use of in Ionic and Tragedy, 13.
ἀκεῖσθαι, 175, 176.
ἀκεστής, 175, 176.
ἀκίς, old word, 25.
ἀκμήν = *ἔτι*, un-Attic, 203.
ἀκολασταίνειν, aorist of, 78.
ἀκολουθεῖν, construction of, 458.
ἀκούειν, perfect of, 96.
ἀκραιφνής, of water, 113.
ἀκρατεύεσθαι, meaning of, 500.
ἄκρατος, comparative of, 224.
ἀκτή, old Ionic word, 11.
ἀλαίνειν, 78.
ἀλγύνειν, old and poetical word, 42.
ἀλγύνεσθαι, in Xenophon, 165.
ἀλεῖν, 240; perfects of, 96, 98.
ἀλείφειν, perfects of, 95, 96.
ἀλέκειν, in Xenophon, 165.
ἀλεκτρυών, 307.
ἀλεκτορίς, 307.
ἀλέκτωρ, 307.
ἀλεξητήρ, in Xenophon, 165.
ἀλέξειν, in Xenophon, 165.
ἀλήθειν, un-Attic, 90, 240.
ἀλήλεκα, ἀλήλεμαι, 96, 98.
ἀλίζειν, in Xenophon, 165.
Ἀλκαικός, or *Ἀλκαϊκός*? 111.
ἀλκή, history of, 25, note 2.
ἄλκιμος, in Xenophon, 165; un-Attic, 50.
ἀλλόθροος, 16, note.
ἁλμάδες ἐλᾶαι, 199.
ἀλύειν, 40.
ἀλφάνειν = *εὑρίσκειν*, 254.
ἀμαξευμένος, 14.
ἀμαυροῦν, in Xenophon, 165.
ἀμβλίσκειν, 288.
ἀμβλωθρίδιον, 288.
ἀμείβειν, history of, 187, note.
ἀμείβεσθαι, 187
ἀμεινότερον, 209.
ἄμεμπτος, 20.
ἁμιλλᾶσθαι, 191–193.
ἀμοῦ, 271, 272.
ἀμπειχόμην, 83–86.

ἀμπεσχόμην, 83-86.
ἀμπέχεσθαι, augmenting of, 83-86.
ἄμυνα, un-Attic, 74.
ἀμύνεσθαι, 74.
ἀμφιγνοεῖν, augment of, 83, 84.
ἀμφιδέξιος, 14.
ἀμφίπολος, old Ionic word, 22.
ἀμφισβητεῖν, augment of, 83, 84.
ἄμωμος, 20.
-ᾶν, verbs in, 153 ff.
ἀναγαργαρίζειν, 396.
ἀναγορεύειν, 328.
ἀναθέσθαι, 292.
ἀναιδεύεσθαι, 140.
ἀναιδίζεσθαι, 140.
ἀναισθητεύεσθαι, 457.
ἀνακάειν, 7.
ἀνακεῖον, 358.
ἀνακεῖσθαι, 294.
ἀνακλάειν, 7.
ἀνάκλιντρον, 207.
ἀνακογχυλιάζειν, 396.
ἀναλίσκειν, augment of, 82.
ἄναλκις, 25, note 2; 166.
ἀναπίπτειν, 293.
ἀνατέλλειν, 204.
ἀνατιθέναι, 292.
ἀνατοιχεῖν, 249.
ἀναχαιτίζειν, 180.
ἀνδάνειν, 29.
ἀνδραγάθημα, 319.
ἀνείλλειν, 89, 90.
ἀνειλεῖν, late form, 89.
ἀνειχόμην, 83 ff.
ἀνέκαθεν, 21, 338.
ἀνεσχόμην, 83-86.
ἀνέχεσθαι, augment of, 83-86.
ἀνεψιός, 361.
ἀνέῳγα, active in meaning, 246.
ἀνιέναι, signification of, 79.
ἀνιμᾶν, 166.
ἄνιππος, 26.
ἀνίστασο, ἀνίστω, 463.
ἀνοήτως, 221.
ἀνοιγνύναι, augment of, 83.
ἀντᾶν, 6.
ἄντεσθαι, 349.
ἀντιάζειν, 21.
ἀντιβάλλειν, 295.
ἀντιβολεῖν, augment of, 83, 84.
ἀντιδικεῖν, augment of, 83, 84.
ἀντικρύ, ἄντικρυς, distinguished, 500.
ἀντιλογία, 326 ff.
ἀντιοῦσθαι, 5.
ἀντίρρησις, 326 ff.
ἀνυπόδετος, 501.
ἀνωγέναι, 29.
ἀνώγεων, 358.
ἄνωθεν, 338.
ἆξαι, 348, 217, 218.
ἀπαμείβεσθαι, 166.
ἀπαναίνεσθαι, aorist of, 78.
ἀπαντᾶν, 21.
ἀπάντεσθαι, 349.
ἀπαράβατος, 367.
ἀπαρτί, 71.
ἀπαρτίζειν, 502.
Ἀπατούρια, 19.
ἀπέκ, 120.
ἀπεκεῖθεν, 120.
ἀπερύκειν, 166.
ἀπό, in composition, 75.
ἀποδεκτήρ, in Xenophon, 165.
ἀποδιδράσκειν, 218, 335.
ἀποδρᾶναι, 335.
ἀποθανεῖν, 38.
ἄποινα, 26.
ἀποκοπή, 158.
ἀποκριθῆναι, 186.
ἀποκρίνεσθαι, 186.
ἀπολαγχάνειν, 7.
ἀπολαύειν, future of, 409.
ἀποκριθήσομαι, 188.
ἀπολογεῖσθαι, 191.
ἀπόνιπτρον, 280.
ἀπόνοσφιν, 120.
ἀπόπαλαι, 117.
ἀποπέφαγκα, 97.
ἀπορεῖσθαι, 191.
ἀποσκυθίζειν, 180.
ἀποτάσσεσθαι, 75.
ἀπότιμος, 14.
ἄπωθεν, not ἄποθεν, 60.
ἀραιός, in Xenophon, 166.
ἀράσσειν, 6.
ἀργός, inflexion of, 185.
ἄρδις, 25.
Ἄρειος πάγος, 12 note.
ἀρέσκειν, 29.
ἀρήγειν, 166.
ἄρθμιος, 14.
ἀριστεύς, 30.
ἁρμόζειν, 14.
ἁρμοστήρ, 58, 59.
ἀρνεῖσθαι, 190, 192.
ἀροῦν, perfects of, 96, 100.
ἄρουρα, old Ionic and poetical word, 14.
ἁρπάζειν, future of, 407.
ἄρτι, limits of its use, 70.
ἀρτίως, coined by Sophocles, 71.
ἀρτοκόπος, 303.
ἀρτοποιός, 303.
ἀρτοπόπος, 303.
ἀρύειν, perfect passive of, 100.
ἀρχαϊκός, or ἀρχαικός? 111.
ἀρχῆθεν, 21, 176.
-ας, substantives in, used in Ionic as adjectives, 21.
ἄσβολος, 197.

ἀσελγαίνειν, aorist of, 78.
-*ασία*, substantives in, 198.
-*άσιον*, diminutives in, 148.
ἀσπαίρειν, 30.
ἀσπάραγος, 196.
ἀστραφιστήρ, 58.
ἀστυφέλικτος, 166
ἀσφάραγος, 196.
ἀτημέλητος, in Xenophon, 166.
ἀτρεκής, 26.
ἄτρυτος, 14.
ἀτταγᾶς, 199.
αὐ-, verbs beginning in, augment of, 245.
αὐδᾶν, 29.
αὐθαδίζεσθαι, 140.
αὐθέκαστος, αὐθεκαστότης, 458.
αὐθέντης, 201.
αὐταύλης, 253.
αὐτομολεῖν, 42.
αὐτόμολος, 42.
αὐτότροφος, 285.
ἀφειλάμην, 215.
ἀφήλιξ, 157.
ἄφθογγος, 26.
ἀφιέναι, augment of, 81.
ἀφιεροῦν, 279.
ἀφορμή, 304.
ἀφρόνιτρον, 361.
ἀφυπνίζειν, 305.
ἀχθεινός, 166.
ἀχθέσομαι, 195.
ἄχος, 166.
ἄχρι, 64.
-*ᾱώ*, verbs in, denoting bodily, &c. states, 152 ff.
-*ᾰω*, verbs in, perfects passive of, 101.

B.

βαδίζειν, future of, 382.
βαθμός, 372.
βάκηλος, 339.
βαλαντιοκλέπτης, 305.
βαλαντοκλέπτης, 305.
βαλβῖδες, meaning of the term, 146, 147.
βάρδιστος, 150.
βασίλεια, 306.
βασιλίς, 306.
βασίλισσα, 306.
βασκαίνειν, aorist of, 78.
βασκάνιον, 159.
βασμός, 372.
βελόνη, 174.
βελονοπώλης, 174, 175.
βῆσαι, in Xenophon, 30; replaced in Attic by *βιβάσαι*, id.
βιάζεσθαι, 144.
βιβλιαγράφος, 158.
βιβλογράφος, 158.
βίβλος, 360.
βιοτή, 166.
βιώσιμος, 20.
βιωτικός, 459.
βιωτός, 20.
βλακικός, 340.
βλάξ, 339.
βλαστάνειν, future of, 395, 406.
βοήθεια, 25.
βοίδιον, orthography of, 159.
βόλβιτον, 462.
βολεών, 253.
βόλιτον, 462.
βούλεσθαι, 189.
βουνός, history of, 459.
βράδιον, 149.
βρέχειν, 352.
βρυάσεσθαι, 405.
βρῶμος, 246.
βρώσεσθαι, 376.
βῶλος, 127.

Γ.

γαμέτης, in Xenophon, 166.
γαγγαλίζειν, 180.
γαργαλίζειν, 180.
γαστρίζειν, 178.
γαστροκνημία, 413.
γαυροῦσθαι, in Xenophon, 167.
γεινάμενοι, οἱ, in Xenophon, 167.
γελάσιμος, 307.
γελοῖος, 307.
γενέθλια, 184.
γενέσια, 184.
γενηθῆναι, 194.
γενηθήσομαι, 194.
γεννήματα, late use of, 348.
γεύεσθαι, 29.
γῆ, compounds of, 356.
γηΐνος, 181.
-*γκα*, a collocation of letters avoided in Attic, 96.
γλωσσίς, 308.
γλωσσόκομον, 181.
γλῶττα, 308.
γλωττοκομεῖον, 181.
γνῶμα, 19.
γνώρισμα, 19.
γνωστήρ, in Xenophon, 165.
γογγύζειν, 463.
γογγύλη, 182.
γογγυλίς, 182.
γογγυσμός, 463.
γονή, 19.
γόνος, 19.
γούνατος, &c., Tragic for *γόνατος*, &c., 5.
γρηγορεῖν, 200.
γρυλίζειν, 182.

γρυλλίζειν, 182.
γρύζειν, future of, 384.
γρυμέα, 309.
γρύτη, 309.
γοᾶσθαι, 167.
γῦρος, 492.
γύψ, 19.

Δ.

δαήμων, 167.
δαινύναι, 29.
δακρύειν, future of, 404.
δαπανᾶσθαι, aorist of, 191.
δάπεδον, in Xenophon, 167.
δαψιλής, in Xenophon, 167.
δέδια, inflexions of, 269 ff.
δέδοικα, inflexions of, 269 ff.
δέῃ, uncontracted, 299.
δεῖν (*bind*), anomalous contraction of, 301.
δειπνίζειν, in Xenophon, 167.
δείρειν, δέρειν, both good Attic, 432.
δειρή, 25.
δεῖσθαι, aorist of, 189.
δεξαμενή, 369.
δεσμοί and δεσμά, distinguished, 353.
δεσπόσυνος, in Xenophon, 167.
δεύειν, 61.
δημοτεύειν, 61.
δημοῦσθαι, reason for middle inflexions of, 193.
διά in compounds influences the inflexions of the verb, 193.
διαιτᾶν, augment of, 83, 86; meaning of, 189.
διαιρεῖν, 330 ff.
διάκρισις, 344.
διαλέγεσθαι, reason for middle inflexions of, 191.
διακονεῖν, augment of, 83, 86.
διανοεῖσθαι, reason for middle inflexions of, 191–193.
διαρρήδην, 329.
διατοιχεῖν, 249.
διαφέρειν, construction of, 483.
διαφθείρειν, 145.
διδόασιν, 315.
διδόναι, inflexions of, 220, 315, 316.
διδοῦσιν, 315.
διείρηκα, 330 ff.
διετετρήνατο, 77.
διέφθορα, 246.
διήρηκα and διείρηκα, confused, 330 ff.
διϊέναι, signification of, 79.
δικαιολογεῖσθαι, reason for middle inflexions of, 193.
δίκρανον, 310.
δικροῦν, 310.
διόρθωσις, 320.
Διόσκοροι, 310.
διπλοίζειν, orthography of, 160.
διψῆν, 132.
διψῆσθαι, 382.
διώκειν, future of, 377.
διωριά, 78.
διώρυξ, inflexions of, 309.
δοκεῖν, 29.
δοτήρ, in Xenophon, 165.
δουπεῖν, in Xenophon, 167.
δράμημα, 19.
δρᾶν, aorist and perfect passive of, 101.
δρόμος, 19.
δρύπτεσθαι, in Xenophon, 168.
δρωπακίζειν, 488.
δυεῖν, 289.
δύνασαι, δύνᾳ, δύνῃ, 463.
δύνασθαι, with neuter adjectives, 189; 2nd pers. sing. pres. ind. of, 463.
δύο, inflexions of, 289, 290.
δυοῖν, not used with the plural, 289, 290.
δύσελπις, in Xenophon, 168.
δυσί, 289.
δυσωπεῖσθαι, 278.
δυσωπία, 278.
δῶμα, 25.
δωμάτιον, 321.
δώρημα, 168.
δωροδοκεῖν, 362.

E

-έας, acc. pl. of substantives in **ευς**, 234.
ἐβουλησάμην, 189, note.
ἔγγαιος, 357.
ἔγγειος, 356.
ἐγγελᾶν, 66.
ἐγγυᾶν, augment of, 82.
ἐγγύς, comparative of, 356.
ἐγείρειν, perfects of, 96, 97.
ἐγκάθετος, 417.
ἐγκοπή, 158.
ἐγκωμιάζειν, augment of, 82.
ἐγρηγορέναι, 200.
ἐγχεῖν, meaning of, 66.
ἐγχρίμπτειν, 14.
ἐδεδίεσαν, 269.
ἐδέδισαν, 269.
ἔδεσθαι, 376.
ἐδήδοκα, ἐδήδεσμαι, 96.
ἔδομαι, not ἐδοῦμαι, 92.
ἐδράσθην, or ἐδράθην? 101.
ἐδυνησάμην, 189 note.
ἔδωκα, 220.
-έειν, verbs in, contraction of, 296 ff.
ἕζεσθαι for **καθέζεσθαι**, 6.
ἔζωμαι, not ἔζωσμαι, 99.
ἔθανον, 39.
ἐθέλειν or **θέλειν** ? 415.

ἐθελοντηδόν, 59.
ἐθελοντήν, 60.
ἐθελοντήρ, 57.
ἐθελοντής, 57.
ἐθελοντί, 59.
ἐθελούσιος, 60.
ἔθηκα, 220.
εἰ-, verbs beginning in, augmentation of, 245.
εἰκάζειν, future of, 409, 410.
εἴλλειν, orthography of, 89, 90.
εἶμι, always future in meaning, 103, 111; infinitive of, 65.
εἶμα, 19.
εἶπα, εἶπον, 219.
εἶπον, 326 ff.
εἴρηκα, 326 ff.
εἰς, with adverbs, 117 ff.; replaces ἐς, 432.
-εις, late form of acc. pl. of substantives in ευς, 234.
εἰσάγαν, 119.
εἰσάπαξ, 118.
εἰσάρτι, 119.
εἰσαῦθις, 118.
εἰσάχρι, 119.
εἰσμάτην, 119.
εἰσότε, 117.
εἶτεν, 204.
ἐκ, with adverbs, 117 ff.; Ionic and poetical compounds of, 7.
ἐκαθήμην, 81.
ἐκάθιζον, 81.
ἔκανον, 217.
ἕκας, old Attic, 28.
ἐκεῖ and ἐκεῖσε, confused, 114.
ἐκεῖθεν, 116.
ἐκεῖνος, only form known to Attic, 4.
ἐκζεῖν, metaphorical use of, 17.
ἐκθεᾶσθαι, 7.
ἔκθεμα, 319.
ἐκθύειν, 7.
ἐκκλησιάζειν, augment of, 82.
ἐκκοπή, 158.
ἐκλαγχάνειν, 7.
ἐκλήγειν, 7.
ἐκμανθάνειν, 7.
ἐκνόμιος, 46.
ἑκοντής, 57.
ἑκοντί, 59.
ἑκούσιος, 60.
ἔκπαγλος, in Xenophon, 168.
ἐκπαγλούμενος, 14.
ἔκπαλαι, 117.
ἐκπείθειν, 7.
ἐκπέρυσι, 119.
ἐκπροτιμᾶν, 7.
ἐκσημαίνειν, 7.
ἐκστέλλεσθαι, 7.
ἐκσώζειν, 7.
ἔκτανον, 217.
ἐκτενής, 365.
ἐκτιμᾶν, 7.
ἔκτοτε, 116.
ἐκτρίβειν, metaphorical use of, 17, 18.
ἔκτρωμα, 288.
ἐκτρῶσαι, 288.
ἐκφοβεῖσθαι, 7.
ἑκὼν εἶναι, rules for the use of in Attic Greek, 340 ff.
ἐλλύχνιον, 250.
ἐλαία, old Attic and Tragic for ἐλάα, 112.
ἔλακον, Euripidean word, 43.
ἐλαστρεῖν, 14.
ἐλαύνειν, perfects of, 96, 100.
ἐλέγχειν, perfects of, 96.
ἔλειψα, never aorist of **λείπειν**, 217.
ἐλεύσομαι, Attic except in Indicative, 103, 110.
Ἑλλάς, as adjective, 21.
ἐμάστιξα, survival of in Attic, 16.
ἔμολον, un-Attic, 41.
ἐμπαίζειν, meaning of, 68.
ἐμπλῆσθαι, survival of in Attic, 63.
ἐμπολᾶν, augment of, 82.
ἐμπολή, 168.
ἐμπρέπειν, 15.
ἐμπρησμός, 419.
ἐμπτύειν, meaning of, 66.
ἐμπυρισμός, un-Attic, 419.
ἐν, force of in composition, 66; intensive, 67; **ἐν χρῷ**, Attic phrase, 132.
ἔναγχος, 70.
ἐνάλλεσθαι, 67.
ἐναντιοῦσθαι, 188; augmentation of, 81.
ἐνάρετος, 412.
ἔνδον, 206.
ἐνδυμενία, un-Attic, 418.
ἔνεγγυς, 120.
ἐνεπλήμην, survival of in Attic, 63.
ἔνερθε, old Attic word, 27.
ἔνεροι, old Attic word, 27.
ἐνέρτεροι, Ionic and old Attic, 27.
ἐνέτεξα, 219.
ἐνεχυριμαῖα, ἐνέχυρα, 468.
ἐνήλατα, 267.
ἐνθήκη, 304.
ἐνθυμεῖσθαι, 191.
ἐνιαυσιαῖος, ἐνιαύσιος, 467.
ἐνορᾶν, meaning of, 67.
ἐνουρεῖν, meaning of, 66.
ἐνοχλεῖν, augment of, 83–85.
ἐντευτλανοῦν, corrupt for ἐντευτλιοῦν, 128.
ἐντέχνως, 457.
ἐντρώγειν, meaning of, 67.
ἐνυβρίζειν, meaning of, 68.

ἔνυστρον, orthography of, 250.
ἐξ, compounds of, 490.
ἐξάδελφος, un-Attic, 361.
ἐξαιτεῖν, 7.
ἐξακούειν, 7.
ἐξαλλάσσειν, meaning of, 467.
ἐξαλαπάζειν, in Xenophon, 168.
ἐξαμβλίσκειν, 288.
ἐξάμβλωμα, 288.
ἐξανάγεσθαι, 7.
ἐξαναγκάζειν, 7.
ἐξανέχεσθαι, 7.
ἐξαπαλλάσσεσθαι, 7.
ἐξαπολλύναι, 7.
ἐξαποφθείρειν, 7.
ἐξείλλειν, orthography of, 89, 90.
ἐξελευθεροστομεῖν, 7.
ἐξατιμάζειν, 7.
ἐξεπιπολῆς, 205.
ἐξεπίστασθαι, 7.
ἐξεργάζεσθαι = *ἀποκτείνειν*, 16 note.
ἐξέτι, 119.
ἐξεφίεσθαι, 7.
ἐξημεροῦν, 7.
ἐξηρήσατο, impossible form in Attic, 216.
ἐξιδιάζεσθαι, 284.
ἐξονυχίζειν, 350.
ἐξυπνίζειν, 305.
-εος, adjectives in, 287, 288.
ἐπακρίζειν, formation of, 127.
ἐπαμφοτερίζειν, 127.
ἐπανορθοῦν, augment of, 86, 87.
ἐπαοιδή, 315.
ἐπαρήγειν, 168.
ἐπαρίστερος, 324.
ἐπαυρέσθαι, survival of in Attic, 30.
ἐπαφᾶν, old word, 392.
ἐπείσθην, 217.
ἔπειτεν, late form, 204.
ἐπέλησα, influence of the *ἐπί*, 216.
ἐπί, in composition, producing a causative meaning, 216.
ἐπὶ κόρρης, 257.
ἐπιγλωττᾶσθαι, 193.
ἐπιδαψιλεύεσθαι, 168.
ἐπιδέξιος, 324.
ἐπίδεσμος, gender of, 353.
ἐπιδήν, 121.
ἐπίδοξος, 208.
ἐπιζεῖν, metaphorical use of, 17.
ἐπιθεάζειν, orthography of, 275.
ἐπιθόμην, 217.
ἔπιθον, 217.
ἐπικηρύσσειν **ἀργύριον** s. **χρήματά τινι**, 329.
ἐπίκλιντρον, 207.
ἐπιλέγειν, 327.
ἐπίλογος, 327.
ἐπιορκεῖν, future of, 409.
ἐπιπολῆς, 205.
ἐπιπρόσω, 120.
ἐπίσημος, 208.
ἐπίστασαι, *ἐπίστα*, *ἐπίστασο*, *ἐπίστω*, 463.
ἐπίστασις, 345.
ἐπιτακτήρ, 165.
ἐπιτέλλειν, 204, 205.
ἐπίτεξ, 417.
ἐπτηδεύειν, augment of, 80.
ἐπίτοκος, un-Attic, 417.
ἐπιτολή, meaning of, 205.
ἐπιτροπιάζειν, 158.
ἐπιψηφίζειν, 216, 217.
ἐπριάμην, 210, 214.
ἐπρίασο, *ἐπρίω*, 463.
ἐπῳδή, 315.
ἐργοδοτεῖν, **ἐργοδότης**, 456.
ἔρδειν, old Attic word, 29; survival of in certain Attic proverbs, 49.
ἐρεῖν, 326 ff.
ἐρείπειν, in Xenophon, 168.
ἐρείπια, old Attic word, 15.
ἐρεύγεσθαι, 138.
ἕρπειν, survival of in Attic, 50.
ἐρρήθην, 326.
ἐρυγγάνειν, 138.
ἐρύκειν, 168.
ἔρχομαι, Attic only in Indic., 103.
ἐς, date of change to *εἰς*, 432.
-εσαν, 3 pers. pl. plupf. act, 229 ff.
ἐσάπαξ, 118.
ἐσαῦθις, 118.
ἐσαυτίκα, 118.
ἐσέπειτα, 118.
ἔσθης, 19.
ἐσθίειν, perfects of, 96.
ἔσθ' ὅπη, 339.
ἐστήξειν, 411.
ἑστιᾶν, 29.
ἑστιᾶσθαι, 188.
ἐσχάτως, 481.
ἐσχατώτατος, 144.
ἑτερόφθαλμος, 209.
εὐ-, verbs beginning in, augmentation of, 245.
εὐαγγελεῖν, Atticicity of, 335.
εὐαγγελίζεσθαι, construction of, 334.
Εὐβοΐδα, orthography of, 160.
εὕειν, 61.
-εύειν, perfects passive of verbs in, 101; origin of verbs in, 61; deponents in, 141.
εὔειρος, 224.
εὐέριος, 224.
εὔερος, 224.
εὔζωρος, 223; comparative of, 224.
εὐθημοσύνη, 168.
εὐθύ and *εὐθύς*, distinguished, 222.
εὔθυνα, 74.

εὐκαιρεῖν, late use of, 205.
εὐκερματεῖν, 467.
εὐκοιτεῖν, late use of, 69.
εὐνάζειν, 169.
εὐνοικῶς, 221.
εὔνους, adverb of, 221.
εὔνως, 221.
εὐξύμβλητος, 20.
εὔρασθαι, un-Attic, 215.
εὕρεμα, εὕρημα, 501.
-*ευς*, nom. and acc. pl. of substantives in, 234 note.
εὐστάθεια, 347.
εὐσταθής, 347.
εὐσύμβολος, 20.
εὐσχήμων, signification of, 417.
εὐφρόνη, old Attic word, 13.
εὐχαριστεῖν, meaning of, 69.
εὐχάριστος, meaning of, 69.
εὐχρηστεῖν, late use of, 487.
-*εύω*, origin of verb-termination, 61.
εὐωχεῖσθαι, 188.
ἐφέστιος, 15.
ἔφευξα, un-Attic as aor. of *φεύγειν*, 217.
ἔφης, 225.
ἔφησθα, 225 ff.
ἔφθασα, 217.
ἐφίορκος, 363.
ἐφιστάναι, meaning of, 345.
ἐφοβησάμην, 189 note.
ἔφρηκα, existence of in Attic, 220, 221.
ἔχεεν, aorist, 300.
ἐχθές, orthography of, 370 ff.
ἐχθραίνειν, in Xenophon, 169.
ἐχρῆν or *χρῆν* ? 81.
ἐωνησάμην, 50, 210.
ἕως, form of in Xenophon, 164.

Z.

ζα, Tragic for *δια-*, 5.
ζεῖν, metaphorical use of, 17.
ζεύγλη, 19.
ζῆν, 133.
ζόη, Ionic and Tragic for *ζωή*, 5.
ζύγον, 19.
ζώνη, 19.
ζωννύναι, perf. pass. of, 99.
ζωρός, 223.
ζωστήρ, 12, 19.

H.

ἦ, true Attic form of first pers. sing. impf. ind. of *εἰμί*, 242 ff.
ᾔδει(ν), 236.
ᾔδεμεν, 238.
ᾔδη, 236.
ᾔδησθα, not *ᾔδης*, the true Attic 2 pers. sing. of *ᾔδη*, 226 ff.
-*ηθήσομαι*, futures in, 189 note.
ἦθος, rules for the use of, 468.
ἠϊών, in Xenophon, 169.
ἧκα, 220.
ᾔκειν, 3 sing. past of *ἔοικα*, 231.
ἠλίβατος, in Xenophon, 169.
ἡμερήσιος, 125.
ἡμερινός, 125.
ἡμέριος, 125.
ἤμην, 240, 241.
-*ήμην*, optatives in, 63.
ἡμίκακος, 419.
ἡμικεφάλαιον, 412.
ἡμίκραιρα, 412.
ἡμίκρανον, 412.
ἡμιμόχθηρος, 419.
ἦμος, old Attic and poetical word, 28.
ἠμπειχόμην, 83–86.
ἠμπεσχόμην, 83–86.
ἦν or *ἦ*, the latter the best Attic form, 242, 243.
ἤνεγκα and *ἤνεγκον*, supplement one another in Attic, 220.
ἠνειχόμην, 83–86.
ἠνεσχόμην, 83–86.
ἡνίκα, uses of in Attic, 122 ff.
ἦνυστρον, orthography of, 250.
ἦξα, early Attic aor. of *ἄγω*, 349.
ἠπήσασθαι, old word, 47, 175.
ἠπητής, old word, 175, 176.
ἠπίστασο, ἠπίστω, 463.
-*ηρ*, substantival termination, 57, 58; used by Xenophon for -*ής*, 59.
ᾐρησάμην, impossible form in Attic, 216.
ἠρινός, 125.
ἥρως, Attic inflexions of, 248.
ἦς, un-Attic for *ἦσθα*, 225.
-*ής*, substantival termination, 57 ff.
ἦσθα, 225 ff.
ἦσθας, a very doubtful form, 228.
-*ήσομαι*, futures in, corrupted, 194, 195.
ἠφευμένος, 81.
ἠφίει, 81.
ἠώς, in Xenophon, 164.

Θ.

-*θα*, in second person sing., 226 ff.
θάλπειν, in Xenophon, 169.
θαμβεῖν, 29.
θανεῖν, old Attic and poetical, 39.
θαυμάζειν, 29.
θεήλατος, 15.
θειάζειν, 275.
θείνειν, survival of in Attic, 10.
θέλειν, un-Attic, 415, 416.
-*θεν*, adverbs in, 177.

θεόθυτος, 249.
θεοπρόπος, 15.
θεράπαινα, history of the word, 22.
θεραπεύειν, 61.
θεραπευτήρ, in Xenophon, 165.
θεράπων, history of the word, 22.
θερμασία, un-Attic, 198.
θέρμα, 3rd declension, not 1st, 414.
θέρμη, 198, 414.
θερμότης, 198.
θεσπίζειν, 29.
θήγειν, in Xenophon, 169.
θηλάζειν, future of, 401.
-θῆναι, aorists in, 186 ff.
-θήσομαι, futures in, 189 note.
θιγγάνειν, in Xenophon, 169; un-Attic, 391.
θοινᾶν, 29.
θριδακίνη, 207.
θρίδαξ, 207.
θρώσκειν, 29.
θυεία, 251.
θυηχοῦς, 196.
θυμέλη, meaning of the term, 250.
θυμοῦσθαι, 29.
θωκεῖν, 15.

I.

-αίνειν, aorist of verbs in, 77.
ἴγδις, history of the word, 251.
ἰδιολογεῖσθαι, 193.
ἴδιος, late use of, 499.
ἰδιοῦσθαι, 284.
ἱεῖς, true Attic form of, 2 pers. sing. pres. ind. of *ἵημι*, 316, 317.
ἱερόθυτος, 249.
ἰέναι, Attic forms of, 65.
ἱέναι, 2nd pers. sing. pres. ind., 316; aorist of, 220.
-ίζειν, verbs in, their meaning often dependent upon context, 178.
-ίζεσθαι, deponents in, 141.
ἵης, un-Attic, 316, 317.
ἰθαγενής, 15.
ἰθύς, 223.
ἱκεσία, history of the word, 61.
ἱκετεία, 61.
ἱκετεύειν, 61.
ἱκνεῖσθαι = *ἀφικνεῖσθαι*, 6.
Ἰλιάς, used as an adjective, 21.
ἴλλειν, orthography of, 89, 90.
ἰλύς, meaning of the term, 147.
ἱμάτιον, meaning of, 22.
ἱππεύς, 19.
ἱππότης = *ἱππεύς*, in Tragedy and Xenophon, 19, 170; as adjective, 21.
ἵπτασθαι, 373.
ἱστών, 252.
ἰσχναίνειν, aorist of, 78.

K.

καθαρός, of water, 113.
καθεδοῦμαι, 336.
καθέζεσθαι, 336.
καθεσθῆναι, 336.
καθεσθήσομαι, 336.
καθήμην, 81.
κάθησθαι, 336; augmentation of, 81.
κάθησο, distinguished from *κάθιζε*, 336.
καθιεροῦν, 279.
καθίζειν, augmention of, 81; uses of in Attic, 336.
καθυβρίζειν, meaning of, 66.
καθώς, a late word, 495.
καίειν, old Attic and Trag. for *κάειν*, 112; future of, 408.
καίνειν, un-Attic, 170.
κακαγγελεῖν, 335.
κακκάβη, **κάκκαβος**, 496.
κακοδαιμονᾶν and **κακοδαιμονεῖν**, distinguished, 152.
κακοδαίμων, meaning of, 152.
καλίνδειν, orthography of, 90.
καλλιγραφεῖν, 203.
καλλιώτερον, 209.
καλχαίνειν, aorist of, 78.
καμμύειν, 426.
κάμνειν = *χαλεπῶς φέρειν*, 16 note.
κανεῖν, un-Attic, 217.
καρατομεῖν, 427.
καρῆναι and *κείρασθαι*, distinguished, 368.
κάρτα, history of the word, 8.
κασίγνητος, 15.
κάτα, force of in composition with verbs, 66; **κατ' ἐκεῖνο καιροῦ**, 345; **κατὰ κοιλίας ποιεῖν**, 363; **κατὰ χειρός**, 375.
καταγελᾶν, 66.
κατακεντεῖν, 296.
καταλογή, meaning of, 498.
καταπροίξεται, orthography of, 160; meaning of the term, 254.
καταπτύειν, 66.
κατάσκοπος, 25.
καταυτόθι, 121.
καταφαγᾶς, un-Attic, 497.
καταφονεύειν, 15.
κατασχάζειν, 296.
καταφερής, meaning of, 498.
καταχεῖν, 66.
κατέθανον, un-Attic, 39.
κατείλλειν, orthography of, 89, 90.
κατεργάζεσθαι = *ἀποκτείνειν*, 16 note.
καθανεῖν, un-Attic, 39.
κατόπτης, 25.
κατορθοῦν, 319.

κατόρθωμα, 319, 320.
κατόρθωσις, 320.
κατουρεῖν, 66.
κεγχρεών, 253.
κεῖνος, Ionic, 4.
κείρειν, aorists of, 368.
κεκραγμός, 423.
κελεύειν, perf. pass. of, 101.
κέκλημαι, 102.
κεκόλουμαι, not *κεκόλουσμαι*, 99.
κέρτομος, 15.
κεφαλαιωδέστατος, 339.
κεφαλοτομεῖν, 427.
κικλήσκειν, un-Attic, 48.
κλαδεύειν, 255.
κλάειν, better than *κλαίειν*, 112; future of, 404.
κλᾶν, 255.
κλαυσοῦμαι, un-Attic, 91, 92.
κλέπτειν, future of, 407, 408.
κλέπτης, 20.
κληδών, 15.
κλῄειν, aorist and perf. pass. of, 102.
κληρονομεῖν, construction of, 206.
κλῄζειν, in Xenophon, 170.
-κλῆς, acc. sing. of substantives in, 246.
κλητήρ, 58.
κλίβανος, orthography of, 267.
κλωπεύειν, poetical word in Xenophon, 170.
κλώψ, old Attic and poetical, 19.
κνέφαλον, 256.
κνήμη, 413.
κνῆν, contraction of, 133, 134.
κοινών, in Xenophon, 170.
κοιτών, 321.
κόλακες, 214.
κόλλαβοι, 280.
κόλλοπες, 280.
κολλυβιστής, **κόλλυβος**, late use of, 499.
κολόκυνθα, **κολοκύντη**, 498.
κολούειν, perf. pass. of, 99.
κολυμβάδες, un-Attic, 199.
κολυμβήθρα, 369.
κομίζειν, 191.
κόνις, 25.
κόπτειν θύραν, 266.
κοράσιον, un-Attic, 148.
κορεῖν, Attic for *σαίρειν*, 156, 157.
κόρημα, Attic for *σάρον*, 156.
κόριον, 148.
κόρις, gender of, 362.
κορίσκη, 148.
κορός, 311.
κορυδαλός, 426.
κόρυδος, 426.
κορυφαιότατος, 143.
κουρίας, 132.
κοῦρος, un-Attic, 311.
κοχλιάριον, 369.
κράββατος, un-Attic, 137, 138.
κραδαίνειν, aorist of, 78.
κραστήρια, 267.
κρατήρ, 58.
κραυγασμός, 423.
κρεισσότερον, 209.
κρίβανος, orthography of, 267.
κροῦσαι θύραν, 266.
κρύβεσθαι, un-Attic, 368.
κτανεῖν, 217.
κῦδος, 25.
κυδρός, in Xenophon, 170.
Κύκλωπες, not all one-eyed, 210.
κυναγός, 496.
κυνάριον, 268.
κυνηγέτης, 496.
κυνίδιον, 268.
κύπτειν, future of, 398.
κωλύφιον, 151.

Λ.

Λαβρός, 26.
λάγνης, 272.
λάγνος, orthography of, 272.
λαγός, **λαγώς**, 272.
λαικάζειν, future of, 402.
-λαίνειν, aorist of verbs in, 77.
Λάκαινα, limitations of usage of, 427.
λακεῖν, un-Attic aorist, 43.
λαλεῖν, future of, 388.
λαμπάς, 131.
λαμπτήρ, 131.
λάμυρος, meaning of, 352.
λάσκειν, un-Attic verb, 43; aorists of, 219.
λάσταυρος, meaning of, 282.
λάφυρα, in Xenophon, 170.
λάχος, in Xenophon, 171.
λέγειν, future of, 388.
λεηλατεῖν, in Xenophon, 171.
λεκάριον, 265.
λεπτόγεως, 357.
λέχριος, in Xenophon, 171.
λεωργός, in Xenophon, 171.
λήθαργος, late use of, 491.
λῄς, 171.
λίβανος, **λιβανωτός**, distinguished, 273.
λιθάριον, 268.
λιθίδιον, 268.
λιμός, gender of, 274.
λιπαίνειν, aorist of, 78.
λίσσεσθαι, 25 note 8.
λίτρον, orthography of, 369.
λισφός, orthography of, 196.
λιταί, 25.
λίτρου ἀφρός, 361.

λόγιος, meaning of, 284.
λοιδορεῖσθαι, 191 ff.
Λολλιανός, 65.
λούειν, Attic inflexions of, 274 ff.
λούεσθαι, &c., late forms of **λοῦσθαι**, &c., 90.
λυμαίνεσθαι, 193.
λυμαντήρ, in Xenophon, 165, 171.
λυχνεῖον, meaning of, 132.
λυχνιά, meaning of, 367.
λυχνοῦχος, meaning of, 367.
λωβᾶσθαι, reason for middle inflexions of, 193, 410.

M.

μαγειρεῖον, 341.
-μαίνειν, verbs in, aorists of, 76.
μάλη, in Attic confined to the phrase ὑπὸ μάλης, 282.
μαλκίειν, orthography of, 155, 156.
μάμμη, 208.
μαμμίον, 208.
μαμμόθρεπτος, 359.
μαστεύειν, in Xenophon, 171.
μαστίξαι, survival of in Attic, 10.
μάχεσθαι, reason for middle inflexions of, 193.
μέγα, used adverbially, 28; *μέγα δύνασθαι*, 283.
μεγιστᾶνες, un-Attic term, 283.
μέθυσος, 240.
μεθυστικός, 240.
μειράκιον, μειρακίσκος, μειρακύλλιον, μεῖραξ, differentiated, 291.
μέλλειν, construction of, 420 ff.
μέμφεσθαι, reason for middle inflexions of, 193.
μὲν οὖν, 428.
μεσεγγυηθῆναι, 202.
μεσημβρία, μεσημβρινός, 125, 126.
μέσης νυκτός, 126.
μεσιδιωθῆναι, 202.
μεσόγαια, orthography of, 358.
μεσοδάκτυλα, 281.
μέσον νυκτῶν, 126.
μεσονύκτιον, un-Attic, 126.
μεσοπορεῖν, late use of, 491.
μεσούσης νυκτός, 126.
μεταῦθις, 21.
μεταχειρίζεσθαι, 190.
μετόπισθεν, 120.
μετριάζειν, meaning of, 494.
μέχρι, orthography of, 64; *μέχρι ἄν* with mood of verb, 65.
μηδὲ εἷς, 271.
μηθείς, 271.
μήκιστος, 171.
μηνίειν, old Attic word, 29; orthography of, 155.
μηρύειν, in Xenophon, 171.
μητρόθεν, 177.
μιαρία, μιαρός, 428.
μιμνήσκεσθαι, aorist of, 190.
μνηστήρ, in Xenophon, 165.
μολεῖν, history of, 41.
μονθυλεύειν, 461.
μονοκοιτεῖν, 69.
μονόμματος, meaning of, 209.
μονόφθαλμος, 209.
μόρος, 15.
μόχθος, in Xenophon, 171.
μόχλος, orthography of, 362.
μυελός, orthography of, 364.
μύκης, 284.
μυκτήρ, 58.
μύνη, 74.
μυσαρός, 15.
μυσάττεσθαι, in Xenophon, 172.
μωμᾶσθαι, reason for middle inflexions of, 193.

N.

ν ἐφελκυστικόν, in pluperfect act., 231, 232.
νᾶπυ, only Attic form, 349.
ναρός, history of word, 114.
ναῦς, Attic inflexions of, 254.
ναύτης, 20.
ναυτίλλεσθαι, 20, note 1; *ναυτίλος*, ib.
νεῖσθαι, in Xenophon, 172.
νεογνός, in Xenophon, 172.
νεομηνία, 225.
νέος, 20.
νεοττός, νεοττίον, orthography of, 287.
νεοχμός, 20.
νέρθε, 27.
νεύειν, 61.
νεύσομαι, not *νευσοῦμαι*, 92.
νεφρός, 359.
νεωστί, 70.
νὴ τὼ θεώ, limitations to use of, 281.
νήθειν, late form of *νῆν*, 90.
νῆν, Attic inflexions of, 133 ff.
νηρός, of water, 113.
νήστης, un-Attic, 375.
νητικός, not *νηστικός*, 135.
νίμμα, 280.
νίτρον, 361.
νίφειν, orthography of, 90.
νομός, 'dwelling-place,' 16 note.
νοσσός, νοσσίον, 287.
νοσφίζειν, in Xenophon, 172.
νουμηνία, 225.
νοῦς καὶ φρένες, 9.
νυκτερήσιος, νυκτερινός, distinguished, 125.
νῶτον, νῶτος, 351.

Ξ.

ξεῖν (to polish), always contracts in Attic, 301.
ξενιτεύεσθαι, anomalous formation of, 62.
ξενοδόκος, 362.
ξηρός, 20.
ξυλάριον, ξυλήφιον, ξυλύφιον, 151.
ξυμβάλλεσθαι γνώμην, retention of ξύν for σύν in this phrase, 24 note 2.
ξύν, date of change to σύν, 24 note 2.
ξύνεγγυς, 119.
ξυνός = κοινός, 5.
ξύστρα, 358.

O.

'Οδμή, orthography of, 160, 164.
ὀδοῦν, 16 note.
οἷ and οὗ, confused, 114.
οἰ-, augment of verbs beginning in, 244.
-οίατο, as optative ending, 431.
οἶδας, doubtful form, 227.
οἰζυρός, orthography of, 160.
οἴκαδε for οἴκοι, 115 ff.
οἰκιστήρ, 58.
οἰκογενής, 285.
οἰκοδεσπότης, 470.
οἰκοδομή, un-Attic, 493.
οἰκόσιτος, 285.
οἰκότριψ, 285.
οἶμαι, οἴομαι, both good Attic, 432.
οἰμώζειν, future of, 384, 385.
οἶς, orthography of, 160.
οἶσθας, a doubtful form, 227, 228.
οἰστίς, orthography of, 160.
ὀκτώ, compounds of, 490.
ὄλβος, 25; in Xenophon, 172.
ὀλλύναι, perfects of, 96.
ὀλοσφύρατος, 286.
ὅμαιμος, 15.
ὁμῆλιξ, 15.
ὀμνύναι, perfects of, 95 ff.
ὁμόνους, adverb of, 221.
ὄμφαξ, 126.
ὄναρ, late usage of, 494.
ὀνθυλεύειν, 461.
ὀνυχίζειν, 350.
ὀπάων, 22.
ὁπηνίκα, 122, 123.
ὄπισθεν, orthography of, 60.
ὅποι, ὅπου, confused, 114.
ὀπτάνιον, meaning of, 341.
ὀπτήρ, in Xenophon, 165.
ὀπωρινός, 125.
ὀπωροπώλης, 286.
ὀπωρώνης, 286.
ὀργαίνειν, aorist of, 78.
ὀργεών, 24.
ὄργια, history of the word, 24.
ὀρθοστάδιος, 312.
ὀρθούμενος = successful, 320.
ὀρθρινός, ὄρθριος, 124.
ὄρθρος, meaning of, 341.
ὅρισμα, 20.
ὁρκίζειν and **ὁρκοῦν**, 466.
ὁρμᾶσθαι, 188.
ὅρμενα, meaning of, 196.
ὁρμίζεσθαι, 190.
ὀρύσσειν, perfects of, 95, 96.
ὀσδηποτοῦν, un-Attic, 471.
ὀσμή, orthography of, 160, 164.
οὐδείς, οὐθείς, 271.
-οῦν, perfects passive of verbs in, 101.
οὖς, inflexions of, 291.
οὐχ οἷον, 470.
ὀφρύη, ὀφρύς, 20.
ὄχημα, ὄχος, 20.
ὄχθος, 25; in Xenophon, 172.
ὀχλεῖν = ἐνοχλεῖν, 5.
ὄψιμος, ὀψινός, ὄψιος, 124.

Π.

πάγχυ, 21.
παιδίσκη, meaning of, 312.
παίειν, Attic forms of, 258 ff.
παίζειν, future of, 91, 313; aorist of, 313.
παλαιστής, 356.
παλαιστικός, παλαιστρικός, 314.
παλαμναῖος, in Xenophon, 172.
παλαστή, orthography of, 356.
πάλι, πάλιν, 347.
πάλλειν, 29.
πάλος, meaning of, 13.
πανδοκεῖον, πανδοχεῖον, 362.
παντὶ σθένει, 10.
πάντοτε, 183.
πανώλεθρος, a Tragic word, 18 note.
παπταίνειν, aorist of, 78.
πάπυρος, 360.
παραβάλλεσθαι, παραβόλιον, 312.
παράδειγμα, 62.
παραθήκη, παρακαταθήκη, 366.
παρακοπή, 158.
παρακορεῖν, 156.
παράσιτος, history of the term, 214.
παρατιθέσθαι, meaning of, 312.
παραυτόθεν, 120.
πάρεγγυς, 120.
παρεκεῖ, 120.
παρεμβολή, late use of, 473.
παρενθήκη, 304.
παρηΐς, 20.
παροινεῖν, augment of, 83, 85.
παροψίς, meaning of, 265.

πατάξαι, only tense of *πατάσσειν* used in Attic, 257.
πατεῖν, future of, 397, 398.
πάτρα, *πατρίς*, 18, 19.
πεινῆν, 132.
πειρᾶν, aorists of, 191, 192.
πελάζειν, 29.
πέλας, 28.
Πελαργός, 195.
πέντε, compounds of, 489.
πεπαίνειν, aorist of, 78.
πεπᾶσθαι, in Xenophon, 173.
πεποίθησις, 355.
πεποτῆσθαι, 373 ff.
πέπρημαι, not *πέπρησμαι*, 102.
πέπων, 323.
πέρ, limitations to use of, 21.
περαιοῦσθαι, 188.
περιείλλειν, 89, 90.
περιέπειν, in Xenophon, 173.
περιέσσευσεν, corrupt form, 79.
περικοπή, 158.
περισπᾶσθαι, meaning of, 491.
περισσεύειν, augment of, 79.
περίστασις, meaning of, 473.
περιστερεών, survival of in Attic, 253.
Περσίς, adjectival, 21.
πέτεσθαι, Attic forms of, 373 ff.
πέτρινος, *πετρώδης*, 20.
πεύσομαι, not *πευσοῦμαι*, 93.
πηδᾶν, 29.
πηλίκος, meaning of, 127.
πηλός, gender of, 126.
πηνίκα, meaning of, 122.
πιεῖσθαι, late form of *πιέσθαι*, 91.
πιθεῖν, 217.
πίνεσθαι = *πίνειν* (?), 382.
πιοῦμαι, late form of *πιόμαι*, 91.
πίσυνος, un-Attic, 21.
πλάζεσθαι, *πλανᾶσθαι*, 21.
πλεονεκτεῖν, future of, 408.
πλεύσομαι, not *πλευσοῦμαι*, 93.
πληγὰς διδόναι, *πληγὴν διδόναι*, 258 ff.
πλήσσειν, limitations to its use in Attic, 258 ff.
πλόκιον, 324.
πνεῖν, future of, 401.
πνεύσομαι, not *πνευσοῦμαι*, 92.
πνῖγος, 185.
ποδανιπτήρ, 58.
ποδαπός, meaning of, 128-130.
ποθεῖν, future of, 404.
ποῖ, **ποῦ**, confused, 114.
ποινή, 25, 26.
πονεῖν, parts of, 191.
πορεύεσθαι, parts of, 189.
πορθμός, 12 note; *πορθμός*, *πόρος*, 20.
πορνοκόπος, 491.
πορσύνειν, in Xenophon, 173.
ποταπός, orthography and meaning, 128-130.
ποτᾶσθαι, Attic usage of, 189.
πραγματεύεσθαι, parts of, 191.
πράκτορες, 58.
πρίασθαι, Attic usage of, 210-214.
πρίασο, *πρίω*, 48, 212 note.
προαλῶς, 317.
προβασκάνιον, 159.
προδωμάτιον, 321.
προειρημένα, τά, 334.
προηγορευμένα, τά, 334.
προθεσμία, 78.
προκοιτών, 321.
προκοπή, **προκόπτειν**, 158.
προνοεῖσθαι, parts of, 190.
πρόνους, 26.
πρόπαλαι, 119.
προπάροιθεν, 120.
προπέρυσιν, 119.
προπηλακίζειν, derivation of, 127; future of, 410.
προσείλλειν, orthography of, 89, 90.
προσέτι, 119.
πρόσφατος, of water, 113; of things generally, 471.
προσφάτως, 70.
πρόσωπα, late use of, 474.
πρώιμος, *πρωινός*, *πρῷος*, 124, 125.
πρώτως, un-Attic, 366.
πτέσθαι, 373 ff.
πτήσσειν, 21.
πτύειν, future of, 394.
πτῶμα, **πτῶσις**, compounds of, 319.
πτῶμα, limitations to use of in Attic, 472.
πτώσσειν, 21.
πύελος, 364, 372.
πυρία, 372.
πωλήσω, an un-Attic form, 48 note 2.

Ρ.

-ραίνειν, aorists of verbs in, 76 ff.
ῥάξ, gender and orthography of, 148, 149.
ῥᾳότερος, 487.
ῥαπίζειν, 264.
ῥάπισμα, 257, 264.
ῥαφανίς, **ῥάφανος**, 221.
ῥαφίς, 174.
ῥεῖθρον, 20; in Xenophon, 173.
ῥεῦμα, 20.
ῥηθήσομαι, 326.
ῥοίδιον, orthography of, 159.
ῥύεσθαι, metaphorical use of, 11.
ῥύμη, late use of, 487.
ῥύπος, 238.
ῥύπτειν, meaning of, 239.

ῥυτήρ, 58.
ῥώξ, gender and orthography of, 148.

Σ.

σ, rules for, in perfect passive, 97–101.
σάκκος, σάκος, 323.
σαλπίζειν, σαλπικτής, 279.
σαπρός, meaning of, 474.
σάρον, σαροῦν, un-Attic, 156.
σαφηνίζειν, in Xenophon, 174.
σαφηνῶς, 21.
σαχυφάντης, 323.
σαώτερος, in Xenophon, 174.
σείειν, 29.
σέλας, 16 note.
σέσωμαι, not σέσωσμαι, 99.
σηκάζειν, in Xenophon, 174.
σθένειν, σθένος, survival of in Attic, 10.
σιδάρεος, 49.
σίκυον, 323.
σικχαίνεσθαι, 307.
σίλφη, orthography of, 359.
σίναπι, an un-Attic form, 349.
σιτομετρεῖσθαι, late use of, 477.
σκαιός, 324.
σκίμπους, 137.
σκληροκοιτεῖν, 69.
σκνιφός, σκνίψ, form and meaning of, 486.
σκοπεῖν, future of, 389.
σκορακίζειν, 127.
σκορπίζεσθαι, 295.
σκώπτειν, future of, 193.
σκώρ, inflexions of, 354.
σμῆγμα, σμῆμα, σμῆν, 321; σμῆν, 133.
σμητρίς, 322.
σμήχειν, un-Attic, 321.
σπιλάς, σπίλος, 87.
σποδός, un-Attic, 25.
σταθερός, meaning of, 293.
σταμνία, meaning of, 486.
στατός, 312.
στείχειν, old Attic and poetical word, 29, 400.
στέμφυλα, meaning of, 489.
στηθίδιον, στηθύνιον, 477.
στιβαδοκοιτεῖν, 69.
στλεγγίς, 358.
στρατάρχης, 16.
στρατηλατεῖν, 15.
στρηνιᾶν, 475.
στρόβιλος, meaning of, 484.
στρογγύλος, 182, 183.
στρωματεύς, meaning of, 487.
στυγεῖν, un-Attic, 40.
στυππεῖνος, στυπεῖον, &c., 325.
σύαγρος, 476.
συγγνωμονεῖν, 476.
συγκαταβαίνειν, late meaning of, 485.
συγκοπή, 158.
συγκρίνειν, σύγκρισις, late use of, 344.
συμπαίστης, orthography of, 313.
συμπολίτης, 255.
σύμπτωμα, 318.
σύν, date of change in spelling of, 24, note 2; in composition with substantives, 256.
συνάντεσθαι, 349.
σύνεγγυς, 119.
συνείλλειν, 89, 90.
συντάσσεσθαι, meaning of in late Greek, 75.
συρίττειν, future of, 387 ff.
σύσσημον, 492.
συσχολαστής, un-Attic, 486.
σφυρήλατος, 286.
σχάζειν, σχᾶν, 296.
σχινδαλμός, orthography of, 196.
σώζειν, perfect passive of, 99.
σώματα, of slaves, 474

T.

τάραχος, 174.
ταυροῦν, pliability of meaning of, 179.
τάχιον, 149.
ταχύτατος, 150.
τεθεληκέναι, 415.
τεθνήξειν, 411.
τεῖσαι, not τῖσαι, the true Attic form, 90.
τελευταιότατος, 143.
τέμαχος and **τόμος**, distinguished, 72.
τέρμα, 26.
τηθελλαδοῦς, 359.
τήθη, 208.
τηνικάδε, τηνικαῦτα, strict meaning of, 122 ff.
τιθεῖς, τίθης, orthography of second pers. sing. pres. ind. act. of τιθέναι, 316, 317.
τιθέναι, inflexions of, 315 ff.; aorist of, 220.
τίκτειν, future of, 403.
τίφη, orthography of, 359.
τόμος and **τέμαχος**, distinguished, 72.
τραυλίζειν, future of, 382.
τράχηλος, 25.
τριπτήρ, 58.
τροπωτήρ, 58.
τροχαϊκός, orthography of, 111.
τρύβλιον, 265.
τρύγοιπος, 360.
τρύξ, 147.
τρυφεραίνεσθαι, aorist of, 77.
τυγχάνειν, construction of, 342; perfect of, 483.

τύλη, 256.
τύπτειν, limitations to its use in Attic, 257 ff.
τωθάζειν, future of, 193, 410.

Υ.

ὕαλος, 363.
ὑβρίζειν, future of, 193, 410.
ὑδρία, history of the word, 23.
υἱός, inflexions of, 141, 142.
ὑλιστήρ, 360.
-ύνειν, verbs in, formation of, 74; have no perfect active, 96.
ὑός, not *υἱός*, 143.
ὑπάγειν τὴν γαστέρα, 363.
ὑπαίθριος, ὕπαιθρος, 321.
ὑπάλλαγμα, meaning of, 362.
ὑπείλλειν, 89, 90.
ὑπέρδριμυς, 478.
ὑπέροχος, 26.
ὑπερτέλλειν, 16 note.
ὑπέρχεσθαι, in metaphorical sense inflected throughout, 109.
ὑπισχνεῖσθαι, aorist of, 190.
ὑπὸ μάλης, 282.
ὑπόδειγμα, 62.
ὑποθημοσύνη, 174.
ὑποστάθμη, meaning of, 147.
ὑπόστασις, meaning of, 348.
ὑποτροπιάζειν, 158.
-υς, substantives in, gen. sing. and pl. of, 318.
ὕσπληξ, gender and meaning, 146.
ὑστερίζειν, late construction of, 311.

Φ.

φάγεσθαι, 376.
φανός, meaning of, 131.
φᾶρος, history of the word, 22.
φάρυγξ, gender of, 139.
φατίζειν, un-Attic, 16.
φάτις, un-Attic, 20.
φεύξομαι, φευξοῦμαι, 93, 94.
φήμη, 20.
φθάνειν, aorists of, 217; future of, 396.
φθείρ, gender of, 362.
φθείρεσθαι, v. **βιάζεσθαι**, 144, 145.
φθίμενοι, οἱ, used by Xenophon, 174.
φιδάκνη, 196.
φιλόλογος, 483.
φιλοπαίσμων, orthography of, 313.
φλεΐνος, φλέως, φλοῦς, 355.
φοβεῖσθαι, passive, not middle, 189.
φοιτᾶν, fut. of, 400.
φοναί, φόνος, 20.
φονεύειν, poetical, 15.
φορβή, 26.
φορμοκοιτεῖν, 69.
φορτίον, φόρτος, 20.
φράζεσθαι, 190.
φραστήρ, 165.
φρενοῦν, in Xenophon, 174.
φρενῶν συμφορά, 9.
φρήν, un-Attic word, 9.
φρονιμεύεσθαι, 479.
φυγαδεύειν, 478.
φυλάττειν, corruption for *φυλάττεσθαι*, 379.
φύρδην, 174.

Χ.

χαλεπαίνειν, aorist of, 78.
χάραξ, gender, 137.
χαριεντίζεσθαι reason for middle inflexions of, 193.
χέζειν, future of, 92.
χειμάμυνα, 75.
χειμερινός, χειμέριος, 125.
χεῖν, aorist act. of, 300.
χείρ, inflexions of, 224.
χειρότερος, 209.
χειρώναξ, 16.
χερειότερος, 209.
χέρσος, 20.
χέσομαι or *χεσοῦμαι* ?, 92.
χήμη, 479.
χθές, orthography of, 370 ff.
χθεσινός, *χθεζινός*, **χθιζός**, 370.
χολάδες, 364.
χολή, χόλος, 20.
χόλικες, gender of, 364.
χολοῦσθαι, 29.
χονδροκοπεῖον, 365.
χονδροκωνεῖον, 365.
χοῦν, Attic inflexions of, 274.
χρεωλυτεῖν, 481.
χρέως, Attic inflexions of, 482.
χρῆν, ἐχρῆν, 81.
χρῆν, anomalous contraction of, 133, 134.
χρῆσθαι, 133.
χρησιμεύειν, 480.
χρίειν, aor. pass. of, 98; perfect pass. of, 98.
χρύσεος, 287.
χωρεῖν, fut. of, 397.

Ψ.

ψαύειν, un-Attic, 391.
ψελλίζεσθαι, 382.
ψῆν, 133, 134, 323.
ψηφοπαιστεῖν, 314.
ψήχειν, 323.
ψίαθος, 363.
ψιλόκουρος, 132.
ψιλός, 253.

ψοία, ψύα, 359.
ψύλλα, ψύλλος, 416.

Ω.

-ων, substantives in, 252.
ὠνάμην, un-Attic, 63.
ὠνεῖσθαι, usage of in Attic, 210–214.
ὠνήμην, 63.
ὠνὴν ποιεῖσθαι, 213, *τίθεσθαι*, 214.
ὠνησάμην, un-Attic, 50.
ὤνιος, 213.
-ωρ, substantival termination, 58.
ὥστε = *ὥσπερ*, *ἅτε*, 28.
ὤτοις, 291.
ὤφλησα, un-Attic, 219.

INDEX II.

Aeschines, 2. 15, p. 122; 14. 18, p. 474; 16. 23, p. 495; 23. 29, p. 471; 51. 5, p. 320; 67. 38, p. 117; 77. 11, p. 227; 82. 23, p. 195; 86. 27, p. 308; 90. 30, p. 387.

Aeschylus, *Agam.* 516, p. 248; 905, p. 85; 1274, p. 85; 1308, p. 217; 1313, p. 384; 1384, p. 290.

Choeph. 184, p. 263; 275, p. 179; 374, p. 465; 523, p. 242; 747, p. 85; 856, p. 275, note.

Eumen. 267, p. 78; 288, p. 112; 299, p. 112; 500, p. 401; 600, p. 290; 614, p. 112; 972, p. 78; 982, p. 436.

Pers. 767, p. 245; 1002, p. 60.

Prom. Vinct. 115, p. 164; 625, p. 422; 988, p. 93.

Sept. 374, p. 501; 520, p. 343; 709, p. 17; 961, p. 263.

Supp. 662, p. 436, 472; 807, p. 451; 983, p. 366; 1052, p. 436.

Andocides, 20. 20, p. 30; 20. 29, p. 9; 26. 7, p. 195; 31. 44, p. 110.

Antiphon, 112. 31, p. 447; 113. 29, p. 301; 115. 9, p. 107; 115. 25, p. 357; 127, p. 262; 130. 29, p. 321; 134. 41, p. 218; 147. 14, p. 58.

Apollon. Rhod., 1. 516, p. 121; 2. 778, p. 121; 4. 738, p. 121.

Aristophanes, *Ach.*, 10, p. 235; 17, p. 239; 33, p. 40; 147, p. 19; 203, p. 95; 278, p. 392; 321, p. 17, note; 410, p 43; 472, p. 40; 544, p. 8; 564, p. 10; 616, p. 280; 659-662, p. 36; 690, p. 41; 709, p. 85; 745, p. 323; 758, p. 213; 778, p. 134; 822, p. 323; 870, p. 465; 883, p. 48; 893, p. 39; 894, p. 128; 905, p. 281; 979, p. 300; 1046, p. 44; 1067, p. 66; 1129, p. 67; 1141, p. 125; 1159, p. 422.

Aves, 9, p. 115; 54, p. 10; 121, p. 224; 204, p. 445; 334, p. 117; 342, p. 8; 366, p. 422; 385, p. 81; 404, p. 41; 511, p. 230, 235; 760, p. 343; 788, p. 374; 832, p. 195; 1148, p. 99; 1350, p. 259; 1470, p. 37; 1498, p. 122; 1568, p. 379; 1586, p. 133.

Eccles., 32, p. 235; 121, p. 301; 155, p. 281; 227, p. 224; 606, p. 73; 650, p. 235; 667, p. 408; 977, p. 6.

Equit., 15–26, p. 41; 51, p. 67; 112, p. 153; 273, p. 178; 283, p. 73; 294, p. 384; 358, p. 180; 360, p. 393; 396, p. 140; 412, p. 85; 435, p 254; 454, p. 178; 480, p. 213; 717, p. 316; 781, p. 180; 973, p. 37; 1018, p. 44; 1033, p. 342; 1090, p. 67; 1131, p. 444; 1153, p. 119; 1177, p. 73; 1206, p. 140; 1247, p 213; 1263, p. 36.

Lys., 225, p. 145; 316, p. 366; 300, p. 379; 506, p. 441; 507, p. 85; 519, p. 135; 553, p. 219; 592, p. 69; 743, p. 41; 831, p 25, note 1; 895, p. 316; 984, p. 42; 1008, p. 70; 1224, p. 245.

Nub., 30, p. 48; 74, p. 67, 300; 107, p. 302; 137, p. 289; 153, p. 9; 339, p. 73; 639, p. 70; 762, p. 90; 776, p. 440; 811, p. 393; 838, p. 275; 883, p. 106; 1237, p. 322; 1240, p. 254; 1347, p. 229; 1363, p. 85; 1373, p. 85; 1409, p. 106; 1441, p. 195.

Pax, 46, p. 4; 176, p. 379; 186, p. 130; 347, p. 85; 366, p. 118; 381, p. 43; 405, p. 440; 541, p. 80; 637, p. 310; 717, p. 364; 775, p. 36; 796, p. 36; 891, p. 342; 1075, p. 47; 1081, p. 91; 1142, p. 124; 1182, p. 231.

Plut. 77, p. 243; 102, p. 327; 106, p. 437; 206, p. 102; 216, p. 299; 369, p. 441; 388, p. 72; 589, p. 301; 696, p. 231; 720, p. 79; 854, p. 45; 894, p. 73; 912, p. 10; 932, p. 379; 981, p. 46; 984, p. 214; 992, p. 46; 1055, p. 408; 1084, p. 360.

Ran., 97, p. 43; 138, p. 189, note; 177, p. 456; 243, p. 355; 259, p. 139; 265, p. 299; 335, p. 314; 468, p. 218; 571, p. 139; 830, p. 379; 941, p. 78; 1082, p.

39; 1163, p. 19; 1221, p. 92; 1235, p. 380; 1309, p. 36; 1339, p. 36; 1380, p. 380; 1384, p. 380; 1393, p. 380; 1427, p. 19; 1450, p. 451; 1477, p. 39.

Thesm. 18, p. 77; 136, p. 19; 246, p. 197; 468, p. 17, note; 504, p. 108; 566, p. 254; 593, p. 85; 719, p. 68; 761, p. 216; 865, p. 39; 1144, p. 40; 1146, p. 41; 1155, p. 41; 1224, p. 378.

Vesp., 36, p. 102; 112, p. 40; 162, p. 220; 262, p. 284; 558, p. 231; 635, p. 230; 646, p. 78; 801, p. 235; 819, p. 441; 1158, p. 301; 1168, p. 302; 1291, p. 137; 1305, pp. 67, 245; 1366, p. 254; 1396, p. 254; 1404, p. 446; 1439, p. 353; 1490, p. 308; 1529, p. 178.

Athenaeus, 1. 21. C, p. 22; 27. D, p. 47; 2. 49. F, p. 46; 54. F, p. 127; 59, p. 346; 60, p. 285; 62, p. 196; 3. 99. D, p. 308; 3. 100. A, p. 302; 110. C, p. 267; 117. B, p. 261; 4. 134. F, p. 375; 139. D, p. 130; 161. D, p. 150; 170. B, p. 79; 172. F, p. 183; 6. 227. A, p. 211; 228. E, p. 355; 235, p. 214; 241. C, p. 44; 247, p. 285; 266. F, p. 50; 6. 268, C, p. 140; 322. A, p. 279; 7. 280. D, p. 40; 293. A, p. 309; 293. D, p. 79; 305. B, p. 449; 322. D, p. 10; 324. B, p. 322; 8. 338. E, p. 70; 347. E, p. 73; 362. C, p. 354; 364. B, p. 47; 9. 367. D, p. 265; 374. D, p. 307; 375. E, p. 81, 268; 383. A, p. 403; 386. A, p. 129, 342; 387. F, p. 199; 400. D, p. 273; 401. p. 476; 409. C, p. 322; 9. 409. E, p. 300; 10. 411. E, p. 139; 423. D, p. 223; 426. F, p. 381; 430. p. 300; 431. B, p. 129; 446. E, p. 91; 11. 463. p. 437; 499. D, p. 65; 502. F, p. 361; 12. 516. D, p. 92; 525. A, p. 84; 13. 568. D, p. 151; 571. A, p. 265; 579. E, p. 366; 14. 623. F, p. 264; 641. p. 437; 642. A, p. 98; 15. 667. A, p. 170, 178; 677. A, p. 308; 699. D, p. 131.

Demosthenes, 13. 26, p. 433; 93. 24, p. 152; 113. p. 389; 120. 7, p. 155; 155. 15, p. 127; 214. 29, p. 100; 235 fin. p. 467; 245. 10, p. 346; 284. 17, p. 401; 297. 11, p. 42; 302. 3, p. 457; 314. 13, p. 286; 315. 24, p. 335; 323. 1, p. 180; 329. 23, p. 123; 332. 20, p. 9; 401. 17, p. 67; 411. 3. p. 294; 430. 21, p. 466; 480. 10, p. 474; 505. 29, p. 97; 537 extr. p. 265; 567. 12, p. 294; 572. p. 262; 623. 22, p. 110; 630. 28, p. 26; 780. 11, p. 9; 782. 8, p. 130; 787. 23, p. 265; 799. 21, p. 477; 845. 23, p. 428; 848. 12, p. 282; 893. 15, p. 357; 990. 4, p. 94; 1010. 15, p. 471; 1021. 20, p. 333, 334; 1057, p. 142; 1062, p. 142; 1075, p. 142; 1077, p. 142; 1170. 27, p. 323; 1295. 20, p. 318; 1295. 20, p. 318; 1303. 14, p. 118; 1304, p. 162; 1392. 4, p. 30.

Dinarchus, 110. 2, p. 11.

Euripides, *Alc.* 757, p. 224.

Andr. 225, p. 456.

Bacch. 798, p. 95; 920, p. 179.

Cycl. 132, p. 455; 172, p. 394; 215, p. 139; 356, p. 139; 406, p. 86.

El. 1032, p. 220.

Hel. 452, p. 89; 587, p. 228; 583, p. 17; 914, p. 126; 930 p. 241; 1010, p. 455; 1602, p. 297.

Heracl. 647, p. 391.

Herc. Fur. 74, p. 115; 158, p. 13; 243, p 387; 340, p. 170; 1054, p. 387; 1136 p. 335; 1266, p. 220; 1319, p. 86; 1368, p. 63.

Hipp. 110, p. 323; 683, p. 18; 687, p. 86; 1093, p. 95; 1197, p. 222; 1391, p. 164.

Ion. 943, p. 455; 1187, p. 232; 1525, p. 317.

I. A. 339, p. 227; 607, p. 99; 769, p. 311.

I. T. 951, p. 78; 987, p. 17; 1410, p. 116.

Med. 60, p. 71; 92, p. 179; 188, p. 180; 237, p. 78; 604, p. 95; 1409, p. 275, note.

Or. 141, p. 316; 504, p. 451; 700, p. 438; 1474, p. 115.

Phoen. 546, p. 38; 1273, p. 13.

Rhes. 25, p. 305; 816, p. 97.

Supp. 442. p. 201.

Troad. 474, p. 241.

Herodotus, 2. 7, p. 147; 158, p. 72; 167, p. 16; 3. 36, p. 254; 62, p. 219; 4. 105, p. 17; 5. 53, p. 72; 94, p. 13; 6. 37 p. 17; 86, p. 18; 126, p. 18; 7. 13, p. 17; 152, p. 13; 9. 82, p. 495.

Hesiod, *Op. et Di.* 528, p. 150; 777, p. 135.

Theog. 144, p. 210; 793, p. 217.

Homer *Iliad*, 9. 203, p. 223; 270, p. 47; 13. 342, p. 322; 15. 128, p. 247; 16. 847, p. 84; 17. 575. p.

214; 17. 575, p. 214; 20. 128, p. 135; 21. 262, p. 317; 318, p. 147; 23. 282, p. 67.
Odyssey, 2. 99, p. 117; 291, p. 57; 3. 298, p. 87; 6. 128, p. 255; 226, p. 322; 7. 198, p. 135; 318, p. 118; 8. 251, p. 313; 9. 10, p. 66; 240, p. 469; 10. 152, p. 197; 361, p. 275; 20. 83, p. 216; 21. 111, p. 74; 22. 198, p. 123; 23. 134, p. 313.
Hyperides, *Ov. Fun.* Col. 13. 3, p. 390; Col. 11. 142, p. 409.
Isaeus, 51. 32, p. 428; 84. 37, p. 332; 86. 10, p. 332.
Isocrates, 1. C, p. 203; 44. B, p. 142; 62. A, p. 78; 203. A, p. 346; 213. D, p. 346.
Lycurgus, 166. 16, p. 218.
Lysias, 93. 43, p. 123; 94. 41, p. 145; 94, p. 262; 102. 12, p. 262; 111. 16, p. 241; 136. 1, p. 219; 147. 34, p. 107; 165. 12, p. 110; 180. 5, p. 63.
Pindar, *Ol.* 13. 43, p. 84.
Pyth. 4 extr. p. 70.
Nem. 9. 46, p. 208.
Plato, *Apol.* 20. A, p. 142.
Axioc. 368. E, p. 418.
Charm. 172. D, p. 70.
Cratyl. 406. C, p. 313.
Critias. 109. D, p. 99; 117. A, p. 369.
Crito. 53. E, p. 110.
Euthyd. 278. C, p. 91; 302. A, p. 398.
Euthyphro. 4. B, p. 227.
Gorg. 477. B, p. 67; 481, p. 456; 492. E, p. 39; 494. C, p. 133; 506. C, p. 195; 510. D, p. 448; 512. E, p. 456; 527. A, p. 410.
Hipp. Maj. 292. B, p. 262.
Laches. 192. E, p. 408.
Legg. 646. C, p. 340; 666. D, p. 377; 687. D, p. 142; 757, p. 329; 800. D, p. 67; 840. D, p. 194; 845. A, p. 149; 913. B, p. 447; 916. A, p. 155.
Parmen. 140. A, p. 449; 141. E, p. 194.
Phaedo, 69. B, p. 213; 99. B, p. 303; 104. A, p. 333.
Phaedr. 242. A, p. 293; 251. A. p. 270; 254. E, p. 146.
Phileb. 62. D, p. 194.
Polit. 282. A, E, p. 135; 289. C, p. 135.
Protag. 321. A, p. 303.
Rep. 371. p. 29; 378. A, p. 142; 378. D, p. 353; 379. p. 301; 398. A, p. 67; 410. E, p. 142; 410. E, p. 142; 432. D, p. 235; 452. F, p. 313; 460. D, p. 402; 470. A, p. 189, note; 539. E. p. 312; 603. E, p. 195.
Symp. 413. B, p. 29.
Theaet. 144. B, p. 335; 147. D, p. 334; 153. E, p. 75; 154. D, p. 9; 178. C, p. 415; 197. C, D, p. 253; 198. B, p. 253; 200. B, p. 253; 200. D, p, 334.
Tim. 26. C, p. 227.
Pollux 1. 79, p. 321; 2. 17, p. 148, 157; 2. 33, p. 132; 2. 41, p. 155; 2. 76, p. 164; 168, p. 178; 3. 17, p. 208; 78, p. 474; 7. 13, p. 213; 40, p. 322; 48, p. 312; 108, p. 159; 191, p. 256; 200, p. 314; 9. 124, p. 37; 10. 12, p. 418; 21, p. 471; 34, p. 207, 267; 35, p. 322; 39, p. 256; 103, p. 251; 136, p. 175.
Sophocles, *Aj.* 312, p. 448; 571, p. 64; 679, p. 241; 786, p. 132; 1185, p. 117; 1373, p. 134.
Ant. 447, p. 226; 571, p. 143; 887, p. 133; 1231, p. 78.
El. 596, p. 317; 606, p. 134; 1306, p. 379.
Oed. Col. 335, p. 115; 505, p. 116; 528, p. 173; 1339, p. 68.
Oed. Rex 246, p. 18; 428, p. 18; 696, p. 465; 840, p. 449; 967, p. 423.
Phil. 666, p. 27; 992, p. 316; 1306, p. 13.
Trach. 24, p. 241; 276, p. 85; 564, p. 242; 675, p. 225; 698, p. 323.
Theocritus 3. 50, p. 93; 8. 78, p. 69; 11. 31, p. 210; 13. 36, p. 93; 14. 55, p. 93.
Thucydides, 1. 2, p. 358; 6, p. 99; 13, p. 142; 62, p. 116; 70, p. 294; 2. 17, p. 195; 20, p. 337; 40, p. 81; 84, p. 132; 97, p. 218; 3. 8, p. 126; 12, p. 110, note; 22, p. 167; 54, p. 101; 61, p. 101; 4. 9, p. 314; 24, p. 119; 26, p. 98; 36, p. 318; 120, p. 108; 4. 121, p. 107; 5. 63, p. 11; 6. 3, p. 107, note; 66, p. 337; 88, p. 358; 96, p. 223; 104, p. 314; 7. 66, p. 99; 81, p. 340; 8. 23, p. 118; 92, p. 262; 107, p. 116.
Xenophon, *Anab.* 1. 2. 17, p. 279; 2. 1. 22, p. 187; 2. 4. 25, p. 109; 2. 5. 15, p. 188; 2. 6. 1, p. 481; 4. 3. 12, p. 92; 4. 3. 13, p. 109; 4. 3. 26, p. 203; 4. 5. 19, p. 357; 4. 6.

22, pp. 109, 200, 238; 4. 7. 12, p. 109; 5. 4. 29, p. 358; 5. 8. 15, p. 198; 6. 2. 19, p. 358; 6. 3. 10, p. 358.

Cyrop. 1. 3. 4, p. 115; 1. 3. 14, p. 314; 1. 3. 17, p. 263; 1. 4. 22, p. 495; 1. 6. 16, p. 176; 2. 2. 1, p. 69; 2. 4. 18, p. 109; 3. 1. 35, p. 456; 3. 2. 19, p. 185; 4. 1. 1, p. 109; 4. 1. 11, p. 172; 4. 5. 56, p. 427; 5. 3. 52, p. 448; 5. 4. 38, p. 399; 5. 5. 39, p. 303; 6. 1. 9, p. 241; 6. 3. 13, p. 378; 7. 1. 30, p. 500; 7. 5. 65, p. 59; 8. 2. 5, p. 456; 8. 5. 12, p. 109.

Eq. 2. 2, p. 62; 3. 3, p. 351; 4. 4, p. 323; 6. 1, p. 323.

Hell. 1. 7. 8, p. 132; 2. 2. 20, p. 218; 2. 3. 49, p. 144; 4. 1. 40, p. 142; 4. 8. 39, p. 59; 5. 1. 27, p. 151; 5. 3. 1, p. 427; 5. 4. 58, p. 296; 6. 5. 20, p. 189, note; 7. 1. 29, p. 428.

Hiero. 2. 4, p. 152; 3. 3, p. 59.

Mem. 2. 1. 3, p. 60; 2. 1. 5, p. 152; 3. 3. 2, p. 427; 4. 3. 13, p. 62.

Oec 16. 14, p. 126; 17. 4, p. 124.

Rep. Ath. 2. 16, p. 367.

Symp. 4. 7, p. 91; 4. 31, p. 357; 4. 43, p. 486; 9. 2, p. 91.

INDEX III.

Accusative plural of substantives in -εύς, 234.
Adverbs in -θεν, 114, 177.
  of place confused, 114, 115.
  compounded with prepositions, 117.
Anapaestic verse, licence in, 51.
Antiphon, his diction, 30, 107, 164, 227.
Aorist, optative forms of, 429 ff.
  rarely a first and second aorist co-existent, 215 ff.
  aorists of verbs in -αίνω and αίρω, 76 ff.
  in -θην, with active signification, 186 ff.
Apollonius Rhodius, diction of, 121.
Aspiration, Attic, 196.
Athenian civilization homogeneous, 32, 33.
Attic dialect, in relation to Athenian civilization, 33.
  early history of illustrated by Tragedy, 3, 4.
  short duration of, 1.
  purity of, 199.
  old words replaced by new creations, 22.
  by new formations from the same stem, 19.
Augmentation, inconsistencies of Attic, 79 ff.
  double, 83 ff.
  of verbs beginning in a diphthong, 244.

Caricature, as affecting the diction of comedy, 46.
Comedy, utility of in deciding questions of Atticism, p. 33 ff.
Comparatives, double, 209.
Compound words, late methods of forming them, 361.
  in Ionic and Tragedy, 6.
Contraction of verbs in -αμαι, 463 ff.
  in -έω, 297 ff.
  of adjectives in -εος, 287.
Cyclops in Homer, prevalent mistake regarding, 209, 210.

Dawes, his work characterized, 229.
Dialects, literary dialects in Greece, 162 ff.
Diminutives in -άσιον, 148.
Dual number, rules regarding, 289 ff.
  true forms of nom. and acc. 3rd declension, 142.

Euripides, diction of, 35, 121.
Futures in -θήσομαι, 189 note.
  middle, Doric, 91 ff.
  futures deponent, 376 ff.

Legal technical terms, 26.
Lysias, diction of, 202.

Metaphor, picturesqueness of in Ionic and Tragedy, 16.
  growth of freedom in the use of, 479 ff.
Middle voice and Active, often confused in MSS., 377 ff.
  direct middle, 368.
  in the future tense, 376 ff.

Nominative plural of substantives in -εύς, 233, 234.

Optative forms discussed, 429 ff.

Parasite, history of the name, 214 ff.
Parody, in the senarii of Comedy, 37 ff.
  in hexameter, 46.
  in Epic, 47.
  in choric metres, 36.
Parsimony, law of, 120.
Perfect tense, original meaning of in Greek, 200.
  optative forms in the active, 449.
Pluperfect, inflexions of, 229 ff.
Prepositions used adverbially, 119.
  governing adverbs, 117.
Proverbial sayings preserve old forms, 49 ff.
Pseudo-oracles in Comedy, 46 ff.

Reduplication, Attic, 95 ff.

Sigma in perfect passive, 97 ff.
Sirens, error regarding the, 210.
Sophocles, fondness for ἐκ in composition, 7.
Substantives used as adjectives, 21.
Superlatives, 144.

Thucydides, diction of, 28, 107, 218.
Tragic dialect explained and discussed, 3, 4, 8, 58, 140, 223.

Verbs in -άω, contracting in -η, 132 ff.
denoting mental states, 152 ff.
in -εύομαι, 141.
in -ίζομαι, 141.
with signification definable by context, 178 ff.
deponent, 192.
denoting rivalry necessarily middle, 192 ff.

Xenophon's diction, 28, 30, 59, 62, 67, 69, 109, 115, 124, 160 ff., 187, 203.